BEYOND
THE INFORMATION
GIVEN

Contributors with Jerome S. Bruner

to papers in this volume

GEORGE AUSTIN	GEORGE KLEIN
BLANCHE M. BRUNER	JEAN M. MANDLER
MICHAEL COLE	GEORGE A. MILLER
EUGENE H. GALANTER	DONALD D. O'DOWD
CECILE C. GOODMAN	ROSE R. OLVER
JACQUELINE S. GOODNOW	LEO J. POSTMAN
PATRICIA GREENFIELD	MARY C. POTTER
HELEN J. KENNEY	MICHAEL A. WALLACH

Jerome S. Bruner

BEYOND
THE INFORMATION
GIVEN

Studies in the Psychology of Knowing

Selected, Edited, and Introduced

by JEREMY M. ANGLIN

 W · W · Norton & Company · Inc · New York

ALL RIGHTS RESERVED
Published simultaneously in Canada
by George J. McLeod Limited, Toronto

Library of Congress Cataloging in Publication Data

Bruner, Jerome Seymour.
  Beyond the information given.

  Includes bibliographies.
  1. Perception. 2. Thought and thinking.
3. Education. 4. Cognition (child psychology)
I. Title.
BF311.B77 1973   153.7   72–13402
ISBN 0–393–01095–3

PRINTED IN THE UNITED STATES OF AMERICA

1 2 3 4 5 6 7 8 9 0

For George Miller

Contents

Author's Foreword

I am deeply grateful to Jeremy Anglin for the care and discernment of his editing and commentary.

I must also express my gratitude to the collaborators with whom I worked on the various papers—companions who added enormously not only to the enterprise but to the quality of life in the laboratory and out:

George Austin   George Klein
Blanche M. Bruner   Jean M. Mandler
Michael Cole   George A. Miller
Eugene H. Galanter   Donald D. O'Dowd
Cecile C. Goodman   Rose R. Olver
Jacqueline S. Goodnow   Leo J. Postman
Patricia Greenfield   Mary C. Potter
Helen J. Kenney   Michael A. Wallach

Finally, this volume is dedicated to George Miller to whom the author and the editor owe so much for instruction and friendship.

October 25, 1971   JEROME S. BRUNER

Editor's Preface

The idea behind this book has been to collect in one place and in an instructive sequence some of Jerome S. Bruner's major ideas in the psychology of knowing. The studies presented cover a great variety of problems—from the perception of a tachistoscopic flash to the development of a scientific theory, from the attainment of an artificial concept in the laboratory to the mastery of a course of study in school, from manual skill in infancy to creativity in adulthood. The diversity of topics is admittedly great, but not, I think, overwhelming. For there are a number of themes which recur throughout this work, and which serve to unite what might at first sight seem to be rather disparate studies in psychology. I have tried to outline these themes in the introduction to this volume. Suffice it to say now that the most fundamental of them is the author's persistent concern with the process of knowing, with what man does with information and, in particular, how he goes beyond it to achieve insight, understanding, and competence.

In selecting the twenty-seven articles of this book I have been guided primarily by a single concern. I chose those papers that I thought might best combine to present Bruner's work on cognition, development, and education as a unified whole. These twenty-seven articles have been divided into five sections corresponding to what I consider to be the five most productive phases of his research and thought. In general, sections begin and end with important theoretical papers which are separated by the research papers best illustrating the theoretical arguments. In brief introductions to the sections I have outlined the reasons for my selections and have tried to indicate certain themes that run through and, to some extent, unify the book.

The sections do not follow in exact chronological order the phases of Bruner's thought in that Bruner's most recent work on skill in infancy appears before the sections on representation in childhood and on education. I chose this ordering for several reasons. Putting the section on infancy before the one on childhood has the advantage of matching the individual's actual sequence of growth. Also the work on education is best understood after a consideration of the studies on skill in infancy and representation in childhood, since they are crucial to Bruner's ideas about instruction. Finally, and perhaps most importantly, the chosen order seemed best in view of the theoretical themes of the book. The first three sections follow the uses to which information is put "inward," moving from the constructions involved in perceptual recognition to those involved in the higher mental processes, and finally "outward" to those involved in converting knowledge into action. These successive phases of dealing with information can be viewed as kinds of problems whose solutions have much in common at a formal level. By presenting the papers on perception, reasoning, and skill in succession I feel these themes may become more apparent. One crucial unifying theme in these three sections is the central idea of an "internal model" or "system of representation." In the fourth section the concept of representation is differentiated and the successive modes of representation in the child's development are described. This section paves the way for the final section on education in which a dominant theme concerns the advantages of tailoring course material in a way that acknowledges the development of the modes of representation depicted in the preceding section.

In organizing this book I have had three groups of people in mind. First, it should be of considerable interest to psychologists and could be used as a text for courses in cognition and development. Second, educators will find in it some of Bruner's important views on pedagogy in the context of the psychological work that has shaped them. Finally, it may be of more than passing interest to philosophers, particularly epistemologists who will find here a psychological and developmental approach to the problem of the growth of knowledge. Philosophers of science will also discover many notions in Bruner's work that may be relevant to their pursuits. To take but one example, Bruner's description of perceptual recognition is remarkably similar to the description of doing "normal science" provided by Thomas Kuhn in his essay *The Structure of Scientific Revolution*. There are also interesting similarities (as well as differences) between Kuhn on the change in the accepted paradigm that occurs in a scientific revolution and Bruner on the developmental changes in the modes of representation.

In putting this volume together I have been most generously assisted by several people. Conversations with George Miller during the early stages of the planning of this book proved to be invaluable. Anita Gill not only helped with the editing of the section on education, but also made several valuable suggestions about the articles to be included. Eleanor Rosenberger was most generous in giving me advice as questions concerning

the fine details of editing arose. G. Thomas Rowland provided the original
impetus and I am grateful for his role in getting this volume started. Donald S. Lamm of W. W. Norton and Company, our publisher, has made
several valuable suggestions and has provided continued support and encouragement. I am most grateful to the following people for their helpful
comments on the introductory material for this book: Eleanor Stephens,
Susan Carey Block, Patricia Greenfield, Maryellen Rulovo, Elizabeth
Smith, Achola Pala, Nelson Goodman, Stephen Mackay, Marvin Cohen,
Frank Sulloway, John Carroll, and Alistaire Mundy-Castle. Margaret
Morse helped proofread the galleys with characteristic perseverance and
care. I would like to thank the distinguished psychologists who were co-
authors with Professor Bruner on the various papers for allowing us to
include their work in this collection. Their contributions are acknowledged specifically by credits on the first page of selections and generally by
the presence of their names on the title page. Finally, there is Jerome Bruner, the author of the papers in this book, who has been for me a great
personal friend and mentor. We are all deeply indebted to him for his
immense contribution to our understanding of the nature and origins of
human cognition.

Cambridge, Massachusetts   JEREMY M. ANGLIN
July 1972

Introduction

Jerome S. Bruner received his doctorate in psychology at Harvard University in 1941. Since then he has surely been one of the world's most productive psychologists with major contributions in at least half a dozen fields and with an average of close to a publication every two months in the thirty years since he received his degree. Though there has been considerable overlap in the various stages of his thought, both in terms of the periods during which important ideas have been produced and of the intellectual themes that have shaped them, it has helped me to think of his work as having developed through six major phases. The ordering of the phases has been roughly as follows: public opinion, perception, thought, education, and concurrently, representation in childhood and skill in infancy. This book concerns all but the first of these phases.

The work on public opinion centered around research conducted during World War II on the social psychology of group attitudes, propaganda, and prejudice. Studies on the relation between America's foreign policy and public opinion, on German propaganda, and on attitudes toward postwar problems were typical of this period. These studies are not represented here, for their inclusion might detract from the book's overall unity. Nonetheless, traces of Bruner's work on social psychology are evident in his later work. For one thing, his investigations of attitudes convinced him that they served important functions for their holders—to align them with reference groups, to externalize their internal systems of beliefs, and to test their hypotheses. The related stress on the functions of perceiving and reasoning was to become a hallmark of the next stages in Bruner's thought. Moreover, his concern with opinions and attitudes led him to study how they affect the process of perceiving. In fact, the study of the influence of such social factors on perceptual recognition was a crucial dimension in the next major phase of his work.

The majority of the papers on perception were published between 1946 and 1958. One of the first, "Value and Need as Organizing Factors in Perception" (Article 2), outlined a program of research which was to be concerned with the behavioral determinants of perceptual recognition. By *behavioral determinants* Bruner and his coauthor, Cecile Goodman, meant to include the laws of learning and motivation, personality dynamics, and of course, social attitudes and opinions. The integrative spirit of this paper and of the ensuing program of research by Bruner, Leo Postman, and their colleagues—the viewing of a process not in isolation, but in combination with other psychological processes—was an important respect in which this approach merited the label, the "New Look in Perception." Another distinguishing feature of the New Look which was present from the beginning and which was increasingly stressed as the program matured, was the emphasis on the continuity between perceptual and conceptual activity. Perception was considered to be an essentially inferential process in which an individual constructed his perceptual world on the basis of information provided by his senses.

His concern with inference in perception soon led Bruner to an investigation of the inferential processes involved in various kinds of reasoning. In 1951, a five-year program of research was begun by Bruner, Jacqueline Goodnow, George Austin, and several other colleagues on the process of concept attainment, culminating with the publication of *A Study of Thinking* (9) in 1956. The concepts with which they were concerned were of a particular sort—they were either conjunctive, disjunctive, or relational concepts, the instances of which achieved category membership by exemplifying experimentally defined and therefore rather arbitrary rules. These concepts were different from most naturally occurring verbal concepts in that there was this kind of precise rule defining them, in that they did not achieve their meaning through their relation to a system of interrelated concepts, and in that they were not likely to be important to people in their day-to-day experiences. Bruner's later developmental work on conservation, on the growth of equivalence relations, with Rose Olver, and on the teaching of mathematical concepts, with Helen Kenney, was concerned with the acquisition of concepts that are more representative of those important to people in everyday life.

Nonetheless, *A Study of Thinking* was an extraordinary achievement in cognitive psychology because of its precise analysis of the processes involved when a subject is faced with the problem of constructing experimentally defined concepts. Bruner, Goodnow, and Austin took as their unit of analysis not the individual response, but rather the sequence of decisions an individual employed in solving the problem. By comparing the patterns among successive decisions that people made in attempting to attain a concept with various rational or ideal patterns, the authors came up with a beautifully precise description of the strategies involved in this kind of conceptual activity.

The work on reasoning was not confined to concept attainment nor to inferential processes in human beings. In the middle and late fifties Bruner and his colleagues conducted several studies on both animals and humans in which the experimental task required processing recurrent sequences of events. A basic finding of these studies was that subjects do not mechanically associate specific responses with specific stimuli, but rather tend to infer principles or rules underlying the patterns which allow them to transfer their learning to different problems. The knowledge achieved by subjects in these studies was often productive, or to borrow a term from linguistics, generative.

Bruner's experimental studies of reasoning were complemented by a set of less empirical and rather more conjectural inquiries into the nature of knowing. Some of these were collected in *On Knowing: Essays for the Left Hand* (4) which appeared in 1962. The book was for the "left hand" because it was concerned with the intuitive and the creative aspects of knowing which complement the more orderly, rational, and methodical skills of the "right hand." It dealt with knowing through art and poetry, through myth and man's image of himself. The essays in this book again reflected Bruner's persistent effort to achieve a more integrated conception of human cognition, in this case by viewing man not only as scientist and logician but also as humanist and artist.

Two important events occurred just over a decade ago which were to influence deeply the next phases of Bruner's work. The first was the Woods Hole Conference on Education. In 1959 some thirty-five scientists, scholars, and educators met under Bruner's direction on Cape Cod for ten days to discuss how education, especially in the sciences, could be improved in primary and secondary schools. The Woods Hole Conference crystallized and gave direction to the next two phases of his research: education and representation in childhood. His interest in both curriculum design and developmental psychology had clearly been present in his earlier studies of reasoning, and in the late fifties he had pursued these concerns substantively in his work with children who displayed learning disabilities. The Woods Hole Conference suggested how these interests might be pursued further. In the opening days of the conference various curriculum projects designed to teach mathematics, biology, and physics were discussed and appraised, and several instructional techniques were demonstrated. The focus of the conference on these kinds of ecologically representative learning situations guided Bruner's later attempts to design and implement courses of study. Moreover, an important theme of the conference, notably stressed by Barbel Inhelder from Geneva, was that instruction must take into account the student's existing stage in development. The importance of considering intellectual development in designing curricula has been emphasized by Bruner ever since the conference, and probably accounts in part for the fact that from 1960 his concern with the process of education has gone hand in hand with his more theoretical explorations of human development.

Since the Woods Hole Conference, three books have appeared which present Bruner's major views on education: *The Process of Education* (3), *Toward a Theory of Instruction* (5), and *The Relevance of Education* (6). Two important notions to emerge from the work on instruction, particularly crucial for this volume, have been that the student should be encouraged to participate actively in the learning process and that curricula should be tailored to the learner's existing mode of representation. These ideas are explored in both theoretical and empirical papers in the last section of this book.

The second event which strongly influenced Jerome Bruner's research occurred in 1960 when he, together with George Miller, founded the Center for Cognitive Studies at Harvard University. The purpose of the center was to foster interdisciplinary studies of the higher mental processes. Each year Miller and Bruner were hosts to a distinguished group of visitors and students from different countries and from different disciplines who shared an interest in the nature of human cognition. Guided by Bruner's concerns with intellectual development and education, and by Miller's concerns with psycholinguistics and human memory, the center soon became an active forum for creating, sharing, and testing ideas. An illustration of the kind of interaction that took place in the Center can be seen in *Studies in Cognitive Growth* (10) which appeared in 1966. This book was written by Bruner, together with eleven postdoctoral fellows and students who had spent time working with him at the center. It presents the most extensive treatment of their research on representation in childhood.

Two messages come through most clearly from this book, and from the empirical work upon which it was based. The first is that a transition takes place in childhood from "iconic representation," based upon a somewhat intractable visual imagery, to "symbolic representation," based upon a more abstract and more flexible system of symbols. The second message is that culture plays a central role in influencing the course of cognitive growth and that schooling is a particularly important instrument of the culture by means of which intellectual skills are amplified.

Both the work on education and the work on representation in childhood led Bruner to study the growth of skill in infancy, the sixth phase in his work. His research in education had convinced him that, in addition to its role as an agent of socialization, the school should equip its students with basic skills. The obviously necessary precursor to the implementation of such a suggestion was to study the origins and development of skilled behavior. Moreover, Bruner's developmental work with older children had convinced him that by the age of three the child had already achieved considerable intellectual competence. To appreciate the origins of human cognition and the nature of the earliest forms of problem solving he decided he would do well to look to infancy.

This work is still in progress and the sample that is presented in this volume should not be viewed as Bruner's final word on the subject. Nonetheless, the topic has been sufficiently developed to convey the elements of a unique theory of the development and structure of human skill. An initial outline of this approach appeared in *Process of Cognitive Growth: Infancy* (7), which contained Bruner's lectures in the Heinz Werner series given at Clark University in 1968. From the beginning of his work on infancy, he has stressed the communality between skills and problem solving in general. The execution of a skill is thought to be guided by an intention that specifies possible serial orders which will result in successful completion of a task. The constituents of the skilled act must be orchestrated into one of these serial orders if the intention is to be fulfilled. Complex skills are slowly mastered in infancy through the integration of simpler constituent skills, a view that has implications for educational policy, as we shall see.

The reader will discover that Bruner's approach to psychology has been affected by a long list of intellectual predecessors. The immediate ancestry would surely include William McDougall and Egon Brunswik, whose stress on the functions served by psychological processes has been extended in Bruner's work. There has been the influence of Edward Tolman and David Krech, both of whom, like Bruner, have been unyielding in their criticism of an overly simple and overly mechanistic behaviorism and in their insistence on the need for theories that postulate internal conceptual structures and processes. Lev Semanovich Vygotsky's book, *Thought and Language* (16) certainly provided important direction for the work on conceptual development. It also provided a necessary background for the studies in education, as did John Dewey's (11) pioneering work. The great developmental psychologist, Heinz Werner (17), had stressed the value of the comparative approach to developmental psychology which has been an important dimension of Bruner's most recent research. Moreover, Werner had described three major periods in intellectual growth which correspond with Bruner's description of the development of enactive, iconic, and symbolic representation. And, of course, Karl Lashley (12) had clearly posed the problem of serial order in behavior in 1951 which has been a dominant concern in Bruner's most recent work on infancy.

Yet of the myriad intellectual figures who have influenced Bruner's thought, two stand out as being most important: Sir Frederick Bartlett and Jean Piaget. Bruner's early work on perception, concept attainment, and problem solving extends a tradition in psychology begun by Bartlett, with his classic book, *Remembering* (1) which appeared in 1932. In a sense, Bartlett had shown how individuals "go beyond the information given" when they perceive and remember, in the same way that Bruner and his colleagues have in the cases of perceiving, attaining concepts, and solving problems. Bartlett's theoretical account of remembering invoked the concept of the "schema," that integrated, organized representation of past behavior and experience which guides an individual in reconstructing previously encountered material. The role of schemata in remembering is very close to the role played by an internal model or a generic coding system in Bruner's account of perceiving and reasoning. Closely related to this, and in some respects the most striking parallel in the theories of the two men, is the emphasis on the constructive nature of the cognitive processes. Bartlett was determined to demonstrate that remembering was not merely the re-excitation of fixed, lifeless traces, but was rather a matter of imaginative reconstruction. In a similar vein, Bruner has doggedly argued against the notion of passive reception in perception, concept attainment, and reasoning and has insisted in each case that the acquisition of knowledge depends upon an active process of construction.

If Bartlett has been a strong influence on Bruner's earlier work with adults, then it has been Piaget's pioneering studies that have probably most deeply affected his later work in development. Although there are several crucial differences in the approach and theory of the two men, the similarities are more fundamental. For both, cognitive development involves qualitative rather than quantitative changes in the cognitive structures presumed to mediate behavior at different ages. At a general level both view the total process of growth as comprising three major epochs. For Piaget these are the sensorimotor period, the period of preparation for and organization of concrete operations, and the period of formal operations; for Bruner, enactive representation, iconic representation, and symbolic representation. Both have been struck by the importance of action in infancy and both view growth in childhood as carrying the individual from a state of being dominated by immediacy and appearance to a state in which he is able to transcend the present and perceptual, to appreciate connectedness over time and invariance in the face of surface change.

As well as the general similarities that link the approaches of these two developmental psychologists, there are also important differences. Piaget's theory of intellectual development is saturated with reference to mathematics and logic and as a result tends to be rather formal. Bruner's, in contrast, is fundamentally psychological. As a case in point one might compare the theoretical constructs employed by Piaget in his description of the achievement of conservation of liquids with those invoked by Bruner to account for the same phenomenon. In the conservation problem one of two identical beakers of water is poured into a taller, thinner beaker and the child is asked whether there is the same amount, or more, or less to drink in each of the beakers containing water. At around six or seven years the child will say, as adults do, that there is the same amount to drink in each of the beakers, whereas a younger child will typically say that there is more in the tall thin beaker. Piaget (13) earlier stressed the notions of compensation (the internal multiplication of dimensions) and, to a lesser extent, reversibility (the realization that although A has been changed to B, B could be changed back to A). More recently, and partially in response to Bruner's point that a necessary though not sufficient condition for conservation is the appreciation of the identity of the transformed substance, Piaget has added "quantitative identity" (which he represents as $+0-0=0$), to the list (14). Compensation, reversibility, and quantitative identity are three of several tightly interrelated logical operations the child is said to have in the subperiod of concrete operations. Each of these terms has a precise logical meaning and can be represented in terms of mathematical symbols and operations.

Bruner, in contrast, prefers more psychological and intuitive constructs to account for such phenomena. For example, he has stressed the ideas that conservation is achieved as the child begins to develop a capacity for reasoning symbolically, a capacity which supplements and empowers his iconic mode of representation, that the conflict which results when the different modes of representation provide discrepant information can hasten the child's ability to conserve, and that it is the appreciation of the phenomenal identity of the transformed substance that is the necessary though not sufficient condition for conservation. In short, Bruner seems to be trying primarily to identify the psychological processes which occur during cognitive development and the forces which impel it; while Piaget, who is obviously concerned with such processes and forces (e.g., assimilation and accommodation), seems equally if not more concerned with representing the knowledge of the child in the various stages of his development formally in terms of mathematical and logical symbols and operations.

Another real difference between Bruner and Piaget concerns the question of whether the changes that do occur in the child's problem-solving skills at around six or seven years of age are mediated by language. Bruner and his colleagues demonstrated in a wide variety of tasks a correlation between the child's performance and the language he used in describing his reasons for that performance. They argued that such demonstrations reflect the important role that symbolic and, specifically, linguistic transformations come to play in guiding thought when the child first uses symbolic representation. Piaget argues that the linguistic correlates of success in these various tasks are correlates only, that they are symptoms of the achievement of concrete operations, but in no way are they causally linked to the young child's increased competence. While it is true that Bruner and his colleagues have not demonstrated unequivocally that language does mediate the increased competence of the conserver for example, the question of whether language serves as an instrument of thought is still an open one. Piaget offers Hermina Sinclair de Zwart's work (15) as evidence for his belief that language is a symptom and not a source of the change. Sinclair de Zwart, in some intriguing studies, attempted to teach preoperational children the language used by operational children to see if they would improve their performance on certain Piagetian tasks. For example, she attempted to teach nonconservers the differentiated and comparative terms of the conserver as well as the ability to give a coordinated description of a difference in two dimensions. She found that only about 10 per cent of the nonconservers achieved conservation following this linguistic training. Now this may mean that language does not mediate conservation; but it may also mean that she was not really effective in teaching the language so that it could be used productively in new situations, or that the language she taught was not appropriate to the task. Indeed, if Bruner is right that the sine qua non for conservation is the appreciation of identity, perhaps she should have been teaching the concept "the same" rather than the verbal concepts that she did choose to teach. The debate between Piaget and Bruner about the relation of language and thought is reminiscent of Piaget's earlier debate with Vygotsky (16) on the subject and is still unresolved.

Perhaps the most critical difference in the work of the two men concerns the power attributed to agents of culture in shaping structures in the course of intellectual development. Compared with Bruner's account, Piaget's description of the course of development seems relatively fixed and prefigured. Not that Piaget's theory is a wholly hereditary account. His central concept of accommodation certainly implies that the environment does bring about changes in cognitive structure. Moreover, the idea that teaching should start "where the learner is," which has been so crucial to Bruner's views on education, is implicit in Piaget's work and was clearly outlined by his long-time colleague, Barbel Inhelder, in her memorandum for the Woods Hole Conference. Nonetheless, in most of his work, Piaget seems little concerned with the pedagogical means of aiding intellectual development, which he calls "the American question." Generally he has presented his analysis of the unfolding stages in conceptual development without a corresponding analysis of possible accelerating educational techniques. In contrast, Bruner, who believes that a theory of development should go hand in hand with a theory of instruction, has argued that "mental growth is in very considerable measure dependent upon growth from the outside in—a mastering of techniques that are embodied in the culture and that are passed on in a contingent dialogue by agents of the culture." In line with this belief he and his colleagues have continually tried to design pedagogical means for accelerating intellectual achievements.

The nature of Bruner's approach to human cognition has changed over the years, not only in terms of the specific content of the areas investigated, but also in terms of the style of inquiry. Two related stylistic changes distinguish the earlier work on perception and reasoning from the later work on education and development. First, the later work relies heavily on the method of contrasts by which the cognitive processes of educated Western adults are compared systematically with the cognitive processes of primates, of members of different cultures, and of immature human beings. The result has been a picture of man's thought processes in the perspective of his phylogenetic, cultural, and ontogenetic heritage, an essentially historical perspective that was absent in the earlier work.

The second stylistic change is closely related to the first. The earlier work tended to be done "in vitro," in somewhat abstracted circumstances though the attempt was always to extrapolate to processes in everyday life. His theory of perception was based primarily on work done with tachistoscopic flashes and his views on reasoning were based on research with somewhat arbitrary experimental puzzles. The later work has tended to be done "in vivo," dependent more upon naturalistic observation and ecologically representative situations. His observations of the effects of various kinds of course material presented to the child in his daily school environment is a case in point. And his most recent studies on grasping, looking, sucking, and social interaction in infants are not so much experimental abstractions as controlled attempts to analyze naturally occurring behavior.

In spite of the changes in both the content and the style of Bruner's approach over the years, there have been several invariant themes that have provided continuity to his studies. In terms of his style of inquiry, his work has always been deeply integrative in spirit. He has continually attempted to combine different specialties to obtain a more complete, and therefore more realistic, picture of human cognition. He studied perception in the light of personality dynamics and social psychology, thought from the perspective of scientist and humanist, development at the interface of biology and anthropology, and education in view of his cognitive and developmental psychology. His work is full of references to such diverse fields as computer science, mathematics, economics, linguistics, philosophy, literature, and art, though always in the context of his approach to cognitive psychology.

A closely related theme has been Bruner's persistent concern with the relevance of his theoretical ideas to practical matters, particularly education. As early as 1946 he had written a paper on educational reform in France. The experimental work on reasoning was always motivated in part by pedagogical concerns, as the reader will see in the first and last articles of Section 2 of this book. And, of course, his study of development has always been closely tied to and deeply affected by his work on education.

An important theoretical theme throughout the work has been the stress on the idea that to understand the acquisition of knowledge one must always keep in mind the exigencies of action and the uses to which knowledge will be put. The selective character of perception to which most of the New Look work pointed was always viewed in terms of the requirements of the activity or the enterprise of the organism at the time of stimulus input. Perception served important functions in guiding action and was to some extent dependent upon those functions. The same stress permeated the work on reasoning. For example, the studies of concept attainment were motivated, in part, by a belief in the great functional utility of this sort of conceptual activity in one's adjustment to his environment, and they consistently emphasized the role played by the consequences of categorical judgments. Most recently this theme has emerged in the work on infancy with its central emphasis on the concept of intention. In fact, Bruner views the earliest forms of problem solving by infants to be biased and selective in ways that acknowledge the requirements of action more directly than the adult cognitive processes which he had studied previously.

For the purposes of this book, perhaps the most important integrating notions in Bruner's work crop up in his theoretical description of the processes involved in the different kinds of conceptual activities he has studied. Though obviously different in basic ways, several modes of acquiring knowledge—including the perception of an event, the attainment of a concept, the solution of a problem, the discovery of a scientific theory, and the mastery of a skill—can be described at a formal level in ways that are strikingly similar. In short, each can be viewed as a kind of problem whose solution is actively, though not necessarily consciously, constructed. Construction usually involves a recursive process in which the first step is an inferential leap from sense data to a tentative hypothesis achieved by relating incoming information to an internally stored model of the world based upon past experience. The second step is essentially a confirmation check in which the tentative hypothesis is tested against further sense data. In the face of a match the hypothesis is maintained; in the face of a mismatch the hypothesis is altered in a way that acknowledges the discrepant evidence. That the sense data might be called cues, clues, instances, or experimental results; that the hypothesis might be called a category, a rule, a principle, or a theory; that the internal model might be called a generic coding system, a focus, a system of representation, a cognitive structure, a schema, or a paradigm; that the recursive process might be called inference and confirmation check, strategy, analysis by synthesis, induction and deduction, conjecture and refutation, or the hypothetico-deductive method—all these should not be allowed to obscure the underlying formal similarity of diverse kinds of mental activities. Bruner himself has described different conceptual processes in different languages, but has depicted many of the communalities clearly in what is perhaps the central article of this book, "Going Beyond the Information Given" (Article 13).

The reader may find that the image of man that emerges from the author's approach is somewhat different from that created by other influential schools in recent psychology. In so doing, Bruner's work and that of certain other cognitive and developmental psychologists redresses a balance. It might not be too far off to say that within the recent history of psychology the three most influential traditions have come from the work on natural selection starting with Darwin, psychoanalysis beginning with Freud, and behaviorism which has developed under the leadership of Thorndike, Watson, Guthrie, Hull, Spence, Skinner, and others. The result has often been a picture that overemphasizes man's similarity with other animals, the emotional, unconscious, and irrational drives that direct his behavior, and the control to which he is susceptible. In contrast, Bruner's view of man as an information processor, thinker, and creator emphasizes both the rationality and the dignity of which human beings are capable. While both views are surely partially valid, the emphasis on human intellectual potential is crucially needed to round out our conception of man if it is to be realistic, particularly in these times of moon walks, genetic surgery, high speed digital computers, and the like. For this reason it is an honor and a pleasure to present at least some of Jerome S. Bruner's major ideas in this volume, for his work is paralleled by only a few in teaching us so much about human intellectual potential.

JEREMY M. ANGLIN

References

1. BARTLETT, F. C. 1932. *Remembering: a study in experimental and social psychology* Cambridge, Eng.: Cambridge University Press (paperback, 1968).
2. BRUNER, J. S. 1957. Going beyond the information given. In *Contemporary approaches to cognition,* ed. H. Gruber, K. R. Hammond, and R. Jesser. Cambridge, Mass.: Harvard University Press.
3. BRUNER, J. S. 1960. *The process of education.* Cambridge, Mass.: Harvard University Press.
4. BRUNER, J. S. 1962. *On knowing: essays for the left hand.* Cambridge, Mass.: Harvard University Press.
5. BRUNER, J. S. 1966. *Toward a theory of instruction.* Cambridge, Mass.: Harvard University Press (paperback, New York: Norton, 1968).
6. BRUNER, J. S. 1971. *The relevance of education.* New York: Norton.
7. BRUNER, J. S. 1968. *Processes of cognitive growth: infancy.* Heinz Werner Lecture Series, vol. 3. Worcester, Mass.: Clark University Press, with Barre.
8. BRUNER, J. S., and GOODMAN, C. C. 1947. Value and need as organizing factors in perception. *Journal of Abnormal and Social Psychology* 42:33–44.
9. BRUNER, J. S.; GOODNOW, J. J.; and AUSTIN, G. A. 1956. *A study of thinking.* New York: Wiley.
10. BRUNER, J. S.; OLVER, R. R.; GREENFIELD, P. M.; et al. 1966. *Studies in cognitive growth.* New York: Wiley.
11. DEWEY, J. 1964. *Democracy and education.* New York: Macmillan.
12. LASHLEY, K. 1951. The problem of serial order in behavior. In *Cerebral mechanisms in behavior: the Hixon symposium,* ed. L. A. Jeffress, pp. 112–46. New York: Wiley.

13. PIAGET, J. 1952. *The child's conception of number.* New York: Humanities Press.
14. PIAGET, J. 1967. *On the development of memory and identity.* Heinz Werner Lecture Series, vol. 2, Worcester, Mass.: Clark University Press, with Barre.
15. SINCLAIR DE ZWART, H. 1966. *Acquisition du langage et developpment de la pensee.* Paris: Dunod.
16. VYGOTSKY, L. S. 1962. *Thought and language.* 2d. and trans. E. Hanfmann and G. Vakar. Cambridge, Mass.: M.I.T. Press, and New York: Wiley.
17. WERNER, H. 1948. *Comparative psychology of mental development.* Rev. ed. Chicago: Follett.

I

PERCEPTION

Introduction

Jerome Bruner was one of the chief architects of a tradition in the study of perceptual identification that came to be called the New Look in perception. His approach, illustrated by the articles in this section, diverged from more traditional approaches to the study of perception in at least three ways. First, a basic tenet of the work of Bruner, his collaborator Leo Postman, and their fellow conspirators, Gardner Murphy, Nevitt Sanford, Muzafer Sherif, George Klein, and others is that perception is not an isolated, independent system but rather one that interacts with a host of other psychological systems. Perception, according to this view, is not only a product of autochthonous or stimulus determinants but also of experiential, motivational, personal, and social factors as well. Second, in the tradition of Egon Brunswik (1), Bruner has underlined the functional nature of perception. The perceiver is not seen as a passive and indifferent organism but rather as one who actively selects information, forms perceptual hypotheses, and on occasion distorts the input in the service of reducing surprise and of attaining valued objects. Third, Bruner has argued that perception is an activity that is fundamentally of the same nature as concept attainment and the other higher mental processes. Thus perception can be viewed as an act of categorization which, though possibly silent or unconscious, is based upon an inferential leap from cue to class identity and which appears to be the product of a strategy comprised of a series of decisions.

In certain respects, Bruner's description of perception is quite similar to the analysis-by-synthesis model that has been gaining credibility as a theory of pattern recognition (for instance, Neisser, 2), although it is couched in somewhat different terms. In both there is explicit rejection of a model based on template matching in favor of one that is more properly constructive. And both involve an iterative process comprised of two essential steps: an inferential leap from some of the features of an object to a category or hypothesis, and a confirmation check in which the category or hypothesis is tested against additional properties of the object. In the first article of this section, "On Perceptual Readiness," Bruner articulates his theory of perceptual recognition in a way that stresses the underlying similarity between perceptual inference and the more traditional cognitive processes to be considered in the next section. He goes on to a treatment of the stages involved in the decision sequence leading to perceptual categorization, then to a discussion of certain mechanisms presumed to mediate perceptual readiness, and, finally, to a consideration of the determinants of nonveridical perception.

The four research articles that follow have been chosen from dozens of possible candidates as best illustrating the empirical foundations upon which such theoretical conjectures are based. "Value and Need as Organizing Factors in Perception" by Bruner and Goodman was one of the first studies in the tradition of the New Look. In it the authors outline a program of research which would be concerned with the behavioral determinants of perceptual recognition and they launch their program by describing a first and particularly influential experiment in the field. They also introduce the notion of a perceptual hypothesis to account for the selective and biased nature of perceptual recognition. The next three articles are similar in that they all point to the significance of past experience as a determinant of such perceptual hypotheses. "Familiarity of Letter Sequences and Tachistoscopic Identification" by Miller, Bruner, and Postman is important because it demonstrated the role of familiarity in the recognition of letter sequences and because it identified the rather vague notion of context with the precisely defined concept of redundancy, thereby creating a link between work in perception and information theory. In "On the Perception of Incongruity: A Paradigm," by Bruner and Postman, the recognition threshold for trick playing cards with suit and color reversed is seen to be markedly higher than the threshold for normal cards. Moreover, an initial identification of an incongruity is seen to facilitate subsequent such identifications. In "Interference in Visual Recognition," by Bruner and Potter, experience in a recognition task is also seen to affect later performance. Subjects were presented blurred pictures of common objects which were gradually brought into focus. Identification was found to be delayed for blurred pictures and, the greater the initial blur, the more delayed the recognition.

As mentioned above, these four studies corroborate a theory that acknowledges the role of hypotheses in perception. Such a theory had, in fact, been described by Bruner as early as 1950 in his article "Personality Dynamics and the Process of Perceiving." Although it was written before many pertinent studies had been conducted or even conceived, it still serves well as a theoretical interpretation of a great deal of research in perceptual recognition. We have chosen to supplement this theoretical article with a general article, "The Functions of Perceiving: New Look Retrospect," by Bruner and Klein, which acknowledges certain oversimplifications found in and confusions caused by earlier research; which relates this kind of work to the classical approach to perception, to the study of attention, to neurophysiology, and to ethology; and which discusses certain areas of conflict that have plagued those who have grappled with the theoretical implications of the New Look.

References

1. BRUNSWIK, E. 1947. *Systematic and representative design of psychological experiments*. Berkeley: University of California Press.
2. NEISSER, U. 1967. *Cognitive psychology*. New York: Appleton-Century-Crofts.

1

On Perceptual Readiness [*]

Perception involves an act of categorization. Put in terms of the antecedent and subsequent conditions from which we make our inferences, we stimulate an organism with some appropriate input and he responds by referring the input to some class of things or events. "That is an orange," he states, or he presses a lever that he has been tuned to press when the object that he perceives is an orange. On the basis of certain defining or criterial attributes in the input—usually called cues although they should be called clues (35)—there is a selective placing of the input in one category of identity rather than another. The category need not be elaborate: A sound, a touch, a pain are also examples of categorized inputs. The use of cues in inferring the categorial identity of a perceived object, most recently treated by Bruner, Goodnow, and Austin (9) and by Binder (4), is as much a feature of perception as the sensory stuff from which percepts are made. What is interesting about the nature of the inference from cue to identity in perception is that it is in no sense different from other kinds of categorial inferences based on defining attributes. "That thing is round and

[*] Jerome S. Bruner, "On Perceptual Readiness" *Psychological Review,* Vol. 64, 1957, pp. 123–152. Copyright 1957 by the American Psychological Association, and reproduced by permission of the publisher.

The present paper was prepared with the invaluable assistance of Michael Wallach. I also benefited from the comments of W. C. H. Prentice, Karl Pribram, and M. E. Bitterman, and from various associates at Princeton University, Kansas University, and the University of Michigan, where versions of this paper were presented.

nubbly in texture and orange in color and of such-and-such size—therefore an orange; let me now test its other properties to be sure." In terms of process, this course of events is no different from the more abstract task of looking at a number, determining that it is divisible only by itself and unity, and thereupon categorizing it in the class of prime numbers. So at the outset, it is evident that one of the principal characteristics of perceiving is a characteristic of cognition generally. There is no reason to assume that the laws governing inferences of this kind are discontinuous as one moves from perceptual to more conceptual activities. In no sense need the process be conscious or deliberate. A theory of perception, we assert, needs a mechanism capable of inference and categorizing as much as one is needed in a theory of cognition.

Let it be plain that no claim is being made for the utter indistinguishability of perceptual and more conceptual inferences. In the first place, the former appear to be notably less docile or reversible than the latter. I may know that the Ames distorted room that looks so rectangular is indeed distorted, but unless conflicting cues are put into the situation, as in experiments to be discussed later, the room still looks rectangular. So, too, with such compelling illusions as the Müller-Lyer: In spite of knowledge to the contrary, the line with the extended arrowheads looks longer than the equal-length line with arrowheads inclined inward. But these differences, interesting in themselves, must not lead us to overlook the common feature of inference underlying so much of cognitive activity.

Is what we have said a denial of the classic doctrine of sense-data? Surely, one may argue (and Hebb [36] has done so effectively) that there must be certain forms of primitive organization within the perceptual field that make possible the differential use of cues in identity categorizing. Both logically and psychologically the point is evident. Yet it seems to me foolish and unnecessary to assume that the sensory stuff on which higher-order categorizations are based is, if you will, of a different sensory order than more evolved identities with which our perceptual world is normally peopled. To argue otherwise is to be forced into the contradictions of Locke's distinction between primary and secondary qualities in perception. The rather bold assumption that we shall make at the outset is that all perceptual experience is necessarily the end product of a categorization process.

And this for two reasons. The first is that all perception is generic, in the sense that whatever is perceived is placed in and achieves its meaning from a class of percepts with which it is grouped. To be sure, in each thing we encounter there is an aspect of uniqueness, but the uniqueness inheres in deviation from the class to which an object is assigned. Analytically, let it be noted, one may make a distinction, as Gestalt theorists have, between a pure stimulus process and the interaction of that stimulus process with an appropriate memory trace—the latter presumably resulting in a percept that has an identity. If indeed there is a pure stimulus process, it is doubt-ful indeed that it is ever represented in perception bereft of identity char-acteristics. The phenomenon of a completely unplaceable object or event or sensation—even unplaceable with respect to modality—is sufficiently far from experience to be uncanny. Categorization of an object or event—placing it or giving it identity—can be likened to what in set theory is the placement of an element from a universe in a subset of that universe of items on the basis of such ordered dimensional pairs, triples, or *n*-tuples as man-woman, mesomorph-endomorph-ectomorph, or height to the nearest inch. In short, when one specifies something more than that an element or object belongs to a universe, and that it belongs in a subset of the universe, one has categorized the element or object. The categorization can be as in-tersecting as "this is a quartz crystal goblet fashioned in Denmark," or as simple as "this is a glassy thing." So long as an operation assigns an input to a subset, it is an act of categorization.

More serious, although it is only a logical issue, is the question of how one could communicate or make public the presence of a nongeneric or completely unique perceptual experience. Neither language nor the tuning that one could give an organism to direct any other form of overt response could provide an account, save in generic or categorial terms. If perceptual experience is ever had raw, that is, free of categorial identity, it is doomed to be a gem, serene, locked in the silence of private experience.

Various writers, among them Gibson (26), Wallach (83), and Pratt (69), have proposed that we make a sharp distinction between the class of per-ceptual phenomena that have to do with the identity or object-meaning of things and the attributive or sensory world from which we derive our cues for inferring identities. Gibson, like Titchener (78) before him, urges a distinction between the visual field and the visual world; the former the world of attributive sense impressions, the latter of objects and things and events. Pratt urges that motivation and set and past experience may affect the things of the visual world but not the stuff of the visual field. And Wallach, too, reflects this ancient tradition of his Gestalt forebears by urg-ing the distinction between a pure stimulus process and the stimulus pro-cess interacting with a memory trace of past experience with which it has made a neural contact on the basis of similarity. The former is the stuff of perception; the latter the finished percept. From shirtsleeves to shirtsleeves in three generations: We are back with the founding and founded content of the pre-Gestalt Gestalters. If one is to study the visual field freed of the things of the visual world, it becomes necessary—as Wallach implies—to free oneself of the stimulus error: dealing with a percept not as an object or as a thing with identity, but as a magnitude or a brightness or a hue or a shape to be matched against a variable test patch.

If we have implied that categorizing is often a silent or unconscious pro-cess, that we do not experience a going-from-no-identity to an arrival-at-identity, but that the first hallmark of any perception is some form of identity, this does not free us of the responsibility of inquiring into the origin of categories. Certainly, Hebb (36) is correct in asserting, like Immanuel Kant, that certain primitive unities or identities within perception must be innate or autochthonous and not learned. The primitive capacity to categorize things from background is very likely one such; and so, too, the capacity to distinguish events in one modality from those in others— although the phenomena of synesthesia would suggest that this is not so complete a juncture as it might seem; for example, von Hornbostel (39). The sound of a buzz saw does rise and fall phenomenally as one switches room illumination on and off. The full repertory of innate categories—a favorite topic for philosophical debate in the nineteenth century—is a topic on which perhaps too much ink and too little empirical effort have been spilled. Motion, causation, intention, identity, equivalence, time, and space, it may be persuasively argued, are categories that must have some primitive counterpart in the neonate. And it may well be, as Piaget (65) implies, that certain primitive capacities to categorize in particular ways depend upon the existence of still more primitive ones. To identify something as having caused something else requires, first, the existence of an identity category such that the two things involved each may conserve identity in the process of cause producing effect. Primitive or unlearned categories—a matter of much concern to such students of instinctive behavior as Lashley (51) and Tinbergen (77)—remain to be explicated. In what follows we shall rather cavalierly take them for granted. As to the development of more elaborated categories in terms of which objects are placed or identified, it involves the process of learning how to isolate, weigh, and use criterial attribute values, or cues for grouping objects in equivalence classes. It is only as mysterious, but no more so, than the learning of any differential discrimination, and we shall have occasion to revisit the problem later.

A second feature of perception, beyond its seemingly categorial and inferential nature, is that it can be described as varyingly veridical. This is what has classically been called the representative function of perception: What is perceived is somehow a representation of the external world—a metaphysical hodgepodge of a statement, but one which we somehow manage to understand in spite of its confusion. We have long since given up simulacral theories of representation. What we generally mean when we speak of representation or veridicality is that perception is predictive in varying degrees. That is to say, the object that we see can also be felt and smelled and there will somehow be a match or a congruity between what we see, feel and smell. Or, to paraphrase a younger Bertrand Russell, what we see will turn out to be the same thing should we take a closer look at it. Or, in still different terms, the categorial placement of the object leads to appropriate consequences in terms of later behavior directed toward the perceived object: It appears as an apple, and indeed it keeps the doctor away if consumed once a day.

Let it be said that philosophers, and notably the pragmatist C. S. Peirce, have been urging such a view for more years than psychologists have taken their urgings seriously. The meaning of a proposition, as Peirce noted in his famous essay on the pragmatic theory of meaning (63), is the set of hypothetical statements one can make about attributes or consequences related to that proposition. "Let us ask what we mean by calling a thing *hard*. Evidently, that it will not be scratched by many other substances" (White, 84). The meaning of a thing, thus, is the placement of an object in a network of hypothetical inference concerning its other observable properties, its effects, and so on.

All of this suggests that veridicality is not so much a matter of representation as it is a matter of what I shall call "model building." In learning to perceive, we are learning the relations that exist between the properties of objects and events that we encounter, learning appropriate categories and category systems, learning to predict and to check what goes with what. A simple example illustrates the point. I present for tachistoscopic recognition two nonsense words, one a zero-order approximation to English constructed according to Shannon's rules, the other a fourth-order approximation: *YRULPZOC* and *VERNALIT*. At 500 milliseconds of exposure, one perceives correctly and in their proper place about 48 per cent of the letters in zero-order words, and about 93 per cent of the letters in fourth-order words. In terms of the amount of information transmitted by these letter arrays, that is, correcting them for redundancy, the subject is actually receiving the same informational input. The difference in reportable perception is a function of the fact that the individual has learned the transitional probability model of what goes with what in English writing. We say that perception in one case is more veridical than in the other—the difference between 93 per cent correct as contrasted with 48 per cent. What we mean is that the model of English with which the individual is working corresponds to the actual events that occur in English, and that if the stimulus input does not conform to the model, the resulting perception will be less veridical. Now let us drop the image of the model and adopt a more sensible terminology. Perceiving accurately under substandard conditions consists in being able to refer stimulus inputs to appropriate coding systems; where the information is fragmentary, one reads the missing properties of the stimulus input from the code to which part of the input has been referred. If the coding system applied does not match the input, what we read off from the coding system will lead to error and nonveridical perception. I would propose that perceptual learning consists not in making finer and finer discriminations, as the Gibsons (27) would have us believe; but that it consists rather in the learning of appropriate modes of coding an environment in terms of its object character, connectedness, or redundancy, and then in allocating stimulus inputs to appropriate categorial coding systems.

The reader will properly ask, as Prentice (70) has, whether the notion of perceptual representation set forth here is appropriate to anything other than situations where the nature of the percept is not clear—perceptual representation under peripheral viewing conditions, in tachistoscopes, under extreme fatigue. If I am given a very good look at an object, under full illumination and with all the viewing time necessary, and end by calling it an orange, is this a different process from one in which the same object is flashed for a millisecond or two on the periphery of my retina with poor illumination? In the first and quite rare case, the cues permitting the identification of the object are superabundant and the inferential mechanism operates with high probability relationships between cues and identities. In the latter, it is less so. The difference is of degree. What I am trying to say is that under any conditions of perception, what is achieved by the perceiver is the categorization of an object or sensory event in terms of more or less abundant and reliable cues. Representation consists in knowing how to utilize cues with reference to a system of categories. It also depends upon the creation of a system of categories-in-relationship that fit the nature of the world in which the person must live. In fine, adequate perceptual representation involves the learning of appropriate categories, the learning of cues useful in placing objects appropriately in such systems of categories, and the learning of what objects are likely to occur in the environment, a matter to which we will turn later.

We have neglected one important feature of perceptual representation in our discussion: representation in perception of the space-time-intensity conditions of the external world. Perceptual magnitudes correspond in some degree to the metrical properties of the physical world that we infer from the nature of our perception. That is to say, when one line looks longer than another, it is likely to be longer as measured by the ruler. There are constant errors and sampling errors in such sensory representation, but on the whole there is enough isomorphism between perceiving without aids (psychology) and perceiving with aids (physics) to make the matter perenially interesting.

Is this form of representation subject to the kinds of considerations we have been passing in review? Does it depend upon categorizing activities and upon the construction of an adequate system of categories against which stimulus inputs can be matched? There is probably one condition where perceptual acts are relatively free of such influences, and that is in the task of discriminating simultaneously presented stimuli as alike or different—provided we do not count the tuning of the organism that leads one to base his judgment on one rather than another feature of the two stimuli. Ask the person to deal with one stimulus at a time, to array it in terms of some magnitude scale, and immediately one is back in the familiar territory of inferential categorizing. Prentice, in his able defense of formalism in the study of perception (70), seems to assume that there is a special status attached to perceptual research that limits the set of the observer to simple binary decisions of like and different or present and absent, as well as to research that provides the subject with optimal stimulus conditions. Graham (31) has expressed the credo that no perceptual laws will be proper or pure laws unless we reduce perceptual experimentation to the kinds of operations used in the method of constant stimuli.

There was at one time a justification for such a claim on the ground that such is the best strategy for getting at the sensory-physiological processes that underlie perception. As we shall see in a later section, current work in neurophysiology brings this contention into serious doubt. In any case, the point must be made that many of the most interesting phenomena in sensory perception are precisely those that have been uncovered by departing from the rigid purism of the method of constants. I have in mind such pioneering studies as those of Stevens on sensory scales, where the organism is treated as an instrument whose sensory categorizations and scalar orderings are the specific object of study (74). Add to this the advances made by Helson on adaptation level (37) and by Volkmann on the anchoring of sensory scales (82)—both using the "sloppy" method of single stimuli—and one realizes that the nature of representation in perception of magnitudes is very much subject to categorizing processes and to perceptual readiness as this is affected by subjective estimates of the likelihood of occurrence of sensory events of different magnitudes. Indeed, Helson's law of adaptation level states that the subjective magnitude of a singly presented stimulus depends upon the weighted geometric mean of the series of stimuli that the subject has worked with; and the ingenious experiments of Donald Brown (7) have indicated that this adaptation level is influenced only by those stimuli that the subject considers to be within the category of objects being considered. Ask the subject to move a weight from one side of the table to the other with the excuse that it is cluttering up the table, and the weight does not serve as an anchor to the series, although it will show a discernible effect if it is directly included in the series being judged. In short, the category systems that are utilized in arraying magnitudes are also affected by the requirement of matching one's model of the world to the actual events that are occurring—even if the categories be no more complicated than heavy, medium, and light.

The work of Stevens (75) on "the direct estimation of sensory magnitudes" highlights the manner in which veridicality in sensory judgment depends upon the prior learning of an adequate category set in terms of which sensory input may be ordered. Subjects are presented a standard tone of 1,000 cycles per second at 80 decibels sound-pressure level and are told that the value of this loudness is 10. Nine variable loudnesses all of the 1,000 cycles per second are then presented, varying 70 decibels on either side of the standard, each one at a time being paired with the standard. "If the standard is called 10, what would you call the variable? Use whatever numbers seem to you appropriate—fractions, decimals, or whole numbers." If one then compares the categorial judgments made with the sound-pressure level of the various tones presented, using a log-log plot (log of the magnitude estimation against log of sound-pressure level), the resulting function is a straight line, described by the empirical formula $L = kI^{0.3}$, where L is loudness and I intensity. In short, categorial sorting of sensory magnitudes provides one with a mapping or representation of physical intensity. There are, to be sure, many problems connected with such a procedure, but the point remains: The magnitude categories in terms of which we scale sensory events represent a good fit to the physical characteristics of the world. Call this veridicality if you wish—although I do not see what is gained thereby; yet, whatever one calls it, one must not lose sight of the fact that the judgments made are predictive of other features of the sensory inputs. Given the empirical conversion formula, one can predict from categorial judgment to physical meter readings.

To summarize, we have proposed that perception is a process of categorization in which organisms move inferentially from cues to categorial identity and that in many cases, as Helmholtz long ago suggested, the process is a silent one. If you will, the inference is often an unconscious one. Moreover, the results of such categorizations are representational in nature: They represent with varying degrees of predictive veridicality the nature of the physical world in which the organism operates. By predictive veridicality, I mean simply that perceptual categorization of an object or event permits one to go beyond the properties of the object or event perceived to a prediction of other properties of the object not yet tested. The more adequate the category systems constructed for coding environmental events in this way, the greater the predictive veridicality that results.

Doubtless, the reader will think of any number of examples of perceptual phenomena not covered by the simple picture we have drawn. Yet a great many of the classic phenomena are covered—psychophysical judgment, constancy, perceptual identification, perceptual learning, and so on. This will become clearer in the following sections. What must now be dealt with are the phenomena having to do with selectivity: attention, set, and the like.

Cue Utilization and Category Accessibility

A fruitful way of thinking of the nature of perceptual readiness is in terms of the accessibility of categories for use in coding or identifying environmental events. Accessibility is a heuristic concept and it may be defined in terms of a set of measures. Conceive of a person who is perceptually ready to encounter a certain object, an apple let us say. How he happens to be in this state we shall consider later. We measure the accessibility of the category apples by the amount of stimulus input of a certain pattern necessary to evoke the perceptual response "there is an apple," or some other standardized response. We can state the minimum input required for such categorization by having our observer operate with two response categories, yes and no, with the likelihood of occurrence of apples and nonapples at 50:50, or by using any other definition of maximum readiness that one wishes to employ. The greater the accessibility of a category, (*a*) the less the input necessary for categorization to occur in terms of this category, (*b*) the wider the range of input characteristics that will be accepted as fitting the category in question, (*c*) the more likely that categories that provide a better or equally good fit for the input will be masked. To put it in more ordinary language: Apples will be more easily and swiftly recognized; a wider range of things will be identified or misidentified as apples; and, in consequence, the correct or best-fitting identity of these other inputs will be masked. This is what is intended by accessibility.

Obviously, categories are not isolated. One has a category apples, to be sure, but it is embedded by past learning in a network of categories: "An apple a day keeps the doctor away" is one such category system. So, too, is "apples are fruits" and other placements of an object in a general classification scheme. Predictive systems are of the same order: for instance, "The apple will rot if not refrigerated." We have spoken of these systems before as the meaning of an object. We mention them again here to indicate that, though we speak analytically of separate or isolated categories as being accessible to inputs, it is quite obvious that category systems vary in accessibility as a whole.

It follows from what has just been said that the most appropriate pattern of readiness at any given moment would be that one which would lead, on the average, to the most veridical guess about the nature of the world around one at the moment—the best guess here being construed, of course, as a response in the absence of the necessary stimulus input. And it follows from this that the most ready perceiver would then have the best chances of estimating situations most adequately and planning accordingly. It is in this general sense that the ready perceiver who can proceed with fairly minimal inputs is also in a position to use his cognitive readiness not only for perceiving what is before him but in foreseeing what is likely to be before him. We shall return to this point shortly.

We must turn now to the question of cue utilization, the strategies in terms of which inferences are made (by the nervous system, of course) from cue to category and thence to other cues. I prefer to use the term *strategy* for several reasons. Perceiving, since it involves inference, rests upon a decision process, as Brunswik (17), Tanner and Swets (76) and others have pointed out. Even in the simplest threshold-measurement test, the subject has the task of deciding whether what he is seeing or hearing is noise only or signal-plus-noise. Given a set of cues, however presented, my nervous system must decide whether the thing is an airplane or a sea gull, a red or a green, or whatever.

There appears, moreover, to be a sequence of such decisions involved in categorizing an object or event. A common-sense example will make this clear. I look across to the mantel opposite my desk and see a rectangular object lying on it. If I continue this pursuit, subsequent decisions are to be made: Is it the block of plastic I purchased for some apparatus or is it a book? In the dim light it can be either. I remember that the plastic is downstairs in one of the experimental rooms: The object *is* a book now, and I search for further cues on its dark red surface. I see what I think is some gold: It is a McGraw-Hill book, probably G. A. Miller's *Language and Communication* that I had been using late this afternoon. If you will, the process is a bracketing one, a gradual narrowing of the category placement of the object.

Let us attempt to analyze the various stages in such a decision sequence:

Primitive Categorization. Before any more elaborate inferential activity can occur, there must be a first, silent process that results in the perceptual isolation of an object or an event with certain characteristic qualities. Whether this is an innate process or one depending upon the prior construction of a cell-assembly, in the manner of Hebb (36), need not concern us. What is required simply is that an environmental event has been perceptually isolated and that the event is marked by certain spatiotemporal-qualitative characteristics. The event may have no more meaning than that it is an object, a sound, or a movement.

Cue Search. In highly practiced cases or in cases of high cue-category probability linkage, a second process of more precise placement based on additional cues may be equally silent or unconscious. An object is seen with phenomenal immediacy as a book or an ash tray. In such instances there is usually a good fit between the specifications of a category and the nature of the cues impinging on the organism—although fit and probability of linkage may stand in a vicarious relation to each other. Where the fit to accessible categories is not precise, or when the linkage between cue and category is low in probability in the past experience of the organism, the conscious experience of cue searching occurs. "What is that thing?" Here, one is scanning the environment for data in order to find cues that permit a more precise placement of the object. Under these circumstances, the organism is open to maximum stimulation, in a manner described below.

Confirmation Check. When a tentative categorization has occurred following cue search, cue search changes. The openness to stimulation decreases

sharply in the sense that now, a tentative placement of identity having occurred, the search is narrowed for additional confirmatory cues to check
this placement. It is this feature of perceptual identification that Woodworth, (85) in his paper, "Reenforcement of Perception," speaks of as
"trial-and-check." We shall speak of a selective gating process coming into
operation in this stage with the effect of reducing the effective input of
stimulation not relevant to the confirmatory process.

Confirmation Completion.   The last stage in the process of perceptual identification is a completion, marked by termination of cue searching. It is
characteristic of this state that openness to additional cues is drastically reduced, and incongruent cues are either normalized or gated out. Experiments on the perception of incongruity (14),[1] error (67), and the like (15),
suggest that once an object has been categorized in a high-probability,
good-fit category, the threshold for recognizing cues contrary to this categorization increases by almost an order of magnitude.

The question of fit between cue and category specification brings us to the
key problem of the nature of categories. By a category we mean a rule for
classing objects as equivalent. The rule specifies the following about the instances that are to be comprised in the category:
    a. The properties or criterial attribute values required of an instance to
be coded in a given class
    b. The manner in which such attribute values are to be combined in
making an inference from properties to category membership: whether
conjunctively (a_i and b_i), relationally (a_i bears a certain relation to b_i),
or disjunctively (a_i or b_i)
    c. The weight assigned various properties in making an inference from
properties to category membership
    d. The acceptance limits within which properties must fall to be cri-
terial; that is to say, from what range of attribute values a_i b_i . . . k_i
may be drawn.

When we speak of rules, again it should be made clear that conscious rules
are not intended. These are the rules that govern the operation of a categorizing mechanism.
    The likelihood that a sensory input will be categorized in terms of a
given category is not only a matter of fit between sensory input and category specifications, it depends also on the accessibility of a category. To
put the matter in an oversimplified way, given a sensory input with equally

[1] See pp. 68–83.

good fit to two nonoverlapping categories, the more accessible of the two categories would capture the input. It is in this sense that mention was earlier made about the vicarious relationship between fit and accessibility.

We have already noted that the accessibility of categories reflects the learned probabilities of occurrence of events in the person's world. The more frequently in a given context instances of a given category occur, the greater the accessibility of the category. Operationally, this means that less stimulus input will be required for the instance or event to be categorized in terms of a frequently used category. In general, the type of probability we are referring to is not absolute probability of occurrence where each event that occurs is independent of each other. Such independence is rare in the environment. Rather, the principal form of probability learning affecting category accessibility is the learning of contingent or transitional probabilities—the redundant structure of the environment. That either the absolute or the contingent probability of events makes a crucial difference in determining ease of perceptual identification is readily supported by research findings: in the former case by studies like those of Howes (40) and Solomon and Postman (73) and in the latter by the work of Miller, Heise, and Lichten (62) and Miller, Bruner, and Postman (61).[2]

But the organism, to operate adequately, must not only be ready for likely events in the environment, the better to represent them and in order to perceive them quickly and without undue cognitive strain; it must also be able to search out unlikely objects and events essential to its maintenance and the pursuit of its enterprises. If I am walking the streets of a strange city and find myself hungry, I must be able to look for restaurants regardless of their likelihood of occurrence in the environment where I now find myself. In short the accessibility of categories I employ for identifying the objects of the world around me must not only reflect the environmental probabilities of objects that fit these categories, but also reflect the search requirements imposed by my needs, my ongoing activities, my defenses, and so forth. And for effective search behavior to occur, the pattern of perceptual readiness during search must be realistic, tempered by what one is likely to find in one's perceptual world at that time and at that place as well as by what one seeks to find.

Let me summarize our considerations about the general properties of perception with a few propositions. The first is that perception is a decision process. Whatever the nature of the task set, the perceiver or his nervous system decides that a thing perceived is one thing and not another. A line is longer or shorter than a standard, a particular object is a snake and not a fallen branch, the incomplete word *l*ve* in the context men l*ve women is the word *love* and not *live*.

The second proposition is that the decision process involves the utiliza-

[2] See pp. 57–67.

tion of discriminatory cues, as do all decision processes. That is to say, the properties of stimulus inputs make it possible to sort these inputs into categories of best fit.

Third, the cue utilization process involves the operation of inference. Going from cue to an inference of identity is probably the most ubiquitous and primitive cognitive activity. The utilization of inference presupposes the learning of environmental probabilities and invariances relating cues to cues, and cues to behavioral consequences. Cue utilization involves various stages: a primitive step of isolating an object or event from the flux of environmental stimulation, stages of cue searching where the task is to find cues that can be fitted to available category specifications, a tentative categorization with more search for confirming cues, and final categorization when cue searching is severely reduced.

Fourth, a category may be regarded as a set of specifications regarding what events will be grouped as equivalent—rules respecting the nature of criterial cues required, the manner of their combining, their inferential weight, and the acceptance limits of their variability.

Fifth, categories vary in terms of their accessibility, the readiness with which a stimulus input with given properties will be coded or identified in terms of a category. The relative accessibility of categories and systems of categories seems to depend upon two factors: the expectancies of the person with regard to the likelihood of events to be encountered in the environment, and the search requirements imposed on the organism by his needs and his ongoing enterprises. To use the functionalist's language, perceptual readiness or accessibility serves two functions: to minimize the surprise value of the environment by matching category accessibility to the probabilities of events in the world about one, and to maximize the attainment of sought-after objects and events.

Veridical perception, so our sixth proposition would run, consists of the coding of stimulus inputs in appropriate categories such that one may go from cue to categorial identification, and thence to the correct inference or prediction of other properties of the object so categorized. Thus, veridical perception requires the learning of categories and category systems appropriate to the events and objects with which the person has commerce in the physical world. When we speak of the representative function of perception, we speak of the adequacy of the categorizing system of the individual in permitting him to infer the nature of events and to go beyond them to the correct prediction of other events.

Seventh, under less than optimal conditions, perception will be veridical in the degree to which the accessibility of categorizing systems reflects the likelihood of occurrence of the events that the person will encounter. Where accessibility of categories reflects environmental probabilities, the organism is in the position of requiring less stimulus input, less redundancy of cues for the appropriate categorization of objects. In like vein, nonveridical perception will be systematic rather than random in its error insofar as it reflects the inappropriate readiness of the perceiver. The more inappropriate the readiness, the greater the input or redundancy of cues required for appropriate categorization to occur—where appropriate means that an input is coded in the category that yields more adequate subsequent predictions.

Mechanisms Mediating Perceptual Readiness

Having considered some of the most general characteristics of perceiving, particularly as these relate to the phenomena of perceptual readiness, we must turn next to a consideration of the kinds of mechanisms that mediate such phenomena. Four general types of mechanisms will be proposed: grouping and integration, access ordering, match-mismatch signaling, and gating. They will be described in such a form that they may be considered as prototypes of neural mechanisms and, where possible, neurophysiological counterparts will be described briefly. In 1949 Edward Tolman (79) proposed that the time was perhaps ripe for reconsidering the neural substrate of perception. Perhaps he was right, or perhaps even now the enterprise is somewhat premature. Yet, the body of perceptual data available makes it worthwhile to consider the kinds of mechanisms that will be required to deal with them. To use Hebb's engaging metaphor, it is worthwhile to build a bridge between neurophysiology and psychology provided we are anchored at both ends, even if the middle of the bridge is very shaky.

GROUPING AND INTEGRATION

It is with the neural basis of the categorizing process that Hebb's *Organization of Behavior* (36) is principally concerned. Little is served by recapitulating his proposals here, for chapters 4 and 5 of that book contain a concise account of the concepts of cell assembly and phase sequence, set forth with a clarity that permits one to distinguish what is neurophysiological fact and what speculation. In essence, Hebb's account attempts to provide an anatomical-physiological theory of how it is that we distinguish classes of events in the environment, and how we come to recognize new events as exemplars of the once-established classes. The theory seeks also to provide a mechanism for integration of sorting activity over time; the formation of phase sequences for the conservation of superordinate classes of events and superordinate sequences. Basically, it is an associational or an enrichment theory of perception at the neural level, requiring that established neural associations facilitate perception of events that have gone together before. The expectancies, the centrally induced facilitations that occur prior to the sensory process for which they are appropriate, are learned expectancies based on the existence of frequency integrators.

These frequency integrators may be neuroanatomical in the form of synaptic knobs, or they may be any process that has the effect of making activity in one locus of the brain increase or decrease the likelihood of activity in another. To be sure, Hebb's theory depends upon some broad assumptions about convergence of firing from area 17 outward, about synchronization of impulses, and about the manner in which reverberatory circuits can carry organization until the much slower process of anatomical change can take place. But this is minor in comparison with the stimulation provided by facing squarely the question of how the known facts of categorization and superordination in perception could be represented in the light of present knowledge.

While it is difficult indeed to propose a plausible neural mediator to account for category formation and the development of elaborated categorial systems (for instance, our knowledge of the relations between classes of events in the physical world which we manipulate in everyday life), it is less difficult to specify what such mechanisms must account for in perceptual behavior.

At the level of the individual category or cell assembly the phenomenon of object identity must be accounted for. Moreover, identity conservation or object constancy requires explanation in terms common with the explanation of identity. Experiments by Piaget (65) suggest that the capacity to maintain the phenomenal identity of an object undergoing change is the hard-won result of maturation and learning. In connection with the later discussion of gating processes, we shall have occasion to consider the manner in which, at different stages in cue utilization, the required fit between an input and a cell assembly changes.

Where integration is concerned there must be a process capable of conserving a record of the likely transitions and contingencies of the environment. The moment-to-moment programming of perceptual readiness depends upon such integrations. In short, the relation between classes of events is conserved in such a way as to be subject to change by learning. Several things can be guessed about integration processes. It is unlikely that it is a simple autocorrelation device. Clearly, the conceptions of transitional probabilities that are established in dealing with sequences of events show biases that no self-respecting autocorrelation computer would be likely to operate with. One of these is a strong and early tendency to treat events as nonindependent of each other over time. In the absence of evidence, or even in the presence of contrary evidence, humans—as their behavior has been observed in choice tasks, for instance, Estes (23), Goodnow (29)—treat random sequences of events as though they were governed by dependent probabilities. The spate of research on two-choice decision behavior has made us quite sharply aware of this characteristic of cognitive functioning. The typical pattern is the gambler's fallacy or, more properly, the negative recency effect. Given two equiprobable events whose occurrences are random, the repetition of one event progressively leads to the expectancy of the other. As in the elegant experiments of Jarvik (44) and Goodnow (29), the probability that a person will predict one of two events increases directly as a function of the number of repetitions of the other event. Such behavior persists over thousands of opportunities for testing, and it appears under a variety of testing conditions (9).

The second feature of sequential probability integration mechanisms is that, in establishing a conception of the probability with which events will occur, the typical human subject will bias his estimate in terms of desired or feared outcomes. As in the experiments of Marks (60) on children and of Irwin (41) on adults, the subjectively estimated probability of strongly desired events will be higher per previous encountered occurrence than the estimated likelihood of less-desired events. Quite clearly, then, the establishment of estimates depends upon more than frequency integrations biased by assumptions of nonindependence. The something more is a motivational or personality process; we shall have more to say about it in considering phenomena of so-called perceptual sensitization and perceptual defense.

ACCESS ORDERING

The term *accessibility* has been used in preceding pages to denote the ease or speed with which a given stimulus input is coded in terms of a given category under varying conditions of instruction, past learning, motivation, and so forth. It has been suggested, moreover, that two general sets of conditions affect accessibility: subjective probability estimates of the likelihood of a given event and certain kinds of search sets induced by needs and by a variety of other factors.

Let us consider a few relevant facts about perception. The first of these is that the threshold of recognition for stimuli presented by visual, auditory, or other means is not only a function of the time, intensity, or fittingness of the stimulus input, but also varies massively as a function of the number of alternatives for which the perceiver is set. The size of the expected array, to say it another way, increases the identification threshold for any item in the array. Typical examples of this general finding are contained in papers by Miller, Heise, and Lichten (62) and by Bruner, Miller, and Zimmerman (10). The actual shape of the function need not concern us, save that it is quite clear that it is not what one would expect from a simple binary system with a fixed channel capacity. What we are saying holds, of course, only for the case where the perceiver has learned that all the items in the expected array are (a) equiprobable and (b) independent, one of the other, in order of appearance.

The first hunch we may propose, then, about access-ordering mechanisms is that degree of accessibility of coding categories to stimulus inputs is related to regulation of the number of preactivated cell assemblies that are operative at the time of input. In an earlier paper (8),[3] in which I discussed factors that strengthen a hypothesis in the sense of making it more easily confirmable, I proposed that one of the major determinants of such strength was monopoly: Where one and only one hypothesis is operative with no competing alternatives, it tends to be more readily confirmable. It is the same general point that is being made here. Accessibility, then, must have something to do with the resolution of competing alternatives.

We may distinguish between two arrays of expected alternatives, each of the same size, on the basis of the bias that exists in terms of expected likelihood of occurrence of each alternative. If one could characterize the expected alternatives in terms of probability values, one could conceive of the array ranging in values from a figure approaching 1.0 at one extreme, to another approaching 0.0 at the other. The findings with respect to perceptual readiness for the alternatives represented in such an array are well known. For a constant-sized array, the greater the estimated likelihood of occurrence of an alternative, the more readily will the alternative be perceived or identified. This is known to be true for large arrays, such as the ensemble of known words in the English language, whose likelihood may be roughly judged by their frequency of occurrence in printed English (for instance, 40). It is not altogether clear that it is the case for arrays of expected alternatives that are within the so-called span of attention—less than seven or eight alternatives. That the principle holds for middling arrays of about 20 items has been shown by Solomon and Postman (73).

What is particularly interesting about change of accessibility, under conditions where estimates of the likelihood of occurrence of alternatives become biased, is that the biasing can be produced either by a gradual learning process akin to probability learning or by instruction. Thus, Bitterman and Kniffin (5), investigating recognition thresholds for taboo and neutral words, show that as the experiment progresses there is a gradual lowering of threshold for the taboo words as the subject comes to expect their occurrence. Bruner and Postman (14) [4] have similarly shown that repeated presentation of stimulus materials containing very low-probability incongruities leads to a marked decrease in threshold time required for recognizing the incongruous features. At the same time, both Cowen and Beier (20) and Postman and Crutchfield (68) have shown that, if a subject is forewarned that taboo words are going to be presented, his threshold for them will tend to be lower than for neutral words, whereas it will be higher if no instruction is given. In short, preactivation of cell assemblies —assuming for a moment that degree of preactivation is the mechanism that represents subjective estimates of likelihood of occurrence of an event —can be produced by gradual learning or quantally by instruction. More-

[3] See pp. 89–113.
[4] See pp. 68–83.

over, biasing may be produced by the nature of the situation in which the perceiver is operating. A study by Bruner and Minturn (11) illustrates the point. Subjects are presented at brief exposure a broken capital *B* with a small separation between the vertical and the curved component of the letter so that it may be perceived as a *B* or as a 13. The manner in which it is reported is determined by whether the subject has previously been presented with letters or with numbers. In short, expectancy of one or the other context preactivates a related array of categories or cell-assemblies, not just a single isolated one.

What the neural correlates of access ordering will look like is anybody's guess. Lashley (52) has remarked that, for all our searching, we have not located a specific memory trace—either in the form of a reverberatory circuit, a definite change in fiber size as proposed by J. Z. Young (88) and Eccles (21), a synaptic knob—in the manner of Lorente de No (57) or in any known form. To be sure, Penfield (64) has activated memories by punctate electrical stimulation of the cortex, but this is far from a definition of the neural properties of the trace. For the time being, one does better to deal in terms of the formal properties that a trace system must exhibit than to rest one's psychological model on any neurophysiological or anatomical conception of the memory trace.

And, quite clearly, one of the formal properties of a trace system is that its elements vary in accessibility to stimulus input with the kinds of conditions we have considered. It is instructive to note that when a theory of traces lacks this feature, it ceases to be useful in dealing with the wide range of perceptual categorizing phenomena of which we now know. Gestalt theory is a case in point. According to Köhler (48), a stimulus process finds its appropriate memory trace, resulting in identification of the stimulus process, on the basis of distinctive similarity between stimulus process and memory trace. The theory has been criticized, justly I think, for failing to specify the nature of this similarity save by saying that it is a neural isomorph of phenomenal similarity. But since similarity may be highly selective—two objects may be alike in color but different in dozens of other respects—there is obviously some tertium quid that determines the basis of similarity. More serious still is the inability of such a theory to deal with the increased likelihood of categorization in terms of particular traces as a function of changes in search set or subjective likelihood estimates. The Bruner-Minturn results would require that, as between two traces with which a stimulus process may make contact, each equally similar to the stimulus, the stimulus process will make contact with the one having a higher probability of being matched by environmental events. This is interesting, but it is far from the spirit of Gestalt theory.

MATCH-MISMATCH PROCESSES

One may readily conceive of and, indeed, build an apparatus that will accept or reject inputs on the basis of whether or not they fulfill certain specifications. Selfridge (71) has constructed a machine to read letters; Fry and Denes (24) have one that will discriminate various phonemes; and Uttley (80) has constructed one that, like Tinbergen's graylag geese, will recognize the flying silhouette of a predator hawk. All such machines have in common that they require a match between a stimulus input and various specifications required by the sorting mechanism of the machine.

In the examples just given there is no consequence generated by whether a given input fulfills the specifications required by the identifying machine. It fits or it does not fit. But now let us build in two other features. The first is that the machine emit a signal to indicate how close any given input comes to fulfilling the specifications required, either by indicating how many attributes the object has in common with the specifications or by indicating how far off the mark on any given attribute dimension a given input is. The second is that the machine do something on the basis of these signals; either increase sensitivity if an object is within a given distance of specifications for a closer look, or decrease it if the object is further than a certain amount from specifications, or stop registering further if the input fits.

In short, one can imagine a nervous system that emits all-or-none match-mismatch signals or graded match-mismatch signals; one can also imagine that these signals could then feed into an effector system to regulate activity relevant to continuing search behavior for a fitting object or to regulate other forms of activity. MacKay (59) has recently proposed such a model.

We must return for a moment to an earlier discussion. In the discussion of cue utilization, a distinction was made between three phases of openness in cue search. The first was one in which a given input was being scanned for its properties so as to place it in one of a relatively large set of possible alternative categories. Here one would register as many features of an object as possible. In a second stage, the input has been tentatively placed, and the search is limited to confirming or infirming criterial cues. Finally, with more definite placement, cue search is suspended and deviations from specification may even be normalized. It is for the regulation of such patterns of search or cue utilization that some mechanism such as match-mismatch signaling is postulated.

Let it be said that while match-mismatch signaling-effector systems are readily conceivable and readily constructed, there is no knowledge available as to how a system like the nervous system might effect such a process. That there is feedback all over the system is quite apparent from its detailed anatomy; and this is the process out of which a larger-scale system such as we have described would be constructed.

GATING PROCESSES

The picture thus far presented is of a conceptual nervous system with a massive afferent intake that manages somehow to sort inputs into appropriate assemblies of varying accessibility. It seems unlikely that this is the nature of the nervous system, that there should be no gating or monitoring of stimulus input short of what occurs at higher centers. It is with this more peripheral form of screening of inputs that we shall now be concerned.

It has long been known that the concept of the adequate stimulus could not simply be defined as a change in environmental energy sufficient to stimulate a receptor. For, quite evidently, a stimulus could be peripherally adequate in this sense and not be centrally adequate at all, either in eliciting electrical activity in the cortex or in producing a verbal report of a change in experience by the subject. Indeed, the very nature of such complex receptor surfaces as the retina argues against such a simple notion of adequate stimulus. For the reactivity of even a retinal cell at the fovea seems to be gated by the state of stimulation of neighboring cells. Thus, if cells A, B, and C lie next to each other in that order, stimulation of B suppresses the sensitivity of C. If A is now stimulated, B is suppressed and C is released or heightened in sensitivity. So, even at the level of the first synapse of a sensory system, there is a mediation outward, or gating, from internuncial to receptor cells that programs the nature of the input that can come into the sensory system. And, to be sure, there are many phenomena in perception itself that speak for this same kind of gating. When we are fixated upon the vase in the Rubin reversible figure, the background recedes, is less surfacy, and in general seems to provide a less centrally adequate form of sensory input. So, too, with the studies of Yokoyama (87) and Chapman (19) where subjects, set to report on one of several attributes of briefly presented stimuli, accomplished their selective task with a loss of ability to discriminate on the attributes for which they had not been set. We shall propose that such phenomena are very likely mediated by a gating process which filters input before it ever reaches the cortex.

There is now a growing body of neurophysiological evidence that part of this screening process is relegated to peripheral levels of the nervous system—even as far out as the second synapse of specialized sensory systems. In the past I have used the rather fanciful phrase that "perception acts sometimes as a welcoming committee and sometimes as a screening committee." It now appears that both these committees are closer to the entrance port than previously conceived.

Consider first the evidence of Kuffler and Hunt (50) on so simple a reflex as the stretch reflex of the biceps femoris muscle of the cat in an isolated spinal nerve-muscle preparation. Recall a little anatomy first. Muscle tissue contains special cells called spindles that are receptors in function, discharging with the contraction or stretch of the muscle in which they are embedded. The muscle itself is innervated by an efferent nerve trunk emerging from the ventral horn of the spinal cord and, in turn, an afferent nerve travels to the dorsal root of the spinal cord. According to the classical law of Bell and Magendie, the ventral root of the spinal cord carries efferent motor impulses down to the muscles, while the dorsal root carries sensory impulses up to the cord. It has been known for a long time that the presumed efferent nerve going to muscles carries fibers of large and of small diameter. In the early 1920s Eccles and Sherrington showed that the ventral nerve branch supplying the biceps femoris of the cat shows a "striking division of the fibers into two diameter groups" (49), one group centering around 5_μ in diameter, the other around $15·_\mu$ or 16_μ. The large fibers are, of course, fast conductors, the small ones slow. Leksell (55) has shown that stimulation of the slow-conducting smaller fibers did not cause detectable contractions or propagated muscle impulses. When the larger and fast-conducting fibers were stimulated, the usual motor-unit twitch occurred. Kuffler and Hunt (50) state that, in the lumbosacral outflow, about two-thirds of the fibers are of the large-diameter, fast-conduction type; the other third are of the small type that, in mammalia, are "ineffective in directly setting up significant muscular contraction." There has been much speculation about what these fibers are there for; the answer is now fairly clear. It is revolutionary in its implications and brings deeply into question both the classical Bell-Magendie law and the simplistic notion of the reflex arc on which so much of American learning theory is based.

It is this: The small fibers of the presumably motor trunk go to the spindle cells and the activity in these fibers serves to modulate or gate the receptivity of these specialized sensory endings. For example, if the small-diameter fibers are firing into the muscle spindle it may speed up the amount of firing from this cell into the afferent nerve that is produced by a given amount of stretch tension on the muscle. We need not go into detail here. It suffices to note that the state of presumed motor discharge does not simply innervate the muscle; it also regulates the amount and kind of kinesthetic sensory discharge that the sensory cells in the muscle will send back to the central nervous system. Instead of thinking of a stimulus-response reflex arc, it becomes necessary, even at this peripheral level, to think of the efferent portion of the arc acting back on sensory receptors to change the nature of the stimulus that can get through.

Two additional pieces of evidence on gating mechanisms at higher levels of integration may be cited. Where vision is concerned, Granit (32) has recently shown that pupillary changes produced by the ciliary muscle of the eye create changes in the pattern of firing of the retina: Changes in muscular state work their way back through the nervous system into the visual system and back outward to the retina. There is also evidence of gating working from the visual system backward in the opposite direction: During binocular rivalry, the nondominant eye shows a less sensitive pupillary reflex than the dominant eye.

Finally, we may cite the evidence of Hernandez-Péon, Scherrer, and Jouvet (38) working in Magoun's laboratory, work confirmed by analogous findings of Galambos, Sheatz, and Vernier (28) at the Walter Reed Hospital. If one stimulates the cat with auditory clicks, it is possible to record an evoked spike potential from the cochlear nucleus. Repetition of the clicks leads to a gradual diminution of the evoked potential, as if the organism were adapting. It is quite extraordinary that such adaptation should be registered as far out peripherally as the cochlear nucleus, which is, after all, only the second synapse of the eighth nerve. Now, if the clicks are previously used as conditioned stimuli signaling shock, the diminution of the evoked potential no longer occurs upon repetition of the clicks. Evidence that the response from the brain is not being produced by the muscular activity produced by the click as a conditioned stimulus is provided by the fact that the same kind of effects are obtained from cats with temporarily induced muscular paralysis. Further, if one takes a cat whose cochlear nucleus is still firing upon click stimulation and introduces a mouse into its visual field, the clicks no longer evoke a spike potential. A fish odor or a shock to the paw has the same effect of inhibiting spike potentials at the cochlear nucleus, if these distracting stimuli occur concurrently with the click. Distraction or shifting of attention appears to work its way outward to the cochlear nucleus.[5]

Perhaps the foregoing account has been needlessly detailed on the side of neurophysiology. Yet, the interesting implications of the findings for perceptual theory make such an excursion worthwhile. That the nervous system accomplishes something like gating is quite clear, even without the neurophysiological evidence. The data of behavior are full of examples, and the phenomena of attention require some such mechanism to be explained. Indeed, it is quite clear that the nervous system must be capable of more selective gating than physiology has yet been able to discover. That is to say, there must be a filter somewhere in the cat's nervous system that will pass the squeak of the mouse in the Hernandez-Péon experiment but not the cough of the experimenter. It is to this problem that we turn now.

I would propose that one of the mechanisms operative in regulating search behavior is some sort of gating or filtering system. In the preceding section, it was proposed that the openness of the first stage of cue utilization, the selectivity of the second stage, and the closedness of the third stage were probably regulated by a match-mismatch mechanism. What may be proposed here is that the degree of openness or closedness to sensory input during different phases of cue utilization is likely effected by the kind of gating processes we have been considering. How these work in in-

---

[5] After the above was written, evidence was presented by Galambos indicating that efferently controlled inhibition operates as far out to the periphery as the hair cells of the organ of Corti and fibers carrying such inhibitory impulses were traced as far centrally as the superior olivary nucleus—not very far, but a start.

timate detail is far from known, yet the work of the fifties in neurophysiology seems to have drawn closer to an answer.

Having considered some general properties of perception and some possible mechanisms underlying these, we turn now to some selected problems in perception in order to explore the implications of what has thus far been proposed.

On Failure of Readiness

From the foregoing discussion, it is clear that veridical perception under viewing or listening conditions that are less than ideal depends upon a state of perceptual readiness that matches the probability of occurrence of events in the world of the perceiver. This is true, of course, only in a statistical sense. What is most likely to occur is not necessarily what will occur, and the perceiver whose readiness is well matched to the likelihoods of his environment may be duped. In Farquhar's handsome seventeenth-century phrase: "I cou'd be mighty foolish, and fancy myself mighty witty; reason still keeps its Throne—but it nods a little, that's all." The only assurance against the nodding of reason or probability, under the circumstances, is the maintenance of a flexibility of readiness, an ability to permit one's hypotheses about what it is that is to be perceptually encountered to be easily infirmed by sensory input. But this is a topic for later.

There appear to be two antidotes to nonveridical perception, two ways of overcoming inappropriate perceptual readinesses. The one is a re-education of the misperceiver's expectancies concerning the events he is to encounter. The other is the constant close look. If the re-education succeeds in producing a better match between internal expectancies and external event-probabilities, the danger of misperception under hurried or substandard conditions of perceiving is lessened. But the matter of re-educating perceptual expectancies is complex. For where consequences are grave, expectancy concerning what may be encountered does not change easily, even with continued opportunity to test the environment. In this concluding section we shall consider some of the factors that contribute to states of perceptual unreadiness that either fail to match the likelihood of environmental events or fail to reflect the requirements of adjustment or both.

Before turning to this task, a word is in order about the constant close look as an antidote to inappropriate perceptual readiness. There is for every category of objects that has been established in the organism a stimulus input of sufficient duration and cue redundancy such that, if the stimulus input fits the specifications of the category, it will eventually be correctly perceived as an exemplar of that category. With enough time and enough testing of defining cues, such best-fit perceiving can be accomplished for most but not all classes of environmental events with which the person has contact. There are some objects whose cues to identity are sufficiently equivocal so that no such resolution can be achieved; these are mostly in the sphere of so-called interpersonal perception: perceiving the states of other people, their characteristics, intentions, and so forth on the basis of external signs. And since this is the domain where misperception can have the most chronic if not the most acute consequences, it is doubtful whether a therapeutic regimen of close looking will aid the misperceiver much in dealing with more complex cue patterns. But the greatest difficulty rests in the fact that the cost of close looks is generally too high under the conditions of speed, risk, and limited capacity imposed upon organisms by their environment or their constitutions. The ability to use minimal cues quickly in categorizing the events of the environment is what gives the organism its lead time in adjusting to events. Pause and close inspection inevitably cut down on this precious interval for adjustment.

INAPPROPRIATE CATEGORIES

Perhaps the most primitive form of perceptual unreadiness for dealing with a particular environment is the case in which the perceiver has a set of categories that are inappropriate for adequate prediction of his environment. A frequently cited example of such a case is Bartlett's account (3) of the African visitors in London who perceived the London bobbies as especially friendly because they frequently raised their right hand, palm forward, to the approaching traffic. The cue-category inference was, of course, incorrect, and they should have identified the cue as a signal for stopping traffic. The example, however, is not particularly interesting because it is a transient phenomenon, soon corrected by instruction.

A more interesting example, because it is far less tractable, is provided by second-language learning and the learning of a new phonemic system. Why is it, we may ask, that a person can learn the structure of a new language, its form classes, morphemes, lexemes, and so on, but still retain a foreign accent which he cannot, after a while, distinguish from the speech flow of native speakers around him? And why is it that a person learning a new language can follow the speech of a person with his own kind of foreign accent more readily than he can follow a native speaker? The answer lies, I think, in the phenomenon of postcategorization sensory gating: Once an utterance has been understood or decoded in appropriate categories, on the basis of some of the diacritica of the speech flow, the remaining features are assimilated or normalized or screened out. The phonemic categories that are used, moreover, are modifications of those in the first language of the speaker. Normalization is in the direction of these first-language phonemic categories. It is only by a special effort that, after having achieved adequate comprehension of the second language, one can remain sensorially open enough to register on the deviation between his own phonemic pattern and that of native speakers. And since there is common categorization of the meaning of utterances by the native speaker and the fluent foreigner, there is no built-in incentive for the foreigner to maintain a cognitively strainful regimen of attending further to speech sounds.

Lenneberg (56) has shown the difficulties involved in learning new modes of categorizing such continua as chromatic colors. He taught subjects various nonsense languages, explaining to them that the words were Hopi names for colors and that their task was to learn what colors they stood for. His stimulus materials were graded Munsell colors going in a circle from brown, through green, through blue, through pink, and then back to brown. A standardizing group was used to find the frequency distribution of color naming over the circle when the English color names mentioned above were used. Experimental groups, six in number, were then run, each being exposed to the use of the nonsense color names "as these are used by the Hopi." Then they were tested on their usage of the names. A first group was taught the nonsense words with exact correspondence to the usage found for the standardizing group on brown, blue, green, and pink. The other groups were given distorted usage training— distorted from English usage. The distortions were both in the slopes of the frequency of usage and in the points on the color continua where the highest usage frequencies fell. That is to say, the mode of a distribution in some cases would fall at a color which in English had no specific name, or fall between two English categories.

The principal results of the experiment are these: If the reference and probability relationship is the same for a nonsense language as it is for English, relearning is very rapid. The slightest deviation from this correspondence increases difficulty of learning quite markedly. It is disturbing either to shift the center of the categories on the color continuum or to change the shape of the frequency-of-calling functions, even when these are made more determinative (that is, rectilinear) than they normally are. A shift in the shape of the frequency-of-calling functions is more disruptive than a shift in placement on the color continuum. What is quite striking is that a highly determinative frequency-of-calling function can be learned much more rapidly than one in which there is a gradual transition in color naming from one color to another on the color continuum.

Now, I suspect that the difficulty in learning a set of neighboring categories with a state of equivocality prevailing in the area between the typical instances of each category comes precisely from the tendency to normalize in the direction of the center of one category or the other. If there is a sharp transition between one color category and another, this tendency aids learning. If the transition is gradual, it hinders it. For it is noteworthy, as in the experiment of Bruner, Postman, and Rodrigues (16) that equivocal colors are readily subject to assimilation in the direction of expected value.

It is perhaps in the realm of social perception, where the problem of validating one's categorizations is severe, that one finds the most striking effects of inappropriate category systems. What is meant here by validation is the testing of the predictions inherent in a categorization. If, on the basis of a few cues of personal appearance, for example, one categorizes another person as dishonest, it is extremely difficult in most cases to check for the other cues that one would predict might be associated with instances of this category. There is either a delay or an absence of opportunity for additional cue checking. Moreover, there is also the likelihood, since cues themselves are so equivocal in such a case, that available equivocal signs will be distorted in such a manner as to confirm the first impression. It is much as in the experiments of Asch (2) and of Haire and Grunes (33) on the formation of first impressions, where later cues encountered are cognitively transformed so as to support the first impression. The reticence of the man we categorize as dishonest is seen as caginess; the honest man's reticence is seen as integrity and good judgment.

It is perhaps because of this difficulty of infirming such categorial judgments that an inappropriate category system can be so hard to change. The slum boy who rises to the top in science can change his categories for coding the events of the physical world quite readily. He has much more difficulty in altering the socially related category system with which he codes the phenomena of the social world around him.

INAPPROPRIATE ACCESSIBILITY ORDERING

Perhaps the most noticeable perceptual unreadiness comes from interference with good probability learning by wishes and fears. I have in mind the kind of distorted expectancies that arise when the desirability or undesirability of events distorts the learning of their probability of occurrence. The experiments of Marks (60) and of Irwin (41), cited earlier, are simplified examples of the way in which desired outcomes increase estimates of their likelihood of occurrence. Certain more persistent general personality tendencies also operate in this sphere. It is indeed the case that some people are readier to expect and therefore quicker to perceive the least desirable event among an array of expected events, and others the most desired. This is quite clearly a learned adjustment to the events one is likely to encounter, even if it may be supported by temperamental characteristics. How such learning occurs and why it is so resistant to correction by exposure to environmental events are hardly clear. But one matter that becomes increasingly clear is that, before we can know much about how appropriate and inappropriate perceptual readiness is produced, we shall have to know much more about how organisms learn the probabilistic structure of their environments. This is a point that Brunswik has made for some years (17), and it is one that has also been taken seriously by such students of probability learning as Bush and Mosteller (18); Bruner, Goodnow, and

Austin (9), Estes (23); Galanter and Gerstenhaber (25); Hake and Hyman (34); Edwards (22); and others.

There is another important feature of learning that effects perceptual readiness. It has to do with the range of alternatives for which organisms learn to be set perceptually. Put the matter this way: It is a common observation that some people are characteristically tuned for a narrow range of alternatives in the situations in which they find themselves. If the environment is banal in the sense of containing only high-probability events and sequences or, more properly, events and sequences that are strongly expected, then the individual will do well and perceive with a minimum of pause for close looking. But should the environment contain unexpected events, unusual sequences, then the result will be a marked slowdown in identification and categorizing. Cue search must begin again. We speak of such people as rigid or stuck. George Klein's work (46) on shifting category judgments suggests that, in general, people who are not able to shift categorization under gradually changing conditions of stimulation tend also to show what he describes as "overcontrol" on other cognitive and motivational tasks. At the other extreme is specialization upon diversity; how such specialization is learned is equally puzzling. I can perhaps best illustrate the phenomenon by a commonly observed pattern found in subjects in tachistoscopic experiments. There are subjects who show rather high thresholds of identification generally, and who seem to be weighing the stimulus in terms of a wide array of interpretive categories. Jenkin (45) has described such perception as "rationalized," the subject describing what he sees as "like a so-and-so" rather than, as in the "projective" response, reporting it "as a so-and-so." It is as if the former type of response involved a greater cue searching of stimulus inputs for a fit to a wide range of things that it could be. It is also very likely that premature sensory gating occurs in individuals with a tendency to be set for a minimum array of alternatives, leading them into error. The topic is one that bears closer investigation. To anyone who has had much experience in observing subjects in tachistoscopic work, it seems intuitively evident that there are large and individual differences possibly worth examining here.

We come finally to the vexing problem of perceptual defense—the manner in which organisms utilize their perceptual readiness to ward off events that are threatening, but about which there is nothing they can do. There has been foolish and some bitter ink spilled over this topic, mostly because of a misunderstanding. The notion of perceptual defense does not require a little homuncular ego, sitting behind a Judas-eye, capable of ruling out any input that is potentially disruptive—as even so able a critic as F. H. Allport (1) seems to think. Any preset filtering device can do all that is required.

Let me begin with the general proposition that failure to perceive is most often not a lack of perceiving but a matter of interference with perceiving. Whence the interference? I would propose that the interference comes from categorizations in highly accessible categories that serve to block alternative categorizations in less accessible categories. As a highly speculative suggestion, the mechanism that seems most likely to mediate such interference is probably the broadening of category acceptance limits when a high state of readiness to perceive prevails; or, in the language of the preceding section, the range of inputs that will produce a match signal for a category increases in such a way that more accessible categories are likely to capture poor-fitting sensory inputs. We have already considered some evidence for increase in acceptance limits under high readiness conditions: the tendency to see a red four of clubs as either a four of diamonds or a four of clubs, with color-suit relationship rectified (14),[6] the difficulty of spotting reversed letters embedded in the middle of a word (67), and so on.

Let us examine some experimental evidence on the role of interference in perceptual failure. Wyatt and Campbell (86) have shown that if a subject develops a wrong hypothesis about the nature of what is being presented to him for perception at suboptimal conditions, the perception of the object in terms of its conventional identity is slowed down. This observation has been repeated in other studies as well. Postman and Bruner (66) for example, have shown that if a subject is put under pressure by the experimenter and given to believe that he is operating below standard, then he will develop premature hypotheses that interfere with correct perception of the word stimuli being presented to him. The authors refer to "perceptual recklessness" as characterizing the stressed subjects in contrast to those who operated under normal experimental conditions. It may well be, just in passing, that stress has not only the specific effect of leading to premature, interfering hypotheses, but that it disrupts the normal operation of match-mismatch signaling systems in the nervous system. Unpublished studies from our own laboratory carried out by Bruner, Postman, and John (15) have shown the manner in which subjects misperceive low-probability contingencies in terms of higher probability categories. For example, a subject in the experimental group is shown tachistoscopically a picture of a discus thrower, wound up and ready to throw. In his balancing arm and placed across the front of him is a large bass viol. A control subject is shown the same picture, the exact space filled by the bass viol now being occupied by the crouching figure of a track official with his back to the camera. The brightness, shading, and area of the viol and the official are almost identical. Subjects begin by identifying the first flash of the picture as an athlete with a shadow across him. The subjects faced with the incongruous picture then go on with reasonable hypotheses—including the hy-

[6] See pp. 68–83.

pothesis of a crouching human figure, "probably an official," as one subject put it. In the process of running through the gamut of likely hypotheses, correct perception is interfered with. It is interesting that the threshold for the incongruous stimulus picture is markedly higher than that for the more conventional one.

Hypotheses and states of readiness may interfere with correct perception in yet another way, by creating a shifting noise background that masks the cues that might be used for identifying an environmental event. At the common-sense level this can best be illustrated by reference to perceptual-motor learning where kinesthetic cues are of importance. In teaching a person how to cast a fly, it is necessary for him to guide his forward delivery by feeling the gentle pressure release that occurs when the line reaches the end of its uncurving on the backcast. If your fly-casting pupil is too eager to spot this cue, he will be rather tense, and his own muscular tension will mask the gentle pressure release that he must use as a signal.

A good instance is provided by the experiment of Goodnow and Pettigrew (30) at Harvard. It is concerned with the ability of subjects to perceive a regularity in a sequence of events—a very simple regularity, like the alternation left-right-left-right. . . . The experiment is done on a conventional two-armed bandit, the subject having the task of betting on whether a light will appear on the left or on the right. The task is simple. A subject is first given some pretraining, in one of four pretraining groups. One is given pretraining by learning a simple alternation pattern of pay-off, another is trained to find the pay-off all on one side (not easy for all subjects), a third is trained to find the pattern *LLRLLR* . . . , and a final group is given no pretraining. Following the pretraining, without pause, all subjects are given a series of 60 choices in which the pay-off is randomly arranged, the two sides totaling out to 50:50. Immediately following this random phase, and again without pause, the pay-offs go into a stage of simple alternation, *LRLR*. . . . How long does it take the subject to perceive the regularity of the final temporal pattern? The speed of discovery depends, it turns out, upon the kinds of behavioral hypotheses a subject develops during the phase of random pay-off. If he develops any regularity of response—like win-stay-lose-shift or win-shift-lose-stay—then he will quickly spot the new pattern. Pretraining on a constant one-side pay-off or on single alternation both produce such regularity, and both forms of pretraining produce equally good results—the subject requiring but eight or nine exposures to the pattern introduced after the random phase to begin responding without error. No pretraining, or pretraining on the pattern *LLRLLR* . . . , does not produce the regularity of response required. Instead, the subject works on odd and constantly shifting hypotheses during the random period. When the single-alternation regularity is introduced, the result is a marked reduction in ability to spot the new pattern—some subjects failing to discover the pattern in 200 trials. What we are dealing with here is interference—hypotheses and responses serve to mask the regularity of events in the environment. In order for an environmental regularity to be perceived, there has to be a certain amount of steadiness in the hypotheses being employed and in the response pattern that is controlled by it. Short of this, masking and clumsy perceptual performance results.

Now what has all this to do with perceptual defense? The concept was introduced by Bruner and Postman (13) as a description of the phenomenon of failure to perceive and/or report material known by independent test to be regarded as inimical by the subject. It was proposed that there was a hierarchy of thresholds, and that an incoming stimulus could be responded to without its reaching the level of reportable experience—as in the McGinnies (58) and Lazarus and McCleary (54) studies, where autonomic response followed presentation of a potentially traumatic stimulus without the subject's being able to give a report of the nature of the stimulus. The study of Bricker and Chapanis (6) threw further light on the concept of a hierarchy of thresholds by demonstrating that, though subjects could not report spontaneously on the identity of the shock syllables used by Lazarus and McCleary, they could guess them well in excess of chance if given a restricted choice regarding what word had been presented.

I would like to propose two additional factors that might lead to a failure of perception of emotionally negative material. It is conceivable that the estimates of probability of occurrence of disvalued events are, in some individuals, reduced—essentially the obverse of what was observed in the experiments of Marks (60) and Irwin (41), where probability estimates were inflated by desirability. If accessibility is decreased by such disvaluation, then a cognitive counterpart of what is clinically called repression can be posited. It is known, however, that not everyone shows this tendency to be unready for objects and events that are anxiety-arousing. Others seem to inflate their estimate of the likelihood of occurrence of inimical events. Certainly one finds clinical evidence for such a pattern among anxiety neurotics. Postman and Bruner (66) have described two types of performance with respect to known anxiety-producing stimuli: defense and vigilance; the former a heightened threshold of identification for such stimuli, the latter a lowered threshold. In a carefully designed experiment contrasting the performance of clinically diagnosed intellectualizers and repressors, Lazarus, Eriksen, and Fonda (53) have shown that the former group indeed are faster in recognizing negatively charged material than they are in recognizing neutral material, while the latter show the reverse tendency. Again, I find it necessary to revert to a point made earlier: I do not think that we are going to get much further ahead in understanding hyper- and hyporeadiness for encountering anxiety-evoking stimuli short of doing studies of the learning of environmental probabilities for sequences containing noxious and beneficial events.

There is one additional mechanism that may be operative in lowering or generally altering readiness to perceive material that in some way may be threatening. I hesitate to speak of it in detail, since it is of such a speculative order, and do so only because some experiments suggest themselves. Conceivably, categories for classes of objects that are pain-arousing are set up with narrow acceptance limits for stimulus inputs related to them. That is to say, what we speak of as repression may be the establishment of very narrow category limits that prevent the evocation of match signals for inputs that do not fit category specifications very precisely. I am mindful that as far as autonomic reactivity is concerned, potentially traumatic stimuli work in quite the reverse direction. If anything, a wide range of objects, appropriate and inappropriate, arouse autonomic reactions, without leading to verbalizable report concerning the categorial identity of the eliciting objects. Yet it is conceivable that with respect to one kind of threshold (autonomic) the acceptance limits are broad, and with respect to another (reportable awareness) very narrow. I think it would be worthwhile in any case to investigate the acceptance limits of inimical stimulus inputs by altering the characteristics of objects so that, in essence, one gets a generalization gradient for recognition. My guess is that the gradient will be much steeper for anxiety-arousing stimuli than for neutral ones. All that remains is to do the experiment.

Finally, it may also be the case that category accessibility reflects the instrumental relevance of the environmental events they represent. There is evidence that the recognition threshold for noxious objects about which one can do something is lower than normal, whereas for ones about which nothing instrumental can be done, the threshold is higher. That is to say, words that signal a shock that can be avoided show lowered thresholds, words signaling unavoidable shock show a threshold rise. One may well speculate whether the instrumental relevance of objects is not a controlling factor in guiding the kind of search behavior that affects category accessibility. The problem needs much more thorough investigation than it has received.

We have touched on various conditions that might lead a person to be inappropriately set for the events he must perceive easily and quickly in his environment. Many other studies could be mentioned. However, the intention has not been to review the rather sprawling literature in the field, but to propose some possible mechanism affecting readiness so that research might be given a clearer theoretical direction.

Conclusions

We have been concerned in these pages with a general view of perception that depends upon the construction of a set of organized categories in terms of which stimulus inputs may be sorted, given identity, and given more elaborated, connotative meaning. Veridical perception, it has been urged, depends upon the construction of such category systems, categories built upon the inference of identity from cues or signs. Identity, in fine, represents the range of inferences about properties, uses, and consequences that can be predicted from the presence of certain criterial cues.

Perceptual readiness refers to the relative accessibility of categories to afferent stimulus inputs. The more accessible a category, the less the stimulus input required for it to be sorted in terms of the category, given a degree of match between the characteristics of the input and the specifications of the category. In rough form, there appear to be two general determinants of category accessibility. One of them is the likelihood of occurrence of events learned by the person in the course of dealing with the world of objects and events and the redundant sequences in which these are embedded. If you will, the person builds a model of the likelihood of events. Again in rough terms, one can think of this activity as achieving a minimization of surprise for the organism. A second determinant of accessibility is the requirements of search dictated by need states and the need to carry out habitual enterprises such as walking, reading, or whatever it is that makes up the round of daily, habitual life.

Failure to achieve a state of perceptual readiness that matches the probability of events in one's world can be dealt with in one of two ways: either by the relearning of categories and expectancies or by constant close inspection of events and objects. Where the latter alternative must be used, an organism is put in the position of losing his lead time for adjusting quickly and smoothly to events under varying conditions of time pressure, risk, and limited capacity. Readiness in the sense that we are using it is not a luxury, but a necessity for smooth adjustment.

The processes involved in sorting sensory inputs into appropriate categories involve cue utilization, varying from sensorially open cue searching under relative uncertainty to selective search for confirming cues under partial certainty, to sensory gating and distortion when an input has been categorized beyond a certain level of certainty.

Four kinds of mechanisms are proposed to deal with known phenomena of perceptual categorizing and differential perceptual readiness: grouping and integration, access ordering, match-mismatch signal utilization, and gating. The psychological evidence leading one to infer such processes were examined and possible neurological analogues considered. The processes are conceived of as mediators of categorizing and its forms of connectivity, the phenomena of differential threshold levels for various environmental events, the guidance of cue search behavior, and lastly, the phenomena of sensory inhibition and filtering.

Finally, we have considered some of the ways in which failure of perceptual readiness comes about: first, through a failure to learn appropriate categories for sorting the environment and for following its sequences and second, through a process of interference whereby more accessible categories with wide acceptance limits serve to mask or prevent the use of less accessible categories for the coding of stimulus inputs. The concept of perceptual defense may be re-examined in the light of these notions.

References

1. ALLPORT, F. H. 1955. *Theories of perception and the concept of structure.* New York: Wiley.
2. ASCH, S. E. 1952. *Social psychology.* New York: Prentice-Hall.
3. BARTLETT, F. C. 1932. *Remembering: a study in experimental and social psychology.* Cambridge, Eng.: Cambridge University Press (paperback, 1968).
4. BINDER, A. 1955. A statistical model for the process of visual recognition. *Psychological Review* 62:119–29.
5. BITTERMAN, M. E., AND KNIFFIN, C. W. 1953. Manifest anxiety and "perceptual defense." *Journal of Abnormal and Social Psychology* 48:248–52.
6. BRICKER, P. D., AND CHAPANIS, A. 1953. Do incorrectly perceived tachistoscopic stimuli convey some information? *Psychological Review* 60:181–88.
7. BROWN, D. R. 1953. Stimulus similarity and the anchoring of subjective scales. *American Journal of Psychology* 66:199–214.
8. BRUNER, J. S. 1951. Personality dynamics and the process of perceiving. In *Perception: an approach to personality,* ed. R. R. Blake and G. V. Ramsey, pp. 121–47. New York: Ronald Press.
9. BRUNER, J. S.; GOODNOW, J. J.; AND AUSTIN, G. A. 1956. *A study of thinking.* New York: Wiley.
10. BRUNER, J. S.; MILLER, G. A.; AND ZIMMERMAN, C. 1955. Discriminative skill and discriminative matching in perceptual recognition. *Journal of Experimental Psychology* 49:187–92.
11. BRUNER, J. S., AND MINTURN, A. L. 1955. Perceptual identification and perceptual organization. *Journal of General Psychology* 53:21–28.
12. BRUNER, J. S., AND POSTMAN, L. 1947. Emotional selectivity in perception and reaction. *Journal of Personality* 16:69–77.
13. BRUNER, J. S., AND POSTMAN, L. 1949. Perception, cognition, and behavior. *Journal of Personality* 18:14–31.
14. BRUNER, J. S., AND POSTMAN, L. 1949. On the perception of incongruity: a paradigm. *Journal of Personality* 18:206–23.
15. BRUNER, J. S.; POSTMAN, L.; AND JOHN, W. 1949. Normalization of incongruity. Research memorandum, Cognition Project, Harvard University.
16. BRUNER, J. S.; POSTMAN, L.; AND RODRIGUES, J. 1951. Expectation and the perception of color. *American Journal of Psychology* 64:216–27.
17. BRUNSWIK, E. 1947. *Systematic and representative design of psychological experiments.* Berkeley: University of California Press.
18. BUSH, R. R., AND MOSTELLER, C. F. 1955. *Stochastic models for learning.* New York: Wiley.
19. CHAPMAN, D. W. 1932. Relative effects of determinate and indeterminate Aufgaben. *American Journal of Psychology* 44:163–74.
20. COWEN, E. L., AND BEIER, E. G. 1951. The influence of "threat expectancy" on perception. *Journal of Personality* 19:85–94.
21. ECCLES, J. C. 1953. *The neurophysiological basis of mind.* Oxford: Oxford University Press.
22. EDWARDS, W. 1954. The theory of decision making. *Psychological Bulletin* 51:380–417.
23. ESTES, W. K. 1954. Individual behavior in uncertain situations: an interpretation in terms of statistical association theory. In *Decision processes,* ed. R. M. Thrall, C. H. Coombs, and R. L. Davis, pp. 127–37. New York: Wiley.

24. FRY, D. P., AND DENES, P. 1953. Mechanical speech recognition. In *Communication theory*, ed. W. Jackson. New York: Academic Press.
25. GALANTER, E., AND GERSTENHABER, M. 1955. On thought: extrinsic theory of insight. *American Psychologist* 10:465.
26. GIBSON, J. J. 1950. *The perception of the visual world*. Boston: Houghton Mifflin.
27. GIBSON, J. J., AND GIBSON, E. J. 1955. Perceptual learning: differentiation or enrichment? *Psychological Review* 62:32–41.
28. GALAMBOS, R.; SHEATZ, G.; AND VERNIER, V. G. 1956. Electrophysiological correlates of a conditioned response in cats. *Science* 123:376–77.
29. GOODNOW, J. J. 1955. Determinants of choice-distribution in two-choice situations. *American Journal of Psychology* 68:106–16.
30. GOODNOW, J. J., AND PETTIGREW, T. E. 1956. Some difficulties in learning a simple pattern of events. Paper presented at annual meeting of the Eastern Psychological Association, March 1956, Atlantic City, N.J.
31. GRAHAM, C. H. 1956. Perception and behavior. Presidential address to the Eastern Psychological Association, March 1956, Atlantic City, N.J.
32. GRANIT, R. 1955. *Receptors and sensory perception*. New Haven, Conn.: Yale University Press.
33. HAIRE, M., AND GRUNES, W. F. 1950. Perceptual defenses: processes protecting an organized perception of another personality. *Human Relations* 3:403–12.
34. HAKE, H. W., AND HYMAN, R. 1953. Perception of the statistical structure of a random series of binary symbols. *Journal of Experimental Psychology* 45:64–74.
35. HARPER, R. S., AND BORING, E. G. 1948. Cues. *American Journal of Psychology* 61:119–23.
36. HEBB, D. O. 1949. *The organization of behavior*. New York: Wiley.
37. HELSON, H. 1948. Adaptation-level as a basis for a quantitative theory of frames of reference. *Psychological Review* 55:297–313.
38. HERNANDEZ-PÉON, R.; SCHERRER, R. H.; AND JOUVET, M. 1956. Modification of electric activity in the cochlear nucleus during "attention" in unanesthetized cats. *Science* 123:331–32.
39. HORNBOSTEL, E. M. VON. 1926. Unity of the senses. *Psyche* 7:83–89.
40. HOWES, D. 1954. On the interpretation of word frequency as a variable affecting speed of recognition. *Journal of Experimental Psychology* 48:106–12.
41. IRWIN, F. W. 1953. Stated expectations as functions of probability and desirability of outcomes. *Journal of Personality* 21:329–35.
42. ITTLESON, W. H. 1952. *The Ames demonstrations in perception*. Princeton: N.J.: Princeton University Press.
43. JARRETT, J. 1951. Strategies in risk-taking situations. Unpublished doctoral dissertation, Harvard University Library.
44. JARVIK, M. E. 1951. Probability learning and a negative recency effect in the serial anticipation of alternative symbols. *Journal of Experimental Psychology* 41:291–97.
45. JENKIN, N. 1956. Two types of perceptual experience. *Journal of Clinical Psychology* 12:44–49.
46. KLEIN, G. S. 1951. The personal world through perception. In *Perception: an approach to personality*, ed. R. R. Blake and G. V. Ramsey, pp. 328–55. New York: Ronald Press.
47. KOHLER, I. 1953. Rehabituation in perception. Published separately in three parts, in German, in *Die Pyramide*, Heft 5, 6, and 7 (Austria), trans. Henry Gleitman and ed. J. J. Gibson. Privately circulated by the editor.
48. KÖHLER, W. 1940. *Dynamics in psychology*. New York: Liveright.
49. KUFFLER, S. W., AND HUNT, C. C. 1952. The mammalian small-nerve fibers: a system for efferent nervous regulation of muscle spindle discharge. *Proceedings of the Association for Research in Nervous and Mental Disease* 30.
50. KUFFLER, S. W.; HUNT, C. C.; AND QUILLIAN, J. P. 1951. Function of medullated small-nerve fibers in mammalian ventral roots: efferent muscle spindle innervation. *Journal of Neurophysiology* 14:29–54.

51. LASHLEY, K. S. 1938. Experimental analysis of instinctive behavior. *Psychological Review* 45:445–71.
52. LASHLEY, K. S. 1950. In search of the engram. *Symposia of the Society for Experimental Biology* 4:454–82.
53. LAZARUS, R. S.; ERIKSEN, C. W.; AND FONDA, C. P. 1951. Personality dynamics and auditory perceptual recognition. *Journal of Personality* 19:471–82.
54. LAZARUS, R. S., AND McCLEARY, R. A. 1951. Autonomic discrimination without awareness: a study of subception. *Psychological Review* 58:113–222.
55. LEKSELL, L. 1945. The action potential and excitatory effects of the small ventral root fibers to skeletal muscles. *Acta Physiologica Scandinavica* 10, suppl. 31.
56. LENNEBERG, E. H. 1956. An empirical investigation into the relationship between language and cognition. Unpublished doctoral dissertation, Harvard University Library.
57. LORENTE DE NO, R. 1939. Transmission of impulses through cranial motor nuclei. *Journal of Neurophysiology* 2:402–64.
58. McGINNIES, E. 1949. Emotionality and perceptual defense. *Psychological Review* 56:244–51.
59. MACKAY, D. M. 1956. Toward an information-flow model of human behavior. *British Journal of Psychology* 47:30–43.
60. MARKS, R. W. 1951. The effect of probability, desirability, and "privilege" on the state of expectations of children. *Journal of Personality* 19:332–51.
61. MILLER, G. A.; BRUNER, J. S.; AND POSTMAN, L. 1954. Familiarity of letter sequences and tachistoscopic identification. *Journal of General Psychology* 50:129–39.
62. MILLER, G. A.; HEISE, G. A.; AND LICHTEN, W. 1951. The intelligibility of speech as a function of the context of the test materials. *Journal of Experimental Psychology* 41:329–35.
63. PEIRCE, C. S. 1878. How to make our ideas clear. *Popular Science Monthly* 12:286–302.
64. PENFIELD, W. 1952. Memory mechanisms. *Archives of Neurology and Psychiatry* 67:178–91.
65. PIAGET, J. 1951. *Play, dreams, and imitation in childhood*. New York: Norton.
66. POSTMAN, L., AND BRUNER, J. S. 1948. Perception under stress. *Psychological Review* 55:314–23.
67. POSTMAN, L.; BRUNER, J. S.; and WALK, R. D. 1951. The perception of error. *British Journal of Psychology* 42:1–10.
68. POSTMAN, L., and CRUTCHFIELD, R. S. 1952. The interaction of need, set, and stimulus structure in a cognitive task. *American Journal of Psychology*, 65:196–217.
69. PRATT, C. C. 1950. The role of past experience in visual perception. *Journal of Psychology* 30:85–107.
70. PRENTICE, W. C. H. 1954. Paper read at the Symposium on Conceptual Trends in Psychology, at the American Psychological Association, September 1954, New York.
71. SELFRIDGE, O. 1955. Pattern recognition and learning. Memorandum of Lincoln Laboratory, M.I.T.
72. SMITH, J. W., and KLEIN, G. S. 1951. Cognitive control in serial behavior patterns. Dittoed manuscript, available from authors.
73. SOLOMON, R. L., and POSTMAN, L. 1952. Frequency of usage as a determinant of recognition thresholds for words. *Journal of Experimental Psychology* 43:195–201.
74. STEVENS, S. S. 1951. Chap. 1 in *Handbook of experimental psychology,* ed. S. S. Stevens. New York: Wiley.
75. STEVENS, S. S. 1956. The direct estimation of sensory magnitudes—loudness. *American Journal of Psychology* 69:1–25.
76. TANNER, W. P., Jr., and SWETS, J. A. 1954. A decision-making theory of human detection. *Psychological Review* 61:401–9.
77. TINBERGEN, N. 1951. *The study of instinct*. Oxford: Oxford University Press.
78. TITCHENER, E. B. 1916. *A beginner's psychology*. New York: Macmillan.

79. TOLMAN, E. C. 1949. Discussion. *Journal of Personality* 18:48–50.
80. UTTLEY, A. M. 1955. *The conditional probability of signals in the nervous system*. Radar Research Establishment, British Ministry of Supply.
81. VERNON, M. D. 1952. *A further study of visual perception*. Cambridge, Eng.: Cambridge University Press.
82. VOLKMANN, J. 1951. Chap. 11, Scales of judgment and their implications for social psychology. In *Social psychology at the crossroads,* ed. M. Sherif and J. H. Rohrer, pp. 273–94. New York: Harper.
83. WALLACH, H. 1949. Some considerations concerning the relation between perception and cognition. *Journal of Personality* 18:6–13.
84. WHITE, M. 1955. *The age of analysis*. New York: New American Library.
85. WOODWORTH, R. S. 1947. Reenforcement of perception. *American Journal of Psychology* 60:119–24.
86. WYATT, D. F., and CAMPBELL, D. T. 1951. On the liability of stereotype or hypothesis. *Journal of Abnormal and Social Psychology* 46:496–500.
87. YOKOYAMA, J. 1954. Reported in *A history of experimental psychology,* E. G. Boring. 2d ed. New York: Appleton-Century.
88. YOUNG, J. Z. 1951. *Doubt and certainty in science*. Oxford: Oxford University Press.

2

Value and Need as Organizing Factors in Perception[*]

Throughout the history of modern psychology, until very recent times, perception has been treated as though the perceiver were a passive recording instrument of rather complex design. One might, in most experiments, describe him in much the same graphical terms as one uses to describe the latest piece of recording apparatus obtainable from Stoelting or the American Optical Company. Such psychology, practiced as it were in vitro, has fallen short of clarifying the nature of perception in everyday life much as the old nerve-muscle psychophysiology fell short of explaining everyday behavior. Both have been monumentally useful—in their place. The names of Weber, Fechner, Wundt, Titchener, Hecht, and Crozier are safely ensconced in any respectable psychological hall of fame. But their work, like the work of the nerve-muscle men, is only a beginning.

* Jerome S. Bruner and Cecile C. Goodman, "Value and Need as Organizing Factors in Perception," *Journal of Abnormal and Social Psychology,* Vol. 42, No. 1, January 1947, pp. 33–44. Copyright 1947 by the American Psychological Association, and reproduced by permission of the publisher and authors.

The writers are greatly indebted to Pauline B. Hahn and Leo J. Postman for invaluable assistance and advice.

For, as L. L. Thurstone (34) has put it, "In these days when we insist so frequently on the interdependence of all aspects of personality, it would be difficult to maintain that any of these functions, such as perception, is isolated from the rest of the dynamical system that constitutes the person." The problem is, indeed, to understand how the process of perception is affected by other concurrent mental functions and how these functions, in their turn, are affected by the operation of perceptual processes.

Given a dark room and a highly motivated subject, one has no difficulty in demonstrating Korte's laws of phenomenal movement. Lead the subject from the dark room to the market place and then find out what it is he sees moving and under what conditions; Korte's laws, though still valid, describe the situation about as well as the laws of color mixture describe one's feelings before an El Greco canvas. The discrepancy between the dark room and the market place we have, in the past, found convenient to dismiss by invoking various *dei ex machina:* attention, apperception, *unbewusster schluss, einstellung,* preparatory set, and so forth. Like the vengeful and unannounced stepbrother from Australia in the poorer murder mysteries, they turn up at the crucial juncture to do the dirty work. Though such constructs are useful, perception itself must remain the primary focus. To shift attention away from it by invoking poorly understood intervening variables does little service. What we must study before invoking such variables are the variations perception itself undergoes when one is hungry, in love, in pain, or solving a problem. These variations are as much a part of the psychology of perception as Korte's laws.

Before considering the evidence that such perceptual phenomena are as scientifically measurable in terms of appropriate metrics as such more hallowed phenomena as flicker fusion, constancy, or tonal attributes, let us pause to construct a sketchy terminology. Let us, in what ensues, distinguish heuristically between two types of perceptual determinants. These we shall call autochthonous and behavioral. Under the former we group those highly predictable properties of the nervous system which account for phenomena like simple pair formation, closure, and contrast; or, at another level, tonal masking, difference and summation tones, flicker fusion, paradoxical cold, and binaural beats. Given ideal dark-room conditions and no compelling distractions, the average organism responds to set physical stimuli in these relatively fixed ways. Autochthonous determinants, in brief, reflect directly the characteristic electrochemical properties of sensory end organs and nervous tissue.

Under the category of behavioral determinants we group those active, adaptive functions of the organism which lead to the governance and control of all higher-level functions, including perception: the laws of learning and motivation, such personality dynamics as repression, the operation of quasi-temperamental characteristics like introversion and extroversion, social needs and attitudes, and so on. Underlying these behavioral determinants, doubtless, are a host of physiological mechanisms. But we can hardly wait until we understand these before tackling experimentally the role of behavioral determinants in perception. The physiology of Weber's law is still more or less obscure, yet the enunciation of it has been recognizably useful—even to the physiologist for whom it has been a challenge to discovery.

While we cannot give any extensive review of the literature on those perceptual dynamics which we have called behavioral, it is necessary to pass rapidly over some of the notable facts and experiments which have forced us to draw certain distinctions and make bold claims about the measurability of behavioral determinants. First, we have the facts of *sensory conditioning,* a term first used by Cason (7). Starting with the work of Perky in 1910 (23), it has been demonstrated repeatedly by Brown (5), Ellson (10), Coffin (8), and others that subjects can be conditioned to see and hear things in much the same way as they can be conditioned to perform such overt acts as knee jerking, eye blinking, or salivating. Pair a sound and a faint image frequently enough, fail to present the image, and the subject sees it anyway when the sound is presented. Any student of suggestion, whether or not he has perused Bird's exhaustive bibliography (3) of the literature on the subject, knows that. Not perception? Why not? The subject sees what he reports as vividly as he sees the Phi phenomenon.

Closely related are such experiments as those of Haggard and Rose (15), Proshansky and Murphy (26), and Schafer and Murphy (30) demonstrating the role of reward and punishment in altering perceptual organization. Haggard and Rose show that the extent of autokinetic movement can be altered by a system of rewards; Proshansky and Murphy that discriminable differences in the perception of lines and weights can be similarly altered; Schafer and Murphy that, given an ambiguous figure-ground configuration, what is seen as figure and what as ground can be altered by a system of reward and punishment.

Another group of researchers has demonstrated that what is seen in a complex configuration is not determined solely by the laws of Gestalt, but by practice. Among experimenters who have confirmed this generalization are Henle (16), Fehrer (13), Braly (4), Leeper (19), and Djang (9). Closely related are the experiments of Thouless (33) showing that phenomenal constancy or, as he calls it, "regression to the real object," reflects the habits of the individual. Art students, for example, see the real object—its color, shape, and brightness—less readily, show greater phenomenal constancy, than matched individuals with no art training. Indeed, von Fieandt (14) has shown that the appearance of light gray in shadow or dark gray in light can be controlled by simple Pavlovian conditioning, the CS being a sound or a button in the visual field. And all of us are fond of citing the work of Haddon in the Torres Straits (27) demonstrating that these primitive island spear fishers are, most likely as a result of their experience with spears, considerably less susceptible to the Müller-Lyer illusion.

Sherif's classic experiments (31) on social factors are too well known to need any elucidation here. Demonstrating further the role of social factors in perception are the experiments of Zuk-Kardos (35) and Fazil (12), students of Egon Brunswik, who showed that the subjective number equation for matching a standard cluster of stamps or coins to a variable depended in part upon the value of the coins or stamps in the standard and variable clusters. With many refinements and extensions, these experiments have been repeated in America by Ansbacher (1).

One can go on to cite many more experiments, but in our brief summary review, that would be impossible. Let us conclude then with two pieces of research, one French, the other Swiss, indicating the possible connection of general personality traits and perception. Binet (2) and Meili and Tobler (21) have suggested that the child is more susceptible to illusions, more a prey to those organizing factors which, as adults, we call distorting. Binet has shown that, as the child grows older, his susceptibility to the Müller-Lyer illusion decreases. The contribution of Meili and Tobler has been to show that, as the child ages, his threshold for seeing stroboscopic movement becomes higher. Whether from these two experiments, plus such incidental observations as Piaget's (24) to the effect that the child sees the moon as following him, we can draw any conclusions about increasing perceptual realism as a function of age is open to question. Yet the way has been opened to those who wish to investigate this area further.

So much for prior research. There exists a fruitful, if slim, body of literature on behavioral factors in perception. Where does one go from here? Two approaches are open. Armed with our slender reed of empirical proof, we can set about the task of systematization, indulging in S-R's topology, or psychoanalytic constructs to suit the taste. There is already one brilliant theoretical structure to account for many of the facts we have been discussing, presented in Egon Brunswik's *Wahrnehmung und Gegenstandswelt* (6). Or we may go on to the empirical demonstration of general hypotheses concerning the relation of behavior dynamics and perception. Both are indispensable activities. At present, however, we are concerned mainly with empirical hypotheses. But certain minimum systematic assumptions must first be made clear to bring these hypotheses into clear focus.

The organism exists in a world of more or less ambiguously organized sensory stimulation. What the organism sees, what is actually there perceptually represents some sort of compromise between what is presented by autochthonous processes and what is selected by behavioral ones. Such selection, we know, is determined not only by learning, as already indicated, but also by motivational factors such as have been indicated for hunger by Sanford (28, 29) and Levine, Chein, and Murphy (20). The selective process in perception we shall refer to as a *perceptual hypothesis,* using the term, with Krechevsky (18), to denote a systematic response tendency. Such a hypothesis may be set into operation by a need, by the requirements of learning a task, or by any internally or externally imposed demands on the organism. If a given perceptual hypothesis is rewarded by leading to food, water, love, fame, or what not, it will become fixated; the experimental literature, notably the work of Ellson (11) and Leeper (19), indicates that the fixation of sensory conditioning is very resistant to extinction. A fixation takes place, the perceptual hypothesis grows stronger, not only in the sense of growing more frequent in the presence of certain types of stimulation, but also more perceptually accentuated. Perceptual objects which are habitually selected become more vivid, have greater clarity or greater brightness or greater apparent size.

Two other systematic matters must concern us before we turn to the experiments. One has to do with perceptual compromise, the other with perceptual equivocality. Frequently, alternative hypotheses operate: A quick glimpse of a man in gray on a European battlefield may leave us in doubt as to whether he is a civilian or a Wehrmacht infantryman. Almost inevitably one or the other hypothesis prevails, and the field is perceived as either one or the other. But, in spite of the dominance of a single hypothesis in perception, compromise also occurs. Using Ansbacher's experiments (1) as an example, a group of small paper squares is seen both in terms of number and in terms of value as stamps. What results, if you will, is a perception of number-value. We know very little about such perceptual compromises, although we shall be discussing experiments demonstrating their operation.

As for equivocality, or ambiguity in the perceptual field, it has generally been supposed that the greater the equivocality the greater the chance for behavioral factors in perception to operate, all other things being equal. Sherif (31) chose the autokinetic phenomenon to work with for this reason. Proshansky and Murphy (26) worked close to threshold illumination with similar intent. Within broad limits, which we shall discuss, the generalization is valid, insofar as equivocality reduces the organizing capacity of autochthonous perceptual determinants. How important this generalization is, we who think so exclusively in terms of the well-controlled dark-room experiment, often forget. For in everyday life, perception is, by and large, a series of quick looks, glances, inattentive listenings, furtive touches. Save for what is at the very focus of interested attention, the world of sense is more equivocal than our textbook writers seem to think.

Empirical Hypotheses

We may turn now to the experiments with which this paper is primarily concerned. Three general hypotheses, growing out of the systematic principles just presented, are under consideration.

   a. The greater the social value of an object, the more it will be susceptible to organization by behavioral determinants. It will be selected perceptually from among alternative perceptual objects, will become fixated as a perceptual response tendency, and will become perceptually accentuated.

b. The greater the individual need for a socially valued object, the more marked will be the operation of behavioral determinants.

c. Perceptual equivocality will facilitate the operation of behavioral determinants only insofar as equivocality reduces the operation of autochthonous determinants without reducing the effectiveness of behavioral determinants.

In the experiments reported here, only one aspect of behavioral determination will be treated, what we have called accentuation—the tendency for sought-after perceptual objects to become more vivid. Perceptual selectivity and fixation have already been demonstrated in other experiments, though they remain poorly systematized. For purposes of economy of exposition we omit consideration of them here, though they constitute important variables in the broader research.

The Subjects and the Apparatus

The subjects were 30 ten-year-old children of normal intelligence, divisible (according to certain characteristics to be discussed shortly) into three groups, two experimental and one control. The apparatus consisted of a rectangular wooden box (9 x 9 x 18 inches) at one end of which was a 5-inch square ground-glass screen and a knob at its lower right-hand corner. At the center of the ground-glass screen was an almost circular patch of light (16.2 apparent foot candles) cast upon the back of the screen by a 60-watt incandescent light shining through an iris diaphragm which could be varied in diameter from ⅛ to 2 inches by turning the knob on the front end of the box. All that was visible to the subject was the box with its ground-glass screen and the circle of light whose diameter he could change by turning the knob. The circle was not truly round, containing the familiar nine elliptoid sides found in the Bausch & Lomb iris diaphragm. It was so close to round, however, that subjects had no difficulty making the subjective equations required of them.

Subjects individually sat in a chair in front of the screen on the box with the light circle slightly below eye level. The box rested on a table behind which sat the experimenter. The child was told that this was a game, and that he was to make the circle of light on the box the same size as various objects he was shown or told about. Before beginning judgments, each child, with no urging, was encouraged to see how large and small the circle of light could be made.

The two experimental groups received the same treatment. Two series were run for these groups, comprising 20 of the children in all. First the child was asked to estimate the sizes of coins from a penny through a half dollar from memory. He did the first in ascending order of value, then in descending order, always making two judgments for each coin named, one from the open, the other from the closed position of the iris diaphragm. Four judgments were made for each coin by each child. No inkling was given the child as to how nearly right he had been.

Following the memory series, and using the same order of presentation, a similar series was then run with coins present. Coins, individually, were held close to the center of the palm of the left hand, at a level with the light circle and 6 inches to its left. The subjects took as much time as suited them.

A control group of ten subjects followed a procedure identical with the one just described. Instead of coins, medium gray cardboard discs of identical size were employed. No mention of money was made to this group.

Results

Let us compare the difference between judgments of size of coins and identically sized cardboard discs. Two things can be noted in Figure 1, which presents judgments of experimentals and controls with coins present. First, coins, socially valued objects, are judged larger in size than gray discs. Second, the greater the value of the coin, the greater is the deviation of apparent size from actual size. The exception to this generalization is the half dollar, overestimation of which is below that of a quarter. By way of the sheerest guess one might explain this reversal of the curve in terms of the lesser reality-value for the ten-year-old of a half dollar compared with a quarter. More likely there is some simple autochthonous reason for the reversal. Yet, no such reversal is found in curves plotted for adults.

The difference between experimentals and controls is, of course, highly significant. The variance in overestimation in the experimental groups introduced by using coins of different value is similarly significant. Our results, as handled by the Postman-Bruner (25) adaptation of the analysis of variance to psychophysical data, show that variances due to coin value and due to using discs versus coins yield F scores convertible to P values of less than .01.[1]

So much for the first hypothesis, that socially valued objects are susceptible to behavioral determinants in proportion to their value. Consider now the second hypothesis, that the greater the subjective need for a socially

---

[1] P values at the .01 level were also found for constant errors introduced by ascending and descending value orders and for judgments made from the open and closed positions of the diaphragm. Since these parameters were controlled and balanced in the judgment data for the groups discussed, nothing further need be said of them here. Analysis of variance was carried out both with percentage scores representing deviation of individual judgments from actual size and with raw scores. Necessary corrections suggested by Snedecor (32) were used in the former method. The values presented here are applicable to both raw and percentage scores.

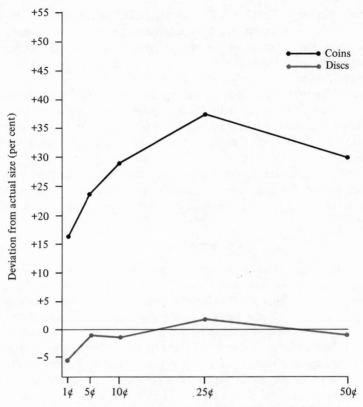

FIGURE 1. Size estimations of coins and discs of same size made by ten-year-olds (method of average error)

valued object, the greater will be the role of behavioral determinants of perception. In the second experimental variation, the experimental group was divided into two component groups. One we call the rich group, the other the poor group, each comprising ten subjects. Well-to-do subjects were drawn from a progressive school in the Boston area, catering to the sons and daughters of prosperous business and professional people. The poor subjects came from a settlement house in one of Boston's slum areas. The reasonable assumption is made that poor children have a greater subjective need for money than rich ones. When the figures presented in Figure 1 are broken down into scores for rich and poor groups, a striking difference will be noted (Figure 2). The poor group overestimates the size of coins considerably more than does the rich. Again there are some irregularities in the curves. The drop-off for the half dollar we have already sought to explain. As for the dip in the rich group's curve at a dime, the explanation is problematical. All curves which we have plotted for adults —more than 2,000 judgments—show this dip. Perhaps it is due to the dis-

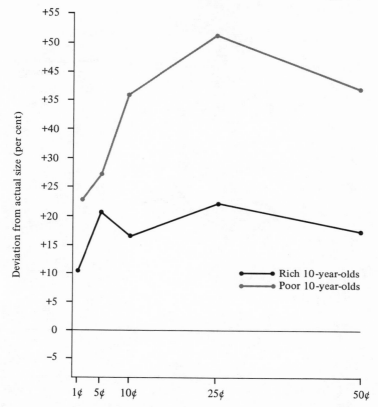

FIGURE 2. Size estimations of coins made by well-to-do and poor ten-year-olds (method of average error)

crepancy between the relative size and value of the dime, perhaps to some inherent characteristic of the coin itself.[2]

The difference between rich and poor is highly significant, analysis of variance showing that the source of variance is significant beyond the *P* level of .01. Our second hypothesis cannot, then, be rejected. It is notable, too, that the interaction between the parameters of economic status and value of coins yields an *F* score convertible to a *P* value between .05 and .01 which leads to a secondary hypothesis: Given perceptual objects of the same class but varying in value, the effect of need for that class of objects will be to accentuate the most valuable objects most, the least valuable least, and so forth.

What of ambiguity of perceptual equivocality? We have arbitrarily as-

[2] If the reader is a smoker, let him ask himself whether a dime will cover the hump on the camel which appears as a trademark on Camel cigarettes. Hold the two six inches apart. In spite of the apparently small size of the coin, it will cover the camel's hump with margin to spare.

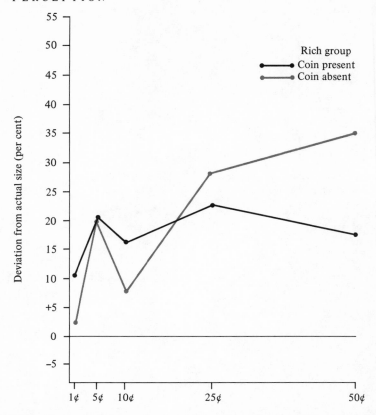

FIGURE 3. Size estimations of coins with coins present and from memory by well-to-do ten-year-olds (method of average error)

sumed that a situation in which one judges size from memory is more equivocal than one in which the object being judged is in clear view 6 inches away from the test patch. The assumption is open to serious question, but let us examine what follows from it experimentally. Compare first the judgments of the rich group under conditions like those described: with the coin present as compared with the coin as a mere memory image. The curves are in Figure 3. It would seem that, for all values below a quarter, equivocality has the effect of making judgments conform more to actual size, aiding, in other words, the operation of autochthonous determinants. For values over a quarter, equivocality favors behavioral factors, making apparent size diverge still more from actual size. For the rich group, with coin present, a half dollar is overjudged by 17.4 per cent; with coin absent, by 34.7 per cent.

This finding is difficult to interpret by itself. Consider now Figure 4, showing the discrepancy in absent and present judgments for the poor

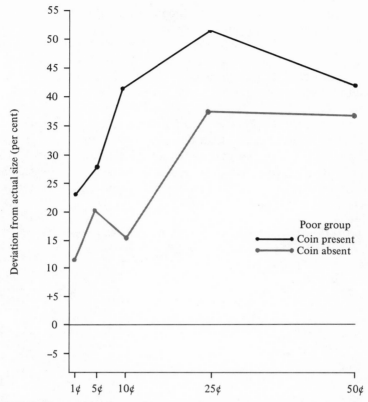

FIGURE 4. Size estimations of coins with coins present and from memory by poor ten-year-olds (method of average error)

group. Here there is no crossing. Equivocality, in this group, seems to have the exclusive effect of bringing judgments down toward actual size. Equivocality even brings out the dime dip in the poor group. How do we account for the difference? Why does equivocality liberate behavioral determinants among the rich children for higher values, and depress these factors for poor children? We can offer nothing but a guess, one which needs confirmation by further research. Some years ago, Oeser (22) reported that in his study of children in Dundee he found the fantasy life of the children of the unemployed strikingly choked off. Asked what they would like to be when grown, normal children of employed parents gave such glamorous replies as cowboys or film stars, while children of the unemployed named the rather lowly occupations traditionally followed by members of their class. The figures just presented suggest that we are witnessing the same phenomenon. In the case of the poor children, judging coin size from memory, a weakened fantasy is substituted for the compelling presence of a valued coin; while among rich children equivocality has the effect of liberating strong and active fantasy.[3]

Are any other explanations available to account for the shape of the curves we have been concerned with here? Weber's law would predict in all cases a straight-line plot parallel to the axis representing actual size. *DL* should be a constant fraction of the stimulus, whatever its magnitude. If one were to treat the slope of the curves by reference to Hollingworth's central-tendency effect (17), one should find a negative rather than a positive slope. All values smaller than the center of all the series should appear larger in size; all larger than the center of the series, smaller. Assuming that the Hollingworth effect is mediated by autochthonous factors, it then represents one more autochthonous factor outweighed by the behavioral determinants we have discussed.

TABLE 1 Deviation from Actual Size of Judgments of Coins and Discs under Various Conditions (per cent)

Group and Condition	Penny	Nickel	Dime	Quarter	Half-dollar	Number Judgments per Coin
20 *O*s coin present	16.5	23.9	29.1	37.0	29.6	80
20 *O*s coin absent	7.2	19.6	11.6	32.8	35.8	80
10 *O*s disc present	− 5.4	− 0.9	− 1.5	1.8	− 0.8	40
10 rich *O*s coin present	10.3	20.4	16.3	22.4	17.4	40
10 rich *O*s coin absent	2.6	19.8	7.8	28.3	34.7	40
10 poor *O*s coin present	22.7	27.3	41.8	51.6	42.0	40
10 poor *O*s coin absent	11.8	19.4	15.4	37.3	36.9	40

In conclusion, only one point need be reiterated. For too long now, perception has been virtually the exclusive domain of the Experimental psychologists (with a capital *E*). If we are to reach an understanding of the way in which perception works in everyday life, we social psychologists and students of personality will have to join with the experimental psychologists and re-explore much of this ancient field of perception whose laws for too long have been taken for granted.

[3] The difference between rich and poor children in their size judgments of absent and present coins as here discussed is statistically significant. The interaction variance for these two parameters (economic status and presence-absence of coins) is at the .01 level of significance.

References

1. ANSBACHER, H. 1937. Perception of number as affected by the monetary value of the objects. *Archives of Psychology*, no. 215.
2. BINET, A. 1895. La mesure des illusions visuelles chez l'enfant. *Revue de Philosophie* 40:11–25.
3. BIRD, C. 1939. Suggestion and suggestibility: a bibliography. *Psychological Bulletin* 36:264–83.
4. BRALY, K. W. 1933. The influence of past experience in visual perception. *Journal of Experimental Psychology* 16:613–43.
5. BROWN, W. 1916. Individual and sex differences in suggestibility. *University of California Publications in Psychology* 2:291–430.
6. BRUNSWIK, E. 1934. *Wahrnehmung und Gegenstandswelt*. Vienna: Deuticke.
7. CASON, H. 1936. Sensory conditioning. *Journal of Experimental Psychology* 19:572–91.
8. COFFIN, T. E. 1941. Some conditions of suggestion and suggestibility: a study of some attitudinal and situational factors influencing the process of suggestion. *Psychological Monographs*, p. 241.
9. DJANG, S. 1937. The role of past experience in the visual apprehension of masked forms. *Journal of Experimental Psychology* 20:29–59.
10. ELLSON, D. G. 1941. Hallucinations produced by sensory conditioning. *Journal of Experimental Psychology* 28:1–20.
11. ELLSON, D. G. 1941. Experimental extinction of an hallucination produced by sensory conditioning. *Journal of Experimental Psychology* 28:350–61.
12. FAZIL, A. Münzenversuche über Anzahl-Grossen , und Wertwahrnehmung. Cited by Ansbacher (1).
13. FEHRER, E. V. 1935. An investigation of the learning of visually perceived forms. *American Journal of Psychology* 47:187–221.
14. FIEANDT, K. von (1938). A new constancy phenomenon in color perception. *Annales Academiae Scientiarun Fennicae* (Finland) 41 (Summary in English). See also, Dressurversuche an der Farbenwahrnehmung. *Archiv für die Gesamte Psychologie* 96 (1936): 467–95.
15. HAGGARD, E. R., and ROSE, G. J. 1944. Some effects of mental set and active participation in the conditioning of the autokinetic phenomenon. *Journal of Experimental Psychology* 34:45–59.
16. HENLE, M. 1942. An experimental investigation of past experience as a determinant of visual form perception. *Journal of Experimental Psychology* 30:1–21.
17. HOLLINGWORTH, H. L. 1909. The inaccuracy of movement. *Archives of Psychology*, no. 13.
18. KRECHEVSKY, I. 1932. "Hypothesis" versus "chance" in the presolution period in sensory discrimination learning. *University of California Publications in Psychology* 6:27–44.
19. LEEPER, R. 1935. A study of a neglected portion of the field of learning—the development of sensory organization. *Journal of General Psychology* 46:41–75.
20. LEVINE, R.; CHEIN, I.; and MURPHY, G. 1942. The relation of the intensity of a need to the amount of perceptual distortion: a preliminary report. *Journal of Psychology* 13:283–93.
21. MEILI, R., and TOBLER, C. 1931. Les mouvements stroboscopiques chez les enfants. *Archives de Psychologie* (Geneva) 23:131–56.
22. OESER, O. A. 1939. Personal communication.
23. PERKY, C. W. 1910. An experimental study of imagination. *American Journal of Psychology* 21:422–52.
24. PIAGET, J. 1932. *Language and thought of the child*. London and New York.
25. POSTMAN, L., and BRUNER, J. S. 1946. The reliability of constant errors in psychophysical measurement. *Journal of Psychology* 21:293–99.

26. PROSHANSKY, H., and MURPHY, G. 1942. The effects of reward and punishment on perception. *Journal of Psychology* 13:295–305.
27. RIVERS, W. H. R. 1901. *Report of the Cambridge Anthropological Expedition to the Torres Straits*, vol. 2.
28. SANFORD, R. N. 1936. The effect of abstinence from food upon imaginal processes: a preliminary experiment. *Journal of Psychology* 2:129–36.
29. SANFORD, R. N. 1937. The effect of abstinence from food upon imaginal processes: a further experiment. *Journal of Psychology* 3:145–59.
30. SCHAFER, R., and MURPHY, G. 1943. The role of autism in a visual figure-ground relationship. *Journal of Experimental Psychology* 32:335–43.
31. SHERIF, M. 1935. A study in some social factors in perception. *Archives of Psychology,* no. 187.
32. SNEDECOR, D. 1940. *Statistical methods.* Ames, Iowa.
33. THOULESS, R. H. 1932. Individual differences in phenomenal regression. *British Journal of Psychology* 22:216–41.
34. THURSTONE, L. L. 1944. *A factorial study of perception.* Chicago.
35. ZUK-KARDOS, I. Perzeptionale Zugänglichkeit von Anzahl, Fläche, und Wert unter verschiedenen Umstandskonstellationen. Cited by Ansbacher (1).

3

Familiarity
of Letter Sequences and
Tachistoscopic Identification*

The Problem

Since Cattell's early studies of tachistoscopic perception (1, 2), it has been recognized that familiarity with an exposed configuration is an important factor in its identification. Cattell discovered that the speed of reading in different languages varies according to the familiarity of the language, and that letters are more easily perceived when they form a word. Cattell compared single letters with short words by measuring the Ss' reaction times and also by determining the shortest exposure times necessary for correct identification. Under exposure conditions where four or five random letters could be recognized it was possible to read as many as three short words that altogether contained more than five letters. These results led to the conclusion that words are perceived as a whole, and are as unitary in character as single letters.

Cattell's results are the visual counterpart of the auditory phenomenon,

* "Familiarity of Letter Sequences and Tachitoscopic Identification," by George A. Miller, Jerome S. Bruner, and Leo J. Postman, in *The Journal of General Psychology*, 1954, *50*, 129–139. Copyright © 1954 by The Journal Press, and reproduced by permission of the publisher and authors.

discovered in tests of the intelligibility of speech, that sentences can be heard correctly under conditions where nonsense syllables are unintelligible. The test score obtained for sentences cannot be predicted directly from a knowledge of the audibility of isolated speech sounds, for one constellation of phonemes may be perceived correctly where the same sounds in a different, less familiar pattern are not.

The explanation of such results usually invokes the fact that a familiar unit can be reconstructed from a bare minimum of perceptual clues because there are only a limited number of ways the ambiguous portions can be filled in. With nonsense materials, every part of the pattern must be correctly perceived; there is little chance that an ambiguously perceived portion can be supplied by S on the basis of its context. This statement is essentially statistical, for it involves an estimate of the relative chances of supplying missing parts to familiar and unfamiliar patterns.

A quantitative formulation of the relative chances of completing the patterns correctly is provided by the theory of communication recently developed by Shannon (3). In its simplest form this theory states that the amount of information carried by a signal is proportional to the logarithm of the number of alternative signals that might have occurred. If the particular symbol is chosen from a wide range of alternatives, then its occurrence conveys more information than would the same symbol chosen from a limited range of alternatives. Thus the quantity of information does not depend upon the particular symbol, but rather upon the size of the set of alternative symbols from which the particular symbol is drawn.

Suppose we wished to construct a language to refer to any one of 64 different objects. This simple pointing language, let us call it language A, will have an alphabet of 64 different letters and each letter will have its own definition relating it to one of the 64 objects. Now for purposes of comparison let us construct a language B, following the same rules, save that this time we shall have only 32 letters, each denoting one of 32 objects. Now we may inquire about the information per letter in these two languages. It is evident that the occurrence of a letter in language A contains more information than the occurrence of a letter in language B. For as we have noted, information increases with the number of alternatives from which a particular symbol is drawn.

Most languages, however, do not have as many different symbols as there are things that the language can point to. Let us now construct a language C, with only eight different letters in its alphabet. Used one at a time, the letters of a language could refer only to eight objects. In order to refer to more than eight objects, we shall have to use more than one letter at a time. If we decide to use letters in pairs, we find that this language of eight letters yields 64 possible pairs. Each of these pairs can now have its own definition relating it to one of 64 different objects. Note that under these conditions two letters in this language contain the same amount of information as did one letter in language *A*. It is in this sense that one can say that there is twice as much information per letter in language *A* as in this eight-letter language.

Once the relation of information to range of alternatives is established it is possible to discuss the effects of context upon information. The argument is that the context operates to reduce the effective range of alternatives and thus to reduce the amount of information that the symbol carries. For example, suppose a pattern is exposed briefly and *S* sees *I* but nothing else. If he knows the pattern is nonsense, he has one chance in 26 of guessing the next letter correctly. If he knows the pattern is a word, his best guess is that *N* follows *I,* for this is the letter that follows most frequently (once in every five appearances of *I*) in ordinary English. He can, therefore, improve his chances from 1 in 26 to 1 in 5 if he knows the pattern is a word. Now suppose he perceives *RI* and so has more contextual information upon which to base a guess as to the next letter. This context reduces still further the range of alternative letters that might follow. If he sees *ERI* he has still more context; and by the time the context has grown to *EXPERI* there are only two likely alternatives left, *EXPERIENCE* and *EXPERIMENT*. As the context grows, the range of alternatives decreases, and the information carried by the next letter also decreases.

When missing or ambiguous portions of a stimulus pattern can be supplied correctly by *S* on the basis of the context alone, the missing portions carry little or no information. This fact is referred to as the redundancy of the language. If a language is highly redundant, the relative information per symbol is much lower than it would be if successive symbols in a message could be chosen independently. The extent to which the context limits the range of possible continuations and makes the next choice depend upon the choices of the preceding symbols is the extent to which the language is redundant and the information per symbol is reduced. The ratio of the average information per symbol to the maximum that could be had with no contextual constraints is the relative information per symbol. The measure of redundancy is one minus the relative information per symbol.

With this theoretical orientation the results of the perceptual experiments suggest a simple hypothesis: Within reasonable limits, the total amount of information received by Ss familiar with the language is constant and unaffected by the redundancy of the language. For example, consider the experimental conditions where only two or three letters can be perceived correctly in a nonsense pattern, but six or eight can be perceived correctly if they form a word. In the nonsense case the information per letter is greater, but fewer letters are perceived correctly. With a familiar word, more letters are perceived, but the information per letter is reduced by redundancy. The hypothesis suggests that the amount of information received is approximately the same in both cases, and that the number of letters perceived correctly is not a direct measure of the amount of information received.

Experimental Design

The purpose of the experiment was to test the hypothesis that the amount of information per exposure is relatively constant (even though the number of letters received varies) as a function of the familiarity of the letter sequences. With this hypothesis in mind the experiment was conducted as follows. Pseudo words were constructed in such a manner as to reflect different degrees of contextual constraint. These words were exposed tachistoscopically to a group of Ss who wrote what they saw. They saw more letters correctly when the pseudo words reflected the contextual constraints of ordinary English than they did when successive letters were independent. These results are then used to test the hypothesis presented above.

The pseudo words were constructed according to the procedure discussed by Shannon (3). The minimal amount of contextual constraint (called a zero-order approximation to English) was obtained by selecting letters from the alphabet according to a table of random numbers. Every letter in the alphabet had an equal opportunity to occur.

More contextual constraint was obtained by selecting letters according to their relative frequencies of occurrence in English (first-order approximation). This is accomplished by selecting letters from printed English according to a table of random numbers. The printed material contains the letters in proportions corresponding to their relative frequencies. Drawing single letters at random from a sample text thus introduces constraints on the choice of letters that makes the first-order more like English than the zero-order approximation.

The third class of pseudo words was constrained by the context of the immediately preceding letter. The pseudo words thus reflected the relative frequencies of occurrence of *pairs* of letters in English (second-order approximation). These were constructed by drawing pairs of letters from printed English according to a simple rule. Suppose the sequence started with *T*. The next letter was selected by searching for the next occurrence of *T* (not in a final position), then recording the letter which followed immediately after. This was, say, *H*. Then the next letter was selected by reading on through the passage until *H* occurred again, then recording the letter that followed. By this procedure the chance of selecting a given letter depends upon its likelihood after the preceding letter in normal English writing. The process might produce the pseudo word *THERARES,* for example.

The final class of pseudo words reflected the relative frequencies of occurrence of sequences of four letters in English (fourth-order approximation). Each letter was chosen according to the three letters that preceded it. For example, the word might begin with *VER*. We search until this sequence occurs again, and note that it is followed by *N*. Now we take *ERN* and search until this pattern occurs again. It is followed by, say, *A*. Then we look for *RNA* and note the letter that follows, and so on. In this way the pseudo word *VERNALIT* might be produced.

All the pseudo words were eight letters long. Fifteen different words were constructed at each order of approximation to English. These sixty pseudo words are presented in Table 1. It is clear that although these sequences become more wordlike when the choice of the successive letters depends upon more context, all were, strictly speaking, nonsense. But they represent degrees of nonsense for which we have a definition.

TABLE 1 Pseudo Words Constructed at Different Orders of Approximation to English

0-Order	1-Order	2-Order	4-Order
YRULPZOC	STANUGOP	WALLYLOF	RICANING
OZHGPMTJ	VTYEHULO	THERARES	VERNALIT
DLEGQMNW	EINOAASE	CHEVADNE	MOSSIANT
GFUJXZAQ	IYDEWAKN	NERMBLIM	POKERSON
WXPAUJVB	RPITCQET	ONESTEVA	ONETICUL
VQWBVIFX	OMNTOHCH	ACOSUNST	ATEDITOL
CVGJCDHM	DNEHHSNO	SERRRTHE	APHYSTER
MFRSIWZE	RSEMPOIN	ROCEDERT	TERVALLE
EJOYOEVZ	ISAAESPW	HEFLINYC	CULATTER
GFXRWMXR	ITYNENEE	EDINGEDL	PREVERAL
BHDTUNQK	OAENSTVT	LIKINERA	FAVORIAL
ANROAHOV	NHIDCFRA	RIPRYPLI	LYMISTIC
HHJHUFSW	YWDNMIIE	UMATSORE	OTATIONS
IJHBWSTT	IODTIRPS	SINEDSIN	INFOREMS
EAPMZCEN	NHGTTEDE	EDESENER	EXPRESPE

The percentage of the letters correctly recognized was determined by the following procedure. A lantern slide was made for each of the pseudo words. Each of the 60 pseudo words was projected tachistoscopically on a large screen for durations of 10, 20, 40, 100, and 500 milliseconds. These durations were obtained with a camera shutter. All 60 of the words were first exposed in a random order for 10 milliseconds each, then the order was scrambled and all 60 were presented again for 20 milliseconds, and so on, up to the 500 millisecond duration which was presented last.

A group of six Harvard undergraduates served as Ss. They were seated about 10 feet from the screen. Uniform fixation was provided by boundary lines above and below the area in which the pseudo words were projected. Measurements with a Macbeth illuminometer showed that the letters were 3.65 apparent foot candles on a background of 3.94 apparent foot candles.

The Ss were provided mimeographed answer sheets with eight blanks to be filled for each of 60 items. At the top of this sheet were the following instructions: "The patterns you see will consist of eight letters from the alphabet. None of the sequences of eight letters forms a word that you could find in the dictionary. Fill in the blanks below with the letters you see. Try to place each letter in its correct position."

Results

The results were scored in two different ways: (*a*) the total number of correct letters, regardless of position, and (*b*) the number of correct letters that were recorded in the proper blank on the answer sheet. For convenience, (*a*) will be called the letter score, and (*b*) the placement score. Both scores were converted into percentages for all six *S*s, and these are presented in Table 2. The placement scores are presented graphically in Figure 1. Letter scores provide functions qualitatively similar to those in Figure 1.

TABLE 2 *The Letter Score and Placement Score
for Four Sets of Pseudo Words at Six
Different Exposure Durations*

Exposure Duration (msec)	Order of Approximation to English			
	0	*1*	*2*	*4*
10	15.8 (5.5)	23.5 (10.8)	19.4 (10.7)	22.7 (12.6)
20	32.9 (19.6)	43.5 (25.7)	46.0 (27.3)	55.8 (37.1)
40	50.2 (31.6)	61.2 (37.8)	69.0 (46.6)	73.0 (57.4)
100	52.8 (36.9)	69.2 (43.0)	77.6 (59.5)	87.1 (70.1)
200	62.5 (41.0)	73.5 (47.5)	83.2 (67.5)	91.2 (79.2)
500	66.0 (49.0)	85.0 (66.2)	90.5 (76.2)	96.0 (91.0)

Note: Scores are given as percentages. The letter score is given first, and beneath it in parentheses is the placement score. Averages for six observers and 15 pseudo words.

The data reveal a consistent difference among the orders of approximation at all exposure durations. The most nonsensical pseudo words (zero-order) yield the lowest scores, and the most sensible pseudo

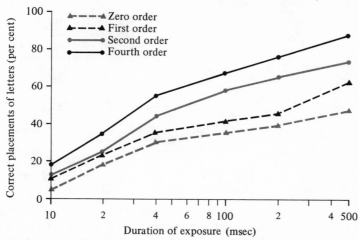

FIGURE 1. Average placement scores plotted against duration of exposure for pseudo words at four orders of approximation to English

words (fourth-order) yield the highest scores. The data do not reveal any significant learning effects at the longer exposure times, so the effects of increasing familiarity with the test materials can be neglected in the discussion.

Discussion

In order to check the hypothesis that a constant amount of information is received under a given exposure duration, we need a measure of the redundancy of sequences of letters in English. Figure 2 summarizes the data currently available. Shannon (4) has calculated the relative information per symbol for sequences up to three in length, and we have made our own count of pairs of letters. There is excellent agreement between these two direct estimates. Shannon has also used an indirect experimental method to determine upper and lower bounds for the amount of information per letter for sequences up to 15 letters in length. These estimates are also shown in Figure 2. Shannon's upper bounds coincide rather well with the actual counts of pairs and triplets, but the lower bounds show far more redundancy than any direct measure has yet indicated. We have taken our estimates of redundancy, therefore, from the solid curve of Figure 2: zero per cent redundancy at the zero order of approximation, 15 per cent at the first order, 29 per cent at the second order, and 43 per cent at the fourth order.

Letters chosen at random are not limited by context in any way. If we regard this case as 100 per cent relative information per letter, then the redundancy of the zero-order approximation is clearly zero per cent. As

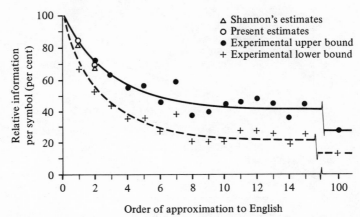

FIGURE 2. Relative amount of information per letter as a function of the order of approximation to the statistical structure of written English (The relative information is the ratio of the average information per symbol to the maximum per symbol obtainable without the operation of contextual constraints.)

soon as we make some letters more likely than others, however, our choice of letters is constrained and we cannot convey as much information per letter. Estimates from guessing experiments and from actual counts of the frequencies of 27-letter English both indicate that we can convey only about 85 per cent as much information per letter with a first-order approximation as we can with a zero-order approximation. That is to say, we need 15 per cent more letters with the first-order approximation in order to encode the same amount of information. When we take into account the fact that some pairs of letters are more frequent than others, we find that our choice of letters is still further constrained by context. At the second order we require 29 per cent more letters to encode the same amount of information. The redundancy of a fourth-order approximation to English has not been directly calculated from counts of four-letter sequences, but an estimate of 43 per cent redundancy seems reasonable from the data of Figure 2.

These values of the information per letter at the different orders of approximation are used to reinterpret the experimental data. For example, at 40 milliseconds the average S got four out of the eight letters correct (letter score) for the zero-order approximation, but got six out of eight correct when the fourth-order words were exposed. The fourth order, however, carries only 57 per cent as much information per letter. Thus the fourth-order information was the equivalent of $6 \times .57 = 3.4$ letters correct at the zero-order approximation. Correcting the score according to the relative information per letter greatly reduces the discrepancy between the different orders of approximation.

Table 3 shows the results when they are corrected for the relative amounts of information per letter. The original scores in Table 2 are simply multiplied by the relative information per letter determined from Figure 2. When this correction is made, the scores for all orders of approximation are reduced to approximately the same values as the scores for the zero-order approximation.

TABLE 3 *Letter and Placement Scores Corrected for Relative Amounts of Information per Letter*

Exposure Duration (msec)	Order of Approximation to English			
	0	1	2	4
10	15.8 (5.5)	20.0 (9.2)	13.8 (7.6)	12.9 (7.2)
20	32.9 (19.6)	37.0 (21.8)	32.7 (19.4)	31.8 (21.2)
40	50.2 (31.6)	52.0 (32.2)	49.0 (33.1)	46.6 (32.7)
100	52.8 (36.9)	58.9 (36.5)	55.1 (42.3)	49.6 (40.0)
200	62.5 (41.0)	62.3 (40.4)	59.1 (48.0)	52.0 (45.1)
500	66.0 (49.0)	72.1 (56.3)	64.3 (54.2)	54.7 (51.8)

Note: The scores given in Table 2 are multiplied by the appropriate values of information per letter taken from Figure 2. The letter score is given first, and beneath it, in parentheses, is the placement score.

In Figure 3 the placement scores, corrected for information value, are replotted for comparison with Figure 1. From Figure 3 it is apparent that all four functions are clustered together. For the placement scores, therefore, we can conclude that our hypothesis is approximately correct to the fourth order. The corrected letter scores, however, are more variable. There is a ceiling of 57 per cent placed over the fourth-order letter scores when they are corrected; they cannot possibly rise as high as the zero-order letter scores at the long durations. The letter scores do not provide a fair test of the hypothesis. In the range up to 100 milliseconds, however, the test is reasonable and the corrected scores tend to support the hypothesis.

We conclude, therefore, that the amount of information obtained from the tachistoscopic exposure under the conditions of this experiment depend upon the conditions of illumination and exposure duration, and are inde-

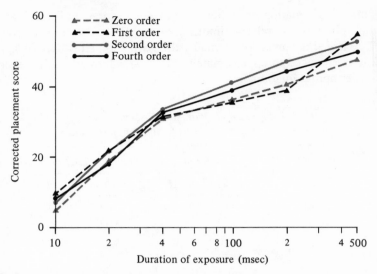

FIGURE 3. Average placement scores multiplied by the relative amounts of information per letter plotted against duration of exposure for pseudo words at four orders of approximation to English

pendent of the order of approximation to English letter sequences. The uncorrected percentage scores are not a direct measure of the amount of information obtained from the exposure, but differences in the percentage of letters correct can be predicted from a knowledge of the statistical structure of English. It follows from the above that the more frequently a trace has been embedded in a trace aggregate, to use the language of Gestalt theory, the greater the probability that the aggregate will be aroused when a component is activated.

Conclusions

Tachistoscopic identification of letter sequences is a function of the conditions of illumination and exposure duration. These factors control the amount of information that is presented to the observer. The number of letters identified correctly increases when the stimulus sequence provides a context familiar to the observer. When the sequence is a word, for example, a larger absolute number of letters is perceived under given exposure conditions than if the sequence is nonsense. Thus it appears that context improves recognition. However, the number of letters perceived correctly is not a measure of the amount of information received from the exposure, since this measure fails to take redundancy into account. When the lower informational value of the contextually constrained sequences is considered, the corrected identification scores for familiar and unfamiliar sequences of letters become essentially equivalent.

References

1. CATTELL, J. McK. 1885. Ueber die Zeit der Erkennung und Benennung von Schriftzeichen, Bildern und Farben. *Philosophische Studien* 2:635–50.
2. CATTELL, J. McK. 1886. Psychometrische Untersuchungen. *Philosophische Studien* 3:452–92.
3. SHANNON, C. E. 1948. A mathematical theory of communication. *Bell System Technical Journal* 27:379–423, 623–56.
4. SHANNON, C. E. 1951. Prediction and entropy of printed English. *Bell System Technical Journal* 30:50–64.

4

On the Perception
of Incongruity: A Paradigm*

Perceiving, for all its nicety of functioning in the dark room under strict instructions for accuracy, comprises a highly complex series of little-understood psychological processes. For, under all conditions, perceiving represents a resultant of two complex sets of specifications. One set describes the conditions of stimulation. This is done either in terms of physical measures such as wave length, or in terms of psychological norms such as in the description of a picture as that picture is seen by normal observers under optimal conditions and with a set for accuracy. This first set of specifications we are used to calling stimulus factors.

Stimuli, however, do not act upon an indifferent organism. There is never, in the old-fashioned language of G. F. Stout, "anoetic sentience." The organism in perception is in one way or another in a state of expectancy about the environment. It is a truism worth repeating that the perceptual effect of a stimulus is necessarily dependent upon the set or expectancy of the organism. And so, in many situations the student of perception must also specify the expectancies of the organism when exposed to stimulation. If we sometimes, in simple sensory experiments, fail

* "On the Perception of Incongruity: A Paradigm," by Jerome S. Bruner and Leo J. Postman, from the *Journal of Personality,* No. 18, September 1949. Reprinted by permission of Duke University Press and the authors.

to do so, the reason is not that we do not care about the attitude of the organism but, rather, that we take it for granted that the observer is attentive to the task and that he is seeking to judge in terms of some required sensory dimension and not some other.

There have been very few systematic efforts to analyze the dimensions of set and to formulate laws regarding the effectiveness of set in perception such as those which describe stimulus-perception relationships. That students of nonsensory or directive factors in perception have thus far refrained from any large-scale statement of principles, while a mark of admirable modesty in the face of a very confusing array of experimental data, is highly regrettable. It has prevented the emergence of new hypotheses which, flowing even from premature principles, might serve to test the utility of theories of perception.

Though empirical in nature, our discussion is essentially an essay on the theory of perception—or at least that part of the theory of perception which deals with directive factors in the perceiving process. Our basic axiom has already been stated—that perceiving is a process which results from the stimulation of a prepared or *eingestellt* organism. A second axiom concerns the operation of such directive factors: Given a stimulus input of certain characteristics, directive processes in the organism operate to organize the perceptual field in such a way as to maximize percepts relevant to current needs and expectations and to minimize percepts inimical to such needs and expectations. This "minimax" axiom we have referred to elsewhere as the construction-defense balance in perceiving (1).

All of which is not to say that perception is always wishful or autistic. Indeed, that is not the point. *Wishfulness* has to do with the nature of the expectations which are at work and is not a term relevant to the perceiving process as such. By *wishful* we mean an expectation with a low probability of being confirmed by events. The construction-defense process operates where expectations are realistic or where they are wishful. In the former case, it is simply a matter of constructing a percept which is relevant, say, to the exigencies of locomotion, defending against percepts which, though potentially wish-fulfilling, are disruptive to the task of locomotion. While directive factors do operate in the interests of locomotion, the skier on the trail does not organize the distant steep hillside in a manner which would make his own path seem less steep and hazardous. Rather, in his perception, the dangers ahead may be sharpened and emphasized. Similarly, although it is the other side of the coin of realism, one smitten by love does rather poorly in perceiving the linear characteristics of his beloved. His perceptual expectancies, so to speak, are elsewhere. The construction-defense balance operates along other lines. One sees softness of the skin, loftiness of brow, lightness of step—but perception of certain physical flaws does not materialize.

Perceptual expectancies, whether realistic or wishful, continue to operate so long as they are reinforced by the outcome of events. In short, expectancies continue to mold perceptual organization in a self-sustaining fashion so long as they are confirmed. It is when well-established expectancies fail of confirmation that the organism may face a task of perceptual reorganization.

Our principal concern here is with the perceptual events which occur when perceptual expectancies fail of confirmation—the problem of incongruity. Incongruity represents a crucial problem for a theory of perception because, by its very nature, its perception represents a violation of expectation. An unexpected concatenation of events, a conspicuous mismatching, an unlikely pairing of cause and effect—all of these have in common a violation of normal expectancy. Yet incongruities are perceived. Through a process of "trial-and-check," to borrow a phrase from Woodworth (8), the organism operates to discover whether any given expectancy will pay off. It is either a very sick organism, an overly motivated one, or one deprived of the opportunity to "try-and-check" which will not give up an expectancy in the face of a contradicting environment.

It is our contention, nonetheless, that for as long as possible and by whatever means available, the organism will ward off the perception of the unexpected, those things which do not fit his prevailing set. Our assumption, and it is hardly extravagant, is simply that most people come to depend upon a certain constancy in their environment and, save under special conditions, attempt to ward off variations from this state of affairs: "Thar ain't no such animal," the hayseed is reputed to have said on seeing his first giraffe.

Turning now to the study itself, our aim was to observe the behavior of intact, normal organisms faced with incongruous situations. How are such situations coped with perceptually? What is seen and under what conditions? We shall not be concerned here with factors making for differences among individuals in their tolerance for incongruity. That is for other studies. It is essential first to examine how incongruity is dealt with, what repertory of responses is available to the organism in incongruous situations.

The Experiment

Twenty-eight subjects, students at Harvard and Radcliffe, were shown successively by tachistoscopic exposure five different playing cards. From one to four of these cards were incongruous—color and suit were reversed. The order of presentation of normal and incongruous cards was random. The normal and trick cards used were the following:

Normal cards (printed in their proper color): five of hearts, ace of hearts, five of spades, seven of spades

Trick cards (printed with color reversed): three of hearts (black), four of hearts (black), two of spades (red), six of spades (red), ace of diamonds (black), six of clubs (red)

Fourteen orders of presentation were worked out, and two subjects were presented the cards in each of these orders. There were three types of stimulus series: (*a*) a single trick card embedded in a series of four normal cards; (*b*) a single normal card embedded in a series of four trick cards; (*c*) a mixed series in which trick and normal cards were in the ratio of 3:2 or 2:3. A summary of the orders of presentation appears in Table 1. The reader will note that the average number value of the trick cards is slightly under 4 (3.94) and slightly over 4 for the normal cards (4.35)—a flaw which operates slightly against the recognition of normal cards since lower value cards are probably more easily recognized.

TABLE 1 Orders of Presentation

Order	Card 1	Card 2	Card 3	Card 4	Card 5
Isolated trick					
1	4H (B)	5H	7S	AH	5S
2	7S	5H	4H (B)	AH	5S
3	5S	AH	7S	5H	3H (B)
Isolated normal					
4	5H	2S (R)	AD (B)	3H (B)	6S (R)
5	6S (R)	3H (B)	7S	6C (R)	2S (R)
6	4H (B)	6C (R)	2S (R)	3H (B)	5H
Mixed					
7	2S (R)	4H (B)	AH	7S	6S (R)
8	5S	2S (R)	4H (B)	6S (R)	AH
9	4H (B)	7S	AH	6S (R)	3H (B)
10	5H	2S (R)	5S	6S (R)	4H (B)
11	5S	AH	6S (R)	4H (B)	5H
12	2S (R)	5H	7S	AH	4H (B)
13	7S	3H (B)	6S (R)	AH	5S
14	3H (B)	5H	6S (R)	7S	AH

Each card was presented successively until correct recognition occurred, three times each at 10, 30, 50, 70, 100, 150, 200, 250, 300, 400, 450, 500, 600, 700, 800, 900, and 1,000 milliseconds. If at 1,000 milliseconds recognition did not occur, the next card was presented. In determining thresholds, correct recognition was defined as two successive correct responses. At each exposure, the subject was asked to report everything he saw or thought he saw.

The cards were mounted on medium gray cardboard and were shown in a Dodge-Gerbrands tachistoscope. The pre-exposure field was of the same gray color and consistency as the exposure field save that it contained no playing card. The light in the tachistoscope was provided by two G.E. daylight fluorescent tubes.

A word about the color of the incongruous cards is in order. Our efforts to have them printed by a playing card company were in vain. We therefore used poster paints to alter the colors of the cards. We had difficulty matching the red of a playing card, our best match being a slightly muddier and less yellow red than that of a regular card. Because of this, all red cards—trick and normal alike—were painted over in this color.

Results

Thresholds.   Perhaps the most central finding is that the recognition threshold for the incongruous playing cards (those with suit and color reversed) is significantly higher than the threshold for normal cards. While normal cards on the average were recognized correctly—here defined as a correct response followed by a second correct response—at 28 milliseconds, the incongruous cards required 114 milliseconds. The difference representing a fourfold increase in threshold, is highly significant statistically, t being 3.76 (confidence level $<.01$).

The threshold data, expressed as the cumulative percentage of stimuli correctly recognized as a function of increasing exposure time, are presented in Figure 1. The curves, generally, are parallel. The reader will note that even at the longest exposure used, 1,000 milliseconds, only 89.7 per cent of the incongruous cards had been correctly recognized while 100 per cent of the normal cards had been recognized by 350 milliseconds.

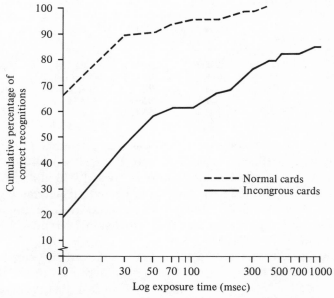

FIGURE 1. Cumulative percentage of normal and incongruous playing cards correctly recognized as a function of increasing exposure time

Our design was such that we might test the hypothesis that the more experience a subject had had in the past with incongruity, the less difficulty he would have in recognizing incongruity of a related nature. Indeed, this is tantamount to saying that when one has experienced an incongruity often enough, it ceases to violate expectancy and hence ceases to be incongruous. Experience with an incongruity is effective insofar as it modifies the set of the subject to prepare him for incongruity. To take an example, the threshold recognition time for incongruous cards presented before the subject has had anything else in the tachistoscope—normal or incongruous —is 360 milliseconds. If he has had experience in the recognition of one or more normal cards before being presented an incongruous stimulus, the threshold rises slightly but insignificantly to 420 milliseconds. Prior experience with normal cards does not lead to better recognition performance with incongruous cards (Table 2). If, however, an observer has had to rec-

TABLE 2 *The Effect of Previous Experience*
with Normal Cards upon the First Recognition
of Incongruous Cards

Previous Practice with Normal Cards	*Mean Recognition Time*	*Number of Threshold Determinations*	*Mean Serial Position of First Incongruous Card*
None	360 msec	14	1.0
One or more normal cards	420 msec	14	2.6
	$t = .38$		
	$P = .68$		

ognize one incongruous card, the threshold for the next trick card he is presented drops to 230 milliseconds. If, finally, the incongruous card comes after experience with two or three previously exposed trick cards, threshold drops still further to 84 milliseconds. These figures, along with relevant tests of significance are summarized in Table 3 and plotted in Figure 2.

The point immediately arises as to how much the decrease in threshold noted above is due to sheer number of trials in the tachistoscope (skill practice) and how much to the heightened expectancy of incongruity. Unfortunately our data are confounded in a complicated way here, and we shall have to depend upon rather broad inferences. We cannot partial out the differential effect of serial position of a card, whether first or third or fifth in the series, independently of the kinds of experience the subject had before being presented any given card. Because of the nature of our design, such a procedure would leave us with groups differing in number and in the difficulty of cards presented. What evidence we have points, however, to the importance of previous experience with incongruity quite apart

TABLE 3 *The Effect of Previous Experience with Incongruous Cards on the Recognition of Subsequent Incongruous Cards*

Nature of Previous Practice with Incongruous Cards	Mean Recognition Time	Threshold Number of Determinations	Mean Serial Position of Incongruous Cards
None	390 msec	28	1.8
One card	230 msec	22	3.3
Two or more cards	84 msec	20	4.2

Tests of significance

None versus one $t = 1.42$, $P = .16$
None versus two or more $t = 3.20$, $P = .001$
One versus two or more $t = 1.72$, $P = .08$

from skill practice. We have remarked already that previous tachistoscopic experience with normal cards serves to raise slightly the threshold for incongruous cards. Sheer skill practice cannot, then, be solely or even largely responsible for decreasing the threshold for incongruous cards.

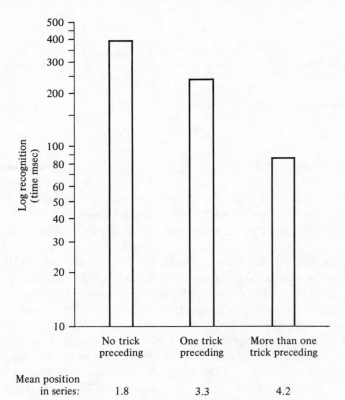

FIGURE 2. *Recognition thresholds for incongruous cards as a function of past experience with such cards*

Reactions to Incongruity. We may ask properly at this point why the recognition threshold for incongruous stimuli was four times as high as the threshold for normal cards. The answer, it appears from an analysis of the data, lies in the manner in which subjects dealt with or coped with incongruity per se.

Generally speaking, there appear to be four kinds of reaction to rapidly presented incongruities. The first of these we have called the dominance reaction. It consists, essentially, of a perceptual denial of the incongruous elements in the stimulus pattern. Faced with a red six of spades, for example, a subject may report with considerable assurance, "the six of spades" or the "six of hearts," depending upon whether he is color- or formbound (vide infra). In the one case the form dominates and the color is assimilated to it; in the other the stimulus color dominates and form is assimilated to it. In both instances the perceptual resultant conforms with past expectations about the normal nature of playing cards.

A second technique of dealing with incongruous stimuli we have called compromise. In the language of Egon Brunswik (2), it is the perception of a *Zwischengegenstand* or compromise object which composes the potential conflict between two or more perceptual intentions. Three examples of color compromise: (*a*) the red six of spades is reported as either the purple six of hearts or the purple six of spades; (*b*) the black four of hearts is reported as a grayish four of spades; (*c*) the red six of clubs is seen as "the six of clubs illuminated by red light."

A third reaction may be called disruption. A subject fails to achieve a perceptual organization at the level of coherence normally attained by him at a given exposure level. Disruption usually follows upon a period in which the subject has failed to resolve the stimulus in terms of his available perceptual expectations. He has failed to confirm any of his repertory of expectancies. Its expression tends to be somewhat bizarre: "I don't know what the hell it is now, not even for sure whether it's a playing card," said one frustrated subject after an exposure well above his normal threshold.

Finally, there is recognition of incongruity, the fourth, and from the experimenter's point of view, most successful reaction. It, too, is marked by some interesting psychological by-products, of which more will be said.

Consider now each of these four reactions, the forms they take, and the way in which they differentiate responses to normal and trick cards.

Dominance Reactions

A first datum is that 27 out of our 28 subjects showed dominance responses to the trick cards in their records, some considerably more than others. Strictly speaking, there is often no determinate way to discover dominance reactions to a normal card. A correct response may be a dominance response—either dominance of color or dominance of form. A few instances of discernible dominance reactions to the normal cards were observed in the case of erroneous perceptions. There were, for example, instances in which a red normal card was seen as black and form was assimilated to match the black color. One subject saw the red five of hearts as the black five of spades for 8 out of the 25 exposures required for full recognition; another saw the red ace of hearts as the black ace of clubs for 3 out of 15 trials required for recognition. In sum, then, 7 per cent of the subjects showed dominance responses to the normal cards—attempting to rectify an incongruity imposed on themselves by seeing our imperfect red cards as black—while 96 per cent of the subjects showed dominance reactions to the incongruous cards.

The nature of the dominance reactions to the trick cards is easily described. First, such reactions occurred with equal frequency to trick black and trick red cards. Two options were available: Either the subject could organize the field in terms of suit, for instance, hearts seen as red regardless of their stimulus color; or the field could be organized in terms of color, for instance, a red card seen as a heart or diamond regardless of its true suit.

It must be said, with whatever bearing it may have for Rorschach theory, that subjects showed a marked preference for one or another of the dominance options. Assuming that a 50:50 distribution of form- and color-dominant responses would be expected by chance, we tested for form and color types among our subjects. Of the 27 subjects showing dominance responses, 19 showed preferences for form or color in excess of chance at the .05 level or better; the remaining 8 being equally prone to both kinds of response.

To sum up, dominance reactions to trick cards were almost universal among our subjects. An incongruous stimulus was rendered congruent with expectancy by the operation of either form or color dominance. Only a small fraction of the responses to the normal cards was of this type; and where such responses occurred, they were always elicited by incongruities imposed by the subject through a failure to perceive correctly one of the attributes of the normal cards—for instance, perceiving a red card as black.

Compromise Reactions

As we have already noted, a compromise perception is one in which the resultant perception embodies elements of both the expected attribute and the attribute provided by stimulation. Compromise reactions are, of course, limited to certain types of stimulus situations where a perceptual middle ground exists between the expectancy and the stimulus contradicting the expectancy. Our situation was one such. The subjects often perceived color in such a way as to make it more in keeping with, or to bring it nearer to, normal expectation about what colors go with what suits. Perhaps the best way to illustrate the point is to list the different colors reported when subjects were presented with red spade and club cards:

Brown	Black on reddish card
Black and red mixed	Olive drab
Black with red edges	Grayish red
Black in red light	Looks reddish, then blackens
Purple	Blackish brown
Black but redness somewhere	Blurred reddish
Rusty color	Near black but not quite
Rusty black	Black in yellow light
Lighter than black, blacker than red	

Several questions arise at once. To what extent can the color compromise reactions be attributed to the action time required for the development of red? To what extent is compromise color due to the fact that our cards were not precisely playing-card red in color? Answers to these questions can be provided in two ways.

First, the normal red cards (hearts and diamonds) were colored in precisely the same manner as the incongruous red cards (trick spades and clubs). This being the case, we would expect (if action time or off-color alone accounted for compromise) that there would be no difference between normal and trick red cards. There is, however, a striking difference. In reacting to trick red cards, 50 per cent of the subjects showed compromise responses; only 15 per cent showed such responses to the normal red cards. It should be noted, moreover, that if action time were a major factor, the normal cards, recognized on the whole at briefer durations, should have been more susceptible to compromise.

We have also checked on the frequency of compromise responses per card for those cards which elicited any compromise responses at all. When compromise responses do occur, will there be a difference in their frequency for normal and incongruous cards? Using percentages of exposures on which compromises occurred, weighted by total number of trials to recognition, we find that the percentage of compromises elicited by incongruous cards averages 63 per cent of the exposures preceding correct recognition. On the other hand, those normal cards which produced compromise responses did so on the average in only 32 per cent of the prerecognition exposures.

In sum, then, it seems highly unlikely that either off-coloredness or action time alone accounted for these interesting responses. The question remains, of course, as to whether these two considerations facilitated the appearance of compromise. Although we lack publishable evidence on the point at this time, it seems to us on the basis of our own direct observations of briefly presented colors that both are important. Color, briefly presented, is subjectively more labile; one is somewhat less subjectively certain about its hue, and saturation is less. Given the decreased stability of the color in our briefly presented cards, it is not surprising that the normal expectation should readily lead to compromise. And when, moreover, the card falls somewhat short of playing card redness, the tendency toward partial assimilation may become even greater.

Compromise reactions to black cards were considerably rarer than such reactions to the red cards. When they did occur, they were always given to trick black cards, never to normal ones. Only 11 per cent of the subjects showed such responses. Where they did appear, they constituted a weighted proportion of only 12 per cent of the prerecognition trials. The quality of the compromise responses to black trick cards was not strikingly different from that already reported for red cards.

Grayish tinged with red
Black with reddish-gray background
Dark red
First black, then red, then black

Why so few compromise responses to the black cards? Several highly conjectural answers are worth examining. The first, and perhaps the most likely, has to do with the greater phenomenal stability of black at rapid exposure. There is, to be sure, a certain graying effect if the black is figural on white, which probably has to do with the poorly defined boundaries of such a figure at brief exposure. But the gray does not have the same quality of lability or instability of the chromatic card when presented for a brief duration (for instance, 10–50 milliseconds).

What, precisely, is involved in perceptual compromise? The most parsimonious assumption, we think, is that we are dealing with a special case of color assimilation, namely, assimilation to expectancy. The effect has been noted before, although it may not have been called compromise. For example, Duncker (3) reports that a green felt leaf in hidden red illumination maintains its greenness better than an identically colored felt donkey in the same illumination. It is apparent from his subjects' color matches that neither stimulus object maintained green perfectly, but that the leaf did so more than the donkey. The color wheel used as the variable stimulus for matching contained green, orange, and white sectors. The green sector for the leaf was 60 degrees, for the donkey, 39 degrees. Like us, Duncker was dealing in his experiment with the problem of "expectancy color"—that is, that leaves are green—and as in our case his subjects were compromising between an expected color (leaf green) and a given color (the resultant of leaf green in hidden red illumination). Very probably other experimenters, to name Heider (5) and Fuchs as but two examples, obtained color compromises at least in part dependent upon their subjects' expectations about the color of the objects being partially obscured by a differently colored episcotister.

Disruption

Disruption is a gross failure of the subject to organize the perceptual field at a level of efficiency usually associated with a given viewing condition. Let us say that for normal cards the subject is able to perceive the color, suit, and number at from 20 to 50 milliseconds. The same subject, faced with an incongruous card at 50 milliseconds may just begin reporting with some degree of confidence and only partial accuracy on the number and suit and color of the card before him. This may go on for several exposures as duration is increased, let us say, to 100 milliseconds—well above his normal threshold range. At this point, the subject loses confidence, becomes perceptually confused. Said our most extremely disrupted subject at 300 milliseconds in response to a red spade card: "I can't make the suit out, whatever it is. It didn't even look like a card that time. I don't know what color it is now or whether it's a spade or heart. I'm not even sure now what a spade looks like! My God!"

Disruption was not frequent in terms of the number of exposures on which it appeared. But it did occur in 16 of our 28 subjects in response to trick cards. Among these 16 subjects and for those cards on which disruption occurred at all, it occurred on the average in 4 per cent of their pre-recognition responses (percentages weighted by number of trials preceding recognition). Disruption typically occurred after the subject had tried out his available hypotheses and failed to come to a satisfactory recognition. In Woodworth's terms (8), the "trial-and-check" procedure had failed to yield a stable percept.

The kinds of disruption varied from subject to subject and even from card to card. In analyzing disorganized reactions, one can find any one or any combination of five disruptive effects. One might well expect that dis-

Color disruption:	4 *S*s
Form disruption:	10 *S*s
Form-color disruption:	3 *S*s
Number* disruption:	2 *S*s
Corner† disruption:	3 *S*s

* Number disruption is a loss of perceptual certainty about the number of symbols on the card.
† Corner disruption refers to confusion about what is in the corner of the card; for instance, reports that the pip in the corner is wrong or displaced or that the number in the corner seems out of place.

ruption would be selective, affecting those attributes of the stimulus with which the subject was having maximum difficulty. Indeed, the figures above point to such selectivity—form and color being the primary loci of incongruity. Having exhausted his resources in trying unsuccessfully to perceive the incongruous pairing of form and color, the subject might indeed be expected to end in the plight characterized by the typical remark: "I'll be damned if I know now whether it's red or what!"

But what of number disruption? How to account for it? Only two subjects, to be sure, seemed to show disruptive uncertainty about the number of pips present—in both cases after they had already perceived number correctly. In these instances one had the impression that the subjects had, so to speak, displaced their uncertainty upon an attribute of the stimulus which was not causing the real perceptual trouble. Indeed, an additional exploratory experiment has indicated that in an extremely difficult incongruity situation such displaced disruptions are more common than in the present experiment. In that experiment a series of normal cards had interspersed at random among them two rather fantastic cards procured from a magic supply house: a card containing 11 diamonds but labeled in the corner with the notation for the 15 of diamonds; the other was made up in the same way but was in the suit of spades and bore the notation of the 14 of spades. In response to both cards subjects not infrequently ran the gamut of displacement, first being uncertain, properly, about the number, then suit, then color, then (though not frequently) about the size of the card.

Tempting though it might be to relate proneness to disruption to such concepts as Frenkel-Brunswik's tolerance for ambiguity (4) or the concept of frustration tolerance (7), we do not at this time have any information which would warrant such an essay. One can, however, point to the phenomenon as a consequence of the frustration attendant upon failure to confirm a series of perceptual hypotheses. In this sense, the frustration is predominantly a perceptual matter (although some subjects grew irritated at their inability to get the stimulus).

A final word disposes of the frequency of disruption responses to the normal cards. There were none.

Recognition

In the perception of the incongruous stimuli, the recognition process is temporarily thwarted and exhibits characteristics which are generally not observable in the recognition of more conventional stimuli.

One specific way in which the recognition process is affected by the thwarting of well-established expectations is the emergence of a sense of wrongness. The subject may either, even while dominance and compromise responses are continuing, suddenly or gradually begin to report that there is something wrong with the stimulus without being able to specify what it is that is wrong. It is not infrequent after such a report to witness the onset of perceptual disruption. But at the same time, such a sense of wrongness may also turn out to be a prelude to veridical recognition, for it often has the effect of making the subject change his hypotheses or give up his previous expectation about the nature of the stimulus.

Occasionally, as in 6 of our 28 subjects, the sense of wrongness may become focused upon a rather tangential but, in point of fact, correct aspect of the incongruous stimuli and in so doing lead to a successful unmasking. These subjects, prior to correct recognition, all reported that the position of the pips on the card was wrong. All these responses were given either to spades printed in red or hearts printed in black at a time when the subject was calling the black hearts spades or the red spades hearts. "What's the matter with the symbols now? They look reversed or something. (*6SR*)" "The spades are turned the wrong way, I think. (*4HB*)" For those who do not have playing cards before them or who cannot remember the position of heart and spade pips, the former are printed with the point down in the top tier of pips and with the points up in the bottom, while spades are up-pointed in the top tier, down-pointed in the bottom.

Four of the six subjects who focused on this odd, and usually overlooked, positional arrangement of pips on a card finally achieved recognition. Two of the subjects failed to recognize their cards correctly in spite of unmasking this telltale feature.

Perhaps the greatest single barrier to the recognition of incongruous stimuli is the tendency for perceptual hypotheses to fixate after receiving a minimum of confirmation. As we have noted, some of our subjects persisted up to 1,000 milliseconds in giving dominance responses to incongruous stimuli. Once there had occurred in these cases a partial confirmation of the hypothesis that the card in the tachistoscope was a black club or a black spade, it seemed that nothing could change the subject's report. One subject gave 24 successive black color-dominant responses to the black three of hearts, another 44 of them (both calling it the three of spades). Another persisted for 16 trials in calling it a red three of hearts. There were 6 instances in which subjects persisted in a color or form dominance response for over 50 exposures up to 1,000 milliseconds, finally failing to recognize the card correctly.

Such fixation tendencies are, one might say, the chief block to perceptual learning. In another article on the effects of stress on perception (6), we pointed out that perceptual recklessness often resulted when a subject had to work under difficulties—the formation and fixation of premature and incorrect perceptual hypotheses. It would appear, indeed, that working in incongruous situations where partial confirmation of expectancy can occur (the form of a spade is not so different from that of a heart, even if the colors are) has the same effect of inducing premature fixation.

As for correct recognition of incongruity following an unsuccessful period of trial and check, we have irreverently come to call the response of some of our subjects the "My God!" reaction. For, to borrow a phrase from a distinguished literary critic, what occurs can well be characterized as "the shock of recognition."

One could, we suppose, liken the process of correct recognition to Köhler's description of insight. Indeed, it has some of the characteristics of sudden solution following unsuccessful attempts to master a situation. When a subject says, "Good Lord, what have I been saying? That's a *red* six of spades," there is no question about the sudden phenomenal emergence of the new perception.

Our reluctance in likening the phenomena to Köhler's description of insight is the suspicion that there is more to the matter than sudden emergence. The uncertainty that sometimes comes before, the sense of wrongness, the disruptions—all these point to the gradual weakening of previous hypotheses before sudden reorganization can occur. Indeed, to match cases of sudden phenomenal emergence, one sometimes finds a very gradual and almost timed approach to the correct recognition of incongruous object color. A subject viewing a red spade may start by reporting a red tint which gradually becomes redder on succeeding trials until he finally asserts that the card is a red spade.

Unfortunately, we have no light to throw on this particular variant of the continuity-noncontinuity sequence in perceptual reorganization.

Conclusions

Our major conclusion is simply a reaffirmation of the general statement that perceptual organization is powerfully determined by expectations built upon past commerce with the environment. When such expectations are violated by the environment, the perceiver's behavior can be described as resistance to the recognition of the unexpected or incongruous. The resistance manifests itself in subtle and complex but nevertheless distinguishable perceptual responses. Among the perceptual processes which implement this resistance are (*a*) the dominance of one principle of organization which prevents the appearance of incongruity and (*b*) a form of partial assimilation to expectancy which we have called compromise. When these responses fail and when correct recognition does not occur, what results may best be described as perceptual disruption. Correct recognition itself results when inappropriate expectancies are discarded after failure of confirmation.

References

1. BRUNER, J. S. 1948. Perceptual theory and the Rorschach test. *Journal of Personality* 17:157–68.
2. BRUNSWIK, E. 1934. *Wahrnehmung und Gegenstandswelt*. Vienna: Deuticke.
3. DUNCKER, K. 1939. The influence of past experience upon perceptual properties. *American Journal of Psychology* 52:255–65.

4. FRENKEL-BRUNSWIK, E. 1949. Intolerance of ambiguity as an emotional and perceptual personality variable. *Journal of Personality* 18:108–43.
5. HEIDER, G. 1932. New studies in transparency, form, and color. *Psychologische Forschung* 17:13–55.
6. POSTMAN, L., AND BRUNER, J. S. 1948. Perception under stress. *Psychological Review* 55:314–23.
7. ROSENZWEIG, S. 1944. Frustration theory. In *Personality and the behavior disorders,* J. McV. Hunt. New York: Ronald Press.
8. WOODWORTH, R. S. 1947. Reenforcement of perception. *American Journal of Psychology* 60:119–24.

5

Interference
in Visual Recognition[*]

Under ordinary conditions, visual recognition operates effortlessly and with no discernible interference. If the clarity of the display is diminished in some manner, however, recognition understandably takes longer. Moreover, studies indicate that if a subject is initially exposed to a blurred image that he cannot recognize, subsequent recognition of the image in clearer form is substantially delayed (1, 2, 3, 5). We are presently concerned with the further investigation of this interference phenomenon.

We varied both the range of blur to which subjects were exposed and the length of time of the exposure. Undergraduate subjects were shown eight ordinary color photographs, projected one at a time. The pictures were initially exposed in a state of blur and brought continuously into better focus. The initial point of focus was varied, as was the amount of time the changing picture was in view. Under all conditions, the picture being exposed was stopped at the same point of focus, regardless of its starting point and its rate of change of focus. At this common terminal point, the projected picture was turned off and the subject was asked to report what it was.

* "Interference in Visual Recognition," by Jerome S. Bruner and Mary C. Potter, from *Science*, Vol. 144, No. 3617, April 24, 1964, pp. 424–425. Copyright 1964 by the American Association for the Advancement of Science and reproduced by permission of the publisher and authors.

Three starting points of focus and the common stopping point were determined as follows. Thirteen subjects were run individually as a standardizing group and were presented the pictures in gradually increasing focus, starting from almost complete blur (very blurred, or *VB*). The point at which they reported correctly the identity of the picture was recorded. For each picture, the point at which it was first recognized by any subject was obtained (light blur, or *LB*), and likewise the point at which a quarter of the subjects recognized the objects (first quartile, or *FQ*); [1] this latter was the stopping point used with all later groups. A fourth point was computed for each picture that was about four-fifths of the way from the out-of-focus point (*VB*) to the point of first recognition (*LB*). This point we refer to as medium blur (*MB*). Each of these points varied, of course, from picture to picture, since some pictures in fact required more clarity for recognition than did others. Each picture, changing toward clearer focus, was exposed for one of three lengths of time, the exposure intervals being chosen in the following manner. A slow but constant rate of change was first selected such that the time between *VB* and *FQ* (the stopping point) averaged 122 seconds per picture (range from 92 to 145 seconds). At this same rate of change, the average time from *MB* to *FQ* was 35 seconds (range from 26 to 49 seconds), and the time from *LB* to *FQ* was 13 seconds (range from 4 to 25 seconds).

Eighty-nine new subjects were then divided into nine groups of approximately equal size. Three of these groups began their viewing of each picture at *VB;* of these three, one group covered the course from *VB* to *FQ* in the long exposure averaging 122 seconds, one covered the same course of focus in the medium exposure of 35 seconds, and one in the short exposure of 13 seconds. Likewise, three other groups viewed the pictures moving from *MB* to *FQ* with the same three exposure times. And a final three groups started at *LB* and were given the same three times of viewing, thus completing a 3 x 3 design.

The pictures, 35 millimeter Kodachrome slides, were of a dog standing on grass, a bird in the sky, an aerial view of a clover-leaf intersection, a pile of bricks, a fire hydrant, silverware on a rug, glass ashtrays piled on a desk, and a set of brass fire irons. A Sawyer projector, model 500 *EE,* was used in a dimly lit room to project the pictures onto a nonglare screen 4.5 meters away. A variable-speed motor controlled the excursion of the lens barrel, allowing focus to be changed at a wide range of rates. Subjects were run in groups up to 12, seated in two semicircular rows averaging 3.5 meters from the screen. All subjects had normal vision or corrected normal vision as tested by a Snellen chart. They wrote their responses to the pictures on prepared sheets.

---

[1] Since 13 subjects were used in the standardizing group, the point at which the fourth subject recognized the object was taken as the first quartile.

The results are shown in Table 1, and an analysis of variance is given in Table 2, based on the number of pictures (out of eight) recognized by each subject.[2] Viewing time has a systematic effect: On average, the longer the viewing time permitted, the more frequently a picture is recognized. Although the interaction between time and focus is not significant, there is a suggestion in Table 1 that viewing time has a greater effect on recognition in the range *LB* to *FQ* than in the other focal ranges. Consider next the recognition scores of the groups that began viewing at different starting levels of focus. Here the interfering effect of viewing on subsequent recognition is striking, ranging from slightly less than a quarter of the subjects recognizing pictures when they began their viewing with a very blurred image, to well over half achieving recognition when viewing began with light blur.

TABLE 1 Pictures Recognized under Various Conditions of Time and Focal Range

Average Viewing Time per Picture (sec)	Focal Range			
	VB–FQ	*MB–FQ*	*LB–FQ*	*Mean*
122	25.0 (N=8)	50.7 (N=9)	72.9 (N=9)	49.5
35	25.4 (N=14)	44.4 (N=9)	63.8 (N=10)	44.5
13	19.4 (N=10)	39.1 (N=8)	42.7 (N=12)	33.7
Mean	23.3	44.7	59.8	

Note: Each subject had eight pictures.

TABLE 2 Analysis of Variance of Number of Pictures Recognized by Each Subject with Different Viewing Times and Focal Ranges

Source	df	Mean Square	F	P
Time	2	1.252	5.70	0.01
Focal range	2	6.463	29.43	0.001
Interaction	4	0.283	1.29	n.s.*
Error	80	0.2196		

* Not significant.

[2] Since there were unequal numbers of subjects in the various conditions, a method of approximation described by Walker and Lev (4) was used.

One way of dramatizing the striking interference effect that comes from early exposure to the blurred version of visual displays is to compare two groups of subjects who were exposed to the same focal range, one group shifting from medium blur (*MB*) to the terminal point (*FQ*), and the other group shifting at the same rate but in the opposite direction, from *FQ* to *MB*. There were nine and ten subjects respectively in the two groups. The group that viewed the pictures coming into focus recognized them in 44 per cent of the cases for the eight pictures. The group that viewed the pictures going out of focus over the same range succeeded in 76 per cent of the cases—a highly reliable difference.

Do individual subjects differ in their ability to recognize pictures? Kendall's measure of concordance, *W,* was used to test the consistency of recognition scores of the 13 standardizing subjects. The result was not significant ($W = .116$, $p > .50$), suggesting that there is no general recognition ability under these experimental conditions.

In summary, exposure to a substandard visual display has the effect of interfering with its subsequent recognition. The shorter the exposure and the worse the display, the greater the effect. Examination of the responses of the standardizing subjects, who reported aloud from the start of each picture, provides a clue as to the nature of the interference effect. Hypotheses about the identity of the picture are made despite the blur. The ambiguity of the stimulus is such that no obvious contradiction appears for a time, and the initial interpretation is maintained, even when the subject is doubtful of its correctness.

An incorrect interpretation of the picture may occur either in the primary figural organization of the picture (for example, an inhomogeneity is seen as concave, whereas it is convex in the full picture when correctly identified), or in the assignment of identity to a visual organization (the convexity is recognized, but is seen as a pile of earth rather than correctly, say, as a dish of chocolate ice cream). The amount of exposure necessary to invalidate an incorrect interpretation seems to exceed that required to set up a first interpretation, so that at any particular clarity of the display, those who see it for the first time are more likely to recognize the objects than those who started viewing at a less clear stage.

When one views a picture going out of focus, both initial clarity and resistance to change of interpretation are pitted in favor of correct recognition, which accounts for the great superiority of this condition. Indeed, it is striking how long one can hang on to the identity of a picture which is going out of focus, considering the difficulty of recognizing the same picture when it is seen for the first time coming into focus.

References

1. CROWELL, A. 1961. Unpublished doctoral dissertation, McGill University.
2. GALLOWAY D. 1946. Unpublished doctoral dissertation, University of California, Berkeley.
3. GUMP, P. 1955. Unpublished doctoral dissertation, University of Colorado.
4. WALKER, H., and LEV, J. 1953. *Statistical inference,* pp. 381–82. New York: Holt.
5. WYATT, D. F., and CAMPBELL, D. T. 1951. *Journal of Abnormal and Social Psychology* 46:496–500.

6

---

*Personality Dynamics
and the Process
of Perceiving* *

Our aim in these pages is to show the interdependence of the dynamics of
personality and the dynamics of perceiving. A theory of personality, I
shall contend, cannot be complete without a complementary theory of perception, and, by the same logic, one cannot account for the full range of
perceptual phenomena without broadening perceptual theory to a point
where it contains personality variables. Our intention is not to show that
perception achieves objectives necessary to personality functioning. This
functionalist analysis has been admirably performed by Hilgard (31),
Brunswik (13), and others. Let us, rather, examine the proposition that
perceptual processes are critical intervening variables for personality

* "Personality Dynamics and the Process of Perceiving," by Jerome S. Bruner,
in *Perception—An Approach to Personality,* edited by Robert R. Blake and Glenn
V. Ramsey. Copyright 1951, The Ronald Press Company, New York and reproduced
by permission of the publisher.

I am particularly grateful to my colleagues, Leo Postman and David McClelland, for the opportunity to clarify many points in the course of preparing this
paper. Members of the Seminar on Perception at Harvard have also provided many
valuable suggestions. The author is indebted to the Laboratory of Social Relations at
Harvard for assistance in carrying out several experiments reported in these pages.

theory and that personality processes are indispensable intervening variables for perceptual theory.

Else Frenkel-Brunswik (26), in a recent article, has drawn a distinction between "personality-centered" and "perception-centered" perceptual research. The perception-centered approach takes as its primary focus of interest the variables of perception and studies the way these are affected by various learnings, motivational states, personological structures, and so forth. A study of the effect of hunger on the recognition of food objects is perception-centered, its main interest being in the variability of recognition limens as a function of need. Insofar as perceptionists make forays into the theory of personality, the result is usually a projection of perception categories onto the nature of personality. Rorschach's work is typical, and we find investigators today who, in conversation if not in print, will refer to a patient as "typically a rare detail kind of personality" or "highly coarted" or "very *CF.*"

The personality-centered approach, perhaps best represented by the work of Frenkel-Brunswik herself (26) as well as by the research of Klein and his associates (for instance, 38) at the Menninger Clinic, is characterized by a primary concern with variables of personality and their manifestation in the perceptual and other spheres. One begins, for example, with the concept of personality rigidity, inquiring whether and how it manifests itself in such areas of functioning as thinking, perceiving, remembering, and so on. A typical example is the following series of experiments carried out under the general direction of Sanford and Frenkel-Brunswik. A preliminary study (24) demonstrates first that personalities can be categorized in terms of certain basic patterns which can best be described in shorthand as the authoritarian, rigid personality and, at the opposite extreme, the flexible, tolerant personality. A variety of projective and life-history methods are used in classifying subjects. A second series of studies (25) then shows that rigid, authoritarian personalities are more prone to exhibit ethnocentric attitudes as measured by a questionnaire dealing with interracial attitudes. Rokeach (49) then carries the research one step further and shows that those high in ethnocentrism are more rigid or less flexible in performing problem-solving tasks involving basically neutral material. Another study (26) demonstrates less perceptual tolerance for ambiguity in the rigid personalities. Throughout the course of these research projects, the major emphasis was upon the representation of certain generalized personality processes in different specific spheres of mental functioning.

While the distinction has had a certain heuristic value, I think that it will not in the long run; for there cannot be one way of thinking about perception when one is interested in personality and another way of thinking about it when one is interested in, say, size constancy. The two approaches must inevitably converge, the result being a set of personality variables useful in perceptual theory and a set of perceptual variables essential in personality theory. At that happy point of convergence, doubtless, personality theory and perceptual theory will themselves merge into a common theory of behavior.[1]

Outline of a Theory of Perception

We seek a theory, then, adequate both to the laboratory and to the clinic. It is a theory which, in the words of Klein (37), makes room for the perceiver in perception. Above all, such a theory of perception should account systematically for individual differences in the perceptual process and not assign them to random error. Perhaps at its most general level, to be sure, certain perceptual laws can be stated without regard to the principles which account for individual difference. But, in the main, the theory we seek must contain within it the possibility of handling the differences in perceiving which characterize different personality constellations. That much is essential if there is to be a rapprochement between the perceptual theorist and the personality theorist. Indeed, if perception is to be regarded as an approach to personality, we will have to come a long way from the period in which Fechner (22) enunciated the dogma that to get at the true state of perceptual affairs, one should seek to cancel out the systematic or constant errors in perception by counterbalancing them. In future research, we must seek to maximize the constant errors and, what is more, cease calling them by the old-fashioned statistical name of *errors*. Let the word *error* apply only to that portion of total variance which can be attributed to no source. This is our error, not the subject's. A personality-oriented perceptual theory needs laws to account for the systematic judgmental and perceptual tendencies of different groups of people displaying different personality patterns—not just general laws of perception, each embellished with a statement of variance.

My work with Leo Postman has led us toward an expectancy or hypothesis theory of perception as one which is adequate for dealing with both the laboratory experiment in perception and the observations of the clinician. Let me sketch briefly the general outlines of the theory on which we have been working and in terms of which we have been trying to interpret experimental results. After that we may turn to the implications of this discussion for personality-oriented perceptual research.

Basically, perceiving involves a three-step cycle. Analytically, we may say that perceiving begins with an expectancy or hypothesis. In the lan-

[1] One may briefly mention a third approach to the study of perception, one best called the culture-centered approach, whose aim is to study the manner in which various cultural forms operate in the modeling of both personality and its subsidiary functions, including cognition. Perhaps the best illustration of this work is to be found in a paper by Whorf (58), whose objective is to show how various linguistic structures place limits to and set the framework of the experience of members of a given culture. Indeed, Dennis (17) has treated some of the research in this field of ethnophenomenology and, better to illustrate some of the points which we must make, we will have recourse to other examples.

guage of Woodworth (60), we not only see, but we look for, not only hear but listen to. In short, perceiving takes place in a tuned organism. The assumption is that we are never randomly set, or *eingestellt,* but rather, we are always to some extent prepared for seeing, hearing, smelling, tasting some particular thing or class of things. What evokes a hypothesis? Any given hypothesis results from the arousal of central cognitive and motivational processes by preceding environmental states of affairs.

The second analytic step in the perceiving process is the input of information from the environment (which environment includes the stimulus complex brought to us by distance receptors and by the somatic senses). Here we purposely use the term *information* to characterize stimulus input, for we are not concerned with the energy characteristics of the stimulus as such but only with its cue or clue characteristics.

The third step in the cycle is a checking or confirmation procedure. Input information is confirmatory to or congruent with the operative hypothesis, or it is in varying degree infirming or incongruous. If confirmation does not occur, the hypothesis shifts in a direction partly determined by internal or personological or experiential factors and partly on the basis of feedback from the learning which occurred in the immediately preceding, partly unsuccessful information-checking cycle. For heuristic purposes we speak of initial and consequent hypotheses, the latter being those which follow upon an infirmed hypothesis.

The reader may object that our model of the information-confirming cycle seems too saccadic, too jumpy, that perception seems to work more smoothly than our model indicates. There are two legitimate answers to this objection. The first is that only under well-practiced conditions of perceiving is the process so smooth. Faced with a strange slide in a microscope, perceiving and recognizing are steplike processes. But this rejoinder is trivial in light of the second one. There need be no phenomenal resemblance, we would insist, between the feeling tone of a psychic process and the conceptual model used to predict or describe it. Nobody would seriously object today, for example, that the atomic theory of matter is an inadequate theory because matter, a rock for instance, does not look or feel like an amalgam of whirling atoms.

A series of theoretical queries pose themselves about the information cycles which constitute the perceiving process. These fall into three broad categories:

a. Queries about the characteristics and dimensions of hypotheses or expectancies which characterize the first stage of perceiving and the conditions which elicit hypotheses of different kinds

b. Queries about the nature of information that may confirm or infirm any given hypothesis

c. Queries about the process whereby a hypothesis is confirmed or infirmed and altered

Although the three sets of problems are analytically separable, they are difficult to keep separated in discussion. In what follows, I shall not attempt to isolate each step but only to highlight these analytic distinctions in the course of general discussion.

THE NATURE OF HYPOTHESIS

The concept of hypothesis is best likened to such terms as *determining tendency, set, Aufgabe,* and *cognitive predisposition.* It may be regarded as a highly generalized state of readiness to respond selectively to classes of events in the environment. We may characterize it as generalized, for it is a form of tuning of the organism that may govern all cognitive activity carried out during its period of operation. The selectivity of remembering, problem solving, perceiving, imagining, insofar as they show a unity or consistency at a given time, are in this formulation assumed to be governed jointly by the intervening variable, the hypothesis. An operational definition of hypothesis can be stated by reference to the specific selectivity of a given perception at a given time. In theory a hypothesis is inferred, of course, from the presence of certain antecedent and consequent events, for instance, prior instruction and consequent reduction in threshold. If, as in the tachistoscopic experiments of Yokoyama (61) and Chapman (15), subjects are presented multiattributive material (containing equally perceptible colors, numbers, sizes, and so on), we may infer the nature of the hypothesis by reference to prior instruction and to the attribute which is reported on most accurately, that is, whether it was a set or hypothesis for color, number, or what not.

As postulated here, a hypothesis is in no sense limited with respect to the substantive nature of its selectivity. A hypothesis can be tuned selectively for the perception of colors of a certain hue; more often it is tuned to the perception of such environmental attributes as personal warmth or threateningness or the need-gratifyingness of objects of a certain kind. This is in no sense to imply that hypotheses about the environment are wishful in nature. They may and do tune the organism to aspects of the environment the perception of which is a guide to the most realistic behavior.

A specific hypothesis is not simply an isolated expectancy about the environment, but rather relates to more integrated systems of belief or expectancy about environmental events in general. Put in terms of current systems of learning, for example, we may think of a hypothesis as dependent upon a "cognitive map" in Tolman's sense (55) or upon an established habit-family hierarchy (32).

HYPOTHESIS STRENGTH

Thus far, we have been completely descriptive or taxonomic in our approach, describing the analytic steps involved in the process of perceiving. One further step is necessary before the implications of the hypothesis-information-confirmation cycle can be made apparent. A basic property of a hypothesis is what we shall refer to as strength. There are three theorems that are contingent upon this concept of strength:

    a. The stronger a hypothesis, the greater its likelihood of arousal in a given situation
    b. The greater the strength of a hypothesis, the less the amount of appropriate information necessary to confirm it
    c. The greater the strength of a hypothesis, the more the amount of inappropriate or contradictory information necessary to infirm it

We see immediately that there is need for defining more precisely how we infer the strength of a hypothesis and how we know what amount of appropriate information has been necessary in confirming it.

I should like to propose that there are five determinants of hypothesis strength that may be used as measures of this variable in an experimental procedure. Let me describe them briefly, and then present some preliminary evidence as to their effect on the processes of hypothesis arousal, hypothesis confirmation and hypothesis rejection.

Frequency of Past Confirmation.   The more frequently a hypothesis or expectancy has been confirmed in the past, the greater will be its strength. Such a frequently confirmed hypothesis will be more readily arousable, will require less environmental information to confirm it, and, conversely, will require more contradictory evidence to infirm it than would be required for a less frequently confirmed hypothesis.

Monopoly.   The smaller the number of alternative hypotheses held by the person concerning his environment at a given moment, the greater their strength will be. If the person faces a perceptual situation with the hypothesis that, in a given situation *A, B* and only *B* will occur, his hypothesis can be described as completely monopolistic. A monopolistic hypothesis is stronger than duopolistic hypotheses, and so on. The closer to monopoly a hypothesis is, the less information will be required to confirm it and the more tenaciously will it be retained in the face of stimulus contradiction.

Cognitive Consequences.   Any given hypothesis, for instance, that infants are generally smaller than grownups, can be conceived of as embedded in a larger system of supporting hypotheses and beliefs. The larger the number of supporting hypotheses or the more integrated the supporting system of hypotheses, the stronger the hypothesis with all that it implies for arousal, confirmation, and infirmation.

Motivational Consequences.   Hypotheses have varying consequences in aiding the organism to the fulfilment of needs. The more basic the confirmation of a hypothesis is to the carrying out of goal-striving activity, the greater will be its strength. It will be more readily aroused, more easily confirmed, less readily infirmed. This must not be taken as a redefinition of autism, for many needs which operate and which are guided by perception to their fulfillment are not simple or infantile strivings for immediate gratification.

Social Consequences.   Where stimulus conditions are such that information for either confirming or infirming a hypothesis is minimal, the hypothesis may be strengthened by virtue of its agreement with the hypotheses of other observers to whom the perceiver may turn.

If we may indulge our fantasies for a moment, let us assume that if a hypothesis, say, if *A* then *B,* had been frequently confirmed in the past, was the only one operative at the moment, was strongly supported by the beliefs of the perceiver, had immense consequences for the individual's adjustment, and was widely agreed on within his circle—if all these strengthening conditions prevailed, the hypothesis would be tediously evident in the behavior of the person, would be confirmed by the very least pip of confirming information, and would be obdurately resistant to rejection by contradictory evidence. If we were dealing with the kind of perception for which stimulus information was inherently poor—for example, the perception of characteristics in persons other than ourselves—we might have here a good description of the bigot, the anti-Semite, the xenophobe, or, for that matter, the starry-eyed idealist who can see only good in all men.

Although we have not yet attempted a definition of appropriateness of information, let us turn away to some very simple supporting laboratory evidence for the series of propositions thus far presented. Frequency of confirmation is a good one to start with, for it is a variable easily manipulated in experiment and one which yields such complex results as to stimulate a proper sense of humility in the student of perception. Bruner and Postman (10) have shown that a shorter exposure is necessary for the recognition of nonsense words whose structure conforms to more probable letter linkages in the English language than for nonsense words whose letter linkages are less likely to occur in our language. In brief, the higher the probableness or likeness to English of our nonsense words, the less the amount of stimulus information (in terms of length of exposure) necessary for recognizing them correctly. We may assume, without too much violence to experience, that English letter linkages such as *th* and *qu* and *ty* have been more frequently confirmed than such bizarre linkages as *rw* or *tx*.

A good transition to the difficulties of the prediction of hypothesis strength from frequency alone is found in an elegantly designed experiment of Henle's (30) in which she found that her subjects were better able to recognize words in printwise position when presented peripherally or tachistoscopically than when these words were presented in reverse face. However, when her subjects were told that both printwise and reverse words were being presented, the superiority of printwise letters disappeared. It would seem that a simple instruction altering the set of her subjects countervailed against a lifetime of frequency training.

Two other instances of the complex effects of frequency can be cited. In an experiment by Bruner and Postman (11),[2] subjects were presented playing cards in a tachistoscope—some of them ordinary, some with suit and color reversed in such bizarre cards as a red six of clubs. The threshold for the full recognition of the incongruous cards was, of course, much higher than the threshold of recognition for the familiar normal cards (28 as compared with 114 milliseconds). But with respect to frequency of confirmation as a principle of expectancy learning, it is interesting that, when a subject had once perceived an incongruous card, the threshold for later incongruous cards was materially reduced. Stated in terms of hypothesis theory: One confirmation of the hypothesis that black suits can be red and vice versa had a very marked effect on the strength of this hypothesis. Certainly frequency does not operate by the addition of small increments of strength.

Ellson (19) has demonstrated a conditioned hallucinatory response in which, by initial pairing of a faint tone of gradual onset with a light, a subject can be brought to hear a physically nonexistent tone when the light alone is flashed on. Ellson points out that the data concerning acquisition of this conditioned hallucinatory response show no evidence "for the progressive acquisition of the response by any one subject" (19, p. 9) as a function of the repetition of training trials. In any event, frequency provides no uniform increments of strength to the response. Moreover, when one examines the data on the extinction of this hallucinatory response (20), again one finds that the number of extinction trials (where there is no adequate and clear-cut condition for checking on the adequacy of the expectancy that a tone will follow the light) seems to have no discernible effect on the course of extinction. If, however, the subject is told that there will be no further pairing of the two stimuli and if the subject accepts this account as true (as revealed by later questioning), then the hallucinatory responses of subjects are markedly diminished. Such instruction need be given only once.

Lest we be left with the feeling that frequency of confirmation is a variable too slippery to deal with, we should point out that there is a host of experiments which do underline the importance of past confirmation as a condition for strengthening expectancies and for reducing the amount of information necessary to confirm expectancies once established. Bartlett's early experiments (2), showing the readiness of his subjects to report the

2 See pp. 68–83.

well-confirmed word *aeroplane* when *aeroplaxe* had been presented tachistoscopically, and many others (see 9) could be cited. We do not wish to belittle the importance of past experience qua past experience in determining our hypotheses, but only to guard against oversimplification.

The confirming evidence on monopoly as a determinant of hypothesis strength is rather scanty, though quite unambiguous. Postman and Bruner (47) have shown, for example, that less exposure is required for recognition of words having to do with food when subjects are set with the simple instruction to find such words than when they are told to find food words or color words, in spite of the fact that, in the series of words, both kinds of words are presented equally often. This experiment has been repeated with other kinds of stimuli with substantially the same results.

Evidence for cognitive support at a simple level is provided in a study at Harvard. Briefly, a reversed letter is embedded in a word. The word may be either a nonsense word or a regular English word. If it is the latter, subjects have more difficulty discovering the reversed letter than if the reversed letter is in a nonsense word. The supporting context of a meaningful word is far greater in disguising the incorrect letter. An incorrect hypothesis that all letters are facing correctly is confirmed by minimal information and is consequently slow in being rejected. Indeed, this experiment, one must confess, goes little beyond what has been known to experts in camouflage for many years. If one sets up or arouses a context of hypotheses about the environment, it is difficult for the observer to see minor details which violate that context. I suspect, by the way, that the best method of training observers to break camouflage is to give them highly multiple hypotheses with which to face stimulus situations, thereby increasing the amount of information necessary for any expectancy to be confirmed.

Various lines of evidence—experimental, observational, and clinical— can be cited in support of the role of motivational support in strengthening hypotheses. Postman, Bruner, and McGinnies (48) and Vanderplas and Blake (57) have reported a positive relationship between an individual's hierarchy of personal values and the ease with which he recognizes words relating to his differently cherished values. And we may cite Thouless's finding (54) that artists come to depend more upon retinal cues of size and brightness, necessary to their occupational tasks. By the same token, microscopists become skillful in evaluating minimal cues in their preparations; and lovers, either for defense or enhancement, see only the good and the beautiful in their chosen ones.

There is also ample evidence to indicate that many complexities are involved in the relationship between hypothesis strength and motivational consequences. Thus, McClelland and Liberman (45) have shown that, where the recognition of negative achievement-related (failure) words are concerned, subjects with moderate need achievement are less quick in their recognition than those who are either high or low in this need. And experiments by McGinnies (46) and by McCleary and Lazarus (44) have indicated that response to stimulus information when one is operating with expectancies of high motivational consequence may not necessarily result in altered recognition but in lowered autonomic response thresholds as measured by galvanic skin responses.

It suffices to mention the results of Sherif's classic experiments (51) on the autokinetic effect as evidence for the effect of social validation on hypothesis strength. It is necessary to recall that in this experiment the possibility of confirming or infirming hypotheses with the kind of stimulus used was virtually nil. Under the circumstances, only social factors could operate.

THE NATURE OF CONFIRMING AND INFIRMING INFORMATION

We have tried in the preceding pages to utilize independent measures of hypothesis strength. Frequency of past confirmation could be controlled, in a typical experiment, and its effect measured by the amount of time necessary, say, in tachistoscopic exposure, for the subject to perceive a stimulus. If threshold is reduced as a function of past confirmation or monopoly, we say that an alteration has occurred in our intervening variable, hypothesis strength. In our discussion, there has been one serious omission: the definition in any given experiment of what constitutes appropriate or relevant information. We shall treat this problem in considerable detail later; here we must pause to examine what is meant by information.

Let us distinguish first between relevant and nonrelevant information. Relevant information, or a relevant cue, refers to stimulus input which can be used by the subject for confirming or infirming an expectancy about the environment. The case is simplest in the area of space perception. Certain information, like perspective lines, parallactic movements, and so on, is clearly relevant as cues for confirming or infirming a hypothesis concerning the distance of a haystack in the valley. Other cues are obviously not relevant; the heat of the day, assorted sounds, and so forth. Among the cues that are relevant, one may distinguish a hierarchy of reliability. The texture of intervening terrain, particularly under circumstances where we do not recognize clearly the composition of the terrain, is a relevant but not very reliable item of stimulus information. The apparent size of a haystack in a section of the country where we do not know the characteristic sizes of haystacks is also a relevant informational cue, but again, not a very reliable one. As dusk falls, the more reliable cues, such as the perspective gained from parallel fences, while still relevant, also become less reliable. We have then a continuum from relevant and reliable information, through relevant and unreliable information, to nonrelevant information.

The words *relevant* and *reliable* are defined in the above example not with respect to the perceiver's experience, but with reference to the experimenter's knowledge about how people, in Brunswik's terms (13), correctly attain objects in their environment. By using what to the experimenter seem like highly unreliable cues, a subject can perceive with great subjective certainty the distance of an object. He may, to be sure, be all wrong. His hypotheses about distance may be psychotic to the point where he may even utilize conventionally nonrelevant, almost magical informational cues. He may see the haystack as his castle and displace it according to the grandiosity of his views about castle sizes.

We must distinguish, then, between the experimenter's definition of relevant and reliable information and the subject's utilization of information. It is of the essence in any given experiment that we define in advance what we as experimenters mean by relevant information and do not depend upon the subject's response to do it for us; otherwise we would be in a complete circle. In any experiment on perception, such a distinction is made implicitly or explicitly, whatever the nature of the stimulus materials dealt with. In short, we set a criterion of what is a correct perception, that is, when the subject has used what we have defined as the relevant cues in coming to a final report about what is there before him on the screen, in the tachistoscope, in the room around him, or elsewhere.

What we study in most perceptual experiments is the extent to which the subject is able to maximize relevant cues (defined by the experimenter) for confirming and/or infirming hypotheses. This maximization depends upon the kind and strength of the hypotheses which he employs in his perception of a situation. Let us take a typical experiment. We have a series of pictures drawn, each depicting one of the six Spranger values: religious, economic, theoretical, social, political, and aesthetic. We choose a group of subjects showing certain scores in these value areas as defined by the Allport-Vernon test. We arbitrarily define in each picture what shall be the correct perception of the activity depicted. In each picture, there is some highly reliable relevant information, some nonrelevant information, and much rather unreliable relevant information. In the religious picture, for example, there is a man with head bowed in prayer or reverence. The outline of the man, however, is rather low grade, ambiguous information, for at rapid exposure, his figure can be seen as tired, dejected, stooped in work, and in many ways other than prayerful. Now if our subject has a strong religious orientation, and if he is prone to approach his perceptual environment armed with hypotheses concerning religious behavior, he will see the figure as in a religious posture and rapidly reconstruct the remainder of the stimulus in terms of his religious hypothesis. This sequence of events has also been referred to as resonance (47). Another subject, economically oriented, will perceive the stooped figure as at work. Before he will be able to perceive the picture for what it is (or what the experimenter says it is), his economic hypothesis will have to be rejected by contradictory information.

Perhaps he will have to see the Gothic window behind the stooped figure.

When a hypothesis is strong, there will be a tendency for it to be confirmed by what is normally considered by the experimenter to be unreliable information. As likely as not, the confirmation may be incorrect from the experimenter's point of view. Whether it is or is not depends upon the relationship which happens to exist between the stimulus information present and the hypothesis employed by the subject.

It is primarily when we are dealing with low-grade or unreliable stimulus information that one gets a clear view of the differences in hypotheses which different individuals normally employ. Given high-grade, reliable information, differences tend to be washed out. Yet this formulation is too facile. For it is also true that, when hypotheses are strong enough, stimulus information considered highly reliable by the experimenter is not utilized by subjects or is utilized in a manner to confirm wrong hypotheses. Subjects in our playing-card experiment reported incongruously colored red cards as black at exposure levels well above their normal thresholds for color discrimination. And at still higher exposure levels, after they had become uncertain of their perceptions, they were unable to tell whether the cards were black or red or any other color (11).[3] In sum, reliable information may for some subjects confirm a correct hypothesis, for others an incorrect one, and for still others it may be subjectively ambiguous in the sense of neither confirming nor infirming any hypothesis. All we can say finally, and it is not very much, is that in any given experiment the experimenter decides what is relevant information and then studies how subjects utilize this information in the course of perceiving.

As Luchins (42), Dennis (17), and others have pointed out, much of the work in the field of perception and personality is done with ambiguous stimuli—dimly illuminated pictures or words, rapidly exposed materials, ambiguous drawings, and the like. The justification, generally, has been that by using less than optimal presentational methods the subject is thrown back on his own resources and that hypothesis arousal is more guided by motivational or experiential factors than by the characteristics of the stimulus immediately present. Another way of stating this is to say that these investigators have been interested in discovering the extent to which hypotheses varying in strength would be able to utilize substandard information, assuming that the greater the strength, the greater would be the utilization. One can name a long list of investigators who have been more or less explicitly guided by such reasoning: McClelland and Liberman (45), Sanford (50), Vanderplas and Blake (57), Sherif (51), Bruner and Postman (7), Luchins (41), and many others.

Let me cite the additional evidence of three related experiments recently completed by Bruner, Postman, and Rodrigues (12) in more specific sup-

[3] See pp. 68–83.

port of this general proposition concerning the utilization of low-grade information. The subject has the task of matching two-dimensional objects, all uniformly colored orange, to a variable color mixer. His task is to perform a simple color match. The objects differ in respect to their normal or everyday color: Some are objects which are normally red (a cooked lobster claw and a tomato), some orange (a tangerine and a carrot), and some normally yellow (a banana and a lemon). In the first experiment, the orange color of the objects is highly unstable, being induced by color contrast (a gray object is placed on a blue-green ground, entirely covered by a ground glass). The variable color wheel and the object to be matched which lies before the subject are separated by 90 degrees of visual arc. In the second experiment the conditions are identical save that the objects to be matched are well-saturated orange paper; but as before objects are separated from the variable color wheel by 90 degrees of visual arc. In the third condition, the orange paper objects are placed immediately adjacent to the color wheel, and object and color wheel appear against a uniform gray background. The three conditions, then, represent steps in decreasing ambiguity. The first step involves highly unstable, ambiguous information. The second step contains more stable or less ambiguous information, but its appropriateness is kept ambiguous by heterogeneous background cues and by the necessity for successive comparison across 90 degrees of arc. In the third experiment, heterogeneous background is replaced by homogeneity, and simultaneous comparison is possible. Again, to use communications engineering language, as we go from the first to the third experiment, the signal-to-noise ratio in our input information steadily increases.

The results can be simply stated. In the first condition, the match for the normally red objects is significantly redder and for the normally yellow objects significantly yellower than is the match for the normally orange objects. The same results hold, though to a considerably lesser degree, for the second condition. In the third condition, when high-grade information is made available, the influence of past experience is wiped out altogether and no significant judgment tendency for the three kinds of objects is noticeable. In sum, the less ambiguous the information, the less the effect of past experience in confirming hypotheses and the greater the use of input information.[4]

Two other experiments underline the dependence of learning and motivational effects on the use of substandard stimulus information. Both Ellson (21) and Kelley (34) have shown that conditioned sensory hallucinations can only be obtained when the onset of the stimulus to be conditioned is gradual to the point of ambiguity.

Does what we have been saying imply that only under conditions of poor perception do the effects of learning and personality show them-

---

[4] Incidentally, in all conditions, subjects insisted that all objects were of the same color and that their color matches were the same for all objects.

selves? Perhaps so. It might be better to say that there are limits imposed by stimulus factors which reduce the effects of past experience and present needs almost to zero when one works with rather simple stimuli. I insist, however, that most complex perception, particularly in our social lives, is dependent upon the integration of information of a far less reliable kind than we normally provide in a tachistoscope at rapid exposure.

Implications for Personality Theory

Our first insistence was that a personality-oriented theory of perception must have systematic means whereby it can account for individual differences in perceiving. Let me mention two points in the theory outlined above at which articulation can be and is being made with personality theory and theories of social behavior: (a) differences in the kinds of hypotheses that different individuals habitually employ, reflecting differences in past history, personality structure, and so forth; (b) differences in strength of hypotheses characterizing different individuals, again reflecting divergent life histories and major personality trends. Bearing these points in mind, we turn to material drawn from the work of social psychologists and personality theorists on the functioning of personality.

Consider first the matter of cultural differences. In the Cambridge Anthropological Expedition to the Torres Straits at the turn of the century, McDougall and Rivers (29) drew a distinction between acuity on the one hand and observational powers on the other. While there appeared to be no difference between the acuity test scores, obtained using standard methods, of Murray Islanders and white Europeans (leaving aside cases where the effects of endemic or epidemic disease were to be noted), the investigators observed a rather striking superiority of the native men over themselves in such matters as being able to spot distant horizon objects looked at from the sea against the background of the island. In like manner, the native men were superior in being able to unmask the camouflage of coral fish against the background of their matching habitat. The natives had learned to use good hypotheses which served to utilize maximally what appropriate information was available. Their hypotheses were strong enough to maximize relevant confirming information, but not so strong as to be confirmed by what to the uninitiated might have been confirming information.

More bizarre examples can be cited in which powers of observation seem to belie the evidence of acuity data. Bogoras (3), who has provided a monumental monographic study of the Chukchee, reports that it was only with the greatest of difficulty that he could force and/or teach these people to carry out anything resembling an adequate sorting of the Holmgren yarns. The Chukchee, of course, have an exceedingly impoverished color nomenclature. Yet these reindeer-herding people can and do apply more than two dozen names to the task of distinguishing the patterns of reindeer hides. Bogoras reports his own considerable difficulty in learning to make such fine distinctions in patterns, many of which at the outset looked identical to him.

One last example suffices. It has often been commented upon that, perhaps for reasons deep in the nature of man's inhibitions about the excretory functions or perhaps because of their inadequacy as locomotion guides, we utilize smell cues to a very minimum in our Western society. Save in matters of high cuisine and high fashion, we are not attentive, have few hypotheses about odors. Hence we notice them rarely, have a barren smell terminolgy, and are generally undiscriminating in this modality. Here again, the Chukchee provide a striking contrast. For reasons which are far from clear, but which might well be rewarding to study, they have an intensely discriminating sense of smell, even to the point of greeting each other by sniffing down the back of the neck. They frequently describe the odor of things where we would use visual, gustatory, or tactual descriptions. Indeed, so strong are these odor hypotheses that certain hysterical phenomena come to be mediated by them. Bogoras reports that strangeness, for example, is translated into bad smell. On one occasion, he brought a strange box into his host's house. The mistress of the house upon spying the box almost went into a faint at its strong and malevolent odor. Bogoras himself could get no smell from the box. So strong, apparently, is this hypothesis that strange things smell badly that this Chukchee woman's hypothesis could be confirmed by the highly ambiguous and inappropriate smell atmosphere of her own house.

Part of the shock of these examples, to be sure, derives from their distance. The exquisite sensitivity of the musician, the tea taster, or the microscopist; the prodigies of observation of the veteran naval lookout, the experienced hunter, the novelists of character—all these are close at hand to challenge us. The fact that some parents see the obstreperous behavior of their children as fatigued, some as naughty, some as expressing sibling rivalry—and that these may differ by social class—is perhaps of the same order. They indicate the utilization of different hypotheses of different strength, depending for their confirmation on different kinds of environmental information, reflecting different adjustmental needs in the perceiver.

Moving one step closer to the functioning of the individual personality, a good continuity is provided by historical reference. Logan Pearsall Smith (52) writes that self-prefixes (self-esteem, self-regard, and the like) do not appear in English usage until the seventeenth century, their introduction coinciding with the rise of individualistic Puritanism. The word *selfish,* for example, was introduced in 1640, and at that date by the Scottish Presbyterians. It is interesting to speculate about the gradual change in the perception of self which resulted from the revolution in hypotheses during the

Reformation. We shall return to this question in the final section. One wonders, too, about the changes that have occurred in our perception of abnormal or aberrant behavior as our hypotheses about mental disease have shifted from a theory of possession, to one of degeneration, and then to a theory of psychic dynamics. Zilboorg's account (62) of the medical rebellion of Cornelius Agrippa against the possession theory of the Middle Ages is as much an essay on social perception as on the history of medicine. Where perceptual evidence or, in our terms, environmental information is so ambiguous in its appropriateness for confirming or infirming hypotheses about cause and effect in behavior, it is not surprising that the battle of diagnosis of behavior is almost as sharply joined today as in Agrippa's day.

It is perhaps in the perception of attributes of the social environment that people vary most strikingly. For in this sphere hypotheses are strong, information is low grade, and adjustmental consequences are serious. We shall, in the final section, refer to a study of the perception of causation in group behavior by extrapunitive and intrapunitive leaders in which intrapunitive leaders more often perceived themselves as sources of causation. Intrapunitiveness may, indeed, be considered a description of the kinds of hypotheses with which an individual approaches frustrating situations. He is set to evaluate normally ambiguous information as confirming his own guilt. The more marked the degree of intrapunitiveness, the less the appropriate information necessary to confirm self-guilt. As the hypothesis attains greater and greater strength, intrapunitiveness attains neurotic proportions, which is to say that self-guilt hypotheses are confirmed by information judged by society to be grossly inappropriate or ambiguous.

Programmatic Implications for Future Research

Thus far we have been speaking rather generally about the manner in which the theory described earlier throws light on various personality processes and cultural differences. What of specific research on personality-perception interdependence, research which has as its object the introduction of personality variables into perceptual theory and perceptual variables into personality theory?

We have already made reference to studies involving the perception of more or less ambiguous stimuli by subjects in varying states of need, with different past experience, and so forth. These studies have been reviewed elsewhere (9, 10) and need not be dealt with in detail here. They have been in the direction of investigating the utilization of different kinds of stimulus information by subjects operating under rather haphazardly selected motivations. By and large, they have been demonstrational in nature in the sense that they represented isolated instances of the operation of needs or other states on perceptual selectivity. Few of these studies have utilized motivational states and stimulus materials, a relation between which is predicted by a coherent theory of personality. More specifically, few studies have started out with a hypothesis which stated explicitly that, according to such and such a theory of personality, we would expect people of such and such a type to handle stimuli of such and such a kind in such and such a manner. Hypotheses of this kind can be stated, but first let us examine a second type of perception-and-personality research.

In this kind of investigation—and here one may name studies by Thouless (54), Duncker (18), Cramer (16), Klein (36, 38), Witkin (59), Bruner and Postman (6), Tresselt (56), Ansbacher (1), and others—the focus is upon judgments of such classical attributes as size, movement, brightness, hue, and so on. Characteristically, one investigates the extent to which subjects show certain systematic errors in judgment, the nature of which errors are then related to ˙past experience, present motivation, and other more or less personal factors. One thing must certainly be said for studies of this kind. They provided an a fortiori demonstration of the fruitfulness of considering the contribution of behavioral or personality factors in perception. To take but a sample of findings for comment, it is an impressive challenge to classical perceptual theory to show (*a*) that the color constancy of artists shows a systematic and occupationally useful verging-away from "phenomenal regression to the real object" (54); (*b*) that dependence on the body for orientation in the gravitational field as compared with dependence on the visual framework increases with age and, in a more complex manner, with degree of adjustment (59); and (*c*) that the appearance of a color depends on one's expectancy concerning the normal color of an object (12, 16, 18). Has not the time passed, however, when we must continue to restrict ourselves to such experiments?

Investigations of motivational or behavioral factors as determinants of apparent size, brightness, hue, shape, and so forth have perhaps obscured a basic theoretical point. Consider, for example, the question of apparent size. Studies by Bruner and Goodman (5),[5] Bruner and Postman (8), and Lambert, Soloman, and Watson (39) have served to support a general principle of accentuation in size judgment: Apparent size is accentuated in judgments of valuable or need-relevant objects. I suspect that there is something adventitious about these results, that they are to some extent misleading because they have never been stated in a proper theoretical context. Several things lead to this conclusion. In the first place, Bruner and Postman (6) have shown that accentuation is absent when the object in question is to be manipulated—that is, when the stimulus information from the object is used in the confirmation of highly accurate manipulative hypotheses. I suspect, moreover, that if a subject is given a highly critical, accuracy-oriented set for judging, size accentuation is markedly dimin-

[5] See pp. 43–56.

ished. Klein, Meister, and Schlesinger (36) have reported results which indicate that if the subject is given a critical judging set, a form of accentuation noted by Bruner and Postman (8) fails to occur. And finally, it appears that the use of optimal viewing conditions can wipe out accentuation of simple attributes in the normal laboratory situation. Certainly the results of the color-judgment experiments cited earlier in some detail show the basic importance of poor viewing conditions as a necessary condition for the operation of behavioral factors in the laboratory setting. Carter and Schooler (14), for example, achieved a considerable reduction in perceptual accentuation of valuable objects when ambiguity was reduced to a minimum, though accentuation appeared in their more ambiguous memory situation.

What is theoretically wrong about most of these studies, both those which have and those which have not found perceptual accentuation, is that there is rarely stated a specific hypothesis about why the attribute being studied should be influenced by behavioral factors. Is it that the attribute studied provides highly appropriate information for the confirmation of an unsuspected hypothesis operative in the judging situation? Take judgments of size, for example. A subject is set to judge the sizes of coins. He comes to the situation with hypotheses about the size of the object (very likely based, as we have indicated in an earlier paper [10], on principles of adaptation level) but also with hypotheses about the value of the coin. In this experiment, size information confirms both size and value hypotheses. For size increases as value increases in the objects being judged, and this linkage is widespread in our culture. There is, therefore, likely to be a maximization of size cues, such cues serving to confirm both the value and the size hypothesis. We would propose that it is this joint maximization of size cues which brings about accentuation in apparent size.

But what is crucial in this line of reasoning is that the conventional size attribute being studied here bears some confirmatory relationship to the value or need-gratification hypothesis that is operating in the situation. In short, if we are to work on the distortion of conventional attributes by behavioral factors or personality factors, we must be explicit in recognizing that such distortions occur because the size or shape or color of the object being studied provides appropriate information for the confirmation of a motivational or personality-related hypothesis. If this is not the case, I would predict that there will be no distortion.

This brings us to the problem of adequate personality-oriented research on perception. It seems to me that the most basic point to be made is this: If we wish to work on personality factors in perceiving, then we must concentrate upon the investigation of those environmental cues which are appropriate to the confirmation of hypotheses which reflect basic personality patterns. By and large, these environmental cues are not size cues or color cues or brightness cues. They are cues which aid more directly in our interpersonal adjustment: the apparent warmth or coldness of people, the apparent threat of situations, the apparent intelligence or apparent sincerity of others. Let me cite a few experiments which have been concerned with such attributes. Kelley (34) has shown that the behavior of a teacher in a group situation is perceived quite differently with respect to its warmth or coldness as a function of prior information given the class about the instructor. If the prior description of the teacher contains elements which maximize the threatening character of the teacher-figure, the perceiver is predisposed or sensitized toward experiencing cues appropriate to spotting such behavior when it appears. Maas (43), to take another example, has shown the manner in which the perception of causation (whether the group or the leader appears to be to blame for an event) varies depending in combination upon (*a*) whether the leader is intrapunitive or extrapunitive on the one hand and (*b*) whether the group is informal and open or formalized and closed. Environmental cues indicating social causation, however ambiguous, are the crucial perceptual attributes here. Lindzey and Rogolsky (40) have suggested, to cite another instance, that the sensitivity of the anti-Semite which results in his readier recognition of Jewish faces stems from the fact that he is more dependent upon such cues for his general adjustment—that, in short, such cues have high appropriateness to him, in confirming hypotheses which guide behavior.

Such environmental cues as Jewishness or personal warmth are, to be sure, highly composite with respect to the myriad of size, movement, color, and other cues that support them. But phenomenologically speaking, they are unitary and not readily reducible. They can no more be dismissed for their compositeness than one can dismiss the dimension of roughness as a tonal attribute—in spite of the fact that it depends upon an intricate temporal interaction of loudness, pitch, and other factors.

Working with such complex adjustment-appropriate attributes of experience as we have been discussing bars one from the comfort of using physical measures as reference points in his experiments. In studying size, for example, we may speak of distortion in terms of deviation of judgments from actual or physically measurable size. There is no such base measurement of apparent personal warmth. What we must do, then, is to utilize instead judgments by different groups or different individuals under different psychological conditions. Our basic metric will involve the comparison of group scores. And where possible we can use ratings of the stimulus by independent judges against which to compare the perceptions of our subjects. The task is difficult, but far from impossible.

THE SELECTION OF PERSONALLY RELEVANT CUES

There are, I believe, two guides to the selection of personally relevant stimulus cues for investigation. One is theoretical. Various theories of personality contain implicit or explicit statements concerning the cues in the environment which guide the individual in maintaining or advancing his personal adjustment. Thus, the psychoanalytic theory of ego defenses contains some implicit suggestions for perceptual investigation and serves well as an example. Consider the classical description of the obsessional-compulsive character structure described in such detail by Fenichel (23). It seems reasonable to pose the hypothesis that the supposedly anal-sadistic, compulsive character, because of his defensive needs, would be highly dependent upon or set to perceive cues to orderliness in his immediate environment. For him the attribute of orderliness (and its many translations into, say, symmetry, cleanliness, and the like) would provide highly appropriate and personally relevant information. We say of him that he notices pictures in a room that hang slightly askew; he has a low threshold for seeing poorly cleaned silverware; and, perhaps at a more basic dynamic level, he is either defensively blind toward, or hypervigilant to, minimally aggressive or sadistic events in his immediate environment (7). Indeed, one might suppose, and the matter can be tested, that his defense of isolation and undoing and his ritual behavior depend upon certain perceptual predispositions for their effectiveness. There are no adequate experimental studies dealing with such a problem—in spite of the fact that Freud early referred to one aspect of the ego as "perceptual consciousness" (28) and despite the title of the first chapter ("The Ego as the Seat of Observation") in Anna Freud's *The Ego and the Mechanisms of Defence* (27).

Another example drawn from psychoanalytic theory relates to the theory of schizophrenia as a regression to primary narcism, a withdrawal from object relationships (23). What might follow perceptually from such a theory? Might not we predict, for example, that a withdrawal from object relations and an increasing concern for the self would lead to a breakdown in such phenomena as size and shape constancy? Might not apparent size and shape conform more toward retinal proportions than toward real object proportions and particularly so if the stimulus objects used were other people?

One could go on and propose perceptual hypotheses stemming from psychoanalytic concepts or from concepts embodied in other theories of personality. That is not our task here. We have simply presented these examples to suggest one approach to research on appropriate, personally relevant stimulus information.

Another approach to the selection of adjustmentally relevant cues for study is frankly phenomenological. We begin by inquiring how the world appears to us. The answer to such a naïve question would be that the world consists of many things, perhaps divisible into our perception of self, of objects and people sensed as related to us in some way, and of objects basically neutral with respect to ourselves. Along the borders of these regions of the perceptual field there might be certain ambiguities. Where the perceived self terminates and the world of objects begins is, under extraordinary conditions, a matter of confusion; and there is also a shading off between those objects which have a self-relating characteristic and those which do not. But we need not concern ourselves here with, say, whether a phantom limb or well-practiced prosthetic aid is part of the self. We will accept simply the naïve distinction between perceived self, objects which have some personal meaning for us, and objects which have little or no personal meaning.[6]

As a highly tentative general theorem—one proposed more in the spirit of starting a discussion than of concluding it—we would propose that variations in the attributes of the perceived self provide the most highly relevant stimulus information for confirming adjustmentally relevant hypotheses, that is, hypotheses the confirmation of which is crucial to adjustment.

What do we mean by the attributes of the perceived self? We mean simply a dimension of variation in terms of which experience can be described and along which judgments can be arrayed. These need not, as Boring (4) and Stevens (53) have pointed out, be independently variable or orthogonal. But will there not be an infinity of attributes characterizing the perceived self? If a pure tone can be systematically described by at least four attributes—pitch, loudness, volume, and density—will not the complex set of stimuli which evokes the experience of self be described by a bewildering array of attributes? If indeed Boring (4) is correct in remarking "that there is theoretically no limit to the number of attributes, except the nature of the nervous system" which can characterize a perception, then again we may expect that the self-experience will be multiattributive in the extreme. For in considerable measure the process of development involves learning to discriminate many different attributes of the self. Let us forget the complexity of the task for the moment. Can we suggest some possible attributes of self which provide particularly crucial information for guiding us in our adjustment?

One obvious dimension is self-salience, what in everyday language is probably called self-consciousness. How well aware is the person of himself, and how differentiated does he feel from his environment? Subjects should be able to rate themselves on this attribute. Again I ask a very naïve question: What kinds of situations increase or decrease self-salience in individuals with different kinds of past developmental histories? A better way of asking the question, one closer to our theoretical scheme, is: What kinds of hypotheses depend for their confirmation on self-saliency cues, and what kinds of individuals characteristically use such hypotheses?

The sense of self-potency is another such attributive dimension of perceived self to be pondered. By it we mean self-confidence, the sense of

---

[6] The reader will note that we are speaking here of the experience of self and not of the psychologist's Ego or the philosopher's Self. Self is here treated as an object of experience rather than as an agent or a knower.

being able to act effectively in a situation, to overcome obstacles, to make out all right. We may ask the same kind of questions about it as we did about self-salience.

Take these two attributes or forms of stimulus information or cues as illustrations and let us examine them. In neither case is it clear what kinds of stimuli evoke the perceptions. Certainly there is still enough lingering of the James-Lange theory for us to assume that part of the stimulus is somatic in nature and that autonomic activity has no small part in mediating these somatic stimulus components. We know, too, I suspect, that self-cues are probably ambiguous in nature, that they rarely are very appropriate for confirming specific hypotheses, that, in short, self-information is a good deal vaguer than the highly salient information we get from the external environment. Beyond this we know little indeed about the stimulus—even less than is known about the stimulus in smell and in the vestibular senses. Here, moreover, we are working with a stimulus where it is impossible to get any independent measure, for even independent judges cannot get inside the skin. This is particularly troublesome, for it seems reasonable to suppose that the base-line state of self-potency in a resting situation differs markedly in different individuals. We are literally limited in measuring self-attributes to the use of carefully constructed self-rating scales. But even with these there is much that can be accomplished, not only in studying differences in these attributes in groups of different past histories, but also in studying intraindividual differences as a person moves from one kind of diagnostic situation to another. Again in theoretical terms, we will find the kinds of personalities which depend upon and maximize self-cues for the confirmation of characteristic hypotheses. Such cues, we can surmise already, will be utilized and maximized more by the introvert, the intrapunitive, the person with inadequately developed object relations, the adolescent, the generally insecure person, and so forth.

However banal such predictions may seem, we must not overlook the fact that it is far from banal to ask what kinds of situations and what kinds of therapy reduce overdependence upon self-salience cues and increase the extent to which an individual maximizes self-potency cues.

A second phenomenological proposition—really a tautology—is that those cues in the environment which confirm or infirm hypotheses derived from basic and enduring needs and values are also crucial in guiding adjustment. What kinds of hypotheses serve such basic needs, and what kinds of environmental information are needed to confirm or infirm them? David McClelland has remarked, half in jest, that it would not be amiss to carry out a phenomenological census to discover what things and attributes in the environment people look for and attend to in guiding their behavior. When we have found out something about the phenomenology of everyday life, perhaps we shall be in a better position to choose the stimulus materials to use in future research on the way in which personality factors affect perception.

References

1. ANSBACHER, H. 1937. Perception of number as affected by the monetary value of the objects. *Archives of Psychology*, no. 215.
2. BARTLETT, F. C. 1916. An experimental study of some problems of perceiving and imaging. *British Journal of Psychology* 8:222–66.
3. BOGORAS, W. 1904–09. *The Chukchee*. New York: G. E. Stechert.
4. BORING, E. G. 1942. *Sensation and perception in the history of experimental psychology*. New York: Appleton-Century-Crofts.
5. BRUNER, J. S., and GOODMAN, C. C. 1947. Value and need as organizing factors in perception. *Journal of Abnormal and Social Psychology* 42:33–44.
6. BRUNER, J. S., and POSTMAN, L. 1947. Tension and tension-release as organizing factors in perception. *Journal of Personality* 15:300–308.
7. BRUNER, J. S., and POSTMAN, L. 1947. Emotional selectivity in perception and reaction. *Journal of Personality* 16:69–77.
8. BRUNER, J. S., and POSTMAN, L. 1948. Symbolic value as an organizing factor in perception. *Journal of Social Psychology* 27:203–8.
9. BRUNER, J. S., and POSTMAN, L. 1948. An approach to social perception. In *Current trends in social psychology,* ed. W. Dennis. Pittsburgh: University of Pittsburgh Press.
10. BRUNER, J. S. and POSTMAN, L. 1949. Perception, cognition, and behavior. *Journal of Personality* 18:14–31.
11. BRUNER, J. S. and POSTMAN, L. 1949. On the perception of incongruity: a paradigm. *Journal of Personality* 18:206–23.
12. BRUNER, J. S.; POSTMAN, L.; and RODRIGUES, J. S. 1950. Stimulus appropriateness and ambiguity as factors in judgment. Presented at the annual meeting of the Eastern Psychological Association, 1950.
13. BRUNSWIK, E. 1947. *Systematic and representative design of psychological experiments*. Berkeley: University of California Press.
14. CARTER, L., and SCHOOLER, E. 1949. Value, need, and other factors in perception. *Psychological Review* 56:200–208.
15. CHAPMAN, D. W. 1932. Relative effects of determinate and indeterminate Aufgaben. *American Journal of Psychology* 44:163–74.
16. CRAMER, T. 1923. Ueber die Beziehung des Zwischenmediums zu den Transformations- und Kontrasterscheinungen. *Zeitschrfit für Sinnesphysiologie* 54:214–42.
17. DENNIS, W. 1951. Cultural and developmental factors in perception. In *Perception: an approach to personality,* ed. R. R. Blake and G. Ramsey, pp. 121–47. New York: Ronald Press.
18. DUNCKER, K. 1939. The influence of past experience upon perceptual properties. *American Journal of Psychology* 52:255–65.
19. ELLSON, D. G. 1941. Hallucinations produced by sensory conditioning. *Journal of Experimental Psychology* 28:1–20.
20. ELLSON, D. G. 1941. Experimental extinction of an hallucination produced by sensory conditioning. *Journal of Experimental Psychology* 28:350–61.
21. ELLSON, D. G. 1942. Critical conditions influencing sensory conditioning. *Journal of Experimental Psychology* 31:333–38.
22. FECHNER, G. T. 1889. *Elemente der Psychophysik*. 2 vols. Leipzig: Breitkopfard Härtel.
23. FENICHEL, O. 1945. *The psychoanalytic theory of neurosis*. New York: Norton.
24. FRENKEL-BRUNSWIK, E. 1948. Dynamic and cognitive categorization of qualitative material. I. General problems and the thematic apperception test. *Journal of Psychology* 24:253–60.
25. FRENKEL-BRUNSWIK, E. 1948. Dynamic and cognitive categorization of qualitative

material. II. Interviews of the ethnically prejudiced. *Journal of Psychology* 25:261–77.
26. FRENKEL-BRUNSWIK, E. 1949. Intolerance of ambiguity as an emotional and perceptual personality variable. *Journal of Personality* 18:108–43.
27. FREUD, A. 1946. *The ego and the mechanisms of defence.* New York: International Universities Press.
28. FREUD, S. 1920. *A general introduction to psychoanalysis.* New York: Boni & Liveright.
29. HADDON, A. C., ed. 1901. *Reports of the Cambridge Anthropological Expedition to Torres Straits. Physiology and psychology,* vol. 2. Cambridge, Eng.: Cambridge University Press.
30. HENLE, M. 1942. An experimental investigation of past experience as a determinant of visual form perception. *Journal of Experimental Psychology* 30:1–21.
31. HILGARD, E. R. 1951. The role of learning in perception. In *Perception: an approach to personality,* ed. R. R. Blake and G. Ramsey, pp. 95–120. New York: Ronald Press.
32. HOLZMAN, P. S., and KLEIN, G. S. 1949. The "schemetizing process": perceptual attitudes and personality qualities in sensitivity to change. *American Psychologist* 5:312 (abstract only).
33. HULL, C. L. 1943. *Principals of behavior.* New York: Appleton-Century-Crofts.
34. KELLEY, E. 1. 1934. An experimental attempt to produce artificial chromesthesia by the technique of the conditioned response. *Journal of Experimental Psychology* 17:315–41.
35. KELLEY, H. H. 1949. The effects of expectations upon first impressions of persons. *American Psychologist* 4:252.
36. KLEIN, G. S.; MEISTER, D.; and SCHLESINGER, H. J. 1949. The effect of personal values on perception: an experimental critique. *American Psychologist* 4:252–53.
37. KLEIN, G. S., and SCHLESINGER, H. J., 1949. Where is the perceiver in perceptual theory? *Journal of Personality* 18:32–47.
38. KLEIN, G. S., and SCHLESINGER, H. J. Studies of the schematizing process: shifting behavior in "paranoid" and "non-paranoid" individuals. Unpublished paper.
39. LAMBERT, W. W.; SOLOMAN, R. L.; and WATSON, P. D. 1949. Reinforcement and extinction as factors in size estimation. *Journal of Experimental Psychology* 39:637–41.
40. LINDZEY, G., and ROGOLSKY, S. 1950. Prejudice and identification of minority group membership. *Journal of Abnormal and Social Psychology* 45:37–53.
41. LUCHINS, A. S. 1945. Social influences on perception of complex drawings. *Journal of Social Psychology* 21:257–73.
42. LUCHINS, A. S. A critique of current research on perception. Unpublished paper.
43. MAAS, H. S. 1950. Personal and group factors in leaders' social perception. *Journal of Abnormal and Social Psychology* 45:54–63.
44. McCLEARY, R. A., and LAZARUS, R. S. 1949. Automatic discrimination without awareness. *Journal of Personality* 18:171–79.
45. McCLELLAND, D. C., and LIBERMAN, A. M. 1949. The effect of need for achievement on recognition of need-related words. *Journal of Personality* 18:236–51.
46. McGINNIES, E. 1949. Emotionality and perceptual defense. *Psychological Review* 56:244–51.
47. POSTMAN, L., and BRUNER, J. S. 1949. Multiplicity of set as a determinant of perceptual organization. *Journal of Experimental Psychology* 39:369–77.
48. POSTMAN, L.; BRUNER, J. S.; and McGINNIES, E. 1948. Personal values as selective factors in perception. *Journal of Abnormal and Social Psychology* 43:142–54.
49. ROKEACH, M. 1943. Generalized mental rigidity as a factor in ethnocentrism. *Journal of Abnormal and Social Psychology* 48:259–78.
50. SANFORD, R. N. 1937. The effect of abstinence from food upon imaginal processes: a further experiment. *Journal of Psychology* 3:145–59.
51. SHERIF, M. 1935. A study in some social factors in perception. *Archives of Psychology,* no. 187.
52. SMITH, L. P. 1912. *The English language.* New York: Holt.

53. STEVENS, S. S. 1934. The attributes of tone. *Proceedings of the National Academy of Science* 20:457–59.
54. THOULESS, R. H. 1932. Individual differences in phenomenal regression. *British Journal of Psychology* 22:216–41.
55. TOLMAN, E. C. 1948. Cognitive maps in rats and men. *Psychological Review* 55:189–208.
56. TRESSELT, M. E. 1949. The shift of a scale of judgment and a personality correlate. *American Psychologist* 4:251–52.
57. VANDERPLAS, J. M. and BLAKE, R. R. 1949. Selective sensitization in auditory perception. *Journal of Personality* 18:252–66.
58. WHORF, B. L. 1947. Science and linguistics. In *Readings in social psychology,* ed. E. L. Hartley and T. M. Newcomb. New York: Holt.
59. WITKIN, H. A. 1949. The nature and importance of individual differences in perception. *Journal of Personality* 18:145–70.
60. WOODWORTH, R. S. 1947. Reinforcement of perception. *American Journal of Psychology* 60:119–24.
61. YOKOYAMA, M. 1924. Reported by E. G. Boring. Attribute and sensation. *American Journal of Psychology* 35:301–4.
62. ZILBOORG, G. 1935. *The medical men and the witch during the Renaissance.* Noguchi Lecture in the History of Medicine. Baltimore, Md.: Johns Hopkins Press.

7

The Functions of Perceiving:
New Look Retrospect *

It is taken for granted that the so-called New Look in perceptual and cognitive theorizing had its developmental beginnings long before 1946, but the postwar years were the period of its most intense development, certainly in its search for identity. It seemed that perhaps the best structure for an accounting might be to examine some of the major sources of stress and antinomy that have plagued the turbulent years in the development of the New Look—or, more properly, the New Looks, for there is indeed a plural and not a singular New Look.

What, to begin with, can be said about the degree to which the renewed activity of the so-called New Look has been helpful and to what degree harmful to the progress of work in the field of perception specifically, and in the study of psychological processes generally? Very likely, the most interesting thing historically about the New Look is that it represented a moment of confluence in psychological theory—a response to a desire or a historical force that was antiseparatist in spirit, possibly too much so. To some extent, the antiseparatism stemmed from a need in social psychology

* "The Functions of Perceiving: New Look Retrospect," by Jerome S. Bruner and George S. Klein, from B. Kaplan and S. Wapner (eds.), *Perspectives in Psychological Theory*. Copyright 1960 by International Universities Press, Inc. and reproduced by permission of the publisher.

and the psychology of personality to recognize the role of perceptual phenomena in guiding action—a development that was a long time growing and slow in finding direct expression in perceptual research. But if it was the case that research began out of an interest in bending perceptual theory to other uses in other fields it has also been the case that the past decade has witnessed an increasing concern for a better understanding of perceptual processes per se. So while the enthusiastic New Lookers have at times confused the issues and muddied the waters with imperfectly designed and executed research, in the end they may also have contributed materially to the outlook and findings that constitute the field of perceptual research. Our aim is to consider some of these contributions—none of them yet clear, but such is the hazard of writing contemporary history.

We would single out first the manner in which the wooly and residual concept of set has been vivified and given substance. Partly as a result of the antidynamic bias of Gestalt theory and partly in reflection of the bias against internal variables that characterizes much of American psychology, the concept of set and the notions surrounding the word *attention* had been allowed to languish. What seemed most important to research workers who were fundamentally concerned with kinds of perception where stimulus constraints did not appear to account for all the variance was that perception was highly selective. So work was begun on the effects of need, of interest, of past experience, on the manner of organization of the perceptual field—or, rather, what one saw when one was set in certain ways and, as Julian Hochberg has amusingly remarked, the price of tachistoscopes began to rise. But while it was the case that the very phenomena the New Lookers studied—identification of complex stimulus patterns presented at relatively high speeds or under dim illumination—rigged results so that they magnified the role of variable sets in perception, it was also the case that the same research often pointed to the areas where set factors were of first importance though previously neglected. We make no brief for the various theoretical positions that were put forth by workers in this tradition—hypothesis theories, theories about the role of regulation or of inhibition, and the like—but only remark on the fact that a balance was redressed, and with important consequences.

A similar point can be made about work on other nonstimulus or behavioral determinants in perception, notably past experience. For if it were the case that needs and interests served to program an organism's selectivity of organization and awareness, it was even more the case that past experience had such an effect. It is not a trivial finding that speed of recognition of stimulus materials could be predicted, for example, on the basis of the likelihood of occurrence of such stimuli in the organism's environment—what, elsewhere, one of us has called the surprise-reducing character of perception. But even more strikingly, subsequent research has shown that early sensory experience and deprivation of such experience has a profound effect on the organism's world as structured in terms of perceived relations, equivalence, constancy, and so forth. While work on early sensory deprivation was inspired by other trends in psychology—notably Hebb's theory of development—it nonetheless tied in closely with the changing outlook in perception brought about by work inspired by the New Look. Indeed, other work also indicated that interruption with the constant bombardment of environmental events has the effect of disrupting the structures so painfully created by the organism's past history.

Perhaps the lesson that has been clearest, where past experience is concerned, is that neither past experience nor the motives and sets that program selectivity influence perception directly, in the sense of providing direct determination of perceptual organization or of selectivity. Rather, they operate by creating structures or rules of operation that mediate in a much subtler, indirect fashion to regulate the cognitive activity of the organism. To this point we shall return later. We mention it here to underline one of the mischievous effects of the early work of the New Lookers, the tendency to talk about the effects of needs or past experience or the rest without reference to the complex of mediating mechanisms that are involved. Yet again there is self-correction in the ways of investigation, for we have seen in the past five years much interesting work at the experimental and theoretical level on the nature of mediators. But more of this later.

Because of the emphasis of New Look perceptual work on selectivity and the rules governing both selectivity of awareness and organization, there is an interesting area of contact between this work and several advances in contemporary biology. The most notable is in the field of the neurophysiology of perception—even the neurophysiology of sensation. Perhaps this connection is clearest in the now-famous Laurentian symposium on consciousness (1954)—or more accurately on the operation of the ascending and descending reticular systems. Two things were apparent in the reports of that symposium and in the work that has followed it. One is the emphasis on the programmed nature of perceptual intake, the other on the role of nonspecific activation as a factor in perceptual organization. The work from Magoun's laboratory and from Granit's, as well as the work of Galambos and many others, indicates that what registers perceptually—or neurophysiologically—is partly a function of where an organism is directing attention. So that, interestingly enough, it was the neurophysiologist who brought the internal variable of attention back into psychology via the back door of physiological research. There has been much less resistance on the part of traditional perceptionists to this backdoor entry by physiologists than there had been to the knocking on the front door by the New Lookers.

In essence, two messages have been contained in the work of the neurophysiologists. The first is that there are corticofugal impulses that go down through the reticular formation to program selectivity of intake by way stations in the sensory system—operating all the way out to peripheral elements like the retinal internuncial fibers or the organ of Corti in the ear. The second is that ascending impulses of a nonspecific type travel up to the cortical areas via the ascending reticular system to serve as boosters or inhibitors of sensory messages, and one can indeed simulate these messages by electrical stimulation, even to the extent of lowering sensory thresholds in tachistoscopic recognition studies by the joint input of a visual stimulus and a jolt to the ascending reticular. Again, the ascending system and its boosting messages seem to be programmed in terms of principles of selectivity that have to do with the general activity or enterprise of the organism at the time of input of the specific stimulus. In general then, though the work of the neurophysiologists has only begun, it would seem as if the model of the nervous system that is now being proposed makes a better fit with the emphasis of the New Look research than with the older conception of a perceptual system completely captive of autochthonous factors programmed once and for all to handle input in terms of certain fixed invariances. But again, when we deal more specifically with the conflicts of the New Look movement, we shall return to this point in discussing the distinction between an emphasis on stimulus domination versus an emphasis on selective programming.

Even the much maligned research and theorizing on perceptual defense, viewed as a specific instance of interference with or facilitation of activation effects, takes on a more general meaning in light of these findings in neurophysiology. Indeed, findings like those of Hernandez-Péon and Galambos would indicate that it is a general characteristic of the nervous system, to speak metaphorically, to program out potential inputs that interfere with or distract an organism from the enterprise on which he is working. Why then should we not expect that, where there is a built-up avoidance pattern, the same programming out or interference should not occur?

The point that has been made about contact with neurophysiology can be paralleled by one about contact with the work of the ethologists. Certainly the emphasis of Tinbergen on the innate releasing mechanism and its effect on selectivity suggests that the general model of internally regulated programs of perceptual registration holds even for the simplest organisms and that the receptive system is scarcely a matter of passive registration once a traditionally adequate stimulus has impinged. Indeed, the concept of adequate stimulus is something that needs restatement, not just in terms of the capacity for reception of end organs, but in terms of the programmed readiness of the entire receptive system.

But it can also be argued that the ethologists, the neurophysiologists, and the New Lookers are throwing the picture off balance by elevating ideas about selectivity and programming to the status of the most central concept in perception. Indeed, we believe this is the case, and though we would plead for tolerance toward enthusiasm, we would also remark that there are still many modes of organizing perceptual input that are highly invariant across changes in program, and that are not only crucial but highly in need of study.

It seems to us, to take up another point, that there has been a steady increase of insight in the New Look work with respect to an understanding of the perception and judgment of sensory attributes and magnitudes. The early experiment of Bruner and Goodman and the various repetitions were not only marked by technical flaws, but also were hobbled by a conception of need factors distorting magnitude judgments—size, weight, brightness, and so on. In time, this emphasis was replaced by one that was more relativistic or scalar in nature: that the relevance of a stimulus dimension changes the nature of the scale of judgment imposed on it by the observer; that overestimation and underestimation were matters of relative or comparative judgment, and not a case of distortion of perception from some veridical state. Thus, Bruner and Rodrigues remarked that it was the subjective scalar separation between sizes in a series of objects where size and value were correlated, and not a matter of the absolute subjective sizes of the objects. Tajfel has taken the matter one step further and shown the manner in which imposed value dimensions that correlate or run counter to magnitude changes affect the scale characteristics that develop in judgment. And finally, Klein and his collaborators have shown that the extent of interaction that takes place between a series of magnitudes and a correlated value scale will depend upon the general flexibility or constrictedness of the perceiver, and that this quality of control is related to certain general cognitive characteristics of the perceiver.

Finally, a word should be said about the reopening of curiosity brought about by the New Look research on the difference between awareness or report on the one hand and nonreportable registration on the other. At the very least, we know that input that does not result in reportable awareness when there are no aids to recognition can, with aids to recognition, yield accurate reports on what is there. Information theory and the work it has generated certainly make that matter clear enough—as in the experiments of Miller, Heise and Lichten, and of Bruner, Miller, and Zimmerman, on the recognition of words presented in noise. With $N/2$ alternative response categories, a word can be recognized correctly, and with N alternatives, say, recognition in terms of a list of alternatives is close to chance. This is indeed a puzzling finding that tells us that we had better be careful in the N-list case about talking of chance-recognition performance. Bricker and Chapanis's findings fit this case as well, and we know from their study that subjects can use fragments of the input to help them make a match, as it were, between input and response alternative. Yet, should the number of alternatives be greatly increased, then the match is not possible. Here we come to the issue of underlying cognitive structures and their accessibility for matching with inputs. It is certainly the case that this match may take place later, as in the experiments of Poetzl and Fisher, where unreported parts of a tachistoscopic input appear later in dreams and imagery. The experiments of Klein and his collaborators also indicate that, though one is not able to report the identity of an input, the input may nonetheless affect the nature of what is reported next when a different and supraliminal input is presented. Indeed, the work of Blackwell in America, and of Dixon in England, suggests strongly that the reportability of a stimulus or awareness of a subject depends upon the nature of response alternatives.

The issues have certainly not been straightened out in this troubled area of inquiry, but it is to the credit of the New Lookers that at least they were bold enough to barge in where virgins feared to tread. It is notable, by the way, that some of our purest perceptual virgins have entered the fray after it was demonstrated that virtue was not automatically to be lost by exposing oneself to the temptations of the unconscious. The less said about subliminal advertising and the clamor it has created, the better—at least at this moment. We have yet to see any evidence about it that mattered terribly much one way or the other.

In sum, then, the New Look has had an activating effect, a disturbing effect; it has created some useful models; it has got part way through some research that shows signs of being better done; and it has been bold enough to look at problems. It has also been naïve and inept and confusing. Its chief contribution has been to explore the nature of selectivity, but it has also violated its limits. A noisy and brawling adolescent, it has at least had the virtue of not taking much for granted, and in so doing, it has often proceeded without enough attention to the lessons learned by its older siblings and parents.

We turn now to the principal areas of conflict that have plagued the New Lookers and led them into family conflict with other perceptual researchers. We single out three of these: (*A*) emphasis on autism versus emphasis upon the programmed nature of perceptual selectivity and organization; (*B*) the distinction between perception pure and cognition; and, finally, (*C*) the relative roles of internally determined selective programs versus determination by external stimulus events.

Autism versus Adaptive Programming

Partly as a result of the early tradition of irrationalism in personality theory and partly out of an impulse to find a simple explanation for complex phenomena, early New Lookers tended to extend the principle of autism into the area of perception: "What looms large in need looms large perceptually"; or in extension of the doctrine of primary process, "Perception is a need-satisfying activity." A corollary of this oversimplification was that the effect of need on perception was to distort the percept away from reality, whatever that might reasonably be expected to be. In brief, the dual principle of some of the earliest work of Murphy, of Sanford, of Bruner, and others, was that (*a*) the greater the need, the greater its intrusion into and distortion of perception; and (*b*) distortion went in the direction of warping reality into something approaching wish fulfillment.

It took the zeal of enthusiasts to promulgate that vast (though heuristically useful) oversimplification in the face of the very special conditions that are necessary to produce wish-fulfilling hallucination. In consequence, there was a failure to appreciate the huge effectiveness (not accuracy necessarily) of perception even under conditions of exigent need. It is not surprising that colleagues who had developed a healthy respect for the stable acuity and finesse of the perceptual system were resistant to the enthusiasts. With time and with the reality-adjusting effect of controversy and corrective research, it soon became apparent that the way in which needs and interests operate is not by any means always or mostly autistic; that the programming of perceptual selectivity was highly stable across changes in need; and that, where not stable, it was often geared to requirements that were anything but wish fulfilling. Attention was drawn, for example, to the vigilance-producing effect of need states. It also became evident that a basic rule of set was its predictive expectancy—that thresholds reflected the organism's prediction concerning the transitional and absolute probabilities with which events occurred. Speed of registration or awareness seemed to depend, in sum, upon a subtle programming that governed what inputs would get in and how they would be organized.

And so with the effects of need—not on perception per se, but on the nature of the program. Not only needs, but modes of handling them, turned out to be critical, and often in indirect ways. Whether hot material was perceived at a lower or higher threshold than psychologically cool material depended not so much on need, but on how a person characteristically dealt with his needs. The reality context of the need—what had to be taken into account in gratifying it—had a large part in how the need was permitted to show in behavior; and people differed in their manner of controlling this reality. The degree to which an effect could be discerned at all depended also upon a host of other considerations that entered into the making of a perceptual expectancy—requirements of locomotion, of surprise regulation, of how well practiced the subject was in dealing with inputs such as those used by the experimenter, and so forth.

But what is amply clear, and it is the subject of the section that follows, is that registration and organization are dependent on a predetermined, though flexible, program—what William James years ago called "preperception"—and such programs seem to vary systematically with many conditions. To argue the contrary on the basis of the results of perceptual experiments where the subject is carefully preset for stability before input is to beg the question, at the very least. It does not suffice for the student of apparent movement or differential sensitivity to proclaim, "But who didn't know that!" For if he knows it and fails to appreciate by the effort of research the highly complex presetting that gets him his beautifully clean results, he is guilty of intellectual pound foolishness, of an order to match his exquisite penny wiseness.

We realize that what we have been saying bypasses the question of what Prentice some years ago described as the distinction between functionalism and formalism in perception. The major emphasis of New Look research has been functional, unblushingly so, concerned principally with the functions served by perceiving, the manner in which organization and selectivity serve these, and with the extraperceptual factors that determine function. What has happened over the past decade is a broadening of the conception of function from an overly simple conception of autism to one that recognizes the variable means by which people cope with the givens of experience. This does not mean that formalism as Prentice described it is not a worth-while approach. Rather, it may be that we should celebrate the fact that there are several approaches to perceptual research now flourishing.

Perception and Cognition

Admittedly, one of the difficulties of the New Look has been its loose use of the concept of perception—and our colleagues in neighboring fields do not make usage easier by speaking, say, of the perception of national character. Yet it seems to us not very profitable to circle endlessly the question as it is usually raised: Is it really perception, or is it inference, judgment, memory, response, or what not? In fact, the New Looker has dealt with a somewhat different concept of perception than, say, the student of absolute-brightness thresholds. To caricature the difference, the perceptual purist is interested in studying the most limited and circumscribed attribute of the perceptual experience that he can get hold of in an experimental setting that will permit him to get a relation between a perceptual response and a stimulus over which he has rigorous control. He must have a *ceteris paribus* and so he adopts conventions about resting state, set, expectancy, need, past experience, and the like. These conventions or fixed parameters he then often chooses to forget. The caricature of the New Looker is based on another source of folly altogether: He tends to use a stimulus input of a relatively complex kind, without being able to specify very rigorously its nature, and then proceeds to vary a great many other conditions that have little directly to do with conventional descriptions of perception. He often ends up very confused. These are caricatures. Most of us do not live at such wildly unthoughtful extremes. But the two extremes perhaps represent our temptations, if not our practices.

It is impossible to say by any criterion that perception in its purest sense is not involved in the final size estimations of the subjects of the Bruner and Goodman experiment. It is also plain that there are many other factors interacting with the purely perceptual. From the first input of light on the subject's eye, through the complex activities that occur before the subject makes his match and says, "Okay, that's it," there are many interacting processes operating which can be teased out analytically, to be sure, but which can also be studied in terms of a final resultant, whether one wants to call that final resultant a perception or whatever. Eventually, if he is serious, the student of size estimation will have to tease out the nature of these processes, both from the point of view of stimulus conditions and behavioral conditions. So, too, the student of the differential threshold. If he is serious, he will have to study the pay-off conditions that affect his phenomenon and all the rest—if ever he is to understand the generality of his effects and not remain a differential-threshold technician.

In the end, the student of the full behavioral context involved in everyday perceiving is bound to set up experiments that involve a wide range of processes over and beyond stimulus input and its variation. For it is precisely in the coming to a decision about the nature of what is present perceptually that past experience and need and the processes of defense and coping come into play. He is doing his research to find out how such processes operate in the making of such decisions for action. To ask him to rule them out of his research in the interest of cleaning up his experiments is as silly as asking the psychophysicist at every turn to replicate his experiments under conditions of inattention or imperious need states, given that his interest is in sensory receptivity under optimal conditions.

In the end, what we are saying is that full explanation of any phenomenon—be it perception or anything else—requires both a close study of the context in which the phenomenon occurs, and also of the intrinsic nature of the phenomenon itself under idealized conditions. The New Lookers have tended to do the former, the researcher raised in psychophysics and sensory physiology the latter.

It may well turn out that there are some phenomena in perception that are governed entirely by invariant ratios on the retina unaffected by any conditions of judgment or need or the other factors that go into programming perceptual operations, that nothing but these invariants matter. We rather hope so. For these phenomena can then become the last retreat of those who do not want to have their composure disturbed by matters other than those that can be specified as stimulation on the sensory surface of the end organ. And for the most rabid New Lookers, we wish them a phenomenon in which the modes of transformation of input stimuli are always overweighed by factors of set and need. For the rest of us, we think the current confusion is rather healthy, given how little we really know about the nature of perception in the large.

Selectivity versus Stimulus Dominance

There is a great deal of pseudo controversy here. When a Gestalt theorist talks about autochthonous factors in perception, when a Gibsonian speaks of the manner in which texture determines apparent distance or tilt, when a psychophysicist like Graham speaks of a set of factors in the stimulus input determining the manner in which brightness or distance or size will be judged either absolutely or with respect to some comparison standard, they surely do not intend that there are no laws of transformation that lead to a conversion of input into a reportable percept or judgment. It is interesting to look at what is required to simulate even the simplest forms of perception with a digital computing system. The most striking thing about the job is that one must set up a program for handling inputs, a program that governs the way in which the elementary processes which it controls will operate. Now it would be a very dumb computer indeed that had only one rigid order of steps for dealing with input, no provision made for handling doubtful cases, for example, as to whether this line is tilted or straight in a tilted background. If one set the program up that rigidly, then we could properly speak of complete stimulus determination, for the program would be such that given the presence of a stimulus pattern at the receptor, it could behave only in one way—the way indicated for that program. It seems highly unlikely that such is the case; and it was certainly never intended by such writers as Gibson and Hochberg that the proximal stimulus was all, dictating the nature of the perceptual response save in instances where there was much equivocality, in which case the program would decide that equivocality was present and signal the system that the time had come for a season in the imaginative sun.

Rather, transformation seems to be all, transformation of inputs by certain interesting rules—for example, that the gradient *lllldddlld* or *lllldddlllddllddld* both stood for a surface extending into the distance and that the first surface was extending more sharply into the distance than the second. Now, nobody who has ever spent the afternoon in a perceptual laboratory would doubt for a moment that there are such rules of transformation operating in the nervous system—call them rules or structures or schemata or whatever you will. And nobody who had extended his stay in the laboratory for over a week would doubt that one could distinguish between the transformation rules that seem to be highly stable across changes in the state of the organism and across changes in the nature of other characteristics of the stimulus field and those that seem to alter under altered conditions. It seems very foolish indeed to take either the model of the invariant transformations or that of the highly variable ones and propose imperialistically that they are all, and that if certain perceptual phenomena do not conform to them, then, be hanged, they are not perception at all.

Even Gibson's beautiful demonstrations of depth effects produced by texture gradients do not tempt us to go for a walk into his photographs, and yet we know that the rules of transformation he has discovered can be counted on to produce what in painting are called *trompe l'oeil* affects— they are indeed good enough to trick the eye. But we already know enough about the rules governing the organization of the third dimension to know that lots of cues can get used and combined in lots of ways by the nervous system so that there must be some stunning, variable higher-order transformation rules yet to be discovered, and the single determinants of depth, the so-called painter's rules first formulated by Leonardo, do not tell the whole story. The higher order transforms substitute cues for each other, and does all sorts of things to prevent their being a simple correlation between proximal stimulus and report. It is a subtle business and is scarcely stimulus determination alone.

That the rules are relatively stable in their operation goes without saying. But that they are also changeable, goes without saying too, for we know that Ivo Kohler's subjects change and develop new rules for dealing with reversed cues by alteration in transformation. We think that this is all that need be said.[1]

In the end, we can only conclude by urging that we wait for the adolescent New Look to become an adult. The real test then will be whether the "New Look" still has to be singled out and contrasted with something else. We hope that it will have been absorbed by then, to the enrichment of itself and the host organism—whether the host organism is the study of perception or some more including organism.

References

1. ALLPORT, F. H. 1955. *Theories of perception and the concept of structure.* New York: Wiley.
2. BLAKE, R. R. and RAMSEY, G. V., eds. 1951. *Perception: an approach to personality.* New York: Ronald Press.
3. BRUNER, J. S. 1957. On Perceptual Readiness. *Psychological Review,* 64:123–52.
4. BRUNER, J. S., and KRECH, D., eds. 1950. *Perception and personality: a symposium.* Durham, N.C.: Duke University Press.
5. GARDNER, R. S.; HOLZMAN, P. S.; KLEIN, G. S.; LINTON H.; and SPENCE, D. P. 1959. Cognitive control: a study of consistencies in cognitive behavior. *Psychological Issues* 1(4).
6. JENKIN, N. 1957. Affective processes in perception. *Psychological Bulletin* 54:100–27.
7. KLEIN, G. S. 1956. Perception, motives, and personality: a clinical perspective. In *Psychology of personality: six modern approaches,* ed. J. L. McCary. New York: Logos Press.
8. TAJFEL, H. 1957. Value and the perceptual judgment of magnitude. *Psychological Review* 64:192–204.
9. VERNON, M. D. 1952. *A further study of visual perception.* Cambridge, Eng.: Cambridge University Press.

[1] Comprehensive bibliographies of New Look research can be found in all the references cited below.

2

THOUGHT

Introduction

Bruner's approach to the study of the higher mental processes is in part a reaction against two schools of thought that seemed to bypass or undermine "the exquisite forms of problem solving that we see in everyday life and may see in our laboratories any time we choose to give our subjects something more challenging than key-pressing to perform" (1). The first of these schools was behaviorism. The stimulus-response bond, whether mediated or otherwise, provided neither the malleability nor the explanatory power to account for the complex behavior of individuals engaged in concept attainment, problem solving, or language production. The second of these schools was psychoanalysis. At least until personality theorists focused their gaze upon the mechanisms whereby the ego comes to terms with reality, the psychoanalytic stress on unconscious drives depicted man as being perhaps excessively emotional and irrational, and failed to underline his capacity for coping deliberately and intelligently with his environment. In contrast with these two traditions, Bruner has stressed both the rationality and the complexity that characterize the thought processes from the outset. His concern has been with the means whereby people actively select, retain, and transform information. His theoretical emphasis has been upon the construction of internal models or generic coding systems which are isomorphic with the redundancy in the environment and by means of which an individual can predict, extrapolate, or go beyond the information given.

In the previous section we saw how the perception of an event could be viewed as an essentially constructive process in which an individual infers a hypothesis by relating sense data to his internal model of the world and then checks that hypothesis against additional properties of the event. In this section different kinds of problem solving or reasoning are described in a similar fashion. The attainment of concepts, the induction of principles, and the development of scientific theories are seen to involve constructive activities that are similar to those that result in perceptual recognition. Again individuals generate hypotheses by relating instances of a concept, patterns of stimulation, or experimental results to a focus, an internal model, or a theory and then check their hypotheses against further properties in the world of sense.

The first two selections in this section are excerpts from *A Study of Thinking* by Bruner, Goodnow, and Austin (1). This book was a landmark in the investigation of categorization, the process of grouping discriminably different things into equivalence classes. The approach taken was to externalize the sequence of decisions employed in the attainment of a concept and to compare the resulting performance strategy with various rational or ideal strategies. In "The Process of Concept Attainment," the notion of a strategy is defined, the objectives of a strategy are outlined, conditions presumed to affect the strategies chosen for concept attainment are discussed, and the decisions involved in such strategies are analyzed in terms of economic theories of choice. The theoretical conjectures of this discussion are made concrete by the research presented in "Reception Strategies in Concept Attainment." In this selection two ideal strategies are described in detail and a precise analysis is given of the extent to which the performance of actual subjects matches those ideal strategies.

Bruner's investigation of cognitive processes has not been confined to the study of concept attainment. The next two articles describe the behavior of subjects when confronted with a different kind of problem, one which requires the induction of a principle in the face of a recurrent pattern of stimulation. In "The Role of Overlearning and Drive Level in Reversal Learning," Bruner, Mandler, O'Dowd, and Wallach have shown that the behavior of rats which face the task of mastering a pattern of single alternation sometimes appears to reflect the appreciation of a principle rather than the conditioning of specific responses to specific stimuli. The ability of humans to infer principles underlying more complex patterns is examined by Bruner, Wallach, and Galanter in "The Identification of Recurrent Regularity." They have investigated the extent to which three sources of interference prevent the construction of a predictive model in the face of recurrent patterns of stimulation.

"The Conditions of Creativity" has been written in an entirely different spirit than the articles that precede it. It is neither a report of research nor an explicit theoretical statement. It is concerned not with the acquisition of an arbitrary concept or principle that the investigator has contrived for the subject to discover, but rather with the act of creativity, with the making of art or poetry or scientific theory. Although there are no cut-and-dried generalizations, the paper is rich in both the questions it raises concerning the creative process and the examples it provides from mathematics, science, literature, and art.

The last article in this section is a programmatic essay that goes some distance in unifying diverse types of conceptual activity, including those discussed in the preceding articles, into a single theoretical framework. In *On Going Beyond the Information Given,* Bruner suggests that such phenomena as the attainment of concepts, the sensitivity to regularities in the environment, the appreciation of redundancy in language, and the development of theories in science all involve the construction of generic coding systems (elsewhere referred to as models), which permit prediction and extrapolation. He goes on to consider the conditions affecting the acquisition of such coding systems, the role they play in creativity, and their implications for education.

Reference

1. BRUNER, J. S.; GOODNOW, J. J.; and AUSTIN, G. A. 1956. *A study of thinking.* New York: Wiley.

8

The Process
of Concept Attainment[*]

It is curiously difficult to recapture preconceptual innocence. Having learned a new language, it is almost impossible to recall the undifferentiated flow of voiced sounds that one heard before one learned to sort the flow into words and phrases. Having mastered the distinction between odd and even numbers, it is a feat to remember what it was like in a mental world where there was no such distinction. In short, the attainment of a concept has about it something of a quantal character. It is as if the mastery of a conceptual distinction were able to mask the preconceptual memory of the things now distinguished. Moreover, the transition experience between not having the distinction and having it seems to be without experiential content. From the point of view of imagery and sensory stuff the act of grasping a conceptual distinction is, if not *unanschaulich* or impalpable, to use the language of the Wurzburg investigators, at least unverbalizable. It is, if you will, an enigmatic process and often a sudden process. The psychologist's "aha" experience singles out this suddenness as does the literary man's shock of recognition. Something happens quickly and one thinks one has found something. Concept attainment seems almost an

* "The Process of Concept Attainment," from *A Study of Thinking* by Jerome S. Bruner, Jacqueline J. Goodnow, and George A. Austin. Copyright © by John Wiley & Sons, Inc., 1956. Reprinted by permission of the publisher and authors.

intrinsically unanalyzable process from an experiential point of view: "Now I understand the distinction, before there was nothing, and in between was only a moment of illumination."

It is perhaps because of the inaccessibility of reportable experience that psychologists have produced such a relatively sparse yield of knowledge when they have sought to investigate concept attainment and the thought processes by techniques of phenomenological analysis. To say, as Graham Wallas (30) did, that thinking or invention is divided into the four stages of "preparation," "incubation," "illumination," and "verification" is helpful only insofar as it serves to indicate that while the experience of "grasping" (illumination or insight) is sudden, it is imbedded in a longer process —still to be described in analytic terms. We do well to heed the lesson of history and look to sources of data additional to the report of direct experience as a basis for understanding what is the process of concept attainment.

Three questions may guide our efforts to discover how people come to grasp conceptual or categorial distinctions:

a. How do people achieve the information necessary for isolating and learning a concept?
b. How do they retain the information gained from encounters with possibly relevant events so that it may be useful later?
c. How is retained information transformed so that it may be rendered useful for testing a hypothesis still unborn at the moment of first encountering new information?

People do manage these vastly complex tasks of achieving, retaining, and transforming information and they do so without exceeding the relatively narrow limits of human cognitive capacity. They do it in a manner that reflects with nicety the requirements of speed, accuracy, and the like that are imposed upon them by circumstances. We look about us and we see people constantly engaged in picking up and using information that enables them to make conceptual distinctions on the basis of appropriate defining attributes, doing it in such a way that they seem neither overwhelmed by the complexity of the task nor much endangered by maladaptive slowness or by reckless speed. People learn to distinguish conceptually between daylight color film and indoor color film, between different cuts of meat, between fresh vegetables and stale ones, between policemen and subway guards, between detergents and soap flakes, between honest and crooked politicians, between bashful children and less timid ones, between a flow of traffic that permits crossing the street safely and a flow that one should not risk. How may one go about analyzing the learning process that leads to such rational behavior?

The Investigation of Concept Attainment

It is more than a casual truism of the operational behaviorist that in order to study a psychological process one must externalize it for observation. Concept attainment is not an exception. How do we get it externalized into observable behavior? Verbal report, as we have noted, provides insufficient data for making generalizations about it. What then?

Consider the chain of events leading up to the learning of a concept; we purposely choose an example from everyday life. Our hypothetical subject is a foreigner who has arrived in town and is being introduced around by an old resident who is a trusted friend. The people to whom he is being introduced are the instances. After each encounter with a new person—an instance, in the jargon of concept studies—his friend remarks either, "He's an influential person" or "He's a nice fellow but not very influential." Our subject has reason to respect his friend's judgment and is, more or less intentionally, trying to learn the basis of his friend's distinction between influential people and nice-but-not-influential people. Looked at more precisely, he encounters instances and then has them labeled categorywise as in one class or another by his tutor-friend. The instances that he encounters vary in the myriad of attributes by which human beings are marked. Some are more educated than others, better traveled, more facile conversationally, richer, more forceful, and so on. His task is to determine which attributes lead reliably to membership in the class influential people. Note one thing: Very early in the round of visits, our subject begins to make tentative judgments of his own, prior to his friend's advice, as to whether the person he is meeting is influential or not, perhaps on the basis of attributes that he would have difficulty in describing even to himself. With respect to these tentative hypotheses, several contingencies may arise: He may consider a person influential and have his judgment confirmed or infirmed by his friend, or he may consider a person not influential with the same two possible outcomes. And, of course, the tutor-friend can also resolve cases of doubt for him. If the friend were also able to give him the proper advice about the defining attributes of the class, the task would be finished. But let us assume that this is not to be the case, that the tutor-friend is somehow reticent on this score.

Our subject as we have described him thus far exists in something of a privileged enclave in which he is protected from the consequences of his own tentative judgments. This is how it is, of course, in most concept-attainment studies—whether a particular Chinese figure is called a *CIV* or a *DAX* by a subject is seemingly without consequence, save that miscalling may hurt one's self-esteem. But it is conceivable that our man may have to act on the basis of his tentative categorization before getting his friend's guidance, and his action may have serious consequences. To what extent will this lead to constant errors in his placement of people and in the tentative hypotheses he develops? Our man's position is privileged too in the sense that there is no limit of time on his learning activity. Suppose that his tutor-friend were only going to be in town for a few days and in that time he had to learn to recognize examples of the category influential people in order to carry out his future business. To what extent would this influence his approach to learning?

We must also ask a question about recordkeeping. How does the person keep track? Each instance he encounters exhibits many attributes, and our man notes the value of some of these and not others upon encountering exemplars and nonexemplars of the class influential people—that more of the influentials were rich than poor, but not that more of them were tall rather than short. He may also want to keep track of the fate of those tentative hypotheses that were checked and found wanting on subsequent encounters. Is the recordkeeping (whether in his head or in a ledger) of such a kind that it insures the ready utilization of information encountered?

Finally, how does the person know when he has learned the concept in a serviceable way? This is a deceptively simple question. The first thing that may come to mind is that the person knows he has learned the concept when he feels he is able to predict the status of new instances with a sufficiently high degree of certainty. But what is a sufficiently high degree of certainty when a person is working with a probabilistic concept where cues do not yield complete prediction of identity? We find that some people, when they are unable to categorize perfectly, will continue to explore obvious attributes and to abstract less obvious ones. Others will stabilize in their behavior and base their categorizations exclusively on partially predictive cues without any further effort to try out new, possibly relevant attributes. Even when a subject is working with a simple conjunctive concept whose defining attributes predict perfectly the status of all instances encountered, he may not be sure that he has the concept even though he is performing perfectly. He will go on testing new instances, just to be sure. We do not mean to obscure what may seem to be a simple matter; but in fact it is very difficult to describe what it is that leads a subject to state that he has now learned the concept. For simplicity's sake, it is often better to bypass the question and to ask instead whether the attributes that are criterial for the subject in his categorizing judgment are also the attributes that are defining of the concept. Let it be clear, however, that some people require many more encounters beyond this point before they feel any degree of certainty; others reach the stage of certainty before their behavior meets this criterion.

The first and most notable thing about the sequence of events set forth is that it can be described as a series of decisions. At the very outset, even before the person has so much as encountered a single instance, he must make a decision about the nature of the task. Will he try to learn the concept influential people or will he concentrate on remembering in rote fashion which people he met were and which people were not influential? There are then decisions to be made, important ones from the point of view of efficiency, as to which attributes and how many attributes he should attend to in attempting to find out how to spot an influential person without having to ask his friend or going through the difficult business of observing the exercise of influence in the community. And should a tentative hypothesis prove wrong, his next decision is how to change it. Indeed, if his hypothesis is correct on one encounter, should he hold to it in toto? The decisions, moreover, are always contingent on the consequences he foresees and he must also make decisions about what consequences seem reasonable. If you will, then, the steps involved in attaining a concept are successive decisions, earlier ones of which affect the degrees of freedom possible for later decisions.

In studying concept attainment it has been our aim to externalize for observation as many of the decisions as could possibly be brought into the open in the hope that regularities in these decisions might provide the basis for making inferences about the processes involved in learning or attaining a concept. These regularities in decision making we shall call strategies.

The phrase *strategies of decision making* is not meant in a metaphorical sense. A strategy refers to a pattern of decisions in the acquisition, retention, and utilization of information that serves to meet certain objectives, that is, to insure certain forms of outcome and to insure against certain others. Among the objectives of a strategy are the following:

    a. To insure that the concept will be attained after the minimum number of encounters with relevant instances
    b. To insure that a concept will be attained with certainty, regardless of the number of instances one must test en route to attainment
    c. To minimize the amount of strain on inference and memory capacity while at the same time insuring that a concept will be attained
    d. To minimize the number of wrong categorizations prior to attaining a concept

Let it be said at the outset that a strategy as we are using the term here does not refer to a conscious plan for achieving and utilizing information. The question whether a person is or is not conscious of his strategy, while interesting, is basically irrelevant to our inquiry. Rather, a strategy is inferred from the pattern of decisions one observes in a problem solver seeking to attain a concept. What instances does he seek to test, what hypotheses does he construct, how does he change these when he meets certain contingencies? These are the data from which strategies are inferred. The manner in which one proceeds to analyze a strategy can be described here only in general terms. Essentially, what is required is that one construct an ideal strategy or a set of ideal strategies that have the formal properties necessary to meet certain demands or objectives with maximum rationality. Such ideal strategies can be stated in quite strict logical terms. For any given concept-attainment task, for example, there is an ideal strategy that can be constructed having the property that by following it one can attain a concept with a minimum number of encounters—but without regard to the cognitive strain involved. There are other ideal strategies having the property of minimizing cognitive strain, but they often are wasteful of the number of instances one must encounter en route to solution. And, indeed, there are also ideal compromise strategies that serve both the purposes of cognitive economy and rapid solution. To put the matter perhaps too simply, the analysis of performance strategy consists in comparing the actual performance of a subject with a set of rational or ideal strategies and determining a best fit. We ask then which ideal strategy does the subject's performance conform to most closely.

Obviously, strategies as employed by people are not fixed things. They alter with the nature of the concept being sought, with the kinds of pressures that exist in the situation, with the consequences of behavior, and so on. This is of the essence, for what is most creative about concept-attainment behavior is that the patterning of decisions does indeed reflect the demands of the situations in which the person finds himself. We do not know how strategies are learned, and the matter does not concern us for the present. Presumably they are learned. What is learned, however, is not of the order of a set of simple responses. The systematic behavior of subjects attaining concepts is a highly patterned, skilled performance. If contemporary theories of learning are to deal with such performances, it is our feeling that the unit of analysis now called the response will have to be broadened considerably to encompass the long, contingent sequence of acts that, more properly speaking, can only be called a performance. Our effort, then, is directed to locating strategies for dealing with information and trying to understand the manner in which they reflect the person's adjustment to the complex environment in which he must move.

Conditions Affecting Concept-Attainment Behavior

The pattern of decisions involved in attaining a concept is affected by a host of factors. Without doing too much violence to this diversity of determinants, it is possible to group them under several rather broad headings.

a. The definition of the task. What does the person take as the objective of his behavior? What does he think he is supposed to do?

b. The nature of instances encountered. How many attributes does each exhibit, and how many of these are defining and how many noisy? Does he encounter instances at random, in a systematic order, and does he have any control over the order in which instances will be tested? Do instances encountered contain sufficient information for learning the concept fully?

c. The nature of validation. Does the person learn each time an instance is encountered whether it is or is not an exemplar of the concept whose definition he is seeking? Or is such validation only available after a series of encounters? Can hypotheses be readily checked or not?

d. The consequences of specific categorizations. What is the price of categorizing a specific instance wrongly and the gain from a correct categorization? What is the price attached to a wrong hypothesis? And do the various contingencies—rightness or wrongness of a categorization of X and not-X—have a different price attached to them?

e. The nature of imposed restrictions. Is it possible to keep a record of instances and contingencies? Is there a price attached to the testing of instances as a means of finding out in which category they belong? Is there pressure of time to contend with, a need for speedy decisions?

We shall consider each of these matters in turn.

THE DEFINITION OF THE TASK

The first consideration here is whether or not the person is consciously or reportedly seeking to attain a concept. Consider our hypothetical subject mentioned in the preceding section. It makes a vast difference in behavior whether he is set to find out the extrapolatable properties of the class of people who are influential or whether he is merely trying to remember in rote fashion which of the people he met were and which were not influential. Many of the classic experiments in concept attainment, beginning with Hull's famous study (16), have employed rote-memory instructions, leading their subjects to believe that their task was to memorize the labels of different figures presented to them rather than to seek to discover what were the defining properties of instances bearing the same labels. Yet we know from the careful studies of Reed (22) that this prior set of the subject makes a considerable difference, even when the concepts to be attained are simple in nature. When a subject is set only to learn names, the rate of success in discovering the basis for grouping was 67 per cent; with instructions to discover the basis for grouping, the figure increased to 86 per cent—and this, let it be noted, with very simple concepts.

Roger Brown (6) proposes that one of the functions of words is to alert people to the possibilities of concept attainment. We say to a class of students in biological chemistry, "Consider now the substance histamine." The function of such a word is to suggest that a concept is about to be presented and that one must be alert to the possible defining attributes in terms of which its exemplars can be differentiated from other things in the world. It may well be, as Goldstein (10) has so vigorously and persuasively suggested, that people are differentially set to handle the events they encounter, some seeking constantly to form conceptual groupings, others to deal with events concretely in terms of simple identity categories. "This thing in all its appearances," rather than "This thing as a member of the class of things alpha." There are many deep and unsolved problems surrounding the question of what it is that alerts people to conceptualizing activity, and it is clear that the full picture of concept-attainment behavior will not emerge until these problems are solved.

A second question concerning the definition of the task is the person's expectancies concerning the nature of the concept with which he must deal. Some of our own studies have indicated that, when the nature of the concept to be sought is not specified, subjects will tend to assume that they are looking for a simple conjunctive concept of the certainty type. Is it indeed the case, as the late Alfred Korzybski (18) urged, that Western man is burdened with a preference for conjunctive classification stemming from the tradition of so-called Aristotelian logic? Does the difficulty of dealing with disjunctive, relational, and probabilistic concepts reflect the difficulty of such concepts or does the difficulty perhaps reflect certain cultural biases in problem solvers?

These are questions that cannot presently be answered. Certainly, there are cultural factors at work, or subcultural ones. The organic chemist, if organic chemistry can be treated as a subculture, develops a taste for relational groupings, at least during his working hours. Benzene rings, for example, are essentially relational groupings. Presumably, the physicist who works in quantum mechanics and nuclear theory will develop a taste for probabilistic concepts by the very nature of the discipline he must use. Though the generalization requires a leap, it is probably the case that most modern science is moving in the direction of probabilistic-relational concepts, classes of events defined in terms of the probability that certain attribute values will represent a kind of relation to each other. In economics, one classes nations over a period of years in terms of an average state of their balance of payments, whether favorable or unfavorable. Botany, a field in which conjunctive classificatory schemata have been classical, now deals with concepts such as a habitat's balance, or with approximations to certain forms of climax in which a special variety of soil, climate, and flora are in a quasi-stationary equilibrium.

Still another feature of defining the task, already alluded to earlier, is the predilection for criterial attributes that a person brings to the task of concept attainment. This is particularly the case when the task is one of constructing a series of systematic categories for continuing use as in geology, zoology, or anthropology. What is striking about such attribute predilection (and the Latin origin, *praedilegere,* "to choose in advance," is indeed the proper word) is that one finds both in the behavior of subjects and of scientists that preferred but nondefining attributes are not readily given up even when one's encounter with instances proves them to be noisy and useless. Insofar as people define the task of attaining a concept as one of proving that their prior hunches about defining attributes were right, it will be reflected in the pattern of decisions about changes in one's hypotheses in the face of infirming contingencies.

One hidden feature of the definition of a task—one of the skeletons in the psychologist's closet—needs some publicity, for it most certainly affects the manner in which people in experiments go about the task of attaining a concept. It is the two-man-game feature of most experimental research on the thought processes. Subjects in psychological experiments tend to define the task as one in which their abilities are under test. As a result, error may come to have a consequence that is different from and perhaps more severe than what usually prevails in more private cognitive activity. The effect may be to lead the subject to play safe in his choice of hypotheses or in the instances he chooses for testing. One countervailing factor, however, may make such a hedgehog strategy less attractive. For the subject in approaching a task also may operate on the assumption that the experimenter would not have chosen an easy task for testing his abilities. So one often finds subjects trying complicated approaches to a problem when easy ones would have served them better, and admitting it sheepishly after they discover that the task was simpler than they had thought. We cannot settle this vexing problem here, but wish only to point it out as a ubiquitous and important factor in determining the behavior of subjects in experiments on the thought processes.

One last point about the subject's definition of the task: his expectations about what constitutes successful solution or successful progress in a problem-solving task. Simmel (24) reports that one of the subjects in her problem-solving experiment asked to be allowed to keep going after he had attained solution on the grounds that his solution was "inelegant." At the other extreme, Smedslund (25) tells of one of his subjects in a multiple-cue probability experiment who was doing badly and showing no improvement. When queried, he replied that his "system" was quite satisfactory and that he was "performing as well as one could possibly do under the given circumstances, and that he was not responsible for his failures because they were unavoidable" (p. 39). The two contrasting cases illustrate nicely the extent to which the objectives of the systematic behavior adopted by a subject will differ as a function of how he defines his task. In one case, the subject wants an elegant solution, in the other he wants to do only somewhat better than chance. What is interesting about these levels of aspiration is that they determine in considerable measure when the person will cease trying, where he will stabilize and end the strainful process of searching out relevant attributes and relations. Thus all the factors that have to do with the setting of the level of aspiration—situational and personological alike—will in some measure affect the definition of a task and in so doing affect the objectives that go into the forming of a behavior strategy.

One other feature of aspiration level is the depth of understanding that the subject seeks to achieve in his solution. We single out this point because it has special relevance to the matter of knowing a concept behaviorally and knowing it at the level of verbal report. The world of mathematics is rife with examples of people who could come up with correct solutions before they ever were able to describe the steps used in attaining them. Many experiments in concept attainment, including our own, have shown that subjects are able to distinguish correctly exemplars from nonexemplars of a concept before being able to name the defining features on which their judgments are based. The studies of Hull (16), Smoke (26), and Walk (29) all provide examples. Indeed, Adkins and Lyerly (1) indicate that different factors contribute to success on two forms of the Progressive Matrices Test, one form requiring the subject to recognize the answer, the other to furnish it. We do not know whether there is a difference in behavior that results when one sees one's task as behavioral attainment in contrast to verbal attainment of a concept. There is evidence, however, that the two forms of attainment come at different points in a sequence of behavior and that good problem solvers show this separation more markedly than poor ones. At least Thurstone (28) suggests, on the basis of Bouthilet's study (4), that creative problem solving may express itself in this way, with the more imaginative problem solver being the one whose actual performance runs well ahead of his ability to state verbal justifications for it. It remains to be seen whether patterns of decisions in problem solving reflect this kind of difference.

THE NATURE OF INSTANCES ENCOUNTERED

Return for a moment to the hypothetical foreign visitor seeking to discover the defining attributes of an influential person. At the outset, he is armed with a certain amount of wisdom. While it is possible for him to distinguish many possible attributes of the people-instances he encounters, he is wise enough to know that certain of these are more likely to be important than others and will not waste his time considering whether shoe size is something worth attending to. But even after he strips the situation down to the most likely factors—factors, of course, that had proved useful in making distinctions between influential and other people in his own country—the number that remain to be tested will make a great deal of difference in terms of the nature of the task and, indeed, in the strategy he will adopt. First, it will make a difference in terms of the number of possible hypotheses he may entertain about the correct basis for inferring the influence of a person. Suppose, for argument's sake, that there were four likely attributes, each with three discriminable values. Let us say one is age (under 35, 35–50, over 50), economic status (high, medium, and low), religion (Catholic, Jew, Protestant), and apparent aggressiveness (high, medium, low). Assuming (quite in the manner of an Aristotle-ridden

Western man) that the concept influential people is conjunctive, the four attributes each with their three values could be compounded in a frighteningly large number of ways. For example, the influential people could be defined in terms of the values of all four attributes and include all those who are, over 50, rich, Protestant, and moderately aggressive. Or they could be defined by values of only two attributes, rich and Protestant; rich and moderately aggressive; over 50 and highly aggressive; and so forth. The larger the number of attributes exhibited by instances and the larger the number of discriminable values they exhibit, the greater will be the number of hypotheses to be entertained. This is the first constraining factor imposed on problem solving by the nature of instances encountered.

Here we may note that one of the principal differences between various strategies is the rate with which they eliminate alternative hypotheses about which attribute values are relevant for identifying exemplars of a concept. Moreover, the larger the number of attributes being considered, and therefore the larger the number of alternative hypotheses to be eliminated, the greater will be the necessity for adopting a quick-elimination strategy if time is short or if the number of encounters permitted is limited by their costliness. In sum, the number or richness of the attributes to be dealt with almost inevitably introduces a factor to be dealt with in attaining concepts.

The nature of the instances that one must bring under conceptual grouping may also vary in terms of the kinds of attributes they exhibit: their immediacy, their familiarity, their status as good systematic differentia, and their value in past conceptualizing. We remarked, for example, that our hypothetical foreigner in search of the defining attributes of influence would adopt certain reasonable attributes as good places for starting his search. This is indeed a rational procedure, although it must be noted that the road to failure in concept attainment is often marked by a sense of verisimilitude created by past experience.

The manner and order of encounter with instances is another factor in determining the behavior of subjects. Does the effort to isolate a conceptual grouping begin with a positive instance or exemplar of the concept being sought? If the concept to be discovered is conjunctive, then from a sheer informational point of view the problem solver is in a position, if he knows how to utilize the information contained in this instance, to eliminate a very great majority of the possible hypotheses that were entertainable before such an encounter. If the concept is disjunctive, a first positive instance often proves the occasion for adopting an altogether incorrect approach to the problem. Hovland (14) has provided an excellent analysis of the potential information to be gained from positive and negative instances of a conjunctive concept when such instances appear at different places in a series of encounters.

The sheer frequency of positive and negative instances, whatever the order in which they are encountered, also governs the likelihood of encountering certain contingencies with respect to the tentative hypotheses one is trying out. That is to say, one may encounter positive or negative instances and each of these is capable of confirming or infirming a hypothesis that the problem solver may have tentatively developed concerning the correct concept. If, for example, one encounters a red instance at a time when one is considering the hypothesis that red is the correct basis for grouping, and if the instance encountered is positive or exemplifying of the concept, then we speak of this as a positive confirming contingency. Each contingency encountered requires an act of decision on the part of the problem solver. Shall he maintain the hypothesis that he is holding tentatively or shall he change it, and if he changes it, how shall this be done? Now, a high proportion of negative instances (at least where conjunctive concepts are concerned) inevitably places a strain on inference capacity whether the instance confirms or infirms the hypothesis in force. (Lest the reader be puzzled, a negative instance, one not exemplifying the concept being sought, is confirming when it is predicted to be negative by the hypothesis in force.) And insofar as negative instances are infirming of a hypothesis, the change that is required in the hypothesis entails considerable strain on memory for reasons that will be apparent presently. Thus a long series of encounters with negative instances often requires the person to adopt modes of solution that are predominantly devoted to reduction of memory strain.

Smoke (27) has made much of the role of negative instances in concept attainment. He contrasted the performance of subjects who worked with a series of instances composed half of positive and half of negative instances in contrast to subjects working with positive instances alone. Success in attainment did not seem to be affected by these two conditions, a questionable finding since the two series were not equated for the amount of information they contained, but a finding that has been properly established by the better-controlled experiment of Hovland and Weiss (15). Smoke makes an exceedingly interesting point about the subjects in the two groups. "There is a tendency for negative instances to discourage 'snap judgments.' . . . The subjects . . . tended to come to an initial wrong conclusion less readily and to subsequent wrong conclusions less frequently, than when they were learning from positive instances alone" (p. 588). This finding suggests that negative instances play some role, yet to be ascertained, in determining the feeling of confidence that leads the subject to believe he has attained the concept.

Are encounters with instances orderly or haphazard? Consider the matter in terms of our useful hypothetical foreigner. Suppose his friend had introduced him to residents of the community in a prearranged order somewhat as follows: He begins by meeting people who are rich, over 50, and Protestant, and who differ only in terms of aggressiveness. He then moves on to people who are rich, over 50, Catholic, and again only differing in aggressiveness, and so on, until he has had a chance to sample each attribute systematically and see its relationship to influence in the community. A properly conscientious guide, if he were of an orderly turn of mind, would doubtless do something like this in educating his friend. If he did, he would find that his pupil arrived far more easily at the correct solution. For the patterns of solution that people adopt in attempting to attain concepts reflect very sensitively the order inherent in the instances they meet. Where order is systematic, the objective of minimizing memory strain becomes notably less, and with a reduction of strain, new modes of attack begin to appear.

The question of the orderliness of encounter and the effort to reduce cognitive strain brings us to a more general problem, one that has to do with methods of reducing disorder and confusion used by a subject in attaining or utilizing concepts. The reader will very soon become aware of the importance of what we call a focus, an exemplar of a concept that the problem solver uses as a reference point or *pied-à-terre*. Virtually all the effective strategies for attaining concepts depend upon the use of some sort of initial focus. Recall your own efforts in learning to distinguish prime numbers from other numbers. It is likely that you will recall the number three as your first association, and this number is very likely the focus point from which you began exploring other exemplars of that interesting class of integers divisible only by themselves and unity. So, too, we would expect that our hypothetical foreign visitor would be likely to take the first positive instance encountered of an influential person and use him as a basis for comparison with new members of the class. The use of such focuses in concept attainment—usually positive instances although not universally so—represents one of the most direct and simple ways of reducing strain on memory and on inference. Reference backward to the focus is perhaps what suggests that under certain circumstances the attaining of a concept is like the construction of a composite photograph, although the image connoted is, we believe, a highly misleading one.

Indeed, after a concept has been attained, the process of keeping order continues by the use of two processes. One of them is represented by the phenomenon of the adaptation level, the formation of a typical instance of the category. This consists essentially of "summarizing" all exemplars of a class that have been encountered in terms of typical or average values of each of the defining attributes of the class. For example, the subjects in an experiment of Bruner and Rodrigues's found no difficulty in setting a color wheel to the typical color of an eating orange, less trouble, indeed, than they had in setting the extremes of the acceptable range. A typical instance of a category is, then, the adaptation level of the values of the defining attributes of the class, whether computed as a weighted geometric mean of instance values as Helson (13) proposes or in some other way. A typical orange, for example, has a typical color, typical size, typical shape, and so on. As Helson suggests, such an adaptation level or typical instance permits one to evaluate exemplars in terms of their "fitness" in the category.[2]

Another order-preserving device used after a concept has been attained, akin in some respects to the typical instance, is the generic instance, a representation of the concept in terms of idealized values of the defining attributes and stripped of all noisy attributes. It is perhaps the kind of schematized imagery that Fisher (9) reports developing in her subjects as they move toward concept attainment. Often they become highly conventionalized, as, for example, the images of the different types of levers described by Archimedes which are represented by idealized fulcra, levers, and weights. The usual isosceles right-angle triangle that one thinks of when the class right-angle triangle is mentioned is another case in point. It is highly doubtful whether the average right-angle triangle we see is indeed marked by two equal sides around the right angle. The function of the generic instance beyond its use as an ordering or simplifying device is obscure, but it may well be that it is used as a search model in problem-solving behavior when a subject is considering what classes of things would be relevant to fill a gap in an unsolved problem.

Another feature of the sequence of instances encountered now needs consideration. There is a specifiable point in any sequential array of information that, formally speaking, can be regarded as informationally sufficient. One can illustrate this by reference to the amount of information necessary for deciding whether A is equal to, greater than, or smaller than C. The informationally sufficient array of information is, $A > B$, $B > C$, and any further data or any repetitions of these data would be redundant. The mystery writer, Ellery Queen, uses the same technique when he informs the reader that at a certain point all the clues necessary are available if the reader wishes to solve the mystery. One can specify the minimum array of instances necessary in order for our hypothetical foreigner to solve the problem of who is influential. But however convincing this may sound as a logical matter, it is grossly misleading from a psychological point of view. Redundancy thus defined has very little to do with psychological redundancy. The point of psychological informational sufficiency depends upon the strategy of information utilization a person has adopted,

[2] An interesting study by D. R. Brown (5) indicates the importance of identifying an instance as a member of a class of relevant instances as a condition for its affecting the adaptation level or typical instance of a category. Making a weight distinctively separate from a class of weights being judged by a subject reduces significantly its effect as an anchor on the series or its contribution to the adaptation level of the series. The role of categorial identity as a factor in adaptation level phenomena is discussed in Brown's paper.

and upon the manner and rate at which he is using the information contained in instances he is encountering. Since more than a few psychological experiments on concept attainment utilizing instances with multiple attributes have failed to take into account either the formal or the psychological point of informational sufficiency, the matter is worth noting in passing. For the way in which people will operate when insufficient information is provided them is not of the same order as their behavior when a sufficient series of instances has been permitted them.

A critical question in determining the kind of strategies that may be employed is whether or not the person can control the order of instances he will encounter or whether they come to him under the control either of chance factors or of some external agency. The difference can be caricatured as similar to that which separates the clinician and the experimentalist. Let us say that each is interested in finding out what areas of the brain mediate (that is, are defining attributes of) intact pattern vision. The experimentalist goes systematically about the task of extirpating now this area, now that, all in a manner dictated by the canons of efficient experimental design, until he arrives at the point where he is ready to publish his paper. The clinician gets his cases as they come, testing for pattern vision and for brain damage. In principle (and if the clinician were patient enough and orderly enough to keep his records elegantly) there is no difference in the situations of the two men. But in fact, the difference in behavior is striking. It is not simply that the experimentalist has cleaner data. When the data are, so to speak, cleaned up, the difference in the kinds of decisions each must make is even more apparent.

Another feature of control versus no control over the order of instances one encounters is whether or not one encounters instances when one is ready for them. In Hull's well-known study (16) in which the defining attributes of the concepts to be attained were radicals embedded in pseudo-Chinese ideograms, he contrasted two orders of presentation, one going from displays containing complex exemplars to ones with simple exemplars, the other from simple to complex. Simple and complex are defined by the number of what we have called noisy attributes contained in exemplars to be grouped. When subjects were allowed only a short and specified time to examine each exemplar, there was no difference in success rates for the two procedures. But if subjects were allowed to proceed at their own pace, "if each individual experience in the series is continued until the reaction to it is just perfected before passing on to the next, there is a distinct advantage in favor of the simple-to-complex method" (p. 38). We shall see in the next selection that the result of readiness for the next instance is not simply that one succeeds more readily, but that it also affects the manner in which a subject goes about the decisions required in his task.

One can go on almost endlessly about the critical role of the nature and order of instances encountered, for example, of the effect of successive encounters with instances as compared with simultaneous encounter with an array of instances that are either laid out in an orderly or in a random fashion. These are problems that are not simply technical in nature. They critically affect the manner in which concept-attainment behavior unfolds and they have notable implications for teaching practice as well. How, for example, should one expose a student to the bewildering array of instances that must be categorized in terms of the concepts of geology or botany or any of the other classificatory sciences? And with respect to the conduct of scientific research, when the scientist has control over the instances being scrutinized or must depend on a random intake as the clinician must, what is the optimal way of ordering one's contact with instances so that one can test them for defining attributes? When a neuroanatomist, using techniques of electrophysiology, attempts to collate the data on localization in order to map those brain areas associated with different behavioral processes, how shall he proceed? One neurologist, Karl Pribram (21), proposes that one pay attention only to "positive instances," reported instances where a given area has been found to be related to the presence of a particular kind of behavior—related either by the evidence of extirpation or the evidence of electrophysiological activity. Is this the best procedure? There is evidence that it may not always be so.

THE NATURE OF VALIDATION

There are various sources of validation of one's categorizations: by reference to a pragmatic criterion, by official or consensual validation, by consistency, and so on. Now we must introduce the question of opportunity for validation in the course of attaining a concept: the frequency of validation, how soon it occurs after a tentative categorization has been made, the ambiguity of validation (since it is not always clear whether we are right or wrong), and the extent to which the validation is direct or indirect.

Usually in psychological experiments we give subjects (be they animal or human) full knowledge of results. In a typical discrimination learning experiment, an animal must learn to make a distinction between, say, black doors and white doors in terms of the pragmatic criterion of whether they are in the class go-throughable or blocked. If the correction method is used, the animal learns which door is correct and may also have an opportunity to check the wrong door if he happens to try it first. Where non-correction procedures are followed, the animal at least gets a chance to test one instance for its positive or negative status. So, too, in concept-attainment experiments. The subject is shown an instance, may be asked to give his best guess about its category membership (usually to be indicated by a label of some sort), and then told the correct label. Only in the test trials is validation withdrawn. To test the animal's conceptual learning, new instances are introduced, say, a light gray and a dark gray door, in place of the black and white ones, and both doors are left unlatched to see whether the animal has learned the relational concept of going to the darker (or the lighter) door. In concept-attainment experiments, the same procedure is followed. Instances other than those used in the original learning are introduced and these the subject must label without benefit of feedback from the experimenter who now changes his role from tutor to that of tester.

Much the same type of procedure prevails when the young child is being taught to distinguish the conceptual entities of the environment. At first, the word *cat* is uttered each time the child is exposed to this animal. Then there is a stage at which the child is asked to name it and if he is correct we validate by approbation; if not we correct him. Eventually, the child comes to operate on his own and validation by an external source is given only on an intermittent basis.

But there are many cases in everyday life where the course of validation is neither so regular, so benign, nor so well designed to help the struggling attainer of concepts. Validation may be absent, may in fact be prevented; it may be greatly delayed and frequently is. Indeed, it is often indirect and ambiguous as well. The pattern of validating clearly, immediately, frequently, and directly, so typical of psychological experimentation, does not by any means heed the caveat of Brunswik (7) that psychological research designs be representative of the life situations to which their results will be generalized.

One feature of opportunity for validation is simply the frequency with which validation is available. Infrequent opportunity for validation may have the effect of increasing the reliance on preferred cues that are considerably less than certain. If, in learning to categorize aircraft silhouettes, attempted identifications are not frequently checkable against external information, the effect may be to lead the learner to utilize excessively some cues that have permitted him to make a few successful identifications in the past. One may, under conditions of restricted opportunity for validation, stabilize one's cue utilization too soon and end with a level of performance that is less efficient than warranted by the goodness of cues available. Or with reduced opportunity, one may turn to some other external criterion for checking one's categorizations. Experiments by Asch (3) and Crutchfield (8) indicate that, if correction is not readily available, subjects will turn to the group consensus as a basis for validation, even though the subject may be utilizing better bases for categorization than can be found in the consensus. In the Asch experiment, for example, the subject is asked to categorize the length of lines in terms of their height. Given no validation by the experimenter and given the fact that the group of which he is a member consists of stooges who are all primed to call out the wrong categorizing answer, the beleaguered subject soon comes to adopt the group norm as the basis of validation and begins to change his own pattern of calls. To be sure, Asch notes that few subjects were tricked to the extent of seeing length of lines in this distorted way. But the fact of the matter is that the actual categorizations made do suffer a marked change under these conditions. If external validation on the actual length of lines had been provided regularly, it is dubious indeed that the effect could have been produced, although Crutchfield's research indicates that even with some external validation, susceptibility to consensual pressures varies widely from subject to subject.

Frequency is only one feature of validation. Immediacy is another. In human relationships one quite often learns and continues to make groupings of people and events in the environment with considerably delayed validation. Consider such categorizations of other people as honest or of high integrity or as a promising young man. Perhaps under the tutelage of parents and peers, we early learn to classify people as, say, honest, somewhat shifty and downright crooked on the basis of a minimum number of defining attribute values. We are often a long time finding out the validity of such categorizations if indeed we ever fully do: "He seemed like an honest man from all I could tell, and I must say I'm suprised that. . . ." The seeming and the validation may be years apart.

It is likely that long delay in the validation of one's categorical inferences also leads to undue reliance on those few cues that have in the past paid off predictively or to reliance upon consensus in much the same manner discussed in connection with reduced frequency of validation. If we are unable to check immediately our bases for classification against a good external criterion, we are readier to use the vicarious criterion of consensus or to rely on rather nonrational cues.

It may also be characteristic of delayed validation that one reconstructs backward from the validation to possible defining attributes that might have been. A man is suddenly found to be an embezzler who for the last ten years has been accepted as a pillar of the community. Immediately the search backward begins as we try to recall signs that might have led us to infer correctly that the man was going to behave in this way. The eventual effectiveness of the search backward will depend of course on what can be called the ecological validity of labels. More likely than not, the cues that are honored in the consensus of folklore will be found: "He did, after all, have shifty eyes," or "He did act rather too piously and one does well to suspect that sort of thing." Or a factor of vividness will operate: "That facial tic probably indicated a not very balanced person."

It is rather unfortunate that one must treat the subject of delayed validation by reference to intuitive examples from everyday life, for it seems apparent that it is a rich area for systematic psychological inquiry. The psychological literature yields little on the subject.

The same complaint can be made about work on the ambiguous validation of categorial inference. Everyday life abounds with examples, yet a literature of experimentation on the subject is virtually nonexistent.

Without meaning to be flippant in illustration, we may take the heavily magical sphere of angling as a prime starting ground of examples. Consider the fly fisherman who is learning a stream, one of the principal components of which is learning to sort his flies into those that are takers on this stream and those that are not. His testing of instances consists of making a series of casts and determining whether the particular fly he is using will or will not raise a fish. If he is serious about his sport, his objective in learning is to be able to emerge with knowledge such a small pattern, tied sparsely, of a dark color, cast slightly upstream will take fish (the presumed criterion) on Yellowjacket Brook. Consider what is involved in validation and what makes for ambiguous validation. There are some days when fish will rise to anything up to and including a discarded cigarette butt. There are other days when fish will rise for nothing that is offered. Somewhere between there are days when, to use the conventional phrase, the fish are *feeding selectively*. Validation under these variable circumstances is hard to estimate. Is failure to get a strike on a particular fly an indication that the fly is inappropriate or simply that no fish are feeding that day? Does a strike mean that the fly used is in the category of takers or simply that the fish are striking at everything offered?

The essence of ambiguous validation is that the validating criterion provides uncertain information as in the example just cited. This may come about in one of two ways. The first is that the validating criterion—whether a pragmatic one, an official one, or what not—itself turns out to have a probabilistic relationship to the concept. Take the category mentally ill as a case in point. We seek prognostic signs of mental illness that may prove useful in predicting mental breakdown. Part of the difficulty in fixing upon useful anticipatory attributes of this sort is the difficulty of finding a validating criterion. Admission to a mental hospital? Clearly not, since many severe neurotics spend their lives without going into a mental hospital. Going to a psychiatrist for treatment? Again, the validating criterion is not certain, for many people seek the aid of a psychiatrist in times of personal troubles without being seriously ill and a good many neurotics avoid the psychiatrist on principle. Under these circumstances, one is faced with a category that is clearly accepted as existing by the society at large but about which there is a lack of full agreement concerning a properly valid criterion. As frequently happens, the consequences of the decision as to whether a particular person is or is not mentally ill are extremely grave, as in establishing responsibility for crimes or when it must be decided whether a will is valid or not. Under these circumstances societies maintain official organs for deciding. One must have recourse to a court of law.

A second condition of ambiguous validation is when the validating criterion is itself equivocal in the sense that it may not be clear whether it indicates one way or the other. The angling example given a moment ago is a sufficient illustration of this case. Does a strike or the absence of a strike provide sure information on whether or not a particular fly is a taker?

The effect of ambiguous validation on the process of concept attainment and concept utilization seems to be much as we have described it under conditions of reduced opportunity for or delay in validation. Quips about the fisherman being the easiest thing to catch are not without justification and the multimillion-dollar fishing-tackle industry is a tribute to the range of nonrational factors that affect the fisherman. The contending claims of laymen and experts alike concerning the predisposing factors leading to mental ailments bespeak the same type of failure to pin down the defining conditions associated with a category whose validating criterion is itself ambiguous.

One last matter remains in considering validation. It has to do with direct and indirect validation. By direct test we mean the chance to test one's hypothesis about what an exemplar of a category is. The child is seeking to find out what is meant by the concept cat. An animal comes along. The child says, "That's a cat." The parent says either "yes" or "no." In either case, a direct test of the hypothesis has been made. An indirect test, of course, is the case in which the same child says, "Oh, that's not a cat." Again the parent will answer in the affirmative or negative. But the child's hypothesis about what a cat *is* will not be tested directly, only his residual hypothesis about what a cat is not. Note that this is not a matter of positive and negative instances. It refers to the direct or indirect test of an hypothesis, regardless of the negative or positive status of the instance that occurs.

Consider a simple experimental procedure used by Goodnow (11) in which the subject must bet either on the left key or the right key of a two-armed bandit. He has a hypothesis that the right key will pay off. Each time, one or the other key pays off, so that whichever way he bets, he will know which one was correct. The subject has a hypothesis that the right key will pay off on the next trial. Under these circumstances, subjects prefer to act out their hypothesis by a choice of the right key, even though in doing so they risk losing by virtue of the fact that they have learned the left key does in fact pay off 70 per cent of the time. To bet on the left and find that the right key paid off "does not give you the same information" as a straight choice of right, as one subject put it. We suspect that such indirect validation is more difficult for the subject because it requires transformation of information and risks the making of errors. Though the transformation is not great, the urge to avoid indirect tests may often lead to risk in the interest of making more direct tests. Under many conditions, this feature of validation can be a critical factor in determining decisions about what instances to test next.

So much, then, for problems raised by the nature of validation. We turn next to the critical question of the consequences of categorizing events in one class or in another while one is in the process of learning a category as well as later when the category has been learned and is being used to group the environment.

THE ANTICIPATED CONSEQUENCES OF CATEGORIZING

The point has already been made that learning a new category can be fruitfully conceived of as the making of a series of interrelated sequential decisions. These decisions include such matters as what instance to test next, or what hypothesis to adopt next. It is in decisions such as these that the anticipated consequences become of major importance.

We begin by stating some of the assumptions we make about the relations between decisions and their expected consequences. The first assumption, already implicit in much of the previous discussion, is that each step in a performance can be usefully regarded as a choice or decision between alternative steps. The second assumption is that in analyzing the expected consequences of a decision it is necessary to consider the expected consequences not only of the step taken by the decision maker but also of the step he did not take. The third assumption is that the expected consequences of a decision can be analyzed into two components. The first is the estimated likelihood of occurrence of alternative outcomes. The second is the value placed by the decision maker on anticipated outcomes. So much by way of introduction. We turn now to the application of these notions, taken principally from outside psychology, to the process of categorization.[3]

Consider first the question: What are the outcomes which have value for an individual in a concept-attainment situation? And how does the individual's performance reflect the value to him of certain kinds of outcome rather than others?

Which particular outcomes are valued depends essentially upon the objectives of the individual. Take as an example the objective of attaining a concept after encountering as few instances as possible. This is a common objective guiding subjects in their decisions about instances to test and hypotheses to try out. We may deliberately set this objective before them by insisting that the concept must be attained within a limited number of choices. Or we may say to a subject, often without realizing the consequences, "Try to discover the nature of the concept as quickly as you can." By either procedure we are telling the subject that each encounter with an instance matters and that as much information as possible must be extracted from each.

[3] The reader familiar with economic theory will see immediately that there is a fair similarity between the assumptions made here and those made in many economic theories of choice (for instance, Arrow, 2). We have, in fact, derived much stimulation from such theories and especially from the arguments of Knight (17), Shackle (23), and Marschak (19, 20), who appear to us to be most aware of the psychological features of choice and decision making.

Suppose one is testing instances to find out whether or not they are exemplars of the concept one is trying to learn, as for example in the Vygotsky test. One chooses an instance at the outset that turns out to be positive. It exhibits values of, say, six attributes. The next decision to be made by the person is, what kind of instance to test next.

This decision is informationally a crucial one. Concretely, shall the person choose an instance that is drastically different from the first positive instance encountered, or shall he choose one that differs only slightly? If our by now somewhat overworked foreigner had met first an influential person who was over 50, rich, Protestant, and aggressive, should he now ask to meet one who is over 50 but poor, Catholic, and meek? Or shall he choose a second case for testing who differs in only one respect from the original influential person encountered? Let us suppose the individual chooses as his second instance one who differs in all respects save one from the previous positive instance. This is a desperate measure in the sense that, should the instance chosen turn out to be negative, it will provide the individual with little or no information. He will not know which one or ones of the many attributes changed made the instance negative. If, however, the instance chosen turns out to be positive, then in one fell swoop the individual will have learned that only the one attribute left unchanged really mattered as far as influence is concerned—a very big yield indeed.

In contrast, what are the consequences if the individual chooses as the second instance to test one which differs in only one respect from the previous positive instance? Whether it turns out to be positive or negative, one is assured of being able to use the information it provides. If positive, the one attribute changed does not matter; if negative, the one attribute changed does matter. Whatever the result, however, only one attribute will have been checked. If there are six or more attributes which may be defining, the task of solution will barely have begun.

Faced with the need to attain the concept within a limited number of instances encountered, which step will the individual take? Shall he choose as his next instance one which differs in all respects save one from the previous positive instance, or one which differs in only one respect? In other words, will he take a chance or adopt the slow-but-sure method?

Presented with such a question, the reader will surely demur. If the individual thinks the next instance is more likely to be positive, then he will be more prone to take a chance and choose a second instance which differs a great deal from the previous positive one. But if he thinks it is very likely to be negative, then he will be more prone to take the surer step and choose an instance which differs little from the previous positive instance. The step taken or the decision made rests upon a resolution of expectations about the values of positive and negative outcomes and the likelihood of occurrence of each of these.

We have introduced this discussion of anticipated consequences and of expected values and likelihoods by reference to a concrete problem. We wish now to talk about consequences in a more general and somewhat more formal manner. As our context, we take the case where the individual is presented with a choice of placing an object or event in one category or another under conditions of uncertainty, and we consider the consequences of placing the object or event in each category and being right or wrong in one's placement.

The basic device in such analysis is the pay-off matrix. Suppose we start with as simple an example as possible: a psychophysical experiment in which a series of lines is being presented, each to be categorized as long or short. The subject at the outset is given a reference line, 10 inches in length, all lines longer than which are to be called long, all lines shorter to be called short. The subject is told to be as careful as possible. He is told, moreover, that for every four short lines presented, there will be six long lines. The matrix can be specified as follows:

Decision Alternatives	Anticipated Events and Outcome Values	
	Longer Than 10 Inches	Shorter Than 10 Inches
Categorize as long	good	bad
Categorize as short	bad	good
Estimated likelihood of events	0.60	0.40

In this accuracy matrix, the outcome values of placement in either category are balanced. Categorizing correctly a line as short is as good as correctly categorizing it as long. Both correct categories are equally valued, and both incorrect placements are equally negatively valued. Since the outcome values are balanced, we would expect to find that estimates of event probability would be the major factor biasing judgment whenever there is uncertainty. We would expect the subject in case of doubt to favor calls of long, since he has been told that long lines are the more likely.

The fact of the matter is that the accuracy matrix with its balanced outcome values is only one of several highly interesting matrices that may govern categorizing decisions. Let us consider what the problems are like when the outcome values of placement in either category are not equal. There is, for example, a matrix that we have come to call a sentry matrix because it is so well illustrated by the plight of a sentry in a combat zone. A sentry is standing at his post. It is his task to categorize oncoming figures in the dark as friend or foe. Enemy intelligence and reconnaissance have been so good that enemy and friend alike now know the password

and it can no longer be used as a basis of discrimination. The sentry estimates that the chances of any given figure being friend or foe are 50:50.
Two alternatives are available to him. He may categorize the approaching
figure as a foe and open fire. Or he may categorize it as a friend and hold
fire. We represent the matrix as follows:

Decision Alternatives	Anticipated Events and Outcome Values	
	Foe	Friend
Categorize foe and fire	Alive and highly regarded	Alive, regretful, but duty fulfilled
Categorize friend and not fire	Dead or wounded	Alive, but feels both lucky and neglectful
Estimated likelihood of events	0.50	0.50

This is a matrix where the events being equally likely we can expect the
decisions to be biased by the unequal outcomes of placement in the two
categories. If the sentry categorizes an approaching figure as foe and is
correct, the outcome is highly favorable (alive and highly regarded); if incorrect, the outcome is not too bad (alive, regretful, but duty fulfilled). If
the sentry categorizes an approaching figure as friend and is correct, the
outcome is middling in value (alive, feels both lucky and neglectful); if incorrect, the outcome is highly unfavorable (dead or wounded). The outcome values are all in favor of categorizing an uncertain figure as foe and
acting accordingly. It is small wonder that sentries are regarded as so dangerous to men returning from patrol.

We have chosen so far two simple cases of categorizing decision: one
where the expected outcome values are balanced, and where the differences in expected event probabilities sway decision; the other, where expected event probabilities are balanced, and where differences in outcome
values bias decision. One need not be limited to such simple cases. In general, the argument can be made that, when outcome values are equal for
placement in one category or another, categorizing decisions will correspond to the expected event probabilities; and when outcome values are
not equal, categorizing decisions will be biased in the direction of the most
favorable alternative.

It must be noted, however, that we are always limited to statements
about the direction that bias will take as long as we remain on the descriptive level. We can make no predictions about the amount of bias or departure from expected event probabilities that will occur. Predictions of
amount call first for replacing our descriptive statements of value with numerical statements. Once such numerical values have been assigned, one
can follow the traditional mathematical technique of multiplying outcome
values by probability estimates to obtain a measure of expected utility, and

one can also argue for a general principle such as maximizing utility to determine which alternative should be chosen. There are, however, a number of problems in determining how the expected values of an outcome for any given individual can be quantitatively stated. We are not yet prepared to develop or to utilize any formal or mathematical model to predict the effect of anticipated consequences on categorizing judgments. We have chosen to be satisfied with less precise prediction and to concern ourselves with the psychological questions which must eventually underlie any model. The most important of these questions concern the objectives determining outcome values and the conditions affecting an individual's estimate of event probability.

For all its present limitation, the concept of a pay-off matrix is a useful and a suggestive one. In the first place, it suggests problems that have far too long been overlooked. Psychophysics, concerned as it is with the categorization of magnitudes, could well be re-examined for the manner in which outcome values and likelihood estimates affect categorizing behavior. It could, we believe, thereby be brought much closer to the judgmental behavior of people in everyday situations.

Analysis of the effects of anticipated consequences in terms of pay-off matrices may also serve as a link between motivational states and judgmental behavior. Specifically, one's set in judging is partially describable in such terms. Again we may benefit by examining the judging acts that prevail in everyday life. One example is the personnel officer who must categorize applicants into acceptable and unacceptable groups and who is punished only when his incorrect categorization takes the form of classing as acceptable a man who later fails. The practices of the progressive school provide another example: There the child is rewarded for his correct categorizations only; the others are overlooked. The situation in the basic training camp is yet another example: Only errors are noted and punished, correct acts are overlooked. Each time a subject walks into an experimental room, he imposes a pay-off matrix on the situation the experimenter presents to him and often the experimenter needs to set him straight.[4]

THE NATURE OF IMPOSED RESTRICTIONS

We end with what may seem like a trivial problem in comparison with the one just discussed: the restrictions imposed upon concept-attainment strategies by the nature of one's working conditions. But in fact, the topic is anything but trivial. Concretely, for example, does the individual have to

[4] An interesting example is provided in a recently reported experiment by Green (12). His subjects operated in a kind of Skinner box situation where, when a positive exemplar of a concept appeared, they were to hit a key as often as they could get points. The experimenter soon discovered that subjects had to be warned not to hit the key when a nonexemplar was shown. So long as there was no penalty for doing so they operated on the principle of not taking any chances: One might be wrong about an instance that seemed like a nonexemplar.

work toward concept attainment without such external aids as paper and pencil? Does he encounter instances visually and concretely or must he work entirely from verbal descriptions of instances? Are the instances with which he must cope concrete and palpable such as the stimulus cards of the psychologist, or are they abstract and only to be inferred like the data of the modern physicist? These are among the things that comprise the conditions of work that impose restrictions on the manner of attaining a concept.

A few words about the problems involved will suffice to introduce the subject. Insofar as one is forced to operate entirely in the head in solving a concept—on a mental problem rather than one in which concrete instances must be sorted—one's method of proceeding may have to take into account the added strain in some way or other. One may literally have to throw away information and proceed more slowly if one is to succeed at all. Indeed, there are certain strategies of concept attainment that are informationally wasteful but which make it possible to work under a restricting work condition. It has been our experience in studying the behavior of our subjects that people who have been trained in mathematics and theoretical physics, where systems of condensed notation make easy the task of carrying along a lot of information, frequently attempt solutions to conceptual problems that, while excellent in principle, cannot succeed because of the impositions they make upon memory.

More often, to be sure, ineffectiveness in concept attainment derives from the use of techniques that are too wasteful of information and do not utilize fully enough the cognitive capacities of our subjects. The use of the dramatic instance as a basis for arriving at the definition of a concept, overextrapolation of attributes found useful in the past with a failure to adopt an adequate information-gathering strategy—these and various other lapses from cognitive rigor are more notable. In the end, the question reduces to one of choosing a mode of attack that is appropriate to the restrictions imposed by the conditions of work provided.

References

1. ADKINS, D. C., and LYERLY, S. B. 1951. Factor analysis of reasoning tests. Adjutant General's Office PRS report no. 878.
2. ARROW, K. J. 1951. Alternative approaches to the theory of choice in risk-taking situations. *Econometrica* 19:404–37.
3. ASCH, S. E. 1951. Effects of group pressure upon the modification and distortion of judgments. In *Groups, leadership, and men,* ed. H. Guetzkow, pp 177–90. Pittsburgh: Carnegie Press.
4. BOUTHILET, L. 1948. The measurement of intuitive thinking. Unpublished doctoral dissertation, University of Chicago.
5. BROWN, D. R. 1953. Stimulus similarity and the anchoring of subjective scales. *American Journal of Psychology* 66:199–214.
6. BROWN, R. 1956. Language and categories. In *A study of thinking,* ed. J. S. Bruner, J. J. Goodnow, and G. A. Austin. New York: Wiley.

7. BRUNSWIK, E. 1947. Systematic and representative design of psychological experiments. Berkeley: University of California Press.
8. CRUTCHFIELD, R. S. Conformity and character. Presidential address to American Psychological Association (Division of Personal and Social Psychology), September 1954, New York.
9. FISHER, S. C. 1916. The process of generalizing abstraction, and its product, the general concept. *Psychological Monographs* 21 (2) (whole no. 90).
10. GOLDSTEIN, K. 1940. *Human nature in the light of psychopathology*. Cambridge, Mass.: Harvard University Press.
11. GOODNOW, J. J. 1955. Determinants of choice-distribution in two-choice situations. *American Journal of Psychology* 68:106–16.
12. GREEN, E. J. 1955. Concept formation: a problem in human operant conditioning. *Journal of Experimental Psychology* 49:175–80.
13. HELSON, H. 1948. Adaptation-level as a basis for a quantitative theory of frames of reference. *Psychological Review* 55:297–313.
14. HOVLAND, C. I. 1952. A "communication analysis" of concept learning. *Psychological Review* 59:461–72.
15. HOVLAND, C. I., and WEISS, W. 1953. Transmission of information concerning concepts through positive and negative instances. *Journal of Experimental Psychology* 45:175–82.
16. HULL, C. L. 1920. Quantitative aspects of the evolution of concepts. *Psychological Monographs* 28(1) (whole no. 123).
17. KNIGHT, F. H. 1921. *Risk, uncertainty, and profit*. Boston: Houghton Mifflin.
18. KORZYBSKI, A. 1951. The role of language in the perceptual processes. In *Perception: an approach to personality*, ed. R. R. Blake and G. V. Ramsay, pp. 170–205. New York: Ronald Press.
19. MARSCHAK, J. 1950. Rational behavior, uncertain prospects, and measurable utility. *Econometrica* 18:111–41.
20. MARSCHAK, J. 1954. Scaling utilities and probabilities. Cowles Commission Discussion Paper econ. no. 216.
21. PRIBRAM, K. 1953. Paper read at annual American Association for the Advancement of Science meeting, Boston, Mass.
22. REED, H. B. 1946. Factors influencing the learning and retention of concepts. I. The influence of set. *Journal of Experimental Psychology* 36:71–87.
23. SHACKLE, G. L. S. 1949. *Expectations in economics*. Cambridge, Eng.: Cambridge University Press.
24. SIMMEL, M. L. 1953. The coin problem: a study in thinking. *American Journal of Psychology* 66:229–41.
25. SMEDSLUND, J. 1955. Multiple-probability learning. *Akademisk Forlag* (Oslo).
26. SMOKE, K. L. 1932. An objective study of concept formation. *Psychological Monographs* 42 (4) (whole no. 191).
27. SMOKE, K. L. 1933. Negative instances in concept learning. *Journal of Experimental Psychology* 16:583–88.
28. THURSTONE, L. L. 1950. Creative talent. Psychometric Lab, University of Chicago, report no. 61.
29. WALK, R. D. 1952. Effect of discrimination reversal on human discrimination learning. *Journal of Experimental Psychology* 44:410–19.
30. WALLAS, G. 1926. *The art of thought*. New York: Harcourt Brace.

9

Reception Strategies in Concept Attainment[*]

Some approaches to the study of concept attainment are concerned with the means whereby an individual may select instances in such a way as to isolate easily and efficiently the attributes that are useful for inferring a conjunctive grouping. What is perhaps most distant from life about this procedure is its Olympian quality. The universe is spread before one and one has freedom of choice as to what one will take as an instance for testing. There are perhaps times when an experimentalist in science has the good fortune to work on problems that have this feature. More likely, his plight is that he must make sense of what happens to come along, to find the significant groupings in the flow of events to which he is exposed and over which he has only partial control. His major area of freedom is in the hypotheses he chooses to adopt, not in the manner in which he can choose instances to test. The clinician's condition is perhaps more typical than that of the experimentalist.

As an example, a clinical neurologist in the course of his practice encounters a patient with a damaged brain exhibiting the set of speech defects called aphasia. The concept of aphasia need not be formed, for it al-

* "Reception Strategies in Concept Attainment," from *A Study of Thinking* by Jerome S. Bruner, Jacqueline J. Goodnow, and George A. Austin. Copyright © by John Wiley & Sons, Inc., 1956. Reprinted by permission of the publisher and authors.

ready exists. The aphasia case is referred to him by an examining diagnostician. The diagnostician's statement that the case shows aphasia is the criterion of a positive instance. The research neurologist is now trying to find out about the neural correlates of aphasia. He must, in other words, seek the neural defining attributes of the class of patients known as aphasics. If one wishes to say that the neurologist is trying to find the causes of aphasia, this in no sense changes the basic problem, which is to find what neural conditions lead to the inference of aphasia with maximum certainty.

If the experimentalist were engaged in such a pursuit and could find laboratory animals capable of speech and on whom surgery might be performed, then he could systematically remove areas of the brain in certain combinatorial orders until the answer was forthcoming. But the clinician has to take his cases as they come. He must employ a reception strategy.

Let us begin at the beginning of modern neurology by taking Paul Broca, a gifted neurologist of the mid nineteenth century, as our subject.[1] He has a chance to carry out an autopsy on an aphasic patient. He finds massive damage in that portion of the brain at the base of the third frontal convolution (since named, in his honor, Broca's area), the speech center. But this describes only part of the properties of the instance. For Broca's exact description of the patient's lesion shows a softening of the brain in the left hemisphere all the way from the frontal lobe dorsally to the parieto-occipital junction, extending downward as far as the superior portion of the temporal lobe. One can sum this up more simply by saying that there is much more destroyed than Broca's area alone. It is at this point that Broca is able to exercise his major freedom, the freedom to formulate a hypothesis. He could attribute the aphasia to all of the destroyed areas or to any part thereof. He takes his option and proposes that aphasia is caused by damage to a speech center, the famous Broca's area. Perhaps there is reason in the fact that this is the area of most concentrated degeneration. Nonetheless, the die is cast. The neural defining attribute of aphasia is this particular speech center.

At the other extreme we have Flourens, who adopts another option. No specific lesion is taken as a defining attribute of aphasia. If the aphasic's brain shows specific damage, it is the interaction of the damaged areas and the intact areas together that create the final common path of aphasia.

What is of great interest about these two innovators is that each has a line of descendants, call them the localists and the totalists. The former seek always a specific area where possible, some set of limited defining attributes, adding new attributes only when forced by the burden of much evidence. The list of localists, requiring oversimplification in its compiling,

---

[1] In the interest of exposition, we shall take certain liberties with the history of this complex field. If the reader finds that our historical license leads us to exaggeration, he will, we hope, forgive us and treat our examples as fictional rather than real figures.

includes such names as Fritsch, Hitzig, Bianchi, Flechsig, and Adrian. The totalists have wanted to stay as close as possible to the whole cortex as an explanation, and it is only with the greatest reluctance that they will subtract any of its attributes as irrelevant. Here, too, we find a distinguished list: Goltz, Munk, Hughlings Jackson, Head, Goldstein, Lashley. The interesting thing about each group is not only that they attempt to proceed as they do but that they urge the absurdity of proceeding in any other way.

In point of fact, one could begin either way—adopting either a part or a whole hypothesis—and arrive at the same conclusion provided one did not become rigidified before the process of proof was completed. What is even more important than the starting hypothesis is what one does with it when one encounters new instances that differ from it. For a hypothesis is not a final declaration so much as it is something to be tried out and altered. We shall be considering in this chapter the manner in which, in the kinds of problems we have been discussing, hypotheses are changed to conform to the arbitrary stream of events to which they are exposed.

The first and obvious thing about a hypothesis is that it can have any one of four fates when exposed to a new event to which it is relevant. Let us bring Paul Broca back on the scene. He has declared his hypothesis on the relevance of the speech center. Each new patient he sees can have his speech center intact or destroyed. Again, each patient he sees must either have the symptoms of aphasia or not have them. Broca's world, then, is made up of four contingencies.

Speech Area	Symptomatology
Destroyed	Aphasia
Intact	Aphasia
Intact	No aphasia
Destroyed	No aphasia

It is apparent that two of the contingencies confirm, or at least fail to infirm, Broca's hypothesis. A patient with the speech center destroyed and the symptoms of aphasia confirms it. One with the center intact and without aphasia at least fails to infirm his hypothesis. Two of the outcomes are damaging to Broca's hypothesis. A patient with speech center intact and aphasia is as infirming as one whose speech center is destroyed but who shows no sign of aphasia. Let us adopt the language of medicine, for the moment, and speak of any case as positive which shows the signs of illness we are investigating; its absence negative. Whether it is positive or negative, a case can confirm or infirm the hypothesis in force. In this fashion of speaking, then, the four contingencies that Broca can meet are:

Positive confirming: aphasic with speech center destroyed.
Positive infirming: aphasic with speech center intact.
Negative confirming: nonaphasic with speech center intact.
Negative infirming: nonaphasic with speech center destroyed.

A good reception strategy consists in being able to alter hypotheses appropriately in the face of each of these contingencies. At an even more primitive level, obviously, it consists in being able to recognize their existence and to formulate hypotheses in such a way that, whatever the contingency met, one will know how and whether to change one's hypothesis.

A Paradigm and Two Strategies

Four things are required to reproduce in the laboratory a task comparable to the examples we have given. First, one must construct an array of instances that are alike in some respects and different in others, so that there are multiple ways in which the instances in the array may be grouped. Second, instances must be encountered by the person in an order over which he has no control. Third, the subject must know whether each instance is positive or negative in the sense of exemplifying or not exemplifying a concept. Fourth, the subject must be given freedom to formulate and reformulate hypotheses on each encounter with an instance. Given these requisites, a task is easily set. A grouping or a concept to be attained is chosen, and the subject is shown in succession exemplars and nonexemplars of this concept. His objective is to formulate a hypothesis that will distinguish an exemplar from a nonexemplar among the instances he encounters.

We begin with instances such as those illustrated in Figure 1, composed of the combinations of three values of each of four attributes—cards each showing four properties, such as two red squares and three borders or one black cross and two borders. We decide upon a concept, say all black figures. We present one instance at a time to the subject, telling him whether or not it exemplifies the concept, whether it is positive or negative. After each card, the subject is asked to indicate his best hypothesis concerning the nature of the correct concept. Thus, following the presentation of any given card, he offers a hypothesis. The experimenter makes no comment. The next card the subject encounters must perforce represent one of the four possible contingencies. It may be positive or it may be negative. Whether it is one or the other, it also has the property that it confirms or infirms the subject's previously held hypothesis about the nature of the correct concept.

Before examining the behavior of subjects dealing with such problems, perhaps we should consider the ideal strategies that are applicable. First, there is a focusing strategy which is useful both for maximizing information yield and for reducing the strain on inference and memory. The surprisingly simple rules for the alteration of hypotheses with this strategy are best presented with the aid of an illustration.

The clinician begins, let us say, with an aphasic showing a badly damaged brain—areas 1 to 6 destroyed. He takes as his first hypothesis that destruction in all six areas must be responsible for aphasia. If he should encounter a positive-confirming instance (another aphasic with like de-

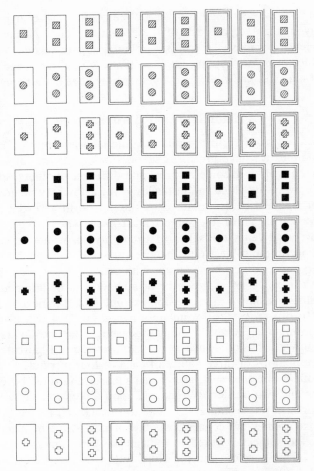

FIGURE 1. Array of instances comprising combinations of four attributes, each exhibiting three values. Plain figures are in green, striped figures in red, solid figures in black

struction), he maintains the hypothesis in force. If he should meet a nega-tive-confirming instance (a nonaphasic with some or all of the areas in-tact), he still maintains his hypothesis. The only time he changes is when he meets a positive-infirming instance. An example of one such would be an aphasic with areas 1 to 3 intact, and areas 4 to 6 destroyed. Under these circumstances, he alters his hypothesis by taking the intersect be-tween his old hypothesis and the new instance, those features common to the two. The features common to the old hypothesis and the new positive instance can be readily seen:

  Old hypothesis: areas 1, 2, 3, 4, 5, 6 destroyed produce aphasia
  New positive instance: aphasic with areas 1, 2, 3, intact; 4, 5, 6 destroyed

Thus the clinician chooses as his new hypothesis: areas 4, 5, and 6 destroyed produce aphasia.

Now consider the rules in their barest form. The first one is of central importance. Take the first positive instance and make it in toto one's initial hypothesis. From here on, the rules can be simply described. They are:

	Positive Instance	*Negative Instance*
Confirming	Maintain the hypothesis now in force	Maintain the hypothesis now in force
Infirming	Take as the next hypothesis what the old hypothesis and the present instance have in common	Impossible unless one has misreckoned. If one has misreckoned, correct from memory of past instances and present hypothesis

By following this procedure, the subject will arrive at the correct concept on the basis of a minimum number of events encountered. The strategy has only two rules in addition to the initial rule that one begin with a positive instance in toto as one's hypothesis. These two rules are:

a Consider what is common to your hypothesis and any positive-infirming instance you may encounter.
b Ignore everything else.

It is apparent, of course, that focusing in the present case is analogous to the focusing strategy under conditions where the subject chooses the order of the instances that he will consider. In both types of problems, the first positive card encountered is used in toto as a guide, in the reception case as the basis for all subsequent hypotheses, and in the selection case as the point of departure for all subsequent choices of instances whose positive or negative character will systematically delimit the concept. In focusing where one chooses instances, the problem solver tests attribute values of the focus card one at a time as a means of seeing which features of the initial focus card are relevant to the concept. In the reception case, one embodies this focus card in one's initial hypothesis and then evaluates its attribute values in the light of subsequent instances encountered.

In the interest of brief nomenclature, we shall refer to the ideal strategy just described as the wholist strategy since it consists in the adoption of a first hypothesis that is based on the whole instance initially encountered, followed by an adherence to the rules of focusing just described. From time to time, we shall also use the expression *focusing* to describe the strategy.

As in the selection case, scanning strategies are also possible here. Again, they may take one of two forms. The first is a simultaneous process in which a person attempts to use each instance to make all possible inferences about the correct concept. A first positive card "eliminates these 240, and renders possible these 15 hypotheses," etc. This is the simultaneous form of the scanning strategy, so called because all alternative possible hypotheses are entertained simultaneously. It is of little interest to us primarily because we find no behavior conforming to it. Nor, for that matter, have we observed the kind of lazy successive scanning that can be described in ideal terms as formulating one hypothesis at a time and holding on to it so long as confirming instances are encountered, changing only when an infirming instance is encountered to a hypothesis not yet tested. Then one starts afresh to test the new hypothesis with no reference to instances used for the test of prior hypotheses. This, of course, is successive scanning in its pure, discontinuous form.

The type of scanning strategy that best describes the behavior of our subjects is a compromise between these two forms. It is a strategy that begins with the choice of a hypothesis about part of the initial exemplar encountered. When this hypothesis fails to be confirmed by some subsequent instance, the person seeks to change it by referring back to all instances previously met and making modifications accordingly. That is to say, he bets on some feature of the exemplar, choosing it as his hypothesis about why the instance is an exemplar of the category—why it is correct. So long as the next exemplars also exhibit this feature, the hypothesis is retained. Or if nonexemplars do not show it, it is also retained. But as soon as an instance infirms the hypothesis, the hypothesis is changed. The change is made with as much reference as possible to what has gone before. He now seeks to formulate a hypothesis that will be consistent with all instances thus far encountered. To do so requires either a system of note-taking or a reliance on memory. Let us look more specifically at the way contingencies are handled.

Confirming contingencies are handled as in the ideal wholist strategy. The subject maintains the hypothesis in force. The two infirming contingencies present a challenge to the strategy in that both of them require him to go back in his memory over past instances encountered.

To sum up, the rules of the scanning strategy are as follows. Begin with part of the first positive instance as a hypothesis. The remaining rules can be put in the familiar fourfold table.

	Positive Instance	*Negative Instance*
Confirming	Maintain hypothesis now in force	Maintain hypothesis now in force
Infirming	Change hypothesis to make it consistent with past instances; that is, choose a hypothesis not previously infirmed	Change hypothesis to make it consistent with past instances; that is, choose a hypothesis not previously infirmed

For describing this procedure we shall use the expression *part-scanning strategy* or, on occasion, *part strategy*.

Let us now briefly sum up the differences between the two strategies:

a Part-scanning obviously makes more demands on memory and inference than does the focusing strategy. The wholist's hypothesis is modified at each step to incorporate the information gained from the instances he has encountered. He need never recall either his past hypotheses or the relation between these. His present hypothesis is a current summary of all these. Only when he must recover from an error is recourse to memory necessary. The part-scanner must fall back on memory or the record every time he encounters an infirming instance.

b The scope of one's initial hypothesis—whether a part or a whole hypothesis—will alter the probability of encountering the four different contingencies. The most dramatic feature of this arithmetical fate of the two strategies is that a wholist who follows all the rules of his strategy will never encounter the most psychologically disrupting of the contingencies, the negative infirming case.

c To succeed, the scanner must remain alert to all the characteristics of the instances he is encountering, for he may have to revise his hypothesis in light of these. Such a degree of alertness and spread of attention is not required of the focuser. If he stays with the rules of focusing, he need pay no heed to the characteristics of the instances encountered after he has used them to correct his hypothesis. If you will, the scanner must keep a continuing interest in nature; the focuser need only be preoccupied with his hypothesis.

So much, then, for the ideal strategies. Specifically, we have three objectives in the research to which we now turn.

a The first is to examine the degree to which performance corresponds to the ideal strategies, the degree to which one acts like a Broca or a Flourens from problem to problem and from contingency to contingency.

b The second is to examine change in performance over a long series of problems varying in the cognitive strain they impose.

c Finally, we wish to raise some questions about the effectiveness of the two strategies under varying work conditions. We know, for example, that scanning is more dependent upon memory and inference than is focusing. What difference does this make for success and failure in attaining concepts?

An Experimental Design

Our experimental operations can be sketched rapidly so that the present design may be contrasted with some of the classical studies. At the outset the nature of the task is fully described for the subject. As noted earlier, an array of instances is constructed. The subject is presented instances from this array one at a time, and each is designated as either positive or negative. The first instance presented is always positive. The subject is asked after each instance to state his hypothesis concerning the correct concept: What it is that the first positive card exemplifies. Instances are presented until the subject has had at least as many instances as would be required logically to eliminate all hypotheses save the correct one. At no time does he have more than one instance before him, and should he ask about instances previously encountered, the experimenter demurs. No such aids as paper and pencil are permitted him. Moreover, it is explained at the outset just what it is about the instances that need be considered: the shape of the figure they contain, the color of these figures, their number, and so on.[2]

For the reader not well acquainted with the literature on concept attainment, we should like to point out here several crucial differences between the conduct of this experiment and of classical experiments in this field which have also used arbitrary sequences. First, no effort was made to conceal the nature of the subject's task. He knew that his job was to discover the correct concept. He knew what a concept was, a grouping of instances in terms of common properties. He knew what properties of instances were worth considering. And he knew, finally, that what he was seeking was a conjunctive concept, and that only one concept was to be attained in each problem.

In these respects, the procedure differed from the procedure originally introduced by Hull (6). In the Hull procedure, the subject was not told what his task was. Rather the task was presented as a study in rote learning. The subject had the task of learning to associate names or nonsense syllables with instances that were presented to him. There might, for example, be five different concepts, illustrated by an array of instances; and the subject's task was to learn that particular cards were labeled *DAX*, others *CIV*, and so on. If he did not figure it out for himself, he might never realize that *DAX* cards were so labeled because they shared certain common attribute values. The test of whether the subject had attained the concept was, at least in Hull's study, whether the nonsense syllables could be applied to a series of new cards that illustrated the various concepts but which had not been presented before. In sum, incidental concept attainment was being studied. William James urged that the psychology of religion begin with the investigation of "the most religious man in his most religious moment." We wanted at the outset to see concept attainment at its best.

There is one other crucial difference between our procedure here and earlier ones, a difference whose importance has already been lucidly remarked upon by Hovland (5). In studies inspired by Hull's procedure, it

[2] We are particularly indebted to Mary Crawford Potter for aid in designing and executing this experiment, as well as devising techniques of analysis for it.

was not made clear to the subjects what it was about the instances presented to them that might be relevant. The different attributes and their values were, in short, left uncontrolled. Thus, Hull used a set of pseudo-Chinese characters, a particular radical of which was the defining attribute of the correct concept. It is apparent that the number of attributes a subject might consider as possibly relevant are close to limitless: any component stroke, angularity, or curvedness of components, thickness of strokes, crowdedness of strokes, number of right angles, number of strokes, number of disconnected lines, width, length, and symmetry of characters, predominance of vertical or horizontal strokes, movement or stillness of the arrangement of strokes.

So long as the experimenter does not know to which and to how many component attributes the subject is attending, it is impossible to control or understand the amount of information being presented to the subject by any one instance or combination of instances. One cannot know when the subject has had an informationally adequate series of instances—adequate to eliminate all but one, the correct concept. Nor is it possible to study the effect of the number of defining attributes in the concept as compared to the number of noisy irrelevant attributes. To be sure, the use of such characters in concept-attainment studies provides highly useful knowledge—knowledge about the manner in which subjects abstract attributes from a complex situation. But the process of how concepts are attained, given the abstraction of attributes, is greatly obscured. Perhaps most serious of all, where the experimenter does not know to what attributes the subject is attending, he cannot know whether the instance he is presenting to a subject is positive confirming, positive infirming, negative confirming, or negative infirming. Moreover, in order to know the contingencies with which the subject is coping, it is necessary to have the subject state his hypothesis after each instance rather than merely respond in terms of a set of labels.

These points of design reflect our concern with the necessity of externalizing the decisions a subject makes en route to the attainment of a concept. It was a deliberate choice on our part to use a known number of attributes, each with a known number of values—known to both the experimenter and the subject. If you will, then, this is concept attainment with the perceptual-abstraction phase bypassed.

DETAILS OF PROCEDURE

The instances were cards containing various shapes, colors, and numbers of figures; and various kinds, colors, and numbers of borders. The six attributes and their values comprising the problems were:

Number of figures: one, two, or three
Kind of figures: square, circle, or cross
Color of figures: red, blue, or green

Number of borders: one, two, or three
Kind of borders: solid, dotted, or wavy
Color of borders: red, blue, or green

Subjects were run in groups of about ten. They were first shown a sample of several stimulus cards and the experimenter pointed out how the cards vary in their attribute values. It was then carefully explained to the subject that a concept is a combination of attribute values; that is, all cards containing crosses, or all cards containing one green figure. Thus, the experimenter points out, certain cards represent positive instances of the concept. For example, the card containing one green circle with three borders $(1G\bigcirc.3B)$ is a positive instance of the concept cards containing one green figure. By the same token, the subject was informed about the meaning of a negative instance as a card not exemplifying the concept.

We then said, "I will now show you a sequence of cards and tell you whether each is a positive or a negative instance of the concept I have in mind. After each card, please write down your best guess of the concept." Each subject was provided with a response sheet. Each problem was done on a single sheet, the last entry on the sheet being the subject's final answer. If the final answer corresponded to the correct concept, the subject was considered to have attained the concept. Cards were presented one at a time for only ten seconds. No hints were given and once a card had been shown and removed, the subject was not reminded of what it had been. The subjects were instructed to write down on their score sheets only their hypotheses and nothing else. It was not possible for them to refer back to previous hypotheses since the subjects were asked to cover them with a card as soon as they were written down. This covering card was also a code card containing abbreviations for the subjects to use in writing their response.

SAMPLING OF SUBJECTS AND PROBLEMS.

The subjects, 46 Harvard and Wellesley undergraduates, were given 14 problems to solve. The problems varied in the number of possibly relevant attributes with which the subject had to deal and in the number of attributes that defined the concept. The number of possibly relevant attributes varied from three to six and the number of attributes that actually defined the correct concepts varied from one to five.

The attributes used for any given problem were chosen at random, with the restriction that all six attributes were used equally often in the 14 problems. When, for example, a problem involved the use of three attributes, subjects were told what these were and the other attributes were kept at a constant value so as not to distract subjects from their task. The attributes that defined a concept were similarly chosen at random, with the same restriction as mentioned before.

The instances used for each problem were such as to approximate as closely as possible the following desiderata: First, that just enough instances be given so that the subject have sufficient information for attaining the concept with no redundant instances included in the series. Second, that the total number of instances presented for each problem be the same. Third, that the ratio of positive to negative instances presented in the various problems be the same. Fourth, that each problem occur equally often in the first, second, third, or fourth quarter of the series of problems. While we were able to come close to these prescriptions, it was combinatorially impossible to realize them completely. Subjects had to be divided into four subgroups and given slightly different sets of problems. The nature of the instances presented in the set of problems given to one subgroup is set forth in Table 1.

TABLE 1 The 14 Problems Given Subjects in One Subgroup

	Problems													
	1	*2*	*3*	*4*	*5*	*6*	*7*	*8*	*9*	*10*	*11*	*12*	*13*	*14*
Attribute values of concept	1	2	1	2	3	3	1	2	3	4	1	2	3	4
Total attributes in array	3	3	4	4	4	4	5	5	5	5	6	6	6	6
Informative positive instances*	3	2	3	3	2	2	3	3	3	2	3	3	3	3
Redundant positive instances	0	1	0	0	0	1	0	0	0	1	0	0	0	0
Informative negative instances	1	2	2	2	3	3	2	2	3	4	1	2	3	4
Redundant negative instances	2	1	1	1	0	0	1	1	0	0	2	1	0	0
Total instances presented	6	6	6	6	5	6	6	6	6	7	6	6	6	7

* This includes the positive instance, that is, the initial card presented.

But the fit to our prescription was not bad at that. All but three of the problems in this set contained six instances, and these three were only one away from this number. Four of the problems involved instances comprising exactly one full informational cycle with no redundant instances; the others contained one positive redundant instance, and sometimes one or two negative redundant instances. The balance of positive and negative instances was practically constant throughout. Finally, nearly all the possible combinations of ratios of defining to total attributes were represented all the way from one defining attribute value for a three-attribute array to four defining attribute values for a six-attribute array.

Adherence to Strategy

Two ideal strategies have been described in terms of a set of rules for constructing a first hypothesis and for changing it upon encountering various contingencies. The general question we wish to ask is whether, on the whole, subjects adhere consistently to the rules of these strategies or whether, if you will, their behavior is random. The question is reminiscent of one asked years ago by Krechevsky (7) about maze learning in the rat: Is it a chance performance or systematic, this process of finding the .way to a correct solution?

Three concrete questions can be put. Problems are begun with either the part hypothesis of the scanner or the whole hypothesis of the focuser. Are subjects consistent from problem to problem in using a whole or a part initial hypothesis? Given an initial hypothesis of one or the other type, to what extent do subjects follow the remaining rules of the ideal strategy that would permit them to reach a correct solution with minimum information? Where does a subject's performance diverge from the ideal strategy?

Regarding consistency in the utilization of part and whole hypotheses on a series of problems done by a single subject, there is a very marked tendency for the subject to use one or the other approach consistently. In this type of problem, at least, people are either consistently like Broca or like Flourens. The relevant data are presented in Figure 2.

We also see in this figure that it is the exception for subjects to use the two forms of initial hypothesis with equal frequency. It is rather interesting, too, that the whole hypothesis is preferred to the part hypothesis. [3] In

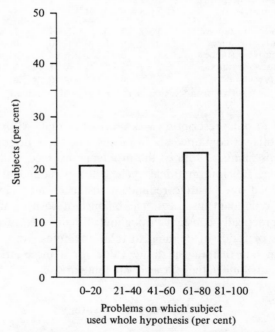

FIGURE 2. Percentage distribution of subjects with respect to the relative frequency with which they used initial whole hypotheses in dealing with problems

[3] In a partial replication of this experiment, with subjects run individually and with no time pressure, the same preference for whole hypotheses was found.

fact, about 62 per cent of the problems were begun with whole hypotheses. A word must be said about the strength of this preference.

Upon being shown an instance exhibiting, say, four attribute values, there are 15 opening hypotheses possible. Of these, one contains all four attribute values, and 14 contain fewer than all four of these. The larger the number of attributes in an instance, the greater the number of alternative hypotheses possible. But always, there is only one of these alternatives that contains all the attribute values of the instance—the so-called whole hypothesis. Thus, the probability of choosing a whole hypothesis by chance alone diminishes as the number of attributes used increases. The best way of showing the strength of our subjects' preference for whole hypotheses is to consider the proportion of whole hypotheses actually used and the number expected by chance.

TABLE 2 Percentage of Problems Begun with Whole Hypotheses and Percentage Expected by Chance

Number of Attributes in Array	Percentage Begun with Whole Hypothesis	Percentage Expected by Chance
3	70	12
4	65	7
5	59	3
6	70	2

The first question posed was whether subjects are consistent from problem to problem in their preference for either part or whole hypotheses. The answer can be given in three parts: (*a*) They are consistent from problem to problem. (*b*) There is a preference for whole hypotheses far in excess of chance. (*c*) Both the consistency and the preference hold for problems of varying complexity.

Why this preference for whole hypotheses? Two explanations suggest themselves. The first is that when the number of attributes to be dealt with is relatively limited, a person may be willing to deal with them all at once. Perhaps had we gone well above the subjects' immediate memory-and-attention span, there might have been a tendency to break the task down by dealing with packets of attributes. A second explanation is that in the kind of abstract material used here, it is not likely that subjects will have any strong preferences about the relevance of particular attributes in the array. They have no favorites to ride. In consequence, there is no preformed tendency to concentrate upon any particular attribute.

So far we have concerned ourselves with the nature of the initial hypotheses adopted after presentation of the illustrative positive card. Consider now the way in which these initial hypotheses are modified in light of contingencies subsequently encountered.

THE MEETING AND HANDLING OF CONTINGENCIES: WHOLISTS

Recall the four rules for the ideal focusing strategy, the ideal ways for a wholist to handle the four contingencies.

Contingency	Ideal Procedure
Positive confirming (*PC*)	Maintain hypothesis now in force
Negative confirming (*NC*)	Maintain hypothesis now in force
Positive infirming (*PI*)	Change hypothesis to whatever the old hypothesis and the new instance have in common
Negative infirming (*NI*)	Change hypothesis on the basis of memory of past instances

How often are these rules followed by subjects who begin with a whole hypothesis—the wholists? The ideal rules are followed on:

> 54 per cent of encounters with *PC* contingencies
> 61 per cent of encounters with *NC* contingencies
> 54 per cent of encounters with *PI* contingencies
> 10 per cent of encounters with *NI* contingencies.

The first three contingencies are handled ideally with a frequency far in excess of chance, and we shall return later to the question of what constitutes chance performance. But ideal handling of the negative infirming contingency is strikingly rare. Why?

For the wholist to deal with the negative infirming contingency, he must change his hypotheses on the basis of his memory of past instances encountered. In short, he must backtrack. This is the only contingency where focusers must use memory in this rote way. In practice, wholists do attempt to remember past instances when they meet a negative infirming contingency, but to remember correctly and to extract the implications from what they have remembered is a task most often beyond them. Actually, the contingency should never arise—if the other rules are followed. Since focusing does not tend to orient the person toward literal remembering of past instances, it is not surprising that the contingency is only dealt with successfully in about 10 per cent of encounters. The scanner, whose behavior we shall examine in detail shortly, is more memory-oriented. He deals successfully with this contingency on 26 per cent of his encounters with it.

The focuser's departure from the rule for handling positive infirming contingencies takes a simple form. The contingency is ideally met with the intersect rule: Take that which is common to the old hypothesis and the infirming positive instances before one. On occasion, subjects are tempted to ignore this rule and to maintain their old hypotheses unchanged. More often, they underintersect. Underintersecting consists in using for one's new hypothesis only some of the features common to the old hypothesis and the new positive infirming instance.

The lack of complete adherence to the ideal rules for handling confirming instances (either positive or negative) brings to light an intriguing feature of subjects' performance. The rule for both confirming contingencies is: Maintain unchanged the hypothesis in force. The fact is that for some subjects, at least, it is difficult to maintain hypotheses in their present state when new instances come along. The involved subject often feels that he is making progress only when he changes his hypothesis in response to new instances. Maintenance seems to be equated with no progress. He is, if you will, too participant, too devoted to the idea that change is progress.

Consider now the frequency with which wholists actually encounter the various contingencies en route to attainment. The average problem contained five contingencies, five instances encountered after the initial illustrative card. Of these,

0.3 were *PC* contingencies
3.0 were *NC* contingencies
1.6 were *PI* contingencies
0.1 were *NI* contingencies

It is quite evident, then, that the principal contingencies to be coped with are negative confirming and positive infirming, constituting 4.6 of the average of 5 instances encountered on each problem.

To determine which of these two important contingencies—positive infirming and negative confirming—created more trouble for users of the wholist strategy, the following analysis was carried out. Problems handled by the wholist strategy are separable into four types:

a. Those in which both contingencies were handled appropriately
b. Those where neither was handled appropriately
c. Those where *PI* contingencies were handled appropriately, but *NC* not
d. Those where *NC* contingencies were handled appropriately, but *PI* not

Table 3 sets forth the number of problems of each type and the proportion of each type successfully solved. In brief summary, handling both contingencies appropriately leads to virtually certain success. Handling neither appropriately always leads to failure. If one does not handle the positive

TABLE 3 *Handling of* PI *and*
NC *Contingencies by Focusers*

Response to Contingencies	*Number of Problems*	*Per cent Solved*
Both contingencies always handled appropriately	103	97
Neither contingency ever handled appropriately	160	20
PI appropriate; *NC* not	54	48
NC appropriate; *PI* not	37	22

infirming contingency properly, failure is as likely as if one violated both critical contingencies. Such a violation is far worse than improper handling of a negative confirming contingency, after a violation of which recovery and success follow half the time.

In brief, then, the handling of the positive infirming contingency by the intersect rule is the heart of the wholist strategy, for it is by this rule that the subject is enabled to alter his hypotheses in a manner such that it summarizes and keeps current all the information he has encountered to date.

THE MEETING AND HANDLING OF CONTINGENCIES: PARTISTS

How do scanners fare when they meet the various contingencies? The rules of the ideal scanning strategy are as follows:

Contingency	Ideal Procedure
PC	Maintain hypothesis now in force
NC	Maintain hypothesis now in force
PI	Change to a hypothesis consistent with memory of past instances
NI	Change on same basis as for positive infirming

How often do partists follow these rules? They follow them on

66 per cent of encounters with *PC* contingencies
52 per cent of encounters with *NC* contingencies
50 per cent of encounters with *PI* contingencies
26 per cent of encounters with *NI* contingencies

As with the wholists, the widest divergence from the rule comes in dealing with the taxing contingency of a negative infirming instance. Consider, as we did before in the case of the wholists, how the partists come to deviate from the ideal strategy.

Faced with confirming contingencies, either positive or negative, a subject should maintain his hypothesis unchanged. As with the wholists, however, many partists find it difficult to maintain a hypothesis unchanged in the presence of a new instance. They, too, feel that change is progress, that use should be made of each instance presented them.

Why is a negative infirming contingency so difficult to deal with for a partist? Adherence to the ideal rule is not striking: 26 per cent as against 50 per cent for an infirming positive instance. For one thing, a negative infirming contingency contains a double negative. The card illustrates what the concept is not, and it also tells you that your present hypothesis is not right. In this sense, a negative infirming contingency provides highly indirect information. Furthermore, such an instance provides one with no new base on which to ground a new hypothesis. A positive infirming contingency provides at least a set of attribute values upon which a new hypothesis can be formed.

Consider now the frequency with which scanners encounter the various contingencies en route to attainment. The average problem contains five contingencies. Of these

0.6 were *PC* contingencies
2.7 were *NC* contingencies
1.3 were *PI* contingencies
0.4 were *NC* contingencies

As with the focusing strategy, the contingencies most frequently encountered are negative confirming and positive infirming, constituting 4.0 of the average of 5 contingencies met per problem per subject.

To determine which of these contingencies was the more crucial for users of the scanning strategy, we again divided problems into the four familiar groups:

a. Those in which both contingencies were handled appropriately
b. Those where neither was handled appropriately
c. Those where *PI* contingencies were handled appropriately, but *NC* not
d. Those where *NC* contingencies were handled appropriately, but *PI* not

Table 4 sets forth the number of problems of each type met and the proportion of each successfully solved.

TABLE 4 Handling of PI *and* NC *Contingencies by Scanners*

Response to Contingencies	*Number of Problems*	*Per Cent Solved*
Both contingencies always handled appropriately	22	73
Neither contingency ever handled appropriately	85	8
PI appropriate; *NC* not	52	31
NC appropriate; *PI* not	29	7

In sum, handling both of these contingencies appropriately is associated with a high rate of success. Handling neither appropriately almost always leads to failure. If one does not handle the positive infirming contingency appropriately, failure is as likely as if neither contingency had been appropriately responded to.

Once again it is the handling of the positive infirming contingency that is the heart of the strategy. For the focuser, its handling in terms of the intersect rule was the way in which he could so modify his hypotheses that each hypothesis was a summary of the information encountered up to that point. For the scanner, the use of the positive infirming contingency is equally crucial. It provides a base on which to build a new hypothesis and a score card against which memory of past instances can be checked.

The Effectiveness of the Two Strategies

Which strategy leads more often and more efficiently to success? Complete adherence to the ideal rules of either, of course, leads inevitably to success. But there are deviations from the ideal rules: All wholists do not always adhere to the rules of focusing, nor partists to scanning.

If one can compare the success of partists and wholists, taking their strategic behavior as we find it, the advantage lies with the wholists. But the real question is: Which strategy is the more effective under what conditions? Does the effectiveness of each strategy vary with the over-all difficulty of the problem to which it is applied, and is there a difference between the two in this effectiveness? Recall that the problems given to subjects varied in difficulty, difficulty depending upon the number of attributes to which one had to attend. For the larger the number of attributes represented by instances to be dealt with, the larger the number of hypothetical concepts in terms of which the instances may be grouped. If A attribute values are present in a first positive instance presented, the number of possible hypotheses about the correct concept will equal the sum of A values taken one at a time (for one-value hypotheses), taken two at a time (for two-value hypotheses), up to A at a time (for A-value hypotheses). The number of possible concepts for each case used, then, is: [4]

3-attribute problems $=$ 7 possible concepts
4-attribute problems $=$ 15 possible concepts
5-attribute problems $=$ 31 possible concepts
6-attribute problems $=$ 63 possible concepts

It is quite evident that the task of keeping track of possible hypotheses increases considerably in difficulty with an increase in the number of attributes in the array.

Figure 3 indicates that the number of attributes in a problem is indeed a source of increasing difficulty. It is not surprising that the wholists were more effective with problems at all levels of difficulty. The fact of the matter is that it is easier for a subject to follow all the rules of focusing, and the superiority of the wholist does indeed derive from this kind of total adherence. For all levels of difficulty, there were more people who seemed able to adhere to all the rules of focusing than those able to follow through with memorybound scanning. The only explanation we can give as to why the

[4] The formula for the number of hypotheses after a first positive instance is:

$$H = \sum_{i=1}^{A} \binom{A}{i},$$ where H is the number of hypothetical concepts possible after a

first positive instance and A is the number of attributes in the array.

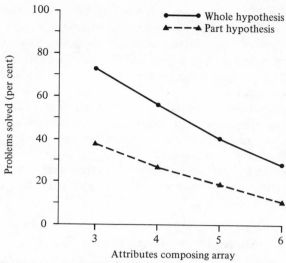

FIGURE 3. Percentage of problems begun with whole and part hypotheses that are solved as a function of the number of attributes represented in the problem.

partists who relied on scanning did not fall apart faster when problems grew more difficult than did wholist focusers was that the pace of the experiment was too fast. With an increased number of attributes in the instances, and with instances coming one after the other at a rapid rate, the focuser was as likely to get confused in remembering his hypothesis as the scanner was in recalling past instances. We have no direct evidence in support of the explanation, but it seems reasonable.

Under what conditions would one expect wholist focusing to show marked superiority to partist scanning? The results thus far presented indicate a general superiority of the former over the latter. It seems reasonable, does it not, that the more difficult one made the task of remembering instances, the more marked would this superiority be. Take, for example, the time strain imposed by the ten-second presentations used in the experiment just described. What if the subjects had been run individually and had been allowed to get instances for testing at their own pace and with as much time registering on instances as they wished? An exploratory study of just this kind has been done (Austin, Bruner, and Seymour, 1). The same strategies emerge, the same proportion of wholists and partists, although the degree of adherence to ideal strategy is greater under these relaxed conditions. It is interesting to compare the behavior of subjects in this experiment with that of the time-pressured subjects with whose behavior we have been principally concerned. Consider the effectiveness of wholists and partists on comparable three- and four-attribute problems. Without time pressure and proceeding at their own pace, wholists and partists do equally well: 80 per cent of problems done by wholists were solved correctly; 79 per cent done by partists. But with time pressure, 63 per cent of problems done by wholists were solved; 31 per cent done by partists. In short, time pressure has a relatively small deleterious effect on the success of focusing, but a major effect on the success of scanning—literally halving its effectiveness.[5]

The reasonable conclusion is that the more a task increases the strain inherent in a strategy, the more hazardous will such a strategy become. If one increases the number of alternatives to be kept in mind (for instance, Bruner, Miller, and Zimmerman, 3), or cuts down redundancy, or increases stress and time pressures, it seems reasonable to expect that a strategy requiring feats of memory and inference will suffer more than one not requiring such feats.

Strategies as Descriptive of Behavior

Early in the chapter the point was made in passing that the behavior of our subjects conformed moderately well to the ideal strategies we had described and that, moreover, the degree of conformance found was massively in excess of what one would expect by chance. It is to this question that we must finally return. How well is behavior described by referring it to the yardstick of ideal strategies?

The first and most obvious point to be made is that the ideal strategies that have served us so steadily are essentially refined versions of what we have observed our subjects doing. They were not invented by us in an a priori manner. Our description of ideal strategies is a description of what, it seemed to us, our subjects were trying to bring off.

There are sources of evidence that are considerably stronger than this mild intuitive point. The first has to do with the agreement that exists between the theoretical frequencies with which various contingencies should be encountered if subjects are conforming to ideal strategies and the actual frequencies with which contingencies were encountered. The second is the analysis of total adherence to ideal strategy, the number of cases in which ideal strategies were followed in their entirety, and the likelihood that such adherence could have occurred by chance.[6]

---

[5] There are several small differences between the major study where time pressure was applied and the pilot study without time pressures: principally that the problems worked under time pressure had fewer redundant instances than the leisurely problems. This probably contributed additionally to the differential effectiveness of the two strategies.

[6] The data presented here are taken from a study by Austin, Bruner, and Seymour (1) in which subjects were allowed to proceed at their own pace and without time pressure. It is with this study that we began our investigation of reception strategies in concept attainment.

EXPECTED AND OBSERVED ENCOUNTERS WITH CONTINGENCIES

For purposes of discussion, we shall concentrate on a problem in which the instances presented to the subject contain four attributes, each of them capable of exhibiting one of three possible values. Let us say that the four attributes are number, color, shape of figures, and number of borders. Given a first positive instance on a problem, one may choose as a hypothesis one, two, three, or four values of the initial positive card. In this experiment the correct concept may in fact be defined by any one, two, or three of these values. No concept is defined by all the attribute values in the initial illustrative card. We know, of course, that the larger the number of values defining a concept, the fewer the positive cards. In our present array, 27 of the 81 cards would be positive if the correct concept were defined, say, by the single value red. Only 3 cards in the 81 possible would be positive if three values defined the concept.

Now the question to be examined is how many instances representing the four contingencies would be expected by chance, given the adoption of an initial hypothesis marked by different numbers of attribute values, when the correct concept itself is defined by different numbers of attribute values. More concretely, what contingencies should a wholist or partist encounter? There may be one-, two-, three-, and four-value hypotheses in the face of one-, two-, or three-value concepts. Begin with the presentation of a first instance, a positive card exhibiting one of three possible values of each of four attributes. The correct concept, let us say, is defined by one of the attribute values on the first card. The first card is $2R\bigcirc1b$ and it exemplifies the concept R. Suppose the subject now adopts a one-value hypothesis consistent with the first instance. This could be either 2, R, $\bigcirc$, or $1b$. Now we ask, what is the chance that a next card, chosen at random from the array of possible instances, will be positive confirming, positive infirming, negative confirming, or negative infirming? We know that one-third or 27 of the cards in the array are positive, that is, contain a red figure. Now the chance that any of these will be positive and confirming will be as follows. If the subject has the right hypothesis, R, all 27 positive instances will be confirming. If he has any of the three wrong one-value hypotheses, say $1b$, only nine of these will be confirming, the nine instances that contain both R and $1b$. Thus, the average theoretical frequency of positive confirming encounters on the first instance after the illustrative card is: $\dfrac{9+9+9+27}{4}=13.5$. It is in this way that the values contained in Table 5 are computed. They represent the average theoretical frequency with which a second instance in a series will fall into one of the contingencies when this second instance has been picked at random from the array of 81 possible instances.

TABLE 5 *Number of Instances in 81-Card Array*
Falling (on the Average) into Each of Four Contingencies
When S Has Adopted Different Numbers of Values
of Initial Positive Card as His Hypothesis

Attribute Values Defining Correct Concept	Contingency	Attribute Values in Hypothesis			
		1	2	3	4*
1	PC	13.5	6.0	2.0	1.0
	PI	13.5	21.0	25.0	26.0
	NC	40.5	51.0	53.5	54.0
	NI	13.5	3.0	0.5	0.0
2	PC	6.75	4.0	2.0	1.0
	PI	2.25	5.0	7.0	8.0
	NC	51.0	66.7	71.0	72.0
	NI	21.0	5.3	1.0	0.0
3	PC	2.5	2.0	1.5	1.0
	PI	0.5	1.0	1.5	2.0
	NC	53.5	71.0	76.5	78.0
	NI	24.5	7.0	1.5	0.0

* For this array adoption of a four-attribute hypothesis constitutes the wholist approach.

It can readily be seen from this table that there is no chance of encountering a negative infirming contingency on the second instance if one begins by adopting a four-value hypothesis (a whole hypothesis). The smaller the number of values in one's initial hypothesis, the greater the likelihood that the next card will be negative infirming. This is true regardless of the number of values actually defining the concept. Contrariwise, the likelihood of encountering a negative confirming instance increases as the number of values in one's hypothesis increases.

If we now examine the behavior of our subjects, it will be apparent that partists do encounter more negative infirming instances than wholists, and that wholists meet more negative confirming instances. Similarly, wholists will show a higher ratio of positive infirming to positive confirming contingencies than will partists. Table 6 shows the average number of different

TABLE 6 *Average Contingencies Encountered per Problem*
by Ss Beginning with Whole
and Part Hypotheses

Contingency	Initial Whole Hypothesis	Initial Part Hypothesis
PC	0.7	1.0
PI	1.3	1.0
NC	3.4	2.8
NI	0.4	1.0
Total	5.8	5.8

Note: Based on 355 problems begun with whole hypotheses; 214 begun with part hypotheses.

contingencies encountered by subjects on problems begun with whole or with part hypotheses.

In general, there is quite fair agreement between the incidence of contingencies we would expect to occur if subjects followed the two ideal strategies and the incidence we observe to occur in the problems begun with part and whole hypotheses.

The major difference lies in the expected and observed frequency of encountering a negative infirming contingency after starting with a whole hypothesis. If the wholist strategy is fully followed, negative infirming contingencies cannot occur. But they are encountered on an average of 0.4 times per problem per subject. These negative infirming contingencies arise from subjects' occasional departures from the rules of the strategy. Aside from this one discrepancy between the general observed and expected incidences of contingency encounters, the agreement is more than sufficient to demonstrate the utility of describing and analyzing performance in terms of its conformance to ideal strategies.

THE INCIDENCE OF COMPLETE ADHERENCE TO STRATEGY RULES

To what degree, given a part or whole hypothesis, do subjects conform respectively to the rules of the scanning and focusing strategies—the strategies ideally suited for modifying such hypotheses? The bare findings can be stated quickly. Of the problems that were begun with a whole hypothesis, 47 per cent were followed up on all subsequent contingencies with complete adherence to the rules of focusing. Of problems begun with a part hypothesis, 38 per cent were followed through with complete adherence to the rules of scanning.

This incidence of complete and correct adherence is strikingly high. It is even more so when we inquire how they compare with what one would expect by chance. What is the chance expectancy for strict adherence?

There are various chance models that one can employ here: robots endowed, if you will, with differing amounts of inference and memory ability. A completely stupid robot, one who is as random as we can make him, would emit a hypothesis after each instance with no bias. For example, he would not even pay attention to the card being presented to him. This means that for a four-attribute array, he would choose indifferently among the 256 possible hypotheses in terms of which the array of instances may be subdivided into categories. If five instances are presented, and he must do something about his hypothesis each time an instance is encountered even if only maintain it, then the chances of obtaining any particular set of five hypotheses over the five instances would be one in 256^5 and this is a very small fraction indeed. And this, of course, is the probability that hypotheses would be changed consistently according to rule over five instances.

But surely this is too stupid a chance model to be anything but trivial.

Let us construct a robot whose only rational property is that he emits an hypothesis upon the presentation of an instance that is consistent with that instance. On the first instance and indeed on every instance, his chances of choosing a particular hypothesis would be a function of the number of consistent hypotheses possible given any one instance. For three-attribute arrays, there are 8 such; for four-attribute arrays, 15; and for five- and six-attribute arrays, 31 and 63 respectively. Thus the chance of a particular hypothesis after any given instance would be $\frac{1}{8}$, $\frac{1}{15}$, $\frac{1}{31}$, and $\frac{1}{63}$ respectively. The chance expectancy that a focuser will follow all the rules consistently on a four-attribute problem containing 5 instances would be $(\frac{1}{15})^5$ or once in 15^5 problems. This is still astronomical, and is considerably greater when one goes to problems based on arrays with still more attributes and still larger numbers of instances. The modest example just taken gives us a prediction that only once in 759,375 problems should we expect to find the rules adhered to strictly throughout a problem. This is for a robot who has good enough sense to emit only hypotheses that are consistent with each instance placed before him.

One could go beyond the last model proposed and construct robots with better inference capacities and with the ability to store information from past instances. But this can end only in the construction of a model that shows the same rate of adherence as our subjects. While this might be a useful exercise in model construction, it is not within the range of our task. Our effort has been to show, simply, that the rate of adherence to the rules of strategy was greatly in excess of what one would obtain from people behaving in a random fashion.

Reception Strategies in Perspective

We began with the contrast between two great figures in the history of brain anatomy, Broca and Flourens, one starting with the assumption that specific areas of the cortex provide one with the proper stuff for hypotheses about brain functioning, the other with the conviction that one must begin with the concept of the whole brain. The burden of the studies reported here is that one can proceed rationally from either initial position to the discovery of what features of the brain are indeed relevant to what kinds of mental functioning. But whichever way one starts, there are certain consequences that follow, for with each initial preference there goes a distinctive and appropriate strategy.

The task one faces in dealing with an arbitrary sequence of instances is one in which the major freedom of the problem solver is in formulating or altering his hypotheses about what is common to an array of instances. Here is a patient with lung cancer: He smokes, lives in a city, has immediate kin with a history of cancer, and has had chest colds frequently during the last ten years. All or some of these must be taken initially as a relevant hypothesis about the cause of cancer of the lung. From then on, freedom consists in the handling of our contingencies: A problem solver will encounter exemplars and nonexemplars of the category for whose definition he is searching, and each of these will perforce confirm or infirm the hypothesis he is entertaining at the time of encounter. What the problem solver must learn is how to modify his initial hypothesis upon encountering each kind of contingency. And this task, we have seen, is bound by the nature of his initial hypothesis. In the main, the focusing strategy appropriate to an initial whole hypothesis is less demanding both on inference and memory than the scanning strategy required to make good an initial part hypothesis.

It appears that far more people prefer to start with a whole hypothesis than with any other form of hypothesis. Moreover, people are consistent from problem to problem in their initial approach. It further appears that, whether one prefers a whole hypothesis or a part one, one is likely thereafter to conform to the rules of the appropriate strategy overwhelmingly in excess of chance.

Because the appropriate scanning follow-up to a part hypothesis is more mnemonically and inferentially demanding than the focusing follow-up to an initial whole hypothesis, the former strategy may be considered more vulnerable to all those conditions that would make recordkeeping difficult. An experiment illustrating one such condition has been reported. The condition is the effect of time pressure, reducing the time available for the subject to weigh, consider, or generally reflect on the nature of instances encountered. When such time pressures are applied, we find that the damage done to the user of the memorybound part hypothesis is more severe than the damage to the wholist. The former cannot apply the rules of his strategy as effectively and one finds a sharp decrement in the proportion of problems that are successfully solved.

We have examined in these pages the manner in which a human being deals with the task of sorting out events that come to him in a haphazard sequence, finding out which of the events are significant and which are not. The experiment has utilized highly stylized materials—slips of cardboard with designs varying in certain properties printed on them—but the task is not so different from the task of the traveler learning what type of inn can be trusted by its externals and without the pain of sampling the service, or of any person who must learn what something is by means short of trying it out directly.

There are certain interesting ways in which our experiments differ from comparable problem solving in everyday life. One of these is in the sheer concentratedness of the task. We are rarely flooded at such a rate with new instances to absorb. On the other hand, our subjects are required to retain only one concept at a time and are shielded from other distractions. Our subjects must also perform without the aid of such enormously important cultural tools as pencils and paper with all that these can do for us in extending the highly limited range of memory and attention. Interestingly enough, however, we find that allowing the use of pencil and paper and easy access to a record of past instances does not necessarily give an advantage in performance (see Goodnow, Bruner, Matter, and Potter, 4). Another difference between our procedures and what happens outside the laboratory is that the materials with which our subjects deal do not lend themselves to thematizing, to encoding in the form of little plots or themas. This abstractness of the materials is, we know, a mixed blessing. On the one hand, it saves the problem solver from his preconceptions as to what is relevant. But on the other hand, it prevents him from using the wonderfully diverse methods of conserving information through assimilation to familiar themes, the methods whose strengths and weaknesses are so vividly told in Bartlett's classic *Remembering* (2) and more rigorously recounted in the studies of Miller and Selfridge (8) and others who have applied information theory to memory phenomena.

Finally, the point will undoubtedly occur to the reader that the motivation of our subjects was either different from or less than what one might expect to find in ordinary life where the consequences or pay off attendant on attaining a concept may be greater. Certainly motivation is different. Intuitively, having watched our subjects struggle and strain, we think it unlikely that it is any less—whatever more and less can be taken to mean. The sense in which the motivation of our subjects is different from what one would be likely to find in a real-life situation is worth a word in passing.

Our subjects were quite clearly trying to succeed and the task obviously aroused achievement needs and other extrinsic motives. But what is more important, they were trying to get information, to attain a concept. That this is a powerful motive, nobody will deny. We need not go into the question of the primary or secondary status of such a need. All we need know is that our subjects were impelled by it. The reinforcement or satisfaction of such a need is the act of acquiring the information sought. This keeps our subjects going. Insofar as other motives are also aroused in the situation, the act of getting information takes on broader significance. It may mean to the subject, "I am a bright fellow" or "I'll show this psychologist!" Such extrinsic consequences of information-getting may, of course, alter the patterning of the behavior observed in our subjects. It is conceivable that had we exposed our subjects to the kind of status stress employed by Postman and Bruner (9) in their study of perceptual recognition, there would have been less incidence of adherence to strategy. We do not know. Obviously, our experiments are neither a proper sampling of real-life situations nor of the kinds of stress that can be applied to subjects. Such research remains to be done. The paradigm we have used will serve, we hope, to make that later research more technically feasible.

One other feature of motivation distinguishes our subjects from, say, the average scientist working on a comparable scientific problem. Our subjects had no passion to prove that a particular attribute was the correct attribute in the sense that Broca was impelled to prove that a particular brain center was responsible for human speech. This is a matter of importance, and it seems not unreasonable to conclude that, had there been such an investment in a particular attribute, there would have been far more part-scanning. The preference for wholist focusing probably reflects a certain dispassion among our subjects with respect to the attributes that were used in the experiment.

Finally, one general point needs to be made. In dealing with the task of conceptualizing arbitrary sequences, human beings behave in a highly patterned, highly rational manner. The concept of strategy has made it possible to describe this sequential patterning. It is only when one departs from the analysis of individual acts-at-a-moment that the sequentially coherent nature of problem solving becomes clear.

References

1. AUSTIN, G. A.; BRUNER, J. S.; and SEYMOUR, R. V. 1953. Fixed-choice strategies in concept attainment. *American Psychologist* 8:314 (abstract).
2. BARTLETT, F. C. 1932. *Remembering: a study in experimental and social psychology*. Cambridge, Eng.: Cambridge University Press (paperback, 1968).
3. BRUNER, J. S.; MILLER, G. A.; and ZIMMERMAN, C. 1955. Discriminative skill and discriminative matching in perceptual recognition. *Journal of Experimental Psychology* 49:187–92.
4. GOODNOW, J. J.; BRUNER, J. S.; MATTER, J.; and POTTER, M. C. Concept determination and concept attainment. Unpublished paper.
5. HOVLAND, C. I. 1952. A "communication analysis" of concept learning. *Psychological Review* 59:461–72.
6. HULL, C. L. 1920. Quantitative aspects of the evolution of concepts. *Psychological Monographs* 28(1) (whole no. 123).
7. KRECHEVSKY, I. 1932. "Hypotheses" versus "chance" in the presolution period in senory discrimination learning." *University of California Publications in Psychology* 6:27–44.
8. MILLER, G. A., and SELFRIDGE, J. 1950. Verbal context and the recall of meaningful material. *American Journal of Psychology* 63:176–85.
9. POSTMAN, L., and BRUNER, J. S. 1948. Perception under stress. *Psychological Review* 55:314–23.

10

The Role of Overlearning and Drive Level in Reversal Learning*

If one trains an organism to traverse a four-unit *T* maze, following the pattern of *LRLR,* the animal learns a series of specific turning responses of the sort, choice point 1, turn left; choice point 2, turn right; choice point 3, turn left; choice point 4, turn right. It is unnecessary to learn more for mastery of the situation. It is possible in this type of maze, however, for the organism to learn as well what might be called the principle of single alternation. By *learning a principle* we mean merely a recording of information such that the number of decisions the organism must make in the task situation is reduced to, choice point 1, turn left; then keep reversing sides.

One way to test whether or not the organism has been able to code information in terms of the principle of single alternation would be to reverse the pattern to its mirror image, *RLRL,* and determine the animal's ability to handle this new form of the same pattern. If there are substantial savings in learning the reversed pattern, this indicates the animal has indeed learned more than a series of specific turning responses, and we may

* Jerome S. Bruner, Jean M. Mandler, Donald D. O'Dowd, and Michael A. Wallach, "The Role of Overlearning and Drive Level in Reversal Learning," *Journal of Comparative Physiological Psychology,* Vol. 51, 1958, pp. 607–613. Copyright 1958 by the American Psychological Association, and reproduced by permission of the publisher and authors.

tentatively say that the principle of single alternation has been learned.

It should be possible to look for factors which might affect the likelihood of an organism's attaining such principle learning. Two such factors have been utilized in the present experiments. The first is degree of overlearning of the original task; the second is degree of motivation. Consider overlearning first: At least two studies indicate that original overlearning has the effect of increasing positive transfer from the original task to its reversal. One of these is a study by McClelland on serial verbal discrimination (3). The other is a study by Reid (4). These findings seem somehow at odds with such well-known experiments as the one by Krechevsky and Honzik (2), which indicated that overtraining produced the sort of rigidity that makes organisms adapt poorly to any changes in the learning situation. The McClelland and Reid studies are, however, in keeping with the bulk of the results in the field of retroactive interference where overtraining on either original or interpolated learning has been shown to have the effect of reducing interference.

Yet there are known conditions in which overlearning has a rigidifying effect, rendering behavior stereotyped. Here it is necessary to introduce the role of motivation. Perhaps drive level is the critical variable in resolving this seeming contradiction. It may well be that overlearning under mild motivational conditions has the effect of increasing the tendency to learn by principle, whereas overlearning under conditions of harsh motivation leads more to rigidification—that is, inability to go beyond the learning of specific responses.

Why should this be the case? Let us operate on the reasonable assumption for the moment that under high drive conditions, the organism seeks to maximize speed of goal attainment. In a paper by Bruner, Matter, and Papanek (1), the point was made that under these conditions the range of alternative cues to which the organism responded would be reduced, given the equal reliability of several possible goal-pointing cues. By the same token, we should expect that high drive would have the effect of reducing the operation of any processes not essential to attaining the immediately present goal as rapidly as possible. This would presumably include any processes that go beyond simple response learning. Since speed of goal attainment is in no way increased by recoding the learned pathway to the goal in terms of a principle—like the principle of single alternation—we may expect that learning under high drive conditions would not be of the principle type.

Experiment

METHOD

Fifty-four naïve male albino rats, between the ages of 80 and 100 days, served as Ss in the experiment. All animals were originally trained to various levels of mastery in running a four-unit straight-alley T maze (1) in a single-alternation pattern, half the animals learning *LRLR,* the remainder *RLRL.* Having reached a specific criterion, animals were then transferred to a single-alternation pattern that was the reverse of what they had originally learned. Throughout the experiment, all animals were run five trials per night, and the nights of running were spaced 48 hours apart. Reward for each run consisted of 10 seconds of feeding on a rich, wet food mash placed in the goal box at the end of the maze, and 1 minute was spent in a waiting box between trials. The animals were divided into six groups of nine rats each. Half of the animals were run throughout the experiment— both on original learning and reversal learning—with 12 hours of food deprivation. The other half operated with 36 hours of deprivation. Animals were fed to satiety on the reward mash on a feeding table at 12-hour intervals, three omitted feedings prior to running constituting 36 hours of deprivation.

The remaining variation in treatment has to do with amount of training given on the original task. One-third of the animals was trained to a criterion of 80 per cent correct—not more than four wrong turns in the 5 trials given on a single night. Upon attaining this criterion, the animals were run on the reversed pattern starting on the next night of runs and trained again to criterion. A second third of the animals was taken to 80 per cent criterion on original learning and then given an additional four nights, or 20 trials, of overlearning. Following the 20 overlearning trials, reversal was carried out as in the other group. The final third of the animals was carried 80 trials beyond the 80 per cent criterion on original learning, 16 additional nights of training. They were then reversed. A correction method was employed, an animal being permitted to try the wrong side as many times as it chose before shifting to the correct side. Only one error per choice was recorded.

RESULTS

The mean numbers of errors made by animals in all groups in reaching a criterion of 80 per cent in original learning and in reversal learning are presented in Table 1. As amount of original training increases, more positive transfer occurs. This tendency is much more notable in the group that operates under mild motivation than among those that operate under 36-hour deprivation. There are marked savings in the learning of reversal by the group that operates with 12 hours of deprivation and receives the maximum amount of original learning. Their counterparts in the 36 hour group do not show positive transfer.

The picture is much the same when one considers the number of trials necessary to reach criterion (Table 1). The same trend toward greater positive transfer with more original learning is present, and again the effect is more marked for the moderately motivated animals.

TABLE 1 *Mean Number of Errors and Trials*
to Attain 80 Per Cent Criterion on Original Learning (OL)
and Transfer Learning (TL)

Hours of Deprivation		Criterion		Criterion +20		Criterion +80	
		Errors	Trials	Errors	Trials	Errors	Trials
12	OL	11.7	9.6	16.2	10.2	15.6	11.3
	TL	17.7	12.2	16.4	10.9	6.9	6.3
36	OL	8.6	7.4	13.8	11.2	11.7	9.0
	TL	18.6	13.1	15.7	11.7	12.9	9.0

To test the significance of these findings it is necessary to equate the performance of different groups on general speed and efficiency of learning, since it is apparent from the data that speed of learning on reversal is correlated with performance on the original task regardless of the treatment given the animals. The equating operation is particularly necessary if one is to compare the performance of highly and moderately motivated groups, since we see from the data that, as one would expect, highly motivated animals learn the original task somewhat (but not significantly) more quickly. The appropriate procedure for achieving such equalization is, of course, analysis of covariance whereby the scores on reversal are corrected for correlation with scores on original learning; in effect, equating all groups on general learning speed.

Consider each of the motivational conditions separately first. We have three groups of animals that operate at 12 hours of food deprivation throughout the experiment, differing only in amount of learning, and three groups that operate at 36 hours of deprivation. There are two hypotheses to be tested. One of them is, simply, do the two levels of motivation affect the benefit derived from overlearning? Specifically, is there positive transfer under moderate motivation but not under high motivation? To test this hypothesis, we perform two one-way analyses of covariance, one on the 12 hour deprived animals, the other on those deprived for 36 hours. Such one-way analyses of covariance on each of these sets of groups show that in the case of 12 hour animals, overlearning is a significant source of variance; for the 36-hour animals it is not. The data for trials to reach an 80 per cent criterion, and converted to $\sqrt{x}$ for homogeneity, resulted in $F = 7.1$ ($p < .01$, df 2,23) for the 12-hour groups, and $F = 1.4$ (ns, [1] df 2,23) for the 36-hour groups. Essentially the same findings are obtained using errors to criterion as the relevant data for analysis, again with the square-root transformation ($F = 8.9$ and 0.7, respectively).

There is a second hypothesis, whether or not the slopes describing de-

[1] Nonsignificant.

gree of savings as a function of overlearning in the moderately and strongly motivated groups are significantly different. To test this hypothesis, a two-way analysis of covariance is required. Such an analysis yields an insignificant interaction term, although the difference is in the expected direction. There are various technical reasons why such an analysis of covariance on all six groups combined happens to come out with an insignificant interaction of motivation and overlearning—notably the increase in error term that results from combining animals operating at different drive levels. But these need not concern us here. It suffices to note only that where a high drive prevails, overlearning does not help transfer; where a moderate drive prevails, it does.

There are other differences that are of central importance as well. The first of these has to do with the amount of time spent by the animals in the different groups in the first unit of the maze on the first transfer trial—a measure of the disturbance created by being introduced to the transfer situation. A second related measure is the amount of vicarious trial and error (*VTE*) on the first unit of the maze following transfer. This too provides a measure of disturbance or doubt. Finally, we may consider repeated errors, repeating an error in a unit of the maze before making the correct response in that unit.

Observing the animals during performance, it was evident that the animals that had received maximum overlearning under moderate motivation were the most surprised when put into the maze with mirror-image turns. Upon finding the first, previously correct door locked on the first transfer trial, they withdrew, showed signs of emotional disturbance, and, in general, showed a marked increase in latency before finally going through the correct door. Indeed, their geometric mean time spent in the first unit was 203.8 seconds, four times as great as that of any other 12-hour group. The 36-hour groups showed no differences. The data are contained in Table 2. Again, one-way analyses of covariance were employed to test whether overlearning under one motivational condition produced effects not obtainable under the other. Amount of overlearning was a significant source of variance in affecting the latency times under discussion for the moderately motivated groups (data transformed to $\log_{10}$, $F = 10.7$, $p < .01$, df 2, 23), but not for those operating under strong motivation ($F = 0.3$, ns, df 2, 23).

Considerable, though statistically unreliable, differences were found for the *VTE* responses of the various groups on the first trial on the first unit of the mirror-image version of the maze. While one-way analyses of covariance on the groups deprived for 12 and for 36 hours show that overlearning is not a significant source in either set of groups, inspection of the data (Table 2) reveals that the one group that showed the greatest transfer also showed a very marked increase in *VTE*.

We come finally to repeated errors made on the first unit of the maze on

TABLE 2 *Time,* VTE,† and Repeated Error Measure ‡*

Hours of Deprivation		Criterion			Criterion +20			Criterion +80		
		Time	VTEs	Errors	Time	VTEs	Errors	Time	VTEs	Errors
12	Last night of *OL*	12.1	1.9		14.0	2.2		5.8	1.7	
	First trial of *TL*	47.1	2.7	1.6	49.0	2.4	2.6	203.8	6.8	6.0
36	Last night of *OL*	7.4	1.6		2.4	1.0		1.4	0.3	
	First trial of *TL*	13.7	0.5	2.3	9.5	0.8	1.6	10.2	1.2	1.7

* Geometric means (in seconds) of time spent in first unit of maze on last trial of original training and first trial of transfer.

† Mean number of *VTE* responses in the first unit of the maze on the first trial of the last night before transfer and the first trial after transfer.

‡ Mean number of repeated errors in the first unit of the maze in the first trial following transfer. An error is scored when an animal physically touched the incorrect release door barring the path.

the first transfer trial. These data are also presented in Table 2, and by now it will be a familiar pattern to the reader. The one group with notable positive transfer persists in trying the formerly correct door. For the moderately motivated groups in a one-way analysis of covariance, amount of overlearning was a significant source of variance in affecting the number of repeated errors (data transformed to $\sqrt{x + .5}$, $F = 15.8$, $p < .01$, $df\,2,23$), but not so for the strongly motivated animals ($F = 0.7$, ns, $df\,2, 23$).

Now we must say a word in a naturalistic vein about the behavior of the animals in the group with maximum transfer—the moderately motivated animals with maximum overlearning. Most of the animals, following a long delay in the first unit marked by the doubt of *VTE* and repeated errors on all four units of that first reversal trial, then proceeded to thread their way through the reversed maze without error and thenceforth made only two or three errors in the succeeding trials before attaining criterion. Their behavior for the first few trials remained highly tense: much rapid approach-withdrawal behavior directed toward the first set of doors. The usual emotional signs—defecation, urination, crouching in the back corners of the first unit—were also present. But the performance, once they got started, was definitely superior to the other groups'.

Compare these animals with the members of the highly motivated group that had had as much opportunity for overlearning. They charged the formerly correct door, were repelled, and paused briefly. Very quickly they shifted to the other door. And so it went in the second, third, and fourth units and on subsequent trials.

It would appear on the basis of what has been presented thus far that moderate motivation provides a condition in which frequently repeated exposure to a specific pattern aids an organism in converting that pattern into a generic, and thus more transferable, form. But before we can explore this matter further, a second experiment must be considered.

Experiment 2

METHOD

The object of the experiment to be reported now was to discern more clearly why a large quantity of overlearning led to effective transfer in a group of moderately motivated animals and none at all in a group that was highly motivated.

The hypothesis, presented in the introduction of this paper, was that acquisition occurring with overlearning under moderate motivation would tend to be more generic, involving a recoding of specific learning into a form approximating a principle. The turns *LRLR* would more likely be recoded into single alternation, thus making the mirror image, *RLRL,* easier to learn as another instance of the general case. High drive, for reasons already stated, would be inimical to such generic recoding.

The difficulty with the hypothesis is that it is not properly tested by the two groups that had received large doses of overlearning. One of them acquired the original learning under high drive conditions, but was also tested for transfer under high drive. So, too, with the moderately motivated group: It was their condition both during acquisition and transfer. Could the effect be due to drive condition during transfer learning and have nothing to do with the nature of drive during acquisition?

To test the matter, two further groups of animals were run, 23 in all, identical in all but one respect to the two groups that had received 80 trials of overlearning after attaining criterion. One of them acquired its original learning under 36 hours of food deprivation and was tested for transfer to a reverse pattern under 12 hours of deprivation. The other learned under a 12-hour regimen of deprivation and was tested for transfer under a 36-hour regimen. In all other respects treatment was the same.

RESULTS

The first result serves to remind that nature rarely takes sides unequivocally about hypotheses. Scores for original learning and transfer learning are set forth in Table 3, which presents both errors made and number of trials before animals attained an 80 per cent learning criterion. In effect, the 12-36, 36-12, and 12-12 animals do equally well, all showing significant positive transfer. The 36-36 animals show no transfer. Highly motivated animals again learn the original task somewhat more quickly, but not significantly so. Analysis of covariance was performed on the data of the four groups. Both for errors and for trials to reach criterion, the interaction of original and transfer motivation was found to be significant. Error scores were transformed for homogeneity to ($\sqrt{x} + \sqrt{x+1}$), and the interaction of drive levels before and after transfer yielded an F of 34.8, $p < .01$, df 1, 31. Trials to criterion, transformed in the same way, yielded an F ratio for interaction of 59.50, $p < .01$, df 1, 31.

*TABLE 3 Mean Errors and Trials to 80 Per Cent
Criterion of Learning in Four Groups
Given 80 Trials of Overlearning*

Transfer Deprivation		Deprivation during Original Learning			
		12 hour		36 hour	
		Errors	Trials	Errors	Trials
12 hour	OL	15.6	11.3	12.6	9.7
	TL	6.9	6.3	4.5	5.3
36 hour	OL	15.3	11.2	11.7	9.0
	TL	4.7	5.5	12.9	9.0

We may ask what such a constellation of results signifies. Given initial overlearning of a pattern, positive transfer to its obverse will occur provided either that original learning occurs under conditions of moderate drive or that transfer is effected under moderate drive conditions. High drive during both original acquisition and transfer seems to prevent transfer from occurring.

What the finding suggests, to pursue the general point with which this paper was introduced, is that apparently generic recoding could occur either during acquisition or when an organism is faced with the task of mastering a new instance of the principle contained in the old set of specific turns; that is, the principle of alternation. What is necessary in any case, it appears, is that there be considerable overlearning of the original task before transfer is undertaken. Before considering the difference between our four overlearning groups, several performance variables need closer inspection.

The first of these is a time measure. Table 4 sets forth the amount of time spent by animals in the four groups, expressed as geometric means, in the various units of the maze on the first run of the night preceding transfer and on the first run following transfer.

We see, first of all, that at the terminal stages of overlearning, the proportion of time spent in the first unit is roughly a quarter. The animals in all groups, in short, are passing through the maze at a quite even clip. Now comes transfer. The ratios change notably, and each group shows a distinctive pattern: 59.4 per cent for the 12-12 group; 48.4 per cent for the 12-36 group; but 30.1 per cent for the 36-36 group; and 26.8 per cent

TABLE 4 *Geometric Mean Time (in Seconds) Spent by Overlearning Groups in Various Units of the Maze on the First Run of the Night Preceding Transfer and on the First Run Following Transfer*

		Deprivation during Original Learning			
		12 hour		36 hour	
Transfer Deprivation		Unit 1	Units 2–4	Unit 1	Units 2–4
12 hour	OL	5.8 (21.2%)	21.6	2.2 (25.9%)	6.3
	TL	203.8 (59.4%)	139.2	113.0 (26.8%)	303.0
36 hour	OL	6.3 (21.4%)	23.2	1.4 (25.9%)	4.0
	TL	140.2 (48.4%)	149.3	10.2 (30.1%)	23.7

for the 36-12 group. In short, the groups that originally acquire the response pattern under moderate drive conditions spend proportionately more time in making decisions at the beginning of the maze; whereas the animals whose original learning occurred under high drive conditions distribute decision time in the maze after transfer in almost the same ratio as before transfer.

The time results just mentioned are statistically reliable. An analysis of covariance carried out on the proportion of time spent in the first unit of the maze, based on the data from which Table 4 is constructed, yields the following results: Using arc-sine transformed data, we find that drive level during original learning is a significant source of variance, and nothing else is—neither posttransfer drive level, nor interaction. (F for drive level during original learning $= 7.9$, $p < .01$; F for posttransfer drive level $= 0.4$, ns; F for interaction $= 0.1$, ns; df 1, 31 in each case.)

Further presumptive evidence of the concept-learning view being here presented is provided by examination of the *VTE*s observed in the four overlearning groups. The relevant data are in Table 5, where *VTE* scores are presented for the first ten trials of original learning, for the first trial of the night before transfer, and for the first transfer trial, again divided into first unit and remaining three units of the maze. There are no striking differences among the four groups during original learning save that, as we know, more highly motivated animals show somewhat less *VTE* behavior. Interesting differences emerge at the time of transfer. All the groups that show positive savings show a marked increase in *VTE* on the first trial after transfer. Paralleling the time data, the two groups that learned originally with a low drive, show a majority of their *VTE* responses in the first unit of the maze; 76 per cent for the 12-12 group, and 53 per cent for the 12-36 group. The group that learned with a high drive and showed positive savings, the 36-12 group, allocates but 40 per cent of *VTE* responses to the first unit.

TABLE 5 *Mean Number of* VTE *Responses in the Various Units of the Maze for the First Ten Trials of Original Learning, the First Trial of the Night before Transfer, and the First Trial after Transfer*

		Deprivation during Original Learning			
		12 hour		36 hour	
Transfer Deprivation		Unit 1	Units 2–4	Unit 1	Units 2–4
12 hour	*OL:* 1–10	1.4	2.2	0.4	1.3
	OL: 76	1.7	3.7	0.0	0.2
	TL: 1	6.8	2.1	11.2	17.0
36 hour	*OL:* 1–10	1.2	2.3	0.8	1.0
	OL: 76	0.5	1.3	0.3	0.4
	TL: 1	7.2	6.5	1.2	1.0

The data on time allocation and *VTE* seem to suggest an interesting difference between animals that learn and overlearn under high and low drive conditions—a difference in deliberation, perhaps. Put anthropomorphically, it is as if the rats that had learned under low drive were spending their time in the first transfer trial trying to figure out, in advance of full testing, what the nature of the new maze might be. The first error, an error on the first unit, leads to a high proportion of time being spent in the first unit, as if the animals could figure out from this error something beyond how it, the specific error, might be corrected. Animals that learned originally operating at high drive, while they too are slowed down generally, seem to be treating the different units much as before. This is true for both groups of such animals. Perhaps the difference between them—one of them shows notable positive transfer, the other not—is that exposure to the reverse pattern now leads one group to recode learning in terms of the principle of single alternation, the other group not. That is to say, for the group that learned with a high drive and transferred under low drive, providing two instances of single alternation, *LRLR* and *RLRL,* leads to attainment of the concept single alternation. Not so the 36-36 group. For the groups operating at 12 hours of deprivation during original learning, generic recoding seems to be effected at least in part before transfer.

One final result will be necessary in evaluating alternative ways of interpreting the data. It has to do with running speed. Older views of the learning of single alternation held that such learning consists of the linking of successive kinesthetic patterns as the animal threads its way through the four units of the maze. It is often argued that fast running gives a more noiseless kinesthetic pattern with no interfering pauses to break up the kinesthetic training. Product-moment correlations were computed for all animals in the four highly overtrained groups between (*a*) mean running speed on the first 15 trials of original learning and errors made in reaching the 80 per cent criterion in original learning, and (b) this mean running time and errors before reaching the 80 per cent criterion on transfer learning. No significant correlations were found for any of these groups. Neither the learning of a specific alternating path nor the learning of single alternation is related to running speed.

Discussion

We have presented a not unfamiliar approach to the problem of transfer: That transfer more easily occurs when learning becomes genericized or recoded into a principle that can be applied to a new instance of the principle. This recoding is greatly aided, we have found, by a considerable amount of overlearning. Where the acquisition and overlearning occur under mild drive conditions, generic recoding occurs then, and transfer is simply a matter of applying the generic principle to new instances. If the principle is relevant, positive savings occur. When acquisition and overlearning occur under high drive conditions, positive savings may occur by reducing drive at the time of transfer, which permits the animal to attain the concept on the basis of encountering a second instance of the pattern. If high drive persists after transfer, no savings occur, which probably means some negative transfer, for there should be a certain amount of saving from sheer mazewiseness. We have marshaled a variety of evidence on time allocation in the maze, repeated errors, and the pattern of *VTE* behavior in support of this view.

There is a variety of alternative explanations that are nourished by the present data, but it is not our object to pass them in review. The only point we would make is that one may state specifiable conditions that affect what may be interpreted as transfer by conceptual extension of original learning. We would urge, in light of the relevance of such interpretations to human problem solving and high-level human intellectual performance, that an effort be made further to pursue this less fashionable approach to transfer. Efficient recoding of information in terms of a generic principle is affected by a host of factors. The present study provides an analysis of two such factors: drive level and degree of overlearning.

Summary

Two experiments were reported. In the first, 54 rats were originally trained to one of three levels of mastery in running a four-unit straight-alley *T* maze in a single-alternation pattern, and then were transferred to a single-alternation pattern that was the reverse of what they had originally learned. Half the animals were run both on original and transfer learning with 12 hours of food deprivation, the other half with 36 hours of deprivation. There were marked savings in the learning of reversal by the group that operated with 12 hours of deprivation and received the maximum amount of original learning, while their counterparts in the 36-hour group showed no transfer. All animals receiving the minimum amount of original learning in turn, exhibited negative transfer, while all receiving the inter-mediate degree of original learning showed no transfer.

In the second experiment, 23 rats were treated in the same fashion as those rats in the above experiment given the highest level of mastery on original learning, the difference being that half the animals were trained originally with 12 and transferred at 36 hours of food deprivation, while the other half had the reverse deprivation schedule. Marked positive trans-fer in learning the reversal was exhibited by both groups.

Thus, given initial overlearning of a pattern, positive transfer to its ob-verse occurred provided that either original learning or transfer learning took place under moderate drive conditions. High drive during both origi-nal learning and transfer, on the other hand, prevented such savings from occurring. From these findings plus further evidence on time in the maze and *VTE* behavior, an interpretation was offered in terms of the genericiz-ing of learning into a principle applicable to new instances.

References

1. BRUNER, J. S.; J. MATTER; and M. L. PAPANEK. 1955. Breadth of learning as a function of drive level and mechanization. *Psychological Review* 62:1–10.
2. KRECHEVSKY, I., and C. H. HONZIK. 1932. Fixation in the rat. *University of California Publications in Psychology* 6:13–26.
3. McCLELLAND, D. C. 1943. Studies in serial verbal discrimination learning: IV. Habit reversal after two degrees of learning. *Journal of Experimental Psychology* 33:457–70.
4. Reid, L. S. 1953. The development of noncontinuity behavior through continuity learning. *Journal of Experimental Psychology* 46:107–12.

11

The Identification of Recurrent Regularity *

Much of what we classify as learning, recognition, and problem solving consists of being able to identify recurrent regularities in the environment (1, 4).[1] What makes such a task a problem is that recurrent regularities—be they turns in a maze, elements in a temporal pattern, or a pattern in successive events—may either be masked by factors that are irrelevant to the regularity, or the regularity itself may be of such a complexity that it exceeds the memory span that an observer brings to the task.

One may think of the task involved in identifying recurrent regularity as requiring the observer to construct a model that is isomorphic with the redundancy of the environment. The case is easily illustrated by reference to the identification of language sequences. If the individual knows a language, that is, has a model of the recurrent regularity of letters or words in the language, his task of identification is rendered easy in proportion to the degree to which a linguistic display approximates the typical sequences of the language (9).[2] So, too, for the rat learning a single-alternation pat-

---

* "The Identification of Recurrent Regularity," by Jerome S. Bruner, Michael A. Wallach, and Eugene H. Galanter, from *The American Journal of Psychology*, June 1959. Reprinted by permission of the University of Illinois Press and the authors.
[1] See pp. 218–38.
[2] See pp. 57–67.

tern; he must construct an adequate, predictive model of the environmental regularity to be identified over time.

Model construction involves the elimination of irrelevancies where such exist or the evolving of methods of recoding stimulus events in such a way as to bring them within the compass of attentional or immediate memory span. An illustration of the first kind of operation is the strategy employed in attaining concepts; the second is exemplified by the recoding of stimulus inputs to conform to the limits imposed on memory (8).

We are here concerned with the sources of interference that prevent rapid and efficient identification of recurrent regularities in the environment. We shall confine ourselves exclusively to regularities of a simple kind that are well within the capacity of people to identify when no interference is present. To illustrate the approach, let us imagine a sequence of events, each of which may take one of two forms—for example, a sequence of binary digits. The sequence is made up of a series of recurrent, fixed, subseries, such as 001001001 . . . or 100110011001 . . . , and the Ss task is to predict each event before it occurs. His task is to identify the regularity by constructing such models as 001 repeated or 1001 repeated and, thereby, to predict subsequent events in the series perfectly. At the outset he knows neither that there is a recurrent sequence nor that it is of any particular length. He is told only whether each of his single predictions is correct or not.

What are the factors that prevent adequate construction of a model in such a simple task? In general terms, we can specify three:

a. Stimulus interference. If the sequence is interfered with by single events that do not conform to the recurrent series, if an element of randomness is added to the series, it is likely that the task of model construction will be difficult in proportion to the amount of randomness introduced. This is a seemingly banal point, but it will appear otherwise when examined later in connection with other matters. Moreover, the variation of irrelevant aspects of the stimuli that do not interfere with the series will have the effect of slowing model construction. Such variation may require S to take time and trials to get information regarding such irrelevancies sufficient to eliminate them from the prediction of the series—as in the case, for example, where the binary digits are presented in different colors.

b. Interference by responses and hypotheses. Heidbreder (6) proposed some years ago a distinction between "spectator" behavior and "participant" behavior in problem solving, the former being simple watching or observing without hypotheses or responses, the latter involving the formulation and test-by-response of hypotheses about the nature of the events before one. Participant behavior in this sense serves to generate response-produced stimuli that may interfere with or mask the recurrent regularity in a problem to be solved. In a gambling experiment with a pattern of pay-off of *RLRL* . . . , we had one S who responded for a long series of trials with an alternating response out of phase with the rewarded choice, *LRLR,* and who finally announced earnestly that he guessed the machine was broken. To use a phrase designed to describe the disrupting effects of premature hypotheses in tachistoscopic recognition, there is a "liability in an hypothesis" (11).

c. Organismic interference. There is obvious interference from inappropriate sets, such as assuming that a series of recurrent regularity is a random series and acting accordingly, but it is not these that are intended here. Rather, we take these as instances of response interference. Our concern here is with nonspecific states of the organism, nonspecific with respect to the recurrent pattern with which an *S* must deal. A trivial example is inattention or fatigue, or a toxic state, but beyond such examples of white noisy organismic variables, one may also expect to find some colored noises operating.

Chief among these is the set of factors usually labeled motivation. Riopelle (10) found, for example, that a reward with food introduced at the beginning of each of a series of discriminative problems had the effect of distracting monkeys from the mastering of later discriminative tasks. It was as if growing preoccupation with the reward interfered with looking for appropriate cues.[3] We should prefer to narrow the issue somewhat by considering the effect of the cost and value of making false and true predictions of events in the sequence. If the cost of error is high relative to the value of correct prediction, it is conceivable that the anxiety generated by the task may be high enough either to goad the person into good performance or to disrupt him. Similarly, a high value for correct prediction relative to the cost of erroneous prediction may serve to concentrate a problem solver on his own response and to distract him from proper attention to stimulus events. Indeed, the point can and has been made that a problem exists only when the cost of error reaches a certain level (7).

In sum, to construct a model adequate to predict a recurrent environmental regularity of a length well within immediate memory span an *S* must overcome sources of disruption and interference of three kinds: stimulus interference, response interference, and organismic interference. Obviously, the three kinds of interference interact. Errors that are costly may lead the individual to test and eliminate more rapidly hypotheses about irrelevant features of a sequence; but these are empirical matters to which we must turn now.

Experiment

The *S*s employed in the experiment, 92 in number, were summer students at Harvard. They were given the basic task of predicting whether a light

---

[3] So, too, in a study of J. S. Bruner, Jean Matter, and M. L. Papanek (3) where drive state seemed to prevent the rats from picking up "superfluous" cue regularities in the learning situation which might be used later.

would appear in the left or the right window of an apparatus. They did this by pressing a key beneath one or the other window. Whichever button was pressed, the light would then appear in one or the other window for four seconds and then be extinguished by the automatic programmer that controlled the sequence of lights.

INSTRUCTIONS

S was told that his task was to predict as many times as he could on which side the light would appear, and that he would be permitted to bet each time, indicating his wager by the button he pressed. He was told that he would have 40 tries at predicting and that the number of points he earned would determine how much more than his base pay of one dollar he would earn.

The following variations in procedure were used with our eight groups.

a. Degree of stimulus interference. Half of the groups received the sequential recurring pattern *LLR* for 40 trials (one trial more than 13 cycles) with no interference. The remaining groups received the same pattern but with some uncertainty added. That is to say, 2 of the 40 appearances of the light, the fourteenth and the twenty-fifth, were out of the pattern. Thus the fifth cycle of the *LLR* pattern became *LRR,* and the ninth cycle *RLR.* In the remaining 11 cycles, the basic pattern was left intact.

b. Degree of response interference. Half of the groups began immediately by responding—pressing the button. The other half was permitted to watch the sequence of lights without responding for the first three presentations. For these *S*s, the light pattern was exhibited by the *E*s pressing the right-hand button three times in a row. They were also instructed by *E* to pay attention to the lights, rather than to their button-pressing activities. The other *S*s were given no such instructions.

c. Cost of error. Above each button were placed two numbers, the upper one of which indicated how many points *S* would win if he predicted that side correctly, the lower indicating the cost in points if he predicted wrongly. Half of the groups worked under high error cost: an error on either side costing five points, a correct prediction earning one point. The groups operating under low error cost earned five points for a correct prediction, lost one point for an error.

Results

The eight groups are summarized in Table 1. The first and most general result is that the larger the number of sources of disruption operative in a group, the greater the difficulty in identifying the recurrent regularity of the series. The simplest way to represent this is to consider the number of erroneous predictions in the 40 presentations of the lights in the one group operating with all three possible sources of disruption (stimulus interference, response interference, and high cost for error), the groups with two

TABLE 1 *Composition and Size*
of the Eight Groups
in the Experiment

Group	No. Ss	Group	No. Ss
SWH	12	SRH	11
SWL	12	SRL	11
NWH	12	NRH	11
NWL	12	NRL	11

Note: S = stimulus noise; N = no stimulus noise;
R = responding from first; W = waiting at first;
H = high error cost; L = low error cost.

sources of disruption, with one source, and with none. The median errors for these groups are, respectively, 15.0 errors in 37 presentations, 9.5 errors, 6.0, and 1.0.[4] Figure 1 presents the results in graphic form.

A better picture is provided by considering the eight groups separately

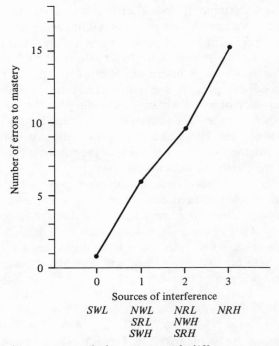

FIGURE 1. *Median errors made by groups with different amounts of potential interference*

[4] Error computations are based on the last 37 of the 40 presentations, for the groups that did not respond on the first three presentations had no opportunity for error on these presentations.

and comparing levels of performance among them. Necessary data on errors and trials for such comparisons are contained in Tables 2 and 3.[5]

EFFECT OF STIMULUS INTERFERENCE

Comparison of the first row of Table 2 with the second row indicates that in all four comparisons, the group without stimulus interference performed with fewer errors. In three of the four comparisons, the difference obtained is highly reliable, the exception being the comparison of the two groups under conditions of response interference (no wait) and low error cost.

TABLE 2 *Median Errors in Each of the Eight Groups Made during 37 Final Presentations of Lights*

	High Cost		Low Cost	
	No Wait	*Wait*	*No Wait*	*Wait*
Stimulus noise	15.0	10.5	12.0	9.0
No noise	3.0	1.5	8.0	1.0

Note: *NRH* versus *NWH*, *NRL* versus *NWL*, and *SRH* versus *SRL* are significant at the 5-per-cent level; *NWH* versus *SWH*, *NRH* versus *SRH*, *NWL* versus *SWL*, and *SRL* versus *SWL* are significant at the 1-per-cent level. Computations made by the Mosteller-Bush version of the Mann-Whitney test, see Gardner Lindsey, ed., *Handbook of Social Psychology* (Cambridge, Mass.: Addison-Wesley, 1954.) 1:315 ff.

TABLE 3 *Median Trials until the Last Error Was Made, in Each of the Eight Groups*

	High Cost		Low Cost	
	No Wait	*Wait*	*No Wait*	*Wait*
Stimulus noise	37.0	37.0	35.0	33.0
No noise	11.0	4.5	25.0	4.5

Note: *SRH* versus *SRL* is significant at the 5-per-cent level; *NWH* versus *SWH*, *NRH* versus *SRH*, *NWL* versus *SWL*, *NRL* versus *SRL*, *SRH* versus *SWH*, and *SRL* versus *SWL* are significant at the 1-per-cent level. If an *S* in a wait group makes no errors, his trial of last error is taken as three.

The first and not very surprising conclusion, then, is that even a small amount of noise thrown into a regularly recurrent pattern seriously inter-

[5] We see in Table 3 that the learning speed for groups *SRH* and *SRL* in the present experiment is considerably more rapid than that in a related experiment reported by Goodnow and Pettigrew (5). We believe this difference is due to the fact that in the present experiment *S* always receives direct information about the correct side since the light appears on the correct side after each response, whereas in Goodnow and Pettigrew's experiment *S* receives indirect information when he errs, since errors are indicated by a chip's failing to drop down a chute in the panel's center.

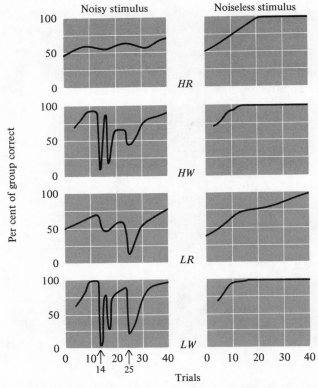

FIGURE 2. Learning curves for each of the eight groups with neighboring pairs equated on all conditions except the nature of the stimulus series to which exposed

feres with the identification of that regularity or, as we would prefer to put it, interferes with the task of constructing a model of this recurrent regularity.

In what does the interference consist? Figure 2 shows graphically the learning curves over the 40 trials of all eight groups. Side by side are curves for groups differing only in whether the stimulus series contained two off-pattern stimuli. The introduction of the off-pattern lights on trials 14 and 25 sharply decreases the percentage of *S*s predicting correctly, following which there is more or less rapid recovery. Up to the point of the first interference, the parallel groups show very similar functions.

Interestingly enough, the interference by the first off-pattern stimulus sequence disrupts the group with an initial period of observation more than the group without it. The explanation is not far to seek; an off-pattern stimulus sequence is more disruptive to an *S* who has already perfected a model of what the stimulus should be. Table 4 shows this difference clearly. The observing groups are doing better than the responding groups by trial 14 and, consequently, make more errors when the required re-

TABLE 4 *Course of Learning, Disruption, and*
Recovery in Ss Presented with a Noisy Stimulus Series
Who Initially Responded to or
Simply Observed the Stimulus Series

	Responding Group	Observing Group
Median errors: trials 4–13*	5.0	2.0
Errors on trial 14†	59.0%	96.0%
Median errors: trials 15–24	4.0	3.0
Errors on trial 25	68.0%	75.0%
Median errors: trials 26–40*	5.5	3.0

Note: Responding group $= NRL + NRH = 22$; observing group $= NWL + NWH = 24$.

* Significant at or beyond 1-per-cent level by Mosteller-Bush version of Mann-Whitney test.

† Significant at 1-per-cent level, by test of difference between two percentages.

sponse is changed, 96 per cent as opposed to 59 per cent, a statistically reliable difference.

Now for the recovery from the first interference. There is no reliable difference between the groups, the responding and the observing *S*s, between the first and second disruptions, errors being almost identical (Table 4).

The second interference is an off-pattern sequence on trial 25. This time there is nothing to choose in the degree of disruption. Errors on this trial are about the same for both groups. Now, however, in the remaining 15 trials (trials 26–40), the observing group shows a statistically reliable increase in mastery, or recovery, in comparison with the noise-producing responding group. Again, the data are contained in Table 4.

In sum, given the presence of stimulus noise, the addition of response noise may have the effect of preventing as rapid initial identification of recurrent regularity, and then prevents rapid recovery from the disruption introduced by an irregular or surprise stimulus.

EFFECT OF RESPONSE INTERFERENCE

A comparison of the first with the second, and the third with the fourth columns of Table 2 contains the relevant comparisons between groups alike in treatment save for difference in responding. In all comparisons, the group which responded from the outset and was not warned to attend to the stimulus made erroneous predictions more often. In three of the four comparisons, the difference is statistically reliable at least at the 5 per cent level; but the effect of response interference is considerably less than the effect of noise in the stimulus series. The mean difference in errors of groups with and without noise in the stimulus series is 8.2, the difference when groups paused to observe three trials was 4.0.

Figure 2 suggests that the effects of not observing were persistent throughout the learning. The observing group shows a more sharply rising learning curve; the responding group reached perfect performance more gradually.

EFFECT OF ERROR COST

A comparison of the right and left halves of Table 2 reveals immediately that error cost does not operate as a simple source of interference, if indeed it may be regarded as a source of interference at all. Neither these figures nor the forms of the learning curves in Figure 2 suggest that there is anything interfering about high error cost. The only significant ·difference between matched groups runs counter to the prediction that high error cost would interfere with identification of a recurrent regularity. Indeed, we are inclined to favor the view that in this condition—where the stimulus series was without interference and S had to overcome the interference of his own responses—high error cost provided incentive to more careful scanning of the stimulus situation.

Discussion

We have presented here what is, in effect, a demonstrational experiment. The point of view may be briefly recapitulated: Much of learning and problem solving can be viewed as a task in identifying recurrent regularities in the environment and this requires either the construction of a model of this regularity or the employment of a model that has previously been constructed by the person. Identification of recurrent regularity is the recognition of pattern complicated by one of two possible factors. Either the recurrent regularity is of a complexity that exceeds the limited cognitive span of the individual, or there are sources of interference either in the stimulus input, in the required pattern of responding, or in the organism, that in effect mask the recurrent regularity to be recognized. Learning, given these interferers, consists, in part, in separating the recurrent regularity to be identified from these interferers. The greater the number of interferers—the more noise there is in the stimulus, the more masking are the responses—the more difficult will identification of regularity be. When these sources are minimized, learning is a matter of immediate recognition, provided the pattern can be handled in immediate memory span. The conditions of no stimulus noise and minimal response interference lead to recognition of a pattern almost immediately.

It seems unlikely to us that the explanation of how a person cuts through the interfering properties of the environment when such exist and when identification is not immediate is to be found in theories of reinforcement. Rather, the answer probably lies in how the organism learns to use techniques for weighing the relevance of different features of input for regularity-to-be-discovered. The simple instruction, "Pay attention to the stimulus and disregard your past responses," for example, is highly effective advice to oneself in identifying environmental regularities that are invariant with respect to the overt responses of the problem solver. It is conceivable that, after such techniques have been mastered, a simple law of frequency might work, but not before. Essentially, as in the case of concept attainment, the first steps in identifying a recurrent regularity require the development of strategies for utilizing potential information from the environment (2). The greater part of contemporary learning theory has tended to overlook this feature of the learning process or has treated such information-using strategies as just another kind of response that gets reinforced, if it happens to be followed by tension reduction. It should be said, however, that those who have worked more directly with problem-solving behavior and thinking have become increasingly mindful of the importance of methods of information utilization.

This study gives evidence, then, that learning and problem solving may be more profitably viewed as identification of temporally or spatially extended patterns and that the process of learning or problem solving be viewed as the development of means for isolating such regularities from the flow of irrelevant events that originate either in the environment, in the organism, or are produced by the organism's response to the environment.

References

1. BRUNER, J. S. 1957. Going beyond the information given. In *Contemporary approaches to cognition,* ed. H. E. Gruber, K. R. Hammond, and R. Jesser. Cambridge, Mass.: Harvard University Press.
2. BRUNER, J. S.; GOODNOW, J. J.: and AUSTIN, G. A. 1956. *A study of thinking.* New York: Wiley.
3. BRUNER, J. S.; MATTER, J.; and PAPANEK, M. L. 1955. Breadth of learning as a function of drive level and mechanization. *Psychological Review* 62:1–10.
4. GALANTER, E. H., and GERSTENHABER, M. 1956. On thought: the extrinsic theory. *Psychological Review* 63:218–27.
5. GOODNOW, J. J., and PETTIGREW, T. F. 1956. Some sources of difficulty in solving simple problems. *Journal of Experimental Psychology* 51:385–92.
6. HEIDBREDER, E. 1924. An experimental study of thinking. *Archives of Psychology* 11 (73):1–175.
7. JOHNSON, D. M. 1955. *The psychology of thought and judgment.* New York: Harper and Brothers.
8. MILLER, G. A. 1956. The magical number seven, plus or minus two: some limits on our capacity for processing information. *Psychological Review* 63:81–97.
9. MILLER, G. A.; BRUNER, J. S.; and POSTMAN, L. 1954. Familiarity of letter sequences and tachistoscopic identification. *Journal of General Psychology* 50:129–39.
10. RIOPELLE, A. J. 1955. Rewards, preferences and learning sets. *Psychological Reports* 1:167–73.
11. WYATT, D. F., and CAMPBELL, D. T. 1951. On the liability of stereotype or hypothesis. *Journal of Abnormal and Social Psychology* 46:496–500.

12

The Conditions of Creativity *

There is something antic about creating, although the enterprise be serious.
And there is a matching antic spirit that goes with writing about it; for, if
ever there were a silent process, it is the creative one. Antic and serious
and silent. Yet there is good reason to inquire about creativity, a reason
beyond practicality; for practicality is not a reason but a justification after
the fact. The reason is the ancient search of the humanist for the excellence of man: The next creative act may bring man to a new dignity.

There is, alas, a shrillness to our contemporary concern with creativity.
Man's search for the sources of dignity changes with the pattern of his
times. In periods during which man saw himself in the image of God, the
creation of works *ad majorem gloriam dei* could provide a sufficient rationale for the dignity of the artist, the artisan, the creative man. But in
an age whose dominant value is a pragmatic one and whose massive
achievement is an intricate technological order, it is not sufficient to be
merely useful. For the servant can pattern himself on the master—and so
he did when God was master and man His servant creating works in His
glory—but the machine is the servant of man, and to pattern one's function on the machine provides no measure for dignity. The machine is use-

* "The Conditions of Creativity," by Jerome S. Bruner. Reprinted by permission of
the publishers from Jerome S. Bruner, *On Knowing: Essays for the Left Hand*, Cambridge, Mass.: The Belknap Press of Harvard University Press, Copyright, 1962, by
the President and Fellows of Harvard College.

ful; the system in terms of which the machines gain their use is efficient; but what is man?

The artist, the writer, and to a new degree the scientist seek an answer in the nature of their acts. They create or they seek to create, and this in itself endows the process with dignity. There is creative writing and pure science, each justifying the work of its producer in its own right. It is implied, I think, that the act of a man creating is the act of a whole man, that it is this rather than the product that makes it good and worthy. So whoever seeks to proclaim his wholeness turns to the new slogan. There is creative advertising, creative engineering, creative problem solving—all lively entries in the struggle for dignity in our time. We, as psychologists, are asked to explicate the process, to lay bare the essence of the creative. Make no mistake about it, it is not simply as technicians that we are being called, but as adjutants to the moralist. My antic sense rises in self-defense. My advice, in the midst of the seriousness, is to keep an eye out for the tinker shuffle, the flying of kites, and kindred sources of surprised amusement.

We had best begin with some minimum working definition that will permit us at least to look at the same set of things. An act that produces effective surprise—this I shall take as the hallmark of a creative enterprise. The content of the surprise can be as various as the enterprises in which men are engaged. It may express itself in one's dealing with children, in making love, in carrying on a business, in formulating physical theory, in painting a picture. I could not care less about the person's intention, whether or not he intended to create. The road to banality is paved with creative intentions. Surprise is not easily defined. It is the unexpected that strikes one with wonder or astonishment. What is curious about effective surprise is that it need not be rare or infrequent or bizarre and is often none of these things. Effective surprises, and we shall spell the matter out in a moment, seem rather to have the quality of obviousness about them when they occur, producing a shock of recognition following which there is no longer astonishment. It is like this with great formulas, as in that for the conservation of energy or for the brilliant insight that makes chemistry possible, the conservation of mass. Weber's stunning insight into the nature of a just noticeable sensory difference is of this order, that before a difference will be noticed it must be a constant fraction of the sensory intensity presently being experienced: $\Delta I / I = K$.

I think it is possible to specify three kinds of effectiveness, three forms of self-evidence implicit in surprise of the kind we have been considering. The first is predictive effectiveness. It is the kind of surprise that yields high predictive value in its wake—as in the instance of the formula for falling bodies or in any good theoretical reformulation in science. You may well argue that predictive effectiveness does not always come through surprise, but through the slow accretion of knowledge and urge—like Newton with his *hypothesis non fingo*. I will reply by agreeing with you and specifying simply that, whether it is the result of intuitive insight or of slow accretion, I will accept it within my definition. The surprise may only come when we look back and see whence we have come.

A second form of effectiveness is best called formal, and its most usual place is in mathematics and logic—possibly in music. One of the most beautiful descriptions of the phenomenon is to be found in G. H. Hardy's engaging *Mathematician's Apology*. It consists of an ordering of elements in such a way that one sees relationships that were not evident before, groupings that were before not present, ways of putting things together not before within reach. Consistency or harmony or depth of relationship is the result. One of the most penetrating essays that has ever been written on the subject is, of course, Henri Poincaré's in his *Science and Method*. He speaks of making combinations that "reveal to us unsuspected kinship between . . . facts, long known, but wrongly believed to be strangers to one another."

Of the final form of effectiveness in surprise it is more difficult to write. I shall call it metaphoric effectiveness. It, too, is effective by connecting domains of experience that were before apart, but with the form of connectedness that has the discipline of art.

It is effective surprise that produces what Melville celebrated as the shock of recognition. Jung speaks of art that can produce such metaphoric connectedness as "visionary" in contrast to the merely psychological. It is, for example, Thomas Mann's achievement in bringing into a single compass the experiences of sickness and beauty, sexuality and restraint in his *Death in Venice*. Or it is the achievement of the French playwright Jean Anouilh who in *Antigone* makes Creon not only a tyrant but a reasonable man. What we are observing is the connecting of diverse experiences by the mediation of symbol and metaphor and image. Experience in literal terms is a categorizing, a placing in a syntax of concepts. Metaphoric combination leaps beyond systematic placement, explores connections that before were unsuspected.

I would propose that all of the forms of effective surprise grow out of combinatorial activity—a placing of things in new perspectives. But it is somehow not simply a taking of known elements and running them together by algorithm into a welter of permutations. One could design a computer to do that, but it would be with some embarrassment, for this is stupid even for a computer; an ingenious computer programmer can show us much more interesting computer models than that. "To create consists precisely in not making useless combinations and in making those which are useful and which are only a small minority. Invention is discernment, choice." If not a brute algorithm, then it must be a heuristic that guides

one to fruitful combinations. What is the heuristic? Poincaré goes on to
urge that it is an emotional sensibility, "the feeling of mathematical
beauty, of the harmony of numbers and forms, of geometric elegance." It
is this that guides one in making combinations in mathematics. But it is
surely not enough. One hears physicists speak of physical intuition as distinguishing the good theorist from the mere formalist, the mathematician. I
suspect that in each empirical field there is developed in the creating scientist a kind of "intuitive familiarity," to use a term that L. J. Henderson was
fond of, that gives him a sense of what combinations are likely to have
predictive effectiveness and which are absurd. What precisely this kind of
heuristic consists of is probably difficult to specify without reference to the
nature of the field in question, which is not to say that the working models
are utterly different in different areas of empirical endeavor, for there is
obviously some generality too.

It seems unlikely that the heuristic either of formal beauty or of intuitive familiarity could serve for the artist, the poet, and the playwright.
What genius leads Faulkner to create and combine a Temple Drake and a
Popeye in *Sanctuary?* How does Dostoevsky hit upon the particular combination of the Grand Inquisitor and the Christ figure in *The Brothers Kara-
mazov?* What leads Picasso to include particular objects in a painting? Picasso says to Christian Zervos:

What a sad thing for a painter who loves blondes but denies himself the
pleasure of putting them in his picture because they don't go well with the bas-
ket of fruit! What misery for a painter who detests apples to have to use them
all the time because they harmonize with the tablecloth! I put in my pictures
everything I like. So much the worse for the things—they have to get along
with one another (2, p. 59).

However maddening such a remark may be coming from a painter, it does
point up the essentially emotive nature of the painter's work and his criteria for judging the fitness of combination. So Yeats may write:

God guard me from those thoughts men think
In the mind alone;
He that sings a lasting song
Thinks in a marrow-bone.

But marrow-bones are not really enough for lasting songs. For if it is true,
as Picasso and many before have said, that "a picture lives only through
him who looks at it," then the artist must speak to the human condition of
the beholder if there is to be effective surprise. I, for one, find myself com-
pelled to believe that there are certain deep sharings of plight among
human beings that make possible the communication of the artist to the
beholder, and, while I object to the paraphernalia that Jung proposes when

he speaks of the collective unconscious, I understand why he feels impelled to proffer the idea. The artist—whatever his medium—must be
close enough to these conditions in himself so that they may guide his
choice among combinations, provide him with the genuine and protect him
from the paste.

The triumph of effective surprise is that it takes one beyond common
ways of experiencing the world. Or perhaps this is simply a restatement of
what we have been meaning by effective surprise. If it is merely that, let
me add only that it is in this sense that life most deeply imitates art or that
nature imitates science. Creative products have this power of reordering
experience and thought in their image. In science, the reordering is much
the same from one beholder of a formula to another. In art, the imitation
is in part self-imitation. It is the case, too, that the effective surprise of the
creative man provides a new instrument for manipulating the world—
physically as with the creation of the wheel or symbolically as with the
creation of $e = mc^2$.

One final point about the combinatorial acts that produce effective surprise: They almost always succeed through the exercise of technique.
Henry Moore, who is usually articulate both as craftsman and artist, tells
us that he was driven to the use of holes in his sculpture by the technical
problem of giving a sense of three-dimensionality to solid forms—"the
hole connects one side to the other, making it immediately more three-dimensional," a discovery made while fretting over the puzzle of how to
avoid relief carving on brittle material like stone. Joseph Conrad and Ford
Madox Ford sat before a scene trying to describe it to each other in the
most economical terms possible. Katherine Anne Porter sat on a camp-
stool before a landscape trying to jot down everything before her—and finally decided that she could not train her memory that way. Technique,
then, and how shall we combine it eventually with the doctrine of inspira-
tion?

As soon as one turns to a consideration of the conditions of creativity,
one is immediately met by paradox and antinomy. A determinant suggests
itself, and in the next pulse its opposite is suggested. I shall honor these
antinomies and what I have to say will, as a result, seem at times paradoxical.

Detachment and commitment—a willingness to divorce one-self from
the obvious is surely a prerequisite for the fresh combinatorial act that
produces effective surprise. There must be as a necessary, if not a sufficient, condition a detachment from the forms as they exist. There are so
many ways in which this expresses itself in creative activity that one can
scarcely enumerate them. Wallace Stevens, among many, has written of the
alienation of the poet from society and reality, and the spirit of this alienation is caught in his searching poem, "Notes towards a Supreme Fiction."
It is in part a condition for exploring one's own individuality, in part a
means of examining the possibilities of human connection. The university

as an institution, protected within its walls, should and sometimes does provide a basis for detachment insofar as it recognizes the inviolate privacy of those who inhabit it. The preoccupation of the scholar, gating out all but what seems relevant to his theme—this, too, is a vehicle of detachment. The creative writer who takes his journey without maps or his voyage into the interior, whether in the subjective Africas of Graham Greene or Joseph Conrad or in the interior jungles of Henry James or Marcel Proust—again it is detachment.

But it is a detachment of commitment. For there is about it a caring, a deep need to understand something, to master a technique, to rerender a meaning. So, while the poet, the mathematician, the scientist must each achieve detachment, they do it in the interest of commitment. And at one stroke they, the creative ones, are disengaged from that which exists conventionally and are engaged deeply in what they construct to replace it.

Passion and decorum—by passion I understand a willingness and ability to let one's impulses express themselves in one's life through one's work. I use it in the sense, he has a passion for painting, or, she has a passion for cooking. I do not wish to raise or explore the Bohemian dilemma—whether the condition for passion in work is its expression in other forms of life. I happen to believe that Freud's fixed quantity of libido (express it here and it must be withdrawn from there) is a kind of first-order nonsense. Passion, like discriminating taste, grows on its use. You more likely act yourself into feeling than feel yourself into action. In any case, it is true of the creative man that he is not indifferent to what he does, that he is moved to it. For the artist, if not for the scientist, there is a tapping of sources of imagery and symbolism that would otherwise not be available —as expressed in the beautiful refrain line of Rimbaud's *Les Illuminations,* "J'ai seul la clef de cette parade sauvage." As for the scientist and the scholar, it is perhaps the eighteenth-century French philosopher, Helvetius, who, in his *Treatise on Man,* has put it best; "A man without *passions* is incapable of that degree of attention to which a superior judgment is annexed: a superiority that is perhaps less the effect of an extraordinary effort than an habitual attention."

But again a paradox: It is not all urgent vitality. There is a decorum in creative activity, a love of form, an etiquette toward the object of our efforts, a respect for materials. Rimbaud's wild beasts in the end are caged. For all that *Lord Jim* is a turbulent book, with the full range of human impulse, its raw power is contained by the decorum of the dispassionate gentlemanly narrator, Marlow. Hercules of the myth was not a hairy ape expressing his mastery indiscriminately. His shrewd trickery is the decorum. The wild flood of ideas that mathematicians like Hardy have described eventually are expressed in the courtesy of equations.

So both are necessary and there must surely be a subtle matter of timing involved—when the impulse, when the taming.

Freedom to be dominated by the object—you begin to write a poem.

Before long it, the poem, begins to develop metrical, stanzaic, symbolical requirements. You, as the writer of the poem, are serving it—it seems. Or you may be pursuing the task of building a formal model to represent the known properties of single nerve fibers and their synapses. Soon the model takes over. Or we say of an experiment in midstream that it needs another control group really to clinch the effect. It is at this point that we get our creative second wind, at the point when the object takes over. I have asked about a dozen of my most creative and productive friends whether they knew what I meant as far as their own work was concerned. All of them replied with one or another form of sheepishness, most of them commenting that one usually did not talk about this kind of personal thing. "This is when you know you're in and—good or bad—the thing will compel you to finish it. In a long piece of work it can come and go several times." The one psychologist among my informants was reminded of the so-called Zeigarnik completion tendency, suggesting that when the watershed was reached the task then had a structure that began to require completeness.

There is something odd about the phenomenon. We externalize an object, a product of our thoughts, treat it as out there. Freud remarked, commenting on projection, that human beings seem better able to deal with stimuli from the outside than from within. So it is with the externalizing of a creative work, permitting it to develop its own being, its own autonomy coming to serve it. It is as if it were easier to cope with there, as if this arrangement permitted the emergence of more unconscious impulse, more material not readily accessible.

There is still another possibility. Observing children in the process of learning mathematics, I have been struck repeatedly by the economical significance of a good mode of representing things to oneself. In group theory, for example, it is extraordinarily difficult to determine whether a set of transformations constitutes a closed group so that any combination of them can be expressed by a single one. The crutch provided by a matrix that gets all the combinations out of the head onto paper or the blackboard makes it possible to look at the group structure as a whole, to go beyond it to the task of seeing whether it has interesting properties and familiar isomorphs. Good representation, then, is a release from intellectual bondage.

I have used the expression *freedom to be dominated* by the object being created. It is a strange choice of words, and I should like to explain it. To be dominated by an object of one's own creation—perhaps its extreme is Pygmalion dominated by Galatea—is to be free of the defenses that keep us hidden from ourselves.

As the object takes over and demands to be completed in its own terms, there is a new opportunity to express a style and an individuality. Likely as not, it is so partly because we are rid of the internal juggling of possibilities, because we have represented them out there where we can look at them, consider them. As one friend, a novelist and critic, put it, "If it doesn't take over and you are foolish enough to go on, what you end up with is contrived and alien."

Deferral and immediacy—there is an immediacy to creating anything, a sense of direction, an objective, a general idea, a feeling. Yet the immediacy is anything but a quick orgasm of completion. Completion is deferred. Let me quote at some length from the conversation of Christian Zervos with Picasso:

> With me a picture is a sum of destructions. I make a picture, and proceed to destroy it. But in the end nothing is lost; the red I have removed from one part shows up in another.
>
> It would be very interesting to record photographically, not the stages of a painting, but its metamorphoses. One would see perhaps by what course a mind finds its way towards the crystallization of its dream. But what is really very curious is to see that the picture does not change basically, that the initial vision remains almost intact in spite of appearance. I see often a light and a dark, when I have put them in my picture, I do everything I can to "break them up," in adding a color that creates a counter effect. I perceive, when the work is photographed, that what I have introduced to correct my first vision has disappeared, and that after all the photographic image corresponds to my first vision, before the occurrence of the transformations brought about by my will (2, pp. 56–57).

This is not to say that there is not the occasional good luck, the piece that comes off lickety-split and finished, the theory hit upon at first fire. If ever Georges Simenon is acclaimed a great writer—and that he is more than simply competent is plain—then we will say he brings it off in a gush, in a quantum of pure energy and with such intensity, Carvel Collins tells us, that he has developed the custom of getting clearance from his doctor before he flings himself into a new novel.

Having read a good many journals and diaries by writers, I have come to the tentative conclusion that the principal guard against precocious completion, in writing at least, is boredom. I have little doubt that the same protection avails the scientist. It is the boredom of conflict, knowing deep down what one wishes to say and knowing that one has not said it. One acts on the impulse to exploit an idea, to begin. One also acts on the impulse of boredom, to defer. Thus Virginia Woolf, trying to finish *Orlando* in February 1928, "Always, always, that last chapter slips out of my hands. One gets bored. One whips oneself up. I still hope for a fresh wind and don't very much bother, except that I miss the fun that was so tremendously lively all October, November, and December"(3, p. 121).

The internal drama—there is within each person his own cast of characters—an ascetic, and perhaps a glutton, a prig, a frightened child, a little man, even an onlooker, sometimes a Renaissance man. The great works of the theater are decompositions of such a cast, the rendering into external drama of the internal one, the conversion of the internal cast into dramatis personae. Freud, in his searching essay on "The Poet and the Daydream," is most discerning about this device of the playwright.[1] There have been times when writers have come too close to their own personal cast in constructing a play; even so able a craftsman of the theater as Goethe stumbled in his *Torquato Tasso,* an embarrassingly transparent autobiographical piece about the conflict between Tasso the poet and Antonio the politician. It is, perhaps, Pirandello among modern playwrights who has most convincingly mastered the technique; although a younger Italian dramatist, Ugo Betti, showed promise of carrying it further before his premature death a few years ago. In his brilliant *The Queen and the Rebels,* Betti includes an unforgettable scene at the political frontier of a mythical fascist state, the frontier guards searching a bus party for the fleeing queen. As the scene progresses, it becomes patent that the queen is a spineless nonentity; it is the prostitute in the party who emerges as the queen.

As in the drama, so too a life can be described as a script, constantly rewritten, guiding the unfolding internal drama. It surely does not do to limit the drama to the stiff characters of the Freudian morality play—the undaunted ego, the brutish id, the censorious and punitive superego. Is the internal cast a reflection of the identifications to which we have been committed? I do not think it is as simple as that. It is a way of grouping our internal demands and there are idealized models over and beyond those with whom we have special identification—figures in myth, in life, in the comics, in history, creations of fantasy.

There are some scripts that are more interesting than others. In some, there is a pre-empting protagonist in the center of the stage, constantly proclaiming, save for those moments when there are screamed intrusions from offstage, at which point the declaimer apologizes by pointing out that the voices are not really in the play. In others there is a richness, an inevitability of relationship, a gripping and constant exchange—or perhaps one should call it inchange. These are dramatic personalities, producers of surprise.

I would like to suggest that it is in the working out of conflict and coalition within the set of identities that compose the person that one finds the source of many of the richest and most surprising combinations. It is not merely the artist and the writer, but the inventor, too, who is the beneficiary.

The dilemma of abilities—we have now looked at some of the paradoxical conditions that one might assume would affect the production of effective surprises—creativity. Nothing has been said about ability, or abilities.

---

[1] For a discussion of Freud's use of the same device in the development of psychoanalysis, see "Freud and the Image of Man" (1).

What shall we say of energy, of combinatorial zest, of intelligence, of alertness, of perseverance? I shall say nothing about them. They are obviously important but, from a deeper point of view, they are also trivial. For at any level of energy or intelligence there can be more or less of creating in our sense. Stupid people create for each other as well as benefiting from what comes from afar. So too do slothful and torpid people. I have been speaking of creativity, not of genius.

The chapter in Henry Adams's *Education,* "The Dynamo and the Virgin," is urbane, but beneath the urbanity there is a deep perplexity about what moves men, what moves history, what makes art. Adams spent the summer and fall of 1900 haunting the Great Exposition in Paris, particularly the hall of dynamos, until the dynamos "became a symbol of infinity . . . a moral force, much as the early Christians felt the Cross." During the same summer he made excursions to Notre Dame of Amiens and to Chartres, and it was then that he came to realize that the Virgin as symbol was also a source of energy, "All the steam in the world could not, like the Virgin, build Chartres." I end with the same perplexity in attempting to find some way of thinking reasonably about the creative process. At the outset I proposed that we define the creative act as effective surprise—the production of novelty. It is reasonable to suppose that we will someday devise a proper scientific theory capable of understanding and predicting such acts. Perhaps we will understand the energies that produce the creative act much as we have come to understand how the dynamo produces its energy. It may be, however, that there is another mode of approach to knowing how the process generates itself, and this will be the way in which we understand how symbols and ideas like the Virgin capture men's thoughts. Often it is the poet who grasps these matters most firmly and communicates them most concisely. Perhaps it is our conceit that there is only one way of understanding a phenomenon. I have argued that just as there is predictive effectiveness, so is there metaphoric effectiveness. For the while, at least, we can do worse than to live with a metaphoric understanding of creativity.

References

1. BRUNER, J. S. 1962. Freud and the image of man. *On knowing: essays for the left hand.* Cambridge, Mass.: Harvard University Press.
2. Conversation with Picasso. 1935. *Cahiers d' Art.* Paris. Trans. Brewster Ghiselin, *The creative process,* New York: Mentor, 1952.
3. WOOLF, V. 1953. *A writer's diary.* New York: Harcourt Brace.

13

Going Beyond
the Information Given*

Many years ago, Charles Spearman (27) undertook the ambitious task of characterizing the basic cognitive processes whose operations might account for the existence of intelligence. He emerged with a triad of noegenetic principles, as he called them, the first of these being simply an affirmation that organisms are capable of apprehending the world they live in. The second and third principles provide us with our starting point. One of these, called "the education of relations," holds that there is an immediate evocation of a sense of relation given the mental presentation of two or more things. "White" and "black" evoke "opposite" or "different." The third principle, the "education of correlates," states that in the presence of a thing and a relation one immediately educes another thing. "White" and "opposite of" evokes "black." I think that Spearman was trying to say that the most characteristic thing about mental life, over and beyond the fact that one apprehends the events of the world around one, is that one constantly goes beyond the information given. With this observation I find

* "Going Beyond the Information Given," by Jerome S. Bruner. Reprinted by permission of the publishers from Jerome S. Bruner, et al., *Contemporary Approaches to Cognition*, Cambridge, Mass.: Harvard University Press, Copyright, 1957, by the President and Fellows of Harvard College.

myself in full agreement, and it is here that my difficulties start. For, as Bartlett (1, p. 1) put it,

Whenever anybody interprets evidence from any source, and his interpretation contains characteristics that cannot be referred wholly to direct sensory observation or perception, this person thinks. The bother is that nobody has ever been able to find any case of the human use of evidence which does not include characters that run beyond what is directly observed by the senses. So, according to this, people think whenever they do anything at all with evidence. If we adopt that view we very soon find ourselves looking out upon a boundless and turbulent ocean of problems.

Bother though it be, there is little else than to plunge right in.

Some Instances of Going Beyond the Information Given

It may help to begin with some rather commonplace examples of the different ways in which people go beyond information that is given to them. The first of these represents the simplest form of utilizing inference. It consists of learning the defining properties of a class of functionally equivalent objects and using the presence of these defining properties as a basis of inferring that a new object encountered is or is not an exemplar of the class. The first form of going beyond, then, is to go beyond sense data to the class identity of the object being perceived. This is more remarkable an achievement when the new object encountered differs from in more respects than it resembles other exemplars of the class that have been previously encountered. A speck on the horizon surmounted by a plume of smoke is identified as a ship, so too a towering transatlantic liner at its dock, so too a few schematic lines in a drawing. Given the presence of a few defining properties or cues, we go beyond them to the inference of identity. Having done so, we infer that the instance so categorized or identified has the other properties characteristic of membership in a category. Given the presence of certain cues of shape, size, and texture, we infer that the thing before us is an apple; therefore, it can be eaten, cut with a knife, it relates by certain principles of classification to other kinds of fruits, and so on. The act of rendering some given event equivalent to a class of other things, placing it in an identity class, provides then one of the most primitive forms of going beyond information given.

William James (13) wrote picturesquely of this process, remarking that cognitive life begins when one is able to exclaim, "Hello! Thingumbob again." The adaptive significance of this capacity for equivalence grouping is, of course, enormous. If we were to respond to each event as unique and to learn anew what to do about it or even what to call it, we would soon be swamped by the complexity of our environment. By last count, there were some 7.5 million discriminable differences in the color solid alone. Yet, for most purposes, we manage by treating them as if there were only a dozen or two classes of colors. No two individuals are alike, yet we get by with perhaps a dozen or so types into which we class others. Equivalence categories or concepts are the most basic currency one can utilize in going beyond the sensory given. They are the first steps toward rendering the environment generic.

Consider a second form of going beyond the information given, one that involves learning the redundancy of the environment. I present the word, *P*YC*OL*GY,* and with no difficulty at all you recognize that the word is *PSYCHOLOGY.* Or the finding of Miller, Heise, and Lichten (19) that words masked by noise are more easily recognized when they are in a meaningful or high-probability context than when they are presented in isolation. Indeed, the missing word in the sentence, "Dwight ———— is currently President of the United States" can be completely masked by noise and yet recognized correctly by anybody who knows the subject matter. Or we find that subjects in some experiments currently in progress check off about an average of 30 trait words from the Gough list as being characteristic of a person who is only described as being either intelligent, or independent, or considerate. Any one of these key traits has at least 30 possible avenues for going beyond it, based on learned probabilities of what things are likely to go with what in another person. Once one learns the probability texture of the environment, one can go beyond the given by predicting its likely concomitants.

We move one step beyond such probabilistic ways of going beyond the information given and come now to certain formal bases for doing so. Two propositions are presented, $A > B$, $B > C$ and with very little difficulty most people can readily go beyond to the inference that $A > C$. Or I present a series of numbers, with one missing one to be supplied: 2, 4, 8, *, 32, 64 and as soon as you are able to see that the numbers are powers of two, or that they represent successive doublings, you will be able to provide the missing number 16. Or in an experiment by Bruner, Mandler, O'Dowd, and Wallach, (5) [1] rats are taught to find their way through a four-unit *T* maze by threading the path *LRLR.* Given the proper conditions (and to these we will return later), an animal readily transfers to the mirror-image pattern of *RLRL*—provided he has learned the path as an instance of single alternation and not as a set of specific turns.

What it is that one learns when one learns to do the sort of thing just described, whether it be learning to do syllogisms or learning the principle of single alternation, is not easily described. It amounts to the learning of certain formal schemata that may be fitted to or may be used to organize arrays of diverse information. We shall use the expression *coding* to de-

[1] See pp. 186–97.

scribe what an organism does to information under such circumstances, leaving its closer examination until later. Thus, we can conceive of an organism capable of rendering things into equivalence classes, capable of learning the probabilistic relationships between events belonging to various classes, and capable of manipulating these classes by the utilization of certain formal coding systems.

We often combine formal codes and probability codes in making inferences beyond the data. Studies such as those by Wilkins (32) provide instructive examples. One finds, for example, that a typical deduction made from the proposition, If all *A* are *B,* is that All *B* are *A,* and to the proposition, If some *A* are not *B* a typical conclusion is that Some *B* are not *A.* Yet none of the subjects ever agrees with the proposition that If all men are mammals, then all mammals are men, or with the proposal that If some men are not criminals, then some criminals are not men. In sum, it may often be the case that common sense—the result of inductive learning of what is what and what goes with what in the environment—may often serve to correct less well-learned formal methods of going beyond information given. In short, one may often have alternative modes of going beyond, sometimes in conflict with each other, sometimes operating to the same effect.

One final case before we turn to the difficult business of trying to specify what is involved in utilizing information in this soaring manner. This time we take a scientist, and we shall take him unprepared with a theory, which, as we know, is a rare state for the scientist and the layman alike. He has been working, let us say, on the effects of sound sleep, and in pursuit of his inquiries has hit on the bright idea of giving his subjects a complete rest for five or six days—just to see what happens. To add to their rest, he places them on a soft bed, covers their eyes with translucent ground-glass goggles, lulls their ears with a soft but persistent homogeneous masking noise, and in general makes life as homogeneously restful as possible for them. At the end of this time, he tests them and finds, lo and behold, that they are incapable of doing simple arithmetic problems, that they cannot concentrate, that their perceptual constancies are impaired, and so on down the list of findings that were reported at McGill by Bexton, Heron, Scott (3), and their collaborators. (Note that the McGill investigators started with a hypothesis about sensory deprivation; our example is a fiction, but it will serve us and may even relate to our Canadian colleagues.) Once one has got some data of this order, one is in a funk unless one can go beyond them. To do so requires a theory. A theory, of course, is something we invent. If it is a good theory—a good formal or probabilistic coding system—it should permit us to go beyond the present data both retrospectively and prospectively. We go backward—turn around on our own schemata—and order data that before seemed unrelated to each other. Old loose ends now become part of a new pattern. We go forward in the sense of having new hypotheses and predictions about other things that should be but that have not been tested. When we have finished the reorganizing by means of the new theoretical coding system, everything then seems obvious, if the thing fits. We mention theory construction as a final example of coding processes largely because it highlights several points that are too easily overlooked in the simpler examples given earlier. Coding may involve inventive behavior and we must be concerned with what is involved in the construction of coding systems. And coding systems may be effective or ineffective in permitting one to go beyond information. Later we shall inquire into the conditions that make for construction of new coding systems and what may lead to the construction of adequate ones.

On Coding Systems

A coding system may be defined as a set of contingently related, nonspecific categories. It is the person's manner of grouping and relating information about his world, and it is constantly subject to change and reorganization. Bartlett's memory schemata are close to what is intended here, and the early work of Piaget (21) on the child's conception of nature represents a naturalistic account of coding systems in the child.

Let it be clear that a coding system as I describe it here is a hypothetical construct. It is inferred from the nature of antecedent and consequent events. For example, in the rat experiment cited earlier, I teach an organism to wend a course that goes *LRLR* through a maze. I wish to discover how the event is coded. I transfer the animal to a maze that goes *RLRL*. He transfers with marked savings. I infer now that he has coded the situation as single alternation. But I must continue to test for the genericalness of the coding system used. Is it alternation in general or alternation only in spatial terms? To test this I set up a situation in the maze where the correct path is defined by taking alternate colors, now a black, now a white member of black-white pairs, without regard to their position. If there is saving here too, I assume that the original learning was coded not as positional alternation but as alternation in general. Of course, I use the appropriate control groups along the way. Note that the technique I am using is identical to the technique we use to discover whether children are learning proper codes in school. We provide training in addition, then we move on to numbers that the child has not yet added, then we move to abstract symbols like $a + a + a$ and see whether $3a$ emerges as the answer. Then we test further to see whether the child has grasped the idea of repeated addition, which we fool him by calling multiplication. We devise techniques of instruction along the way to aid the child in building a generic code to use for all sorts of quantities. If we fail to do this, we say that the child has learned in rote fashion or that, in Wertheimer's (30) moralistic way of putting it, we have given the child "mechanical" rather than "insightful" ways of solving the problem. The distinction is not between mechanical and insightful, really, but whether or not the child has grasped and can use the generic code we have set out to teach him.

You will sense immediately that what I have been describing are examples of transfer of training, so-called. But nothing is being transferred, really. The organism is learning codes that have narrower or wider applicability.

Let me give you some examples of how one uses the transfer paradigm to investigate what kind of coding systems are being learned. William Hull, a teacher in a Cambridge school, raised the question whether the learning of spelling involved simply the learning by rote of specific words or whether instead it did not also involve learning the general coding system for English words from which the child might then be able to reconstruct the letters of a word. He took children of the fifth grade and separated them into those who had done well and those who had done poorly on a standard spelling achievement test, taking as subjects those who fell in the highest and lowest quartile of the class. He then presented these children brief exposures of pseudo words, which they were to write down immediately after the card bearing each word was removed. Some of the words were first-order approximations to English, essentially random strings of letters that had the same frequency distribution of letters as does English. Some were third- and fourth-order approximations to English constructed by Miller, Bruner, and Postman, (18) [2] in connection with another experiment, words like *MOSSIANT, VERNALIT, POKERSON, ONETICUL, APHYSTER,* which reflected the probability structure of English very closely and which, but for the grace of God, might have been in the dictionary. Take the case for five-letter and six-letter pseudo words. For the first-order or random words, there was little difference between good and poor spellers. But for nonsense approximations to English, there was a great difference between the two, the good spellers showing a much superior performance.

The difference between the two groups is in what they had been learning while learning to spell English words. One group had been learning words more by rote, the others had been learning a general coding system based on the transitional probabilities that characterize letter sequences in English. Along the same lines, Robert Harcourt and I tested Italian, German, Swedish, French, Dutch, and English speakers on their ability to reproduce random strings of letters presented briefly (that is, zero-order approximations to any language), and third-order approximations to each of these languages. As you would expect, there was no difference in ability to handle random strings, but a real difference in ability, favoring one's

[2] See pp. 57–67.

mother tongue, in reproducing nonsense in one's own language. You will sense immediately to what language stock each of the following nonsense words belong: *MAJÖLKKOR, KLOOK, GERLANCH, OTIVANCHE, TRIANODE, FATTOLONI,* and so on. When one learns a language one learns a coding system that goes beyond words. If Benjamin Lee Whorf is right, the coding system goes well beyond even such matters as we have described.

Let us sum up the matter to this point. We propose that when one goes beyond the information given, one does so by virtue of being able to place the present given in a more generic coding system and that one essentially reads off from the coding system additional information either on the basis of learned contingent probabilities or learned principles of relating material. Much of what has been called transfer of training can be fruitfully considered a case of applying learned coding systems to new events. Positive transfer represents a case where an appropriate coding system is applied to a new array of events, negative transfer being a case either of misapplication of a coding system to new events or of the absence of a coding system that may be applied. It follows from this that it is of the utmost importance in studying learning to understand systematically what it is that an organism has learned. This is the cognitive problem in learning.

There is perhaps one additional thing that is learned by an organism when he acquires information generically, and this must be mentioned in passing although it is not directly germane to our line of inquiry. Once a situation has been mastered, it would seem that the organism alters the way in which new situations are approached in search of information. A mazewise rat, for example, even when put into a new learning situation, seems not to nose about quite so randomly. In an experiment by Goodnow and Pettigrew (9), for example, once their subjects have learned one pattern of pay-off on a two-armed bandit, they approach the task of finding other patterns by responding more systematically to the alternatives in the situation. Even when they are trying to discover a pattern in what is essentially a random series of pay-offs, their sequential choice behavior shows less haphazardness. It is interesting that this acquired regularity of response makes it possible for them to locate new regularities in pay-off pattern when these are introduced after a long exposure to random positional pay-offs. Even though the behavior is designed to discover whether the old pattern will recur again, its regularity makes it possible to discover new patterns.

Three general problems now emerge. The first problem concerns the conditions under which efficient and generalizable coding systems will be acquired. What will lead a rat to learn the sequence *LRLR* in such a generic way that it will be transferable to the sequence of turns *RLRL?* What will lead a child to learn the sequence 2, 4, 8, 16, 32 . . . in such a way that it transfers to the sequence 3, 9, 27, 81 . . . ? This we shall call the conditions of code acquisition.

The second we may label the problem of creativity. It has two aspects. The first has to do with the inventive activity involved in constructing highly generic and widely appropriate coding systems, armed with which a person will subsequently, in a highly predictive way, be able to deal with and go beyond much of the information he encounters in his environment. The other aspect of the problem of creativity is the development of a readiness to utilize appropriately already acquired coding systems. James long ago called this "the electric sense of analogy" and it consists in being able to recognize something before one fits it into or finds it to be a case of some more generic class of things that one has dealt with before—being able to see, for example, that laws that were originally related to statistical physics also fit the case of the analysis of transmitted information, the leap that carries us from Boltzmann's turn-of-the-century conception of entropy to modern theories of communication as initiated by Claude Shannon (25). The equation of entropy with information was a creative analogical leap indeed, even if it did not require any new invention. Very well, the problem of creativity involves then the invention of efficient and applicable coding systems to apply to the information given and also the proper sense of knowing when it is appropriate to apply them.

The third and final problem to be considered is the problem of instruction, and it is a practical one. It concerns the best coding system in terms of which to present various subject matters so as to guarantee maximum ability to generalize. For example, the statement $S = \frac{1}{2} gt^2$ is an efficient and highly generalizable coding system for learning about falling bodies, and by using the code one can go beyond any partial data given about falling bodies. But how does one teach somebody about a country in general so that given some new specific knowledge about the country he can effectively go beyond it by appropriate inferences based on an effective coding system?

We consider each of these problems in turn.

Conditions Affecting the Acquisition of Coding Systems

Essentially, we are asking under what conditions will an organism learn something or, as we put it, code something in a generic manner so as to maximize the transferability of the learning to new situations?

Let me propose four general sets of conditions that may be relevant here. The first of these is set or attitude. The second is need state. The third is degree of mastery of the original learning from which a more generic coding system must be derived. The fourth is diversity of training.

THE ROLE OF SET

It is a perennial source of embarrassment to psychologists interested in the learning process that set to learn is such a massive source of variance in most experiments on human learning. We make the distinction between incidental learning and intentional learning. What is the difference between the two?

Take typical experiments in the field of concept attainment as a case in point. In most such experiments since Hull's classic study (11), the subject is given the task of memorizing what nonsense syllables go with what figures or pictures or words. One subset of pictures in the array presented—ones that all contain, unbeknownst to the subject, a certain common defining property—will have the label *CIV* and another subset, let us say, will have the label *DAX*. The task as presented is one in which the subject is to learn which label goes with which pictures. Insofar as the task is understood as one involving the memorization of labels, the subject is engaged in what can only be called incidental concept attainment. An interesting experiment by Reed (23) shows that when subjects operate under such a set, they attain concepts more slowly and remember them less well than under instruction conditions where the subject is told frankly what is the real objective of the experiment—that is, to find what makes certain designs *CIV*s and others *DAX*s. In an extensive series of experiments by Bruner, Goodnow, and Austin (4), moreover, it is evident that the search for the defining attributes of a class of objects—the search for a generic code in terms of which a class of objects may be rendered equivalent—leads to certain forms of behavior strategies or learning sets that are absent when the task is seen as one of rote memorization. The subject learns ways of testing instances to gather an optimum amount of information leading him to final discovery of the defining attributes of *CIV*s and *DAX*s. Once success has been achieved in this way, new instances can be recognized with no further learning and the memory of the instances already encountered need no longer depend upon sheer retention. For now, knowing the code, the subject can reconstruct the fact that all positive instances encountered were all marked by certain critical attributes.

In short, an induced set can guide the person to proceed nongenerically and by rote or to proceed as if what was to be learned was a principle or a generic method of coding events. Instructions serve, if you will, as a switching mechanism or set producer that brings different forms of coding into play and tunes the organism to the kind and level of generic activity that seem appropriate to the situation.

Obviously, the principal giver of instruction is our own past history. For, by virtue of living in a certain kind of professional or social setting, our approach to new experience becomes constrained—we develop, if you will, a professional deformation with respect to ways of coding events. The mathematician tends with time to code more and more events in terms of certain formal codes that are the stock in trade of his profession. The historian has his particular deformations, and so too the psychologist. With experience, Harlow's (10) monkeys gradually develop a deformation too and attempt to solve all discrimination problems as exemplars of the oddity principle.

It is perhaps Kurt Goldstein (8) who has insisted most strongly that one may in general characterize the typical sets a person brings to problems along the dimensions of abstractness and concreteness. The person who is high in concreteness deals with information or events in terms of their own specific identity and does not tend to genericize what is learned. The abstract attitude is one in which the individual can not only tear himself away from the given, but actually may not deal with the given save as an exemplar of more generic categories. How people get to be one way and the other or how they maintain an ability to operate at both levels is something we do not understand with any clarity, although some tentative proposals will be put forth in the following section.

To sum up, the manner and the degree with which newly learned knowledge is coded generically can be influenced in a transient way by situational instruction and in a more permanent way by the regimen of one's past experience. One's attitude toward learning, whether a transient or an enduring thing, will then determine the degree to which one is equipped with coding systems that can be brought to bear on new situations and permit one to go beyond them.

NEED STATE

I should like to dust off the Yerkes-Dodson law at this point and propose that the generality of the coding system in terms of which newly acquired information is organized depends upon the presence of an optimum motivational state. Very high and very low drive lead, I think, to an increase in concreteness of cognitive activity. There is a middle state of drive level that produces the strongest tendency toward generic learning.

Let me illustrate this by going back to the experiment of Bruner, Mandler, O'Dowd, and Wallach previously referred to (pp. 186–97). Consider two of their groups. Each group was given enough training to reach a criterion in learning the turn pattern *LRLR* and then given 80 additional trials of overlearning. The only difference between the groups was that one group did its learning under 36 hours of food deprivation, the other under 12 hours of deprivation. When the two groups were then transferred to the reversal pattern, *RLRL,* the moderately motivated group showed positive transfer, learning the new single alternation pattern significantly faster than they had learned the original pattern. The very hungry group showed marked negative transfer.

The behavior of the two groups at the time of transfer is revealing. When transferred, the moderately motivated groups showed much more disturbance in behavior. When these highly trained animals found the old reliable door at the first turn blocked, they drew back from the choice point and sometimes took as long as 20 minutes before they could make up their minds about what to do next. They defecated, seemed upset, and spent a great deal of time looking back and forth at the two doors. Several of the animals, at the end of this period of delay, then charged through the now correct first door and continued to charge right through the now correct single alternation pattern and made no errors from then on. Others made somewhat more errors, but on the whole, their learning was rapid.

The other group, the highly skilled and highly motivated rats of the 36-hour deprived group, showed quite different behavior. Finding the first door locked, they barged right over and took the alternative door, and then attempted unsuccessfully at each successive alley to make their old turn. Some of these animals persisted in this for many trials and then shifted to other forms of systematic response—such as one-sided position habits—that were not single alternation. In sum, it seemed as if they had to unlearn the old pattern of *LRLR* responses and then relearn a new one.

There is one particular feature of the behavior of the animals in the two groups that wants special attention. It is the amount of looking around or *VTE*-ing or scanning that went on in the two groups. As Tolman (29) has observed, highly motivated organisms show less *VTE* behavior, less looking back and forth at choice points. So, too, our 36-hour hungry animals during original learning in contrast with the 12-hour ones. The difference in *VTE* was particularly marked during the early transfer trials as well, and it was exhibited by the less hungry rats predominantly in the first unit of the maze, at the choice point that was the only real alternative, for once the first turn was correctly mastered, the rest of the pattern followed.

It would seem, then, that under conditions of high drive, if a path to the goal has been learned, it is learned, so to speak, as this path to this goal and is not coded or acquired as an example of a more generic pattern, this kind of path to this kind of goal. In consequence, when a new situation arises, the driven creature does not have a generic coding system that permits him to go beyond it insightfully. It is as if one of the students of geometry in Wertheimer's study (30) had learned to do the operations necessary for solving the area of this parallelogram but had not generalized the knowledge into a coding system for handling parallelograms of slightly different size, shape, or position.

Impelling drive states seem also to affect the extent to which a person is able to apply already very firmly acquired coding systems to new material encountered, permitting him to go appropriately beyond the information given. An illustrative study is provided by the experiment of Postman and Bruner (22) on perception under stress. Two groups of subjects were used. They began by having to recognize brief, three-word sentences presented tachistoscopically under usual laboratory conditions. Then the stress group was given an impossible perceptual recognition task to perform (reporting on the details of a complex picture presented at an exposure level too brief in duration for adequate performance). During these stress trials they were rather mercilessly badgered by the experimenter for performing so poorly and were urged to try harder. The other group was given a simple task of judging the illumination level at which the same picture was presented at the same exposure levels. And they were not badgered. Then additional sentences were given subjects in both groups. The stress group showed no further improvement in their sentence-and-word-recognition thresholds, the nonstress group continued to improve. What was striking about the performance of the two groups in the latter half of the experiment was that the stress subjects either overshot the information given and made wild inferences about the nature of the briefly presented words, or they undershot and seemed unable to make words out of the briefly presented data at all. In terms of the Jamesian electric sense of analogy, it was as if the stress introduced either too many ohms of resistance into the circuit or removed too many of them. The stress subjects, let it be noted, did not behave consistently in the overshoot or the undershoot fashion, but seemed to go back and forth between the two.

Let me note finally in connection with code acquisition and/or the transfer of acquired codes to new situations that there is one interesting feature of the Harlow experiments (10) on the acquisition of learning sets that is not often enough remarked. Recall that in the typical experiment of this kind, an animal is trained to choose the odd member of a set of stimuli, and that after training on a variety of such problems he is able to do so regardless of what characteristics the stimuli have: the odd one of several shapes, of several colors, of several junk stimuli, and so on. These experiments are carried out with animals who are only very lightly motivated. They are well fed before they are run, the reward used consists of a half or even a quarter of a peanut, and it would almost be fair to say that the most impelling drive operative is the manipulative-curiosity drive that Harlow has rightly made so much of in his recent writing. The use of such a mild motivational regimen is well advised. The fact of the matter is that one does not get such elegant principle learning in more highly motivated animals. A very hungry monkey may not develop such learning sets at all. Again, more generic coding seems to be inhibited by a condition in which the information to be acquired has too great instrumental relevance to a need state then in being.

Let me conclude this section on the role of need states in acquiring and utilizing coding systems with an important caveat, one that has been insisted upon particularly by George Klein (15). One cannot specify the cognitive or behavioral resultants of need states without specifying the manner in which the organism has learned to deal with his need states. The resultant of learning to deal with needs is the establishment in behavior of what Klein calls "general regulatory systems." In a sense, we have been implying such systems in the rat and monkey when we speak of the fact that a high need state has the effect of specializing the organism to deal with the here-and-now without regard to the more generic significance of what is being learned. It is conceivable that in some higher organisms this may not always be the case.

DEGREE OF MASTERY AND ITS RELATIONSHIP
TO GENERIC CODING

Let me begin again with that overworked species, the rat. Starling Reed (24) reports that animals who have been overtrained on a black-white discrimination, with black the positive stimulus, are able to transfer more easily to a black-white discrimination with white positive than are animals trained simply to criterion and then reversed. In the Bruner, Mandler, O'Dowd, and Wallach study already referred to (pp. 186–97), three groups of 12-hour and three groups of 36-hour hungry animals were used. High- and low-motivation groups were paired in terms of amount of original training given. One pair of groups was given original training on an *LRLR* pattern until they just reached criterion; a second pair was given 20 additional trials of practice beyond criterion; and the third pair was given 80 additional overtraining trials. The biggest effect in the study was in the interaction of drive level and amount of overtraining. For the 12-hour groups, the more their overtraining, the better they did on transfer to the reverse pattern. But only the highly overtrained group showed positive transfer. All the strongly motivated animals showed about the same amount of negative transfer. We may take as a tentative conclusion that overtraining and mastery aids generic coding provided motivation is not severe.

We are in the midst of a controversial area, for the wisdom of common sense and of the psychologist divides sharply on the matter of practice and drill. "Practice makes perfect" is a well-thumbed proverb and the darling of practically all *S-R* learning theory. To be sure, it is a moot point in these theories just what it is that practice makes one perfect at. Nobody denies that it makes one perfect at the thing being practiced, but there is still debate on whether it also improves one at things beyond what one has practiced. The position of most *S-R* theorists has been that it does not make one perfect at anything save the thing itself and that transfer to other things depends upon whether the other things contain elements identical to those that existed in the first task. We shall leave aside the question of how fast and loose one can play with the word *identical* in the expression *identical elements,* for it is obvious that exploring its usage will be a discouraging venture. Even in the original monograph of Thorndike (28) it was claimed that one form of identical element shared by two problems was that they could be solved by the same principle.

In any case, to return to the main issue at hand, there is another school of thought that proposed insight and understanding as a more important factor than drill in improving both performance of a particular task and in guaranteeing wider generalization of the learning to other situations. The names of Wertheimer (30), Katona (14), Duncker (7), and Köhler (16) are associated with this position, and the modern proverb has been provided by International Business Machines, "THINK." The progressive school and its apostles have perhaps been the chief carriers of the practical banner.

I think the issue is a pseudo issue. The nature and effect of drill and overtraining is a function of what has to be learned. Moreover, one cannot speak of drill without specifying the nature of the set and the drive conditions under which it takes place. We cannot talk about practice or training as if it were being administered to an indifferently constructed black box.

First about the nature of materials to be learned. Take Katona's example of the string of numbers: 58121519222629. If subjects are asked to remember it, the amount of practice required to become perfect depends upon their method of recoding the numbers. If they recognize that the numbers are grouped as follows: 5–8–12–15–19–22–26–29 and that this series begins with 5 and is made up of successive additions of 3 and 4, then what they had better practice is, 5 then add 3 and then 4 and keep repeating this alternation. Mastering this coding system requires less practice and it is different practice than trying to remember the series by rote. As George Miller (17) puts it in his delightful discussion of recoding systems,

Suppose that we want to know how far a body falls through space when it has been falling freely for a given number of seconds. One way to tackle this problem is to make measurements, summarize the measurements in a table, and then memorize the table. . . . This is a very stupid way to proceed because we memorize each number as if it were unrelated to all the other numbers. . . . All the measurements can be recoded into a simple rule that says the distance fallen at the end of t seconds is $gt^2/2$. The value of g is about 32. All we need remember is $16t^2$. Now we store all the measurements away in memory by storing this simple formula (p. 234).

Again, we had better practice remembering the formula and the value of g, and never mind practicing on the table of measurements from which it was produced.

But yet this fails to meet the question squarely. For where we do not know the appropriate coding system in advance, what is the best practice procedure for discovering it? Our rats and those of Starling Reed obviously had to do a fair amount of drilling at their task before they learned it in a generic way. And it seems to be frequently the case that a certain amount of skill development is necessary at a simpler level of coding before more generic recoding of the learning can occur. The earliest studies of code learning, the classic study by Bryan and Harter (6) of telegraphic code learning, can be reproduced in many later studies: One first learns to code the messages in terms of letters, then in terms of words, then in terms of sentences. Later methods of regrouping or recoding depend upon prior mastery of less generic methods of coding. One's limited immediate memory span requires one to deal first with the dits and dahs of single letters. Then gradually when the dit-dah arrangement of a letter takes on unitary properties, that is, can be categorized as a unit, it may be grouped with other unitary dit-dah arrangements into words. When words are codable as units, then one goes to sentences. So, too, with the rats; they must master the regularity of a set of turns before it becomes possible to reorganize or recode in terms of a single-alternation principle.

In sum, then, the question of mastery comes down to this. Learning often cannot be translated into a generic form until there has been enough mastery of the specifics of the situation to permit the discovery of lower-order regularities which can then be recombined into higher-order, more generic coding systems. Once a system of recoding has been worked out whereby information is condensed into more generic codes, the problem of mastery becomes one of mastering the recoding system rather than mastering the original set of events. Moreover, the nature of practice cannot be simply specified in terms of repetition to and beyond mastery of a specific task. Rather, one must specify the conditions under which practice takes place, whether with the auxiliary intention to search out a generic coding system or whether simply with a rote learning intention. Finally, the need level at which the organism is practicing a task must also be specified. Practice at a high rate of drive may produce no generic learning. Low-drive practice may.

DIVERSITY OF TRAINING

I think that we know intuitively that if we wish to make a group of students understand the Pythagorean theorem in plane geometry, it helps to illustrate the intuitive proof of the theorem to use several right triangles of different dimensions, and indeed it might also help to demonstrate that the theorem does not apply to nonrectilinear triangles. It also seems intuitively right that if monkeys are to be taught Harlow's oddity problem it helps or indeed may be essential to give them training choosing the odd member of several different arrays. So, too, when we play the original word game with children, we point to several exemplars of the word *dog* and several exemplars of *cat* in demonstrating the linguistic code utterance, cats and dogs are different. The quantitative informational importance of diversity of instances in concept attainment has been dealt with elsewhere and I would only like to consider some of the common-sense implications of the matter here.

The process of finding out what is generic about a given situation so that one can then deal with similar situations later—know their solution without having to go through the tedious business of learning all over again—consists essentially of being able to isolate the defining properties of the class of events to which the present situation belongs. In a concept-formation experiment, for example, if a subject is trying to discover what makes certain cards positive and certain ones negative, his task is to discover which of the discriminable atttibutes or which combination of discriminable attributes are present in the positive instances and absent in the negative ones. I think one can think of the matter of diversity in terms of the interesting old proverb, "The fish will be the last to discover water," as indeed man was very late in discovering the atmosphere. Unless one is exposed to some changes, genericizing does not seem to be stimulated. Kurt Lewin had a subtle point when he urged that the best way to understand the nature of a social process was to try to change it, for only in the face of changes in events does one begin to have the information necessary to abstract generic properties.

This suggests a rather simple but rather startling conclusion. If we are to study the conditions under which generic learning occurs, the pattern of much of present learning research needs drastic change. The present approach is to study the speed of acquisition of new learning and, possibly, to study the conditions that produce extinction. When we have carried our experimental subjects through these steps, we either dismiss them or, if they are animal subjects, dispose of them. The exception, of course, is the clinician; but even his research on learning and cognition is of the cross-sectional type. We have been accustomed to speaking of mazewise rats and testwise human beings, but in the spirit of being annoyed by an inconvenience. The fact of the matter is, as Beach and Jaynes (2) have pointed out, that early and diverse training of lower organisms seems to be one of the conditions for producing intelligent behavior in the more mature organism. If we really intend to study the conditions of generic learning by the use of the transfer-of-training paradigm I have proposed, then we shall have to keep our organisms far longer and teach them original tasks of greater diversity than we now do.

The Invention or Creation of Coding Systems

The past half century has witnessed a profound revolution against the conception of science inherited from the Newtonian period. Newton saw the task of the scientist as a journey on the sea of discovery whose objective was to discover the islands of truth. The conception was essentially Baconian. Newton's *Principia* was not proposed as a theoretical system but as a description of discoveries about nature. His *Opticks* was, in like vein, a disquisition into the secrets of light. Indeed, Jonathan Edwards preached to his parishioners in western Massachusetts on Newton's discovery of the spectral composition of white light as an instance of the fact that God had given man sufficient capacities to see through to some of the deepest secrets of God's design. To a considerable extent, the layman's view of science is still dominated by the spirit of discovery, by the spirit of naturalistic realism.

The temper of modern science is more nominalistic. The scientist constructs formal models or theories that have predictive value, that have a value in going beyond the information available. One works with sets of observations that one fits into a theory. If the theory cannot take one beyond one's observations, if it does not have the surplus value that is demanded of a theory, then the theory is trivial. The universe is a set of perspectives devised by scientists for understanding and rendering predictable the array of observations that are possible. Whoever has read Robert Oppenheimer's account of "Lord Rutherford's World" in his Rieth Lectures (20) or whoever has read Max Wertheimer's account (30) of his conversations with Einstein on the formulation of the special and general theories of relativity cannot but be struck by the emphasis on the constructive, nominalistic, and essentially subjective conception of science-making that prevails in modern physical theory.

The activity of constructing formal models and theoretical constructs is a prototype of what we mean by the creation of generic coding systems that permit one to go beyond the data to new and possibly fruitful predictions.

Let us consider the creative acts by which a person constructs a theory for dealing with a problem. The given, let us say, is as it is in a Duncker type of problem. Here is X-ray apparatus capable of destroying a tumor in the center of a body. The difficulty is that the amount of radiation sufficient to destroy the tumor is also sufficient to destroy the healthy tissue through which it must pass in reaching the tumor. How to solve the difficulty? Let us assume that the problem solver did not learn a routine technique in medical school for dealing with this problem.

We will assume (and it is not an outrageous assumption, as we shall see) that the person has had experiences that provide the elements out of which a solution may be fashioned. The child knows, for example, that if a plank is too weak to take two children across a gap simultaneously, the children can get across one at a time in successive order or get across the gap at the same time if they can find two planks to throw across it. This is highly relevant knowledge. But this is not a theory, nor by remembering it does one either solve the problem or create a relevant coding system.

Suppose now that the person comes, through whatever processes are involved, to a solution of the problem: using two X-ray beams, each of less than lethal dose, to converge at some angle upon the tumor. This solution, insofar as it is specific to the single problem at hand, is still not a theory; indeed it is not altogether clear that anything new has been produced or created. What we mean by a theory or model or generic coding system is a representation of the criterial characteristics of the situation just described, a contentless depiction of the ideal case, empty in the sense that geometry is empty of particulars. It is this emptying operation, I would propose, that constitutes the creative step in inventing or producing a coding system. It is also the step that is involved when one learns something generically. In this sense there is only a difference in degree between what we have spoken of as generic learning and what we here call the production of a generic coding system.

Pursue the matter a bit further. The problem solver says to himself, "This must be a general characteristic of loads, media, and destinations within the medium. Every medium has an array of paths to a destination within it and each path has a capacity. The number of paths required for the simultaneous transmission of a load to a destination is the size of the load divided by the capacity of any single path." Now we say the person has a theory, he has to some degree emptied the problem of specific content.

When we ask what leads to such an emptying operation (or abstraction, if one prefers the more conventional term), we are forced to answer by describing the conditions that inhibit it. What, then, inhibits theory construction? I would submit that the conditions inhibiting theory construction of this kind are the same ones that inhibit generic learning—the conditions of code acquisition described in the preceding section. For generic learning and the abstracting or emptying operation are, I think, the same thing.

But consider one other aspect of the creation or acquisition of generic coding systems. It consists of a form of combining activity that is made possible by the use of abstracted or empty codes. Take the formulation just given—the theory of loads, media, destinations, and path capacities. It now becomes possible to combine this formalized system with other formalized systems to generate new predictions. For example, suppose the problem solver goes on to combine his new formulation with the equally abstract formulations of analytic geometry. The number of paths converging through a medium to an enclosed destination is infinity. Therefore, the combined path capacity of an over-all medium is infinity, and, therefore, in principle, an infinite load (radiation or what not) can be delivered to a destination. In principle, then, one may go beyond to the hypothesis that no load is too large to deliver simultaneously across a medium, given the solution of technical limitations.

It seems to me that the principal creative activity over and beyond the construction of abstracted coding systems is the combination of different systems into new and more general systems that permit additional prediction. It is perhaps because of this that, in Whitehead's picturesque phrase, progress in science seems to occur on the margins between fields. There is virtually no research available on this type of combinatorial creativity. How, for example, do physiological psychologists combine the coding systems of biology and psychology, or biophysicists their component disciplines to derive a new emergent? We might begin by looking.

The Problem of Instruction

What we have said thus far obviously has implications for educational practice, and it is with one of these that we wish to conclude. How shall we teach a subject matter? If the subject matter were geometry we readily would answer that we teach the person those axioms and theorems—a formal coding system—that will maximize the ability of the individual to go beyond the information given in any problem he might encounter. A problem in geometry is simply an incomplete statement, one that has unknowns in it. We say, "Here is a three-sided figure: one side measures x, and the other y, the angle between them is z degrees and the problem is to find the length of the other side and the size of the other two angles as well as the area of the triangle." One must, in short, go beyond what is given. We know intuitively that, if the person has learned the formal coding system, he will be able to perform such feats.

But how to describe the history of a people or, say, Navaho culture? I would propose that much the same criterion should prevail here as we apply to geometry. The best description of a people's history is that set of propositions that permits a given individual to go beyond the information given to him. This, if you will, is the history of a people, the information that is necessary to make all other information as redundant or predictable as possible. So, too, in characterizing Navaho culture: that minimum set of propositions that will permit the largest reconstruction of unknowns by people to whom the propositions are revealed.

Let me in general propose this test as a measure of the adequacy of any set of instructional propositions—that once they are grasped, they permit the maximum reconstruction of material unknown to the reconstructor. Morton White (31) argues persuasively for this position when he says,

We ought to start by observing that a history contains true statements about the whole course of . . . [an] object's existence. True statements about the future of the object will be as much part of its history as true statements about its remote past. We must observe that some of these statements have causal implications whereas others do not . . . The next thing to observe is that there are two kinds of historians, two kinds of students who *want* to approximate the whole truth about a given object. First there are those who conceive it as their task to amass as many true singular statements as can be amassed at a given moment, and in this way approximate the ideal of the historian. Clearly this seems like the way to approach an infinite or very large number of statements —gather as many as you can. But then there are historians who are more discriminating, who recognize that some singular statements are historically more important than others, not because they fit in with some moral point of view, but because they are more useful for achieving the history of the object as here defined. The first group is near-sighted. It tries to amass everything in sight on the theory that this is a sure method of getting close to the whole truth. But it fails to realize that those who select facts which seem to have causal significance are more apt to come to know things about the future and past of the object (pp. 718–19).

White then goes on to compare the criterion of "causal fertility" in history with the criterion of "deductive fertility" in logic, noting that "both attempts at brevity . . . are motivated by a desire for intellectual economy." In the broadest sense, the economy is a predictive economy—to be able to go beyond givens to a prediction of unknowns.

I would submit that it is only by imparting "causally fertile" propositions or generic codes that general education in the broad range of human knowledge is made possible. General education does best to aim at being generic education, training men to be good guessers, stimulating the ability to go beyond the information given to probable reconstructions of other events.

Conclusion

The foregoing has been a programmatic discussion of the conditions by which it becomes possible for people to go beyond the information given them or, as Bartlett (1) has put it, to go beyond evidence, to fill in gaps, to extrapolate. We have posed the problem as one involving the learning of coding systems that have applicability beyond the situation in which they were learned. In essence, our proposal is that we emphasize those conditions that maximize the transferability of learning; in pursuit of that we have urged that psychologists examine more closely what is involved when we learn generically—the motivational conditions, the kinds of practice required, the nature of the set designed for gaining an optimally generic grasp of materials. Rate of acquisition and rate of extinction in learning have occupied us for a generation. Perhaps in the coming generation we can concern ourselves more directly with the utility of learning: whether, one thing having been learned, other things can be solved with no further learning required. When we have achieved this leap, we will have passed from the psychology of learning to the psychology of problem solving.

References

1. BARTLETT, F. C. 1951. Thinking. *Manchester memoirs* 93 (3), The Clayton Memorial Lecture.
2. BEACH, F. A., and JAYNES, J. 1954. The effects of early experience on the behavior of animals. *Psychological Bulletin* 51:239–63.
3. BEXTON, W. H.; HERON, W.; and SCOTT, T. H. 1954. Effects of decreased variation in the sensory environment. *Canadian Journal of Psychology* 8:70–76.
4. BRUNER, J. S.; GOODNOW, J. J.; and AUSTIN, G. A. 1956. *A study of thinking.* New York: Wiley.
5. BRUNER, J. S.; MANDLER, J.; O'DOWD, D.; and WALLACH, M. A. 1958. The role of overlearning and drive level in reversal learning. *Journal of Comparative Physiological Psychology* 51:607–13.
6. BRYAN, W. L., and HARTER, N. 1897. Studies on the telegraphic language. The acquisition of a hierarchy of habits. *Psychological Review* 6:345–75.
7. DUNCKER, K. 1945. On problem-solving. Trans. L. S. Lees. *Psychological Monographs* 58:1–112 (whole no. 248).
8. GOLDSTEIN, K. 1939. *The organism.* New York: American Book Co.
9. GOODNOW, J. J., and PETTIGREW, T. 1955. Responding to change and regularity in environmental events (in preparation).

10. HARLOW, H. F. 1949. The formation of learning sets. *Psychological Review* 56:51–65.
11. HULL C. L. 1920. Quantitative aspects of the evolution of concepts. *Psychological Monographs* (1) (whole no. 123).
12. HUMPHREY, G. 1941. *Thinking*. New York: Wiley.
13. JAMES, W. 1890. *The principles of psychology*. New York: Holt.
14. KATONA, G. 1940. *Organizing and memorizing*. New York: Columbia University Press.
15. KLEIN, G. S. 1951. The personal world through perception. In *Perception: an approach to personality,* ed. R. R. Blake and G. V. Ramsey. New York: Ronald Press.
16. KÖHLER, W. 1925. *The mentality of apes*. New York: Harcourt Brace.
17. MILLER, G. A. 1951. *Language and communication*. New York: McGraw-Hill.
18. MILLER, G. A.; BRUNER, J. S.; and POSTMAN, L. 1954. Familiarity of letter sequences and tachistoscopic identification. *Journal of General Psychology* 50:129–39.
19. MILLER, G. A.; HEISE, G. A.; and LICHTEN, W. 1951. The intelligibility of speech as a function of the context of the test materials. *Journal of Experimental Psychology* 41:329–35.
20. OPPENHEIMER, J. R. 1954. *Science and the common understanding*. New York: Simon and Schuster.
21. PIAGET, J. 1930. *The child's conception of physical causality*. London: Kegan, Paul.
22. POSTMAN, L., and BRUNER, J. S. 1948. Perception under stress. *Psychological Review* 55:314–23.
23. REED, H. B. 1946. Factors influencing the learning and retention of concepts. I. The influence of set. *Journal of Experimental Psychology* 36:71–87.
24. REID, S. 1953. The development of noncontinuity behavior through continuity learning. *Journal of Experimental Psychology* 46:107–12.
25. SHANNON, C. E. 1948. A mathematical theory of communication. *Bell System Technological Journal* 27:379–423, 623–56. Also in *The mathematical theory of communication,* C. E. Shannon and Weaver. Urbana: University of Illinois Press, 1949.
26. SMITH, S. Studies of recoding. Reported by G. A. Miller, The magic number seven plus or minus two. Address given at the meetings of the Eastern Psychological Association, Philadelphia, 1955.
27. SPEARMAN, C. 1923. *The nature of intelligence and principles of cognition*. London: Macmillan.
28. THORNDIKE, E. L. 1903. *Educational psychology*. New York: Teachers College, Columbia University.
29. TOLMAN, E. C. 1938. The determiners of behavior at a choice point. *Psychological Review* 45:1–41.
30. WERTHEIMER, M. 1945. *Productive thinking*. New York and London: Harper.
31. WHITE, M. G. 1950. Toward an analytic philosophy of history. In *Philosophical thought in France and the United States,* M. Farber. Buffalo: University of Buffalo Press.
32. WILKINS, M. C. 1928. The effect of changed material on ability to do formal syllogistic reasoning. *Archives of Psychology,* no. 102.

3

SKILL IN INFANCY

Introduction

Bruner has most recently focused his attention on seemingly simple skills such as reaching, feeding, and looking in infants. This may seem somewhat inconsistent for a man who for so long has been concerned with such higher mental processes as concept attainment, problem solving, and use of symbols. However, when the theory of skill that underlies these investigations is considered, the continuity between the infancy work and the earlier studies on adult cognition becomes more apparent. This theory is clearly in the same spirit as the models espoused by Miller, Galanter, and Pribram (3); by Bernstein (1); and by Lashley (2). It is also clearly in opposition to a stimulus-response or chaining conception of skill. Three key features distinguish Bruner's account of skill from a strictly behavioristic or associationistic description. The first is intention. Skilled behavior is thought to involve a "persistent intention that precedes, directs, and provides a criterion for terminating an act." The second is feedback. Throughout the execution of a skilled act the results of behavior are compared with the intended state, and activity continues to reduce the discrepancy between the two. The third is structure. Skilled behavior can be viewed as being comprised of constituent modular acts whose appearance in serial order implies an organizing program or set of rules which are hierarchically arranged.

When skill is viewed in this way, its formal similarity to certain types of cognitive processes becomes evident. In his writing, Bruner has specifically stressed that skilled behavior has much in common with language production on the one hand and problem solving on the other. Skilled behavior and language production are similar in the ways in which they achieve their flexibility and power. Functionally equivalent but morphologically distinct modules of action can be substituted for one another in the execution of a given skill, just as semantically equivalent but phonologically distinct words and phrases can replace one another in a given sentence.

Moreover, like language, skilled behavior is productive or generative in that acquired constituent acts can be combined in new ways to achieve different goals, just as familiar words can be combined in new ways to produce novel sentences.

The relation between skilled behavior and problem solving is more direct than the analogy that binds action and language. Indeed, skilled behavior can be viewed as a kind of problem solving. Both skills and problems are mastered when an objective has been attained and both usually require a series of constituent operations. What makes a skill or a problem difficult is not so often the execution of a single constituent, but rather the orchestration of constituents to achieve a goal. Given that infants neither produce sentences nor solve abstract problems in their first months, and given the parallels between skill and cognition outlined above, the rationale for Bruner's approach to infancy becomes comprehensible. Simple skill may provide some of the only accessible clues to the mystery of the beginnings of human cognition.

The relation between skill and problem solving serves to link the work in this section with that of the two previous sections. As we have seen, perception, concept attainment, sensitivity to environmental regularities, and the development of scientific theories can be described as acts of construction. The execution of a given skill is also a constructive process in which the modules of the skill are orchestrated in a way that meets the task requirements. Again there is the role of internal representation, in this case the representation of the goal or intended state. And again, skills are executed in a way that is similar to analysis by synthesis. The results of behavior are continually compared with the intended state. If there is a match the act has been completed. If there is a mismatch behavior continues until the discrepancy is eliminated.

In his investigation of the development of skill, Bruner has been primarily interested in visually guided reaching. To a lesser degree he has also been concerned with comparing this gradually acquired skill with others, such as sucking and looking, that appear to have much of their organization built in from the start. His concern with the hands of man stems from a conviction that it is manual or enactive intelligence that has distinguished the human species by allowing for the use and manufacture of tools and, indeed, by establishing the conditions necessary for the creation of culture.

The mastery of certain complex skills when viewed developmentally is a gradual process that begins with the mastery of suitable subskills. The constituents to be included in a given subskill undergo a process of modularization in which they are integrated into a sequence which becomes progressively less variable, more fluid, more uniform, more automatic. In short, they gradually achieve the unity of a single constituent. Once all the required subskills have achieved this unity, competence in the complex skill requires orchestrating them in a way that meets the task requirements. Such a view has implications for educational practice as we shall see in the last section of the book.

The first article in this section, "The Growth and Structure of Skill," consists of two major parts. The first part, which is theoretical, presents the model and describes growth as the increasing ability to orchestrate the modules of skill into a program of action. In the second part, several empirical studies are described which lend support to the theoretical description. This paper is complemented by "Eye, Hand, and Mind" in which the visually guided attainment of objects by infants is analyzed into the components of reaching, grasping, retrieving, and mouthing which, it is argued, eventually become subroutines able to fit into a variety of other behavior sequences.

In the next article a system which has more organization built in from the start and which develops more rapidly is compared with the manual skills already considered. "On Voluntary Action and Its Hierarchical Structure" by Professor and Mrs. Bruner compares the transition from reflexive to voluntary sucking with the growth of visually guided reaching. Although the former is mastered more rapidly than the latter, the achievement of both can be viewed as requiring the differentiation of constituent routines and the establishment of a guiding hierarchical structure.

The last article, "Competence in Infants," is a programmatic essay in which Bruner begins by reviewing and elaborating the theory of the growth of skill already considered. He proceeds to suggest various complexities in the account, some of which may represent new directions for his research in the near future. Specifically, he stresses the roles of mastery play, modeling, and imitation in the development of skilled behavior and the social conditions that can sustain or impede the growth of competence.

References

1. BERNSTEIN, N. 1967. *The coordination and regulation of movement*. London: Pergamon.
2. LASHLEY, K. S. 1951. The problem of serial order in behavior. In *Cerebral mechanisms in behavior: the Hixon symposium,* ed. L. A. Jeffress, pp. 112–46. New York: Wiley.
3. MILLER, G. A.; GALANTER, E.; and PRIBRAM, K. H. 1960. *Plans and the structure of behavior*. New York: Holt.

14

The Growth and Structure of Skill *

I should like to explore what it is that may be species-specific about human sensorimotor skill. My eventual hope is to understand how human skill eventuates in human tool use. Lest the discussion become too abstruse, I should like to concentrate upon a few manifestations of skill which develop during the first 18 months of life, all of them studied in our laboratory at Harvard. You will forgive me this geocentrism, for it is necessary in this case. There is simply no adequate literature on skill development in infancy, and such as there is tends in the main to be concerned with the achievement of norms rather than with the close description of behavior, whether a norm is achieved or not.

The skills in question are all pathetically simple, and in all but one case they involve the use of the hand or hands under visual guidance. The exception deals with skill in following an object with the head-eye system as it appears in a regular sequence in one or another of two windows directly before the infant. The hand skills are:

a. Taking possession of several objects handed successively at the midline— control of multiple objects

* "The Growth and Structure of Skill," by Jerome S. Bruner, from *Motor Skills in Infancy,* K. J. Connolly (ed.), Academic Press Inc., London and New York, 1971. Reprinted by permission of the Developmental Sciences Trust.

b. Raising a weighted sliding transparent lid and removing a desirable toy
—complementary use of the hands

c. Reaching for an object that has been placed behind a barrier screen—
detour reaching

d. Holding a gross object so that a fine object attached to it can be taken—
differentiation of power and precision grips

I shall, in passing, contrast these clumsily achieved skills with a quite
different skill that makes its appearance much earlier and in a highly organized form—visual scanning. We have only begun to study scanning and
search and the manner in which they are adapted to the changing requirements of manipulation. But though this work is still unfinished, it can suggest hypotheses.[1]

In spite of the early promise of learning theory, we know very little
about systems of skilled action that acquire their organization slowly, in
contrast to those that have much of it built in from the start. The hands of
man are a slow-growing system, and it is many years before humans can
exhibit the kind of manual intelligence that has distinguished our species
from others—the using and making of tools. Indeed, historically, the
hands were regarded even by students of primate evolution as of no particular interest. Wood Jones (11) would have us believe that there was little
morphological difference between the monkey hand and that of man, but
that the difference was in the function to which they were put by the central nervous system. Yet, as Clark (7) and Napier (15) have pointed out, it
is the evolutionary direction of morphological change in the hand, from
tree shrews through tarsiers through New World monkeys through Old
World monkeys to man, that should reveal how the function of the hand
has changed and, with it, the nature of the implementation of human intelligence. That change has been steadily in the direction of a very special
form of despecialization. The hand is freed from its locomotor function,
from its brachiating function, and from such specialized requirements as
were answered by claws and by exotic forms of finger pads. Becoming
more despecialized in function means becoming more varied in the functions that can be fulfilled. Without losing its capacity for phalangeal divergence needed for weight-bearing, convergence for cupping food, prehensil-
ity for holding and climbing, or opposability—all part of an early primate
heritage—the hand in later primate evolution achieves several new functional capacities while undergoing appropriate morphological change as
well. A combined capacity for power and precision grip is added. The flexibility of palm and thumb increases through changes in the hamate and
trapezium bones and their articulation. The thumb lengthens and its resting angle to the hand increases. The terminal phalanges broaden and

[1] This work was conducted in one context by Alastair Mundy-Castle and Jeremy
Anglin, and in another by Eric Aronson and Edward Tronick.

strengthen, particularly the thumb. Napier may exaggerate when he says, "The present evidence suggests that the stone implements of early man were as good (or as bad) as the hands that made them" (15, p. 62). For surely, initially stupid hands become clever when employed in a clever program devised by the culture. But the issue becomes interesting when we inquire how the virtuoso morphology achieved by man's hands comes to be employed by clever programs of action and, indeed, makes such clever programs possible. Vygotsky (18) was fond of an epigram from Bacon, *"Nec manus, nisi intellectus, sibi permissus, multum valent"* (Neither hand nor intellect left each to itself is worth much).

In the same spirit, my interest is not in the hands by themselves, but in how they both shape and express human instrumental intelligence. For it is my conviction, to state the issue prematurely, that the manner in which the hands are mastered by skill, how they achieve their full adaptive application, can tell us much about the nature of human problem solving and thought. I believe that the programmatic nature of human problem solving reflects the basic fact of primate evolution: that primates, increasingly, were able to use their hands as instruments of intelligence, that selection favored those that could, and that evolution favored in a variety of ways those organisms with a close link between hand and mind (see Washburn and Howell, 19).

In rough outline, the theory of skill and its development toward which our observations lead is as follows. Skilled activity is a program specifying an objective or terminal state to be achieved, and requiring the serial ordering of a set of constituent, modular subroutines. Functionally equivalent variations in serial order and substitution rules for constituent subroutines both are features of skilled activity and render skill productive in the sense that language is productive. Variations in serial order assure flexibility or productivity by making possible appropriate changes in the order with which constituent subroutines are used. The more a skill is linked in real time with such physical requirements as gravitation, constraining velocities, and so on, the fewer the functionally equivalent variations in order that will be possible; the order of steps involved in batting a ball thrown at high speed or juggling two balls is highly constrained. Where the real time constraints are reduced—as in tying a rope splice or fastening a complex lashing—there will be a variety of functionally adequate serial orders that lead to the objective. A developed skill has rules that include appropriate variant orders and exclude inappropriate ones.

With respect to substitution rules, they constitute one of the most intriguing features of any skilled behavior. We have all seen the equivalent of the outfielder, thrown off balance by his effort to catch a fly ball, yet able, not only to hold onto it, but to throw it to an appropriate base while still crazily off balance. When humans can do this type of substitution in real time, we say they are good athletes; there are situations not so constrained by timing where we would be more likely to say that the performer who showed a flair for appropriate substitutions was clever rather than a good athlete.

These sources of productivity in skilled activity are crucial. To quote Bartlett,

skilled performance must all the time submit to receptor control, and be initiated and directed by the signals which the performer must pick up from his environment, in combination with the other signals, internal to his own body, which tell him something about his own movements as he makes them. These are the main reasons why all forms of skill, expertly carried out, possess an outstanding character of rapid adaptation. For the items in the series have, within wide limits, a fluid order of occurrence and varying qualities. So what is called the same operation is done now in one way and now in another, but each way is, as we say, "fitted to the occasion" (1, p. 14).

Another quotation from Bartlett serves to underline the modular quality of skill. He is, of course, referring to real-time rapid skills; but that is not so crucial, as we shall see shortly.

By far the most important characteristic of expert bodily skill is "timing" [which] . . . has nothing to do with the absolute speed at which any component response in the skill sequence is performed. Efficiency depends, more than anything else, upon the regulation of the flow from component to component in such a way that nowhere in the whole series is there any appearance of hurry, and nowhere unnecessarily prolonged delay. . . . The operator has "all the time in the world to do what he wants" (1, p. 15).

All writers on skill would agree that the secret of such smoothly flowing action is not only anticipation of what is coming next, but a sense of how what one is doing now and what one anticipates next fit into the objective of the serial program in operation. There is guidance—and the parallel is quite striking—by an operation resembling analysis-by-synthesis. That is to say, each component is evaluated and corrected in terms of how well it fits into the over-all performance. The components in a serially organized act of skill have not only an arrow of immediate directionality, a pointing ahead to the next component, mere chaining, but also this regulation in terms of requirements of the over-all performance. Indeed, there is a point in most skilled acts (whether severely constrained by real-time requirements or not) where nothing further can be done about the act-as-a-whole, where, to use Bartlett's felicitous term, the behavior has reached a *"point of no return."*

Indeed, Woodworth (20) makes much of the two-phase and polyphase sensorimotor serial patterns, with simple or complex preparatory and effective phases, the two phases being marked off by a boundary much like the point of no return. Of these components, he says, "The small but highly integrated units reveal a fundamental characteristic of organisms: their ability to integrate their behaviour into time sequences. . . . They may have to learn most of these behaviour sequences, but they do not have to learn 'from scratch,' for their ability and tendency to integrate their behaviour over time gives them a running start." And then he notes, "The child's developing purposiveness . . . is visible first in the little two-phase and polyphase acts, their time span being only a few seconds. Long-range purpose calls for experience and intellectual grasp" (20, p. 39). Woodworth's emphasis upon the "context-proneness" of small units of behavior is an attractive idea, and indeed he may be rather more conservatively an empiricist than he need be in assuming that "purpose," or what I should prefer to call the intentionality of behavior, comes only through experience. This brings us squarely to the issue of the development of skilled behavior, to which we turn in a moment, but only after the issue of intention has been more fully considered.

The crucial issue in the regulation of intentional action is the opportunity to compare what was intended with what in fact resulted, using the difference between the two as a basis of correction. It is immediately apparent that this is the concept of reafference as a source of regulation in behavior—an idea dating from the pioneering work of von Holst and Mittelstaedt (10), and Bernstein (2).

For Bernstein activity is contrasted with mere movement, in that the former requires the co-ordination and regulation of the latter in the attainment of some particular objective; a ball is to be thrown a certain distance and has a certain weight; or a screwdriver to be turned requires the application through the hand and arm of a certain torque. He says,

All systems which are self-regulating for any given parameter, constant or variable, must incorporate the following elements as minimum requirements:
(1) *effector* (motor) activity, which is to be regulated along the given parameter; (2) *a control element,* which conveys to the system in one way or another the *required value* (S_w) of the parameter which is to be regulated: (3) *a receptor* which perceives the *factual* course of the *value* of the parameter (I_w) and signals it by some means to (4) *a comparator device,* which perceives the discrepancy between the *factual* and *required* values with its magnitude and sign (Δ_w); (5) *an apparatus* which encodes the data provided by the comparator device into correctional impulses which are transmitted by feedback linkages to (6) *a regulator* which controls the function of the *effector* along the given parameter (2, pp. 128–29).

His diagrammatic representation of such a system is shown in Figure 1. Quite plainly, a system of this sort requires the constant comparison of intended action (Bernstein's S_w, or *Sollwert*) with feedback from action accomplished (I_w, or *Istwert*), the two being used to generate the crucial Δ_w,

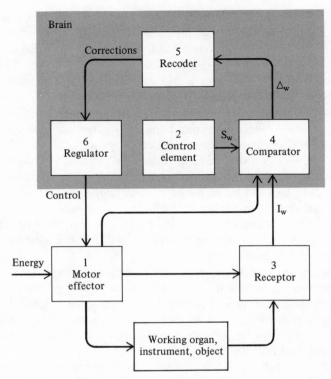

FIGURE 1. Bernstein's model for a system capable of voluntary activity directed toward objects or states of the environment (Modified after Bernstein [2] with permission of Pergamon Press, London.)

or *Deltawert,* that is then converted to a necessary correction. At the center of this system is the course of programs, the control element that signals intention, S_w.

When one observes the early behavior of infants—say at the onset of visually guided reaching at about four months of age—one is struck by the extent to which intentionality precedes skill. Arousal of intention, I would urge, is the initial reaction to an appropriate stimulus. We shall postpone until later how one may determine what constitutes appropriateness. Often, in response to an appropriate stimulus, there are evoked preparatory activities that later will make possible the performance of an adaptive act toward an object. Before the infant can reach, the presentation of an object with sharp contours and good binocular and movement parallax will induce antigravitational activity in the arms, opening and closing of the hands, and even working of the mouth. The last is particularly interesting, since it is to the mouth that the first object grasped under visual guidance will be taken.

It is under the control of an object-directed intention that the modular acts of a skill are serially organized. It is this persistent intention that precedes, directs, and provides a criterion for terminating an act. In this sense, the serial structure of skilled action is, in Lashley's (13) celebrated term, *"atemporal."* Recall that Lashley was particularly concerned to dismiss the idea of chaining as a basis for the organization of serial skilled action, and his general proposal was that it had the properties of syntactically controlled language. "Syntax is not inherent in the words employed or in the idea to be expressed. It is a generalized pattern imposed upon the specific acts as they occur" (13, p. 119). For Lashley, this is one of the three sets of events to be accounted for:

First, the activation of the expressive elements (the individual words or adaptive acts) which do not contain the temporal relations. Second, the determining tendency, the set, or idea. This masquerades under many names in contemporary psychology, but is, in every case, an inference from the restriction of behaviour within definite limits. Third, the syntax of the act (13, p. 122).

It is the second of Lashley's trio, the determining tendency, that we have been considering under the label, intention. The issues of activation of component acts and the syntax of skill remain to be considered.

The constituents of skilled action, the component acts that are contained in the larger pattern, appear to come in their earliest development from two sources. A third source (discussed below) is completely ruled out. One source is the innate repertoire of action patterns that are evoked by appropriate interaction with the environment: the shifting of an object from one hand to another, the use of index finger to touch and explore small inhomogeneities, and so forth. These acts appear in full but awkward completeness, gradually are shaped in a fashion described below, and then are incorporated into longer sequences. A second source of constituents is the differentiation of initially gross acts into component elements, the infant adapting these gross acts by segmentation, to the spatiotemporal structure of new tasks. The segments then achieve independence from their original context and become available for inclusion in new sequences (Bruner, 3, 4).

The one source from which component acts in early skilled behavior do not come is from the repertory of hand-arm reflexes. The skilled behavior we are describing is not effected by the beautifully precise set of reflexes described so carefully by Twitchell (17)—traction grasping, touch-evoked grasp reflex, touch-evoked avoidance-withdrawal, nonvisual groping, and tonic-neck reflex. One can observe the dissolution of these reflex patterns, I believe, in the diffuse, athetoid motion of the infant's arms and hands as an object enters his manipulatory space, motions that are pointed in the general direction of the object, as is the gaze. The beginning of manual skill is this diffusely directional awkwardness, minimally constrained. It is from this early pattern that specific patterns emerge, sometimes as specific bits of behavior, sometimes in more orderly and predictable forms of differentiation.

For Bernstein (2) the achievement of control always involves a reduction of, or "mastery" over, degrees of freedom in the action system being regulated. There are joints and tendons in fingers, wrists, elbows, shoulders, and trunk that can operate independently of each other. A tool can slip this way or that. We shall shortly see instances in which mastery in a given task requires the reduction of such freedom. Within this reduced range, with its characteristic awkwardness, there is a gradual consolidation and mastery. This is the process of modularization, whereby an act is made more automatic, less variable, and achieves a predictable spatiotemporal patterning. Bruner, Bruner, and Kahneman (6) find, for example, that as the child progresses in his reaching for objects, the time required for different kinds of reaches becomes uniform—whether one-handed or two, near reach or far, large object or small. This is the modularization through which innate or differentiated action patterns go.

It is when modularization is achieved and the act becomes smoothly organized, that it then goes through a process of being incorporated into new, more inclusive, and more complex serial patterns. It becomes awkward in its new context. (It is, by the way, hard to escape the conclusion that infant ungainliness or awkwardness is a highly species-specific pattern in human beings as well as the adult response of being touched by a display of such awkwardness.) Why is modularization so essential a preliminary to the inclusion of an act in a more inclusive, more extended routine? I believe it is a matter of attentional capacity. Prior to modularization, an act simply takes up all available attention, as we shall see from time data. We note almost on a week-to-week basis how differently infants behave in a task requiring skilled control of behavior. One week a task such as holding a plastic plaque in one hand while capturing a pearl attached to its center consumes an extraordinary amount of concentrated energy for as long as 30 seconds, even when it leads to failure (the infant handing the plaque from the power grip of one hand to that of the other, unable to form a precision grip or a probe with forefinger); a fortnight later the infant can bring the whole feat off effortlessly in a few seconds.

Once attention is freed, then a new pattern emerges. The new pattern appears in general to take one of three forms. It may be in the form of a more inclusive, rather grossly regulated repetitive sequence of which the previously perfected subroutine is a part. Instead of taking possession of one object with a single hand while the other remains inactive, now the infant takes one and then another object, first with one hand, then with the other. It is a striking change toward inclusion of the single element in a syntactically organized sequence. The objective changes from singular concentration on getting an object to getting both objects. Usually at the outset, the single component acts are more clumsily performed, principally because attention appears to be distributed over a longer sequence and too little is available for the single act.[2]

More typically, a larger act with a more remote goal takes control of the newly modularized acts. Again, we shall see examples, one of the most interesting being the emergence of deposit-and-storage techniques in taking possession of objects, where the taking of an object is not for possession, but for possession within a sphere of control.

Finally, the process of inclusion consists of a virtual decomposition and recomposition of the modular act. It consists, in effect, of the initial breaking up of an organized act into more restricted components with pauses between, and then a regrouping of these components into a modified pattern. A striking example is the transformation of initial cup use from a one-step transport of cup edge to mouth, with neither pauses nor readjustments of the cup en route. This is altered to include several pause points for readjusting the surface of the cup to a position parallel to sea level, so to speak, with subsequent moving of the head to meet the cup, and so on. By the time the act has been perfected, it has gone to the point where adjustment of cup to water level and head requirement is continuously monitored and has no pause points at all.

Wherever we have seen the three modes of reorganization—by repetition, by integration, by differentiated elaboration—we have been struck by the complete, if gross, nature of the new form upon its first observed appearance. I find myself deeply impressed, rereading the account that Coghill (8) gives of the emergence of behavior patterns in growth. In the third lecture of his *Anatomy and the Problem of Behaviour,* he writes,

a nervous mechanism is established in *Amblystoma* for some time before the animal responds to stimulation, that this mechanism is such as to conduct impulses to the muscles from the head tailward, and that this order of conduction to the muscles gives the resulting movement locomotor value and thereby becomes the basic principle of both aquatic and terrestrial locomotion. The general pattern of the primary mechanism of walking is, therefore, laid down before the animal can in the least respond to its environment. . . . Accordingly, the normal experience of the animal with respect to the outside world appears to have nothing specifically to do with the determination of the form into which the behaviour of the animal is cast. On the other hand, experience has much to do with determining when and to what extent the potentiality of behaviour shall rise into action (8, pp. 86–87).

[2] The exception seems to be when a new repetitive pattern becomes organized rhythmically—as with banging, where a single bang on the table is followed by a rhythmic series of bangs. Under these circumstances, the behavior appears to be better controlled. But I would not include this rhythmic patterning in the phenomenon here described.

Indeed, the new patterns appear in a preadapted form, a form whose dimensions are laid down in evolutionary history by the selective processes that brought primate evolution to the point of producing *Homo sapiens*. It is for this reason that we must examine early behavior, not only from the point of view of its neurophysiology and its underlying logic, but also from the point of view of its evolutionary function.

Consider now the close detail of some skilled behavior as it first appears.

Taking Possession of Objects

This experiment had as its objective the discovery of the manner in which infants progressed from the first appearance of visually guided reaching for an object at 4 months to the sophisticated control of several objects simultaneously a year later. Forty-nine normal infants served as our subjects, about equally divided in five age groups: 4–5, 6–8, 9–11, 12–14, and 15–17 months.

The procedure was a simple handling task, similar to an item of the Cattell Infant Intelligence Test. A small toy was handed to the right or left hand. When it was taken, a second toy was immediately presented on the side of the full hand. If not taken after 15 or 20 seconds, the second toy was shifted to the midline. A third and then a fourth object was presented at the midline if the child had taken and retained preceding objects handed to him. When, at any point in the four presentations, the child indicated clearly that he would not take the next object, the trial was ended. Each infant at each age had his four trials divided so that half would be done with the left hand initially and half with the right.

The 4- to 5-month-olds were just crossing the threshold from rather diffuse reaching accompanied by swiping, to effective, visually directed reaching. Two of the subjects in this group, though intensely attracted by the toy and visibly activated by its presence, were never able to achieve an adequately co-ordinated reach-grasp to get the toy. Others could direct their reaches precisely enough to get the object, but could not hold it for more than a brief moment. Children of this age were, for the most part, unable to deal with more than one object at a time. A second toy would either be ignored or, more probably, would so pre-empt attention that the child would drop the toy already in hand as he fastened visually on the new one being presented. The loss of grasp seemed inadvertent, appearing to take place when the child's attention went to the new object. The original object was retained most often when it had begun a journey to the mouth. On two-thirds of the presentations, where capture occurred, the infant took the toy to his mouth and often the mouth was open during reaching or retrieving. The role of the mouth is nicely illustrated in Figure 2 which attests to the sharp decline during the year in the times the mouth is

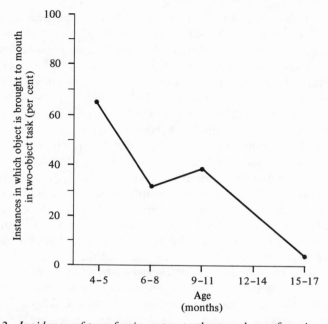

FIGURE 2. Incidence of transferring a toy to the mouth as a function of age

used as destination—a decline from two-thirds at 4.5 months to less than 5 per cent at 16 months.

Six- to eight-month-olds present a sharp contrast to the younger children. All of them had clear command of simple reaching and grasping in their initial performance and were not only able to take and hold a single object, but were able to maintain control of that first object while taking and holding a second as well. The simple reach and grasp could now be embedded in several modes of approaching the toy. They could, for one, transfer an object to the empty hand in order to free the full hand for another reach. This would most often occur after the new object had been presented several times on the side of the initially full hand. Hand-to-hand transfer had a precursor: The child would take a first object to the midline, holding it with both hands. When a second was presented, he would reach for it with the nearest hand. Gradually, this would often differentiate into anticipatory hand-over. Infants also took the second object by reaching across with the empty opposite hand, either traversing the midline slightly or reorienting it. But while all the children were able to deal eventually with two objects on at least two of their four trials, only one of them was ever able to deal with three objects successfully and then only on one of the four trials. If the barrier for the youngest subject was in going beyond one object, the barrier for our six- to eight-month-olds was in going beyond two objects.

But note that the old program of coping with objects has not been stamped out. It is very much there. On a third of the presentations of a second object, the infant drops the one he is holding. Yet, a new program has emerged, and its rules are strikingly powerful by comparison with the old one. It includes features for holding an object in one hand while reaching with the other, handing an object off from one hand to the other, and so on. But for all its productivity in dealing with objects placed now on one side of the midline, now on the other, it is limited to a very small store of constituents, involving two hands and one mouth.

With 9- to 11-month-olds, it is immediately apparent that something new has been acquired. While a majority is not able to take up a third object initially, a significant minority is eventually able to push through to success in taking a third and even a fourth object into possession. In about one in five trials the initial response to a third or fourth object is to deposit one object from the hand either into the lap or onto one of the armrest shelves of the chair. Let it be noted, however, that this response of putting an object in reserve is sporadic and that the length of the storage is not very long. Indeed, half of the deposited toys were retrieved immediately after being deposited. For the use of storage involves, at the outset, several conflicting elements that are amenable to inclusion in one of two continuing programs. As part of the deposit-and-store routine, the object must be put down. But the put down object then evokes a visually guided reach, particularly since it is adjacent to the hand that has deposited it. The factor that finally resolves the conflict is, of course, capacity to delay. Before a deposited object can be stored, there must be capacity to delay

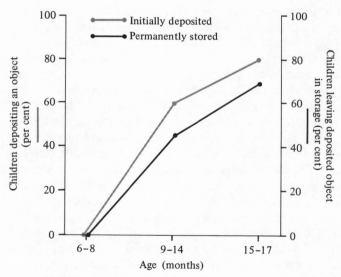

FIGURE 3. Number of objects initially deposited and permanently stored by children of different ages

responding to it and a carry-over of the intention to take an object that had been presented elsewhere and that must be re-engaged now. It is much like the phenomenon of embedding in sentence formation, where an embedded clause is uttered, and then the embedded sentence resumed. It is not surprising then that only a third of the 9- to 11-month-olds dealt successfully through storage with more than two objects.

By 12 months, storage is far better developed and has become so well established that it serves (as the mouth did earlier) as a terminus of expectations. Not only do we find one-year-old infants handing off the toy to the hand on the other side of the midline, but doing so before a second object is presented, in preparation for its appearance on a predicted side. These children, moreover, place an object in storage before the third or the fourth object is handed to them.

Note in Figure 3 that not only does the incidence of deposit increase with age, but that the proportion of objects deposited that remain stored to the end of the task similarly increases until finally more than three-quarters are left. Yet, the one-year-olds still have their old routines and, given the wrong circumstances, they still can slip back into an earlier program.

But there are some real differences between the two oldest groups. The 15- to 17-month-olds are much more consistently successful than the immediately younger subjects. The 12- to 14-month-olds handle a mean of 3.0 objects successfully while the oldest subjects handle 3.7 objects. That much is not surprising; another change is less obvious and more interesting. It is a change in mode of storage. The oldest subjects not only store consistently from trial to trial but store in one way consistently, unlike the 12- to 14-month-olds who use any mode at any time.

One additional feature of the program is added with the two oldest groups, more general substitution rules for deposit and storage that can now include another human being. Of objects stored by the 9- to 12-month-olds, 94 per cent are deposited in the lap or on the arm of a chair. This figure drops sharply to one-quarter for the 12- to 14-month-olds; with them, over three-quarters of objects stored are handed for safekeeping either to the experimenter or to the mother. The same preference is found in the oldest group, some of whom have gone back to using a chair arm, possibly now finding agents less of a novelty.

By the time the child reaches 1.5 years, the behavior in the task we used has the appearance of great skill, even aplomb. In fact, it has gone through a long process of transformation, involving a series of constituent acts embedded in a program that governs their serial order. Much in this progress is the result of learning, particularly the anticipatory elements; but much involves the appearance of routines that clearly could not have been learned in any conventional sense, though they needed to be shaped (as with anticipation) or integrated (as with leaving an object in storage rather than retrieving it immediately).

But before we become too deeply involved in interpreting these data, let us consider another set in which the picture is much less one of integration of constituent acts, and much more of the order of differentiation of constituents, followed by their reintegration.

Acquisition of Complementary Two-Handedness

The skill we examine now is one that is both convenient experimentally and of interest in its own right from a biological and evolutionary point of view. It is the infant's acquisition of the complementary use of his two hands with a division of labor between them. In our experiment the child is presented with a box having a transparent lid that reveals a toy inside it. The lid is mounted on sliding ball bushings so that, in order to remove the toy, the child must slide the lid up its track (which is tilted 30 degrees from horizontal) and hold it open. The interior of the box is well illuminated by a concealed cove light. The box is pictured in Figure 4. The most expedient way for the child to get the toy is to slide the lid up and hold it

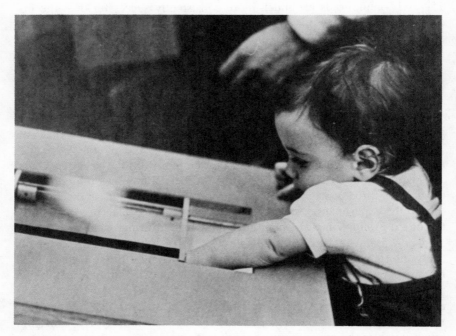

FIGURE 4. Two-handed obstacle box for studying the complementary role of right and left hands (Dimensions of the box: length, 22–25 inches; width, 16 inches; maximum height, 5 inches; minimum height, 1.25 inches. Dimensions of the sliding lid: 8.5 x 6 inches.)

with one hand and to reach inside for the toy with the other. Thus, the skillful child uses one hand as the holder, the other as retriever, the work of the two being sequenced with all constituents in order.

The same subjects studied before (with the exception of the four- to five-month-olds) were used again. Each infant came into the laboratory with his mother and was seated in her lap before the apparatus. A small toy was visible inside the box. The temptation invariably succeeded; the infant attempted as best he could to get the toy. If the infant got the toy from the box, he was permitted to play with it for 15 to 30 seconds, after which it was gently taken from him and replaced in the box. If retrieval was again successful, four further trials were given, for a total of six. The same toy was used throughout—a brightly colored plastic shape. No limit of time was placed on the trials, and they might last as long as 3 minutes. Six trials were given to each child.

It will come as no surprise that success increased with age, from less than a fifth of the trials ending well in the youngest subjects, to somewhat better than half in the next group, to close to nine in ten in the two oldest groups. But much more interesting than the changing frequency of success is the morphology of failure at different points in skill development. For it is in the altered nature of failure that one sees most vividly the differentiation of a gross act into a set of recombinable constituents.

The first approach to the object in the box is direct, a generalized approach behavior that takes little account of the manipulable features of the barrier. It consisted in clawing and banging at the barrier, on a direct line to the object—a matter to be discussed at greater length in a later section. Eloquent testimony to the decline in such behavior is contained in Figure 5, where episodes of barrier banging are plotted for different age groups. Note that barrier banging among the young may become autonomous—a new end in itself. So often our youngest subject, presented with a task, will deal with failure by redefining the nature of the task, varying the end objective rather than holding it constant while varying the means. I believe this to be the heart of play, and its function is to explore means-end relationships without undue commitment. But that is a matter beyond the scope of this paper.

A second form of failure consisted in opening and closing the sliding lid without reaching for the object; each opening and return to the closed position of the sliding lid with no intervening reach counted as an incident. The average number of such incidents is shown in Table 1. We believe this opening and closing also becomes autonomous since the child is diverted from the goal.

Note that autonomous opening was most frequent in the second youngest group of subjects—some four episodes per trial. There were two children in this group who never succeeded in retrieving the toy from beneath the sliding barrier; and it is an interesting fact that the same two showed

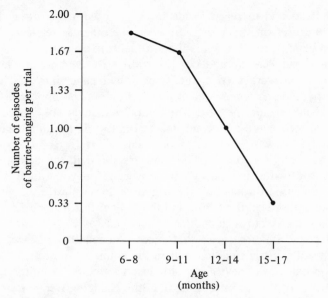

FIGURE 5. Changes in frequency of barrier banging as a function of age

no autonomous opening of the box. If we take the children in this group who were most successful on the task, they too showed relatively little autonomous opening (an average of 16 instances over the 6 trials). It was the five middlingly successful children in this group who were most prone to autonomous opening (an average of 26 instances per child).

The significance of this autonomous activity is in the extent to which it breaks away from the original intention of object capture. Requiring much concentrated attention as it does, it seems in process to achieve its own end. It is not, as with banging at the barrier, a response in failure—but rather an isolation of a step toward success.

Perhaps the simplest or most primitive successful approach to the task is one that, in effect, involves only a single hand, the other remaining inac-

TABLE 1 Mean Number of Incidents of
Autonomous Opening per Child
as a Function of Age

Age (months)	Average Number of Incidents of Autonomous Opening per Child Per Trial
6–8	2.7
9–11	4.1
12–14	1.7
15–17	1.9

tive. The lid is slid up and the toy captured by the same hand. The hand which raised the lid must be inserted in the opening before the lid falls. This is usually accomplished with a kind of worming action rather than a darting one, extricating the toy against the wedging action of the free-sliding lid. The frequency of such one-handed attempts is shown in Table 2. Note that the highest frequency is seen in the second group.

TABLE 2 Mean Number of One-Handed Reaches per Child per Trial as a Function of Age

Age (months)	Average Number of One-Handed Reaches per Child per Trial
6–8	0.27
9–11	0.95
12–14	0.48
15–17	0.42

But as is so often the case, in spite of the fact that the two oldest groups can use many more proficient techniques (as we shall see), they still occasionally use the one-handed worming technique. It is still very much part of their repertoire, although we have little idea of what conditions evoke it.

The least adept of the two-handed strategies appears in several variants. In effect, the general approach involves raising the lid with one or two hands, then going for the toy inside the box with one or two hands, but not holding the lid in the open position long enough to get in and out of the box efficiently. Both hands are involved, but with an inadequate sequencing of component acts. The incidence is not great—a little over one in six reaches in the 12- to 14-month range—but it is interesting as a case where the constituents are present, but the sequence of their execution is either confused or badly timed. It is, in a word, slightly apraxic.

Complementary two-handed reaching is much more prevalent where virtually all the necessary constituents have become differentiated and reintegrated into an effective performance. It involves the joint use of both hands to slide the lid, retaining it in an open position with one hand, while the toy is retrieved from the box with the other. The incidence of this partially complementary two-handed reach is seen in Table 3. The sequence is well organized, but the differentiation is not yet complete. Differentiation is achieved when the infant raises the lid with one hand and holds it open while the other hand retrieves the object. Not surprisingly, it shows a sharp rise in incidence after the first birthday.

From here on, the improvement that occurs with age is not one of strategy, but one of consolidating the complementary two-handed strategy, rendering it less effortful and quicker by the increasing use of the tips of the

TABLE 3 *Mean Number of Partially Complementary Two-Handed Reaches per Child per Trial as a Function of Age*

Age (months)	Average Number of Partially Complementary Two-Handed Reaches per Child per Trial
6–8	0.06
9–11	0.15
12–14	0.20
15–17	0.37

fingers and hands with an attendant decrease in the involvement of arms and trunk for lifting. In effect, by 1.5 years, the act we have studied is well structured, and differentiated, if not yet well mastered: It still exhibits striking variability in time required. Because it still requires a considerable concentration of effort, it probably is not readily embedded into a more complex act of which it might become a component.

For the most part, the children do not gradually improve their approach, but rather increase the skill with which they perform old routines. Learning over the six trials seems to take the form of consolidating or perfecting constituent acts over which the child already has some mastery at the start. Two-handed efforts made their appearance abruptly rather than by some gradual route and seemed to be ready for triggering. It is only after a new response appears that it goes through consolidation and shaping by the opportunities provided by practice. Its initial emergence on the scene as an organized response—in any of the forms of strategy we have reported—seems independent of the practice of that organization. Some of the components, indeed, have been practiced, but not the new pattern. It is in this respect, we believe, that the long evolutionary history of complementary bimanual skill provides a set of preadaptive patterns that emerge, not by trial and error, but in response to appropriate environmental events. These events are not so much releasers as operative requirements that are finally appreciated. Given the intention of capturing an object, it is not until a certain level of skill has been attained that the requirement of two hands is apprehended. Two-handedness then occurs in organized form, if somewhat crudely. Perhaps this is the only way so much skill can be achieved so soon with effector organs (like the hands) marked by so many degrees of freedom of movement and challenged by such a wide range of tasks.

Detour Reaching

An infant sits in an adult's lap before a table, with a screen extending halfway across the field to approximately the infant's midline. A toy is presented to the infant in the open space and then put behind the screen, where its jingling identifies its position if the screen is not transparent. This simple outline of our experiment we varied in many ways to check a number of hypotheses about detour reaching. (These concern us here only incidentally.) As a result, 120 infants were needed as subjects, equally divided into three groups: young with median age of 34 weeks, middle with a median of 51 weeks, and oldest with a median of 69 weeks.

Several evident changes occur with growth. One is, of course, that the older the child the greater the likelihood of direct success—reaching in behind the barrier with the hand on the open side of the screen and getting the toy. The difference between ages is modulated by the depth of the object behind the screen. In general, the middle positions distinguish the different ages the most sharply, since objects in the open are easy for all, and deeply embedded objects rather more difficult for all. Figure 6 demonstrates this point.

Again we learn more about the acquisition of skill from clumsiness en route to perfection. The first locus of clumsiness is in activation; Figure 7 indicates a source of difficulty that comes precisely from the nature of activation in this task. It shows that initial activation in the task comes on the side where the toy has been placed—either heard jingling or seen through the transparent screen.

What the activated hand is trying to do is to get directly at the objective

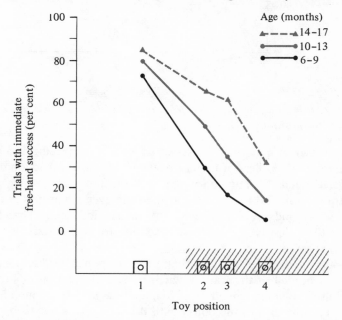

FIGURE 6. Success on detour reaching problem as a function of toy position and age

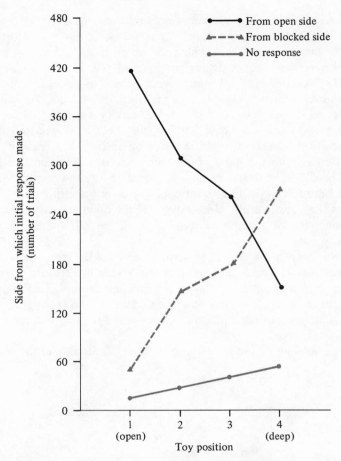

FIGURE 7. Frequency of approach from open and blocked side of detour as a function of toy position

—and in the great majority of cases when the object is well off to one side of the midline, regardless of the age of the child. Again, reaction differs at each age, depending upon the width of the detour. The young start by going straight forward at the toy half the time even when it is at the edge of the screen: and they do so with the screen-side hand. That figure is halved in the oldest children. These reactions are summarized in Figure 8 for the transparent screen.

To understand better what the pattern of response is like, a closer description is needed of the way in which infants proceed on this task. The typical initial response, found most frequently among the 8-month-olds, is a direct reaching toward the object with the screen-side hand, followed by initial scratching or banging at the barrier, followed by quitting. The contralateral hand may even be brought in to help in scrabbling against the

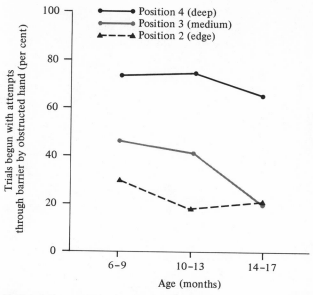

FIGURE 8. *Trials begun with direct approach to toy by screen-side hand as a function of age*

barrier, though it could easily pass behind the barrier and take the object. Sometimes the screen-side ipsilateral hand will move to the edge of the screen, go around it in a clumsy backhand and capture the object while the contralateral hand sits idly by. In the next stage, there is initial activation again of the hand ipsilateral to the toy, a move at the barrier, and then recruitment of the contralateral hand that moves behind the screen to take the toy. About a third of the trials of the 1-year-olds are of this pattern and a quarter of the 17 monthers. There is a decreasing lag in time between ipsilateral activation and contralateral execution of the intention to capture. Finally, there is a pattern of direct reaching for the object with the hand on the open side of the screen, by far the majority response among the oldest infants. The three response patterns are summed up in Figure 9.

Plainly, then, the acquisition of detour reaching begins from a baseline of visual straight-line reaching with the hand nearest the object sought. Three factors work against the replacement of this initial reaching rule. One is the continued power of ipsilateral activation which, when combined with a second rule, crowds out a contralateral approach. The second rule is to keep in operation the program that has been started—hence the awkward backhand reaching as well as the recruitment of the contralateral hand for attacking the boundary. Third, there is conflict (particularly with the transparent screen) from the tendency to be guided by visual criteria rather than by instrumental ones. In this case, the visual display (including

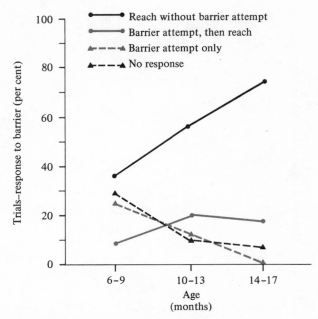

FIGURE 9. Types of reach pattern in relation to age

one's hands) counteracts the tendency to use the instrumentally relevant hand.

It is important to note that there are two programs operating, both fairly open to adaptation—the direct visual ipsilateral program and the operational contralateral one. Each uses, in effect, the same set of constituent subroutines of reaching, grasping, and so forth. We have no basis for believing that learning in any conventional sense of the word leads to a shift from one strategic program to the other. We have counterbalanced our design in such a way that some 24 infants served to randomize out screentype used, order of screen position, age, and so on. Each child in the experiment received 16 trials. There is no indication whatsoever of any learning curve for any age, any position, any screen. The data for the completely counterbalanced subgroup are contained in Figure 10.

I am not proposing that learning or experience affects eventual mastery of the detour task. Rather, the effect of experience is to mature new response systems which at first are slow and crude so that they may be evoked by appropriate tasks. Experience also serves to shape them; but it does not create them. Indeed, the anomaly is this; it is at the point where the old system begins to work smoothly and achieve goals sought that it is most likely to be superseded by a new, initially more clumsy one.

Finally, let me note that, in the present task, strategies or programs continue to coexist and occasionally to get into conflict. There is one element

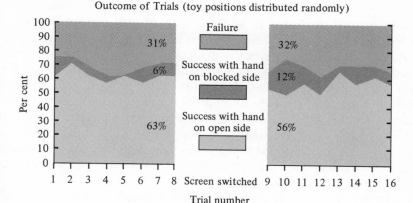

FIGURE 10. *Results of experiment with subgroup where age, screen type used, and screen position were randomized* (The results provide no evidence of learning.)

in skill acquisition that is best called inhibition, suppressing old reaction patterns that continue to intrude. In the present instance, where two programs (visually dominant reaching and indirect instrumental reaching) share common constituents, the requirement of such inhibition is the greater. If our task had had the requirement of real-time operation in the millisecond range, performance would have been doomed by the conflict that existed even in successful performance.

The Tracking of Events

At the outset, we remarked upon the difference in precocity between head-eye tracking and the visually guided manipulation, noting the early evident preadaptation if the former case (see Salapatek, 16; Kessen, 12; Fantz, 9). Yet, though there is a difference in precocity, there are certain likenesses in program that are of some interest. The following experiment, a joint effort of Mundy-Castle and Anglin (14), makes this clearer.

A baby, from ten days to five months, is comfortably seated in The Harvard chair (described briefly on page 273) 20 degrees reclining from upright and well supported by breech-and-belly cloth. Before him at eye level and 12 inches away are two windows side by side, each subtending about 30 degrees of visual arc with 10 degrees between. In these windows a beautifully jeweled ball makes successive appearances—6 seconds in one window, then after a disappearance of 3.5 seconds, 6 seconds in the other window. Record is kept of where the infant is looking, as well as of some measures such as heart rate, breathing, and gross movement.

Between ten days and three months, three separate patterns emerge. The first is one in which the baby simply looks more at the windows than else-where in the room, but with the discernible correlation between where he is looking and where the jeweled ball is appearing. The second pattern is one in which initially the infant's gaze is directed to where the ball is until, finally, the gaze anticipates where the ball will be. During this phase there is a stuck quality—the baby shifts to the other window and stays there waiting if ahead of the ball. There the gaze remains until the ball disap-pears, when he shifts again. Finally there emerges a pattern in which the baby is plainly monitoring both windows. When no ball is in sight, he may spend the 3.5 second period looking back and forth between the windows; and even, when looking at a ball in one window, he may glance over to the other momentarily as if to check up.

Now, let me urge that this development is comparable to one we have observed in the multiple-object manual task. At the outset the infants in this looking study have an intention to orient, but at first this expresses it-self by the glance staying in the vicinity of the recurring stimulus. It is comparable to orienting to an object, arms raised and working, but with no capability of effecting a specific reach. In the second strategy, they are dealing with one stimulus at a time, "stuck" on it, to use Mundy-Castle and Anglin's phrase. In the third strategy, they are dealing with two alter-native loci and objects at those loci simultaneously.

To be sure, the parallelism is not complete, for indeed we have some in-dication that looking and manipulating have some interesting discontinui-ties. But the formal similarities, I believe, are not accidents. I would urge, as Bernstein (2) has, that all action systems have access to a common stock of programs, programs related to resolving spatial, temporal, relational, and identity problems. Many of these programs are, in Coghill's (8) phrase, "preadapted." And as *Amblystoma's* neural "solution" of locomo-tion in water turns out to be formally identical to the solution of locomo-tion on land, so the solution of the problem of multiplicity has formal identities whether it is the head-eye tracking system or the hand system that is in operation.

As noted at the start, then, the management of skill may be considered as the first realization or embodiment of programs that will be used throughout the life of the organisms, not only for mastery of skilled tasks, but also for problem solving of a kind not usually thought of as skill in the bodily sense. Indeed, the proof of the matter is that, from the infant's perspective, it is difficult to say whether the tasks reported in these pages were instances of skill or of problem solving. Perhaps we would do well in the future to explore wherein they are identical, and what makes them sep-arate. I cannot believe that it suffices to argue simply that thought is action internalized or rendered into symbolic form. The task, rather, is to explore the range of development from the attainment of skill in action to the at-tainment of acumen; in problem solving, to explore in detail the kinship between them and the discontinuities as well. I believe that the skill of the hand, given its place in evolutionary history, may provide the ideal vehicle for such a voyage of exploration.

References

1. BARTLETT, F. C. 1958. *Thinking.* New York: Basic Books.
2. BERNSTEIN, N. A. 1967. *The coordination and regulation of movement.* London: Pergamon.
3. BRUNER, J. S. 1969. *Processes of cognitive growth: infancy.* vol. 3. Heinz Werner Lecture Series, Worcester, Mass.: Clark University Press.
4. BRUNER, J. S. 1971. Origins of problem solving strategies in skill acquisition. In *Logic and art: essays in honor of Roman Jakobson,* ed. R. S. Rudner and I. Scheffler. Indianapolis: Bobbs-Merrill.
5. BRUNER, J. S., and BRUNER, B. M. 1968. On voluntary action and its hierarchical structure. *International Journal of Psychology, 3:*239–55.
6. BRUNER, J. S.; BRUNER, B. M.; and KAHNEMAN, I. The growth of manual intelligence. IV. The psychophysics of cup use. Unpublished study, Center for Cognitive Studies, Harvard University.
7. CLARK, W. E. LeGros. 1959. *The antecedents of man.* Edinburgh, Scot.: Edinburgh University Press.
8. COGHILL, G. E. 1929. *Anatomy and the problem of behaviour.* Cambridge, Eng.: Cambridge University Press.
9. FANTZ, R. L. 1961. The origin of form perception. *Scientific American* 204:66–72.
10. HOLST, E. VON, and MITTELSTAEDT, H. 1950. Das Reafferenzprinzip. *Naturwissenschaften* 37:464–76.
11. JONES, F. W. 1917. *Arboreal man.* New York: Hafner.
12. KESSEN, W. 1967. Sucking and looking: two organized congenital patterns of behavior in the human newborn. In *Early behavior: comparative and developmental approaches,* ed. H. W. Stevenson, E. H. Hess, and H. L. Rheingold, pp. 147–79. New York: Wiley.
13. LASHLEY, K. S. 1951. The problem of serial order in behavior. In *Cerebral mechanisms in behavior: the Hixon symposium,* ed. L. A. Jeffress, pp. 112–46. New York: Wiley.
14. MUNDY-CASTLE, A. C., and ANGLIN, J. M. In press. Looking strategies in infants. In *The competent infant: a handbook of readings,* ed. J. L. Stone, H. T. Smith, and L. B. Murphy. New York: Basic Books.
15. NAPIER, J. R. 1962. The evolution of the hand. *Scientific American* 207:56–62.
16. SALAPATEK, P. 1968. Visual scanning of geometric figures by the human newborn. *Journal of Comparative and Physiological Psychology* 66:247–58.
17. TWITCHELL, T. E. 1965. The automatic grasping response of infants. *Neuropsychologia* 3:247–59.
18. VYGOTSKY, L. S. 1962. *Thought and language,* ed. and trans. E. Hanfmann and G. Vakar. Cambridge, Mass.: MIT Press, and New York: Wiley.
19. WASHBURN, S. L., and HOWELL, F. C. 1960. Human evolution and culture. In *The evolution of man,* vol. 2, ed. S. Tax. Chicago: University of Chicago Press.
20. WOODWORTH, R. S. 1958. *Dynamics of behavior.* New York: Holt.

15

Eye, Hand, and Mind[*]

Six years of research on intellectual and perceptual development in children from the third year of life culminated in the publication of a book, *Studies in Cognitive Growth* (1). In the course of these studies it became apparent that by the time a child has entered his third year, he has developed certain characteristic strategies of processing information. More recently, we have been at work on the first two years of life. Our hope is to explore some of the preliminaries to the growth of mind—to explore that unique set of processes that makes it possible for human beings and no other species to make and use tools and to use language not only for communication but also as an instrument of thought. We are occupied with the growth of those capacities that enable humans to utilize culture as an amplifier of their capacities.

A task of this order would break the spirit unless tamed to manageable and testable proportions. We begin with four traditional, initially intractable questions in the hope of converting them into experimental form. Let me mention them in rough terms to establish our context and then turn to the specific problem with which we shall cope—the integration of eye and hand. All four questions enter into our problem.

The first question concerns the growth of voluntary self-initiated activity, and is as much an issue of neurophysiology as of psychology since it concerns the regulation of anticipatory behavior by corollary discharge or feed-forward mechanisms.

The second question centers on the growth of skill and on the forms of growth and learning that permit the child to overcome the three major sources of human awkwardness—grossness of movement that violates the fine structure of a task, contradictory systems of action clamoring for a single common path, and imperfect or faltering sequencing of component acts required to carry out a skilled task. We shall have a little to say about each of them.

Our third concern is with the organization of perception and attention, particularly with one critical issue: how the perceptual world of the infant, first governed by the features of stimulation, comes eventually to reflect the requirements of manipulation—how, in short, the play of attention alters in time from being afferently dominated to being efferently relevant.

Finally, and perforce, we are concerned with how the growing infant learns in time to orchestrate several previously separate enterprises synergically, whereas at the outset he is so one-track that he can scarcely both look and suck at once (a special matter that relates to the integration of an appetitive and an orientative system).

Let me say that these matters in aggregate—intention, skill, attention, and integration—do not sum to either language or tool use. We think of them as preliminaries to the use of uniquely human cognitive activity and are searching for clues in their development that presage those higher-order functions that link the child with his culture.

The problem we address ourselves to now has to do with the process whereby an infant comes to guide visually the voluntary movement of his hands and, indeed, how he comes to relate the activity of one hand to that of the other under the guidance of vision. It is a process of integration that takes at least two years to complete and the very length and clumsiness of the process may be one important respect in which human beings go beyond their primate ancestry to a uniquely human estate. We have been greatly aided in our studies by the existence of four fine works on the topic, each rather different in objective and approach, but all of great value: the pioneer observations of Piaget on the visually guided reaching of his three children (14); the painstaking analyses of Halverson (7) and of McGraw (13) on infantile prehension; and the controlled observational sampling of White, Castle, and Held (16) on the development of visually directed reaching.

Before treating directly the integration of the world of the hand and the world of vision, there are two preliminaries to be described. The first has to do with the development of human visual attention during the period when prehension is a very primitive and, in the main, autonomous operation unrelated to vision. Let me characterize that growth briefly as moving from a diffuse distractibility in the weeks immediately following birth to a stage of stuckness where attention has an "obligatory character," to use Stechler's phrase (15), to a stage in which it becomes anticipatory and predictive. In the first phase, the infant tends to be pulled hither and yon by objects in the field and particularly by movement in the periphery. Head movements and eye movements at this stage are very coarsely related and compensation between them poor. But as Kessen (10) has so elegantly shown, the ballistic movement of the eye itself is exquisitely accurate even shortly after birth, given a steady head. Though there is distractibility from the outside during the opening weeks of life, the child will show preferences for certain concentric stimulus forms (Koopman and Ames, 11; Fantz, 3), for movement, and for human faces (if not their two-dimensional representations, see Koopman and Ames, 11). To observe these preferences, however, the stimulus field needs considerable stripping down to prevent the infant's distractibility from taking over.

By six weeks, often earlier, an obligatory or stuck pattern has emerged. The infant is now caught by targets that have good figure-ground properties and yield binocular and movement parallax. Head-eye compensation is much improved, and we have seen eight-week-olds trying to pull away from a target (a red ball with black-edged white rings, a black velvet bull's-eye surmounted by a glossy pearl, all well illuminated against a plain background), turning their heads, only to have their eyes remain fastened on the target, eventually drawing their heads back to the midline. When they move off, it is to scan in a rather crudely patterned way until some other target catches them. The attention is directed outward to the stimulus world, in search of something on which to fasten.

Gradually, this pattern changes and the infant, to condense the matter, begins to move easily to anticipated objects—pulling away from one target and going to another that is located many visual degrees away without much intermediate drifting. The child, to use Piaget's term (14), seems to be using a visual schema, placing objects with respect to each other. His attention has now become biphasic in nature—directed outward to the good targets, but guided in change by a primitive internalized schema. Work by Haith (6) suggests that anticipatory looking begins to be learned at birth; and the work of Lipsitt and his colleagues (12) suggests early S-S association or habituation. But it does not seem to be until about 15 or 16 weeks that the child seems well able to detach from one aspect of the stimulus field and move to another with a plan that is geared to finding what was intended rather than coming to rest on what is merely encountered. It is this aspect of functioning that I should like to call biphasic attention. Indeed, work by Graham and Clifton (5) suggests that the biphasic autonomic pattern of the orienting response (indicated, for example, by initial acceleration and subsequent deceleration of heart rate in response to a nonsignal stimulus) does not appear until about the sixth month of life, stimulation producing only the first, accelerated response. There is now some reason to believe that it is the second phase of this orienting that is given over to information processing (rather than information receipt). Kahneman's work suggests that during the second phase (he used pupillary dilation as his measure, which he found to be closely correlated with car- diac deceleration), there may actually be a blocking of information receipt while previously obtained information is being processed. I believe this early development of biphasic attention during the first four or five months of life is crucial, involving as it does not only the regulation of attention placing but also the withdrawing and shifting of attention. These develop- ments occur before there is much precise coordination between hand and eye.

The burden of all this is to suggest that there develops first, before vi- sually guided reaching, an orientative visual matrix in which the seen move- ment of the hand can be appreciated. This matrix involves not only vision proper, but the line of sight as regulated in a compensatory fashion by eye movements and head movements. It is in the light of such a matrix that early hand watching should be understood, for the infant is not only recog- nizing what the hand is, but where it is visually. Two other things are also developing during these opening months. One is the hand-mouth coordina- tion, the baby being able to get hand to mouth in some erratic path by the fifth or sixth day and having the movement well perfected even before guided prehension is on the scene. The other is the vision-mouth anticipa- tion, again the baby's learning very early to open his mouth when the ap- propriate object is visually apprehended. So the mouth, in the classic sense, early can serve as a tertium quid between vision and the hand and, as we shall see, plays an important role as the terminus of guided reaching activity.

Now consider some of the steps en route to manipulative prehension. Let me tell you at the outset that our observations on even the youngest children (six weeks) are made with the child in a slightly reclining (about 30 degrees) but sitting position, in a special, cushioned chair that has a wide, soft elastic band to support the abdomen and another around the chest to support the trunk. This gives great freedom to the head and leaves the arms very much unencumbered. The observations are from approxi- mately six weeks to about eighteen months, always in a supported-sitting or, for the older children, in a free-sitting position.

The first analogue of reaching that we observe when an attractive object is presented to the six- to eight-week-old infant and moved back and forth horizontally through 30 degrees of visual arc at about 10 inches distance from him is a general pumping up or activation response, in which he brings his hands up to the midline but with little bimanual coordination. There are rough swiping movements that constitute a diffuse reaching and that ride atop the massive pumping up of activation. If the child's hand (or hands) happens to strike an object while unfisted, there will be a grasping and a retrieval of the object to the mouth.

If the child touches with a single hand, there is somewhat faster bringing forward of the hand in question a second time when the object is immediately presented again. The unattended hand hangs rather limp. Where there is massive activation, achieved by moving the object between the two raised hands, now touching one and now the other, the child, by the sheer anatomy of outward reaching, will close on the object with both hands and immediately bring it to the mouth, insertion into which terminates the act. Repeating this kind of stimulation facilitates its appearance until activation is too high and there is crying. I should like to emphasize that the two hands are not acting to complement each other, but are in synchrony at the midline. One hand will not cross over the midline to help the other get an object to the mouth or even to get a grasp on it.

Our preliminary observations lead us to believe that a successful carrying out of the sequence, reach-capture-retrieve-mouth, seems to preactivate repetition of the sequence through a corollary discharge or feed forward to the components of the act. Its threshold seems lowered and its components more smoothly articulated. Note that what is grasped is brought directly to the mouth under visual inspection. Let me illustrate the role of the mouth by reference to the protocol of a 16-week-old baby. The baby, having closed both hands around an attractive object held in my hand, brought it to his opened mouth. Before he could get the object into his mouth, I inserted the middle finger of my ball-holding hand between his lips, and he immediately began to suck it, holding firmly to the ball all the while. I removed my finger and the ball after several seconds, holding the ball before him again and moving it from extended hand to extended hand until he closed on it again and drew it to his mouth. But before he could get it there, one hand broke away from the ball and was thrust into his mouth, terminating the retrieving act. The anticipatory mouthing aspect of the retrieval short-circuited the retrieval act, so to speak. The child's mouth had opened typically just as he began to approach the object and served as a kind of anticipatory binding to the grasp and retrieval.

Over the succeeding weeks, indeed until the sixth month or so, there is a better and better coordination of the four-part invariant sequence, reach-grasp-retrieve-mouth, all with visual inspection. The sequence has several interesting features. It is at first mainly successive, with little anticipatory priming of movements. With time, there is more feed forward and priming so that the hand is shaped to grasping as the reach is going forward. One has the strong impression that the mouth, before described as the tertium quid, is priming the sequence by opening in advance.

Moreover, the sequence always ends at the mouth—never, be it noted, before the eyes for closer inspection or for bimanual manipulation. That does not come for another month save in a kind of fortuitous conflict between the two hands asymmetrically holding an object in bimanual possession.

Further, the sequence seems to require for its completion a constant visual surveillance. At seven months, for example, we do the following experiment. The child reaches for an object placed on one side of the midline with the ipsilateral hand. As his hand arrives at the object, we drop a light cloth over his hand and the object. He withdraws his hand empty and begins the reach again, but it is interrupted by the visual absence of the object. By nine months, loss of visual contact will not interrupt the act and the infant's hand emerges from under the masking cloth with the object firmly in hand.

During development, the sequential acts of reaching and grasping seem to require cessation of all other enterprises. Like so much of the child's complex behavior, it involves a total commitment. What is interesting, once visually guided reaching achieves some rough competence, is that attention enters a new phase in its deployment. From diffuse distractibility, through stuckness, through anticipation, attention now moves (usually around seven or eight months) to a phase where it is alternately leading and tracking the moving hand toward objects and in its retrieval of objects —again, with the mouth almost invariably the terminus.

I believe that it is at this stage (about eight months) that the final maturing of visually guided manipulation begins, and it requires several forms of mastery to get there. The first of these has to do with rendering the sequence, reach-grasp-retrieve-mouth, less successive and more anticipatory on the one hand and more differentiated on the other—in a word, less *awkward*. There are, from eight or nine months on, fewer distinctive steps in the sequence and each successive step is primed one or two steps ahead. The steps, moreover, overlap in time and give an increasing sense of smoothness and speed. With respect to differentiation, there is first a gradual dropping out of the first activation or pumping-up, and the baby, by eight months, can begin a reach without tensing the whole torso. There is also an end to little bimanual tugs of war.

Second, there is a freeing of the sequence from mouthing as its terminal phase. When an object is to be brought to the mouth at seven months (or even at fourteen months) the mouth opens wide early in the sequence. But there are occasions at eight or nine months when the infant retrieves so as to explore tactually or visually or kinesthetically (using an object for rhythmic banging, for example). The mouth, having served as tertium quid, by helping knit eye and hand systems, now dominates the sequence less.

Third, there is a gradual freeing of the act from the redundancy of input that was originally needed to sustain it. From one year on, the object does not have to be watched so constantly and visual attention, once the hand starts toward its destination, now moves to a next anticipated locus of action. When we compare the time looking at the hand with object of a 14-month-old with that of a 27-month-old baby during visually directed reaching and retrieving, the proportion drops from nearly three-quarter time to less than quarter time. The difference at 27 months is spent, literally, in looking ahead. But both ages, 14 and 27 months, share a certainty in the joint handling of visual and kinesthetic-proprioceptive information from the hand. At 7 months, our specially made films show many episodes in which, while the infant is trying to get hold of a moderately heavy drinking cup, he will literally shut his eyes while bringing his hands together on the cup, particularly if a previous, visually guided effort has failed. So we can say that the first effort is to map the kinesthetic-proprioceptive field of the hand on the visual orientation field (with the help of the mouth), and the second task is to utilize the redundancy of the two fields to free the task from constant visual supervision, so that visual anticipation of action may develop.

Fourth, there is a gradual process of learning bimanual, complementary activity. This is indeed a mysterious process. Piaget (14) urges that it is produced by the clasped hands pulling against each other. I think this is a necessary but not a sufficient condition. It leads to their conjugate or antagonist action, but not to the kind of complementary action where one hand holds something for the other to pick up. Here a word must be said about the mysterious midline barrier. It is a strict one at seven months. If a toy is held before the hand of an infant after he has already grasped something in that hand, the contralateral hand will not reach across the midline to get it. The ipsilateral hand will tense and the infant will bang the new object with a clenched hand holding the original object. Or if an object is hidden beneath a cloth on one side of the midline, the infant will struggle for it with the hand on that side, the contralateral hand lying on its side unattended and unaiding. Perhaps there is what Geschwind (4) calls a "disconnexion syndrome" with insufficient commissural fibers. But I suggest there is exercise needed even after the fibers are connected. The nature of this exercise remains uncertain. It is well to remember a few salient facts about bimanual operations before taking its development too much for granted as mere maturation. Held and Bauer (8) have shown that when infant monkeys are reared without view of their hands, they are not able to reach for and grasp visible objects with the newly seen limb. Moreover, if the experience is given to the animal that is requisite for learning how to reach and grasp with one hand, there is minimum transfer to the other hand when it is brought out from under the masking ruff. This had been found previously in studies of adaptation to prismatic displacement in adult humans, adaptation of one hand's not crossing over to the other (Efstathiou, Bauer, Greene, and Held, 2). Moreover, when both hands of the specially reared infant monkeys were freed and were open to visual guidance, the first one trained was favored and little or no complementary activity was observed. Recall that these animals had previously carried out visually unguided bimanual activities under the masking ruff, and also that the experimental monkeys, when tested, were twice as old as normally reared monkeys who had visually guided bimanual reaching completely under control.

Fifth, from about seven months onward there is a slow but steady dissociation of the gestural components involved in visually guided reaching from the goal-directed sequence noted before as beginning with activation and ending with mouthing. These gestural components might almost be considered the elements to be combined in a syntax of action. Consider some examples. We present an infant with a grasping toy, to one or another side of the midline so as to reduce conflict. As he begins to reach, we cover the toy from view with a dropcloth that is attached to the table along the edge opposite to the one at which the infant is seated. The only way that the child can remove the cloth from over the object is either to lift it directly up and reach under, or to push the cloth away from him. We know from other experiments that both acts are in the repertory of children of the ages we observe. Now, with a seven- to nine-month-old, neither of these acts occurs (or very rarely occurs and then only in precocious children). In infants of this age, to begin with, the whole act of removing the cloth and getting the toy is carried out unilaterally (as already noted), and this precludes success in lifting, though attempts at lifting are quite rare at that. What one never observes is pushing away of the covering cloth—whether one uses an opaque or a semitransparent dropcloth. The response in the great majority of instances is an attempt to pull the cloth toward one—in much the same way as one draws the object toward one. Indeed, one is struck by the fact that in the seven-month-old, the act of attempting to remove the screen is hardly distinguishable from the act of reaching for the object. Pushing away is a response that is tied to rejection (as any parent can testify who has attempted to feed the child an unfavored food). It cannot be dissociated from that goal-directed sequence and inserted in a sequence involved in retrieving a desired object. In this sense we may speak of growth's involving a dissociation of gestural components from goal-directed sequences. The fourteen- to sixteen-month-old has begun to master such dissociation.

Yet it is interesting that en route to this achievement there is an awkward stage in which there seems to be conflict between the retrieve and uncover responses—looking for all the world like a flailing of the arm back and forth in the frontal-lateral line, firmly gripping the dropcloth in hand.

Let me now sum up in a few words. At the outset, there is a growth of biphasic attention that permits the child to register on salient object cues and to anticipate where other objects are so that one can move to them directly. This makes possible not only attention to a specific object but also orderly withdrawal and shift of attention to other objects. This development during the first three or four months involves not only the purely visual field, but also the orientation of the eyes, head, and body toward visual objects. Concurrently, the mouth becomes a kind of common terminus for both visual and manual-kinesthetic anticipation. The child learns to anticipate the visual approach of objects to the mouth, and learns to put his own hands in his mouth. The mouth now becomes a kind of tertium quid between vision and manual movement. As the child's initially gross activation response to visual objects becomes sufficiently differentiated to yield a successful open-handed reach-with-contact, he begins visually guided reaching-grasping-retrieving—the sequence always culminating in mouthing. The act and its components are now dominated by mouthing as an anticipated goal response. Learning during this stage leads to better anticipation, a more integrated act, and finer differentiation.

Full development of visually guided reaching begins with freeing the sequence of reaching-grasping-retrieving from its terminal phase of mouthing. It is freed, also, from the requirement of full visual inspection and control, freed by feed forward of its slow successiveness, and its component gestures are freed from a fixed sequence. The component acts of reaching, grasping, and retrieving now become subroutines able to fit into a variety of other activities with which they can become integrated. An infant's visually guided prehensile career starts in the service of hand-to-mouth operations and gradually acquires a freedom for use in a variety of contexts that the environment has to offer.

References

1. BRUNER, J. S.; OLVER, R. R.; GREENFIELD, P. M.; et al. 1966. *Studies in cognitive growth*. New York: Wiley.
2. EFSTATHIOU, A.; BAUER, J.; GREENE, M.; and HELD, R. 1967. Altered reaching following adaptation to optical displacement of the hand. *Journal of Experimental Psychology* 73:113–20.
3. FANTZ, R. L. 1965. Ontogeny of perception. In *Behavior of nonhuman primates,* vol. 2, ed. A. M. Schrier, H. F. Harlow, and F. Stollnitz. New York: Academic Press.
4. GESCHWIND, N. 1965. Disconnexion syndromes in animals and man, parts 1 and 2. *Brain* 88:237–94, 585–644.
5. GRAHAM, F. K., and CLIFTON, R. K. 1966. Heart rate change as a component of the orienting response. *Psychological Bulletin* 65:305–20.
6. Haith, M. M. 1966. The response of the human newborn to visual movement. *Journal of Experimental Psychology* 3:235–43.
7. HALVERSON, H. M. 1931. An experimental study of prehension in infants by means of systematic cinema records. *Genetic Psychology Monographs* 10:107–284.
8. HELD, R., and BAUER, J. A., JR. 1967. Visually guided reaching in infant monkeys after restricted rearing. *Science* 155:718–20.
9. KAHNEMAN, D.; TURSKY, B.; SHAPIRO, D.; and CRIDER, A. 1969. Pupillary dilation, heart rate, skin resistance changes during a mental task. *Journal of Experimental Psychology* 70(1):164–67.

10. KESSEN, W. 1967. Sucking and looking: two organized congenital patterns of behavior in the human infant. In *Early behavior: comparative and developmental approaches,* ed. H. W. Stevenson, E. H. Hess, and H. L. Rheingold. New York: Wiley.

11. KOOPMAN, P. R., and AMES, E. W. 1967. Infants' preferences for facial arrangements: a failure to replicate. Presented at Biennial Meeting of the Society for Research in Child Development, New York, 1967.

12. LIPSITT, L. 1967. Learning in the human infant. In *Early behavior: comparative and developmental approaches,* ed. H. W. Stevenson, E. H. Hess, and H. L. Rheingold. New York: Wiley.

13. McGRAW, M. B. 1941. Neural maturation as exemplified in the reaching-prehensile behavior of the human infant. *Journal of Psychology* 11:127–41.

14. PIAGET, J. 1952. *The origins of intelligence in children.* New York: International Universities Press.

15. STECHLER, G., and LATZ, E. 1966. Some observations on attention and arousal in the human infant. *Journal of the American Academy of Child Psychiatry* 5(3):517–25.

16. WHITE, B. L.; CASTLE, P.; and HELD, R. 1964. Observations on the development of visually-directed reaching. *Child Development* 35:349–64.

16

On Voluntary Action
and Its Hierarchical Structure*

It is quite apparent that many biological systems operate from the outset as hierarchically organized wholes by their very nature. But it is also true that some systems achieve such structure slowly and haltingly. In early human growth, the initially well-organized systems seem to be predominantly of the automatic or overcontrolled type as with breathing, swallowing, and initial sucking. With a minimum of initial priming, all three of these are potentiated easily and go off in appropriate ways to appropriate stimulation. Moreover, from the start they appear to be embedded smoothly into a larger context of action. A newborn can suck, swallow, and breathe, not contemporaneously, but in a fashion that is beautifully intercalated as to leave little doubt of the role of a pre-established central nervous system in the production of this synergy. Indeed, it can properly be argued without unseemly teleology that crucial biological systems requiring little plasticity generally have such pre-established organization,

* "On Voluntary Action and Its Hierarchical Structure," by Jerome S. Bruner and Blanche M. Bruner. Reprinted from the *International Journal of Psychology,* 1968, *3,* 239–255, by permission of the International Union of Psychological Science and DUNOD, Publisher, France.

Paper presented at the Symposium on New Perspectives in the Sciences of Man, Alpbach, Austria, June, 1968.

selected precisely to assure regulation of functions crucial for gross survival within fairly narrow limits of environmental variability. They are, in the main, systems involving relatively little information processing and in their most specialized version are regulated by the autonomic nervous system. Such systems characteristically show little awkwardness during growth.

Obviously, certain general principles of action do not vary from one type of system to the other. Even at the lowest level, it is necessary to distinguish between exafference and reafference. Von Holst (6) put the matter well,

> If I shake the branch of a tree, various receptors of my skin and joints produce a reafference, but if I place my hand on a branch shaken by the wind, the stimuli of the same receptors produce an exafference. We can see that this distinction has nothing to do with the difference between the so-called proprio- and extero-receptors. The same receptor can serve both the reafference and exafferance. The central nervous system, however, must possess the ability to distinguish one from the other. . . . Stimuli resulting from its own movements must not be interpreted as movements of the environment.

And, of course, it is to the credit of von Holst and Mittelstaedt (6), of Sperry (19), and others to have demonstrated that even the primitive nervous system of the fish can in fact distinguish the stimulation produced on a receptor by the self-induced action and by environmentally induced change.

But plainly, there are some systems of action in which the reafference system, its capacity for control by corollary discharge to related systems and therefore its skill, is virtually zero at the outset. The visually guided use of the hands in human beings is somewhat like this, and it is particularly interesting to examine its growth because it reaches such delicate virtuosity after so awkward a start. It appears to be based on the development of programs of action that are plainly quite different from those, for example, that characterize such a system as eye movements which, virtually at birth, are smooth and controlled by reafference principles and corollary discharge. Obviously the central nervous system can distinguish from the start the movement of objects across the stationary retinal field from the movement of objects across this field produced by the eye itself moving, the former producing an optokinetic pursuit, the latter not. The hand, on the contrary, cannot be so distinguished and an infant is capable of startling himself by a quick swipe of the hand into the central visual field. The corollary discharge from the effector is plainly not getting a wide distribution in the case of the hand movement, but is in the case of the eye movement.

We know extraordinarily little about systems that acquire their organization in contrast to those that have much of it built in. We believe that it is of great importance to examine the former type of system with especial care, for it is in such systems that one finds maximum plasticity, a maximum modeling of the most variable features of the environment, and a maximum amount of information processing. These are the systems of action that, we believe, become generative in the linguistic sense, that is, capable of being employed in a variety of contexts by the use of a minimum set of elementary operations combined and recombined by rule-governed programs. We believe that it is the open quality of these systems that allows for their incorporation of prosthetic devices and tools on the one side, and of language as a medium for programming action on the other.

In the following pages, we shall explore some of the features of organization of a couple of highly plastic, voluntary systems of action that we have been studying with a view to examining something about their growth and structure. Our plan is simple. We shall begin with some behavior that initially seems to be quite automatic and reflexive and is gradually converted to voluntary control. We have chosen the phenomenon of nutritive and comfort-giving sucking as the vehicle for this discussion. The exercise will, perhaps, give us an idea of what happens in the transition from a low to a high information-processing system. Then we shall sample some episodes in the growth of visually guided manipulation of objects, better to appreciate how a program of skilled action may be put together from the outset. Our progress will be from mouth to hand rather than from hand to mouth.

Consider now the growth and integration of human nutritional activity during the early months of human life. First let us briefly review the facts of sucking and the role of the mouth in early infancy.

Functions of Sucking

Sucking serves several functions. It can be observed as early as the third gestational month (Peiper, 14). Though it is instinctive, it requires some priming to get started in the neonate, as we know from the work of Gunther (5), and if not early exercised, may become difficult to evoke. At birth the infant may have certain difficulties beginning to suck, grinding jaws back and forth, missing the pressure, and the like. Once he has connected, so to speak (and it can take as many as four five-second periods of trying before he does), the sucking is immediately highly expert. In addition to its role in feeding, sucking serves nonnutritively to fulfill an antidistractant or analgesic function or both, according to the studies of Jensen (7) and Wolff and Simmons (24). Pinpricks and tickling of the face by a feather increase the sucking rate or lead to initiation of sucking. Indeed, it is now standard practice in some hospitals to carry out circumcision while the child is sucking on a favored pacifier. Sucking also inhibits the newborn infant's level of general activity which may help relieve distress (Kes-

sen and Leutzendorff, 9), with effective suckers showing the greatest qui-
etening (Kessen, 8). A variety of studies indicate that infants suck
nonnutritively at about a constant individual rate of 48–80 per minute
whether hungry or not (Balint, 1; Bridger, 3). The third function of mouthing is for exploration, and its importance in the organization of behavior
will concern us later.

The mouth, from the start, is embedded functionally in several systems.
For one thing, it is the aiming point in the head-turning system. A touch
to the edge of the jaw or the side of the cheek will produce a rooting reflex
with mouth moved toward the touch. It is also mapped into the arm-and-
trunk system, as indicated by the Babkin and the palmomental reflexes;
pressing the palm will produce mouth movements in the newborn, as will
pressure on the ball at the base of the thumb produce contractions in the
mentalis muscle of the jaw.

There is little question either in detail or in general functional terms
that sucking is part of a hierarchical structure or, indeed, of several hierarchically organized systems. At the outset, it has about it a captive quality
within a digestive system that renders it quite inseparable and rigid, the
sucking of the premature, for example, being part of a general digestive
activity of stomach and gut that can be observed easily through the almost
translucent abdominal wall not yet obstructed by the fatty omentum. Sucking can be observed to be one part of a general action of the digestive system, and a quite inseparable part. In the full-term infant as well, the role
of sucking is crucial for maintaining a proper motility in the stomach, even
when the baby is fed through a gastrostomy tube because the connection
from the mouth to stomach has been interrupted by pathology or defect.

But, over and beyond this autonomic and reflexive embedding, sucking
is also destined to become a highly voluntary activity. It plainly becomes
detached from the obligatory and compulsive sucking-feeding-comfort
cycle and, in time, becomes part of such symbolic actions as lifting iced
tea from glass to mouth through a straw or partaking in such physiologically exotic activities as the smoking of marijuana, tobacco, or opium. We
have been much interested in this transition.

Consider a few observations. The first has to do with the nature of the
flexibility and voluntary control that gradually permeates this originally
quite reflexive system of action. While at the outset sucking has a very
compulsive property, closer examination of it shows in what measure, even
in the first day of life, it is also quite sensitive to changes in the environment that relate to it.

Method of Recording Sucking

Figure 1 provides a diagrammatic sketch of a system which measures suctioning pressure on a polygraph, as well as the positive pressure of mouth-

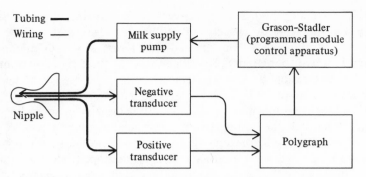

Reinforcement can be switched between negative and positive sucking

FIGURE 1. Diagram of sucking apparatus

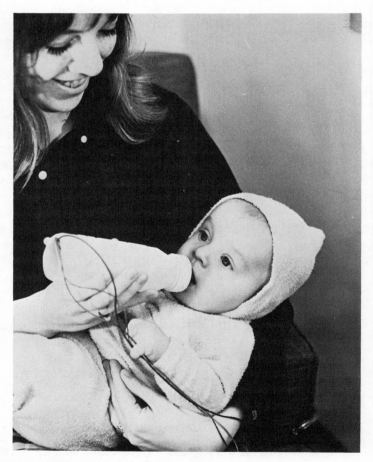

FIGURE 2. Mother and infant with bottle part of sucking apparatus

ing and pressing the nipple with the gums and tongue. At the same time we are able to deliver milk directly through the nipple to the baby in response either to positive or negative sucking or to some combination, and with whatever contingency we choose. For, not only does a record of the baby's sucking register on the polygraph, but also on a programming device that can be set to activate a milk-pulsing system each time the baby sucks in a specified way, every other time, or at specified intervals of time after the baby has sucked. The device builds upon similar devices that have been used in recent years by Kron, Stein, and Goddard (10) and by Sameroff (17). Complicated though the instrument may seem in the context of infancy as lived, it is quite indistinguishable from an ordinary nursing bottle to the infant and mother, as Figure 2 indicates.

Adaptation of Sucking to the Environment

When closely examined, sucking appears to have two modes of control, one quite automatic, rhythmic, and relatively invariable; the other very much more open to the variations of the environment. The best way of picturing the automatic component is to show you the beautiful sucking record of a sleeping infant of four weeks of postnatal age, physiologically closer to one week, since this baby was three weeks premature (Figure 3). This splendid performance went on for minutes on end, accompanied by regular breathing and swallowing.

Yet, for all this automatic quality of sucking, it is also capable from the start of prodigies of adaptation. Sameroff (17) has shown that, when milk is delivered exclusively for mouthing, the neonate will diminish the negative or suctioning component of his sucking. Indeed, if one establishes a certain level of required mouthing pressure to get milk, the infant within a minute or two will adapt to that level. But the adaptation will not carry over to the next feeding. The infant will begin anew at his own natural or

W. Smethurst 4 weeks

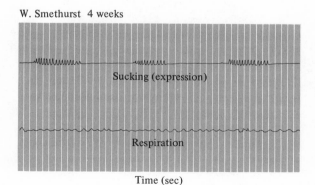

Sucking (expression)

Respiration

Time (sec)

FIGURE 3. Sucking pattern of a sleeping infant

signature level of pressure (or with mouthing and suctioning at original level). In our own laboratory, working with children a month of age and older, Hillman found that over a period of 15 minutes suctioning will virtually drop out if mouthing alone produces milk (Figure 4). He has also investigated the infant's adaptation to rather unusual milk delivery patterns that are correlated, but not directly, with the infant's sucking: The child receives a pulse of his own formula milk at the end of a second if there has been any sucking during that second, or for every other suck or every third suck. The learning that ensues is very interesting indeed, being much more akin to strategy learning than to specific response acquisition. When a pulse of milk is delivered each second, or every two seconds in which a suck has occurred, the effect on some babies is to shorten their sucking bursts, while the pauses between lengthen.

But what is especially interesting for our present purposes is that when the requirements of the task exceed the infant's capacity to adapt, the pattern goes back to the full-fledged, automatized sucking pattern with no account taken of the nature of the environmental situation. If, for example, the adaptation has involved the dropping out of suctioning and the modulation of the mouthing pattern, frustration will induce full rhythmic activity at a signature rate, involving both mouthing and suctioning again. It is as if the automatic system provides something akin to a shield or emergency system.

J. Stafford 17 weeks

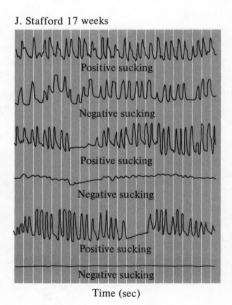

Time (sec)

FIGURE 4. Change in negative sucking when positive sucking alone produces milk

Can we say then that voluntary control is a modulation of an initially reflex system, a modulation that requires confirming feedback to continue? We think not. We believe that reflex sucking is integral and is differently controlled and paced. We shall return to this issue in a moment.

Intercalation of Sucking with Another System

Consider another route to the capture of sucking by a voluntary system, its intercalation with another system. Normal sucking, we know from observations by Kessen (8) and Wolff (23) can be observed in brain-stem infants. What does it take to intercalate this primitive activity with such a higher-order information-processing system as visual scanning? Let me report some observations.

At birth, and for some days after, the infant sucks with eyes tightly shut. If the infant looks or tracks, sucking is disrupted; indeed, the disruption has been used as a measure of attending, as in the classic study by Bronshtein and Petrova (4). With the 3- to 5-week-old baby, the eyes may be open while the infant is sucking, but there is a high likelihood that, when fixation or tracking occurs, sucking stops.

There is a new pattern usually by nine weeks based on the phenomenon of sucking in bursts interspersed by pauses. The child now sucks in bursts and looks during pauses. He remains generally oriented toward the stimulation while sucking, but not fixated or locked on while sucking goes on. Around this age a stimulus change occurring during a sucking burst will disrupt the burst or bring it to an end sooner. But if the stimulus is presented during a pause, it will have no effect on subsequent bursts (Figure 5). It appears that the pauses are being used to process information, a matter that we shall wish to investigate much more thoroughly before letting it rest at that.

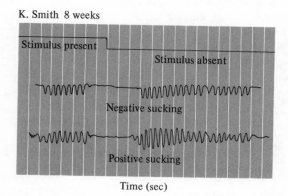

Time (sec)

FIGURE 5. Absence of any disruption of sucking when stimulus disappears during a pause

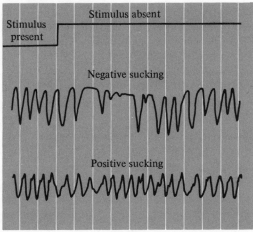

M. Johnson 9 weeks

Time (sec)

FIGURE 6. Positive sucking being used as place holder during disruption of negative sucking by a stimulus

Finally, usually before four months and often as early as two months, the baby appears to be able to suck and look at once. But when one examines the sucking record, it turns out not to be the case. For now, the act of looking inhibits suctioning, while mouthing or positive sucking goes right on through, though with reduced amplitude (Figure 6). We refer to this phenomenon as place holding, maintenance of the structure of a more inclusive act while the various parts of it are separately executed. Once the infant has inspected and has become habituated to the object that has caught his regard, the suctioning returns.

So we may say that the integration of sucking and looking goes through at least three stages: (a) initial suppression of one by the other, (b) an arrangement whereby there can be a succession of the two without interferences, and, finally (c) a place-holding operation where the two can hold their places in a larger act. Note that the achievement of intercalation of this kind requires that the autonomy of sucking is no longer complete, that it becomes part of a new program of action. Note also that this new system of action is quite separate from the original systemic embedding of sucking in the feeding-comfort complex.

Voluntary Sucking

This brings us directly to a final experiment concerned with the voluntarization of sucking, sucking in the interest of a quite arbitrary goal. We can properly argue that one of the features of voluntary control of an action system is the degree to which it can be utilized as a means of a new end.

We had been impressed by experiments conducted by Siqueland (18) indicating that infants of three months were quite capable of sucking to increase the illumination of a picture on a back-lighted screen in an otherwise darkened room. In an experiment done in our laboratory, Kalnins has altered this procedure in one crucial respect to assure that what was involved was not the comfort of the young child provided by a lighted environment. Her infants, varying from one month through three months in age, are shown a motion picture that is initially out of focus. By sucking on a pacifier, the child can bring the picture into focus. If his sucking should fall below the rate of one suck per two seconds, the picture starts back out of focus. The brightness remains virtually constant throughout. In a second experimental condition the picture is in focus, and sucking drives it out of focus at the rate mentioned above. Refraining from sucking at the prescribed rate lets the picture come back into focus.

First let me say that a four-week-old infant can in fact learn to suck to bring the picture into focus and to desist when his sucking blurs the display. Infants plainly will work for visual clarity. What is especially interesting is how the child learns to co-ordinate the two ordinarily independent or even conflicting activities of sucking and looking. He may learn first to suck the picture into focus; but, the moment it is in focus, sucking is inhibited by looking and the attractive motion picture is allowed back out of focus. Or the picture may be in focus and the irresistible pacifier leads him to suck, which drives the picture into a fog. Gradually, the amount of time during which he can suck and look or desist from sucking increases. The child seems to be learning not so much a specific response

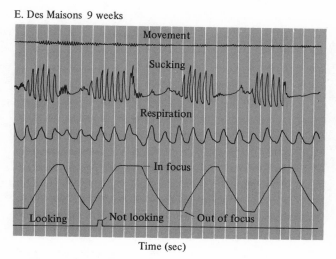

E. Des Maisons 9 weeks

Time (sec)

FIGURE 7. Sucking into focus by means of short, frequent bursts of sucking

E. Levy 9 weeks

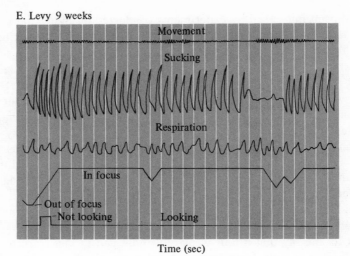

Time (sec)

FIGURE 8. Sucking into focus; focus maintained by long bursts of sucking

as a hierarchically organized, adaptive strategy of responses. He shows a quite individual pattern in achieving this competence, no mere matter of gradual, incremental change. One nine-week-old keeps a picture in focus by a series of short bursts (Figure 7); another achieves his ends by a long, sustained burst that holds the focus (Figure 8); and yet another manages the task by shifting his approach to a mouthing pattern (Figure 9). Or com-

M. Schimke 8 weeks

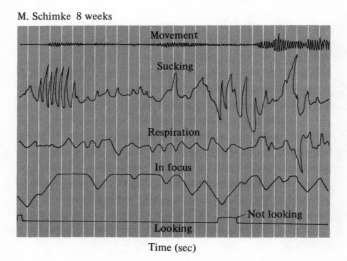

Time (sec)

FIGURE 9. Sucking into focus; change from regular sucking to mouthing

N. Nicholson 6 weeks

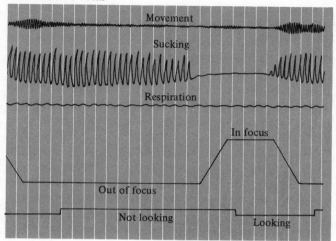

Time (sec)

FIGURE 10. Sucking out of focus; no inhibition of sucking, but baby averts gaze during nonfocus

pare these two infants dealing with the inhibition of sucking that is required to keep the picture in focus: The first sucks compulsively while looking away (Figure 10), then stops sucking and looks; the second, to the accompaniment of much wriggling, inhibits sucking almost totally, inspecting the picture the while (Figure 11).

R. Booth 5 weeks

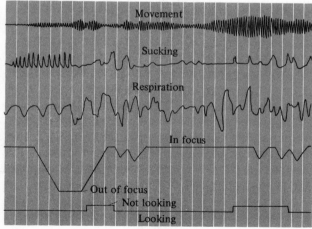

Time (sec)

FIGURE 11. Sucking out of focus; inhibition of sucking

Process of Organization for Voluntary Control

Let me draw a few simple conclusions from this series of experiments. The first and most obvious is that there are discernible steps in the process of organization for voluntary control. What Piaget (15) referred to as the *'structure d'ensemble'* of an operation does not emerge in one great leap forward but in several smaller ones. The second feature of the genesis of organization is inhibition as a resolution of conflict between systems, a matter that Mott and Sherrington (13) understood particularly clearly. This is well illustrated by the pattern of succession already noted. Finally, the establishment of higher-order organization involves, in the most general terms, what linguists call privilege of occurrence, that is, a place in a sequence where an act can fit. Place holding in the present instance is a highly simplified form of this principle, and we shall encounter more interesting examples shortly. Let us comment, before moving on, that there is something strikingly nonspecific about the response that emerges once new organization is achieved; it is as if a generic way of responding is being learned rather than simply a specific reaction.

The Organized Skill System of Eye and Hand

Nicolai Bernstein (2) contrasted voluntary activity with mere movement, noting that the former requires the co-ordination and regulation of the latter. His theoretical model for a self-regulating system is summarized in "The Growth and Structure of Skill" and diagrammed in Figure 1 (p. 250). For Bernstein, the achievement of control always involves a reduction of degrees of freedom in the action system being regulated.

We shall argue in what follows that the mastery of intelligent, visually guided manipulation in infancy and childhood involves a cycle of brute restriction of forms of movement and of programmatic skill formation within the limits of that restriction, with skill moving to a next step only when restriction is altered. Any given program of skilled voluntary action is gradually consolidated within its own restrictions. Its consolidation is signaled by the well-known plateau in the learning curve. Progress points in the infant's development are qualitative rather than quantitative changes of skill. These involve not consolidation, but the formulation of new strategies of programs of action which in turn must be consolidated. Each new program of action involves an increment of actuation of degrees of freedom. The process, moreover, continues throughout life. The difference between good skiing and bad skiing is, alas, qualitative, not quantitative.

Now return to Bernstein's diagram. What it lacks is some specifications about the nature of programs in the so-called command system. These must be generative in several ways. They must contain equivalence rules concerning substitutable types of acts. They must specify sequence, types of acts to be carried out in certain privileged orders. They must specify delay procedures and rules for bracketing, in the event of encountering difficulty. As Piaget (16) would also rightly insist, the programs must be premised on some stored and/or innate model of space and objects.

But before such programmatic voluntary action can get underway, I believe that there must first be a recession of reflex control over the acts that are governed by a program. One sees this recession from the age of one month onward, with the emergence of athetoid, diffuse, undifferentiated action of the infant's arms, hands, and trunk when visual objects approach his participatory space, of about 15 inches away and closer. There are also present the beautifully precise reflex patterns so carefully described by Twitchell (21): shoulder-traction grasping, the touch-evoked grasp reflex, touch-evoked avoidance-withdrawal, pronating and supinating groping without visual guidance. But in no sense are these the paving blocks from which skilled programs of visually guided action are constructed. The beginning of skill is diffusely organized awkwardness guided by a small number of directional specifications.

Diffuse awkwardness is then supplanted by stiff awkwardness. There is, for example, a restriction in the fluid action of joints; fingers are now spread wide, elbow rigid. The midline becomes dominant. Reaching more likely occurs when head and trunk are in line at the midline and in line with a near object. Eye closing and gaze aversion are the reactions to trouble in reaching. The system gets stiff, but it gets vastly more effective. And when it does so, when it becomes reinforced, it then changes. It is this that led R. W. White (22) to postulate a competence motive as crucial to growth. Reaching, in keeping with this stiffness, initially serves the retrieval of objects to the mouth. In time it serves other goals (banging, dropping, and so on). When this multipurpose reaching gets started, there also occurs a modularization of the components of that act: reach, hand close, lift, retrieve, and so forth. The time and effort per component approach uniformity. By eight or nine months, a reach takes about the same time for near or for far objects, the lift of objects is about equal in time whether the object is heavy or light, one-handed or two-handed, or whatever. Does this modularization permit more predictable incorporation of acts into different plans? We think so, although it is still hard to prove it.

Consider the infant of five or six months, reaching now with hands spread wide open and mouth wide open. The open mouth during this early reaching keeps the terminus of the act in evidence while the component parts are run off. In Lashley's terms (11), it maintains an "atemporal" organization through the sequence of the act. The rigidly opened hand is a measure against intrusive, anticipatory fist-closing. As with so much early development, processes that later become internal have initially an external and motoric representation.

We have done close analyses of a seven-month-old child coping with a cup for the first time. It is a film record shot at 50 frames per second. The child's cup-using behavior seems more playful than purposeful. In play, ends are altered to suit means, rather than means being altered to achieve an end held constant, as in problem solving. Thorndike (20) long ago, and others since, believe that the child's early behavior is shaped by trial and error; but that is surely an adult-centered view. Trial and error implies the capacity to hold an end constant while varying means. The segments in which this is possible are very short in duration for the child. What thwarts him is distraction, not error. The place-holding techniques only slowly extend in time. And new sequences are only slowly established with the aid of what Miller, Galanter, and Pribram (12) described as external memory devices, strategically positioned external place holders for the task at hand.

Conclusions

We have tried to illustrate by examples some of the ways in which man achieves adaptive, voluntary control of his interaction with the environment. In doing so, we have concentrated on the initially helpless, reflex-protected infant and his various vicissitudes en route to becoming a strategist and problem solver. I have purposely left out of the account the central role of language and of its internalization in achieving this end, since I would like to argue strongly that there are many species-specific features of human behavior that precede the acquisition of language proper.

There is adaptive, generic, intelligent organization of behavior at every age. It is attained neither by an unfolding of mysterious inner structures nor by the gradual accretion of shaping through reinforcement. It is instead uneven, imperfect, spasmodic, incomplete. The programs that guide voluntary action do not achieve full control. Even spoken language, treated by linguists as if based upon a totally mastered competence, is in fact a faltering performance and, in its internalized version, is even more loosely controlling. Skinner attributes such order as there is to control of behavior by orderly stimuli in the world. Piaget sees more order than Skinner, so he attributes it to the inherent logical structures of mind, accommodating only slightly to the lessons of the environment. Skinner's solution has some of the monotony of nature. But it is much more fortuitous than nature could afford to be. The generativeness in behavior that makes it economical vanishes at Skinner's touch, even from language. With Piaget it is the opposite. The order and generativeness are all there from the start, like the shape of the mollusk, ready to eat so long as nutriment enters the system.

We have no complaint either against universality in human intellectual functioning, or against the shaping power of the environment. But we do have a complaint about theories that opt for internal universality in surfeit, or for environmental shaping as the mold of such uniformity. Human beings are the most awkward species on earth, the most uneven in development, the most beset by obstacles that are not intrinsic to the task. We urge a new functional analysis of what it takes to grow up intelligent, a job description of growing up. It is no obvious matter. It does not suffice to say that the central issue is the question of how we achieve deeper and deeper power over the idea of invariance across transformations in surface properties, for that leaves the issue of action and control unattended. Nor does it do to say that internal processes are so much phantasmagorical nonsense, and action selected by reinforcement is the real thing. That leaves order to fortuity. Rather, the questions are more mixed: How do strategies for coping with complexity develop? How are limited resources used for achieving goals, the means to which vary? How do we sustain action over sufficiently long trains of striving? How do we recognize (when we do) invariant features of events so that we are not constantly ensnared in learning? We suggest we proceed not with a bang, not with a whimper, but with a good close look.

References

1. BALINT, M. 1948. Individual differences of behavior in early infancy, and an objective method for recording them. *Journal of Genetic Psychology* 73:57–117.
2. BERNSTEIN, N. 1967. *The coordination and regulation of movement.* London: Pergamon.
3. BRIDGER, W. H. 1962. Ethological concepts and human development. *Recent advances in biological psychiatry* 4:95–107.
4. BRONSHTEIN, A. I., and PETROVA, E. P. 1967. The auditory analyzer in young infants. In *Behavior in infancy and early childhood*, ed. Y. Brackbill and G. G. Thompson, pp. 163–72. New York: Free Press.
5. GUNTHER, M. 1961. Infant behavior at the breast. In *Determinants of infant behavior*, vol. 1, ed. B. M. Foss, pp. 37–44. New York: Wiley.
6. HOLST, E. VON, and MITTELSTAEDT, H. 1950. Das Reafferenzprinzip. *Naturwissenschaften*, 37:464–76.
7. JENSEN, K. 1932. Differential reactions to taste and temperature stimuli in newborn infants. *Genetic Psychology Monographs* 12:361–479.
8. KESSEN, W. 1967. Sucking and looking: two organized congenital patterns of behavior in the human newborn. In *Early behavior: comparative and developmental approaches*, ed. H. W. Stevenson, E. H. Hess, and H. L. Rheingold, pp. 147–79. New York: Wiley.
9. KESSEN, W., and LEUTZENDORFF, A.-M. 1963. The effect of nonnutritive sucking on movement in the human newborn. *Journal of Comparative and Physiological Psychology* 56:69–72.
10. KRON, R. E.; STEIN, M.; GODDARD, K. E. 1963. A method of measuring sucking behavior of newborn infants. *Psychosomatic Medicine* 25:181–91.
11. LASHLEY, K. S. 1951. The problem of serial order in behavior. In *Cerebral mechanisms in behavior: the Hixon symposium*, ed. L. A. Jeffress, pp. 112–46. New York: Wiley.
12. MILLER, G. A.; GALANTER, E.; and PRIBRAM, K. H. 1960. *Plans and the structure of behavior.* New York: Holt.
13. MOTT, F. W., and SHERRINGTON, C. S. 1895. Experiments on the influence of sen-

sory nerves upon movement and nutrition of the limbs. *Protocol of the Royal Society* 57:481–88.
14. PEIPER, A. 1963. *Cerebral function in infancy and childhood*. New York: Consultants Bureau.
15. PIAGET, J. 1952. *The origins of intelligence in children*. New York: International Universities Press.
16. PIAGET, J. 1954. *The construction of reality in the child*. Trans. M. Cook. New York: Basic Books.
17. SAMEROFF, A. J. 1965. An experimental study of the response components of sucking in the human newborn. Unpublished doctoral dissertation, Yale University.
18. SIQUELAND, E. R. 1968. Conditioned sucking and visual reinforcers with human infants. Paper presented at Eastern Regional Meeting, Society for Research in Child Development, Worcester, Mass, 1968.
19. SPERRY, R. W. 1950. Neural basis of the spontaneous optokinetic response produced by visual inversion. *Journal of Comparative and Physiological Psychology* 43:482–89.
20. THORNDIKE, E. L. 1903. *Educational psychology*. New York: Teachers College, Columbia University.
21. TWITCHELL, T. E. 1965. The automatic grasping response of infants. *Neuropsychologia* 3:247–59.
22. WHITE, R. W. 1959. Motivation reconsidered: the concept of competence. *Psychological Review* 66:297–333.
23. WOLFF, P. H. 1968. Personal communication.
24. WOLFF, P. H., and SIMMONS, M. A. 1967. Nonnutritive sucking and response thresholds in young infants. *Child Development* 38:631–38.

17

Competence in Infants *

In the growth of competence in infants, three themes are central—
intention, feedback, and the patterns of action that mediate between them.
These are the themes that will concern us. We shall have more to say
about intention and the structure of action presently. Feedback is now
known to have at least three aspects: (*a*) internal feedback that signals an
intended action within the nervous system (sometimes called feed forward
for it occurs prior to overt action); (*b*) feedback proper from the effector
system during action; and (*c*) knowledge of results that may occur only
after action has been completed.

We shall concentrate upon infants during the first year of life, starting at
about the third week when sedation and shock and the inevitable initial
difficulties of the sleep-wake cycle are ironed out. The competences
achieved during the first year of life fall roughly into five broad headings
of which four are quite straightforward: feeding, perceiving or attending,
manipulating the world, and interacting with members of the species.
There is another that is somewhat more subtle; it has to do with control of
internal state. In each of these enterprises, the infant initially comes to
solve problems of high complexity and does so on the basis of encounters
with the environment that are too few in number, too unrepresentative, or

* "Competence in Infants," by Jerome S. Bruner, a paper presented at the meeting
of the Society for Research in Child Development in Minneapolis, Minnesota on
March 30, 1971.

too erratic in consequence, to be accounted for either on the basis of concept attainment or by the shaping effects of reinforcement. Initial learning has a large element of preadaptation that reflects species-typical genetic instructions. But it is highly flexible preadaptation, as we shall see. The initial patterns of action that emerge through exercise then become the constituents for new patterns of action directed at more remote or complex objectives. Here, too, the role of learning in the conventional sense is not clear. Indeed, what is striking about the opening year of life is how specialized and circumscribed the role of learning turns out to be.

Let me describe this progress in programmatic terms and then instance it with some quite specific examples. We begin with the initial arousal of an intention in the infant by an appropriate object. *Intention* as here used involves an internal discharge in the nervous system whereby an act about to occur is not only produced in the effectors by the usual motor volley, but is also signaled to related sensory and co-ordination systems by a corollary discharge (Sperry, 38) or efference copy (von Holst and Mittelstaedt, 24), or, as Evarts (15) now proposes to call it, by internal feedback preceding action. Even at the simplest level of postural adjustment or effector movement, it is impossible to conceive of directed action without the compensation made possible by such prior signaling of intention. Oscarsson (32) has in the last years gone so far as to show the internal feedback loops that connect cortex to cerebellum and back to cortex, whereby voluntary motor discharges from precentral gyrus downward are signaled to the cerebellum to regulate balance and, in turn, are modulated by the most recent input from balance organs better to generate an appropriate motor command. Intention viewed abstractly may be at issue philosophically, but it is a necessity for the biology of complex behavior, by whatever label we wish to call it.

The characteristic initial accompaniment of aroused intention in the infant is prolonged orienting accompanied by triggering of anticipatory consummatory activity. It is the nature of objects or states that arouse such intentionality that they operate like triggers or releasers, more like threshold phenomena than like reflexes in which stimulus magnitude determines response magnitude.

Initial arousal is often followed by a loosely ordered sequence of constituent acts that will later occur in an appropriate serial order to achieve the end state toward which the intention appears to be steering. Meanwhile, during this clumsy athetoid phase, the consummatory response will continue, and even the wrongly orchestrated constituent acts can be shown to have an appropriate adjustment with respect to the goal. The development of visually guided reaching is typical of this pattern. An appropriate freestanding object, of appropriate size and texture and at an appropriate distance (and these can be quite specifically described) first produces prolonged looking and, very shortly after, there is action of the mouth and tongue and jaws—the area to which a captured object will be transported once effective, visually guided reaching develops. If the intent persists, one can then observe antigravitational activity of arms and shoulders, clenching of fists in a grab pattern, movement of arms, ballistic flinging of clenched fist, and the like (Bruner, May, and Koslowski, 9).

These constituent acts or subroutines are aroused, but they do not yet occur in the correct order for successful object capture. Yet it can be shown that, in a diffuse way, each of the components is adapted to the goal though there has been no feedback from the effectors during the consummatory act (which has not occurred) nor can there be said to be knowledge of results (for the same reason). Alt (2) has shown, for example, that the ballistic flinging of the arm is well aimed, even when a blinder is placed at the side of the infant's eye, preventing a view of his active hand. And Koslowski and Bruner (25) have found that the hand and arm movements, though unsuccessful, are roughly appropriate to the size of the object evoking the movement.

In time, and probably by virtue of sheer practice of the act in the presence of the releasing stimulus, which permits the co-ordination of internal and peripheral feedback, the act is successfully executed. An object is captured and brought to the mouth. Doubtless some of this progress depends on morphological maturation of relevant tracts in the nervous system, particularly tracts in the corpus callosum, for much of the activity involves bilateral hand use, and the maturation of relevant callosum tracts is known to be slow (Conel, 11). But we also know from the work of White, Castle, and Held (45) and of Held (21) that practice is crucial in maturing such reaching. It is this practice that makes possible the form of co-ordination noted above, allowing the development of appropriate synchrony between feed-forward corollary discharges and feedback from the effectors, finding out how to put them into an orchestrated form much as the kittens in the Held and Hein (22) experiments required active practice to put prismatically displaced visual input into synchrony with efferent discharges to the muscles and to the sense organs regulating the muscles, representing the intended as well as the completed action in the sensory system.

Here we come to a puzzle. Once the act is successfully executed and repeated with success, that is, constituents are put stably into proper serial order, there often appears a sharp alteration in the structure of the act used for achieving an intended outcome. For example, shortly after the first successful taking of an object, the fist rather than being closed early in the reach, thus often producing premature closure, now remains open at maximum extension until the object being sought is touched. There appears to be a reorganization of components, with a substitution of a hyper-extended hand for a clenching hand. A constituent is drastically altered to fit the task requirements.

At this point in the progress, the effects of reinforcement seem to take over. Completion of the act with wide-open hand is now frequent enough to be effective. But reinforcement produces a modification of the action pattern-in-being rather than, as sometimes suggested, selecting elements from a trial-and-error pattern. Its effects are threefold, the first two quite unexceptional, the last puzzling. The first effect is to increase the anticipatory patterning of the act: thus, the hand now begins to close gradually to the shape of the object as it approaches, rather than after it gets there. (We know from the work of Twitchell [41] that the tactile-dominated "instinctive groping reaction" shows months earlier a comparably patterned pronation and supination to fit the shape of objects touched, but not looked at.) The second effect is what we have come to call modularization: The act gradually becomes less variable in latency and in execution time and more economical in expenditure of energy. The third and puzzling effect is that the now increasingly successful act is soon supplanted by a new pattern of action which may in fact include it. Thus, in place of the by now well-modularized bilateral pounce reach, the infant, now six or seven months old, reaches in two steps: One, extends the hands out to the plane of the object, and second, closes in with the familiar anticipatory hand-closure pattern, a pause of some hundreds of milliseconds separating the two. The old program does not disappear; under stress, with overload, in unfamiliar surroundings it appears intact, as also when the more complex act fails of attainment.

Again, reinforcement operates to modularize this newest pattern. However, there is still a question of what brought the new act into being. It is a question that is constantly forced upon us in many of the studies we conduct on reaching under visual guidance, on search patterns involving looking, on social interaction, and, indeed, in our research on nutritive behavior as well. A new act is mastered, only to be supplanted by a higher-order action that usually encompasses it as a subroutine. It is very much like the pattern found in the classical studies of Bryan and Harter on code learning: Once a lower-order pattern begins to work effectively, there is a shift to a higher-order pattern—individual letters, then words, then phrases, and so on.

What leads to the emergence of particular higher-order action programs is a puzzle many of us share. They do not seem to get established by a process of reinforcement that selects a set of constituents from a random or near-random response output. The puzzle has an analogue in linguistic development where the child goes from one level of syntactic complexity to a higher one. Practice is necessary, to be sure, but not in a specific sense of successful practice with reinforcement selecting constituents or rules (see Brown, Cazden, and Bellugi, 6). When, in our studies, for example (Bruner, Lyons, and Kaye, 8) the child has routinized the task of holding two objects, one in each hand, there then occurs a first storage activity for dealing with a third object placed before him—placing blocks in the crook of the arm or in the lap, and then recovering them. It is no more nor less mysterious than the presumably unprovoked first occurrence of embedding in speech, which it formally resembles.

Our speculation about what makes possible these quantum jumps in performance is very much in line with information-processing theories of development as noted above. Modularization frees available information-processing capacity for further use in task analysis, by virtue of constitutent subroutines requiring less attention. The reduction in attention is accomplished when co-ordination is achieved between internal feedback, peripheral feedback, and knowledge of results involving not only the co-ordination between different sense modalities, as Birch and Lefford (4) have proposed, but also synchrony within modalities as Evarts (15) and Hess (23), among many have pointed out. If there are structures that make possible an appropriate anticipatory serial order in behavior, it seems highly likely that the crucial and ubiquitous feed-forward loops mentioned earlier are the hardware that make it possible. Once co-ordination and synchrony become stabilized and response-as-a-unit is possible, as Hess (23) has found, then acts can become combinable constituents in wider, more inclusive patterns of action. It is a limit on the information-processing capacity of the system that prevents the growth of complexity.

What about further task analysis being made possible by more available information processing capacity? Welford (44) in his excellent book on skill suggests there is a translation activity by which a perceptually scanned task is converted into requirements for a plan of action. It involves registering on the relevant features of a task, and formulating a plan for guiding action to an intended goal in light of these features. All that we can say is that as the child develops, his skill in task analysis improves markedly, as attested to by the increasing appropriateness of his initial efforts at dealing with new tasks. We shall return later to this crucial point. We know very little about such activity, though monographs on problem-solving behavior like Duncker's (13) and Maier's (29) and studies like Saugstad's (33) provide interesting leads concerning the combinatory nature of hypotheses in problem solving—whether involving external objects used in a task or internal thought elements.

Goal-directed action, then, may be conceived of as the construction in serial order of constituent acts, the performance output then undergoing modification toward less variability, more anticipation, and greater economy by benefit of reinforcement, feedback, and integration. The stock of constituents from which such action is constructed is in no sense (save initially) to be thought of as fixed-action patterns in the ethological sense or fixed in the linguistic sense like phonemes, morphemes, and lexemes to be used in the construction of utterance. Rather they represent a repertory of combinable, well-practiced acts (some with a preadapted history) from which behavior is put together to meet analyzed task requirements under the control of intention.

One final point about the competence of infants. Intentional programs of action have a remarkable generic character, in the sense of being adaptable to a wide range of conditions. They are, in linguistic terms, highly productive. Given the intention to take an object, it can be done with one hand or the other or the mouth, backhand or fore, through sand or from the surface. Indeed, the substitution rules for constituent acts are such that even alien objects and sticks and containers can be inserted as tools in the program of action. Perhaps skilled human manual behavior, even without alien objects, is akin to tool behavior in its structure, as Schiller (34) has suggested.

The picture of development drawn thus far is much too task-directed, too playless to be characteristic of the first year of life. For it is not until we consider early play that we understand more fully how the child achieves his growing competence. There is, of course, much problem solving in the first year, episodes where an intention is held invariant while the means used to attain its objective are varied. But there is also much behavior that seems to be without clear-cut means-end structure, where the activity seems more playful, where ends are changed to fit available means, and means and ends become admixed.

Vygotsky (43), speaking of somewhat older children, remarks that "a child's play must always be interpreted as the imaginary, illusory realization of unrealizable desires." Play at this higher level is wish fulfillment of a displaced or diffuse kind, often helped by what Vygotsky calls a "pivot" —some prop that carries externally a feature of the wished-for state—for example, a stick serves as a horse to ride on. While agreeing with Vygotsky, I think that the achievement of this kind of symbolic play in late infancy and early childhood is preceded by an earlier type of play, the exercise of which is crucial for development during the first year or year and a half. I shall call it mastery play, and its form is playful means-end matching. Rather than taking the form of "illusory realization of unrealizable desires" it consists precisely in extending to new limits already achieved skills. Several examples drawn from our studies at Harvard will illustrate what appear to be pleasure-giving variations of newly acquired routines. The six-month-old infant, having learned to hold on to an object and get it easily to his mouth, now begins a program of variation; when he takes the object now, he holds it to look at, he shakes it, he bangs it on his high chair, he drops it over the edge, and he manages shortly to fit the object into every activity into which it can be put. Inversely, when the young infant masters a new step in sensorimotor development, as in the conjoint use of power and precision grips with pincer grip directed to an object that is held in the contralateral hand, he very soon uses this new act on any object that has a loose end or "pick-at-able" property. In the first case, a new object is fitted into as many routines as available; in the second, a newly mastered act is addressed to as many different objects as available. Both are absorbing work (or play) for the child. It has been surprising to us how long the infant will stay with such variation of activity—a six- to eight-month-old up to half an hour.

This type of mastery play is particularly characteristic of higher primates. Indeed, elements of it can be found throughout *Mammalia*. Eibl-Eibesfeldt (14) has shown the way in which the red squirrel acquires nut-cracking skill and the role of play in such mastery. But there is a puzzle here. Paul Schiller (34) puts it well in his highly important, but overlooked, "Innate Constituents of Complex Responses in Primates."

Just which response is complex and which simple is not easily decided in the light of embryological behavior studies. Elements of complex responses are admitted to be ready prior to specific learning, but the question is whether the organism is not producing the compounds we observe without any training, just as its effectors mature. Experiments on maturational factors *versus* experience have led to contrasting results with various species and various tasks. In a long forgotten study Spaulding (1875) [37] has shown that flying in birds was unimpeded after he prevented early practice. Essentially the same was found by Carmichael (1926) [10] in the swimming of tadpoles, by Gesell (1929) [18] in the climbing behavior of human twins. On the other hand, Shepard and Breed (1913) [36] recorded that chicks have to learn how to peck seed in a few days of practice, whether freshly hatched or fed artificially for a considerable period allowing for maturation. Similarly Stone (1926) [39] and later Beach (1942) [3] have found severe impairment of copulating behavior in rats isolated from early contact with mates.

The contradiction in these results can be resolved by a dichotomy. The *constituents* of the motor pattern themselves mature. Due to internal, prefunctional factors, they appear at a certain stage of development (many of them traced in embryos) ready formed. Their *application* to external stimulus configurations is something that must be learned. Such a dichotomy was reported by Moseley (1925) [30] who found that pecking, striking, and swallowing were unlearned responses whereas seizing of the grain was formed by practice.

Or one other instance from the Oxford group of ethologists. Cullen (12) reports that the fledgling common tern is early capable of running along hard sand and taking wing in low flight, provided it is actively carried out in isolation from a broader program of goal-directed behavior. If now one moves a dummy predator overhead at a speed that requires flying to escape, the young bird resorts to the earlier developed form of running. So, too, if one tempts the bird with food moved along at a speed such that it could be caught by flying pursuit but not by running. The initial flying of the bird appears to be flying in play.

Play, then, has the effect of maturing some modular routines for later incorporation in more encompassing programs of action. It also seems to trial run a range of possible routines for employing already established subroutines. Not all forms of activity need such exercise, as we know from such pioneering studies as those by McGraw (28) on Johnny and Jimmy, particularly where such tightly knit synergies as walking are involved. But certainly manipulation does require it, and certainly complex oculomotor scanning of visual displays (for instance, Mundy-Castle and Anglin, 31; Mackworth and Bruner, 27; Vurpillot, 42; and Gardner, 17), and certainly social interaction (for instance, Harlow, 20; Ainsworth, 1; Bowlby, 5). And as Schiller remarks, whenever action involves the serial application of constituents to external stimuli with the objective of altering a state of the world, then exercise is particularly needed. For exercise to be highly flexible, play must precede it.

I shall speculate that the more productive the programs of action of the adult of the species, the greater the likelihood of mastery play earlier on in development in that species, with higher primates and man being at the top of the scale.

I know I have left out of my account many crucial factors in the development of early competence, but one omission is unpardonable. The human infant is, above all else, helpless and reliant upon caretaking by a mother or somebody standing in that role. There is an enormous reliance upon adequate social relationships if the child is to get on with the kind of skill development we have been considering. This is the sort of diffuse, affective, yet critical support the child needs in order to thrive. Without it, the sustained intention-directed behavior flags and we have an infant failing to thrive. I am taking this for granted, though I know quite well that it could equally well be the subject of a paper entitled "The Competence of Infants."

What I should like to concentrate upon briefly is an issue that is peculiarly social, affecting the development of the child's competence. It is modeling. Modeling is potentially a very powerful means for transmitting highly patterned behavior. We know as psychologists how difficult the phenomena of modeling and imitation are to understand. It is a subject I do not propose to analyze now. Let me comment, as Hamburg (19) has, on the widespread occurrence of the pattern among young primates, from the pongid apes through man, of observation of adult behavior followed by the incorporation of observed patterns into play among the young. Careful studies of the young in simple hunter-gatherer human societies (Thomas,

40; Lee, 26; Fortes, 16) all highlight this same pattern. I should like to comment, in passing, that in order to do such observational learning the child must be able to construct complex behavior to match to sample. A major accomplishment of the kind of initial skill learning we have been discussing is precisely that it provides the means for the young to enter such observation-play activity. Studies by Wood and Ross (46) indicate that the child's skill at a complex construction task per se determine to what extent he is capable of taking advantage of skilled behavior being modeled by the experimenter. The task involves putting together flats of four blocks by a moderately difficult peg system, then arranging these flats into a pyramid. The child skilled only in putting together pairs will often take apart the experimenter's preferred four-block constructions to follow her way of putting together pairs. So we do well to recognize that preliminary skill mastery provides the basis for utilizing modeling and for carrying out imitation.

While much has been left out of this programmatic account of the beginnings of skill, I hope that the point of view, in any case, has been clear. I should like to mention one crucial point of practical significance in closing. There is inherent in the description given of the growth of infant skill an emphasis on self-initiated behavior. Surely, the chief recommendation one would have to make on the basis of what has been said thus far is that the infant should be encouraged to venture, rewarded for venturing his own acts, sustained against distraction or premature interferences in carrying them out. It is a point of view very alien from such ideas as deprivation and enrichment, both of which are highly passive conceptions. From a practical point of view, the controlling conceptions in this account of skill acquisition are opportunity to initiate and sustain action and encouragement in the diffuse form of affective support for enterprise as well as the specific form of such feedback from the environment as would provide the basis for achieving knowledge of results.

Elsewhere I have argued (7) that "cultures of failure" resulting from persistent poverty often have the effect of signaling very early to the young and to the caretakers of the young a discouragement with or a face-saving reduction in the setting of goals, the mobilizing of means, the cultivation of delay in gratification. The effects are very widespread in terms of development, and there is reason to believe that they begin early, though they may not show up until later testing. Poverty does not necessarily produce the conditions that promote a sense of powerlessness and defeat that then signals to the young, though the important work of Schoggen and Schoggen (35) suggests that in the economically depressed home there are fewer challenging "environmental force units" (EFU's) tempting the child into activity on his own.

Children in middle-income homes as compared to children in low-income homes had EFU characterized by a higher percent of units in which they were (1) *given or asked for information,* (2) *engaged in more extended interaction,* (3) *given an obligation to perform* some specific action, (4) *in harmony* with the goal of the agent, and (5) receiving and giving messages through a *verbal medium.* By contrast, the children in low-income homes, as compared to children in middle-income homes had higher percents of EFU in which they were (1) asked to do *or to stop doing* something, (2) given *negative feedback* and prohibiting obligation, (3) utilizing signals or *physical contacts* in communication, and (4) *in conflict with* and receiving negative affect from the EFU agents.

A further useful study would be the examination not only by experimental means the factors that affect the kind of skill acquisition that has concerned us, but also the social ecology that sustains or impedes it.

References

1. AINSWORTH, M. D. S., and BELL, S. M. 1969. Some contemporary patterns of mother-infant interaction in the feeding situation. In *Stimulation in early infancy,* ed. A. Ambrose. New York: Academic Press.
2. ALT, J. 1968. The use of vision in early reaching. Unpublished honors thesis, Department of Psychology, Harvard University.
3. BEACH, F. A. 1942. Comparison of copulatory behavior of male rats raised in isolation, cohabitation, and segregation. *Journal of Genetic Psychology* 60:121–36.
4. BIRCH, H. G., and LEFFORD, A. 1967. Visual differentiation, intersensory integration, and voluntary motor control. *Monographs of the Society for Research in Child Development* 32(2):1–87.
5. BOWLBY, J. 1969. *Attachment and loss,* vol. 1, *Attachment.* New York: Basic Books.
6. BROWN, R.; CAZDEN, C. B.; and BELLUGI, U. 1969. The child's grammar from I to III. In *1967 Minnesota Symposium on Child Psychology,* ed. J. P. Hill. Minneapolis: University of Minnesota Press.
7. BRUNER, J. S. 1970. *Poverty and childhood.* Detroit, Mich.: Merrill-Palmer Institute.
8. BRUNER, J. S.; LYONS, K.; and KAYE, K. In preparation. Studies in manual intelligence. Center for Cognitive Studies, Harvard University.
9. BRUNER, J. S.; MAY, A.; KOSLOWSKI. 1971. The intention to take. (Film) Center for Cognitive Studies, Harvard University.
10. CARMICHAEL, L. 1926. The development of behavior in vertebrates experimentally removed from the influence of external stimulation. *Psychological Review* 33:51–58.
11. CONEL, J. LEROY. 1939–63. *The postnatal development of the human cerebral cortex,* vols. 1–6. Cambridge, Mass.: Harvard University Press.
12. CULLEN, M. 1971. Personal communication.
13. DUNCKER, K. 1945. On problem solving. Trans. L. S. Lees. *Psychological Monographs* 58 (whole no. 248).
14. EIBL-EIBESFELDT, I. 1967. Concepts of ethology and their significance in the study of human behavior. In *Early behavior: comparative and developmental approaches,* ed. H. W. Stevenson, E. H. Hess, and H. L. Rheingold. New York: Wiley.
15. EVARTS, E. V. 1971. Feedback and corollary discharge: a merging of the concepts. *Neurosciences Research Program Bulletin* 9(1):86–112.

16. FORTES, M. 1938. Social and psychological aspects of education in Taleland. Supple. to *Africa 11*(4).

17. GARDNER, JUDITH. 1971. The development of object identity in the first six months of human infancy. Unpublished doctoral dissertation, Harvard University.

18. GESELL, A. 1926. Maturation and infant behavior pattern. *Psychological Review* 36:307–19.

19. HAMBURG, D. 1968. Evolution of emotional responses: evidence from recent research on nonhuman primates. *Science and Psychoanalysis* 12:39–54.

20. HARLOW, H. F. 1959. Love in infant monkeys. *Scientific American* 200(6):68–74.

21. HELD, R. 1965. Plasticity in sensory-motor systems. *Scientific American* 213(5):84–94.

22. HELD, R., and HEIN, A. 1963. Movement-produced stimulation in the development of visually guided behavior. *Journal of Comparative and Physiological Psychology* 56(5):872–76.

23. HESS, W. R. 1964. *The biology of mind*. Trans. Gerhardt von Bonin. Chicago and London: University of Chicago Press.

24. HOLST, E. VON, and MITTELSTAEDT, H. 1950. Das Reafferenzprinzip. *Naturwissenschaften* 37:464–76.

25. KOSLOWSKI, B., and BRUNER, J. S. 1972. Visually preadapted constituents of manipulatory action. *Perception* 1 (no. 1):3–14.

26. LEE, RICHARD. 1965. Subsistence ecology of !Kung bushmen. Unpublished doctoral dissertation, University of California, Berkeley.

27. MACKWORTH, N. H., and BRUNER, J. S. 1970. How adults and children search and recognize pictures. *Human Development* 13:149–77.

28. McGRAW, MYRTLE. 1935. A study of Johnny and Jimmy. New York: Appleton-Century-Crofts.

29. MAIER, N. R. F. 1937. Reasoning in rats and human beings. *Psychological Review* 44:365–78.

30. MOSELEY, D. 1925. The accuracy of the pecking responses in chicks. *Journal of Comparative and Physiological Psychology* 5:75–97.

31. MUNDY-CASTLE, A. C., and ANGLIN, J. In press. Looking strategies in infants. In *The competent infant: a handbook of readings*, ed. J. L. Stone, H. T. Smith, and L. B. Murphy. New York: Basic Books.

32. OSCARSSON, O. 1970. Functional organization of spinocerebellar paths. In *Handbook of sensory physiology: II. Somatosensory system*, ed. A. Iggo, pp. 121–27. Berlin: Springer-Verlag.

33. SAUGSTAD, P. 1952. Incidental memory and problem-solving. *Psychological Review* 59:221–26.

34. SCHILLER, PAUL H. 1952. Innate constituents of complex responses in primates. *Psychological Review* 59(3):177–91.

35. SCHOGGEN, M., and SCHOGGEN, P. 1971. Environmental forces in the home lives of three-year-old children in three population subgroups. DARCEE Papers and Reports, vol. 5 (2). John F. Kennedy Center for Research on Education and Human Development, George Peabody College for Teachers, Nashville, Tenn.

36. SHEPARD, J. F., and BREED, F. S. 1913. Maturation and use in the development of an instinct. *Journal of Animal Behavior* 3:274–85.

37. SPAULDING, D. 1875. Instinct and acquisition. *Nature* 12:507–8.

38. SPERRY, R. W. 1950. Neural basis of the spontaneous optokinetic response produced by visual inversion. *Journal of Comparative and Physiological Psychology* 43:482–89.

39. STONE, C. P. 1926. The initial copulatory response of female rats reared in isolation from the age of twenty days to the age of puberty. *Journal of Comparative and Physiological Psychology* 6:73–83.

40. THOMAS, E. M. 1963. Bushmen of the Kalahari. *National Geographic* 123(6):866–88.

41. TWITCHELL, T. E. 1965. The automatic grasping response of infants. *Neuropsychologia* 3:247–59.

42. VURPILLOT, E. 1968. The development of scanning strategies and their relation to visual differentiation. *Journal of Experimental Child Psychology,* 6:632–50.

43. VYGOTSKY, L. S. 1967. Play and its role in the mental development of the child. *Soviet Psychology* 5(3):6–18. From *Voprosy psikhologii* 12(6)(1966):62–76.

44. WELFORD, A. T. 1968. *Fundamentals of skill*. London: Methuen.

45. WHITE, B. L.; CASTLE, P.; and HELD, R. 1964. Observations on the development of visually-directed reaching. *Child Development* 35:349–64.

46. WOOD, D., and ROSS, G. In preparation 1971. Planning in three- to five-year-olds: a developmental study. Center for Cognitive Studies, Harvard University.

4

REPRESENTATION
IN CHILDHOOD

Introduction

A sense of man's history permeates all of Bruner's work on development. The educated Western adult is seen as an event defined by the intersection of several historical progressions or trends. First, he is seen as the product of a phylogenetic history. According to this view his approach to problems, characterized by a notable reliance on symbols and language, has been to a large extent shaped by the events of primate evolution beginning with bipedalism and tool use. Second, he is seen as the product of an ontogenetic history. A full understanding of his mature cognitive capacities is thought to require an understanding of the origins of those capacities in infancy and of their transformations in childhood and adolescence. Inextricably linked with these stresses on phylogeny and ontogeny is a third historical emphasis upon man's cultural heritage. Bruner argues that a culture provides the technologies by means of which human cognitive capacities are amplified and the educational systems that profoundly alter the course of cognitive growth.

The stress on man's cognitive heritage distinguishes Bruner's work on development from his earlier work on thought and perception in which these historical progressions were never explicitly elaborated. Nonetheless, there exists an important theoretical communality between Bruner's developmental investigations and his earlier studies. A key theoretical concept in his approach to intellectual growth is that of representation, the system of rules by means of which an individual conserves in a manageable way the recurrent features of his environment. The concept of a representational system can be roughly identified with the notion of an internal model that was seen to be so important in Bruner's approach to perception and thought described in sections 1 and 2. Yet the concept of representation has been differentiated and articulated in the developmental work in a way that the notion of a model had not been. Bruner distinguishes three systems of representation, based upon action, imagery, and language.

These are called enactive representation, iconic representation, and symbolic representation, respectively. He argues that their appearance in the course of growth is in that order, although one system of representation is not replaced but rather supplemented by subsequent systems.

The preceding section on infancy was concerned primarily with the development of enactive or manual intelligence. The major emphasis in Bruner's earlier developmental work on childhood (for instance, 2) which will be considered in this section was not so much on enactive representation as it was on the transition from iconic to symbolic reckoning. In the first article, "The Growth of Representational Processes in Childhood," Bruner elaborates the notion of representation, identifies its three forms, and argues that such a concept satisfies several criteria that must be met by an adequate theory of growth. He then goes on to describe two experiments which suggest that young children depend on images, while older children employ symbolic manipulation in their approach to problems. This paper is supplemented by "The Course of Cognitive Growth" in which several studies are described which suggest again that young children are dominated and often misled by perceptual appearance, whereas older children seem less bound by surface structure and more facile in solving problems, presumably because of their ability to make use of symbolic transformations. In "The Development of Equivalence Transformations in Childhood" by Bruner and Olver, the growth of a specific symbolic transformation, the one involved in verbalizing the equivalence relation among a group of concepts, is examined in detail.

We close this section with "Culture and Cognitive Growth" by Greenfield and Bruner in order to establish a link between Bruner's work on childhood and his work in education exemplified by the articles in section 5. In this selection, the concern is with "what it means, intellectually, to grow up in one cultural milieu and not another." As we shall see in his work on education, Bruner (1) views mental growth as "a mastering of techniques that are embodied in the culture and that are passed on in a contingent dialogue by agents of the culture." As the last article of this section suggests, school is one such cultural agent that is extremely important in shaping the intellectual structures of an individual in the course of his growth.

References

1. BRUNER, J. S. 1966. *Toward a theory of instruction.* Cambridge, Mass.: Harvard University Press.
2. BRUNER, J. S.; OLVER, R. R.; GREENFIELD, P. M.; et al. 1966. *Studies in cognitive growth.* New York: Wiley.

18

The Growth of Representational
Processes in Childhood *

There are, of course, many ways to look at the growth of human intellect, for many processes are involved in going from the early impotence of childhood to the enormous powers of the thinking, talking, coping adult who participates in a culture that serves further to amplify and effectuate his cognitive powers. One way has been to look classically at the course of this growth in terms of increased effectiveness in performance, using as a measure of this increase some set of testing tasks to supply a metric of progress. However useful this normative approach for such practical purposes as school placement and the like, it fails to give us a close enough view of the psychological processes involved in growth and of the cultural conditions that shape such growth.

But let us not criticize our ancestors. They were bold enough at least to open the frontier. It was a beginning. How shall we now most fruitfully conceive of the growth of cognitive powers—of intellect, most broadly viewed as man's capacity to achieve, retain, and transform knowledge to his own uses? Let me begin by urging a set of criteria for answering a question of this kind. Then, I shall present a brief sketch of an answer

* "The Growth of Representational Processes in Childhood," by Jerome S. Bruner, a paper presented at the meeting of the 18th International Congress of Psychology in Moscow in August 1966.

along with some experiments to illustrate.[1] The criteria are in the form of antinomies, in which conceptual virtue and vice live side by side, the one being either an excess or a containment of the other.

Any theory of intellectual growth, to take the first criterion, must characterize the operations of mind in some formal and precise fashion. Such a theory cannot, for example, ignore the basic logical categories in terms of which epistemology, logic, and the fundamentals of mathematics are concerned. The description of what a child has done when he is thinking through or thinking about a problem must include as close an analytic account of his operations from a logical point of view as possible. This is as necessary for adequate description as is the centimeters-grams-seconds description of overt action when describing, say, motor behavior. We owe much to Piaget (10) for bringing this matter more clearly to view and arguing its merits. But each virtue has its defect, and the defect in this case is an empty formalism. For one does not account for or explain a train of intellectual activity by describing its underlying logic any more than one accounts for space perception by describing the geometry of the situation, yet the former is a necessary step for achieving the latter. I do not know whether we have achieved the formulation of a logical notation that is adequate to the task—a proper syntax of thought—though I rather doubt it. Whether it will look like the algebras of Boole (1) and of Whitehead and Russell (14) or the programming languages and compilers of today's computational science, we cannot yet know. But it is crucial that there be a precise mode of describing the products of thought, at least as good as what is available for describing the products of the speech flow of language that is to be explained by psychological theory. In a word, the future of theories of intellectual growth depends as much upon our cousins, the logicians, mathematicians, and other formal analysts, as it does upon us. Vague descriptions will never give birth to powerful theories. Psychological theories of cognitive functioning will have to take account of the formal structure of the acts of thought and account for these in psychological terms. We cannot first reduce what we wish to describe either to some trivial level—reduce reasoning to associations or *S-R* bonds without examining reasoning further—or simply leave thought in the status of some globally defined tendency.

A second criterion: A theory of intellectual growth must take account of the natural ways of thought, the ones that seem ordinary or intuitively obvious or *lebensnah* and give these some special status. It was Wertheimer's (13) great contribution as well as a feature of Gestalt theory to recognize this point. But we must also bear in mind that much of thinking is carried out with culturally invented instruments, and that what is artificial before one has mastered the use of a tool may be nothing of the sort once

[1] For a fuller account see Bruner et al. (2).

the tool has become our servant. Mathematical analysis is not natural for one who is ignorant of algebra, just as driving nails is unnatural to the bare hand without a hammer. Perhaps man's principal tool is language and the symbolic techniques that underlie it. It was Pavlov's (8) genius to recognize and Vygotsky's (12) to exploit the distinction between classical conditioning prior to the growth of symbolic function and thought after the intrusion of the so-called second signal system. For what is natural after one has come to use a particular tool is determined as much or more by the tool as by the user; this is as true for language users as for users of other tools.

A third criterion, implied by what has just been said, is that any account of cognitive growth (or any form of human growth, perhaps) should take into account the nature of the culture in which a human being grows. For, as we have already noted, a culture is, among other things, a system of techniques for giving shape and power to human capacities. The values, tools, and ways of knowing of a culture equip its members. Yet, the danger of this view is, of course, that it can be converted into a cheap cultural relativism that elevates to significance all instances of cultural difference and overlooks the many deep universals in both human nature and in all cultures. In every culture in the world, for example, each and every human being has a name and bears a classificatory kinship relation to others in the culture, a fact that affects the name by which he is known. This is not to say that different kinship systems may not affect ways of viewing the world. Rather, it would be insane to overlook the importance of the universal character of names and kinship by concentrating exclusively on cultural differences. Perhaps perspective can be maintained by comparing human and cultural universals with the universal characteristics of another, nonhuman primate species, a matter that concerns us now in enunciating a fourth and final criterion for a theory of intellectual growth.

A theory must take into account man's primate ancestry and consider the manner in which the evolution of primates and of man imposes a pattern on his growth. Bipedalism, neoteny, tool use, language, certain forms of space perception and spatial intuition, cortical dominance—all of these have evolutionary sequelae relevant to understanding man and his growth. The penetrating work of scholars like Le Gros Clark (6) on the systematic changes from tree shrew, to lemur, to tarsier, to monkey, to ape, to man has hardly been appreciated for its relevance to the growth of human functioning. Yet, for all the importance that may be attached to the shaping forces of man's evolution, we must also beware lest we fall into sophisticated versions of old recapitulation theories of human growth. But while we may laugh at the old enthusiasm for the biogenetic law, our laughter had better not drown out the more sober fact that perceptually, intellectually, emotionally, man is very much a primate.

Let me add one final point in the spirit of a hope rather than a criterion.

Once we have formulated a view of man's intellectual growth that takes into account the formal properties of the products of thought, considers the instrumental nature of thought, responds to the cultural patterning of intelligence, and places man in an evolutionary context, let us also ask whether we have contributed to our understanding of how to educate man to the point where he can use his intellectual heritage to the full. For if a theory of the growth of mind cannot help in that enterprise, nor contribute to the understanding of education, it must surely be at fault.

Representation and Cognitive Development

A useful concept for conceiving of the growth of intellect is the idea of representation. There is no need here for a long discussion of representation; only a few of the features of the concept need concern us. In effect, representation or a system of representation is a set of rules in terms of which one conserves one's encounters with events. A representation of the world or of some segment of one's experience has several interesting features. For one thing, it is in some medium. We may represent some events by the actions they require, by some form of picture, or in words or other symbols. There are many subvarieties within each of these three media—the enactive, the iconic, or the symbolic. A representation of an event is selective. In constructing a model of something, we do not include everything about it. The principle of selectivity is usually determined by the ends to which a representation is put—what we are going to do with what has been retained in this ordered way. Representations, by virtue of their summary nature, are rulebound in the sense that each representation is not an arbitrary or random sampling of what it stands for. That is to say, a representation of a spatially extended event uses a spatial notation that is common to a larger set of extended events. Much of spontaneous learning consists of inducing more general rules for more economical or more effective ways of representing similar events. And much of this learning consists of a kind of translation of one representational system into another, as when we become capable not only of following a given path habitually, but of representing it by an image in our mind's eye.

There are three kinds of representational systems that are operative during the growth of human intellect and whose interaction is central to growth. All of them are amenable to specification in fairly precise terms, all can be shown to be affected and shaped by linkage with tool or instrumental systems, all of them are within important limits affected by cultural conditioning and by man's evolution. They are, as already indicated, enactive representation, iconic representation, and symbolic representation—knowing something through doing it, through a picture or image of it, and through some such symbolic means as language. With respect to a particular knot, we learn the act of tying it; when we know the knot, we know it by some habitual act we have mastered and can repeat. The habit by which the knot is organized is serially organized, governed by some schema that holds its successive segments together, and is in some important sense related to other habitual acts that facilitate or interfere with its learning and execution. What is crucial is that the representation is expressed in the medium of action with many features constrained by the nature of action, for example, its sequential and irreversible nature.

An image of a knot carried in your mind or on a page is not the same thing as the knot being tied, although the image can provide a schema around which action can be sequentially organized. An image is a selective, simultaneous, and often highly stylized analogue of an event experienced. Yet it is not arbitrary in its manner of referring to events as is a word. You can recognize an image of something, once having seen the something in question. You cannot recognize the appropriate word by knowing only the event it signifies. Linguistic signification is, in the main, arbitrary and depends upon the mastery of a symbolic code. A linguistic description, therefore, involves knowing not only the referents of words, but the rules for forming and transforming utterances. These rules, like the rules of image formation and habitual action, are distinctive to the medium of language.

Growth involves not a series of stages, but rather a successive mastering of three forms of representation along with their partial translation each into the others. The child in the early months of life literally defines events by the actions they evoke. Piaget's brilliant descriptions of the six- and seven-month-old child are readily replicated (9). The child has great difficulty at this age separating a percept and an act. To restore an object lost from view, he will perform an act appropriate to it. In time, perception becomes autonomous or relatively autonomous from action, and the child now has two semi-independent systems for representing things and a task of translation to master—to bring action and appearance into some correspondence.[2]

Symbolic representation is clearly the most mysterious of the three. Present evidence suggests that much of human syntax—rules of stunning power —is learned in the two or three years between the ages of two and four or five. There must be a huge innate component in this learning, in this unlocking of a syntactic component. It is not only mastered very swiftly and effortlessly, but first acquired in certain universal forms not to be found in the diverse adult speech communities into which children enter, so that pure imitation is hardly the relevant answer. Nor does syntactic competence bear much relation to the child's capacities on the semantic level. The child can say it correctly long before he can use his words and sen-

---

[2] See Bruner et al. (2) for a fuller account of the process whereby a world of imagery comes first to be abstracted from action and then comes to be coordinated with it in a fashion that permits higher-order integration of sensorimotor behavior.

tences in a fashion realistically appropriate to the situation. Only slowly does he learn to relate the language he speaks to his thoughts about things, to order his representation of the world by the syntactical logic inherent in his speech. As he makes progress in that direction, again there is the task of translating from one mode of representation to another, of resolving the conflicts and contradictions that characterize the difference between how one does it, how it looks, and how one says it.

How does the idea of representation measure up to our four criteria? The formal properties of a representational system are, I believe, amenable to close and precise description, notably the languages in terms of which symbolic and iconic representations are effected. The description of action patterns remains obscure, though concepts of backput (Drever, 3), the *TOTE* unit (Miller, Galanter, and Pribram, 7), and reafference (Held, 4) help to clear up our understanding of action patterns as modes of representing events. It is also plain that the notion of representation does not, so to speak, stop at the human skin. The technologies that a culture provides through language, myths and explanations, metrical and reckoning systems, tools, and its disciplines of knowledge, all reinforce, amplify, and enrich human representational capacities. With respect to a biological and evolutionary perspective, let me only comment that modern ethnological conceptions are centrally concerned with representation in such mechanisms as releasers and imprinting, much of it deriving from the originating idea of the *Umwelt* first proposed by von Uexküll (11). Finally, if education is not concerned with instilling skill and zest for representing one's experience and knowledge in some balance between rich particularity and economical generality, then I am not sure what else it is about.

Experiments

An experiment by Olson [3] was carried out with the aid of a simple piece of apparatus: a rectangular board of five columns and five rows of small light bulbs. Each bulb, upon being pressed by the child, either lights up in brilliant scarlet red or remains unlit, depending upon whether the bulb is part of a pattern or not. The child's task is to discover, by pressing as few bulbs as possible, which one of several patterns presented to him are hidden in the bulb board. Only one bulb can be pressed at a time. Figure 1 shows the board with two alternative patterns. The child must press to determine which of the two is on the board.

Children are introduced to the task by being shown the correspondence between a single model and the board and then tested for their comprehension of the task. Different patterns, varying in difficulty and in number of alternatives, are presented to the child, his task always being the same: to

[3] See chapter 6, "On Conceptual Strategies" (2).

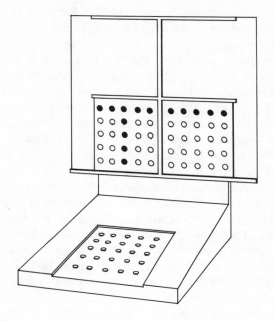

FIGURE 1. Apparatus used in the Olson experiment

press the bulbs that will tell him which alternative pattern lights up on the board. For ease and brevity, we consider now the pair of alternatives on the board in Figure 1: a *T* and a top horizontal bar.

The best way to describe the general course of development in the handling of this task is in terms of the strategies characteristic of the three-year-old, the five-year-old, and the eight-year-old. Their performance characterizes major turning points in development. The three-year-old is, in effect, searching the board for bulbs that will light up—his conception of positive instances. His search is not random. Likely he will start at an edge and, having pressed a bulb, the chances are that he will press one of its immediate neighbors. To put it figuratively in the interest of brevity, he is hoping that a perceptual pattern will spring from the board and often he must be restrained from pressing more than a single bulb at a time. His actions, he hopes, will produce the figure that can then be recognized as corresponding to one of the two before him. Needless to say, three-year-olds rarely succeed.

By age five, it is quite different. Now the child is quite capable of carrying an image representation to the task. But the procedure is striking in one special feature. No matter how many alternatives are presented, the five-year-old will try out one at a time, testing it and eliminating or accepting it, the latter often on insufficient evidence. Each test of an alternative model is of that model and does not use priorly encountered information. In the task of discriminating the *T* from the top horizontal line, a five-year-old, for example, will check the five bulbs across the top and announce it is the horizontal bar. If you then urge him on to check whether it might possibly be the *T,* he will check the vertical as well. But if these should prove not to light, it is almost certain that the child will simply go back to checking the horizontal one again. Confirmation seems to involve direct test of a hypothesis presently in force about a particular image, or perhaps it is better to say direct test of an image.

What is striking about the eight-year-old is that he seems to be able to deal with information properly defined rather than simply in terms of single images. He can deal simultaneously with the patterns before him by dealing with their inclusion, exclusion, and overlap, in order to isolate distinctive features. The older child characteristically takes much longer to decide which bulb to press, though by age nine the choice time begins to speed up again as the child becomes master of the task of using symbolic operations as a basis for dealing simultaneously with many alternative images.

What are we to make of this shift from an active search strategy, to a pattern-matching strategy, and finally to an information-selection strategy? What does this tell us of the growth of representation? The initial search strategy shows a strong carry-over of an early interdependence of action and percept, as if the child were trying to create a response-produced stimulus, to get it all out there by his acts so that it may be discriminated. By the fifth year, the child's choice of bulbs to be pressed is controlled by the patterns before him—but one pattern at a time—and he is not able to embed the alternatives into the hierarchial structure that is the essence of symbolic representation. Only when the apparatus of symbolism can be applied to the task can the set of alternative images be fused into what can be described as an information space, characterized by distinctive features.

We now turn to a second experiment that illustrates the growth of representation in a quite different context. Here our vehicle is the beautiful paradigm experiment on conservation developed at Geneva by Inhelder and Piaget (5). In the classic study, a child begins with two balls of plasticine which the child agrees are equal in amount of material. One of the balls is then deformed in a certain manner, and the child is asked if they still contain the same amount of clay. Under a fairly wide range of circumstances, a five- or six-year-old will say that if one ball has been deformed into the shape of a pancake or a sausage it is "less than the other." We will leave out of the account here the Genevan explanation of the phenomenon and will describe an experiment done with a variant of it by Sonstroem.[4]

4 See chapter 10, "On the Conservation of Solids" (2).

The experiment was carried out with six- and seven-year-olds and began with a pretest to determine that the children showed no conservation in the Piagetian sense. This was followed by some training trials and then there was a posttest. Two major factors were studied in the training procedure: the effect of active manipulation of the materials and the effect of labeling the shapes produced. Four groups were formed: those who altered the second ball of clay themselves and also had to characterize the shapes produced (both labeling and manipulating); those who labeled but did not manipulate the material (the clay was altered by the experimenter); those who manipulated and did not label; and those who did neither.

For example, the training with the child doing the manipulating would go like this:

After the subject had made a pencil (or whatever he chose) from one of the balls and had judged their relative amounts, the experimenter said to him, "O.K., now will you please take that pencil you made and make it back into a ball again, just like it was before (the underscored phrase was always empha-sized). As the child made the pencil back into a ball, the experimenter asked him several times, "Is it just like it was before yet?" When the child asserted that it was just like it was before, he was asked to judge the relative amounts of the two pieces again.

The identical procedure for training, but with labeling added, was as fol-lows:

After the subject had made a pencil, he was asked, "Which one is the long-est?" If he indicated that the pencil was the longer, the experimenter then said, "Now tell me which one is the fattest?" If the child indicated the ball, the ex-perimenter said, "O.K., the pencil is longest, but the ball is the fattest; now tell me, does one of them have more clay than the other or do they have the same?" After the child had given his judgment, the experimenter said, "O.K., you told me the pencil is the longest and the ball is the fattest. Now I want you to take this long pencil and make it just as fat as the ball for me." As the child rolled the pencil back into a ball (which he usually did to make it just as fat), the experimenter asked him several times, "Is it as fat yet?" and "Is it still longer?" When the child asserted that it was just as fat, he was asked to judge the relative amount of the two pieces again. In the second half of these trials, when the subject made a pencil from the other ball, he was asked to "make the fat ball just as long as the pencil," instead of the other way around as in the first half.

Before turning to the rationale and significance of these procedures, let me quickly outline the results. Only about a quarter of the children who went through the experiment without labeling and without handling the materials improved on the posttest. What is interesting is that not many more of them (not significantly more) improved by virtue of having the la-beling training alone or the manipulation training alone. But when both

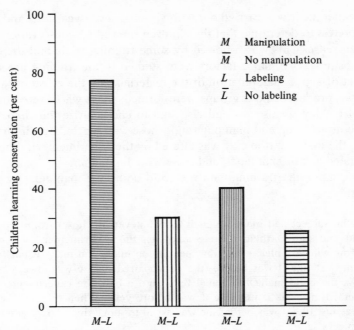

FIGURE 2. Per cent of children learning conservation with labeling and manipulation variables combined

kinds of training are given together, over three-quarters of the children show conservation on the posttest. Figure 2 sums up the results in graphic form. Now let me explain.

There are by now a sufficient number of experiments from our own and other laboratories to indicate that failure of conservation involves not so much failure but, rather, another way of reckoning equivalence by a standard of appearance—iconic reckoning which operates on the principle that if there is inequality between two events in a salient perceptual property, then equality is violated. The distinction between surface structure and deep structure is not grasped when appearance is the sole basis of judgment. Frank[5] had found that if judgments could be made in a conservation task literally behind a screen and in the form of a prediction before the child saw the quantities involved, conservation could often be produced by virtue of the conflict established between the child saying, "It's the same 'cause you only poured it," and the subsequent appearance of water in one tall, thin beaker being greater in height.

The present experiment, by the joint use of labeling and manipulating, offered the child ways of representing the problem that conflicted with the

[5] See the description of Frank's experiment in chapter 9, "On the Conservation of Liquids" (2).

iconic mode. By offering him manipulation, Sonstroem was encouraging enactive representation; and by offering him dimensionalized verbal labeling as she did, she encouraged symbolic representation by linguistic encoding. Manipulation and language were both pitted against appearance. The interesting fact is that neither of the other modes of representation alone was able to induce enough conflict to produce appreciable learning. This is not so surprising, given the enormous power of perceptual cues in the six- and seven-year-old. Perhaps the psychology of conservation, indeed, all forms of invariance, involve a recognition that the same thing can take many guises and still be the same thing. It is probably a peculiarity of the perceptual or iconic sphere that it succumbs most to the error of taking a change in appearance to signal a change in identity.

Indeed, each culture has certain unique ways of dealing with the relation of the three systems. In Greenfield's field studies in Senegal,[6] she found that Frank's screening procedure, so successful in a Western setting, had little effect with Senegalese children. What could produce change was giving the children conservation tasks in which they themselves rather than adults manipulated the materials, largely because the children expected magic powers of adults, but not of themselves.

This is only an introduction to a topic with many more experiments worth mentioning and many more theoretical issues still to be explicated. I am convinced that we shall do better to conceive of growth as an empowering of the individual by multiple means for representing his world, multiple means that often conflict and create the dilemmas that stimulate growth. It is not the whole story of growth and increased competence, but it is, I believe, very close to the center of what is involved when a human being equipped with the gifts of action, imagery, and symbolism, comes to know and to master his world.

References

1. BOOLE, G. 1953. *Laws of thought.* New York: Dover.
2. BRUNER, J. S.; OLVER, R. R.; GREENFIELD, P. M.; et al. 1966. *Studies in cognitive growth.* New York: Wiley.
3. DREVER, J. 1962. Perception and Action. *Bulletin of the British Psychological Society,* no. 45, p. 1.
4. HELD, R. 1965. Plasticity in sensory-motor systems. *Scientific American,* 213(5):84–94.
5. INHELDER, B., and PIAGET, J. 1964. *The early growth of logic in the child.* New York: Harper.
6. LE GROS CLARK, W. E. 1963. *The antecedents of man.* New York: Harper.
7. MILLER, G. A.; GALANTER, E.; and PRIBRAM, K. H. 1960. *Plans and the structure of behavior.* New York: Holt.
8. PAVLOV, I. P. 1929. *Lectures on conditioned reflexes.* New York: International Publishers.

[6] See chapters 11 and 13, "On Culture and Conservation" and "On Culture and Equivalence-II" (2).

324   REPRESENTATION IN CHILDHOOD

9. Piaget, J. 1954. *The construction of reality in the child*. Trans. M. Cook. New York: Basic Books.
10. Piaget, J. 1957. *Logic and psychology*. New York: Basic Books.
11. Uexküll, J. von. 1909. *Umwelt und Innenwelt der Tiere*. 2d ed. Berlin: J. Springer.
12. Vygotsky, L. S. 1962. *Thought and language*. Ed. and trans. E. Hanfmann and G. Vakar. Cambridge, Mass.: MIT Press, and New York: Wiley.
13. Wertheimer, M. 1959. *Productive thinking*. Rev. ed. New York: Harper.
14. Whitehead, A. N., and Russell, B. 1925–1927. *Principia mathematica*. 2d ed. 3 vols. New York: Cambridge University Press.

19

The Course of Cognitive Growth*

The development of human intellectual functioning from infancy to such perfection as it may reach is shaped by a series of technological advances in the use of mind. Growth depends upon the mastery of techniques and cannot be understood without reference to such mastery. These techniques are not, in the main, inventions of the individuals who are growing up; they are, rather, skills transmitted with varying efficiency and success by the culture—language being a prime example. Cognitive growth, then, is in a major way from the outside in as well as from the inside out.

Two matters will concern us. The first has to do with the techniques or technologies that aid growing human beings to represent in a manageable way the recurrent features of the complex environments in which they live. It is fruitful, I think, to distinguish three systems for processing information by which human beings construct models of their world: through action, through imagery, and through language. A second concern is with integration, the means whereby acts are organized into higher-order ensembles, making possible the use of larger and larger units of information for the solution of particular problems.

* Jerome S. Bruner, "The Course of Cognitive Growth," *American Psychologist,* Vol. 19, 1964, pp. 1–15. Copyright 1964 by the American Psychological Association, and reproduced by permission of the publisher.

The assistance of R. R. Olver and Mrs. Blythe Clinchy in the preparation of this paper is gratefully acknowledged.

Let me first elucidate these two theoretical matters, and then turn to an examination of the research upon which they are based.

On the occasion of the One Hundredth Anniversary of the publication of Darwin's *The Origin of Species,* S. L. Washburn and F. Clark Howell presented a paper at the Chicago Centennial celebration containing the following passage:

> It would now appear . . . that the large size of the brain of certain hominids was a relatively late development and that the brain evolved due to new selection pressures *after* bipedalism and consequent upon the use of tools. The tool-using, ground-living, hunting way of life created the large human brain rather than a large brained man discovering certain new ways of life. [We] believe this conclusion is the most important result of the recent fossil hominid discoveries and is one which carries far-reaching implications for the interpretation of human behavior and its origins. . . . The important point is that size of brain, insofar as it can be measured by cranial capacity, has increased some threefold subsequent to the use and manufacture of implements. . . . The uniqueness of modern man is seen as the result of a technical-social life which tripled the size of the brain, reduced the face, and modified many other structures of the body (30, p. 49 f.).

This implies that the principal change in man over a long period of years—perhaps 500,000—has been alloplastic rather than autoplastic. That is to say, he has changed by linking himself with new, external implementation systems rather than by any conspicuous change in morphology —"evolution-by-prosthesis," as Weston La Barre (14) puts it. The implement systems seem to have been of three general kinds: (*a*) amplifiers of human motor capacities ranging from the cutting tool through the lever and wheel to the wide variety of modern devices; (*b*) amplifiers of sensory capacities that include primitive devices such as smoke signaling and modern ones such as magnification and radar sensing, but also likely include such software as those conventionalized perceptual shortcuts that can be applied to the redundant sensory environment; and finally (*c*) amplifiers of human ratiocinative capacities of infinite variety ranging from language systems to myth and theory and explanation. All of these forms of amplification are in major or minor degree conventionalized and transmitted by the culture, the last of them probably the most, since ratiocinative amplfiers involve symbol systems governed by rules that must, for effective use, be shared.

Any implement system, to be effective, must produce an appropriate internal counterpart, an appropriate skill necessary for organizing sensorimotor acts, for organizing percepts, and for organizing our thoughts in a way that matches them to the requirements of implement systems. These internal skills, represented genetically as capacities, are slowly selected in evolution. In the deepest sense, then, man can be described as a species that has become specialized by the use of technological implements. His selection and survival have depended upon a morphology and set of capacities that could be linked with the alloplastic devices that have made his later evolution possible. We move, perceive, and think in a fashion that depends upon techniques rather than upon wired-in arrangements in our nervous system.

Where representation of the environment is concerned, it too depends upon techniques that are learned—and these are precisely the techniques that serve to amplify our motor acts, our perceptions, and our ratiocinative activities. We know and respond to recurrent regularities in our environment by skilled and patterned acts, by conventionalized spatioqualitative imagery and selective perceptual organization, and through linguistic encoding which, as so many writers have remarked, places a selective lattice between us and the physical environment. In short, the capacities that have been shaped by our evolution as tool users are the ones that we rely upon in the primary task of representation—the nature of which we shall consider in more detail directly.

As for integration, it is a truism that there are very few single or simple adult acts that cannot be performed by a young child. In short, any more highly skilled activity can be decomposed into simpler components, each of which can be carried out by a less-skilled operator. What higher skills require is that the component operations be combined. Maturation consists of an orchestration of these components into an integrated sequence. The distractability, so-called, of much early behavior may reflect each act's lack of embeddedness in what Miller, Galanter, and Pribram (21) speak of as "plans." These integrated plans, in turn, reflect the routines and subroutines that one learns in the course of mastering the patterned nature of a social environment. So that integration, too, depends upon patterns that come from the outside in—an internalization of what Roger Barker (2) has called environmental "behavior settings."

If we are to benefit from contact with recurrent regularities in the environment, we must represent them in some manner. To dismiss this problem as mere memory is to misunderstand it. For the most important thing about memory is not storage of past experience, but rather the retrieval of what is relevant in some usable form. This depends upon how past experience is coded and processed so that it may indeed be relevant and usable in the present when needed. The end product of such a system of coding and processing is what we may speak of as a representation.

I shall call the three modes of representation mentioned earlier enactive representation, iconic representation, and symbolic representation. Their appearance in the life of the child is in that order, each depending upon the previous one for its development, yet all of them remaining more or less intact throughout life—barring such early accidents as blindness or deafness or cortical injury. By enactive representation I mean a mode of representing past events through appropriate motor response. We cannot, for example, give an adequate description of familiar sidewalks or floors over which we habitually walk, nor do we have much of an image of what they are like. Yet we get about them without tripping or even looking much. Such segments of our environment—bicycle riding, tying knots, aspects of driving—get represented in our muscles, so to speak. Iconic representation summarizes events by the selective organization of percepts and of images, by the spatial, temporal, and qualitative structures of the perceptual field and their transformed images. Images stand for perceptual events in the close but conventionally selective way that a picture stands for the object pictured. Finally, a symbol system represents things by design features that include remoteness and arbitrariness. A word neither points directly to its referent here and now, nor does it resemble it as a picture. The lexeme *Philadelphia* looks no more like the city so designated than does a nonsense syllable. The other property of language that is crucial is its productiveness in combination, far beyond what can be done with images or acts. Philadelphia is a lavendar sachet in Grandmother's linen closet, or $(x+2)^2 = x^2 + 4x + 4 = x(x+4) + 4$.

An example or two of enactive representation underlines its importance in infancy and in disturbed functioning, while illustrating its limitations. Piaget (25) provides us with an observation from the closing weeks of the first year of life. The child is playing with a rattle in his crib. The rattle drops over the side. The child moves his clenched hand before his face, opens it, looks for the rattle. Not finding it there, he moves his hand, closed again, back to the edge of the crib, shakes it with movements like those he uses in shaking the rattle. Thereupon he moves his closed hand back toward his face, opens it, and looks. Again no rattle; and so he tries again. In several months, the child has benefited from experience to the degree that the rattle and action become separated. Whereas earlier he would not show signs of missing the rattle when it was removed unless he had begun reaching for it, now he cries and searches when the rattle is presented for a moment and hidden by a cover. He no longer repeats a movement to restore the rattle. In place of representation by action alone —where existence is defined by the compass of present action—it is now defined by an image that persists autonomously.

A second example is provided by the results of injury to the occipital and temporal cortex in man (Hanfmann, Rickers-Ovsiankina, and Goldstein, 9). A patient is presented with a hard-boiled egg intact in its shell, and asked what it is. Holding it in his hand, he is embarrassed, for he cannot name it. He makes a motion as if to throw it and halts himself. Then he brings it to his mouth as if to bite it and stops before he gets there. He brings it to his ear and shakes it gently. He is puzzled. The experimenter takes the egg from him and cracks it on the table, handing it back. The patient then begins to peel the egg and announces what it is. He cannot identify objects without reference to the action he directs toward them.

The disadvantages of such a system are illustrated by Emerson's (7) experiment in which children are told to place a ring on a board with seven rows and six columns of pegs, copying the position of a ring put on an identical board by the experimenter. Children ranging from 3 to 12 were examined in this experiment and in an extension of it carried out by Werner (32). The child's board could be placed in various positions relative to the experimenter's: right next to it, 90 degrees rotated away from it, 180 degrees rotated, placed face to face with it so that the child has to turn full around to make his placement, and so on. The older the child, the better his performance. But the younger children could do about as well as the oldest so long as they did not have to change their own position vis-à-vis the experimenter's board in order to make a match on their own board. The more they had to turn, the more difficult the task. They were clearly depending upon their bodily orientation toward the experimenter's board to guide them. When this orientation is disturbed by having to turn, they lose the position on the board. Older children succeed even when they must turn, either by the use of imagery that is invariant across bodily displacements, or, later, by specifying column and row of the experimenter's ring and carrying the symbolized self-instruction back to their own board. It is a limited world, the world of enactive representation.

We know little about the conditions necessary for the growth of imagery and iconic representation, or to what extent parental or environmental intervention affects it during the earliest years. In ordinary adult learning a certain amount of motoric skill and practice seems to be a necessary precondition for the development of a simultaneous image to represent the sequence of acts involved. If an adult subject is made to choose a path through a complex bank of toggle switches, he does not form an image of the path, according to Mandler (18), until he has mastered and overpracticed the task by successive manipulation. Then, finally, he reports that an image of the path has developed and that he is now using it rather than groping his way through.

Our main concern in what follows is not with the growth of iconic representation, but with the transition from it to symbolic representation. For it is in the development of symbolic representation that one finds, perhaps, the greatest thicket of psychological problems. The puzzle begins when the child first achieves the use of productive grammar, usually late in the second year of life. Toward the end of the second year, the child is master of the single-word, agrammatical utterance, the so-called holophrase. In the months following, there occurs a profound change in the use of language. Two classes of words appear—a pivot class and an open class—and the child launches forth on his career in combinatorial talking and, perhaps, thinking. Whereas before, lexemes like *allgone* and *mummy* and *sticky* and *bye-bye* were used singly, now, for example, *allgone* becomes a pivot word and is used in combination. Mother washes jam off the child's hands; he says *allgone sticky*. In the next days, if his speech is carefully followed (Braine, 3), it will be apparent that he is trying out the limits of the pivot combinations, and one will even find constructions that have an extraordinary capacity for representing complex sequences—like *allgone bye-bye* after a visitor has departed. A recent and ingenious observation by Weir (31) on her two-and-a-half-year-old son, recording his speech musings after he was in bed with lights out, indicates that at this stage there is a great deal of metalinguistic combinatorial play with words in which the child is exploring the limits of grammatical productiveness.

In effect, language provides a means, not only for representing experience, but also for transforming it. As Chomsky (6) and Miller (20) have both made clear in the last few years, the transformational rules of grammar provide a syntactic means of reworking the realities one has encountered. Not only, if you will, did the dog bite the man, but the man was bitten by the dog and perhaps the man was not bitten by the dog or was the man not bitten by the dog. The range of reworking that is made possible even by the three transformations of the passive, the negative, and the query is very striking indeed. Or the ordering device whereby the comparative mode makes it possible to connect what is heavy and what is light into the ordinal array of heavy and less heavy is again striking. Or, to take a final example, there is the discrimination that is made possible by the growth of attribute language such that the global dimension big and little can now be decomposed into tall and short on the one hand and fat and skinny on the other.

Once the child has succeeded in internalizing language as a cognitive instrument, it becomes possible for him to represent and systematically transform the regularities of experience with far greater flexibility and power than before. Interestingly enough, it is the recent Russian literature, particularly Vygotsky's (29) book on language and thought, and the work of his disciple, Luria (17), and his students (Abramyan, 1; Martsinovskaya, 19) that has high-lighted these phenomena by calling attention to the so-called second signal system which replaces classical conditioning with an internalized linguistic system for shaping and transforming experience itself.

If all these matters were not of such complexity and human import, I would apologize for taking so much time in speculation. We turn now to some new experiments designed to shed some light on the nature of representation and particularly upon the transition from its iconic to its symbolic form.

Let me begin with an experiment by Bruner and Kenney (5) on the manner in which children between five and seven handle a double classification matrix. The materials of the experiment are nine plastic glasses, arranged so that they vary in 3 degrees of diameter and 3 degrees of height. They are set before the child initially, as in Figure 1, on a 3x3 grid marked on a large piece of cardboard. To acquaint the child with the matrix, we first remove one, then two, and then three glasses from the matrix, asking the child to replace them. We also ask the children to describe how the glasses in the columns and rows are alike and how they differ. Then the glasses are scrambled and we ask the child to make something like what was there before by placing the glasses on the same grid that was used when the task was introduced. Now we scramble the glasses once more, but this time we place the glass that was formerly in the southwest corner of the grid in the southeast corner (it is the shortest, thinnest glass) and ask the child if he can make something like what was there before, leaving the one glass where we have just put it. That is the experiment.

The results can be quickly told. To begin with, there is no difference between ages five, six, and seven either in terms of ability to replace glasses taken from the matrix or in building a matrix once it has been scrambled (but without the transposed glass). Virtually all the children succeed. Interestingly enough, all the children rebuild the matrix to match the original, almost as if they were copying what was there before. The only difference is that the older children are quicker.

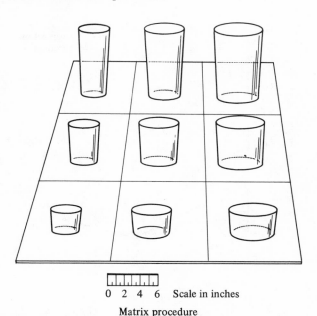

0 2 4 6   Scale in inches

Matrix procedure

FIGURE 1. Array of glasses used in study of matrix ordering (5)

Now compare the performance of the three ages in constructing the matrix with a single member transposed. Most of the seven-year-olds succeed in the transposed task, but hardly any of the youngest children. Figure 2 presents the results graphically. The youngest children seem to be dominated by an image of the original matrix. They try to put the transposed glass "back where it belongs," to rotate the cardboard so that "it will be like before," and sometimes they will start placing a few glasses neighboring the transposed glass correctly only to revert to the original arrangement. In several instances, five- or six-year-olds will simply try to reconstitute the old matrix, building right over the transposed glass. The seven-year-old, on the other hand, is more likely to pause, to treat the transposition as a problem, to talk to himself about "where this should go." The relation of place and size is for him a problem that requires reckoning, not simply copying.

Now consider the language children use for describing the dimensions of the matrix. Recall that the children were asked how glasses in a row and in a column were alike and how they differed. Children answered in three distinctive linguistic modes. One was dimensional, singling out two ends of an attribute—for example, "That one is higher, and that one is shorter." A second was global in nature. Of glasses differing only in height the child says, "That one is bigger and that one is little." The same words could be used equally well for diameter or for nearly any other magnitude. Finally, there was confounded usage, "That one is tall and that one is little," where

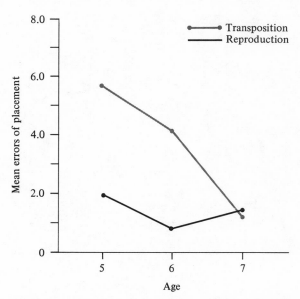

FIGURE 2. Mean number of errors made by children in reproducing and transposing a 3 x 3 matrix

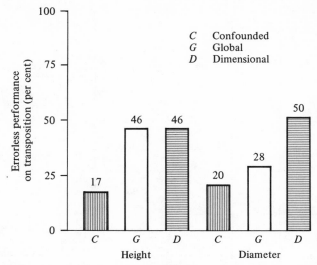

FIGURE 3. *Percentage of children (aged 5–7) using different language patterns who reproduced transposed matrix errorlessly*

a dimensional term is used for one end of the continuum and a global term for the other. The children who used confounded descriptions had the most difficulty with the transposed matrix. Lumping all ages together, the children who used confounded descriptions were twice as likely to fail on the transposition task as those who used either dimensional or global terms. But the language the children used had no relation whatsoever to their performance in reproducing the first untransposed matrix. Inhelder and Sinclair in a recent communication (12) also report that confounded language of this kind is associated with failure on conservation tasks in children of the same age, a subject to which we shall turn shortly.

The findings of this experiment suggest two things. First, that children who use iconic representation are more highly sensitized to the spatial-qualitative organization of experience and less to the ordering principles governing such organization. They can recognize and reproduce, but cannot produce new structures based on rule. And second, there is a suspicion that the language they bring to bear on the task is insufficient as a tool for ordering. If these notions are correct, then certain things should follow. For one thing, improvement in language should aid this type of problem solving. This remains to be investigated. But it is also reasonable to suppose that activation of language habits that the child has already mastered might improve performance as well—a hypothesis already suggested by the findings of Luria's students (for instance, Abramyan, 1). Now, activation can be achieved by two means: One is by having the child say the de-

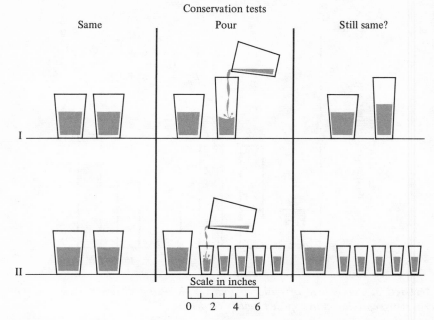

FIGURE 4. *Two Geneva tests for conservation of liquid volume across trans-formations in its appearance* (26)

scription of something before him that he must deal with symbolically. The other is to take advantage of the remoteness of reference that is a feature of language, and have the child say his description in the absence of the things to be described. In this way, there would be less likelihood of a perceptual-iconic representation becoming dominant and inhibiting the operation of symbolic processes. An experiment by Frank (8) illustrates this latter approach—the effects of saying before seeing.

Piaget and Inhelder (26) have shown that if children between ages four and seven are presented two identical beakers which they judge equally full of water, they will no longer consider the water equal if the contents of one of the beakers is now poured into a beaker that is either wider or thinner than the original. If the second beaker is thinner, they will say it has more to drink because the water is higher; if the second beaker is wider, they will say it has less because the water is lower. Comparable results can be obtained by pouring the contents of one glass into several smaller beakers. In Geneva terms, the child is not yet able to conserve liquid volume across transformations in its appearance. Consider how this behavior can be altered.

Françoise Frank first did the classic conservation tests to determine which children exhibited conservation and which did not. Her subjects were four, five, six, and seven years old. She then went on to other procedures, among which was the following: Two standard beakers are partly

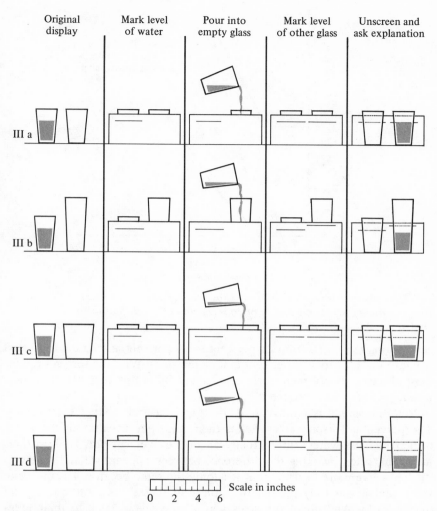

FIGURE 5. *One procedure used in study of effect of language activation on conservation*

filled so that the child judges them to contain equal amounts of water. A wider beaker of the same height is introduced and the three beakers are now, except for their tops, hidden by a screen. The experimenter pours from a standard beaker into the wider beaker. The child, without seeing the water, is asked which has more to drink, or do they have the same amount, the standard or the wider beaker. The results are in Figure 6. In comparison with the unscreened pretest, there is a striking increase in correct equality judgments. Correct responses jump from 0 per cent to 50 per

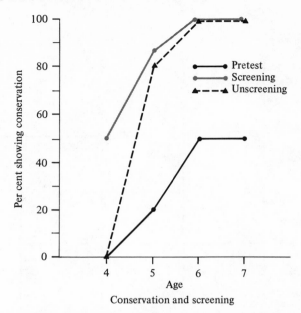

Conservation and screening

FIGURE 6. Percentage of children showing conservation of liquid volume before and during screening and upon unscreening of the displays (8)

cent among the fours, from 20 per cent to 90 per cent among the fives, and from 50 per cent to 100 per cent among the sixes. With the screen present, most children justify their correct judgment by noting that "It's the same water," or "You only poured it."

Now the screen is removed. All the four-year-olds change their minds. The perceptual display overwhelms them and they decide that the wider beaker has less water. But virtually all of the five-year-olds stick to their judgment, often invoking the difference between appearance and reality— "It looks like more to drink, but it is only the same because it is the same water and it was only poured from there to there," to quote one typical five-year-old. And all of the sixes and all the sevens stick to their judgment. Now, some minutes later, Frank does a posttest on the children using a tall thin beaker along with the standard ones, and no screen, of course. The fours are unaffected by their prior experience: None of them is able to grasp the idea of invariant quantity in the new task. With the fives instead of 20 per cent showing conservation, as in the pretest, 70 per cent do. With both sixes and sevens, conservation increases from 50 per cent to 90 per cent. I should mention that control groups doing just a pretest and posttest show no significant improvement in performance.

A related experiment of Nair's (23) explores the arguments children use when they solve a conservation task correctly and when they do not. Her subjects were all five-year-olds. She transferred water from one rectangular clear plastic tank to another that was both longer and wider than the first. Ordinarily, a five-year-old will say there is less water in the second tank. The water is, of course, lower in the second tank. She had a toy duck swimming in the first container, and when the water was poured into the new container, she told the child that, "The duck was taking his water with him."

Three kinds of arguments were set forth by the children to support their judgments. One is perceptual—having to do with the height, width, or apparent bigness of the water. A second type has to do with action: The duck took the water along, or the water was only poured. A third one, transformational argument, invokes the reversibility principle: If you poured the water back into the first container, it would look the same again.[1] Of the children who thought the water was not equal in amount after pouring, 15 per cent used nonperceptual arguments to justify their judgment. Of those who recognized the equality of the water, two-thirds used nonperceptual arguments. It is plain that if a child is to succeed in the conservation task, he must have some internalized verbal formula that shields him from the overpowering appearance of the visual displays much as in the Frank ex-

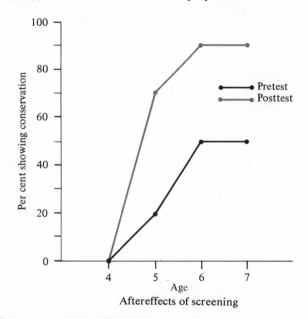

Aftereffects of screening

FIGURE 7. Percentage of children showing conservation of liquid volume in identical pretest and posttest run after completion of experiment

[1] Not one of the 40 children who participated in this experiment used the compensation argument—that though the water was lower it was correspondingly wider and was, therefore, the same amount of water. This type of reasoning by compensation is said by Piaget and Inhelder (26) to be the basis of conservation.

periment. The explanations of the children who lacked conservation suggest how strongly they were oriented to the visual appearance of the displays they had to deal with.

Consider now another experiment by Bruner and Kenney (5) also designed to explore the border between iconic and symbolic representation. Children aged five, six, and seven were asked to say which of two glasses in a pair was fuller and which emptier. Fullness is an interesting concept to work with, for it involves in its very definition a ratio or proportion between the volume of a container and the volume of a substance contained. It is difficult for the iconically oriented child to see a half-full barrel and a half-filled thimble as equally full, since the former looms larger in every one of the attributes that might be perceptually associated with volume. It is like the old riddle of which is heavier, a pound of lead or a pound of feathers. To make a correct judgment of fullness or emptiness, the child must use a symbolic operation, somewhat like computing a ratio, and resist the temptation to use perceptual appearance—that is, unless he finds some happy heuristic to save him the labor of such a computation. Figure 8 contains the 11 pairs of glasses used, and they were selected with a certain malice aforethought.

There are four types of pairs. In Type I (displays 4, 9a, and 9b), the glasses are of unequal volume, but equally, though fractionally, full. In Type II (displays 2, 7a, and 7b) again the glasses are of unequal volume, but they are completely full. Type III (displays 3, 8a, and 8b) consists of two glasses of unequal volume, one filled and the other partly filled. Type IV consists of identical glasses, in one case equally filled, in another unequally (displays 1 and 5).

All the children in the age range we have studied use pretty much the same criteria for judging fullness, and these criteria are based on directly observable sensory indexes rather than upon proportion. That glass is judged fuller that has the greater apparent volume of water, and the favored indication of greater volume is water level; or where that is equated, then width of glass will do; and when width and water level are the same, then height of glass will prevail. But now consider the judgments made by the three age groups with respect to which glass in each pair is emptier. The older children have developed an interesting consistency based on an appreciation of the complementary relation of filled and empty space— albeit an incorrect one. For them emptier means the glass that has the largest apparent volume of unfilled space, just as fuller means the glass that has the largest volume of filled space. In consequence, their responses seem logically contradictory. For the glass that is judged fuller also turns out to be the glass that is judged emptier—given a large glass and a small glass, both half full. The younger children, on the other hand, equate emptiness with littleness: That glass is emptier that gives the impression of being smaller in volume of liquid. If we take the three pairs of glasses of

Ratio procedure

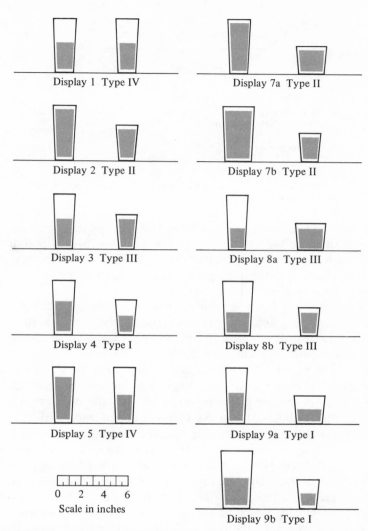

FIGURE 8. Eleven pairs of glasses to be judged in terms of which glass is fuller and which emptier (5)

Type I (unequal volumes, half filled) we can see how the judgments typically distribute themselves. Consider only the errors. The glass with the larger volume of empty space is called emptier by 27 per cent of the erring five-year-olds, by 53 per cent of the erring six-year-olds, and by 72 per cent of erring seven-year-olds. But the glass with the smallest volume of water is called emptier by 73 per cent of the five-year-olds who err, 47 per cent of the sixes, and only 28 per cent of the sevens. When the children

TABLE 1 Percentage of Erroneous Judgments
of Which of Two Glasses Is Emptier
Based on Two Criteria for
Defining the Concept

Criterion for Emptier Judgment	Age		
	5	6	7
Greater empty space	27%	53%	72%
Smaller volume of liquid	73%	47%	28%
	100%	100%	100%
Percentage correct	9%	8%	17%
N =	30	30	30

Note: Criteria are greater volume of empty space and lesser volume of water.

are asked for their reasons for judging one glass as emptier, there is further confirmation: Most of the younger children justify it by pointing to littleness or less water or some other aspect of diminutiveness. And most of the older children justify their judgments of emptiness by reference to the amount of empty space in the vessel.

The result of all this is, of course, that the logical structure of the older children seems to go increasingly awry. But surely, though Figure 9 shows that contradictory errors steadily increase with age (calling the same glass fuller and emptier or equally full but not equally empty or vice versa), the contradiction is a by-product of the method of dealing with attributes. How shall we interpret these findings? Let me suggest that what is involved is a translation difficulty in going from the perceptual or iconic realm to the symbolic. If you ask children of this age whether something can be fuller and also emptier, they will smile and think that you are playing riddles. They are aware of the contrastive nature of the two terms. Indeed, even the very young child has a good working language for the two poles of the contrast: all gone for completely empty and spill or tippy top for completely full. Recall too that from five to seven, there is perfect performance in judging which of two identical beakers is fuller and emptier. The difference between the younger and the older child is in the number of attributes that are being attended to in situations involving fullness and emptiness: The younger child is attending to one—the volume of water; the older to two—the volume of filled space and the volume of empty space. The young child is applying a single contrast pair—full-empty—to a single feature of the situation. The older child can attend to two features, but he does not yet have the means for relating them to a third, the volume of the container per se. To do so involves being able to deal with a relation in the perceptual field that does not have a "point-at-able" or ostensive definition. Once the third term is introduced—the volume of the glass

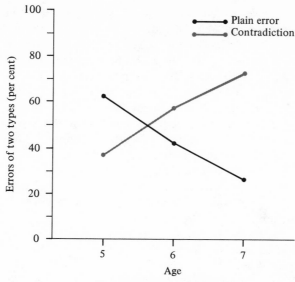

Proportion of two types of error

FIGURE 9. Percentage of children at three ages who make contradictory and plain errors in judging which of two glasses is fuller and which emptier (A contradictory error is calling the same glass both fuller or emptier or calling them equally full but not equally empty or vice versa. A plain error is calling one glass fuller and the other emptier, but incorrectly.) (5)

—then the symbolic concept of proportion can come to stand for something that is not present perceptually. The older child is on the way to achieving the insight, in spite of his contradictions. And, interestingly enough, if we count the number of children who justify their judgments of fuller and emptier by pointing to several rather than a single attribute, we find that the proportion triples in both cases between age five and age seven. The older child, it would seem, is ordering his perceptual world in such a way that, shortly, he will be able to apply concepts of relationship that are not dependent upon simple ostensive definition. As he moves to-

TABLE 2 *Percentage of Children Who Justify Judgments of Fuller and Emptier by Mentioning More Than a Single Attribute*

Age	Fuller Judgments	Emptier Judgments	N
5	7.2%	4.1%	30
6	15.6%	9.3%	30
7	22.2%	15.6%	30

ward this more powerful technology of reckoning, he is led into errors that seem to be contradictory. What is particularly telltale is the fact, for example, that in the Type III displays, younger children sometimes seem to find the judgment easier than older children—pointing to the fuller by placing their finger on the rim of the full member and pointing to the emptier with the remark that "It is not to the top." The older child (and virtually never the younger one) gets all involved in the judgment of fuller by apparent filled volume and then equally involved in the judgment of emptier by apparent empty volume and such are his efforts that he fails to note his contradiction when dealing with a pair like display 8b.

Turn now to a quite different experimental procedure that deals with the related concept of equivalence—how seemingly different objects are grouped into equivalence classes. In the two experiments to be cited, one by Olver (24), the other by Rigney (28), children are given words or pictures to sort into groups or to characterize in terms of how they are alike. The two sets of results, one for words, the other for pictures, obtained for children between 6 and 14, can be summarized together. One may distinguish two aspects of grouping—the first has to do with the features or attributes that children use as a criterion for grouping objects: perceptual features (the color, size, pattern, and so on), arbitrary functional features (what I can do with the objects regardless of their usual use: You can make noise with a newspaper by crumpling it and with a book by slamming it shut, and so forth), appropriate functional features (potato, peach, banana, and milk are characterized, you can eat them). But grouping behavior can also be characterized in terms of the syntactical structure of the equivalence sets that the child develops. There are, first, what Vygotsky (29) has called "heaps," collections put together in an arbitrary way simply because the child has decided to put them together that way. Then there are complexes. The various members of a complex are included in the class in accordance with a rule that does not account uniformly for the inclusion of all the members. Edge matching is one such rule: Each object is grouped into a class on the basis of its similarity with a neighboring object. Yet no two neighboring pieces may be joined by the same similarity. Another type of complexive grouping is thematic: Here objects are put together by virtue of participating in a sentence or a little story. More sophisticated is a key ring in which one organizing object is related to all others but none of those to each other. And finally, considerably more sophisticated than heaps and complexes, there are superordinate concepts, in which one universal rule of inclusion accounts for all the objects in the set —all men and women over 21 are included in the class of voters provided they meet certain residence requirements.

The pattern of growth is revealing of many of the trends we have already discussed, and provides in addition a new clue. Consider first the attributes or features of objects that children at different ages use as a basis

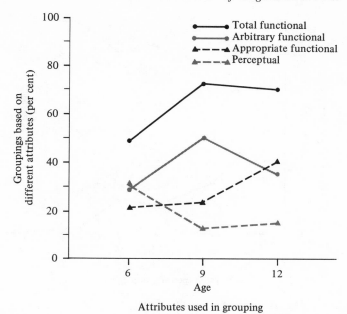

FIGURE 10. Features of objects used by children of different ages as a basis for placing the objects in equivalence groups (24)

for forming equivalence groups. As Figure 10 indicates, the youngest children rely more heavily on perceptual attributes than do the others. As they grow older, grouping comes to depend increasingly upon the functional properties of things—but the transitional phase is worth some attention, for it raises anew the issue of the significance of egocentrism. The first functional groupings to appear are of an arbitrary type—what I or you can do to objects that renders them alike rather than what is the conventional use or function to which objects can be put. During this stage of egocentric functionalism, there is a corresponding rise in the use of first- and second-person personal pronouns: "I can do thus and so to this object; I can do the same to this one," and so on. Gradually, with increasing maturity the child shifts to an appropriate and less egocentric form of using functional groupings. The shift from perceptual to functional groupings is accompanied by a corresponding shift in the syntactical structure of the groups formed. Complexive groupings steadily dwindle; superordinate groupings rise, until the latter almost replace the former in late adolescence. It is difficult to tell which is the pacemaker in this growth—syntax or the semantic basis of grouping.

Rigney reports one other matter of some interest. Her young subjects formed groups of any size they wished, choosing pictures from a display board of several dozen little water colors. She observed that the most perceptually based groups and the ones most often based on complexive

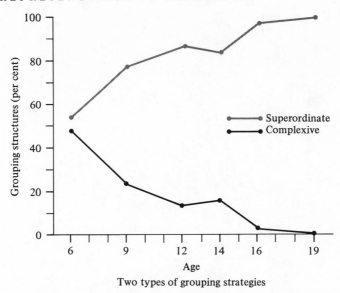

FIGURE 11. The use of two rules of equivalence grouping found in children of different ages (24)

grouping principles were pairs. A count of these revealed that 61 per cent of all the groups made by 6-year-olds were such pairs, 36 per cent of those made by 8-year-olds, and only 25 per cent of the groupings of 11-year-olds.

On the surface, this set of findings—Olver's and Rigney's alike—seems to point more to the decline of a preference for perceptual and iconic ways of dealing with objects and events, particularly with their grouping. But closer inspection suggests still another factor that is operating. In both cases, there is evidence of the development of hierarchical structure and rules for including objects in superordinate hierarchies. Hierarchical classification is surely one of the most evident properties of the structure of language—hierarchical grouping that goes beyond mere perceptual inclusion. Complexive structures of the kind described earlier are much more dominated by the sorts of associative principles by which the appearance of objects leads to their spontaneous grouping in terms of similarity or contiguity. As language becomes more internalized, more guiding as a set of rules for organizing events, there is a shift from the associative principles that operate in classical perceptual organization to the increasingly abstract rules for grouping events by the principles of inclusion, exclusion, and overlap, the most basic characteristics of any hierarchical system.

We have said that cognitive growth consists in part in the development of systems of representation as means for dealing with information. The growing child begins with a strong reliance upon learned action patterns to represent the world around him. In time, there is added to this technology a means for simultanizing regularities in experience into images that stand for events in the way that pictures do. To this is finally added a technology of translating experience into a symbol system that can be operated upon by rules of transformation that greatly increase the possible range of problem solving. One of the effects of this development, or possibly one of its causes, is the power for organizing acts of information processing into more integrated and long-range problem-solving efforts. To this matter we turn next.

Consider in rapid succession three related experiments. All of them point, I think, to the same conclusion.

The first is by Huttenlocher (11), a strikingly simple study, performed with children between the ages of 6 and 12. Two light switches are before the child; each can be in one of two positions. A light bulb is also visible. The child is asked to tell, on the basis of turning only one switch, what turns the light on. There are four ways in which the presentations are made. In the first, the light is off initially and when the child turns a switch the light comes on. In the second, the light is on and when the child turns a switch, it goes off. In the third, the light is on and when the child turns a switch, it stays on. In the fourth and final condition, the light is off and when the child turns a switch, it stays off. Now what is intriguing about this arrangement is that there are different numbers of inductive steps required to make a correct inference in each task. The simplest condition is the off-on case. The position to which the switch has just been moved is responsible for the light going on. Intermediate difficulty should be experienced with the on-off condition. In the on-off case, two connected inferences are required: The present position achieved is rejected and the original position of the switch that has been turned is responsible for lighting the bulb. An even larger number of consecutive acts is required for success in the on-on case: The present position for the turned switch is rejected, the original position as well and the present position of the other switch is responsible. The off-off case requires four steps: rejecting the present position of the turned switch, its original position, and the present position of the other switch, finally accepting the alternative position of the unturned switch. The natures of the individual steps are all the same. Success in the more complex cases depends upon being able to integrate them consecutively.

Huttenlocher's results show that the 6-year-olds are just as capable as their elders of performing the elementary operation involved in the one-step case: the on-off display. They, like the nines and twelves, make nearly perfect scores. But in general, the more inferential steps the 6-year-old must make, the poorer his performance. By age 12, on the other hand, there is an insignificant difference between the tasks requiring one, two, three, or four connected inferences.

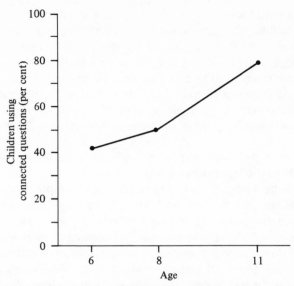

Use of connected questions in twenty questions game

FIGURE 12. The proportion of children at different ages who use connected questions in a Twenty Questions game (22)

An experiment by Mosher (22) underlines the same point. He was concerned with the strategies used by children from 6 to 11 for getting information in the game of Twenty Questions. They were to find out by yes-no questions what caused a car to go off the road and hit a tree. One may distinguish between connected constraint-locating questions ("Was it nighttime?" followed up appropriately) and direct hypothesis-testing questions ("Did a bee fly in the window and sting the man on the eye and make him go off the road and hit the tree?"). From 6 to 11, more and more children use constraint-locating, connected questioning. Let me quote from Mosher's account.

We have asked children . . . after they have played their games, to tell us which of two questions they would rather have the answer to, if they were playing the games again—one of them a typical constraint-seeking question ("Was there anything wrong with the man?") and the other a typical discrete test of an hypothesis ("Did the man have a heart attack?"). All the eleven-year-olds and all the eight-year-olds choose the constraint-seeking question, but only 29% of the six-year-olds do (p. 6).

The questions of the younger children are all one-step substitutes for direct sense experience. They are looking for knowledge by single questions that provide the answer in a finished form. When they succeed they do so by a lucky question that hits an immediate, perceptible cause. When the older child receives a yes answer to one of his constraint-locating questions, he most often follows up by asking another. When, on the rare occasions that a younger child asks a constraint question and it is answered yes, he almost invariably follows it up with a specific question to test a concrete hypothesis. The older child can accrete his information in a structure governed by consecutive inference. The younger child cannot.

Potter's (27) study of the development of perceptual recognition bears on the same point. Ordinary colored photographs of familiar scenes are presented to children between 6 and 12, the pictures coming gradually into focus. Let me sum up one part of the results very briefly. Six-year-olds produce an abundance of hypotheses. But they rarely try to match new hypotheses to previous ones. "There is a big tower in the middle and a road over there and a big ice cream cone through the middle of the tower and a pumpkin on top." It is like a random collage. The 9-year-old's torrent of hypotheses, on the other hand, shows a sense of consistency about what is likely to appear with what. Things are in a context of likelihood, a frame of reference that demands internal consistency. Something is seen as a merry-go-round, and the child then restricts later hypotheses to the other things to be found in an amusement park. The adolescent operates under even more highly organized sequential constraints: He occasionally develops his initial hypotheses from what is implied by the properties of the picture, almost by intersection—"It is red and shiny and metallic: It must be a coffee-pot." Once such constraints are established, the order of hypotheses reflects even more the need to build up a consistent world of objects—even to the point of failing to recognize things that do not fit it.

What shall we make of these three sets of findings—that older children are able to cumulate information by asking questions in a directed sequence leading to a final goal, and that they are capable of recognizing visual displays in a manner governed by a dominating frame of reference that transcends momentary and isolated bits of information? Several points seem apparent. The first is that as children mature, they are able to use indirect information based on forms of information processing other than the act of pointing to what is immediately present. They seem, in short, to make remote reference to states and constraints that are not given by the immediate situation, to go beyond the information given. Second, and this is a matter that has already been discussed, they seem to be able to cumulate information into a structure that can be operated upon by rules that transcend simple association by similarity and contiguity. In the case of Twenty Questions, the rule is best described as implication—that knowing one thing implies certain other things and eliminates still others. In the experiments with the light switches, it is that if the present state does not produce the effect, then there is a system for tracing back to the other states that cause the light to go on. Where perceptual recognition is concerned, the rule is that a piece of information from one part of the display implies what other parts might be. The child, in sum, is translating redundancy into a manipulable model of the environment that is governed by rules of implication. It is this model of the environment that permits him to go beyond the information before him. I would suggest that it is this new array of cognitive equipment that permits the child to transcend momentaneity, to integrate longer sequences of events.

Let me urge, moreover, that such a system of processing environmental events depends upon the translation of experience into symbolic form. Such a translation is necessary in order for there to be the kind of remoteness of reference as is required when one deals with indirect information. To transcend the immediately perceptual, to get beyond what is vividly present to a more extended model of the environment, the child needs a system that permits him to deal with the nonpresent, with things that are remote in space, qualitative similarity, and time, from the present situation. Hockett (10), in describing the design features of language includes this feature as crucial. He is referring to human speech as a system of communication. The same point can be made about language as an instrument of thought. That humans have the capacity for using speech in this way is only part of the point. What is critical is that the capacity is not used until it is coupled with the technology of language in the cognitive operations of the child.

The same can be said for the models of the environment that the child constructs to go beyond present information. This is not to say that nonverbal animals cannot make inferences that go beyond the present stimulus: Anticipatory activity is the rule in vertebrates. But the models that the growing child constructs seem not to be anticipatory, or inferential, or probabilistic-frequency models. They seem to be governed by rules that can more properly be called syntactical rather than associative.

My major concern has been to examine afresh the nature of intellectual growth. The account has surely done violence to the richness of the subject. It seems to me that growth depends upon the emergence of two forms of competence. Children, as they grow, must acquire ways of representing the recurrent regularities in their environment, and they must transcend the momentary by developing ways of linking past to present to future—representation and integration. I have suggested that we can conceive of growth in both of these domains as the emergence of new technologies for the unlocking and amplification of human intellectual powers. Like the growth of technology, the growth of intellect is not smoothly monotonic. Rather, it moves forward in spurts as innovations are adopted. Most of the innovations are transmitted to the child in some prototypic form by agents of the culture: ways of responding, ways of looking and imaging, and most important, ways of translating what one has encountered into language.

I have relied heavily in this account on the successive emergence of action, image, and word as the vehicles of representation, a reliance based both upon our observations and upon modern readings of man's alloplastic evolution. Our attention has been directed largely to the transition between iconic and symbolic representation.

In children between 4 and 12, language comes to play an increasingly powerful role as an implement of knowing. Through simple experiments, I have tried to show how language shapes, augments, and even supercedes the child's earlier modes of processing information. Translation of experience into symbolic form, with its attendant means of achieving remote reference, transformation, and combination, opens up realms of intellectual possibility that are orders of magnitude beyond the most powerful image-forming system.

What of the integration of intellectual activity into more coherent and interconnected acts? It has been the fashion, since Freud, to see delay of gratification as the prinicipal dynamism behind this development—from primary process to secondary process, or from assimilation to accommodation, as Piaget would put it today. Without intending to question the depth of this insight, let me suggest that delay of immediate gratification, the ability to go beyond the moment, also depends upon techniques, and again they are techniques of representation. Perhaps representation exclusively by imagery and perceptual organization has built into it one basic operation that ties it to the immediate present. It is the operation of pointing—ostensiveness, as logicians call it. (This is not to say that highly evolved images do not go beyond immediate time and given place. Maps and flow charts are iconic in nature, but they are images that translate prior linguistic and mathematical renderings into a visual form.) Iconic representation, in the beginning, is built upon a perceptual organization that is tied to the "point-at-able" spatioqualitative properties of events. I have suggested that, for all its limitations, such representation is an achievement beyond the earlier stage where percepts are not autonomous of action. But so long as perceptual representation dominates, it is difficult to develop higher-order techniques for processing information by consecutive inferential steps that take one beyond what can be pointed at.

Once language becomes a medium for the translation of experience, there is a progressive release from immediacy. For language, as we have commented, has the new and powerful features of remoteness and arbitrariness: It permits productive, combinatorial operations in the absence of what is represented. With this achievement, the child can delay gratification by virtue of representing to himself what lies beyond the present, what other possibilities exist beyond the clue that is under his nose. The child may be ready for delay of gratification, but he is no more able to bring it off than somebody ready to build a house, save that he has not yet heard of tools.

The discussion leaves two obvious questions begging. What of the integration of behavior in organisms without language? And how does language become internalized as a vehicle for organizing experience? The first question has to be answered briefly and somewhat cryptically. Wherever integrated behavior has been studied—as in Lehrman's (16) careful work on integrated instinctive patterns in the ring dove, it has turned out that a sustaining external stimulus was needed to keep the highly integrated behavior going. The best way to control behavior in subhuman species is to control the stimulus situation. Surely this is the lesson of Lashley's (15) classic account of instinctive behavior. Where animal learning is concerned, particularly in the primates, there is, to be sure, considerable plasticity. But it too depends upon the development of complex forms of stimulus substitution and organization—as in Klüver's (13) work on equivalence reactions in monkeys. If it should seem that I am urging that the growth of symbolic functioning links a unique set of powers to man's capacity, the appearance is quite as it should be.

As for how language becomes internalized as a program for ordering experience, I join those who despair for an answer. My speculation, for whatever it is worth, is that the process of internalization depends upon interaction with others, upon the need to develop corresponding categories and transformations for communal action. It is the need for cognitive coin that can be exchanged with those on whom we depend. What Roger Brown (4) has called the "Original Word Game" ends up by being the Human Thinking Game.

If I have seemed to underemphasize the importance of inner capacities —for example, the capacity for language or for imagery—it is because I believe that this part of the story is given by the nature of man's evolution. What is significant about the growth of mind in the child is to what degree it depends not upon capacity but upon the unlocking of capacity by techniques that come from exposure to the specialized environment of a culture. Romantic clichés, like the veneer of culture or natural man, are as misleading if not as damaging as the view that the course of human development can be viewed independently of the educational process we arrange to make that development possible.

References

1. ABRAMYAN, L. A. 1958. Organization of the voluntary activity of the child with the help of verbal instruction. Unpublished diploma thesis, Moscow University. Cited by A. R. Luria, *The role of speech in the regulation of normal and abnormal behavior*. New York: Liveright, 1961.
2. BARKER, R. G. 1963. On the nature of the environment. *Journal of Social Issues* 19:17–38.
3. BRAINE, M. D. 1963. On learning the grammatical order of words. *Psychological Review* 70:323–48.
4. BROWN, R. 1958. *Words and things*. Glencoe, Ill.: Free Press.

5. BRUNER, J. S., and KENNEY, H. 1966. The development of the concepts of order and proportion in children. In *Studies in Cognitive Growth,* ed. J. S. Bruner, R. R. Olver, P. M. Greenfield, et al. New York: Wiley.
6. CHOMSKY, N. 1957. *Syntactic structures.* The Hague, Netherlands: Mouton.
7. EMERSON, L. L. 1931. The effect of bodily orientation upon the young child's memory for position of objects. *Child Development* 2:125–42.
8. FRANK, F. 1966. Perception and language in conservation. In *Studies in cognitive growth,* ed. J. S. Bruner, R. R. Olver, P. M. Greenfield, et al. New York: Wiley.
9. HANFMANN, E.; RICKERS-OVSIANKINA, M.; and GOLDSTEIN, K. 1944. Case Lanuti: extreme concretization of behavior due to damage of the brain cortex. *Psychological Monographs* 57(4)(whole no. 264).
10. HOCKETT, C. F. 1959. Animal "languages" and human language. In *The evolution of man's capacity for culture,* ed. J. N. Spuhler, pp. 32–39. Detroit: Wayne State University Press.
11. HUTTENLOCHER, J. 1966. The growth of conceptual strategies. In *Studies in cognitive growth,* ed. J. S. Bruner, R. R. Olver, P. M. Greenfield, et al. New York: Wiley.
12. INHELDER, B., and SINCLAIR, M. 1963. Personal communication.
13. KLÜVER, H. 1933. *Behavior mechanisms in monkeys.* Chicago: University of Chicago Press.
14. LA BARRE, W. 1954. *The human animal.* Chicago: University of Chicago Press.
15. LASHLEY, K. S. 1938. Experimental analysis of instinctive behavior. *Psychological Review* 45:445–72.
16. LEHRMAN, D. S. 1955. The physiological basis of parental feeding behavior in the ring dove (*Streptopelia risoria*). *Behavior* 7:241–86.
17. LURIA A. R. 1961. *The role of speech in the regulation of normal and abnormal behavior.* New York: Liveright.
18. MANDLER, G. 1962. From association to structure. *Psychological Review* 69:415–27.
19. MARTSINOVSKAYA, E. N. Research into the reflective and regulatory role of the second signalling system of pre-school age. Collected papers of the Department of Psychology, Moscow University, undated. Cited by A. R. Luria, *The role of speech in the regulation of normal and abnormal behavior.* New York: Liveright, 1961.
20. MILLER, G. A. 1962. Some psychological studies of grammar. *American Psychologist* 17:748–62.
21. MILLER, G. A.; GALANTER, E.; and PRIBRAM, K. H. 1960. *Plans and the structure of behavior.* New York: Holt.
22. MOSHER, F. A. 1962. Strategies for information gathering. Paper read at Eastern Psychological Association, Atlantic City, N.J., April 1962.
23. NAIR, P. 1963. An experiment in conservation. In Center for Cognitive Studies *Annual Report,* Harvard University.
24. OLVER, R. R. 1961. A developmental study of cognitive equivalence. Unpublished doctoral dissertation, Radcliffe College.
25. PIAGET, J. 1954. *The construction of reality in the child.* Trans. M. Cook. New York: Basic Books.
26. PIAGET, J., and INHELDER, B. 1962. *Le développment des quantités physiques chez l'enfant.* 2d rev. ed. Neuchâtel, Switzerland: Delachaux & Niestlé.
27. POTTER, M. C. 1966. The growth of perceptual recognition. In *Studies in cognitive growth,* ed. J. S. Bruner, R. R. Olver, P. M. Greenfield, et al. New York: Wiley.
28. RIGNEY, J. C. 1962. A developmental study of cognitive equivalence transformations and their use in the acquisition and processing of information. Unpublished honors thesis, Radcliffe College, Department of Social Relations.
29. VYGOTSKY, L. S., 1962. *Thought and language.* Ed. and trans. E. Hanfmann and G. Vakar. Cambridge, Mass.: MIT Press, and New York: Wiley.
30. WASHBURN, S. L., and HOWELL, F. C. 1960. Human evolution and culture. In *The evolution of man,* vol. 2, ed. S. Tax. Chicago: University of Chicago Press.
31. WEIR, R. H. 1962. *Language in the crib.* The Hague: Mouton.
32. WERNER, H. 1948. *Comparative psychology of mental development.* Rev. ed. Chicago: Follett.

20

Development of Equivalence
Transformations in Children*

We would like to devote our attention exclusively to the problem of what people do when they relate one thing to another, when they are faced with the problem of grouping two or more words, events, or objects, occurring either simultaneously or in succession. We shall purposely avoid the explicit form of grouping involved in the process we call sentence making, for we are concerned with the more traditional type of associative grouping.

The usual approaches to the problem of association are two in number. In the first, one simply invokes the passive principle of association. The question of what happens in associative grouping is answered by saying, "It happens." The words, objects, or events are said to get linked, bonded, or hitched by virtue of the fact that they exhibit certain qualities of similarity, contiguity in space or time, or some other form of communality. Under this passive regimen, associative clusters are alleged to form, much as concepts are formed. Indeed, once these clusters have formed, it is then

* "Development of Equivalence Transformations in Children," by Jerome S. Bruner and Rose R. Olver, from Wright and Kagan (Eds.), "Basic Cognitive Processes in Children." *Monographs of the Society for Research in Child Development,* 1963, Serial 86, Vol. 28, No. 2, 125–142. Copyright © 1963 by the Society for Research in Child Development. Reproduced by permission of the publisher and authors.

possible for there to be mediated associations. Things get linked because they share membership in the same associative cluster.

It is all very neat and it is all very automatic, but the difficulty with the scheme is that it explains too many things that do not happen. One example is the contiguous association between the period at the end of a sentence and the word, *the,* in that order. This is one of the most frequent juxtapositions in the English language. Thorndike attempted to handle this exception by invoking the principle of belongingness, implying, but never quite saying, that only those things are naturally associated by the proper associative laws that are seen as belonging together. His hope was that the property of belongingness could eventually be derived from the principles of association as well, like Bishop Berkeley's coach.

Mental development in the cognitive sense in this rather old-fashioned view, was assumed to be the progressive forging of associations and associative clusters. Possibly, too, there was room in such a view for the bases of association to change as the child grew, but this was usually due to the intervention or mediation of newly formed associative clusters.

A second approach to the problem of association is sufficiently powerful to stand exaggeration and still seem reasonable. It is the grammatical approach. It holds that most grouping is determined by gradually emerging, learned rules of morphemic and syntactic ordering of the speech flow, aided and abetted by the formation of conceptual rules for grouping classes of objects in the world of experience and memory. A prediction of grouping could be made in this sytem from one's knowledge of the emerging conceptual geography.

The sequence of rule learning under these circumstances could be variously put as to what kinds of rules are formed first and on the basis of what clues. For example, Piaget (3), who is an eminent example of this particular view of the development of associative grouping, assumes that at the earliest stage there is sensorimotor patterning based essentially on a rule of action, with the gradual development of representation and reversibility, the stage of concrete operations, and finally a set of rules having to do with the generation of the possible, when the child is capable of spinning out what Piaget calls "full combinatorial ensembles."

Other people have a different conception of the order of rule learning. Vygotsky (4), for example, takes a quite different view from that of Piaget. Roger Brown (1) has implicitly still a different view.

We happen to be of the school that assumes that associations do not just happen, that they are governed by certain rules, and that these are the result of certain rather complex transformations imposed on data by active, collective, limitbound, talking organisms. What, in fact, does happen when we observe association? Can we observe something that we could call transformational activity? Can this be observed to change in a systematic way with development? I do not mean the usual transformational activities of converting a set of unrelated words into sentences by grouping. Rather I am talking about a more primitive rule of transforming input that underlies what we refer to as association in our textbooks.

A disparate collection of words or objects, each discriminably different from the others, is presented to a person. It is not automatically the case that he will group or associate them. Whether he will or will not group a given set depends on a variety of circumstances. It will depend, if you will, on what he is up to. Indeed, it is a nice question as to what will lead an individual to group things, or to form an association. He may have to pack them in the same suitcase, for example. Or he may want to assemble them in order to build a shelter. Or he may want to warn somebody of their presence on the grounds that they are contaminating or dangerous. Or he may be a journalist or an anthropologist who plans to report that they were present at the same time and place. There may not, on the other hand, be any reason for him to group the disparate things; and, under these circumstances, there will be a very sharp and quick loss in the ability to report what things were conjointly present just a few minutes before.

Generally speaking, if there is arousal of a strategy or plan for grouping, granted that we know little about what arouses such behavior, it usually exhibits two features. The first is that, however the grouping proceeds, it usually achieves a reduction in load. The grouping rule is simpler than the elements in the collection that are grouped. That is to say, the grouping is less complex than the sum of all the distinguishable features of all the elements in the collection. In this sense, the group always has the property (if it is to achieve any economy at all) of being less than the sum of the elements that compose it. Such load reduction is achieved first by a selection of a fraction of the properties available for forming a group. If one groups oranges, apples, bananas, pears, and grapes as fruit, one ignores all the attributes having to do with color, skin texture, missileworthiness, and so on, and subordinates them to the function that could be served by all of the elements.

Second, the grouping rule always has the property of being a generalizing rule such that, if none of the instances in the group were known, knowledge of the grouping rule would permit one to regenerate the elements in excess of chance, defined as what would be predicted if one did not know the rule. Thus, the second feature of grouping, or of a grouping strategy, is that the grouping rule used usually relates to previous rules of grouping that the organism has used. That is to say that we place things in a context that has been established. Perhaps human beings learn to extend all groupings to new situations in the interest of maximizing connectivity and transfer, and perhaps for other reasons which do not concern us here. In any case, we know that when people associate things with each other they most often do it by the extension or combination of groupings previously formed.

In sum, it can be said that a grouping is always less than the sum of its discriminable elements. It can also be said that a grouping is more than the instances it is used to encompass here and now. The more represents not so much a content of things as a way in which things can be related to prior groupings. Let us emphasize again that we are referring to the forms of grouping that are not sentencial, in the sense that we may group man, bites, and hat into the grammatical form, man bites hat, or hat bites man. Rather, in discussing the set of experiments conducted by Rose Olver at the Harvard Center for Cognitive Studies, we shall limit ourselves to associations formed within collections in terms of their similarities.

One last point before turning to our data. Associating things according to their similarity involves, as we have said, some act of selection with respect to attributes. Most things are alike and different in more than a single way. In most real-life situations the objective of the behavior in force will determine the basis of selection. Short of that, there may be tendencies of various kinds operating in the actual grammar of the grouping. We shall be concerned with these tendencies as they change with growth and development.

An Experiment on Associative Grouping

The task set for the subjects was especially designed to measure the manner in which subjects of different ages impose a similarity transformation on a set of verbally presented materials and the way in which this transformation is conserved or altered in the face of difficulties. The materials used were made up of series of nine sequentially presented nouns, first spoken aloud and then laid out on cards on a table, one at a time. Two sequences were presented to three groups of young subjects made up of equal numbers of boys and girls, ten to a group. Subjects were drawn from a public school in the Boston area. The first-grade group had a mean age of 6 years, 3 months; a fourth-grade group of 9 years, 6 months; and a sixth-grade group of 11 years, 7 months. The same experimental procedure was administered to an additional group of 62 sixth-grade children to give us norms for comparing our more carefully matched groups of ten. The two lists used on the three smaller groups are shown in Table 1.

The first two words, *bell* and *horn,* for example, were presented together, and each child, tested individually, was asked in what way they were

TABLE 1 Lists of Words Used in the Study

Banana—Peach	Water	Bell-Horn	Book
Potato	Air	Telephone	Painting
Meat	Germs	Radio	Education
Milk	Stones	Newspaper	Confusion

alike. He was then presented a third word, along with the first two, and asked in what way the third word differed from the first two and then how all three of them were alike. A fourth word was then added to the list, and the child was asked to tell how it differed from the first three and then how all four were alike. The experiment continued through the list until all nine words had been presented. The subjects were under no time pressure; they could take as long as they wanted. They were not pressed for further responses; and, if additional responses were given, they were excluded from the analysis. When the ninth word was given, they were asked only how it was different from the rest, not how it was similar. At best the last word served to crystallize their concept by contrast. At worst, it served as a negative instance of what might have been a concept if they had formed one.

By using the difference instruction as well as the similarity instruction, we sought to give them as much of a prod as possible toward seeing the likeness in the preceding groups. The use of contrast was intended to elicit their best possible grouping response. Note that the lists are made up of successively more distant items. In generating these logarithmically increasing disparities, we found that none of the lists generated by the mechanical procedures we tried yielded as good agreement among judges as those lists made up by our own intuition.

Grouping Strategies

I would like to describe some of the different forms of grouping that have nothing to do with the content used in the grouping.

SUPERORDINATE CONCEPT FORMATION

The first form of grouping is called superordination. Items are grouped on the basis of one or more attributes common to them all. The basis is one of genuine conceptual grouping. The attributes can be functional properties, perceptible qualities, some common affective reaction, and the like.

Table 2 shows the general superordinate grouping. For example, the bell and the horn are, "Both things that make noises," or "You can get information from all of them," or "They all communicate ideas," a rather fancy sixth-grade response. That is one type of superordinate concept formed for grouping the set.

 TABLE 2 General Superordinate

Grade I	"Both something that makes noise."
Grade IV	"You can get information from all of them."
Grade VI	"They all communicate ideas."

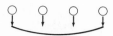

TABLE 3 *Itemized Superordinate*

Grade I	"Bell makes noise; horn makes noise too—bell says 'ding ding'; horn says 'doo doo'."
Grade IV	"They're all alike because you learn something from each one of them—telephone you learn by talking, bell you learn, horn you learn how to use them, book you learn news from, newspaper you learn from."
Grade VI	"You hear things from them—bell, horn, telephone, radio hear things by doing something to them, newspaper you have to read."

Table 3 shows the itemized superordinate grouping, where the elements have a generalized property that ties them all together, but where there is explicitly stated the basis on which each term qualifies: "Bell makes noise; horn makes noise, too. Bell says 'ding ding'; horn says 'doo doo'." In short, itemization is added to superordinate grouping as a means of specifying communalities.

COMPLEX FORMATION

The examples of superordination given are to be contrasted with a range of responses that we refer to as complex formations. The characteristic of complex formation as a general strategy is that the subject uses selected attributes of the array without subordinating the entire array to any one attribute or to any set of attributes. We have been able to distinguish five clearly discernible complex-forming maneuvers, and these five can be used with a wide range of filler content.

The first one, shown in Table 4, is the association complex. What the subject does is to make an association between the first two elements. For example, "Bell and horn are music things." Then, "When you dial a telephone, it's music a little." The subject uses the bond between two elements as the nucleus to form a group. As can be seen from Table 4, they get more complicated. "Bell, horn, telephone, and radio make noises. If you fold back a newspaper, then it will crackle and make a noise."

TABLE 4 *Association Complex*

Grade I	"Bell and horn are music things, when you dial telephone it's music a little."
Grade IV	"Bell, horn, telephone, radio make sound you can hear, when a person talks from a newspaper it is actually a sound too."
Grade VI	"Bell, horn, telephone, radio all make noises, if you fold back a newspaper then it will crackle and make a noise."

The key-ring complex (Table 5) consists of taking an element and ringing all of the others on it by choosing attributes that form relations between one item in the list and each of the others, in a special way:

"Painting—well, one thing is a book has got some painting in it, a news-paper has got some black painting, a radio and a telephone have painting on them, and a horn—well, there's a little painting on it. And a bell is also the color of paints." The author of this example looked a lit-tle shamefaced, but also defiant as he gave the latter instances. Another example, "Germs are in banana, peach, potato, meat, milk, water, and air," which is another, but more sophisticated form of key-ringing.

 TABLE 5 Key-Ring Complex

Grade I	"Painting, one thing is book's got some painting in it, newspaper's got some black paintings—printings, radio's got painting on it, telephone's got paint-ing on it, horn well there's a little painting on it, bell is also the color of paints."
Grade IV	"In an education you learn how to do painting, you read books and gradually you learn how to read newspaper, how to use radio, how to use telephone, and horn and bell the same way."
Grade VI	"Germs are in banana, peach, potato, meat, milk, water and air."

The edge-matching complex (Table 6) is also an interesting one. We were surprised to discover that the patterning we call edge matching was reported in Hughlings-Jackson's (Head, 2) description of sorting behavior in various kinds of brain-injured patients. It consists of forming associative links between neighboring items: "Banana and peach are both yellow. Peach and potato are both round. Potato and meat are served together. Meat and milk both come from cows." The associations pile up in linked pairs.

 TABLE 6 Edge-Matching Complex

Grade I	"Banana and peach look alike—yellow, potato and peach are round."
Grade IV	"Telephone is like a bell because telephone has bell inside it, it's like a horn because you put your mouth up to a telephone and you put your mouth up to a horn."
Grade VI	None

The collection (Table 7) consists essentially in finding complementary, contrasting, or otherwise related properties that all the things have but not quite tying them together in terms of the attributes that are shared by the form of complementarity: "Bell is black, horn is brown, telephone is blue, radio is red." Or "Newspaper you can read, book you can read, telephone you get messages over, radio you get messages over, and a horn you can blow." We failed to get this kind of complex from sixth graders, aged 11 to 12, in either of our samples. It is a sort of putative brand of concept in which they are exploring the specificity. They are providing the itemization, but they cannot quite bring off the superordinate concept.

TABLE 7 Collection Complex

Grade I	"Bell is black, horn is brown, telephone is sometimes blue, radio is red."
Grade IV	"Newspaper you can read, book you can read, telephone you get messages over, radio you get messages over, you can blow a horn and ring a bell."
Grade VI	None

Last is the multiple-grouping complex (Table 8) where several sub-groupings are formed: "A telephone is like a radio—I know that. A horn and a bell both make sounds, but I don't know about a newspaper." Multiple groups are thus formed within the list. The child will draw the line at some point, forming two or more separate groups, but refusing to bridge the gap between them.

TABLE 8 Multiple-Grouping Complex

Grade I	"Telephone is like a radio, I know that, bell is like a horn because they both make sounds, but I don't know about a newspaper."
Grade IV	"Newspaper, book, painting tell stories; bell, horn, telephone, radio make sounds."
Grade VI	"You eat banana, peach, meat; you drink milk."

THEMATIC GROUPING

The last form of grouping (Table 9) yields very beautiful structures, of course, that are about as uneconomical as anything the subject could do with the stimuli. The sequence coat-sweater-umbrella-house-infection yielded the following example of thematic grouping: "If you get an infection, you wouldn't go out of the house, but if you did, you'd take an umbrella if it were drizzling and wear a coat and sweater." The story, of course, can continue to incorporate almost any additional items that are provided on the list.

TABLE 9 Thematic

Grade VI	"It all fits in with fabrics and cotton—if you got hit in the head by a rock you'd get a bandage."
	"If you got an infection you wouldn't go out of the house, but if you did, you'd take an umbrella if it were drizzling and wear a coat and sweater."
	"Earphones you can hear like when you land at an airport."

There are many things that can be said about the differences between the groupings, but we have time to mention only a few. In the first place, it is apparent that, if each were considered a rule for forming a group, the complexity of the instruction for forming the rule increases at a marked rate as one goes from superordinating strategies, through complex-forming strategies, to thematic strategies. Indeed, the number of attributes one needs for stating the rule of grouping or associating rises quite sharply as one goes from general to itemizing superordination, to the various maneuvers for forming complexes. Key-ringing, for example, requires the use of at least $n-1$ different attributes, where n is the number of elements in the set. Edge-matching similarly requires $n-1$ attributes at a minimum.

It can also be seen that to extend the groupings emerging from complex formation requires a steady increment of cognitive work, with the possibility of overload always present. In a sense, then, it is characteristic of groups formed by strategies other than superordination that they are often not much less than the sum of their parts in the sense of economy. Nor are they much more than the sum of their parts in the sense of generalization. In order to combine a grouping formed by a complexive strategy with another grouping already formed, a considerable amount of additional cognitive work is required. To join two key-ring complexes, for example, means finding a way of relating the nucleus of one to the nucleus of another, which is quite a trick if one takes some of the key-rings actually given and tries to link them. Contrast this with the logical addition and subtraction of classes that is possible in categories formed by superordination, that tremendous generator of the possible. One can create a group with superordinate concepts by logical addition no mater how complicated the concept. Female presidents of the United States under 40 with blonde curls and size eight shoes is an example, illustrating the great power of the superordinate concept.

Let us state a first developmental theorem, emerging from these investigations: The development of intelligence, given intervening opportunity for problem solving in the life of the growing organism, moves in the direction of reducing the strain of information processing by the growth of strategies of grouping that encode information in a manner (a) that chunks information in simpler form, (b) that gains connectedness with rules of grouping already formed, and (c) that is designed to maximize the possibility of combinatorial operations such that groupings already formed can be combined and detached from other forms of grouping. In a word, then, what distinguishes the young child from the older child is the fact that the young one is more complicated than the older one, not the reverse. The effect of the complexity is not only to produce a cognitive overload, once the child attempts to operate effectively in settings of a type not familiar to him, but also to establish structures that are less amenable to change through experience and learning. Herein lies the significance of the distinction drawn by both Piaget and Vygotsky between spontaneous concepts and systematic concepts. The virtues inherent in replacing the former (complexes in our language) by the latter, or in supplementing the former with the latter, are that the child is able to use his intellectual resources over a wider range of events by mastering strategies that permit of generality, as well as economy of operations.

You will note that the point we are making here goes quite counter to the picture of development that grows out of association theories of the old kind, and even of the newer type of *S-R* theories, both of which regard growth as a matter of increasing complexity and range of associations, with various devices thrown in presumably to take care of clustering.

If we look at the chronological ages between 6 and 12, as the child is emerging from the final stages of preoperational thought and advancing to well-structured and formal operations, we note a steady change in behavior. Tables 10 and 11 show a steady increase in the use of general superordinate concepts with age. The complexes, however, all decline with age. These results for boys show the most striking changes. It is interesting to notice that the first-grade girls are at about the level of fourth-grade boys, and this is not surprising in view of various findings showing general age advantages for girls in many areas of performance. By the sixth grade, they are about at the same level.

Notice that the lists proceed from near to far items, from easily associated to almost unrelatable elements, and, incidentally, from more specific and concrete to more collective and abstract instances. In short, the second half of the list is more difficult than the first, and we have analyzed separately responses to the first three items in the list and the second four

TABLE 10 *Frequencies of Grouping Strategies by Grade Level*

	I	IV	VI
Superordinate			
Itemized	12	7	8
General	53	96	113
Complex			
Key-ring	10	5	6
Association	5	4	4
Collection	15	5	0
Edge-matching	10	2	0
Multiple-grouping	17	14	8
No grouping	18	7	1
Totals			
Superordinate	65	103	121
Complex	57	30	18
No grouping	18	7	1

TABLE 11 Frequencies of Grouping Strategies by Grade Level and Sex

	Boys			Girls		
	I	IV	VI	I	IV	VI
Superordinate						
Itemized	6	6	5	6	1	3
General	13	44	57	40	52	56
Complex						
Key-ring	10	3	2	0	0	4
Association	3	1	0	2	3	4
Collection	4	5	0	11	0	0
Edge-matching	10	2	0	0	1	0
Multiple-grouping	11	5	5	6	10	3
No grouping	13	4	1	5	3	0
Totals						
Superordinate	19	50	62	46	53	59
Complex	38	16	7	19	14	11
No grouping	13	4	1	5	3	0

items. Table 12 shows the percentage of responses representing each of the different grouping strategies by sex, grade, and difficulty. Notice that superordinate responses decline as *S* proceeds from the first item in the list to the later and more difficult items, in each grade. The opposite occurs for the complexes and the failures.

TABLE 12 Percentage of Responses Governed by Different Grouping Strategies as Task Grows in Difficulty

	Grade I		Grade IV		Grade VI	
	1–3 (easy)	4–7 (hard)	1–3 (easy)	4–7 (hard)	1–3 (easy)	4–7 (hard)
Superordinate	67	31	83	66	100	76
Complexive	28	50	15	26	0	23
Failure	5	19	2	8	0	1
Total	100	100	100	100	100	100
No. of responses	60	80	60	80	60	80

We would like to comment on the intrusion of action into the complex-forming strategies we have discussed. Both Piaget and Vygotsky have noted that, at the early stages, a concept is essentially governed by the action appropriate to it. There is no "decentration" of the concept from the action and affect that go along with it. We became very interested in the extent to which subjects generated attributes for grouping based on action with respect to the object. An example from children's literature is, "A hole is to dig." Another from our data is, "A newspaper makes a noise when you crinkle it." Generating attributes by action is a trememdously complicated form of self-instruction. About half of the first-grade children generate at least one instance of action-produced attributes; the incidence drops very sharply to about 10 to 15 per cent in fourth-grade children, though it never completely disappears, even in the few college students we have tested.

Language Framework

We have also analyzed the content or language frames of the strategies children use in carrying out these groupings. A language frame is defined as a sentence form appropriate to the answering of a particular question. The question, "Where are they?" is appropriately answered by the frame, "They are $X - Y$," where Y is a place, and X is a preposition of the class including at, by, in, near, on, and so forth. Table 13 is a list of the lan-

TABLE 13 Language Frames

Perceptible
  Intrinsic
    They are _____. (X: adjective: ". . . both yellow.")
    They have _____. (X: noun: ". . . writing on them.")
    They are made of _____. (X: noun: ". . . paper.")
  Extrinsic
    They are (preposition) _____. (X: position in time or space: ". . . in a house.")

Functional
  Intrinsic
    They _____. (X: verb: ". . . make noise.")
  Extrinsic
    You _____ them. (X: verb: ". . . can turn them on.")

Affective
    You _____ them. (X: value or internal state: ". . . like them both.")

Linguistic Convention
  Positive
    They are _____. (X: noun: ". . . both fruit.")
  Negative
    They are not _____. (X: noun: ". . . food.")

Fiat Equivalence
  Positive
    "A" is _____ "B." (X: like, similar to, the same thing as: "They are the same thing.")
  Negative
    "A" is not _____ "B." (X: like, the same as: "They are not alike.")

Defeat
    "I don't know."

guage frames we were able to distinguish in the responses of the children studied.

First, we have a set of intrinsic perceptible language frames: "They are X," where X has an adjectival quality of a kind that can be pointed to directly. Another example is, "They have Y," or "They are made of Y," where Y is usually a noun or noun phrase.

Second, there are extrinsic perceptible language frames, such as, "They are X," where X is a position in time or space, where the items are commonly assembled.

A third frame is the intrinsic functional. "They X," is of this class if X is a verb phrase describing their general or intended purposes. An example is, "They are for sending messages."

A fourth frame, the extrinsic functional, is distinguished from the third in that the verb phrase has a subject. "You, we, or people X them," is an example. Others are, "You can eat them," or "We turn them on."

In the affective language frame, the operative phrase accomplishes a preference or value scaling of the items.

Sixth, there is a frame having to do with linguistic convention, in either positive or negative form. These frames are infrequent and sometimes involve vague usages having to do with mass, class, or collective nouns that are applied to a class. An example is, "They are (or are not) X," where X is a class noun such as *things,* or *inventions,* or *instruments,* where because the grouping term exists ready-made in the language, it is impossible to judge its attribute basis with any certainty.

The seventh frame involves equivalences essentially accomplished by fiat. For example, "They are alike," or "are essentially the same thing as X."

Finally, there are a series of statements that are equivalent to the defeat reaction, "I don't know," or "I can't tell," and the like, which conveys the signal that there is no further information forthcoming.

Table 14 shows the responses given by the three age groups in each language frame. The great bulk of the responses given was in the first four

TABLE 14 *Responses in Different Language Frames*
(per cent)

	Grade I	Grade IV	Grade VI
Intrinsic perceptible	24	8	6
Extrinsic perceptible	5	6	10
Functional	49	73	75
Affective	1	1	
Failure	14	5	
Other	11	13	11
No. of Responses	140	140	140

Note: Columns total to 100 per cent or greater since some double classifications of responses were made.

categories: the perceptible and the functional language frames. Of the 140 responses made by the children in each of the three age groups, 14 per cent were failures in the first grade, 5 per cent in the fourth grade, and virtually none in the sixth grade. There is a decline in the use of perceptible qualities of objects from grade one to six. There is a rise in the use of functional grouping. In a word, growth brings a decline in the apparent qualities of objects as a basis for grouping and an increase in the use of functional bases for grouping.

One comment is in order here. The increase in the use of functional groupings, very marked in all of the groups we have studied, including the large sixth-grade sample, indicates that the first major shift in the economy of grouping comes with the adoption of the use of functional techniques for combining or associating items. Perhaps it is American functionalism that is reflected here, but we doubt it. We lack cross-cultural data, but we would be surprised if the findings were culturally limited.

The surface qualities of things have, on the whole, begun to be abandoned as bases for grouping even before children reach the first grade. Is it not reasonable to suppose that functionalism is perhaps a first major step along the way toward being free of the diversity of impressions that the environment loads upon us? To deal with function is perhaps the first way of packaging properties into nonperceptible units of belonging. A coach with this chunking transformation of functions is a coach, and not the smell of the leather, the sound of the hooves, the rolling motion, and so on, through the rest of Bishop Berkeley's catalogue.

An interesting point can be made about the change in the use of language frames as a function of the difficulty of the task. Once more we can examine the change as the children go from the first three groupings to the much more difficult final four (Table 15).

TABLE 15 *Responses Cast in Different Language Frames for Grouping Tasks of Varying Difficulty (per cent)*

	Grade I		Grade IV		Grade VI	
	1–3 (easier)	4–7 (harder)	1–3 (easier)	4–7 (harder)	1–3 (easier)	4–7 (harder)
Intrinsic perceptible	33	16	10	8	7	4
Extrinsic perceptible	2	8	2	10		17
Intrinsic functional	32	15	30	16	45	38
Extrinsic functional	13	38	37	59	27	41
Affective		3		3		
Linguistic convention	17	4	22	6	22	3
Fiat equivalence	2	5		3		1
Failure	5	21	2	8		1
No. of responses	60	80	60	80	60	80

The contents of Table 15 can be summed up in this way: When the going gets rough, the young children shift from their preferred mode of dealing with the surface attributes as a basis of grouping and either fail to group or adopt the frame of extrinsic functional grouping. There also occurs a scattering of fiat equivalance and affective groupings. In the older children the shift with increasing difficulty seems to be from intrinsic functional to extrinsic functional. At all ages the use of linguistic convention occurs with moderate frequency when the going is easy, but drops to a negligible level when the more difficult items are presented. The only group in which intrinsic functional modes hold up under the more difficult items is the oldest class, the sixth graders.

Language and Strategy

Finally, we want to discuss the relationship between these two forms of analysis, the grouping strategies and the conceptual modes or language frames in terms of which groupings are made. In principle there is no reason to expect any canonical relationship at all, save in respect to the so-called failure categories. Complexes and superordination patterns can be constructed on any basis: locus, perceptible attributes, intrinsic or extrinsic functioning, affect, linguistic convention, even fiat. We consider now the linguistic mode in which complexes and superordinations are constructed (Table 16). The first and most striking finding is that for the youngest children, the six-year-olds, the great majority of the superordinate groupings are constructed by means of the functional mode. Very few of these more efficient groupings are carried out in terms of perceptible attributes. When we examine the complexes formed by the younger children, however, we find that a considerable proportion of these less-efficient forms are constructed by reliance on the apparent or perceptible properties of objects. Indeed, nearly two-thirds of the complexes produced by the youngest group are constructed on the basis of perceptible properties, locus, affect, or fiat declaration. Where superordinate groupings are concerned, the figure is less than two in ten formed on this basis.

In the older children there is an increasing tendency for both complexes and superordinate concepts to be formed by the use of the functional mode. In short, then, the functional mode of analyzing events seems to develop before there is a full development of the superordinate strategies, and one is tempted to speculate that the shift from the consideration of surface, perceptible properties to more embracing functional properties may be the vehicle that makes possible the development of efficient and simpler grouping strategies. Indeed, to go back to an earlier mention of Piaget's conception of decentration, one may argue that to consider objects in terms of their potential use represents a step away from immediate concentration upon the ego-object relation, expressed in terms of what I

TABLE 16 Each Grouping Type Stated in Terms
of Different Linguistic Frames (per cent)

	Superordinate Concept			Complexive Grouping		
	I	IV	VI	I	IV	VI
Intrinsic perceptible	15	11	6	39		
Extrinsic perceptible		3	8	13	16	29
Intrinsic functional	40	23	45	5	29	12
Extrinsic functional	29	50	32	36	55	59
Affective		2		4		
Linguistic convention	18	18	12	2		
Fiat equivalence				4	6	
Failure				4		
No. of responses	65	101	120	56	31	17

Note: Since double classification was necessary, columns total either 100 per cent or greater.

see when I examine this set of objects that is before me here and now.

In sum, then, our analysis of these far too scant data suggests that the development of a mode of functionally analyzing the world permits the child to be free of the myriad and changing appearances of things. It makes possible the development of more efficient modes of grouping, the emergence of true concepts rather than complexes. In turn, the child is equipped with simpler modes of grouping that fulfill the dual function of being less than the sum of the items grouped where economy is concerned and more than the sum of the elements grouped in terms of generalization value and combinatorial possibility. We close by repeating the conjecture with which we started: May it not be the case that development consists of finding techniques for being simple with respect to information?

References

1. BROWN, R. 1958. *Words and things.* Glencoe, Ill.: Free Press.
2. HEAD, H. 1926. *Aphasia and kindred disorders of speech.* New York: Macmillan.
3. INHELDER, B., and PIAGET, J. 1958. *The growth of logical thinking from childhood to adolescence.* New York: Basic Books.
4. VYGOTSKY, L. 1962. *Thought and language.* Ed. and trans. E. Hanfmann and G. Vakar. Cambridge, Mass.: MIT Press, and New York: Wiley.

21

Culture and Cognitive Growth*

We shall ask, in the pages that follow, what it means, intellectually, to grow up in one cultural milieu and not another. It is, of course, a form of the old question of how heredity and environment relate: How, in this case, does intellectual development depend upon external influences; in what respects is it a series of unfolding maturational states? But the question is now in qualitative terms. The older debate on heredity versus environment was without a possible solution. For there is no psychological phenomenon without a biologically given organism nor one that takes place outside an environment. But we can, nevertheless, study the intersect in growth of biological background and cultural milieu with the more modest aim of learning what kinds of cultural difference make an intellectual difference at what points in development and how it comes about in some particular way.

It is not a new idea that cultural variation yields variation in modes of thought. It is a persistent theme in anthropology (for example, Boas, 7;

* Patricia Marks Greenfield and Jerome S. Bruner, "Culture and Cognitive Growth," in David A. Goslin (ed.), *Handbook of Socialization Theory and Research,* © by Rand McNally and Company, Chicago, pp. 633–654. Reproduced by permission of the publisher and authors.

This article was supported in part by a grant from the Carnegie Corporation of New York, No. B-3004 and a contract from the United States Office of Education, No. 4–10–136, to Harvard University, Center for Cognitive Studies. Also by a predoctoral fellowship from the Public Health Service, No. 5–F1–MH–15, 200–02, to Patricia Marks Greenfield.

Mead, 43; Whorf, 62). Psychologists have also interested themselves in cultural influences on cognitive development. However, the methods used have rarely been equal to the task at hand. Anthropology's most recent and most promising approach, ethnoscience, explores qualitative cognitive variation by exploring the native terminology used for the particular objectively definable domain such as plants or disease or kinship (Sturtevant, 57). Ethnoscience is limited as a method for investigating cognitive processes precisely because it does not deal with processes at all but with intellectual products as embodied in language. Like the older anthropological strategy of inferring living cognitive processes from static cultural products such as myth, ritual and social life (for instance, Durkheim and Mauss, 19; Lévi-Strauss, 37), ethnoscience infers the mind of the language user from the lexicon he uses. When we know the culturally standard system for kinship or disease classification we still do not know how the system developed or how it is used in novel situations. It is a bit like studying the growth of logic and thought in children of our own society through an analysis of grammar or logic in the books found in the library. It may help to define the idealized version of logical thought in the culture to do this. But it can tell little about the processes involved. In this respect, it is somewhat like some contemporary efforts to found psycholinguistics on the assumption that the rules underlying grammatical competence are the same as the laws that govern the production of grammatical sentences by native speakers. The laws governing the production of sentences may or may not be the same as the rules of grammar that are used to describe the correct combinations in the language.

In the 1930s and 1940s psychologists carried IQ tests around the world. They had learned little more than that natives fared worse than standardization groups at home when projective tests came into vogue in the fifties (Lindzey, 38), and cross-cultural attention shifted from intellect to affect. Again, the intrinsic value of intelligence tests was limited, abroad as at home, by the fact that the IQ is not a process, but the product of many complex cognitive processes that other methods would have to unravel— and a product closely geared to school achievement in Western European culture at that. An ideological factor further complicated this work. As Strodtbeck (56) points out, you can "prove" the power of heredity if you assume your test is "culture-free" (for example, Porteus's maze); whereas differences are due to environmental factors on the assumption of a "culturally relative" test. The assumption in a particular study probably reflected personal bias more than any other factor. Later the absurdity of this distinction, parallel to that of choosing between heredity and environment, became evident.

The point of view animating the present discussion is that intelligence is to a great extent the internalization of tools provided by a given culture. Thus, culture-free means intelligence-free. Such a view of cognitive development has been put forth elsewhere (Bruner, 12).[1] Here we shall examine it by comparing intellectual development in cultures with radically different technologies.

One of the most interesting and oldest lines of cross-cultural work in cognition is through the study of sensation and perception. More than one intelligence tester noted that performance tests often seemed to put foreigners at as much of a disadvantage as verbal tests and were forced to conclude that perceptual as well as verbal habits could vary radically from culture to culture (Cryns, 16; Jahoda, 25; Wintringer, 63). If this were so, then the study of perception could be fundamental in understanding any psychological process involving a response to the outside world.

The classical work on perception was done by the Cambridge Anthropological Expedition to the Torres Straits in 1901–05. A famous and intriguing finding was that of Rivers (52) concerning the lesser susceptibility of the Murray Islanders to the Müller-Lyer illusions. The Todas of India yield a similar finding. This result has been interpreted to mean that the Todas, unaccustomed to inferring three dimensions from two-dimensional displays, were less subject to the illusion; for as soon as three-dimensional stimulus materials were used, cultural differences disappeared (Bonte, 9).

This work—suggesting the effect of particular cultural conditions such as the absence of pictures—has been followed up with studies of illusions in new places (for instance, Allport and Pettigrew in South Africa, 1) and by carefully controlled experimentation with line drawings. The latter studies have shown the interpretation of Rivers's work to be a correct one (Hudson, 23). The effects obtained appear to depend upon perceptual inference; members of different cultures differ in the inferences they draw from perceptual cues, not in the cues they are able to distinguish. Such an interpretation suggests the value of studying more directly the way in which the cues are assimilated to different schemata in different cultures with the effect of producing large cultural differences. It is conceivable that one can also find differences in the cues most likely to be used in organizing percepts, given sufficiently complex stimulus fields. This is to say that, given complex input, the principles of selectivity will vary from culture to culture. This was certainly the point of the Cambridge studies under Rivers and of the careful observations of Bogoras in his work among the Chukchee (8).

Our own cross-cultural work has followed other lines, lines of more recent historical development. We have asked first the naïve question: Where in a culture should one find differences in the processes of thought? The anthropological linguists (for instance, Whorf, 62) suggested a concrete answer: Where there are language differences there may (or should?) be cognitive differences. Our results have led us away from the parallelism of

[1] See pp. 325–51.

Whorf toward the instrumentalism that is more typical of Vygotsky (60) and Luria (39). Language as a tool and a constraint on cognitive development will be discussed below in more detail.

We, like most others who work on development, were strongly influenced by Piaget. But, although Piaget has given us our richest picture of cognitive development, it is one that is based almost entirely on experiments in which age alone is varied. While he admits that environmental influences play a role, the admission is pro forma, and inventive experiments remain confined to Western European children, usually middle-class children at that. Where Piaget's work has been extended to non-Western societies, the emphasis has been almost entirely quantitative. Such work has been confined largely to timetable studies, to the time lag in the development of foreign children in contrast to children in Geneva or Pittsburgh or London (Flavell, 20). A series of experiments carried out by the Harvard Center for Cognitive Studies has explored the role of culturally transmitted technologies in intellectual growth by the use of instructional techniques and cross-cultural studies (Bruner, Olver, Greenfield et al., 13). By comparing children of different ages in extremely different cultures we ask the developmental question in its most radical form. We are not the only ones to have gone abroad with such an intention, and we shall also use the work of others in specifying the impact of culture on growth.

We shall, in what follows, focus on two kinds of cultural constraints operating in development: value orientation and language. They seem fruitful for organizing our findings and illustrating the problems involved.

Value Complexes and Cognitive Growth

Let us, in the interest of specificity, limit our discussion of value orientations to the cognitive implications of one particular value contrast: collective versus individualistic orientation. Kluckhohn (28) in her studies of basic value orientations, attests to the fundamental nature of such a decision about orientation, commenting upon its importance for individual coping as well as for social solidarity. This value contrast represents more than alternate ways of seeing how things ought to be. Rather it reflects a contrast in how things are—a matter of world view about origins and existence and not merely a normative matter.

We begin with a series of studies carried out by Greenfield (13) in Senegal, the westernmost tip of former French West Africa in 1963–64. These studies explored two main areas of cognitive development: concept formation and conservation in the classic Piagetian sense. The two areas complement each other nicely, for much of intellectual growth can be summarized as the development of equivalence or conservation, the equivalence rule of concepts being more internal and that of conservation more external in orientation. The subjects in both sets of experiments were all Wolof, members of the country's dominant ethnic group. The children were constituted into nine groups, better to discern the effect of cultural differences—three degrees of urbanization and education were represented, with three age levels within each.

The cultural milieu of our first group, rural unschooled children and adults, had neither schools nor urban influence. Although their traditional Wolof village had an elementary school, they had never attended it. The three age groups were: six- and seven-year-olds, eight- and nine-year-olds, and eleven- to thirteen-year-olds. There was also a group of adults.

The second major group—the bush school children—attended school in the same village or in a nearby village. This group was partitioned among first graders, third graders, and sixth graders, corresponding as closely as possible to the three age levels of the unschooled groups.

The third major group comprised city school children. These children lived in Dakar, Senegal's cosmopolitan capital and, like the second group, included first, third, and sixth graders. All the children were interrogated in Wolof, although French was the official language of instruction.

Returning now to the question of collective and individualistic orientations, we find that they have cognitive manifestations so basic as to render certain experimental procedures possible or impossible. In both the conservation and the concept experiments, the children were asked to give reasons for their answers. With both American and European children this type of question is usually put something like, "Why do you say (or think) that thus and such is true?" Specifically, in a conservation problem, a child might be asked, "Why do you say that this glass has more water than this one?" But this type of question would meet with uncomprehending silence when addressed to the unschooled children. If, however, the same question were changed in form to "Why is thus and such true?" it could often be answered quite easily. It would seem that the unschooled Wolof children lack Western self-consciousness; they do not distinguish between their own thought or statement about something and the thing itself. Thought and the object of thought seem to be one. Consequently, the idea of explaining a statement is meaningless; it is the external event that is to be explained. We might expect from all this that the relativistic notion that events can vary according to point of view may be absent to a greater degree than in Western culture. This expectation is confirmed in Greenfield's concept formation studies, where the unschooled children can group a given set of objects or pictures according to only one attribute although there are several other possible bases of classification. Let it be noted that the Wolof school children do not differ essentially from Western children in this respect. It appears that school tends to give them something akin to Western self-consciousness, for they can answer questions implying a distinction between their own psychological reactions and external events; and, as they advance in school, they become increasingly capable of categorizing the same stimuli according to several different criteria or points of view.

Piaget (47) has proposed that intellectual growth begins with an egocentric stage, based on the inability to make a distinction between internal and external. This stage is then followed by a more developed egocentrism in which inner and outer are distinguished but confused. When inner psychological phenomena are attributed to inanimate features of the external environment, we have animism; when psychological processes are given characteristics of the inanimate, external world, we speak of realism. These two tendencies are supposed to be complementary and universal forms of childish thought. Their mutual presence indicates a preliminary distinction between inner and outer.

In contrast to this formulation, we should like to propose that in traditional, collectively oriented societies this distinction never gets made, that the world stays on one level of reality, and that this level is realistic rather than animistic. Animism, we realize, has often been considered the characteristic of primitive thought par excellence. We rather suspect it is only the powerful, well-cared for, competent child who sees the world in the pattern of his own feelings, and not the malnourished child of many traditional subsistence cultures like the Wolof. Kardiner (26), too, has made this point with respect to the psychoanalytic conception of the "omnipotence of thought," noting that it is only where the child's every whim is satisfied that he is led to believe his thought omnipotent. Our claim is more severe. It is that animism does not develop where there is no support given for individualistic orientation. The argument would be that the child is not cognizant of his own psychological properties, does not differentiate these from properties of the physical world, and is therefore not cognizant of any psychological properties—far be it from him to attribute such properties to inanimate objects. In place of the cultivation of individual subjectivity, there is instead a reinforcing of the idea of reality, people-in-a-world-as-a-unity.

Consider the following evidence in support of this point. In an equivalence experiment done in the United States by Olver and Hornsby (13), children were shown an assortment of pictures and asked to put the similar ones together. They were then asked the reasons for their groupings. Children as they grow older form groups increasingly by the rule of superordinate grouping (those things go together that share a common attribute). The earlier pattern is more complexive in the sense that things go together because they fit into a story together or what not. The transition from the earlier to the later mode of grouping is handled by egocentrism. Things are alike by virtue of the relationship that I or you have to them, or the action taken toward them by I or you. This is the picture in the United States. But Reich (13), using parallel techniques with Eskimo children in Anchorage, Alaska, finds that they do not express the function of things in terms of personal interaction with them nearly so often as do the American children of European descent. The Eskimo value system stresses self-reliance, but strongly suppresses any expression of individualism as an attitude toward life. The Eskimos are a subsistence culture that requires group action in its major forms of activity—sealing, caribou hunting, stone weir fishing. Eskimo children develop their superordinate structures without the intervention of the kind of egocentrism we observed in European children. Thus, such egocentrism cannot be a universal stage, not even in the development of superordination. Instead, it appears clearly relative to cultural conditions and values.

It should be clear by now that the kind of implicit egocentrism where one cannot distinguish different personal viewpoints, the kind that we have been calling realism, is strikingly different from the type that explicitly relates everything to oneself. Indeed, an explicit concept of self implies some sort of idea of not-self, for every concept must be defined as much by what it excludes as by what it includes. Or, to use Piaget's terminology, we could say equally well that an undifferentiated egocentrism that ends in realism is diametrically opposed to the kind that ends in artificialism, the tendency to see all physical phenomena as made by and for men. This tendency is closely related to animism. It is the artificialistic type of egocentrism that appears in Olver and Hornsby's experiments and is probably typical of individualistically oriented industrial societies.

Unself-conscious realism was clear at yet another point in the Senegalese experiments. Here, too, one sensed its origin in the absence of control over the inanimate world characteristic of indigenous societies. In the classic experiment on the conservation of a continuous quantity (Piaget, 48), one of two identical beakers was filled with water to a certain level. The Wolof child poured an equal amount into the second beaker. Then the experimenter poured the water from one beaker into a longer, thinner beaker, causing the water level to rise. The child was then asked if the two beakers contained the same amount of water or if one had more than the other and why. He was then asked for a reason. A type of reason in support of nonconservation judgments appeared that we had not seen before among American children (13), although Piaget (48) reports one example in a Swiss four-year-old. This was the magical action reason: The child would say, "It's not the same" because "you poured it." The shift from equality to inequality was being resolved and justified by recourse to the experimenter's action. A natural phenomenon was being explained by attributing special magical powers to intervening human agents. More likely, as Köhler (31) points out, this as well as other cases of magical causation are made possible by realism in which animate and inanimate phenomena occupy a single plane of reality. That is, the child in the conservation experiment is faced with the following sequence of events: (a) water a certain way, (*b*) experimenter's action, (*c*) water changed. When the child says the amount is not the same because the experimenter poured it, he is basing his causal inference on contiguity—the usual procedure even in our society. But under ordinary circumstances, we would accept an explanation in terms of contiguous physical events or contiguous social events, but not a causal chain that included both kinds of event. Thus, magic only exists from the perspective of a dualistic ontology.

Note well that school suppresses this mode of thinking with astonishing absoluteness. There is not one instance of such reasoning among either bush or city Senegalese children who have been in school seven months or longer. Once again school seems to promote the self-consciousness born of a distinction between human processes and physical phenomena.

We can argue that just as soon as a child is endowed with control in the situation, his realism and magical reasoning will disappear. And so it turned out to be. The experiment was done again; everything remained basically the same with one exception: this time the child did all the pouring himself. Would he find yet another magical explanation for the seeming inequality of the water? Or, indeed, would he be as likely to believe that the water in the two beakers was uneven? We would reason that he would not. For while the child would be perfectly willing to attribute magical powers to an authority figure like the experimenter, the child would not attribute any special powers to himself for his experience had taught him that he had none.

Our suspicion was well confirmed by the results. Among the younger children, two-thirds of the group who transferred the water themselves achieved conservation, in contrast to only one-quarter of the children who had only watched the experimenter pour. Among the older children, the contrast was equally dramatic; eight in ten of those who did the pouring themselves, as compared with slightly less than half of the others, achieved conservation. When the child poured himself, his reasons were dramatically different from those given when an adult was pouring. Magical action virtually disappears when the unschooled children themselves pour. What emerges instead are identity reasons—reference to the initial state of the system. The child who pours on his own now uses his initial equalizing operation as the basis for his justification of conservation, "They were equal at the beginning."

Price-Williams's (49) study of conservation among Tiv children in Nigeria lends further weight to the point. He found that all of the Tiv children had achieved conservation of both continuous and discrete quantity by age eight, in sharp contrast to our upper limit of 50 per cent with much older Senegalese children. The description given by Price-Williams of the children's behavior during the experiments indicates that Tiv culture is quite different from Wolof in promoting an active manipulative approach to the physical world. He describes the children's behavior like this:

"These children would spontaneously actually perform the operation themselves. . . . Furthermore, they would reverse the sequence of operations, by, for example, pouring back the earth from the second container to the first" (49, p. 302). Such self-initiated action was never observed among unschooled Wolof children and may well be the key to the great disparity between the two cultures in spontaneous conservation results.

It may be that a collective, rather than individual, value orientation develops where the individual lacks power over the physical world. Lacking personal power, he has no notion of personal importance. In terms of his cognitive categories, now, he will be less likely to set himself apart from others and the physical world, he will be less self-conscious at the same time that he places less value on himself. Thus, mastery over the physical world and individualistic self-consciousness will appear together in a culture, in contrast to a collective orientation and a realistic world view in which people's attitudes and actions are not placed in separate conceptual pigeonholes from physical events.

This formulation is commonsensical; absence of personal mastery over the world is consonant with a collective orientation. And, indeed, we have observed empirically that the very same Wolof children who lack self-consciousness when questioned about their thoughts also seem to be hindered by a lack of experience in manipulating the physical world when they approach a problem relating to the conservation of quantity across transformations in its appearance.

Is there, however, developmental reason for this dichotomy between individual mastery and a collective or social value orientation? How does each come about? Is there a point in child rearing at which a choice is made? Rabain-Zempléni (50) has studied the fundamental ways in which the Wolof child (in his traditional bush setting) relates to the world of animate and inanimate things around him from the time of his weaning (age two) to his integration into a peer group (age four). Her findings confirm the preceding interpretation of later intellectual development among Wolof children and elucidate in a most dramatic fashion the antecedents of these developments in terms of child training practice and infant experience. Her work suggests that there is a developmental reason for the dichotomy between physical mastery and a collective orientation and that it appears at the very beginning of life. We learn that: "In a general way, motor manifestations of the child are, from the first year of life, not treated as productions existing for themselves in their capacity of exercising nascent functions, but already are interpreted as signifying a desire on the part of the child oriented in relation to some person" (50, p. 17, our translation). So it seems as if adult members of a family evaluate and interpret the child's emergent motor activity either in terms of the relation of this activity to the people around him or in terms of motor competence per se, depending on the culture to which they belong. The child's attention must therefore be turned toward one or the other of these facets of physical activity. If, as in the Wolof case, the child's activity is not evaluated per se but in terms of its relation to group members, then one would expect both less mastery of physical acts and less differentiation of the physical from the social, that is, a realistic world view. Thus, adult interpretation of the child's first actions would seem to be paradigmatic for the choice between an individualistic and a collective orientation; for a social interpretation of an act not only relates the actor to the group but also relates the group, including actor, to physical events. When, on the one hand, acts are given an interpretation in terms of motoric competence, other people are irrelevant, and the act is separated, moreover, from the motivations, intentions, and desires of the actor himself.

Let us return once more to the Wolof to trace a more complete developmental sequence in a collectively oriented culture. Rabain-Zempléni's naturalistic observations confirm our hypothesis, derived from the conservation behavior of the unschooled children, that Wolof children lack manipulatory experience, for she notes that manipulation of objects is an occasional and secondary activity for the child from two to four and that, furthermore, the Wolof child's "self image does not have to rest in the same way as in Europe on the power which he has over objects, but rather on that which he has over other bodies" (50, p. 13). She also notes that verbal interchanges between children and adults often concern the relations which are supposed to exist between people but rarely concern explanations of natural phenomena.

At the same time as the Wolof child's manipulation of the physical, inanimate world fails to be encouraged in isolation from social relations, the personal desires and intentions which would isolate him from the group are also discouraged. Thus, a collective orientation does not arise simply as a by-product of individual powerlessness vis-à-vis the inanimate world, but is systematically encouraged as socialization progresses. Western society recognizes individual intention and desire as a positive function of age. According to Rabain-Zempléni, Wolof society does the reverse: The newborn child is treated as a person full of personal desire and intention; after he reaches the age of two, the adults in his milieu increasingly subordinate his desires to the ends of the group; he becomes less and less an individual, more and more a member of a collectivity.

When the social and physical constitute but a single level of reality, neither type of explanation should take precedence. To us who give precedence to physicalistic explanations, however, it may often appear that traditional peoples emphasize the social. This impression may be exaggerated by the fact that they often have greater knowledge about the social than the physical realm. Since a social explanation is considered perfectly adequate, we would not expect such people to press on for a physical account.

Gay and Cole's (21, 22) research among the Kpelle of Liberia furnish many other indications of the way in which people-as-causative-agents can play an extraordinary role in the traditional structure of knowledge. In school, facts are true because the teacher says them, and so there is often no attempt at understanding other reasons why or proving the fact for one-self. This same observation has been noted many places in Africa, for example, by Lapp (34) in Cameroun. His experience was similar to ours in this respect, for he found that the way to combat this tendency in teaching natural sciences was to have the students rather than the teacher do the demonstrations.

One other example from Cole and Gay. Among the Kpelle, arguments are won when they are unanswerable. Again, the ultimate criterion is social—does the other person have a comeback?—rather than objective or external. What is being argued about takes a back seat to the arguers.

Most intriguing is Rabain-Zempléni's observation that in the natural situation of sharing a quantity among several persons, a situation not too different from the second half of the conservation experiment where a quantity is divided among six beakers, more attention is paid to which person receives the substance at what point in the distribution than to the amount received. It is like their conservation explanations: More attention is focused on the person pouring—the social aspect of the situation—than on the purely physical aspect, the amount of water.

What is most interesting is the fact that, on a broader cultural level, this very same quality has been recognized by the poets of *négritude* or the African personality as setting off black from white. Lilyan Kesteloof (27) in her book on Aimé Césaire, the originator of the concept of *négritude,* contrasts its elements with the *"valeurs-clef"* of Western civilization. In opposition to *"l'Individualisme (pour la vie sociale)"* of European cultures she places *"solidarité, née de la cohésion du clan primitif"* (27, p. 84). Leopold Sédar Senghor, poet and president of Senegal, defines *négritude* in more psychological terms as *"participation du sujet à l'objet, participation de l'homme aux forces cosmiques, communion de l'homme avec tous les autres hommes"* (45, p. 31).

This complex, moreover, is held to be found in all African societies and to stem from common cultural features. The strong element of collective or social values is particularly clear in the modern concept of African socialism which, unlike Western socialism, is supposed to be a mere modernization of existing ideals and social conditions rather than a radical revolution.

We have come far afield from intellectual development, but what is so intriguing about these world views and ideologies is that they should be so strongly reflected in the details of cognitive growth. Bear in mind, however, that the distinctions we are proposing are not all-or-none, although they have been so presented for the sake of clarity. Our evidence, furthermore, is thus far all from Africa. It is interesting that many different ethnic groups should seem to have so much in common, but on the other hand, we do not really know to what extent this social or collective orientation may be typical of all nonindustrial, traditional, or, perhaps, oral cultures. It is not certain that it is even a valid description for every African society. Finally, although we started out talking about the ramifications of a social or collective orientation, we do not really know what causes what in the whole complex of features that we have ended up discussing.

Language and Cognitive Growth

Our second cultural constraint is language. What does it mean intellectually to speak one language rather than another? What does it mean to write a language as well as to speak it?

Language at the highest level of generality can be divided into two components, semantic and syntactic. Most experiments attempting to relate language to thought have emphasized the semantic side in the style of Benjamin Lee Whorf (62). Here the linguistic variable is the richness of the lexicon that a language has available to represent a given domain. Implicitly, but not explicitly, these experiments deal with the vocabulary of any one language at a single level of generality—its words rather than any structural relation among them.

A second kind of semantic linguistic variable is more structural. It deals with the number of levels of generality that can be encoded by the lexicon of a given language for a particular domain. We shall be interested in the relation of both these kinds of semantic variables to concept formation.

Finally, there are the syntactic properties of language to relate to the logical structure of thought. Hitherto, the cross-cultural study of the relation between syntax and thought has been sorely neglected, although a recent paper (McNeill, 41) suggests that there is reason to believe that the lexical encoding of events is but a special (and perhaps trivial) case of grammatical encoding. Sapir (53) may have been the earliest to think explicitly and clearly about the manner in which syntax can shape thought.

In the view of linguistic relativity inspired by Whorf, language is seen as a system of related categories that both incorporates and perpetuates a particular world view. On the lexical level, every language codes certain domains of experience in more detail than others. It has been suggested that when a given language symbolizes a phenomenon in a single word, it is readily available as a classifying principle to speakers of that language. Although any familiar experience can be coded in any language through the simple expedient of a paraphrase, experiences that must be expressed in this way are supposed to be less available to speakers of the language (Brown, 10). Some experiments have focused on this sort of difference between languages. Others have focused on the fact that grammatical considerations force certain classificatory dimensions on speakers of a given language (for instance, time for speakers of English, shape for speakers of

Navaho) and derive the hypothesis that the dimensions thus emphasized should be more available for cognitive use in categorization, discrimination, and the like to speakers of that language than for speakers of another language without such obligatory distinctions.

Why have experiments generated by these ideas yielded such diverse and confusing results? Under what conditions (if any) can a relatively rich or poor lexicon defined only by number of terms affect nonlinguistic cognitive activity? These are the issues that concern us in this section.

Now, hypotheses about the effect of numerical richness can be based on a comparison of different languages with respect to the same domain or a comparison of different areas within a single language. Research has for the most part yielded ambiguous or negative results for studies of the first kind (interlingual) while a good number of the intralingual studies have confirmed the richness hypothesis. A close look reveals, however, that these two types of research differ in other ways than their results. The intracultural studies have used as their cognitive measure some memory task such as recognition of the identity of denoted stimuli earlier encountered. One classic experiment, done by Brown and Lenneberg (11), showed, for example, that ease in naming colors made recognizing them easier when they appeared in a larger array. The cross-cultural studies, on the other hand, have usually dealt with judgments of similarity among several stimuli rather than with the identity of a single stimulus over time. A classic experiment was done by Carroll and Casagrande (15) in which children were asked which of two stimuli (for instance, a yellow block and a blue rope) would go best with a third item which was like one of the pair in color and like the other in shape. The subjects were Navaho-dominant and English-dominant Navaho children and white children from three to ten years of age. The Navaho-dominant children were expected to be more sensitive to form than the other groups, because Navaho has an obligatory distinction in its verbs: The form of an object dictates the verb of handling. The Navaho-dominant Indian children did indeed classify by form more frequently than did the English-dominant ones, but, alas, the white children who knew no Navaho used form most frequently of all! Other experiments have found much the same kind of anomaly (for instance, Doob, 18; Maclay, 40).

McNeill (41), in reviewing this literature, concludes that language does not influence perception but only memory. He proposes that a perceptual representation consists of both a schema—the linguistic label—and a correction—the visual image, but with time the correction and its label tend to be lost, thus accounting for the influence of language on memory.[2]

[2] The expression *tend to get lost* is advisable, for it is sometimes the case that the correction is not lost but magnified, producing exaggeration in memory—the familiar opposition between "leveling" and "sharpening" introduced long ago by Bartlett (2) and the Gestalt theorists (for instance, Koffka, 30).

The implication is that the cross-cultural studies mentioned above were unsuccessful because they dealt with present perceptual processes. Indeed, the one unambiguously successful cross-cultural study (Lenneberg and Roberts, 36) involved a memory task. Before evaluating this formulation, consider one of our own experiments (13). Children were presented with pictures in sets of three. They were asked to choose the two out of each three that were most alike and to give a reason for their choice. In each of the triads, two pictures were similar in color, two were similar in form, and two were similar in the function of the object pictured. French or Wolof was the language of our subjects who took part in the experiment in a manner presently to be related.

But consider first the Wolof and French lexicons available for dealing with the task. Only words at a single level of generality—the most specific —will be considered at this point. In Wolof, it is impossible to make explicit the three color groupings possible in the experiment without the supplementary aid of French words. Specifically, in the last set of three pictures, the French word *bleu* (blue) must be used if one is to specify the basis of grouping by naming the color, for there is no single word for this color in Wolof. In the second set, color grouping involves contrasting a pair of predominantly orange pictures with a predominantly red one. The Wolof language codes both colors with a single word (*honka*), so that verbalizing the basis of the grouping by means of the Wolof word could not be as satisfactory as using the French word *orange,* for it would not contrast the pair with the third member of the set. For the first set of three pictures, Wolof does almost as well with coding the relevant colors as French, although yellow, the color involved in forming the color pair, is not as codable by Wolof according to the criterion (suggested by Brown, 10) of agreement between speakers of the language. In fact, the same word is sometimes used to name both yellow and orange, the contrasting color of the third picture in the triad.

Let us pass over a comparison of the coding of shapes by the French and Wolof languages, for the relative strength of the two languages is much less clear, and this comparison is not necessary for present purposes. With regard to functional grouping, both easily find ways of saying, "These things are to eat, to wear, to ride in." One cannot say that Wolof is superior to French in this regard, but unlike the color case, it is not clearly inferior in its ability to code at least those aspects of function demanded by the functional groups in this experiment.

On lexical grounds, then, one would at very least expect that monolingual Wolofs would be less color-oriented and more functionally oriented in the content of their groupings than bilinguals, and that both of these groups would form fewer color and more functional groups than monolingual French children, in a forced-choice situation, where one type of attribute must be used at the expense of others.

The results, however, were unambiguously contrary to these expectations. The Wolof monolinguals, that is, the unschooled bush Wolofs, could use nothing but color as a grouping principle even when given a chance to make second choice groupings. The other groups of children, in sharp contrast, used color less and less with age and increasingly turned to the other types of attribute. Obviously, the lack of color words does not stop monolingual Wolofs from grouping by color.

But does it make their color discriminations less accurate? In asking this question, our experiment becomes in one respect like the intracultural tests of the Whorfian hypothesis described above; the task now involves the accuracy of color discriminations. It is no longer a matter of choice between color or form as bases of grouping. It is quite a straightforward matter to identify errors in color discrimination that can be directly related to lexical structuring. For example, the second set of pictures consists of two predominantly orange pictures and one predominantly red one. The orange colors are in fact identical. An error was counted when a child who claimed to be grouping according to color would select one orange and one red picture as being most similar. This choice was clearly wrong from an objective point of view, for he could have chosen the two orange ones that were of identical color. If such errors of discrimination are due to lexical coding, Wolof monolinguals should make them most frequently, Wolof bilinguals next most frequently, and French monolinguals not at all. The results are exactly as predicted. At every age, bilinguals make fewer errors of this kind than Wolof monolinguals, and the French monolingual children make no such errors at all.

These errors, by absolute standards, are infrequent, even in those groups of children where they occur most often. There are never more than three color discrimination errors in any single group (comprising about 20 children). These relatively rare mistakes are not a major conceptual feature in the total context of Wolof equivalence grouping. We begin to wonder whether the lexical features of language should be assigned as large a role in thought as has been claimed by Whorf and even others who have spoken of covariation rather than determinism.

Of great theoretical interest is the fact that these perceptual errors decrease with age until at last they are completely eliminated in all groups. It appears that age brings increasingly accurate perceptual discriminations. This would appear to be a universal trend, even when the lexicon of a culture hinders rather than facilitates such discrimination. We may conclude that with age the constraints of reality increasingly overcome language if they are opposed.

Is it, as McNeill (42) suggests, that such findings prove merely that people learn to see? Clearly language influences perception and not just memory, at least during childhood. As early as 1915, Peters (cited in Smith, 55) experimentally produced color-matching errors in children through teaching them an artificial vocabulary in which certain colors were lexically indistinguishable. Later, when the children were taught these lexical distinctions, the corresponding perceptual discriminations also appeared. Even earlier, Tucker (58) observed this same situation naturally and intraculturally; he found that children would group together different colored wools called by the same name. Lenneberg, on the other hand, confirms the notion that this influence of lexicon on perception diminishes with age; for he finds that the absence of certain terminological color distinctions adversely affects color memory in Zuni adults (Lenneberg and Roberts, 36) and present color perception in Wolof children but does not affect present perception in Zuni adults (Lenneberg, 35). Even adults, however, may fall back on language to aid perception when conditions become particularly difficult, as, for example, when all the relevant stimuli are present but spatially separated (Bruner, Postman, and Rodrigues, 14). Indeed, in terms of the eye movements necessary to visual perception, spatial separation may be translated into a mild form of temporal separation.

McNeill's hypothesis about language affecting only the memory pattern is plainly false. Yet his notions of schema plus correction may still hold. In fact, Ranken (51) shows that linguistic coding in the form of assigning names can help when it is a matter of ordering shapes relative to one another where it is not necessary to remember their exact form, but that it can hinder performance in tasks where the precise image of the same stimuli must be utilized (as in a mental jigsaw puzzle). We interpret this outcome to mean that the label helps where a general scheme suffices for the cognitive task in question, but that it produces deceptive vagueness where the task actually involves both schema and correction, that is, an exact image.

A schema can operate only where called into play; language affects cognition only if a linguistic coding occurs, that is, only if the stimulus is given a verbal representation. It is possible that these conditions prevail only when a task is difficult to perform by means other than linguistic coding. But that is a moot point much in need of further investigation. Perhaps, too, different cultures vary in their tendency to use such linguistic encoding. Unschooled Wolof children in our experiment, for instance, showed a much stronger tendency to use ostensive, as opposed to verbal, reasons for their groupings. That is, they would explain their grouping choice by pointing to the common pictorial elements. Such ostensive definition may have counteracted the detrimental effects of an inexact vocabulary by bypassing language altogether. We do well to remember, in assessing cross-cultural studies, that most cultures are nontechnically traditional, less verbally oriented than our own.

In summary, it appears from our own and other work that linguistic encoding of the stimuli relevant to a given problem situation can affect the ordering of stimuli by providing a formula for relating them across time

(Brown and Lenneberg, 11; Van de Geer and Frijda, 59; Lantz, 32; Lantz and Stefflre, 33; Koen, 29) or space, as our Wolof results and the Bruner, Postman and Rodrigues (14) experiments show. The influence of encoding becomes stronger as cognitive conditions become more difficult, making an iconic approach to the problem increasingly ineffective and a symbolic approach more crucial. Such conditions are produced as the situation becomes less simultaneous and more a matter of memory and as the number of stimuli to be dealt with simultaneously approaches 7 ± 2, the limit of immediate perception and memory (Miller, 44; Brown and Lenneberg, 11). These generalizations about the conditions under which linguistic encoding will affect other cognitive operations must be further qualified. They hold only if a linguistic representation is available to the person in question and has been activated.

Whether or not the linguistic effect will be positive or negative depends on the fit between linguistic representation and situation. If linguistic encoding is inappropriate to the task at hand, either because the labels do not encode all the necessary information (the mental jigsaw puzzle in Ranken's experiment), or because the labels cut the domain in places other than those the task demands, linguistic organization can have an adverse affect on task performance (for instance, Lenneberg and Roberts, 36). Whether or not a label encodes all the necessary information depends not only on the task but also on the array of stimuli. A given label becomes ineffective in distinguishing a given stimulus if it must be discriminated from others to which the name could also apply (Lantz and Stefflre, 33).

We began by considering the part that a lexicon plays in determining the content of equivalence groupings. We have emerged with the conclusion that factors other than lexicon determine the bases or dimensions of equivalence but that a specific lexicon may influence the band width of the individual categories that constitute the dimension. In the end, we have seen that the equivalence of two spatially separated stimuli is affected similarly by lexical conditions as that of two temporally separated stimuli. Thus, equivalence and recognition have much in common.

Let us turn now from the role of labels per se to the role of a set of hierarchically organized labels, that is, to the role of lexical richness defined in structural terms. There has been much controversy about the role of superordinate words in conceptual thought. The Wolof language, in contrast to French (and to English), has neither the word *color* nor the word *shape*. It is clear from the results reported above that the lack of the word *color* does not hinder color groupings from being formed. Does the absence of the general word, however, mean that the Wolofs have no general concept of color? If not, is there much consequence in this seemingly grievous deficit?

Consider Figure 1. It is one possible representation of the hierarchical structure of the first set of three pictures used in the present experiment.

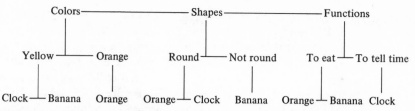

FIGURE 1. Representation of hierarchical structure of one set of three pictures used in grouping experiment

If this hierarchical organization corresponds to the type of structure generated by the subject to deal with the task, then his use of the superordinate words *color* or *shape* should indicate that the person is operating at the top of the hierarchy and has access to the entire hierarchy. One would predict, then, that he would be able to supply more than one kind of attribute if pressed. For he is plainly contrasting, say, color with shape or with use. By the same reasoning, his exclusive use of shape names or color names alone (for instance, round, yellow) would mean that he was operating one level lower in the hierarchy. He would be cut off from the top of the hierarchy and its connections with other branches. He would, therefore, be less likely to operate in branches other than the one in which he found himself. A concept (a consciously or explicitly recognized concept) is defined as much by what it excludes as by what it includes, by its contrast class. The concept of color per se comes into being through contrast with an opposing idea. An opposing concept to color per se cannot be a specific color; just as round is related only to other shapes, so yellow relates only to other colors.

If this reasoning is correct, then one would expect that, if a subject ever used an abstract word like *color* or *shape,* he would also vary his choice of grouping attributes when asked to make a first and second choice of pairs for each of the three sets of pictures. But if he used only a concrete word like *red,* then one would expect him to form nothing but color groupings in all six tasks. Our results do indeed indicate that there is a significant association between use of superordinate words like *color* and *shape* and the number of different types of attribute used for grouping. This relationship also holds when all other factors such as knowledge of French and school grade are held constant. Thus, if a Wolof child uses a superordinate word, his chances of grouping by a variety of attributes are twice as great as those of a child who utilizes no superordinate vocabulary. Recall that when a Wolof child uses the word *color,* it is a French word that he is introducing into a Wolof linguistic context.

Although all our experimentation was carried out in Wolof, we also ran additional sixth-grade Wolof groups in French in order to assess the effect of using one language or another when all other factors are held constant.

The relationship between use of superordinate words and variety of attribute used is weakest under this condition. But before interpreting this finding, consider one further observation. The experiment was also carried out in French with French children in the sixth grade. It is in this experiment that the strongest relationship is found. If a French child uses an abstract top-of-the-hierarchy label, he is almost certain to vary his basis of grouping at least once. So we must conclude that access to the pure conceptual hierarchy as diagrammed is indicated by the use of abstract terms only if the linguistic terms have been thoroughly mastered in all their semantic implications. Our results indicate that such is the case under normal conditions of spontaneous use in the context of one's native language. But when the Wolof children are interrogated in French, their use of superordinate language seems to have a forced character and indicates little about hierarchical structure and where they are in that structure.

The reasons for color preference among the Wolof are too complicated to discuss here. What needs emphasis is that the basis of equivalence is not an either/or phenomenon, as so much experimentation has assumed. It is, rather, a matter of adding new bases to old and of integrating them in a hierarchically organized structure. Everybody is more or less limited in the range of classificatory bases available to him. It is not that one person uses color, the other shape. Rather, one can use color, the other can use shape and color. It is the structure of the lexicon and not simply its list of terms that is crucial.

Superordinate class words are not just a luxury for people who do not have to deal with concrete phenomena, as Roger Brown (10) hypothesizes. In a way quite different from that envisaged by Whorf in the lexical version of his hypothesis, we seem to have found an important correspondence between linguistic and conceptual structure. But it relates not to words in isolation but to their depth of hierarchical embedding both in the language and in thought. This correspondence has to do not with quantitative richness of vocabulary in different domains or with accessibility but with the presence or absence of higher-order words that can be used to integrate different domains of words and objects into hierarchical structures. No matter how rich the vocabulary available to describe a given domain, it is of limited use as an instrument of thought if it is not organized into a hierarchy that can be activated as a whole.

Consider now the grammatical aspect of language. In previous work (Vygotsky, 60; Bruner et al., 13) the structure of equivalence groupings was found to become increasingly superordinate with age and less complexive and thematic. Superordinate structure is not the same as the use of a general or superordinate word. The attribute that organizes a superordinate group may be general or specific, but it must be explicitly stated to be shared by every member of the group in question. Thus, "They are all the same color" would have the same structural status as "They are all red."

In terms of this structural criterion, all the children studied in Senegal conform to the usual development trend. Although the grouping choices of our unschooled Wolof group got increasingly systematic with age, their explanations showed a somewhat different form. Instead of explicitly connecting the common attribute to every member of their groupings in the manner described above, they would explain their grouping with a single word, saying, for example, nothing more than "red." What may we make of this?

Consider the matter in purely grammatical terms. For perhaps we can find a connection between conceptual organization and grammatical rules. Let us posit, first, three stages of symbolic reference. The first is the ostensive mode, mere pointing at the object of reference. The second, the labeling mode, consists of nothing more than a verbal tag. This tag replaces or accompanies the operation of pointing. The third mode is sentential. Here the label is integrated into a complete sentence. In the present experiment, these three modes were defined as follows, and the definitions applied to grouping reasons: (*a*) pointing—no verbal response; (*b*) labeling—label only; no verb in utterance, for example, red; (*c*) sentential placement—complete sentence, for example, "This is red."

Among French monolinguals, pointing is nonexistent even among first graders. Pointing, however, occupies a definite position in the reasoning of all the youngest Wolof groups, especially the unschooled, but disappears in all the groups with advancing age. The other differences set the unschooled children apart from all the school children. In the unschooled groups, labeling, the simple paradigmatic mode, increases with age. But the use of sentential placement does not increase with age but remains at a constantly low level. In all the school groups, both Wolof-French bilingual and French monolingual, the ostensive mode gives way to sentential placement with age and increased schooling. There is, let it be noted, virtually no difference on any criterion between the oldest French monolinguals and the oldest Wolof-French bilinguals when the experiment is run in French. The superiority is slightly on the side of the French when the experiment is carried out in the native language of each group. The contrast that is most dramatic is between Wolof children in school speaking French and those not in school speaking Wolof, with virtually no overlap in the distributions. Some 97 per cent of the 11- to 13-year-old Wolof monolinguals (the unschooled Wolof children) use the labeling mode; 90 per cent of the Wolof sixth graders doing the experiment in French use the sentential mode.

These results using grammatical criteria reveal larger differences between the groups who know French and those who do not than those using the earlier, more semantic verbal measure of grouping structure. Is there, however, any direct relation between grammatical and conceptual structure? A child can frame an explicit superordinate structure in either the labeling or sentential mode. This superordinate structure can be of a general or itemized type. An example of a general superordinate language structure in the labeling mode would be "These—round." Expressed sententially, this structure would be "These (or they) are round." An itemized superordinate in labeling form might be "This—round; this—round." An example of the same structure expressed in the sentential mode would be "This (or it) is round; this (or it) is round." Obviously, a limitless variety of nonsuperordinate structures may be expressed either as labels or as complete sentences. It is valid, then, to ask whether the use of a particular mode of reference is associated with a particular conceptual structure. The answer is a strong affirmative for both schooled and unschooled Wolof children. When a school child frames a reason in the sentential mode, the probability that he will form a superordinate structure of either the itemized or general type is on the average almost three times as great as when he uses simple labeling. For an unschooled child, this same probability of a superordinate structure is almost six times as great when his reasons are sentences rather than labels.

For a school child, moreover, the probability that a superordinate structure will be in a general (rather than itemized) form is more than four times as great when a grouping reason is expressed in the sentential mode. In the unschooled groups, the number of reasons falling into these categories is very small. If, however, all four unschooled groups are combined, the relationship does hold: superordinate reasons expressed as labels take the general form about half as often as do those expressed as complete sentences.

We are led to the hypothesis that school is operating on grouping operations through the training embodied in the written language. This hypothesis has a good theoretical basis. The written language, as Vygotsky (60) points out, provides an occasion in which one must deploy language out of the immediate context of reference. Writing virtually forces a remoteness of reference on the language user. Consequently, he cannot use simple pointing as an aid, nor can he count on labeling that depends on the present context to make clear what his label refers to. Writing, then, is training in the use of linguistic contexts that are independent of the immediate referents. Thus, the embedding of a label in a sentence structure indicates that it is less tied to its situational context and more related to its linguistic context. The implications of this fact for manipulability are great; linguistic contexts can be turned upside down more easily than real ones can. Indeed, the linguistic independence of context achieved by certain grammatical modes appears to favor the development of the more self-contained superordinate structure used by the school children.

Note the recurrence of a theme that has been running through all of our results: It is always the schooling variable that makes qualitative differences in directions of growth. Wolof children who have been to school are more different intellectually from unschooled children living in the same bush village than they are from city children in the same country or from Mexico City, Anchorage, Alaska, or Brookline, Massachusetts (Bruner et al., 13). Similar results demonstrating the huge impact of school have emerged from the Belgian Congo (Cryns, 16) and South Africa (Biesheuvel, 4; Schmidt, 54).

How, then, do school and language interrelate? We may hypothesize that it is the fact of being a written language that makes French such a powerful factor in the cognitive growth of the children we have studied. For all of the semantic and syntactic features that we have discussed in relation to concept formation—a rich vocabulary that is hierarchically organized, syntactical embedding of labels, and so on—become necessary when one must communicate out of the context of immediate reference. It is precisely in this respect that written language differs from spoken. But school itself provides the same opportunity to use language out of context—even spoken language—for, to a very high degree, what one talks about are things not immediately present.

School, Language, and Individualism

In the last section, the final emphasis was on the role of school in establishing context-independent modes of thinking through the separation of the written word from the thing it stands for and the separation of school from life. How exactly does this process relate to the decline of a realistic world view and the correlative rise in self-consciousness discussed in the section before? Realism, as a world view, can characterize a person's concept of language and words, as well as his concept of thought in general. When a word is considered to be as real as the thing for which it stands, the psychological attitude (and philosophical position) is called nominal or verbal realism. School separates word and thing and destroys verbal realism by presenting for the first time a situation where words are systematically and continually there without their referents. The rules of the Original Word Game, described by Brown (10) in which the tutor acts as though things are but signs of their names, are for the first time systematically and thoroughly broken. That is, the sequence object-name no longer is invariant. When names, or symbols in general, no longer inhere in their referents, they must go somewhere; and the logical place is the psyche of the language user. Thus, the separation of word and thing demands a notion that words are in people's heads, not in their referents. (This point has been well made by Ogden and Richards, 46.) The concepts thinker and thought processes thus become important in the shedding of nominal realism. Meaning is seen to vary with the particular speaker, and the notion of psychological relativity is born. Implicit in this notion is the distinctness of oneself and one's own point of view. Thus, the individual must conceptually separate himself from the group; he must become self-conscious, aware of having a particular slant on things, a certain individuality.

The destruction of nominal or verbal realism may thus be the wedge that ultimately fragments the unitary solidarity of a realistic world view. Once thought has been dissociated from its objects, the stage is set for symbolic processes to run ahead of concrete fact, for thought to be in terms of possibility rather than actuality. At this point, symbolic representation can go beyond the capacities of an iconic system, to use Bruner's (12) [3] terms, and the way is open for Piaget's stage of formal operations, where the real becomes but a subset of the possible (Inhelder and Piaget, 24). So school and the written language may have a privileged position in the shift from a collective to an individualistic orientation chronicled above.

Culture and Biological Growth

Lest it be thought that we espouse a view of complete cultural determinism, which we do not, we conclude with some remarks on the interaction of cultural constraints and universal biological maturation.

Because the doctrine that ontogeny recapitulates phylogeny was given too literal a form in biology, a more sophisticated consideration of the relation between phylogeny and ontogeny was also given up. Species-specific behavior does not appear out of the blue. It has evolutionary history, and that history reflects itself in the early growth of the young. We are primates, and our primate heritage affects our growth. All cultures must work on the stuff of the biological organism, specifically on man's primate constraints.

One of the huge discontinuities in man's evolution was his capacity for language and symbolism, and this only gradually achieves realization through training. Sapir (53) may have been quite right in pointing out that no human language can be shown to be more sophisticated than any other and that the speech used by the member of the Academy is no more complex than that of a Hottentot. But again it was Sapir who pointed out that it is in extracting from our use of language the powerful tools for organizing thought that peoples differ from each other. The intellectual nurturing that makes it possible eventually to use language as a tool of thought requires long years and complex training.

It is here that the difference comes. If that intellectual training is not forthcoming, if language is not freely employed in its pragmatic function of guiding thought and action, then one finds forms of intellectual functioning that are adequate for concrete tasks, but not so for matters involving abstract conception. As Werner (61) pointed out, "Development

[3] See pp. 325–51.

among primitive people is characterized on the one hand by precocity and, on the other, by a relatively early arrest of the process of intellectual growth" (p. 27). His remark is telling with respect to the difference we find between school children and those who have not been to school. The latter stabilize earlier and do not go on to new levels of operation. The same early arrest characterizes the differences between culturally-deprived and other American children (for instance, 17).

In short, some environments push cognitive growth better, earlier, and longer than others. What does not seem to happen is that different cultures produce completely divergent and unrelated modes of thought. The reason for this must be the constraint of our biological heritage.[4] That heritage makes it possible for man to reach a form of intellectual maturity that is capable of elaborating a highly technical society. Less demanding societies —less demanding intellectually—do not produce so much symbolic embedding and elaboration of first ways of looking and thinking. Whether one wishes to judge these differences on some universal human scale as favoring an intellectually more evolved man is a matter of one's values. But however one judges, let it be clear that a decision not to aid the intellectual maturation of those who live in less technically developed societies can not be premised on the careless claim that it makes little difference; it makes a huge difference to the intellectual life of a child simply that he was in school.

References

1. ALLPORT, G. W., and PETTIGREW, T. F. 1957. Cultural influence on the perception of movement: the trapezoidal illusion among Zulus. *Journal of Abnormal and Social Psychology* 55:104–13.
2. BARTLETT, F. C. 1932. *Remembering.* Cambridge, Eng.: Cambridge University Press (paperback, 1968).
3. BIESHEUVAL, S. 1943. *African intelligence.* Johannesburg: South African Institute of Race Relations.
4. BIESHEUVEL, S. 1949. Psychological tests and their application to non-European peoples. *Yearbook of Education,* pp. 87–126. London: Evans.
5. BIESHEUVEL, S. 1956. Aspects of Africa. *The Listener* 55:447–49.
6. BIESHEUVEL, S. 1963. *The human resources of the Republic of South Africa and their development.* Johannesburg: Witwatersrand University Press.
7. BOAS, F. 1938. *The mind of primitive man.* New York: Macmillan.
8. BOGORAS, W. G. 1904–09. *The Chukchee.* New York: G. E. Stechert. Part 1, *Material culture,* 1904; part 3, *Social organization,* 1909.
9. BONTE, M. 1962. The reaction of two African societies to the Müller-Lyer illusion. *Journal of Social Psychology* 58:265–68.
10. BROWN, R. 1958. *Words and things.* Glencoe, Ill.: Free Press.
11. BROWN, R., and LENNEBERG, E. H. 1954. A study in language and cognition. *Journal of Abnormal and Social Psychology* 49:454–62. Reprinted in *Psycho-*

---

[4] This constraint is, however, somewhat variable in that widespread malnutrition can affect the neurological and mental functions of large groups of people (Biesheuvel, 3, 4, 5, 6).

linguistics: a book of readings, ed. S. Saporta, pp. 480–92. New York: Holt, 1961.

12. BRUNER, J. S. 1964. The course of cognitive growth. *American Psychologist* 19:1–15.
13. BRUNER, J. S.; OLVER, R. R.; GREENFIELD, P. M.; ET AL. 1966. *Studies in cognitive growth.* New York: Wiley.
14. BRUNER, J. S.; POSTMAN, L.; and RODRIGUES, J. 1951. Expectation and the perception of color. *American Journal of Psychology* 64:216–27.
15. CARROLL, J. B., and CASAGRANDE, J. B. 1958. The function of language classifications in behavior. In *Readings in social psychology,* ed. Eleanor Maccoby, T. M. Newcomb, E. L. Hartley, pp. 18–32. New York: Holt.
16. CRYNS, A. G. J. 1964. African intelligence: a critical survey of cross-cultural intelligence research in Africa south of the Sahara. *Journal of Social Psychology* 57:283–301.
17. DEUTSCH, M. 1965. The role of social class in language development and cognition. *American Journal of Orthopsychiatry* 35:78–88.
18. DOOB, L. W. 1960. The effect of codability upon the afferent and efferent functioning of language. *Journal of Social Psychology* 52:3–15.
19. DURKHEIM, E., and MAUSS, M. 1963. *Primitive classification.* Chicago: University of Chicago Press.
20. FLAVELL, J. 1963. *The developmental psychology of Jean Piaget.* Princeton, N.J.: Van Nostrand.
21. GAY, J. H. 1965. Education and mathematics among the Kpelle of Liberia. Paper read at Commission Interunions de l'Enseignement des Sciences, Dakar, January 1965.
22. GAY, J. H., and COLE, M. 1967. *The new mathematics and an old culture: a study of learning among the Kpelle.* New York: Holt.
23. HUDSON, W. 1960. Pictorial depth perception in subcultural groups in Africa. *Journal of Social Psychology* 52:183–208.
24. INHELDER, B., and PIAGET, J. 1958. *Growth of logical thinking from childhood to adolescence.* New York: Basic Books.
25. JAHODA, J. 1956. Assessment of abstract behaviour in a non-Western culture. *Journal of Abnormal and Social Psychology* 53:237–43.
26. KARDINER, A. 1965. Lecture at Harvard University, Cambridge, Mass., April 1965.
27. KESTELOOF, L. 1962. *Aimé Césaire.* Paris: Editions Presse Seghers.
28. KLUCKHOHN, F. R., and STRODTBECK, F. L. 1961. *Variations in value orientations.* Evanston, Ill.: Row, Peterson.
29. KOEN, F. 1965. The codability of complex stimuli: three modes of representation. Unpublished paper, University of Michigan, Ann Arbor, Mich.
30. KOFFKA, K. 1935. *Principles of Gestalt psychology.* New York: Harcourt Brace.
31. KÖHLER, W. 1937. Psychological remarks on some questions of anthropology. *American Journal of Psychology* 58:271–88. Reprinted in *Documents of Gestalt psychology,* ed. Mary Henle, pp. 203–21. Berkeley, Calif.: University of California Press, 1961.
32. LANTZ, D. L. 1963. Color naming and color recognition: a study in the psychology of language. Unpublished doctoral dissertation, Harvard University.
33. LANTZ, D. L., and STEFFLRE, V. 1964. Language and cognition revisited. *Journal of Abnormal and Social Psychology* 69:472–81.
34. LAPP, D. 1965. Personal communication.
35. LENNEBERG, E. H. 1961. Color naming, color recognition, color discrimination: a reappraisal. *Perceptual and Motor Skills* 12:375–82.
36. LENNEBERG, E. H., and ROBERTS, J. M. 1956. The language of experience: a study in methodology. *International Journal of American Living,* suppl. 22 (memoir 13).
37. LÉVI-STRAUSS, C. 1962. *La Pensée sauvage.* Paris: Plon.
38. LINDZEY, G. 1961. *Projective techniques and cross-cultural research.* New York: Appleton-Century-Crofts.

39. LURIA, A. R. 1961. *The role of speech in regulation of normal and abnormal behavior.* New York: Liveright.
40. MACLAY, H. 1958. An experimental study of language and non-linguistic behavior. *Southwestern Journal of Anthropology* 14:220–29.
41. McNEILL, D. 1965. Anthropological psycholinguistics. Unpublished paper, Harvard University.
42. McNEILL, D. 1966. Personal communication.
43. MEAD, M. 1946. Research on primitive children. In *Manual of child psychology,* ed. L. Carmichael, pp. 735–80. New York: Wiley.
44. MILLER, G. A. 1956. The magical number seven, plus or minus two: some limits on our capacity for processing information. *Psychological Review* 63:81–97.
45. MONTEIL, V. 1964. *L'Islam noir.* Paris: Editions du Seuil.
46. OGDEN, C. K., and RICHARDS, I. A. 1930. *The meaning of meaning.* 3d rev. ed. New York: Harcourt Brace.
47. PIAGET, J. 1930. *The child's conception of physical causality.* London: Kegan Paul.
48. PIAGET, J. 1952. *The child's conception of number.* New York: Humanities Press.
49. PRICE-WILLIAMS, D. R. 1961. A study concerning concepts of conservation of quantities among primitive children. *Acta Psychologica* 18:297–305.
50. RABAIN-ZEMPLÉNI, J. 1965. Quelques réfléxions sur les modes fondamentaux de relations chez l'enfant wolof du sevrage à l'intégration dans la classe d'âge. Paris: Association Universitaire pour le Développement de l'Enseignement et de la culture en Afrique et à Madagascar.
51. RANKEN, H. B. 1963. Language and thinking: positive and negative effects of naming. *Science* 141:48–50.
52. RIVERS, W. H. R. 1905. Observations on the senses of the Todas. *British Journal of Psychology* 1:322–96.
53. SAPIR, E. 1921. *Language: an introduction to the study of speech.* New York: Harcourt Brace.
54. SCHMIDT, W. H. O. 1965. Personal communication.
55. SMITH, H. C. 1943. Age differences in color discrimination. *Journal of General Psychology* 29:191–226.
56. STRODTBECK, F. L. 1964. Considerations of meta-method in cross-cultural studies. In Trans-cultural studies in cognition, ed. A. K. Romney and R. G. D'Andrade, *American Anthropologist,* spec. publ., 66:223–29.
57. STURTEVANT, W. C. 1964. Studies in ethnoscience. In Trans-cultural studies in cognition, ed. A. K. Romney and R. G. D'Andrade, *American Anthropologist,* spec. publ., 66:99–131.
58. TUCKER, A. W. 1911. Observations on the color vision of school children. *British Journal of Psychology* 4:33–43.
59. VAN DE GEER, J. P., and FRIJDA, N. H. 1961. Codability and recognition: an experiment with facial expressions. *Acta Psychologica* 18:360–67.
60. VYGOTSKY, L. S. 1962. *Thought and language.* Ed. and trans. E. Hanfmann and G. Vakar. Cambridge, Mass.: MIT Press, and New York: Wiley.
61. WERNER, H. 1948. *Comparative psychology of mental development.* Rev. ed. Chicago: Follett.
62. WHORF, B. L. 1956. *Language, thought, and reality,* ed. J. B. Carroll. Cambridge, Mass.: Technology Press.
63. WINTRINGER, J. 1955. Considérations sur l'intelligence du Noir africain. *Revue de Psychologie des Peuples* 10:37–55.

5

EDUCATION

Introduction

Two recurrent themes in Bruner's cognitive psychology, considered in the first four sections, have been particularly crucial in shaping his view of education. The first is the notion that the acquisition of knowledge, be it the recognition of a pattern, the attainment of a concept, the solution of a problem, or the development of a scientific theory, is an active process. The individual is best viewed neither as a passive recipient of information nor as a bundle of stimulus-response connections. Rather he should be regarded as an active participant in the knowledge getting process, one who selects and transforms information, who constructs hypotheses and who alters those hypotheses in the face of inconsistent or discrepant evidence. It is not surprising then that one important feature of Bruner's approach to education is to encourage the learner to participate actively in the process of learning. The instructor according to this view should emulate Socrates and where possible should rely on teaching in what Bruner calls the hypothetical mode so that he and the student might coexist in a more co-operative position with respect to the transmission and discovery of knowledge. And the student should be encouraged to work things out for himself, to organize evidence so that he is able to go beyond it to novel conjectures and insights, and to participate in an active dialogue with his teacher.

The second recurrent theme that is particularly germane to Bruner's views on pedagogy is closely related to the first. When a person actively constructs knowledge he does so by relating incoming information to a previously acquired psychological frame of reference. This frame of reference which has been variously labeled cognitive structure, theory, generic coding system, internal model, and system of representation, gives meaning and organization to the regularities in experience, and allows the individual to go beyond the information given. It is in connection with the concept of an internal model that Bruner's work on cognitive development has important implications for a theory of instruction. For, as we saw in the preceding section, the predominant form of this internal model changes qualitatively in the course of growth. The implication of this notion is that the task of the instructor is to translate or to convert knowledge into a form that fits growing minds. The material to be transmitted in a course of study should be tailored, sequenced, and embodied in a form appropriate to the young learner's existing mode of representation so that he will be better able to assimilate it. An understanding of the important epistemological notion that knowledge can be embodied in several different forms, some of which may be more in line with the skills of a child at a certain age, is crucial for an appreciation of Bruner's famous hypothesis that "any subject can be taught effectively in some intellectually honest form to any child at any stage of development." It is also a notion that argues for the feasibility of the spiral curriculum in which the child is introduced "at an early age to the ideas and styles that in later life make an educated man."

The articles of this section were chosen with two aims in mind: first, to present Bruner's initial arguments for curricula that acknowledge the notions outlined above, and, second, to back up those initial arguments with a description of some of his successful efforts to employ these principles in the teaching of advanced material to grade-school students. In "The Act of Discovery" Bruner argues that a student's participation should be as active as possible and that an instructor should teach in what he calls the hypothetical mode. He goes on to describe the benefits that might derive from such an approach to education. In "Readiness for Learning," which constitutes part of *The Process of Education,* his report of the ramifications of the Woods Hole Conference on Education, he defines the task of the educator as one of translation of course material in a way that acknowledges the stages of intellectual development. He also suggests that the courses offered by a school should be re-examined with an emphasis on continuity and development and he proposes the notion of the spiral curriculum.

These theories and proposals are applied in "Representation and Mathematics Learning," which shows how some of the fundamental concepts of mathematics, including primes, factoring, commutativity, associativity, quadratic functions, and group theory can be embodied in very concrete material such as balance beams and wooden blocks. Third grade children can grasp these mathematical concepts when they are presented with such instructional aids and when they are encouraged to participate actively in the learning process by generating hypotheses and by manipulating the material. In "The Growth of Mind," after discussing at a general level what a culture must do in transmitting its amplifying skills to its people, Bruner describes a specific course of study which he and his colleagues designed to teach ten-year-olds some of the fundamental concepts of anthropology, psychology, and sociology. In this course, which is currently being used in some 1,500 schools, abstract ideas are rendered concrete in the form of films, and students are continually induced to participate by presenting their thoughts and conjectures concerning the behavior of humans and other species.

These articles illustrate that there are certain contexts in which the young child will learn and use seemingly advanced cognitive skills, provided that the situations in which these skills are called for are appropriate to his existing level of development. In "Cultural Differences and Inferences about Psychological Processes" by Cole and Bruner, this argument is extended to comparative studies of groups from different cultures and subcultures. Cole and Bruner point out that group differences in achievement, and even in aptitude tests, may not be so much the result of innate differences in capacity as the fact that certain test situations may favor one group more than another. According to this view, the teacher's task is not to create new intellectual structures in the disadvantaged student but rather to "get the child to transfer skills he already possesses to the task at hand."

In the last selection, "Education as Social Invention," a searching essay in which Bruner is concerned with a redefinition of the goals of instruction, he begins by noting that the psychologist's function is not to determine educational objectives but rather to provide the range of possible alternatives from which the society might choose. In view of recently acquired knowledge of man as a species, of the course of intellectual growth, and the process of education, and in view of the rate of technological change within society, he proposes one such alternative. He suggests that in addition to its role as an agent of socialization, which was the function stressed so heavily by Dewey (1), the school should equip its students with basic skills. This emphasis on education as the transmission of skills suggests another way in which students might be introduced to a discipline at a very early age. For as we saw in section 3 a complex skill can be viewed as composed of a set of simpler constituent skills. If such constituent skills are taught in the early stages of education, they might be combined more readily into their complex forms later on. If this conjecture is sound, it constitutes additional support for the merits of Bruner's argument for the spiral curriculum.

Reference

1. DEWEY, J. 1964. *Democracy and Education.* New York: Macmillan.

22

The Act of Discovery *

Maimonides, in his *Guide for the Perplexed* (6), speaks of four forms of perfection that men might seek. The first and lowest form is perfection in the acquisition of worldly goods. The great philosopher dismisses such perfection on the ground that the possessions one acquires bear no meaningful relation to the possessor, "A great king may one morning find that there is no difference between him and the lowest person." A second perfection is of the body, its conformation and skills. Its failing is that it does not reflect on what is uniquely human about man, "He could [in any case] not be as strong as a mule." Moral perfection is the third, "the highest degree of excellency in man's character." Of this perfection Maimonides says, "Imagine a person being alone, and having no connection whatever with any other person; all his good moral principles are at rest, they are not required and give man no perfection whatever. These principles are only necessary and useful when man comes in contact with others." "The fourth kind of perfection is the true perfection of man; the possession of the highest intellectual faculties." In justification of his assertion, the extraordinary Spanish-Judaic philosopher urges, "Examine the first three kinds of perfection; you will find that if you possess them, they are

* "The Act of Discovery," by Jerome S. Bruner, from *Harvard Educational Review*, Vol. 31, No. 1, 1961. Reprinted by permission of the *Harvard Educational Review*. Originally entitled "Human Problem Solving."

not your property, but the property of others. . . . But the last kind of perfection is exclusively yours; no one else owns any part of it."

It is a conjecture much like that of Maimonides that leads me to examine the act of discovery in man's intellectual life. For if man's intellectual excellence is the most his own among his perfections, it is also the case that the most uniquely personal of all that he knows is that which he has discovered for himself. What difference does it make, then, that we encourage discovery in the learning of the young? Does it, as Maimonides would say, create a special and unique relation between knowledge possessed and the possessor? And what may such a unique relation do for a man—or for a child, if you will, for our concern is with the education of the young?

The immediate occasion for my concern with discovery—and I do not restrict discovery to the act of finding out something that before was unknown to mankind, but rather include all forms of obtaining knowledge for oneself by the use of one's own mind—the immediate occasion is the work of the various new curriculum projects that have grown up in America during the late fifties. For whether one speaks to mathematicians or physicists or historians, one encounters repeatedly an expression of faith in the powerful effects that come from permitting the student to put things together for himself, to be his own discoverer.

First, let it be clear what the act of discovery entails. It is rarely, on the frontier of knowledge or elsewhere, that new facts are discovered, in the sense of being encountered as Newton suggested in the form of islands of truth in an uncharted sea of ignorance. Or if they appear to be discovered in this way, it is almost always thanks to some happy hypotheses about where to navigate. Discovery, like surprise, favors the well-prepared mind. In playing bridge, one is surprised by a hand with no honors in it at all and also by hands that are all in one suit. Yet all hands in bridge are equiprobable: One must know to be surprised. So, too, in discovery. The history of science is studded with examples of men finding out something and not knowing it. I shall operate on the assumption that discovery, whether by a schoolboy going it on his own or by a scientist cultivating the growing edge of his field, is in its essence a matter of rearranging or transforming evidence in such a way that one is enabled to go beyond the evidence so reassembled to additional new insights. It may well be that an additional fact or shred of evidence makes this larger transformation of evidence possible. But it is often not even dependent on new information.

It goes without saying that, left to himself, the child will go about discovering things for himself within limits. It also goes without saying that there are certain forms of child rearing, certain home atmospheres that lead some children to be their own discoverers more than other children. These are both topics of great interest, but I shall not be discussing them. Rather, I should like to confine myself to the consideration of discovery and finding-out-for-oneself within an educational setting—specifically the

school. Our aim as teachers is to give our student as firm a grasp of a subject as we can, and to make him as autonomous and self-propelled a
thinker as we can—one who will go along on his own after formal schooling has ended. I shall return in the end to the question of the kind of classroom and the style of teaching that encourages an attitude of wanting to
discover. For purposes of orienting the discussion, however, I would like
to make an overly simplified distinction between teaching that takes place
in the expository mode and teaching that utilizes the hypothetical mode. In
the former, the decisions concerning the mode and pace and style of exposition are principally determined by the teacher as expositor; the student is
the listener. If I can put the matter in terms of structural linguistics, the
speaker has a quite different set of decisions to make than the listener. The
former has a wide choice of alternatives for structuring; he is anticipating
paragraph content while the listener is still intent on the words, he is manipulating the content of the material by various transformations while the
listener is quite unaware of these internal manipulations. In the hypothetical mode, the teacher and the student are in a more co-operative position
with respect to what in linguistics would be called speaker's decisions. The
student is not a benchbound listener, but is taking a part in the formulation and at times may play the principal role in it. He will be aware of alternatives and may even have an as-if attitude toward them; and, as he receives information he may evaluate it as it comes. One cannot describe the
process in either mode with great precision as to detail, but I think the
foregoing may serve to illustrate what is meant.

Consider now what benefit might be derived from the experience of
learning through discoveries that one makes for oneself.

Intellectual Potency

If you will permit me, I would like to consider the difference between subjects in a highly constrained psychological experiment involving a two-
choice apparatus. In order to win chips, they must depress a key either on
the right or the left side of the machine. A pattern of pay-off is designed
such that, say, they will be paid off on the right side 70 per cent of the
time, on the left 30 per cent, although this detail is not important. What is
important is that the pay-off sequence is arranged at random, and there is
no pattern. I should like to contrast the behavior of subjects who think that
there is some pattern to be found in the sequence—who think that regularities are discoverable—in contrast to subjects who think that things are
happening quite by chance. The former group adopts what is called an
event-matching strategy in which the number of responses given to each
side is roughly equal to the proportion of times it pays off: In the present
case $R70:L30$. The group that believes there is no pattern very soon re-
verts to a much more primitive strategy wherein all responses are allocated

to the side that has the greater pay-off. A little arithmetic will show you that the lazy all-and-none strategy pays off more if indeed the environment is random; namely, they win 70 per cent of the time. The event-matching subjects win about 70 per cent on the 70 per cent pay-off side (or 49 per cent of the time there) and 30 per cent of the time on the side that pays off 30 per cent of the time (another 9 per cent for total take-home wage of 58 per cent in return for their labors of decision). But the world is not always or not even frequently random, and if one analyzes carefully what the event-matchers are doing, it turns out that they are trying out hypotheses one after the other, all of them containing a term such that they distribute bets on the two sides with a frequency to match the actual occurrence of events. If it should turn out that there is a pattern to be discovered, their pay-off would become 100 per cent. The other group would go on at the middling rate of 70 per cent.

What has this to do with the subject at hand? For the person to search out and find regularities and relationships in his environment, he must be armed with an expectancy that there will be something to find and, once aroused by expectancy, he must devise ways of searching and finding. One of the chief enemies of such expectancy is the assumption that there is nothing one can find in the environment by way of regularity or relationship. In the experiment just cited, subjects often fall into a habitual attitude that there is either nothing to be found or that they can find a pattern by looking. There is an important sequel in behavior to the two attitudes, and to this I should like to turn now.

We have been conducting a series of experimental studies on a group of some 70 school children over the last four years. The studies have led us to distinguish an interesting dimension of cognitive activity that can be described as ranging from episodic empiricism at one end to cumulative constructionism at the other. The two attitudes in the choice experiments just cited are illustrative of the extremes of the dimension. I might mention some other illustrations. One of the experiments employs the game of Twenty Questions. A child—in this case he is between 10 and 12—is told that a car has gone off the road and hit a tree. He is to ask questions that can be answered by yes or no to discover the cause of the accident. After completing the problem, the same task is given him again, though he is told that the accident had a different cause this time. In all, the procedure is repeated four times. Children enjoy playing the game. They also differ quite markedly in the approach or strategy they bring to the task. There are various elements in the strategies employed. In the first place, one may distinguish clearly between two types of questions asked: One is designed for locating constraints in the problem, constraints that will eventually give shape to a hypothesis; the other is the hypothesis as question. It is the difference between, "Was there anything wrong with the driver?" and "Was the driver rushing to the doctor's office for an appointment and the car got out of control?" There are children who precede hypotheses with efforts to locate constraint and there are those who, to use our local slang, are "potshotters," who string out hypotheses noncumulatively one after the other. A second element of strategy is its connectivity of information gathering, the extent to which questions asked utilize or ignore or violate information previously obtained. The questions asked by children tend to be organized in cycles, each cycle of questions usually being given over to the pursuit of some particular notion. Both within cycles and between cycles one can discern a marked difference in the connectivity of the child's performance. Needless to say, children who employ constraint location as a technique preliminary to the formulation of hypotheses tend to be far more connected in their harvesting of information. Persistence is another feature of strategy, a characteristic compounded of what appear to be two components: a sheer doggedness component and a persistence that stems from the sequential organization that a child brings to the task. Doggedness is probably just animal spirits or the need for achievement—what has come to be called "n-ach." Organized persistence is a maneuver for protecting our fragile cognitive apparatus from overload. The child who has flooded himself with disorganized information from unconnected hypotheses will become discouraged and confused sooner than the child who has shown a certain cunning in his strategy of getting information—a cunning whose principal component is the recognition that the value of information is not simply in getting it but in being able to carry it. The persistence of the organized child stems from his knowledge of how to organize questions in cycles, how to summarize things to himself, and the like.

Episodic empiricism is illustrated by information gathering that is unbound by prior constraints, that lacks connectivity, and that is deficient in organizational persistence. The opposite extreme is illustrated by an approach that is characterized by constraint sensitivity, by connective maneuvers, and by organized persistence. Persistence seems to be one of those gifts from the gods that make people more exaggeratedly what they are.[1]

Before returning to the issue of discovery and its role in the development of thinking, let me say a word more about the ways in which information may get transformed when the problem solver has actively processed it. There is, first of all, a pragmatic question: What does it take to get information processed into a form best designed to fit some future use? Take an experiment by Zajonc (13) as a case in point. He gives groups of subjects information of a controlled kind, some groups being told that their task is to transmit the information to others, others that it is merely to be kept in mind. In general, he finds more differentiation and

---

[1] I should also remark in passing that the two extremes also characterize concept attainment strategies as reported in Bruner et al. (1). Successive scanning illustrates well what is meant here by episodic empiricism; conservative focusing is an example of cumulative constructionism.

organization of the information received passively. An active set leads to a transformation related to a task to be performed. The risk, to be sure, is in possible overspecialization of information processing that may lead to such a high degree of specific organization that information is lost for general use.

I would urge now in the spirit of a hypothesis that emphasis upon discovery in learning has precisely the effect upon the learner of leading him to be a constructionist, to organize what he is encountering in a manner not only designed to discover regularity and relatedness, but also to avoid the kind of information drift that fails to keep account of the uses to which information might have to be put. It is, if you will, a necessary condition for learning the variety of techniques of problem solving, of transforming information for better use, indeed for learning how to go about the very task of learning. Practice in discovering for oneself teaches one to acquire information in a way that makes that information more readily viable in problem solving. So goes the hypothesis. It is still in need of testing. But it is a hypothesis of such important human implications that we cannot afford not to test it—and testing will have to be in the schools.

Intrinsic and Extrinsic Motives

Much of the problem in leading a child to effective cognitive activity is to free him from the immediate control of environmental rewards and punishments. That is to say, learning that starts in response to the rewards of parental or teacher approval or the avoidance of failure can too readily develop a pattern in which the child is seeking cues as to how to conform to what is expected of him. We know from studies of children who tend to be early overachievers in school that they are likely to be seekers after the right way to do it and that their capacity for transforming their learning into viable thought structures tends to be lower than children merely achieving at levels predicted by intelligence tests. Our tests on such children show them to be lower in analytic ability than those who are not conspicuous in overachievement. As we shall see later, they develop rote abilities and depend upon being able to give back what is expected rather than to make it into something that relates to the rest of their cognitive life. As Maimonides would say, their learning is not their own.

The hypothesis that I would propose here is that to the degree that one is able to approach learning as a task of discovering something rather than learning about it, to that degree will there be a tendency for the child to carry out his learning activities with the autonomy of self-reward or, more properly by reward that is discovery itself.

To those of you familiar with the battles of the last half-century in the field of motivation, the above hypothesis will be recognized as controversial. For the classic view of motivation in learning has been, until very recently, couched in terms of a theory of drives and reinforcement—that learning occurred by virtue of the fact that a response produced by a stimulus was followed by the reduction in a primary drive state. The doctrine is greatly extended by the idea of secondary reinforcement; any state associated even remotely with the reduction of a primary drive could also have the effect of producing learning. There has recently appeared a most searching and important criticism of this position by Robert White (12), reviewing the evidence of recently published animal studies, of work in the field of psychoanalysis, and of research on the development of cognitive processes in children. White comes to the conclusion, quite rightly I think, that the drive-reduction model of learning runs counter to too many important phenomena of learning and development to be regarded as either general in its applicability or even correct in its general approach. Let me summarize some of his principal conclusions and explore their applicability to the hypothesis stated above.

I now propose that we gather the various kinds of behavior just mentioned, all of which have to do with effective interaction with the environment, under the general heading of competence. According to Webster, competence means fitness or ability, and the suggested synonyms include capability, capacity, efficiency, proficiency, and skill. It is therefore a suitable word to describe such things as grasping and exploring, crawling and walking, attention and perception, language and thinking, manipulating and changing the surroundings, all of which promote an effective—a competent—interaction with the environment. It is true, of course, that maturation plays a part in all these developments, but this part is heavily overshadowed by learning in all the more complex accomplishments like speech or skilled manipulation. I shall argue that it is necessary to make competence a motivational concept; there is *competence motivation* as well as competence in its more familiar sense of achieved capacity. The behavior that leads to the building up of effective grasping, handling, and letting go of objects, to take one example, is not random behavior that is produced by an overflow of energy. It is directed, selective, and persistent, and it continues not because it serves primary drives, which indeed it cannot serve until it is almost perfected, but because it satisfies an intrinsic need to deal with the environment (pp. 317–18).

I am suggesting that there are forms of activity that serve to enlist and develop the competence motive, that serve to make it the driving force behind behavior. I should like to add to White's general premise that the exercise of competence motives has the effect of strengthening the degree to which they gain control over behavior and thereby reduce the effects of extrinsic rewards or drive gratification.

The brilliant Russian psychologist Vygotsky (11) characterizes the growth of thought processes as starting with a dialogue of speech and gesture between child and parent; autonomous thinking begins at the stage when the child is first able to internalize these conversations and run them off himself. This is a typical sequence in the development of competence. So, too, in instruction. The narrative of teaching is of the order of the conversation. The next move in the development of competence is the internalization of the narrative and its rules of generation so that the child is now capable of running off the narrative on his own. The hypothetical mode in teaching by encouraging the child to participate in speaker's decisions speeds this process along. Once internalization has occurred, the child is in a vastly improved position from several obvious points of view —notably that he is able to go beyond the information he has been given to generate additional ideas that can either be checked immediately from experience or can, at least, be used as a basis for formulating reasonable hypotheses. But over and beyond that, the child is now in a position to experience success and failure not as reward and punishment, but as information. For when the task is his own rather than a matter of matching environmental demands, he becomes his own paymaster in a certain measure. Seeking to gain control over his environment, he can now treat success as indicating that he is on the right track, failure as indicating he is on the wrong one.

In the end, this development has the effect of freeing learning from immediate stimulus control. When learning in the short run leads only to pellets of this or that rather than to mastery in the long run, then behavior can be readily shaped by extrinsic rewards. When behavior becomes more long range and competence-oriented, it comes under the control of more complex cognitive structures, plans and the like, and operates more from the inside out. It is interesting that even Pavlov, whose early account of the learning process was based entirely on a notion of stimulus control of behavior through the conditioning mechanism in which, through contiguity, a new conditioned stimulus was substituted for an old unconditioned stimulus by the mechanism of stimulus substitution, recognized his account as insufficient to deal with higher forms of learning. To supplement the account, he introduced the idea of the second signaling system, with central importance placed on symbolic systems such as language in mediating and giving shape to mental life. Or as Luria (5) has put it, "the first signal system [is] concerned with directly perceived stimuli, the second with systems of verbal elaboration." Luria, commenting on the importance of the transition from first to second signal system, says,

It would be mistaken to suppose that verbal intercourse with adults merely changes the contents of the child's conscious activity without changing its form. . . . The word has a basic function not only because it indicates a corresponding object in the external world, but also because it abstracts, isolates the necessary signal, generalizes perceived signals and relates them to certain categories; it is this systematization of direct experience that makes the role of the word in the formation of mental processes so exceptionally important (p. 12).

It is interesting that the final rejection of the universality of the doctrine of reinforcement in direct conditioning came from some of Pavlov's own students. Ivanov-Smolensky (3) and Krasnogorsky (4) published papers showing the manner in which symbolized linguistic messages could take over the place of the unconditioned stimulus and of the unconditioned response (gratification of hunger) in children. In all instances, they speak of these as replacements of lower, first-system mental or neural processes by higher-order or second-system controls. A strange irony, then, that Russian psychology that gave us the notion of the conditioned response and the assumption that higher-order activities are built up out of colligations or structurings of such primitive units, rejected this notion while much of American learning psychology has stayed until quite recently within the early Pavlovian fold (see, for example, a recent article by Spence [9] or Skinner's treatment of langage [8] and the attacks that have been made upon it by linguists such as Chomsky [2] who have become concerned with the relation of language and cognitive activity). What is even more interesting is that Russian pedagogical theory has become deeply influenced by this new trend and is now placing much stress upon the importance of building up a more active symbolical approach to problem solving among children.

To sum up the matter of the control of learning, then, I am proposing that to the degree that competence or mastery motives come to control behavior, the role of reinforcement or extrinsic pleasure wanes in shaping behavior. The child comes to manipulate his environment more actively and achieves his gratification from coping with problems. Symbolic modes of representing and transforming the environment arise and the importance of stimulus-response-reward sequences declines. To use the metaphor that David Riesman developed in a quite different context, mental life moves from a state of outer-directedness in which the fortuity of stimuli and reinforcement are crucial, to a state of inner-directedness in which the growth and maintenance of mastery become central and dominant.

Learning the Heuristics of Discovery

Lincoln Steffens (10), reflecting in his *Autobiography* on his undergraduate education at Berkeley, comments that his schooling was overly specialized on learning about the known and that too little attention was given to the task of finding out about what was not known. But how does one train a student in the techniques of discovery? Again I would like to offer some hypotheses. There are many ways of coming to the arts of inquiry. One of them is by careful study of its formalization in logic, statistics, mathematics, and the like. If a person is going to pursue inquiry as a way of life, particularly in the sciences, certainly such study is essential. Yet, whoever has taught kindergarten and the early primary grades or has had graduate students working with him on their theses—I choose the two extremes for they are both periods of intense inquiry—knows that an understanding of the formal aspect of inquiry is not sufficient. There appear to be, rather, a series of activities and attitudes, some directly related to a particular subject and some of them fairly generalized, that go with inquiry and research. These have to do with the process of trying to find out something and while they provide no guarantee that the product will be any great discovery, their absence is likely to lead to awkwardness or aridity or confusion. How difficult it is to describe these matters—the heuristics of inquiry. There is one set of attitudes or ways of doing that has to do with sensing the relevance of variables—how to avoid getting stuck with edge effects and getting instead to the big sources of variance. Partly this gift comes from intuitive familiarity with a range of phenomena, sheer knowing the stuff. But it also comes out of a sense of what things among an ensemble of things smell right, in the sense of being of the right order of magnitude or scope or severity.

The English philosopher Weldon describes problem solving in an interesting and picturesque way. He distinguishes between difficulties, puzzles, and problems. We solve a problem or make a discovery when we impose a puzzle form on a difficulty that converts it into a problem that can be solved in such a way that it gets us where we want to be. That is to say, we recast the difficulty into a form that we know how to work with, then work it. Much of what we speak of as discovery consists of knowing how to impose what kind of form on various kinds of difficulties. A small, but crucial part of discovery of the highest order is to invent and develop models or puzzle forms that can be imposed on difficulties with good effect. It is in this area that the truly powerful mind shines. But it is interesting to what degree perfectly ordinary people, given the benefit of instruction, can construct quite interesting and what, a century ago, would have been considered greatly original models.

Now to the hypothesis. It is my hunch that it is only through the exercise of problem solving and the effort of discovery that one learns the working heuristic of discovery; and, the more one has practice, the more likely is one to generalize what one has learned into a style of problem solving or inquiry that serves for any kind of task one may encounter—or almost any kind of task. I think the matter is self-evident, but what is unclear is what kinds of training and teaching produce the best effects. How do we teach a child to, say, cut his losses but at the same time be persistent in trying out an idea; to risk forming an early hunch without at the same time formulating one so early and with so little evidence as to be stuck with it waiting for appropriate evidence to materialize; to pose good testable guesses that are neither too brittle nor too sinuously incorrigible; and so on. Practice in inquiry, in trying to figure out things for oneself is indeed what is needed, but in what form? Of only one thing I am convinced: I have never seen anybody improve in the art and technique of inquiry by any means other than engaging in inquiry.

Conservation of Memory

I should like to take what some psychologists might consider a rather drastic view of the memory process. It is a view that in large measure derives from the work of George Miller (7). Its first premise is that the principal problem of human memory is not storage, but retrieval. In spite of the biological unlikelihood of it, we seem to be able to store a huge quantity of information, a great sufficiency of impressions. We may infer this from the fact that recognition (that is, recall with the aid of maximum prompts) is so extraordinarily good in human beings—particularly in comparison with spontaneous recall where, so to speak, we must get out stored information without external aids or prompts. The key to retrieval is organization or, in even simpler terms, knowing where to find information and how to get there.

Let me illustrate the point with a simple experiment. We present pairs of words to 12-year-old children. One group is simply told to remember the pairs, that they will be asked to repeat them later. Another is told to remember them by producing a word or idea that will tie the pair together in a way that will make sense to them. A third group is given the mediators used by the second group when presented with the pairs to aid them in tying the pairs into working units. The word pairs include such juxtapositions as chair-forest, sidewalk-square, and the like. One can distinguish three styles of mediators, and children can be scaled in terms of their relative preference for each: generic mediation in which a pair is tied together by a superordinate idea: "Chair and forest are both made of wood"; thematic mediation in which the two terms are embedded in a theme or little story: "The lost child sat on a chair in the middle of the forest"; and part-whole mediation where "Chairs are made from trees in the forest" is typical. Now, the chief result, as one would predict, is that children who provide their own mediators do best—indeed, one time through a set of 30 pairs, they recover up to 95 per cent of the second words when presented with the first ones of the pairs, whereas the uninstructed children reach a maximum of less than 50 per cent recovered. Interestingly enough, children do best in recovering materials tied together by the form of mediator they most often use.

One can cite a myriad of findings to indicate that any organization of information that reduces the aggregate complexity of material by embedding it into a cognitive structure a person has constructed will make that material more accessible for retrieval. In short, we may say that the process of memory, looked at from the retrieval side, is also a process of problem solving: How can material be placed in memory so that it can be gotten on demand?

We can take as a point of departure the example of the children who developed their own technique for relating the members of each word pair. You will recall that they did better than the children who were given by exposition the mediators they had developed. Let me suggest that, in general, material that is organized in terms of a person's own interests and cognitive structures is material that has the best chance of being accessible in memory. That is to say, it is more likely to be placed along routes that are connected to one's own ways of intellectual travel.

In sum, the very attitudes and activities that characterize figuring out or discovering things for oneself also seem to have the effect of making material more readily accessible in memory.

References

1. BRUNER, J. S.; GOODNOW, J. J.; and AUSTIN, G. A. 1956. *A study of thinking.* New York: Wiley.
2. CHOMSKY, N. 1957. *Syntactic structures.* The Hague, Netherlands: Mouton.
3. IVANOV-SMOLENSKY, A. G. 1951. Concerning the study of the joint activity of the first and second signal systems. *Journal of Higher Nervous Activity* 1:1.
4. KRASNOGORSKY, N. D. 1954. *Studies of higher nervous activity in animals and man,* vol. 1. Moscow.
5. LURIA, A. L. 1959. The directive function of speech in development and dissolution. *Word* 15(12):341–464.
6. MAIMONIDES. 1956. *Guide for the perplexed.* New York: Dover.
7. MILLER, G. A. 1956. The magical number seven, plus or minus two: some limits on our capacity for processing information. *Psychological Review* 63:81–97.
8. SKINNER, B. F. 1957. *Verbal behavior.* New York: Appleton-Century-Crofts.
9. SPENCE, K. W. 1959. The relation of learning theory to the technique of education. *Harvard Educational Review* 29:84–95.
10. STEFFENS, L. 1931. *Autobiography of Lincoln Steffens.* New York: Harcourt Brace.
11. VYGOTSKY, L. S. 1962. *Thought and language.* Ed. and trans. E. Hanfmann and G. Vakar. Cambridge, Mass.: MIT Press, and New York: Wiley.
12. WHITE, R. W. 1959. Motivation reconsidered: the concept of competence. *Psychological Review* 66:297–333.
13. ZAJONC, R. B. 1957. Personal communication.

23

Readiness for Learning *

We begin with the hypothesis that any subject can be taught effectively in some intellectually honest form to any child at any stage of development. It is a bold hypothesis and an essential one in thinking about the nature of a curriculum. No evidence exists to contradict it; considerable evidence is being amassed that supports it.

To make clear what is implied, let us examine three general ideas. The first has to do with the process of intellectual development in children, the second with the act of learning, and the third with the notion of a spiral curriculum.

Intellectual Development

Research on the intellectual development of the child highlights the fact that at each stage of development the child has a characteristic way of viewing the world and explaining it to himself. The task of teaching a subject to a child at any particular age is one of representing the structure of that subject in terms of the child's way of viewing things. The task can be thought of as one of translation. The general hypothesis that has just been stated is premised on the considered judgment that any idea can be represented honestly and usefully in the thought forms of children of school age, and that these first representations can later be made more powerful and precise more easily by virtue of this early learning. To illustrate and support this view, we present here a somewhat detailed picture of the course of intellectual development, along with some suggestions about teaching at different stages of it.

The work of Piaget and others suggests that, roughly speaking, one may distinguish three stages in the intellectual development of the child. The first stage need not concern us in detail, for it is characteristic principally of the preschool child. In this stage, which ends (at least for Swiss school children) around the fifth or sixth year, the child's mental work consists principally in establishing relationships between experience and action; his concern is with manipulating the world through action. This stage corresponds roughly to the period from the first development of language to the point at which the child learns to manipulate symbols. In this so-called preoperational stage, the principal symbolic achievement is that the child learns how to represent the external world through symbols established by simple generalization; things are represented as equivalent in terms of sharing some common property. But the child's symbolic world does not make a clear separation between internal motives and feelings on the one hand and external reality on the other. The sun moves because God pushes it, and the stars, like himself, have to go to bed. The child is little able to separate his own goals from the means for achieving them, and when he has to make corrections in his activity after unsuccessful attempts at manipulating reality, he does so by what are called intuitive regulations rather than by symbolic operations, the former being of a crude trial-and-error nature rather than the result of taking thought.

What is principally lacking at this stage of development is what the Geneva school has called the concept of reversibility. When the shape of an object is changed, as when one changes the shape of a plasticine ball, the preoperational child cannot grasp the idea that it can be brought back readily to its original state. Because of this fundamental lack the child cannot understand certain fundamental ideas that lie at the basis of mathematics and physics—the mathematical idea that one conserves quantity even when one partitions a set of things into subgroups, or the physical idea that one conserves mass and weight even though one transforms the shape of an object. It goes without saying that teachers are severely limited in transmitting concepts to a child at this stage, even in a highly intuitive manner.

The second stage of development—and now the child is in school—is called the stage of concrete operations. This stage is operational in contrast to the preceding stage, which is merely active. An operation is a type of action, it can be carried out rather directly by the manipulation of objects, or internally, as when one manipulates the symbols that represent things and relations in one's mind. Roughly, an operation is a means of getting data about the real world into the mind and there transforming them so that they can be organized and used selectively in the solution of problems. Assume a child is presented with a pinball machine which bounces a ball off a wall at an angle. Let us find out what he appreciates about the relation between the angle of incidence and the angle of reflection. The young child sees no problem. For him, the ball travels in an arc, touching the wall on the way. The somewhat older child, say age 10, sees the two angles as roughly related—as one changes so does the other. The still older child begins to grasp that there is a fixed relation between the two, and usually says it is a right angle. Finally, the 13- or 14-year-old, often by pointing the ejector directly at the wall and seeing the ball come back at the ejector, gets the idea that the two angles are equal. Each way of looking at the phenomenon represents the result of an operation in this sense, and the child's thinking is constrained by his way of pulling his observations together.

An operation differs from simple action or goal-directed behavior in that it is internalized and reversible. Internalized means that the child does not have to go about his problem solving any longer by overt trial and error, but can actually carry out trial and error in his head. Reversibility is present because operations are seen as characterized where appropriate by what is called complete compensation; that is to say, an operation can be compensated for by an inverse operation. If marbles, for example, are divided into subgroups, the child can grasp intuitively that the original collection of marbles can be restored by being added back together again. The child tips a balance scale too far with a weight and then searches systematically for a lighter weight or for something with which to get the scale rebalanced. He may carry reversibility too far by assuming that a piece of paper, once burned, can also be restored.

With the advent of concrete operations, the child develops an internalized structure with which to operate. In the example of the balance scale, the structure is a serial order of weights that the child has in his mind. Such internal structures are of the essence. They are the internalized symbolic systems by which the child represents the world, as in the example of the pinball machine and the angles of incidence and reflection. It is into the language of these internal structures that one must translate ideas if the child is to grasp them.

But concrete operations, though they are guided by the logic of classes and the logic of relations, are means for structuring only immediately present reality. The child is able to give structure to the things he encounters, but he is not yet readily able to deal with possibilities not directly before him or not already experienced. This is not to say that children operating concretely are not able to anticipate things that are not present. Rather, it is that they do not command the operations for conjuring up systematically the full range of alternative possibilities that could exist at any given time. They cannot go systematically beyond the information given them to a description of what else might occur. Somewhere between 10 and 14 years of age the child passes into a third stage, which is called the stage of formal operations by the Geneva school.

Now the child's intellectual activity seems to be based upon an ability to operate on hypothetical propositions rather than being constrained to what he has experienced or what is before him. The child can now think of possible variables and even deduce potential relationships that can later be verified by experiment or observation. Intellectual operations now appear to be predicated upon the same kinds of logical operations that are the stock in trade of the logician, the scientist, or the abstract thinker. It is at this point that the child is able to give formal or axiomatic expression to the concrete ideas that before guided his problem solving but could not be described or formally understood.

Earlier, while the child is in the stage of concrete operations, he is capable of grasping intuitively and concretely a great many of the basic ideas of mathematics, the sciences, the humanities, and the social sciences. But he can do so only in terms of concrete operations. It can be demonstrated that fifth-grade children can play mathematical games with rules modeled on highly advanced mathematics; indeed, they can arrive at these rules inductively and learn how to work with them. They will flounder, however, if one attempts to force upon them a formal mathematical description of what they have been doing, though they are perfectly capable of guiding their behavior by these rules. At the Woods Hole Conference we were privileged to see a demonstration of teaching in which fifth-grade children very rapidly grasped central ideas from the theory of functions, although had the teacher attempted to explain to them what the theory of functions was, he would have drawn a blank. Later, at the appropriate stage of development, and given a certain amount of practice in concrete operations, the time would be ripe for introducing them to the necessary formalism.

What is most important for teaching basic concepts is that the child be helped to pass progressively from concrete thinking to the utilization of more conceptually adequate modes of thought. But it is futile to attempt this by presenting formal explanations based on a logic that is distant from the child's manner of thinking and sterile in its implications for him. Much teaching in mathematics is of this sort. The child learns not to understand mathematical order but rather to apply certain devices or recipes without understanding their significance and connectedness. They are not translated into his way of thinking. Given this inappropriate start, he is easily led to believe that the important thing is for him to be accurate—though accuracy has less to do with mathematics than with computation. Perhaps the most striking example of this type of thing is to be found in the manner in which the high school student meets Euclidian geometry for the first time, as a set of axioms and theorems, without having had some experience with simple geometric configurations and the intuitive means whereby one deals with them. If the child were earlier given the concepts and strategies in the form of intuitive geometry at a level that he could easily follow, he might be far better able to grasp deeply the meaning of the theorems and axioms to which he is exposed later.

But the intellectual development of the child is no clockwork sequence of events; it also responds to influences from the environment, notably the school environment. Thus instruction in scientific ideas, even at the elementary level, need not follow slavishly the natural course of cognitive development in the child. It can also lead intellectual development by providing challenging but usable opportunities for the child to forge ahead in his development. Experience has shown that it is worth the effort to provide the growing child with problems that tempt him into next stages of development. As David Page, one of the most experienced teachers of elementary mathematics, has commented,

In teaching from kindergarten to graduate school, I have been amazed at the intellectual similarity of human beings at all ages, although children are perhaps more spontaneous, creative, and energetic than adults. As far as I am concerned, young children learn almost anything faster than adults do if it can be given to them in terms they understand. Giving the material to them in terms they understand, interestingly enough, turns out to involve knowing the mathematics oneself, and the better one knows it, the better it can be taught. It is appropriate that we warn ourselves to be careful of assigning an absolute level of difficulty to any particular topic. When I tell mathematicians that fourth-grade students can go a long way into "set theory" a few of them reply: "Of course." Most of them are startled. The latter ones are completely wrong in assuming that "set theory" is intrinsically difficult. Of course it may be that nothing is intrinsically difficult. We just have to wait until the proper point of view and corresponding language for presenting it are revealed. Given particular subject matter or a particular concept, it is easy to ask trivial questions or to lead the child to ask trivial questions. It is also easy to ask impossibly difficult questions. The trick is to find the medium questions that can be answered and that take you somewhere. This is the big job of teachers and textbooks.

One leads the child by the well-wrought medium questions to move more rapidly through the stages of intellectual development, to a deeper understanding of mathematical, physical, and historical principles. We must know far more about the ways in which this can be done.

Bärbel Inhelder was asked to suggest ways in which the child could be moved along faster through the various stages of intellectual development in mathematics and physics. What follows is part of a memorandum she prepared for the conference.

The most elementary forms of reasoning—whether logical, arithmetical, geo-metrical, or physical—rest on the principle of the invariance of quantities: that the whole remains, whatever may be the arrangement of its parts, the change of its form, or its displacement in space or time. The principle of invariance is no *a priori* datum of the mind, nor is it the product of purely empirical obser-vation. The child discovers invariance in a manner comparable to scientific dis-coveries generally. Grasping the idea of invariance is beset with difficulties for the child, often unsuspected by teachers. To the young child, numerical wholes, spatial dimensions, and physical quantities do not seem to remain constant but to dilate or contract as they are operated upon. The total number of beads in a box remains the same whether subdivided into two, three, or ten piles. It is this that is so hard for the child to understand. The young child perceives changes as operating in one direction without being able to grasp the idea that certain fundamental features of things remain constant over change, or that if they change the change is reversible.

A few examples among many used in studying the child's concept of invari-ance will illustrate the kinds of materials one could use to help him to learn the concept more easily. The child transfers beads of a known quantity or liq-uids of a known volume from one receptacle to another, one receptacle being tall and narrow, the other flat and wide. The young child believes there is more in the tall receptacle than the flat one. Now the child can be confronted con-cretely with the nature of one-to-one correspondence between two versions of the same quantity. For there is an easy technique of checking: the beads can be counted or the liquid measured in some standard way. The same operations work for the conservation of spatial quantity if one uses a set of sticks for length or a set of tiles for surface, or by having the child transform the shape of volumes made up of the same number of blocks. In physics, dissolving sugar or transforming the shapes of balls of plasticene while conserving volume pro-vides comparable instruction. If teaching fails to bring the child properly from his perceptual, primitive notions to a proper intuition of the idea of invariance, the result is that he will count without having acquired the idea of the invari-ance of numerical quantities. Or he will use geometrical measures while re-maining ignorant of the operation of transitivity—that if A includes B, and B includes C, then A also includes C. In physics he will apply calculations to im-perfectly understood physical notions such as weight, volume, speed, and time. A teaching method that takes into account the natural thought processes will allow the child to discover such principles of invariance by giving him an op-portunity to progress beyond his own primitive mode of thinking through con-frontation by concrete data—as when he notes that liquid that looks greater in volume in a tall, thin receptacle is in fact the same as that quantity in a flat, low vessel. Concrete activity that becomes increasingly formal is what leads the child to the kind of mental mobility that approaches the naturally reversible operations of mathematics and logic. The child gradually comes to sense that any change may be mentally cancelled out by the reverse operation—addition by subtraction—or that a change may be counterbalanced by a reciprocal change.

A child often focuses on only one aspect of a phenomenon at a time, and this interferes with his understanding. We can set up little teaching experiments in such a way that he is forced to pay attention to other aspects. Thus, children up to about age seven estimate the speed of two automobiles by assuming that the one that gets there first is the faster, or that if one passes the other it is faster. To overcome such errors, one can, by using toy automobiles, show that two objects starting at different distances from a finish line cannot be judged by which one arrives first, or show that one car can pass another by circling it and still not finish first. These are simple exercises, but they speed the child toward attending to several features of a situation at once.

In view of all this it seems highly arbitrary and very likely incorrect to delay the teaching, for example, of Euclidian or metric geometry until the end of the primary grades, particularly when projective geometry has not been given earlier. So too with the teaching of physics, which has much in it that can be profitably taught at an inductive or intuitive level much earlier. Basic notions in these fields are perfectly accessible to children of seven to ten years of age, *provided that they are divorced from their mathematical expression and studied through materials that the child can handle himself.*

Another matter relates particularly to the ordering of a mathematics curriculum. Often the sequence of psychological development follows more closely the axiomatic order of a subject matter than it does the historical order of development of concepts within the field. One observes, for instance, that certain topological notions, such as connection, separation, being interior to, and so forth, precede the formation of Euclidian and projective notions in geometry, though the former ideas are newer in their formalism in the history of mathematics than the latter. If any special justification were needed for teaching the structure of a subject in its proper logical or axiomatic order rather than its order of historical development, this should provide it. This is not to say that there may not be situations where the historical order is important from the point of view of its cultural or pedagogical relevance.

As for teaching geometrical notions of perspective and projection, again there is much that can be done by the use of experiments and demonstrations that rest on the child's operational capacity to analyze concrete experience. We have watched children work with an apparatus in which rings of different diameter are placed at different positions between a candle and a screen with a fixed distance between them so that the rings cast shadows of varying sizes on the screen. The child learns how the cast shadow changes size as a function of the distance of the ring from the light source. By bringing to the child such concrete experience of light in revealing situations, we teach him maneuvers that in the end permit him to understand the general ideas underlying projective geometry.

These examples lead us to think that it is possible to draw up methods of teaching the basic ideas in science and mathematics to children considerably younger than the traditional age. It is at this earlier age that systematic instruction can lay a groundwork in the fundamentals that can be used later and with great profit at the secondary level.

The teaching of probabilistic reasoning, so very common and important a feature of modern science, is hardly developed in our educational system before college. The omission is probably due to the fact that school syllabi in nearly all countries follow scientific progress with a near-disastrous time lag. But it may also be due to the widespread belief that the understanding of random phenomena depends on the learner's grasp of the meaning of the rarity or commonness of events. And admittedly, such ideas are hard to get across to the young. Our research indicates that the understanding of random phenomena requires, rather, the use of certain concrete logical operations well within the grasp of the young child—provided these operations are free of awkward mathematical expression. Principal among these logical operations are disjunction ("either A *or* B is true") and combination. Games in which lots are drawn, games of roulette, and games involving a Gaussian distribution of outcomes are all ideal for giving the child a basic grasp of the logical operation needed for thinking about probability. In such games, children first discover an entirely qualitative notion of chance defined as an uncertain event, contrasted with deductive certainty. The notion of probability as a fraction of certainty is discovered only later. Each of these discoveries can be made before the child ever learns the techniques of the calculus of probabilities or the formal expressions that normally go with probability theory. Interest in problems of a probabilistic nature could easily be awakened and developed before the introduction of any statistical processes or computation. Statistical manipulation and computation are only tools to be used *after* intuitive understanding has been established. If the array of computational paraphernalia is introduced first, then more likely than not it will inhibit or kill the development of probabilistic reasoning.

One wonders in the light of all this whether it might not be interesting to devote the first two years of school to a series of exercises in manipulating, classifying, and ordering objects in ways that highlight basic operations of logical addition, multiplication, inclusion, serial ordering, and the like. For surely these logical operations are the basis of more specific operations and concepts of all mathematics and science. It may indeed be the case that such an early science and mathematics "pre-curriculum" might go a long way toward building up in the child the kind of intuitive and more inductive understanding that could be given embodiment later in formal courses in mathematics and science. The effect of such an approach would be, we think, to put more continuity into science and mathematics and also to give the child a much better and firmer comprehension of the concepts which, unless he has this early foundation, he will mouth later without being able to use them in any effective way.

A comparable approach can surely be taken to the teaching of social studies and literature. There has been little research done on the kinds of concepts that a child brings to these subjects, although there is a wealth of observation and anecdote. Can one teach the structure of literary forms by presenting the child with the first part of a story and then having him complete it in the form of a comedy, a tragedy, or a farce—without ever using such words? When, for example, does the idea of historical trend develop, and what are its precursors in the child? How does one make a child aware of literary style? Perhaps the child can discover the idea of style through the presentation of the same content written in drastically different styles, in the manner of Beerbohm's *Christmas Garland*. Again, there is no reason to believe that any subject cannot be taught to any child at virtually any age in some form.

Here one is immediately faced with the question of the economy of teaching. One can argue that it might be better to wait until the child is 13 or 14 before beginning geometry so that the projective and intuitive first steps can immediately be followed up by a full formal presentation of the subject. Is it worthwhile to train the young inductively so that they may discover the basic order of knowledge before they can appreciate its formalism? In Inhelder's memorandum, it was suggested that the first two grades might be given over to training the child in the basic logical operations that underlie instruction in mathematics and science. There is evidence to indicate that such rigorous and relevant early training has the effect of making later learning easier. Indeed the experiments on learning set seem to indicate just that—one not only learns specifics but in so doing learns how to learn. So important is training per se that monkeys who have been given extensive training in problem solving suffer considerably less loss and recover more quickly after induced brain damage than animals who had not been previously thus educated. But the danger of such early training may be that it has the effect of training out original but deviant ideas. There is no evidence available on the subject, and much is needed.

The Act of Learning

Learning a subject seems to involve three almost simultaneous processes. First there is acquisition of new information—often information that runs counter to or is a replacement for what the person has previously known implicitly or explicitly. At the very least it is a refinement of previous knowledge. Thus one teaches a student Newton's laws of motion, which violate the testimony of the senses. Or in teaching a student about wave mechanics, one violates the student's belief in mechanical impact as the sole source of real-energy transfer. Or one bucks the language and its built-in way of thinking in terms of wasting energy by introducing the student to the conservation theorem in physics which asserts that no energy is lost. More often the situation is less drastic, as when one teaches the details of the circulatory system to a student who already knows vaguely or intuitively that blood circulates.

A second aspect of learning may be called transformation—the process of manipulating knowledge to make it fit new tasks. We learn to unmask or analyze information, to order it in a way that permits extrapolation or interpolation or conversion into another form. Transformation comprises the ways we deal with information in order to go beyond it.

A third aspect of learning is evaluation, checking whether the way we have manipulated information is adequate to the task. Is the generalization fitting, have we extrapolated appropriately, are we operating properly? Often a teacher is crucial in helping with evaluation, but much of it takes place by judgments of plausibility without our actually being able to check rigorously whether we are correct in our efforts.

In the learning of any subject matter, there is usually a series of episodes, each episode involving the three processes. Photosynthesis might reasonably comprise material for a learning episode in biology, fitted into a more comprehensive learning experience such as learning about the conversion of energy generally. At its best a learning episode reflects what has gone before it and permits one to generalize beyond it.

A learning episode can be brief or long, contain many ideas or a few. How sustained an episode a learner is willing to undergo depends upon what the person expects to get from his efforts, in the sense of such external things as grades but also in the sense of a gain in understanding.

We usually tailor material to the capacities and needs of students by manipulating learning episodes in several ways: by shortening or lengthening the episode, by piling on extrinsic rewards in the form of praise and gold stars, or by dramatizing the shock of recognition of what the material means when fully understood. The unit in a curriculum is meant to be a recognition of the importance of learning episodes, though many units drag on with no climax in understanding. There is a surprising lack of research on how one most wisely devises adequate learning episodes for children at different ages and in different subject matters. There are many questions that need answers based on careful research, and to some of these we turn now.

There is, to begin with, the question of the balance between extrinsic rewards and intrinsic ones. There has been much written on the role of reward and punishment in learning, but very little indeed on the role of interest and curiosity and the lure of discovery. If it is our intention as teachers to inure the child to longer and longer episodes of learning, it may well be that intrinsic rewards in the form of quickened awareness and understanding will have to be emphasized far more in the detailed design of curricula. One of the least discussed ways of carrying a student through a hard unit of material is to challenge him with a chance to exercise his full powers so that he may discover the pleasure of full and effective functioning. Good teachers know the power of this lure. Students should know what it feels like to be completely absorbed in a problem. They seldom experience this feeling in school. Given enough absorption in class, some students may be able to carry over the feeling to work done on their own.

There is a range of problems that have to do with how much emphasis should be placed on acquisition, transformation, and evaluation in a learning episode—getting facts, manipulating them, and checking one's ideas. Is it the case, for example, that it is best to give the young child a minimum set of facts first and then encourage him to draw the fullest set of implications possible from this knowledge? In short, should an episode for a young child contain little new information but emphasize what can be done to go beyond that bit on one's own? One teacher of social studies has had great success with fourth graders through this approach: He begins, for example, with the fact that civilizations have most often begun in fertile river valleys—the only fact. The students are encouraged in class discussion to figure out why this is the case and why it would be less likely for civilizations to start in mountainous country. The effect of this approach, essentially the technique of discovery, is that the child generates information on his own, which he can then check or evaluate against the sources, getting more new information in the process. This obviously is one kind of learning episode, and doubtless it has limited applicability. What other kinds are there, and are some more appropriate to certain topics and ages than others? It is not the case that to learn is to learn is to learn, yet in the research literature there appears to be little recognition of differences in learning episodes.

With respect to the optimum length of a learning episode, there are a few common-sense things one can say about it, and these are perhaps interesting enough to suggest fruitful research possibilities. It seems fairly obvious, for example, that the longer and more packed the episode, the greater the pay-off must be in terms of increased power and understanding if the person is to be encouraged to move to a next episode with zest. Where grades are used as a substitute for the reward of understanding, it may well be that learning will cease as soon as grades are no longer given —at graduation.

It also seems reasonable that the more one has a sense of the structure of a subject, the more densely packed and longer a learning episode one can get through without fatigue. Indeed, the amount of new information in any learning episode is really the amount that we cannot quite fit into place at once. And there is a severe limit, as we have already noted, on how much of such unassimilated information we can keep in mind. The estimate is that adults can handle about seven independent items of information at a time. No norms are available for children—a deplorable lack.

There are many details one can discuss concerning the shaping of learning episodes for children, but the problems that have been mentioned will suffice to give their flavor. Inasmuch as the topic is central to an understanding of how one arranges a curriculum, it seems obvious that here is an area of research that is of the first importance.

The Spiral Curriculum

If one respects the ways of thought of the growing child, if one is courteous enough to translate material into his logical forms and challenging enough to tempt him to advance, then it is possible to introduce him at an early age to the ideas and styles that in later life make an educated man. We might ask, as a criterion for any subject taught in primary school, whether, when fully developed, it is worth an adult's knowing, and whether having known it as a child makes a person a better adult. If the answer to both questions is negative or ambiguous, then the material is cluttering the curriculum.

If the hypothesis with which this section was introduced is true—that any subject can be taught to any child in some honest form—then it should follow that a curriculum ought to be built around the great issues, principles, and values that a society deems worthy of the continual concern of its members. Consider two examples—the teaching of literature and of science. If it is granted, for example, that it is desirable to give children an awareness of the meaning of human tragedy and a sense of compassion for it, is it not possible at the earliest appropriate age to teach the literature of tragedy in a manner that illuminates but does not threaten? There are many possible ways to begin: through a retelling of the great myths, through the use of children's classics, through presentation of and commentary on selected films that have proved themselves. Precisely what kinds of materials should be used at what age with what effect is a subject for research—research of several kinds. We may ask first about the child's conception of the tragic, and here one might proceed in much the same way that Piaget and his colleagues have proceeded in studying the child's conception of physical causality, of morality, of number, and the rest. It is only when we are equipped with such knowledge that we will be in a position to know how the child will translate whatever we present to him into his own subjective terms. Nor need we wait for all the research findings to be in before proceeding, for a skillful teacher can also experiment by attempting to teach what seems to be intuitively right for children of different ages, correcting as he goes. In time, one goes beyond to more complex versions of the same kind of literature or simply revisits some of the same books used earlier. What matters is that later teaching build upon earlier reactions to literature, that it seek to create an ever more explicit and mature understanding of the literature of tragedy. Any of the great literary forms can be handled in the same way, or any of the great themes—be it the form of comedy or the theme of identity, personal loyalty, or what not.

So, too, in science. If the understanding of number, measure, and probability is judged crucial in the pursuit of science, then instruction in these subjects should begin as intellectually honestly and as early as possible in a manner consistent with the child's forms of thought. Let the topics be developed and redeveloped in later grades. Thus, if most children are to take a tenth-grade unit in biology, need they approach the subject cold? Is it not possible, with a minimum of formal laboratory work if necessary, to introduce them to some of the major biological ideas earlier, in a spirit perhaps less exact and more intuitive?

Many curricula are originally planned with a guiding idea much like the one set forth here. But as curricula are actually executed, as they grow and change, they often lose their original form and suffer a relapse into a certain shapelessness. It is not amiss to urge that actual curricula be re-examined with an eye to the issues of continuity and development referred to in the preceding pages. One cannot predict the exact forms that revision might take; indeed, it is plain that there is now available too little research to provide adequate answers. One can only propose that appropriate research be undertaken with the greatest vigor and as soon as possible.

24

Representation
and Mathematics Learning[*]

Our central concern is the psychological processes involved in the learning of mathematics by children who, in Piaget's sense, are in the stage of concrete operations and are not, presumably, yet able to deal readily with formal propositions. To understand better how mathematics learning of a highly symbolized type might occur, we worked with a small number of children, observing them in minute detail to determine the steps involved in grasping mathematical ideas. Such an approach is closely akin to the detailed study of the naturalist and clinician. Perhaps such study can serve to aid more large-scale psychometric testing or, indeed, to elucidate the nature of instruction. It would be disingenuous to say that we (or any naturalist, for that matter) worked without due regard to some theory. Our theoretical predilections were, we should say, far clearer when we finished than when we started. They will also be plain to the reader as our account progresses.

The observations to be reported were made on four eight-year-old children, two boys and two girls, who were given an hour of daily instruction

* "Representation and Mathematics Learning," by Jerome S. Bruner and Helen J. Kenney, from "Mathematical Learning." *Monographs of the Society for Research in Child Development,* Morrisett and Vinsonhaler (Eds.), 1965, Serial 99, Vol. 30, No. 1, 50–59. Copyright © 1965 by the Society for Research in Child Development. Reproduced by permission of the publisher and the authors.

in mathematics four times a week for six weeks. The children were in the IQ range of 120–130 and were enrolled in the third grade of a private school that emphasized instruction designed to foster independent problem solving. They were from middle-class professional homes. The teacher of the class was a well-known research mathematician (Z. P. Dienes); his assistant was a professor of psychology at Harvard who has worked long and hard on human thought processes.

Each child worked at a corner table in a generously sized room. Next to each child sat a tutor-observer trained in psychology and with sufficient background in college mathematics to understand the underlying mathematics being taught. In the middle of the room was a large table with a supply of the blocks and balance beams and cups and beans and chalk that served as instructional aids. In the course of six weeks, the children were given instruction in factoring, the distributive and commutative properties of addition and multiplication, and, finally, in quadratic functions.

Each child had available a series of graded problem cards to go through at his own pace. The cards gave directions for different kinds of exercises, using the materials described above. The instructor and his assistant circulated from table to table, helping as needed, and each observer-tutor similarly assisted as needed. The problem sequences were designed to provide, first, an appreciation of mathematical ideas through concrete constructions using materials of various kinds for these constructions. From such constructions, the child was encouraged to form perceptual images of the mathematical idea in terms of the forms that had been constructed. The child was then further encouraged to develop or adopt a notation to describe his construction. After such a cycle, a child moved on to the construction of a further embodiment of the idea on which he was working, one that was mathematically isomorphic with what he had learned although expressed in different materials and with altered appearance. When such a new topic was introduced, the children were given a chance to discover its connection with what had gone before and were shown how to extend the notational system used before. Careful minute-by-minute records were kept of the proceedings, along with photographs of the children's constructions.

In no sense can the children, the teachers, the classroom, or the mathematics be said to be typical of what normally occurs in third grade. Four children rarely have six teachers nor do eight-year-olds ordinarily get into quadratic functions. But our concern is with the processes involved in mathematical learning and not with typicality. We would be foolish to claim that the achievements of the children were typical. But it seems quite reasonable to suppose that the thought processes going on in the children were quite ordinary among eight-year-old human beings.

As we have noted, the instruction emphasized concrete construction and embodiment of mathematical concepts. It could have been more axiomatic, less dependent upon visual intuition of forms. It is highly unlikely that there is one optimum procedure for teaching or learning mathematics. The observations obviously reflect the approach of the study as well as the nature of mathematical learning.

Four aspects of the learning seem worth special comment: the role of construction, the uses of notation, the place of contrast and variation, and the character of insight.

The Role of Construction

In mathematical factoring, to start with an example, the concept of prime numbers appears to be more readily grasped when the child, through construction, discovers that certain handfuls of beans cannot be laid out in completed multiple rows and columns. Such quantities have either to be laid out in a single file or in an incomplete row-column design in which there is always one extra or one too few to fill the pattern. These patterns, the child learns, happen to be called prime, but they could be called unarrangeable. It is easy for the child to go from this step to the recognition that a multiplication table, so called, is a record sheet of quantities in completed multiple rows and columns. Here is factoring, multiplication, and primes in a construction that can also be visualized. Take the matter of factoring in another physical embodiment: a balance beam with hooks placed equidistant from a central fulcrum is the construction vehicle this time (Figure 1). Contrast this with factoring as the usual computational exercise—as in the problem, "What are the factors of 18?" Conventionally, the child parrots the correct set of factors with the usual uncertainty about whether 9 and 2 are different from 2 and 9, or 6 and 3 from 3 and 6. On the balance beam, we place 2 rings on hook 9; the child is encouraged to find and write down every combination of rings on hooks on the opposite side that will balance it. It is a beautiful discovery that 2 rings on

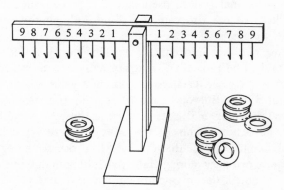

FIGURE 1. Balance beam and rings used on quadratic construction

hook 9 balances 9 rings on hook 2—and an introduction to the idea of commutativity. Note again that the construction produces a basis for imagery. Before long some startlingly abstract principles couched in elegant terms emerge: "You can exchange rings for hooks if you want." Factors are now events. When notation is applied now, there is a referent.

Note that constructions can be unconstructed and reconstructed, even when the child does not yet have a ready symbol system for doing so abstractly. In short, construction, unconstruction, and reconstruction provides reversibility in overt operations until the child, in Piaget's sense, can internalize such operations in symbolized form.

Now consider quadratic functions. Each child was provided with building materials. These were large flat squares made of wood whose dimensions were unspecified and described simply as unknown or x long and x wide (Figure 2). There were also a large number of strips of wood that were as long as the sides of the square and described arbitrarily as having a width of 1 or simply 1 by x. And there was a supply of little squares with sides equal to the width 1 of the strips, thus 1 by 1. The reader should be warned that the presentation of these materials is not as simple as all that. To begin with, it is necessary to convince the children that we really do not know and do not care what is the metric size of the big squares, that rulers are of no interest. A certain humor helps establish in the pupils a proper contempt for measuring in this context, and the snob appeal of simply calling an unknown by the name x is very great. From there on, the children readily discover for themselves that the long strips are x long—by correspondence. They take on faith (as they should) that the narrow dimension is 1, but that they grasp its arbitrariness is clear from one child's declaration of the number of such 1 lengths that make an

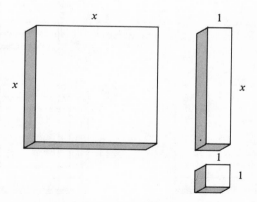

FIGURE 2. Three components for quadratic constructions

x. As for 1 by 1 little squares, that too is established by simple correspondence with the narrow dimension of the 1 by x strips. It is horseback method but quite good mathematics.

The child is asked whether he can make a square bigger than the x by x square, using the materials at hand. He very quickly builds squares with designs like those in Figure 3. We ask him to record how much wood is needed for each larger square and how long and wide each square is.

The Use of Notation

He describes one of his constructed squares; very concretely the pieces are counted out: an x-square, two x-strips, and a one square; or an x-square, four x-strips, and four ones; or an x-square, six x-strips and nine ones; and so on. We help him with language and show him a way to write it down. The big square is an $x^{\square}$, the long strips are 1 x or simply x, and the little squares are one squares, or one by one, or better still simply 1. And the expression *and* can be shortened to $+$. And so he can write out the recipe for a constructed square as $x^{\square} + 4x + 4$. At this stage, these are merely names put together in little sentences. How wide and long is the square in question? This the child can readily measure off—an x and 2 or $x + 2$—and so the whole thing is $(x + 2)^{\square}$. Brackets are not so easily grasped. And so the child is able to put down his first equality: $(x + 2)^{\square} = x^{\square} + 4x + 4$. Virtually everything has a referent that can be pointed to with a finger. He has a notational system into which he can translate the image he has constructed.

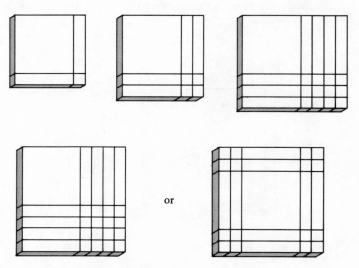

or

FIGURE 3. Squares of ever-increasing size constructed with components

Now we go on to making bigger squares, and each square the child makes he describes in terms of what wood went into it and how wide and how long it is. It takes some ruled sheets to get the child to keep his record so that he can go back and inspect it for what it may reveal, and he is encouraged to go back and look at the record and at the constructions they stand for.

Imagine now a list such as the following, again a product of the child's own construction:

$$x + 2x + 1 \text{ is } x+1 \text{ by } x+1$$
$$x + 4x + 4 \text{ is } x+2 \text{ by } x+2$$
$$x + 6x + 9 \text{ is } x+3 \text{ by } x+3$$
$$x + 8x + 16 \text{ is } x+4 \text{ by } x+4$$

It is almost impossible for him not to make some discoveries about the numbers: that the x values go up 2, 4, 6, 8 . . . and the unit values go up 1, 4, 9, 16 . . . and the dimensions increase by additions to x of 1, 2, 3, 4. . . . The syntactical insights about regularity in notation are matched by perceptual-manipulative insights about the material referents.

After a while, some new manipulations occur that provide the child with a further basis for notational progress. He takes the square, $(x+2)^2$, and reconstructs it in a new way (Figure 4). One may ask whether this is constructive manipulation or whether it is proper factoring. But the child is learning that the same amount of wood can build quite strikingly different patterns and remain the same amount of wood—although it also has a different notational expression. Where does the language begin and the

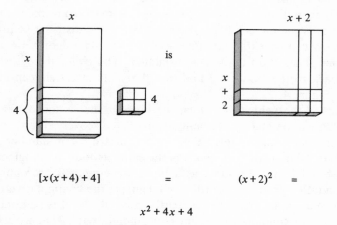

$$[x(x+4)+4] \qquad = \qquad (x+2)^2 \quad =$$

$$x^2 + 4x + 4$$

FIGURE 4. Syntactic exercise supported by construction

manipulation of materials stop? The interplay is continuous. We shall return to this same example in a later section.

But the problem now is how to detach the notation that the child has learned from the concrete, visible, manipulable embodiment to which it refers—the wood. For if the child is to deal with mathematical properties he will have to deal with symbols per se, or else he will be limited to the narrow and rather trivial range of symbolism that can be given direct (and only partial) visual embodiment. Concepts such as x^2 and x^3 may be given a visualizable referent, but what of x^n?

Why do children wean themselves from the perceptual embodiment to the symbolic notation? Perhaps it is partly explained in the nature of variation and contrast.

Variation and Contrast

The child is shown the balance beam again and told, "Choose any hook on one side and put the same number of rings on it as the number the hook is away from the middle. Now balance it with rings placed on the other side. Keep a record." Recall that the balance beam is familiar from work on factoring and that the child knows that 2 rings on 9 balances 9 on 2 or m rings on n balances n on m. He is back to construction. Can anything be constructed on the balance beam that is like the squares? With little effort, the following translation is made. Suppose x is 5. Then 5 rings on hook 5 is x^2, 5 rings on hook 4 is $4x$, and 4 rings on hook 1 is 4: $x^2 + 4x + 4$. How can we find whether this is like a square that is $x+2$ wide by $x+2$ long as before? Well, if x is 5, then $x+2$ is 7, and so 7 rings on hook 7. And nature obliges—the beam balances. One notation works for two strikingly different constructions and perceptual events. Notation, with its broader equivalency, is clearly more economical than reference to embodiments. There is little resistance to using this more convenient language. And now construction can begin—commutative and distributive properties of equations can be explored: $x(x+4) + 4 = x^2 + 4x + 4$ or $x+4$ rings on hook x and 4 rings on hook 1 will balance. The child, if he wishes, can also go back to the wood and find that the same materials can make the design in Figure 4.

Contrast is the vehicle by which the obvious that is too obvious to be appreciated can be made noticeable again. The discovery of an eight-year-old girl illustrates the matter. "Yes, 4×6 equals 6×4 in numbers, like in one way six eskimos in four igloos is the same as four in six igloos. But a venetian blind is not the same as a blind Venetian." By recognizing the noncommutative property of ordinary language, the commutative property of a mathematical language can be partly grasped. But it is still only a partial insight into commutativity and noncommutativity. Had we wished to develop the distinction more deeply we might have proceeded concretely to a contrast between sets of operations that can be carried out in any sequence—like the order of eating courses at a dinner or of going to different movies—and operations that have a noncommutative order—like putting on shoes and socks—where one must precede the other. Then the child could be taken from there to a more general idea of commutative and noncommutative cases and ways of dealing with a notation, perhaps by identical sets and ordered identical sets.

Insight and Development

What was so striking in the performance of the children was their initial inability to represent things to themselves in a way that transcended immediate perceptual grasp. The achievement of more comprehensive insight requires, we think, the building of a mediating representational structure that transcends such immediate imagery, that renders a sequence of acts and image unitary and simultaneous. The children always began by constructing an embodiment of some concept, building a concrete form of operational definition. The fruit of the construction was an image and some operations that stood for the concept. From there on, the task was to provide means of representation that were free of particular manipulations and specific images. Only symbolic operations provide the means of representing an idea in this way. But consider this matter for a moment.

We have already commented upon the fact that by giving the child multiple embodiments of the same general idea expressed in a common notation we lead him to empty the concept of specific sensory properties until he is able to grasp its abstract properties. But surely this is not the best way of describing the child's increasing development of insight. The growth of such abstractions is important. But what struck us about the children, as we observed them, is that they had not only understood the abstractions they had learned but also had a store of concrete images that served to exemplify the abstractions. When they searched for a way to deal with new problems, the task was usually carried out not simply by abstract means but also by matching up images. An example will help here. In going from the wood-blocks embodiment of the quadratic to the balance-beam embodiment, it was interesting that the children equated concrete features of one with concrete features of another. One side of the balance beam stood for the amount of wood, the other side for the sides of the square. These were important concrete props on which they leaned. We have been told by research mathematicians that the same use of props—heuristics—holds for them, that they have preferred ways of imagining certain problems while other problems are handled silently or in terms of an imagery of the symbolism on a page.

We reached the tentative conclusion that it was probably necessary for a child learning mathematics not only to have as firm a sense of the abstraction underlying what he was working on but, also, a good stock of visual images for embodying them. For without the latter, it is difficult to track correspondences and to check what one is doing symbolically. Here an example will help again. We had occasion to teach a group of ten nine-year-olds the elements of group theory. To embody the idea of a mathematical group initially, we gave them the example of a four-group made up of the following four maneuvers (a book was the vehicle, a book with an arrow up the middle of its front cover); rotating the book a quarter turn to the left, rotating it a quarter turn to the right, rotating it a half turn (without regard to direction of rotation), and letting it stay in the position it was in. They were quick to grasp the important property of such a mathematical group, that any sequence of maneuvers made could be reproduced from the starting position by a single move. This is not the usual way in which this property is described mathematically, but it served well for the children. We contrasted this elegant property with a series of our moves that did not constitute a mathematical group—indeed, they provided the counterexample themselves by proposing the one-third turn left, one-third turn right, half turn either way, and stay. It was soon apparent that it did not work. We set the children the task of making games of four maneuvers, six maneuvers, and so on that had the property of a closed game, as we called it. They were, of course, highly ingenious. But what soon became apparent was that they needed some aid in imagery—in this case an imagery notation—that would allow them to keep track and then to discover whether some new game was an isomorph of one they had already developed. The prop in this case was, of course, the matrix, listing the moves possible across the top and then listing them down the side, thus making it easily possible to check whether each combination of pairs of moves could be reproduced by a single move. The matrix in this case is a crutch or heuristic and as such has nothing to do with the abstraction of the mathematical group, yet it was enormously useful to them not only for keeping track but also for comparing one group with another for correspondence. Thus the matrix with which they started had the property of

	s	a	b	c
s	s	a	b	c
a	a	c	s	b
b	b	s	c	a
c	c	b	a	s

Are there any four groups with a different structure? It is extremely difficult to deal with such a question without the aid of this housekeeping matrix as a vehicle for spotting correspondence.

A still better example is provided by a colleague, pointing to the role of imagery in dealing with certain formal properties.[1] Suppose we specify the

[1] We are grateful for this example to Richard Hays.

permissible moves in a finite state structure consisting of the states *A, B, C, D, E.* One may list the permissible transitions between states as follows:

$$
\begin{array}{c}
AB \\
AD \\
BC \\
BE \\
CE \\
DD \\
ED \\
EA
\end{array}
$$

Suppose we now ask of someone who has this set of rules for moving among the five states what is the shortest path from *A* to *E* that moves through *C*. Even with the ordered information in the list, it takes a moment to figure it out. How much easier the task becomes when one produces an image to carry the information, such as,

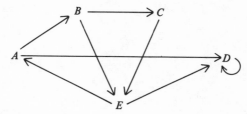

or better, the following:

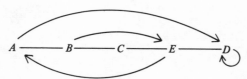

Much of mathematics is carried out with just such less-than-rigorous technique, and it is likely as important as abstraction in the actual doing of mathematical problems. One can use highly concrete embodiments to serve such uses. The building blocks used in teaching quadratic functions can serve as a source image for checking and rethinking just as readily as the diagraming of finite state structures noted directly above.

In sum, then, while the development of insight into mathematics in our group of children depended upon their development of example-free abstractions, this did not lead them to give up their imagery. Quite to the contrary, we had the impression that their enriched imagery was very useful to them in dealing with new problems.

We would suggest that learning mathematics may be viewed as a microcosm of intellectual development. It begins with instrumental activity, a kind of definition of things by doing. Such operations become represented and summarized in the form of particular images. Finally, and with the help of a symbolic notation that remains invariant across transformations in imagery, the learner comes to grasp the formal or abstract properties of the things he is dealing with. But while, once abstraction is achieved, the learner becomes free in a certain measure of the surface appearance of things, he nonetheless continues to rely upon the stock of imagery he has built en route to abstract mastery. It is this stock of imagery that permits him to work at the level of heuristic, through convenient and nonrigorous means of exploring problems and relating them to problems already mastered.

25

*The Growth of Mind**

What is unique about man is that his growth as an individual depends upon the history of his species—not upon a history reflected in genes and chromosomes but, rather, reflected in a culture external to man's tissue and wider in scope than is embodied in any one man's competency. Perforce, then, the growth of mind is always growth assisted from the outside. Since a culture, particularly an advanced one, transcends the bounds of individual competence, the limits for individual growth are by definition greater than what any single person has previously attained; the limits of growth depend on how a culture assists the individual to use such intellectual potential as he may possess. It seems highly unlikely—either empirically or canonically—that we have any realistic sense of the furthest reach of such assistance to growth.

The evidence today is that the full evolution of intelligence came as a result of bipedalism and tool using. The large human brain gradually evolved as a sequel to the first use of pebble tools by early near-man. To condense the story, a near-man, or hominid, with a slightly superior brain, using a pebble tool, could make out better in the niche provided by nature

* Jerome S. Bruner, "The Growth of Mind," *American Psychologist,* Vol. 20, No. 17, December 1965, pp. 1007–1017. Copyright 1965 by the American Psychological Association, and reproduced by permission of the publisher.

Address of the President to the Seventy-Third Annual Convention of the American Psychological Association, Chicago, September 4, 1965.

than a near-man who depended not on tools but on sheer strength and formidable jaws. Natural selection favored the primitive tool user. In time, thanks to his better chance of surviving and breeding, he became more so: The ones who survived had larger brains, smaller jaws, less ferocious teeth. In place of belligerent anatomy, they developed tools and a brain that made it possible to use them. Human evolution thereafter became less a matter of having appropriate fangs or claws and more one of using and later fashioning tools to express the powers of the larger brain that was also emerging. Without tools the brain was of little use, no matter how many hundred cubic centimeters of it there might be. Let it also be said that without the original programmatic capacity for fitting tools into a sequence of acts, early hominids would never have started the epigenetic progress that brought them to their present state. And as human groups stabilized, tools became more complex and shaped to pattern, so that it was no longer a matter of reinventing tools in order to survive, but rather of mastering the skills necessary for using them. In short, after a certain point in human evolution, the only means whereby man could fill his evolutionary niche was through the cultural transmission of the skills necessary for the use of priorly invented techniques, implements, and devices.

Two crucial parallel developments seem also to have occurred. As hominids became increasingly bipedal, with the freed hands necessary for using spontaneous pebble tools, selection also favored those with a heavier pelvic bony structure that could sustain the impacting strain of bipedal locomotion. The added strength came, of course, from a gradual closing down of the birth canal. There is an obstetrical paradox here, a creature with an increasingly larger brain but with a smaller and smaller birth canal to get through. The resolution seems to have been achieved through the immaturity of the human neonate, particularly cerebral immaturity that assures not only a smaller head, but also a longer period of transmitting the necessary skills required by human culture. During this same period, human language must have emerged, giving man not only a new and powerful way of representing reality but also increasing his power to assist the mental growth of the young to a degree beyond anything before seen in nature.

It is impossible, of course, to reconstruct the evolution in techniques of instruction in the shadow zone between hominids and man. I have tried to compensate by observing contemporary analogues of earlier forms, knowing full well that the pursuit of analogy can be dangerously misleading.[1]

---

[1] I have spent many hours observing uncut films of the behavior of free-ranging baboons, films shot in East Africa by Irven DeVore for Educational Services, Inc. with a very generous footage devoted to infants and juveniles. I have also had access to the unedited film archives of a hunting-gathering people living under roughly analogous ecological conditions, the !Kung Bushman of the Kalahari, recorded by Laurance and Lorna Marshall, aided by their son John and daughter Elizabeth. DeVore and the Marshalls have been generous in their counsel as well. I have also worked directly but informally with the Wolof of Senegal, observing children in the bush and

Let me describe very briefly some salient differences in the free-learning patterns of immature baboons and among !Kung children. Baboons have a highly developed social life in their troops, with well-organized and stable dominance patterns. They live within a territory, protecting themselves from predators by joint action of the strongly built, adult males. It is striking that the behavior of baboon juveniles is shaped principally by play with their peer group, play that provides opportunity for the spontaneous expression and practice of the component acts that, in maturity, will be orchestrated into either the behavior of the dominant male or of the infant-protective female. All this seems to be accomplished with little participation by any mature animals in the play of the juveniles. We know from the important experiments of Harlow and his colleagues (Harlow and Harlow, 15) how devastating a disruption in development can be produced in sub-human primates by interfering with their opportunity for peer-group play and social interaction.

Among hunting-gathering humans, on the other hand, there is constant interaction between adult and child, or adult and adolescent, or adolescent and child. !Kung adults and children play and dance together, sit together, participate in minor hunting together, join in song and storytelling together. At very frequent intervals, moreover, children are party to rituals presided over by adults—minor, as in the first haircutting, or major, as when a boy kills his first Kudu buck and goes through the proud but painful process of scarification. Children, besides, are constantly playing imitatively with the rituals, implements, tools, and weapons of the adult world. Young juvenile baboons, on the other hand, virtually never play with things or imitate directly large and significant sequences of adult behavior.

Note, though, that in tens of thousands of feet of !Kung film, one virtually never sees an instance of teaching taking place outside the situation where the behavior to be learned is relevant. Nobody teaches in our prepared sense of the word. There is nothing like school, nothing like lessons. Indeed, among the !Kung children there is very little telling. Most of what we would call instruction is through showing. There is no practice or drill as such save in the form of play modeled directly on adult models—play hunting, play bossing, play exchanging, play baby tending, play housemaking. In the end, every man in the culture knows nearly all there is to know about how to get on with life as a man, and every woman as a woman—the skills, the rituals and myths, the obligations and rights.

The change in the instruction of children in more complex societies is twofold. First of all, there is knowledge and skill in the culture far in excess of what any one individual knows. And so, increasingly, there develops an economical technique of instructing the young based heavily on

in French-style schools. Even more valuable than my own informal observations in Senegal were the systematic experiments carried out later by Patricia Marks Greenfield (14).

telling out of context rather than showing in context. In literate societies, the practice becomes institutionalized in the school or the teacher. Both promote this necessarily abstract way of instructing the young. The result of teaching the culture can, at its worst, lead to the ritual, rote nonsense that has led a generation of critics, from Max Wertheimer (29) to Mary Alice White (30), to despair. For in the detached school, what is imparted often has little to do with life as lived in the society except insofar as the demands of school are of a kind that reflect indirectly the demands of life in a technical society. But these indirectly imposed demands may be the most important feature of the detached school. For school is a sharp departure from indigenous practice. It takes learning, as we have noted, out of the context of immediate action just by dint of putting it into a school. This very extirpation makes learning become an act in itself, freed from the immediate ends of action, preparing the learner for the chain of reckoning remote from pay-off that is needed for the formulation of complex ideas. At the same time, the school (if successful) frees the child from the pace-setting of the round of daily activity. If the school succeeds in avoiding a pace-setting round of its own, it may be one of the great agents for promoting reflectiveness. Moreover, in school, one must follow the lesson, which means one must learn to follow either the abstraction of written speech—abstract in the sense that it is divorced from the concrete situation to which the speech might originally have been related—or the abstraction of language delivered orally but out of the context of an ongoing action. Both of these are highly abstract uses of language.

It is no wonder, then, that many recent studies report large differences between primitive children who are in schools and their brothers who are not: differences in perception, abstraction, time perspective, and so on. I need only cite the work of Biesheuvel (4) in South Africa, Gay and Cole (12) in Liberia, Greenfield (14) in Senegal, Maccoby and Modiano (23) in rural Mexico, and Reich (26) among Alaskan Eskimos.

What a culture does to assist the development of the powers of mind of its members is, in effect, to provide amplification systems to which human beings, equipped with appropriate skills, can link themselves. There are, first, the amplifiers of action—hammers, levers, digging sticks, wheels—but more important, the programs of action into which such implements can be substituted. Second, there are amplifiers of the senses, ways of looking and noticing that can take advantage of devices ranging from smoke signals and hailers to diagrams and pictures that stop the action or microscopes that enlarge it. Finally and most powerfully, there are amplifiers of the thought processes, ways of thinking that employ language and formation of explanation, and later use such languages as mathematics and logic and even find automatic servants to crank out the consequences. A culture is, then, a deviser, a repository, and a transmitter of amplification systems and of the devices that fit into such systems. We know very little in a deep sense about the transmission function, how people are trained to get the most from their potential by use of a culture's resources.

But it is reasonably clear that there is a major difference between the mode of transmission in a technical society, with its schools, and an indigenous one where cultural transmission is in the context of action. It is not just that an indigenous society falls apart at a most terrifying rate when its action pattern becomes disrupted—as in uncontrolled urbanization in some parts of Africa—rather, it is that the institution of a school serves to convert knowledge and skill into more symbolic, more abstract, more verbal form. It is this process of transmission—admittedly very new in human history—that is so poorly understood and to which, finally, we shall return.

There are certain obvious specifications that can be stated about how a society must proceed in order to equip its young. It must convert what is to be known—whether a skill or a belief system or a connected body of knowledge—into a form capable of being mastered by a beginner. The more we know of the process of growth, the better we shall be at such conversion. The failure of modern man to understand mathematics and science may be less a matter of stunted abilities than our failure to understand how to teach such subjects. Second, given the limited amount of time available for learning, there must be a due regard for saving the learner from needless learning. There must be some emphasis placed on economy and transfer and the learning of general rules. All societies must (and virtually all do) distinguish those who are clever from those who are stupid —though few of them generalize this trait across all activities. Cleverness in a particular activity almost universally connotes strategy, economy, heuristics, highly generalized skills. A society must also place emphasis upon how one derives a course of action from what one has learned. Indeed, in an indigenous society, it is almost impossible to separate what one does from what one knows. More advanced societies often have not found a way of dealing with the separation of knowledge and action—probably a result of the emphasis they place upon telling in their instruction. All societies must maintain interest among the young in the learning process, a minor problem when learning is in the context of life and action, but harder when it becomes more abstracted. Finally, and perhaps most obviously, a society must assure that its necessary skills and procedures remain intact from one generation to the next—which does not always happen, as witnessed by Easter Islanders, Incas, Aztecs, and Mayas.[2]

---

[2] I have purposely left out of the discussion the problems of impulse regulation and socialization of motives, topics that have received extended treatment in the voluminous literature on culture and personality. The omission is dictated by emphasis rather than evaluation. Obviously the shaping of character by culture is of great im-

Unfortunately, psychology has not concerned itself much with any of these five requisites of cultural transmission—or at least not much with four of them. We have too easily assumed that learning is learning is learning—that the early version of what was taught did not matter much, one thing being much like another and reducible to a pattern of association, to stimulus-response connections, or to our favorite molecular componentry. We denied there was a problem of development beyond the quantitative one of providing more experience, and with the denial, closed our eyes to the pedagogic problem of how to represent knowledge, how to sequence it, how to embody it in a form appropriate to young learners. We expended more passion on the part-whole controversy than on what whole or what part of it was to be presented first. I should except Piaget (25), Köhler (20), and Vygotsky (28) from these complaints.

Our neglect of the economy of learning stems, ironically, from the heritage of Ebbinghaus (10), who was vastly interested in savings. Our nonsense syllables, our random mazes failed to take into account how we reduce complexity and strangeness to simplicity and the familiar, how we convert what we have learned into rules and procedures, how, to use Bartlett's (3) term, we turn around on our own schemata to reorganize what we have mastered into more manageable form.

Nor have we taken naturally to the issue of knowledge and action. Its apparent mentalism has repelled us. Tolman (27), who bravely made the distinction, was accused of leaving his organisms rapt in thought. But he recognized the problem and if he insisted on the idea that knowledge might be organized in cognitive maps, it was in recognition (as a great functionalist) that organisms go somewhere on the basis of what they have learned. I believe we are getting closer to the problem of how knowledge affects action and vice versa, and offer in testimony of my conviction the provocative book by Miller, Galanter, and Pribram, *Plans and the Structure of Behavior* (24).

Where the maintenance of the learner's interest is concerned, I remind you of what Gordon Allport (1) has long warned. We have been so concerned with the model of driven behavior, with drive reduction and the vis a tergo that, again, until recently, we have tended to overlook the question of what keeps learners interested in the activity of learning, in the achievement of competence beyond bare necessity and first pay-off. The work of R. W. White (31) on effectance motivation, of Harlow and his colleagues (Butler, 9; Harlow, 16) on curiosity, and of Heider (17) and Festinger (11) on consistency begins to redress the balance.

portance for an understanding of our topic as it bears, for example, upon culture-instilled attitudes toward the uses of mind. Since our emphasis is upon human potential and its amplification by culturally patterned instrumental skills, we mention the problem of character formation in passing and in recognition of its importance in a complete treatment of the issues under discussion.

The invention of antidegradation devices, guarantors that skill and knowledge will be maintained intact, is an exception to our oversight. We psychologists have been up to our ears in it. Our special contribution is the achievement test. But the achievement test has, in the main, reflected the timidity of the educational enterprise as a whole. I believe we know how to determine, though we have not yet devised tests to determine, how pupils use what they learn to think with later in life—for there is the real issue.

I have tried to examine briefly what a culture must do in passing on its amplifying skills and knowledge to a new generation and, even more briefly, how we as psychologists have dealt or failed to deal with the problems. I think the situation is fast changing—with a sharp increase in interest in the conversion problem, the problems of economy of learning, the nature of interest, the relation of knowledge and action. We are, I believe, at a major turning point where psychology will once again concern itself with the design of methods of assisting cognitive growth, be it through the invention of a rational technology of toys, of ways of enriching the environment of the crib and nursery, of organizing the activity of a school, or of devising a curriculum whereby we transmit an organized body of knowledge and skill to a new generation to amplify their powers of mind.

I commented earlier that there was strikingly little knowledge available about the third way of training the skills of the young: the first being the play practice of component skills in prehuman primates; the second the teaching-in-context of indigenous societies; and the third the abstracted, detached method of the school.

Let me now become highly specific. Let me consider a particular course of study, one given in a school, one we ourselves constructed, tried out and, in a highly qualitative way, evaluated. It is for schools of the kind that exist in Western culture. The experience we have had with this effort may serve to highlight the kinds of problems and conjectures one encounters in studying how to assist the growth of intellect in this third way.

There is a dilemma in describing a course of study. One begins by setting forth the intellectual substance of what is to be taught. Yet if such a recounting tempts one to get across the subject, the ingredient of pedagogy is in jeopardy. For only in a trivial sense is a course designed to get something across, merely to impart information. There are better means to that end than teaching. Unless the learner develops his skills, disciplines his taste, deepens his view of the world, the something that is gotten across is hardly worth the effort of transmission.

The more elementary a course and the younger its students, the more serious must be its pedagogic aim of forming the intellectual powers of those whom it serves. It is as important to justify a good mathematics course by the intellectual discipline it provides or the honesty it promotes as by the mathematics it transmits. Indeed, neither can be accomplished without the other. The content of this particular course is man: his nature as a species, the forces that shaped and continue to shape his humanity. Three questions recur throughout: What is human about human beings? How did they get that way? How can they be made more so?

In pursuit of our questions we explored five matters, each closely associated with the evolution of man as a species, each defining at once the distinctiveness of man and his potentiality for further evolution. The five great humanizing forces are, of course, tool making, language, social organization, the management of man's prolonged childhood, and man's urge to explain. It has been our first lesson in teaching that no pupil, however eager, can appreciate the relevance of, say, tool making or language in human evolution without first grasping the fundamental concept of a tool or what a language is. These are not self-evident matters, even to the expert. So we are involved in teaching not only the role of tools or language in the emergence of man but, as a necessary precondition for doing so, setting forth the fundamentals of linguistics or the theory of tools. And it is as often the case as not that (as in the case of the theory of tools) we must solve a formidable intellectual problem ourselves in order to be able to help our pupils do the same.

While one readily singles out five sources of man's humanization, under no circumstances can they be put into airtight compartments. Human kinship is distinctively different from primate mating patterns precisely because it is classificatory and rests on man's ability to use language. Or, if you will, tool use enhances the division of labor in a society which in turn affects kinship. So while each domain can be treated as a separate set of ideas, their teaching must make it possible for the children to have a sense of their interaction. We have leaned heavily on the use of contrast, highly controlled contrast, to help children achieve detachment from the all too familiar matrix of social life: the contrasts of man versus higher primates, man versus prehistoric man, contemporary technological man versus primitive man, and man versus child. The primates are principally baboons, the prehistoric materials mostly from the Olduvai Gorge and Les Eyzies, the primitive peoples mostly the Netsilik Eskimos of Pelly Bay and the !Kung Bushmen. The materials, collected for our purposes, are on film, in story, in ethnography, in pictures and drawings, and principally in ideas embodied in exercises.

We hoped to achieve five goals:

a. To give our pupils respect for and confidence in the powers of their own minds

b. To give them respect, moreover, for the powers of thought concerning the human condition, man's plight, and his social life

c. To provide them with a set of workable models that make it simpler to analyze the nature of the social world in which they live and the condition in which man finds himself

d. To impart a sense of respect for the capacities and plight of man as a species, for his origins, for his potential, for his humanity

e. To leave the student with a sense of the unfinished business of man's evolution

Let me now try to describe some of the major problems one encounters in trying to construct a course of study. I shall not try to translate the problems into refined theoretical form, for they do not merit such translation. They are more difficulties than problems. I chose them because they are vividly typical of what one encounters in such enterprises. The course is designed for ten-year-olds in the fifth grade of elementary school, but we have tried it out as well on the fourth and sixth grades better to bracket our difficulties.

One special point about these difficulties. They were born of trying to achieve an objective and were as much policybound as theorybound. It is like the difference between building an economic theory about monopolistic practices and constructing policies for controlling monopoly. Let me remind you that modern economic theory has been reformulated, refined, and revived by having a season in policy. I am convinced that the psychology of assisted growth, pedagogy, will have to be forged in the policy crucible of curriculum-making before it can reach its full descriptive power as theory. Economics was first through the cycle from theory to policy to theory to policy; it is happening now to psychology, anthropology, and sociology.

Now the difficulties. The first is what might be called the psychology of a subject matter. A learned discipline can be conceived as a way of thinking about certain phenomena. Mathematics is one way of thinking about order without reference to what is being ordered. The behavioral sciences provide one or perhaps several ways of thinking about man and his society —about regularities, origins, causes, effects. They are probably special (and suspect) because they permit man to look at himself from a perspective that is outside his own skin and beyond his own preferences—at least for awhile.

Underlying a discipline's way of thought, there is a set of connected, varyingly implicit, generative propositions. In physics and mathematics, most of the underlying generative propositions, like the conservation theorems, or the axioms of geometry, or the associative, distributive, and commutative rules of analysis, are by now very explicit indeed. In the behavioral sciences we must be content with more implicitness. We traffic in inductive propositions; for instance, the different activities of a society are interconnected such that if you know something about the technological response of a society to an environment, you will be able to make some shrewd guesses about its myths or about the things it values, and so on. We use the device of a significant contrast as in linguistics when we describe the territoriality of a baboon troop in order to help us recognize the system of reciprocal exchange of a human group, the former somehow provoking awareness of the latter.

There is nothing more central to a discipline than its way of thinking. There is nothing more important in its teaching than to provide the child the earliest opportunity to learn that way of thinking—the forms of connection, the attitudes, hopes, jokes, and frustrations that go with it. In a word, the best introduction to a subject is the subject itself. At the very first breath, the young learner should, we think, be given the chance to solve problems, to conjecture, to quarrel as these are done at the heart of the discipline. But, you will ask, how can this be arranged?

Here again the problem of conversion. There exist ways of thinking characteristic of different stages of development. We are acquainted with Inhelder and Piaget's (18) account of the transition from preoperational, through concrete operational, to propositional thought in the years from preschool through, say, high school. If you have an eventual pedagogic objective in mind, you can translate the way of thought of a discipline into its Piagetian (or other) equivalent appropriate to a given level of development and take the child onward from there. The Cambridge Mathematics Project of Educational Services, Incorporated, argues that if the child is to master the calculus early in his high school years, he should start work early with the idea of limits, the earliest work being manipulative, later going on to images and diagrams, and finally moving on to the more abstract notation needed for delineating the more precise idea of limits.

In "Man: A Course of Study" (Bruner, 7), there are also versions of the subject appropriate to a particular age that can at a later age be given a more powerful rendering. We tried to choose topics with this in mind: The analysis of kinship that begins with children using sticks and blocks and colors and what not to represent their own families, goes on to the conventional kinship diagrams by a meandering but, as you can imagine, interesting path, and then can move on to more formal and powerful componential analysis. So, too, with myth. We begin with the excitement of a powerful myth (like the Netsilik Nuliajik myth), then have the children construct some myths of their own, then examine what a set of Netsilik myths have in common, which takes us finally to Lévi-Strauss's (21) analysis of contrastive features in myth construction. A variorum text of a myth or corpus of myths put together by sixth graders can be quite an extraordinary document.

This approach to the psychology of a learned discipline turns out to illuminate another problem raised earlier: the maintenance of interest. There is, in this approach, a reward in understanding that grows from the subject matter itself. It is easier to engineer this satisfaction in mathematics, for understanding is so utter in a formal discipline—a balance beam balances or it does not, therefore there is an equality or there is not. In the behavioral sciences the pay-off in understanding cannot be so obviously and startlingly self-revealing. Yet, one can design exercises in the understanding of man, too—as when children figure out the ways in which, given limits of ecology, skills, and materials, Bushmen hunt different animals, and then compare their predictions with the real thing on film.

Consider now a second problem: how to stimulate thought in the setting of a school. We know from experimental studies like those of Bloom and Broder (5), and of Goodnow and Pettigrew (13), that there is a striking difference in the acts of a person who thinks that the task before him represents a problem to be solved rather than being controlled by random forces. School is a particular subculture where these matters are concerned. By school age, children have come to expect quite arbitrary and, from their point of view, meaningless demands to be made upon them by adults—the result, most likely, of the fact that adults often fail to recognize the task of conversion necessary to make their questions have some intrinsic significance for the child. Children, of course, will try to solve problems if they recognize them as such. But they are not often either predisposed to or skillful in problem finding, in recognizing the hidden conjectural feature in tasks set them. But we know now that children in school can quite quickly be led to such problem finding by encouragement and instruction.

The need for this instruction and encouragement and its relatively swift success relates, I suspect, to what psychoanalysts refer to as the guilt-ridden oversuppression of primary process and its public replacement by secondary process. Children, like adults, need reassurance that it is all right to entertain and express highly subjective ideas, to treat a task as a problem where you invent an answer rather than finding one out there in the book or on the blackboard. With children in elementary school, there is often a need to devise emotionally vivid special games, story-making episodes, or construction projects to re-establish in the child's mind his right not only to have his own private ideas but to express them in the public setting of a classroom.

But there is another, perhaps more serious difficulty: the interference of intrinsic problem solving by extrinsic. Young children in school expend extraordinary time and effort figuring out what it is that the teacher wants —and usually coming to the conclusion that she or he wants tidiness or remembering or to do things at a certain time in a certain way. This I refer to as extrinsic problem solving. There is a great deal of it in school.

There are several quite straightforward ways of stimulating problem solving. One is to train teachers to want it and that will come in time. But teachers can be encouraged to like it, interestingly enough, by providing them and their children with materials and lessons that permit legitimate problem solving and permit the teacher to recognize it. Exercises with such materials create an atmosphere by treating things as instances of what might have occurred rather than simply as what did occur. Let me illustrate by a concrete instance. A fifth-grade class was working on the organization of a baboon troop—on this particular day, specifically on how they might protect against predators. They saw a brief sequence of film in which six or seven adult males go forward to intimidate and hold off three cheetahs. The teacher asked what the baboons had done to keep the cheetahs off, and there ensued a lively discussion of how the dominant adult males, by showing their formidable mouthful of teeth and making threatening gestures had turned the trick. A boy raised a tentative hand and asked whether cheetahs always attacked together. Yes, though a single cheetah sometimes followed behind a moving troop and picked off an older, weakened straggler or an unwary, straying juvenile. "Well, what if there were four cheetahs and two of them attacked from behind and two from in front. What would the baboons do then?" The question could have been answered empirically—and the inquiry ended: Cheetahs do not attack that way, and so we do not know what baboons might do. Fortunately, it was not, for the question opens up the deep issues of what might be and why it is not. Is there a necessary relation between predators and prey that share a common ecological niche? Must their encounters have a sporting-chance outcome? It is such conjecture, in this case quite unanswerable, that produces rational, self-consciously problem-finding behavior so crucial to the growth of intellectual power. Given the materials, given some background and encouragement, teachers like it as much as the students.

I should like to turn now to the personalization of knowledge. A generation ago, the progressive movement urged that knowledge be related to the child's own experience and brought out of the realm of empty abstractions. A good idea was translated into banalities about the home, then the friendly postman and trashman, then the community, and so on. It is a poor way to compete with the child's own dramas and mysteries. Clyde Kluckhohn (19) wrote a prize-winning popular book on anthropology with the entrancing title *Mirror for Man*. In some deep way, there is extraordinary power in "that mirror which other civilizations still hold up to us to recognize and study . . . [the] image of ourselves" (Lévi-Strauss, 21). The psychological bases of the power are not obvious. Is it as in discrimination learning, where increasing the degree of contrast helps in the learning of a discrimination, or as in studies of concept attainment where a negative instance demonstrably defines the domain of a conceptual rule? Or is it some primitive identification? All these miss one thing that seemed to come up frequently in our interviews with the children. It is the experience of discovering kinship and likeness in what at first seemed bizarre, exotic, and even a little repellent.

Consider two examples, both involving film of the Netsilik. In the films, a single nuclear family, Zachary, Marta, and their four-year-old Alexi, is followed through the year—spring sealing, summer fishing at the stone weir, fall caribou hunting, early winter fishing through the ice, winter at the big ceremonial igloo. Children report that at first the three members of the family look weird and uncouth. In time, they look normal, and eventually, as when Marta finds sticks around which to wrap her braids, the girls speak of how pretty she is. That much is superficial—or so it seems. But consider a second episode.

It has to do with Alexi who, with his father's help, devises a snare and catches a gull. There is a scene in which he stones the gull to death. Our children watched, horror struck. One girl, Kathy, blurted out, "He's not even human, doing that to the seagull." The class was silent. Then another girl, Jennine, said quietly, "He's got to grow up to be a hunter. His mother was smiling when he was doing that." And then an extended discussion about how people have to do things to learn and even do things to learn how to feel appropriately. "What would you do if you had to live there? Would you be as smart about getting along as they are with what they've got?" said one boy, going back to the accusation that Alexi was inhuman to stone the bird.

In other words, to personalize knowledge one does not simply link it to the familiar. Rather one makes the familiar an instance of a more general case and thereby produces awareness of it. What the children were learning about was not seagulls and Eskimos, but about their own feelings and preconceptions that, up to then, were too implicit to be recognizable to them.

Consider finally the problem of self-conscious reflectiveness. It is an epistemological mystery why traditional education has so often emphasized extensiveness and coverage over intensiveness and depth. We have already commented on the fact that memorizing was usually perceived by children as one of the high-priority tasks, but rarely did children sense an emphasis upon ratiocination with a view toward redefining what had been encountered, reshaping it, reordering it. The cultivation of reflectiveness, or whatever you choose to call it, is one of the great problems one faces in devising curricula: how to lead children to discover the powers and pleasures that await the exercise of retrospection?

Let me suggest one answer that grew from what we have done. It is the use of the organizing conjecture. We have used three such conjectures— what is human about human beings, how they got that way, how they could become more so. They serve two functions, one of them the very obvious though important one of putting perspective back into the particulars. The second is less obvious and considerably more surprising. The questions often seemed to serve as criteria for determining where they were getting, how well they were understanding, whether anything new was emerging. Recall Kathy's cry, "He's not human doing that to the seagull." She was hard at work in her rage on the conjecture what makes human beings human.

There, in brief, are four problems that provide some sense of what a psychologist encounters when he takes a hand in assisting the growth of mind in children in the special setting of a school. The problems look quite different from those we encounter in formulating classic developmental theory with the aid of typical laboratory research. They also look very different from those that one would find in an indigenous society, describing how children picked up skills and knowledge and values in the context of action and daily life. We clearly do not have a theory of the school that is sufficient to the task of running schools—just as we have no adequate theory of toys, or of readiness building, or whatever the jargon is for preparing children to do a better job the next round. It only obscures the issue to urge that someday our classic theories of learning will fill the gap. They show no sign of doing so.

But I am deeply convinced that the psychologist cannot alone construct a theory of how to assist cognitive development and cannot alone learn how to enrich and amplify the powers of a growing human mind. The task belongs to the whole intellectual community: the behavioral scientists and the artists, scientists, and scholars who are the custodians of skill, taste, and knowledge in our culture. Our special task as psychologists is to convert skills and knowledge to forms and exercises that fit growing minds—and it is a task ranging from how to keep children free from anxiety and how to translate physics for the very young child into a set of playground maneuvers that, later, the child can turn around upon and convert into a sense of inertial regularities.

References

1. ALLPORT, G. W. 1946. Effect: a secondary principle of learning. *Psychological Review* 53:335–47.
2. BARKER, R. 1963. On the nature of the environment. *Journal of Social Issues* 19:17–38.
3. BARTLETT, F. C. 1932. *Remembering*. Cambridge, Eng.: Cambridge University Press.
4. BIESHEUVEL, S. 1949. Psychological tests and their application to non-European peoples. *Yearbook of Education*, pp. 87–126. London: Evans.
5. BLOOM, B., and BRODER, L. 1950. Problem solving processes of college students. *Supplementary Educational Monograph*, no. 73. Chicago: University of Chicago Press.
6. BRUNER, J. 1964. The course of cognitive growth. *American Psychologist* 19:1–15.
7. BRUNER, J. 1965. Man: a course of study. *Educational Services, Inc., Quarterly Report* (Spring-Summer), pp. 3–13.
8. BRUNER, J. 1966. *Toward a theory of instruction*. Cambridge, Mass.: Harvard University Press.

9. BUTLER, R. A. 1954. Incentive conditions which influence visual exploration. *Journal of Experimental Psychology* 48:19–23.
10. EBBINGHAUS, H. 1913. *Memory: a contribution to experimental psychology*. New York: Teachers College, Columbia University.
11. FESTINGER, L. 1962. A theory of cognitive dissonance. Stanford, Calif.: Stanford University Press.
12. GAY, J., and COLE, M. Outline of general report on Kpelle mathematics project. Stanford University, Institute for Mathematical Social Studies, undated (mimeo).
13. GOODNOW, J., and PETTIGREW, T. 1955. Effect of prior patterns of experience on strategies and learning sets. *Journal of Experimental Psychology* 49:381–89.
14. GREENFIELD, P. M. 1966. Culture and conservation. In *Studies in cognitive growth*, J. S. Bruner, R. R. Olver, P. M. Greenfield et al. New York: Wiley.
15. HARLOW, H., and HARLOW, M. 1962. Social deprivation in monkeys. *Scientific American* 136 (November).
16. HARLOW, H. F. 1953. Mice, monkeys, men, and motives. *Psychological Review* 60:23–32.
17. HEIDER, F. 1958. *The psychology of interpersonal relations*. New York: Wiley.
18. INHELDER, B. and PIAGET, J. 1958. *The growth of logical thinking from childhood to adolescence*. New York: Basic Books.
19. KLUCKHOHN, C. 1949. *Mirror for man*. New York: Whittlesey House.
20. KÖHLER, W. 1940. *Dynamics in psychology*. New York: Liveright.
21. LÉVI-STRAUSS, C. 1963. The structural study of myth. *Structural anthropology*. Trans. C. Jacobson and B. Grundfest Scharpf, pp. 206–31. New York: Basic Books.
22. LÉVI-STRAUSS, C. 1965. Anthropology: its achievements and future. Lecture presented at Bicentennial Celebration, Smithsonian Institution, Washington, D.C., September 1965.
23. MACCOBY, M., and MODIANO, N. 1966. On culture and equivalence. In *Studies in cognitive growth,* ed. J. S. Bruner, R. R. Olver, P. M. Greenfield et al. New York: Wiley.
24. MILLER, G.; GALANTER, E.; and PRIBRAM, K. 1960. *Plans and the structure of behavior*. New York: Holt.
25. PIAGET, J. 1954. *The construction of reality in the child*. Trans. M. Cook. New York: Basic Books.
26. REICH, L. 1966. On culture and grouping. In *Studies in cognitive growth*, ed. J. S. Bruner, R. R. Olver, P. M. Greenfield et al. New York: Wiley.
27. TOLMAN, E. 1951. Cognitive maps in rats and men. *Collected papers in psychology*, pp. 241–64. Berkeley and Los Angeles: University of California Press.
28. VYGOTSKY, L. 1962. *Thought and language*. Ed. and trans. E. Hanfmann and G. Vakar. New York: Wiley, and Cambridge, Mass.: MIT Press.
29. WERTHEIMER, M. 1945. *Productive thinking*. New York and London: Harper.
30. WHITE, M. A. The child's world of learning. Teachers College, Columbia University, undated (mimeo).
31. WHITE, R. W. 1959. Motivation reconsidered: the concept of competence. *Psychological Review* 66:297–333.

26

Cultural Differences and Inferences about Psychological Processes *

Deficit Interpretation

Perhaps the most prevalent view of the source of ethnic and social class differences in intellectual performance is what might be summed up under the label deficit hypothesis. It can be stated briefly, without risk of gross exaggeration. It rests on the assumption that a community under conditions of poverty (for it is the poor who are the focus of attention, and a disproportionate number of the poor are members of minority ethnic groups) is a disorganized community, and this disorganization expresses itself in various forms of deficit. One widely agreed-upon source of deficit is mothering; the child of poverty is assumed to lack adequate parental attention. Given the illegitimacy rate in the urban ghetto, the most conspicuous deficit is a missing father and, consequently, a missing father model. The mother is away at work or, in any case, less involved with raising her children than she should be by white middle-class standards. There is said to be less regularity, less mutuality in interaction with her. There are said

* Michael Cole and Jerome S. Bruner, "Cultural Differences and Inferences about Psychological Processes," *American Psychologist,* Vol. 26, No. 10, October 1971, pp. 867–876. Copyright 1971 by the American Psychological Association, and reproduced by permission of the authors and publisher.

to be specialized deficits in interaction as well—less guidance in goal seeking from the parents (39), less emphasis upon means and ends in maternal instruction (23), or less positive and more negative reinforcement (1, 40).

More particularly, the deficit hypothesis has been applied to the symbolic and linguistic environment of the growing child. His linguistic community as portrayed in the early work of Basil Bernstein (3), for example, is characterized by a restricted code, dealing more in the stereotype of interaction than in language that explains and elaborates upon social and material events. The games that are played by poor children and to which they are exposed are less strategybound than those of more advantaged children (15); their homes are said to have a more confused noise background, permitting less opportunity for figure-ground formation (29); and the certainty of the environment is sufficiently reduced so that children have difficulty in delaying reinforcement (35) or in accepting verbal reinforcement instead of the real article (44).

The theory of intervention that grew from this view was the idea of early stimulation, modeled on a conception of supplying nutriment for those with a protein deficiency or avitaminosis. The nature of the needed early stimulation was never explained systematically, save in rare cases (40), but it variously took the form of practice in using abstractions (5), in having dialogue where the referent objects were not present, as through the use of telephones (14, 26), or in providing secure mothering by substitution (9, 29).

A primary result of these various deficits was believed to express itself in the lowered test scores and academic performance among children from poverty backgrounds. The issue was most often left moot as to whether or not this lowered test performance was easily reversible, but the standard reference was to a monograph by Bloom (6) indicating that cognitive performance on a battery of tests, given to poor and middle-class children, yielded the result that nearly 80 per cent of the variance in intellectual performance was accounted for by age three.

Difference Interpretation

Such data seem to compel the conclusion that as a consequence of various factors arising from minority group status (factors affecting motivation, linguistic ability, goal orientation, hereditary proclivities to learn in certain ways—the particular mix of factors depends on the writer), minority group children suffer intellectual deficits when compared with their more advantaged peers.

In this section, we review a body of data and theory that controverts this contention, casts doubt on the conclusion that a deficit exists in minority group children, and even raises doubts as to whether any nonsuperficial differences exist among different cultural groups.

There are two long-standing precedents for the view that different groups (defined in terms of cultural, linguistic, and ethnic criteria) do not differ intellectually from each other in any important way.[1] First, there is the anthropological doctrine of psychic unity (31) which, on the basis of the run of total experience, is said to warrant the assumption of intellectual equality as a sufficient approximation to the truth. This view is compatible with current linguistic anthropological theorizing, which concentrates on describing the way in which different cultural/linguistic groups categorize familiar areas of experience (42). By this view, different conclusions about the world are the result of arbitrary and different, but equally logical, ways of cutting up the world of experience. From this perspective, descriptions of the disorganization of minorities would be highly suspect, this suspicion arising in connection with questions like, Disorganized from whose point of view?

Anthropological critiques of psychological experimentation have never carried much weight with psychologists, nor have anthropologists been very impressed with conclusions from psychological tests. We have hypothesized elsewhere (13) that their mutual indifference stems in part from a difference in opinion about the inferences that are warranted from testing and experimentation, and in part because the anthropologist relies mainly on data that the psychologist completely fails to consider: the mundane social life of the people he studies. As we shall see, these issues carry over into our criticism of the deficit theory of cultural deprivation.

A second tradition that calls into question culturally determined group difference in intelligence is the linguist's assertion that languages do not differ in their degree of development (21), buttressed by the transformationalist's caution that one cannot attribute to people a cognitive capacity that is less than is required to produce the complex rule-governed activity called language (12).

Although Chomskian linguistics has had a profound effect on psychological theories of language and cognitive development in recent years, psychological views of language still are considered hopelessly inadequate by working linguists. This criticism applies not only to psycholinguistic theory but to the actual description of linguistic performance on which theory is based. Needless to say, the accusation of misunderstanding at the descriptive level leads to accusations of absurdity at the theoretical level.

A third tradition that leads to rejection of the deficit theory has many sources in recent social sciences. This view holds that even when attempts

[1] It is assumed here that it is permissible to speak of minority group or poverty group culture using as our criterion Lévi-Strauss's (33) definition: "What is called 'culture' is a fragment of humanity which, from the point of view of the research at hand . . . presents significant discontinuities in relation to the rest of humanity" (p. 295). We do not intend to enter into arguments over the existence or nature of a culture of poverty, although such an idea seems implicit in the view of most deficit theorists.

have been made to provide reasonable anthropological and linguistic foundations, the conclusions about cognitive capacity from psychological experiments are unfounded because the performance produced represents a complex interaction of the formal characteristics of the experiment and the social/environmental context that determines the subject's interpretation of the situation in which it occurs. The need for situationbound interpretations of experiments is emphasized in such diverse sources as sociology (20), psychology (8), and psycholinguistics (11). This is an important issue, which we will return to once illustrations of the antideficit view have been explored.

Perhaps the most coherent denial of the deficit position, coupled with compelling illustrations of the resourcefulness of the supposedly deprived and incompetent person, is contained in Labov's attack on the concept of linguistic deprivation and its accompanying assumption of cognitive incapacity (32).

It is not possible here to review all of Labov's evidence. Rather, we have abstracted what we take to be the major points in his attack.

An Assertion of the Functional Equality of All Languages. This assertion is applied specifically to his analysis of nonstandard Negro English, which has been the object of his study for several years. Labov provided a series of examples where young blacks who would be assessed as linguistically retarded and academically hopeless by standard test procedures enter conversations in a way that leaves little doubt that they can speak perfectly adequately and produce very clever arguments in the process.

An Assertion of the Psychologist's Ignorance of Language in General and Nonstandard Dialects in Particular. Labov's particular target is Carl Bereiter (2) whose remedial teaching technique is partly rationalized in terms of the inability of young black children to use language either as an effective tool of communication or thinking. Part of Labov's attack is aimed at misinterpretations of such phrases as "They mine," which Labov analyzed in terms of rules of contraction, but which Bereiter made the mistake of referring to as a "series of badly connected words" (32, p. 171). This psychologist's deficit has a clear remedy. It is roughly equivalent to the anthropological caveat that the psychologist has to know more about the people he studies.

The Inadequacy of Present Experimentation. More serious criticism of the psychologist's interpretation of language deprivation and, by extension, his whole concept of cultural deprivation is contained in the following, rather extensive quote:

this and the preceding section are designed to convince the reader that the controlled experiments that have been offered in evidence [of Negro lack of competence] are misleading. The only thing that is controlled is the superficial form of the stimulus. All children are asked, "What do you think of capital punishment?" or "Tell me everything you can about this." But the speaker's interpretation of these requests, and the action he believes is appropriate in response is completely uncontrolled. One can view these test stimuli as requests for information, commands for action, or meaningless sequences of words. . . . With human subjects it is absurd to believe that identical stimuli are obtained by asking everyone the same question. Since the crucial intervening variables of interpretation and motivation are uncontrolled, most of the literature on verbal deprivation tells us nothing of the capacities of children (32, p. 171).

Here Labov is attacking the experimental method as usually applied to the problem of subcultural differences in cognitive capacity. We can abstract several assertions from this key passage: (a) formal experimental equivalence of operations does not insure de facto equivalence of experimental treatments; (b) different subcultural groups are predisposed to interpret the experimental stimuli (situations) differently; (c) different subcultural groups are motivated by different concerns relevant to the experimental task; (d) in view of the inadequacies of experimentation, inferences about lack of competence among black children are unwarranted.

These criticisms, when combined with linguistic misinterpretation, constitute Labov's attack on the deficit theory of cultural deprivation and represent the rationale underlying his demonstrations of competence where its lack had previously been inferred.

One example of Labov's approach is to conduct a rather standard interview of the type often used for assessment of language competence. The situation is designed to be minimally threatening; the interviewer is a neighborhood figure, and black. Yet, the black eight-year-old interviewee's behavior is monosyllabic. He is a candidate for the diagnosis of linguistically and culturally deprived.

But this diagnosis is very much situation dependent. For at a later time, this same interviewer goes to the boy's apartment, brings one of the boy's friends with him, lies down on the floor, and produces some potato chips. He then begins talking about clearly taboo subjects in dialect. Under these circumstances, the mute interviewee becomes an excited participant in the general conversation.

In similar examples, Labov demonstrated powerful reasoning and debating skills in a school dropout and nonlogical verbosity in an acceptable, normal black who has mastered the forms of standard English. Labov's conclusion is that the usual assessment situations, including IQ and reading tests, elicit deliberate, defensive behavior on the part of the child who has realistic expectations that to talk openly is to expose oneself to insult and harm. As a consequence, such situations cannot measure the child's competence. Labov went even further to assert that, far from being verbally deprived, the typical ghetto child is bathed in verbal stimulation from morning to night. We see many speech events which depend upon the competitive exhibition of verbal skills—sounding, singing, toasts, rifting, louding—a whole range of activities in which the individual gains status through the use of language. . . . We see no connection between the verbal skill in the speech events characteristic of the street culture and success in the school room (32, p. 163).

Labov is not the only linguist to offer such a critique of current theories of cultural deprivation (see, e.g., Stewart [41]). However, Labov's criticism raises larger issues concerning the logic of comparative research designs of which the work in cultural/linguistic deprivation is only a part. It is to this general question that we now turn.

Competence and Performance in Psychological Research

The major thrusts of Labov's argument, that situational factors are important components of psychological experiments and that it is difficult if not impossible to infer competence directly from performance, are not new ideas to psychologists. Indeed, a concern with the relation between psychological processes on the one hand and situational factors on the other has long been a kind of shadow issue in psychology, surfacing most often in the context of comparative research.

It is this question that underlies the oft-berated question, What do IQ tests measure? and has been prominent in attacks on Jensen's (25) argument that group differences in IQ test performance are reflective of innate differences in capacity.

Kagan (27), for example, pointed to the work of Palmer, who regularly delays testing until the child is relaxed and has established rapport with the tester. Jensen (25, p. 100) himself reported that significant differences in test performance can be caused by differential adaptation to the test situation.

Hertzig, Birch, Thomas, and Mendez (22) made a direct study of social class/ethnic differences in response to the test situation and demonstrated stable differences in situational responses that were correlated with test performance and were present even when measured IQ was equivalent for subgroups chosen from the major comparison groups.

Concern with the particular content of tests and experiments as they relate to inferences about cognitive capacity occurs within the same context. The search for a culture-free IQ test has emphasized the use of universally familiar material, and various investigators have found that significant differences in performance can be related to the content of the experimental materials. Price-Williams (36), for example, demonstrated earlier acquisition of conservation concepts in Nigerian children using traditional instead

of imported stimulus materials, and Gay and Cole (18) made a similar
point with respect to Liberian classification behavior and learning.

Contemporary psychology's awareness of the task and situation-specific
determinants of performance is reflected in a recent article by Kagan and
Kogan (28). In a section of their paper titled "The Significance of Public
Performance," they are concerned with the fact that "differences in quality
of style of public performance, although striking, may be misleading in-
dices of competence" (p. 1322).

Although such misgivings abound, they have not yet crystallized into a
coherent program of research and theory nor have the implications of accepting the need to incorporate an analysis of situations in addition to
traditional experimental manipulations been fully appreciated.

Extended Idea of Competence

Labov and others have argued forcefully that we cannot distinguish on the
basis of traditional experimental approaches between the underlying competence of those who have had a poor opportunity to participate in a particular culture and those who have had a good opportunity, between those
who have not had their share of wealth and respect and those who have.
The crux of the argument, when applied to the problem of cultural deprivation, is that those groups ordinarily diagnosed as culturally deprived
have the same underlying competence as those in the mainstream of the
dominant culture, the differences in performance being accounted for by
the situations and contexts in which the competence is expressed. To put
the matter most rigorously, one can find a corresponding situation in which
the member of the out culture, the victim of poverty, can perform on the
basis of a given competence in a fashion equal to or superior to the standard achieved by a member of the dominant culture.

A prosaic example taken from the work of Gay and Cole (18) concerns
the ability to make estimates of volume. The case in question is to estimate the number of cups of rice in each of several bowls. Comparisons of
rice-estimation accuracy were made among several groups of subjects, including nonliterate Kpelle rice farmers from North Central Liberia and
Yale sophomores. The rice farmers manifested significantly greater accuracy than the Yale students, the difference increasing with the amount of
rice presented for estimation. In many other situations, measurement skills
are bound to be superior among educated subjects in the Gay and Cole
study. Just as Kpelle superiority at making rice estimates is clearly not a
universal manifestation of their superior underlying competence, the superiority of Yale students in, for example, distance judgments is no basis for
inferring that their competence is superior.

We think the existence of demonstrations such as those presented by
Labov has been salutary in forcing closer examination of testing situations

used for comparing the children of poverty with their more advantaged peers. And, as the illustration from Gay and Cole suggests, the argument may have quite general implications. Obviously, it is not sufficient to use a simple equivalence-of-test procedure to make inferences about the competence of the two groups being compared. In fact, a two-groups design is almost useless for making any important inferences in cross-cultural research, as Campbell (10) has suggested. From a logical view, however, the conclusion of equal cognitive competence in those who are not members of the prestige culture and those who are its beneficiaries is often equally unwarranted. While it is very proper to criticize the logic of assuming that poor performance implies lack of competence, the contention that poor performance is of no relevance to a theory of cognitive development and to a theory of cultural differences in cognitive development also seems an oversimplification.

Assuming that we can find test situations in which comparably good performance can be elicited from the groups being contrasted, there is plainly an issue having to do with the range and nature of the situations in which performance for any two groups can be found to be equal.

We have noted Labov's conclusion that the usual assessment of linguistic competence in the black child elicits deliberate defensive behavior and that he can respond effectively in familiar nonthreatening surroundings. It may be, however (this possibility is discussed in Bruner, 7), that he is unable to utilize language of a decentered type, taken out of the context of social interaction, used in an abstract way to deal with hypothetical possibilities and to spell out hypothetical plans (see also Gladwin, 19). If such were the case, we could not dismiss the question of different kinds of language usage by saying simply that decontextualized talk is not part of the natural milieu of the black child in the urban ghetto. If it should turn out to be the case that mastery of the culture depends on one's capacity to perform well on the basis of competence one has stored up, and to perform well in particular settings and in particular ways, then plainly the question of differences in the way language enters the problem-solving process cannot be dismissed. It has been argued, for example, by Bernstein (4) that it is in the nature of the very social life of the urban ghetto that there develops a kind of particularism in which communication usually takes place only along concrete personal lines. The ghetto child, who by training is likely to use an idiosyncratic mode of communication, may become locked into the life of his own cultural group, and his migration into other groups consequently becomes the more difficult. Bernstein made clear in his most recent work that this is not a question of capacity but, rather, a matter of what he calls "orientation." Nevertheless, it may very well be that a ghetto dweller's language training unfits him for taking jobs in the power- and prestige-endowing pursuits of middle-class culture. If such is the case, then the issue of representativeness of the situations to which he can apply his competence becomes something more than a matter of test procedure.

A major difficulty with this line of speculation is that at present we have almost no knowledge of the day-to-day representativeness of different situations and the behaviors that are seen as appropriate to them by different cultural groups. For example, the idea that language use must be considered outside of social interactions in order to qualify as abstract, as involving cognition, is almost certainly a psychologist's fiction. The work of contemporary sociologists and ethnolinguists (17, 24, 38) seems conclusively to demonstrate the presence of complex contingent thinking in situations that are all too often characterized by psychologists as consisting of syncretic, affective interactions. Until we have better knowledge of the cognitive components that are part of social interactions (the same applies to many spheres of activity), speculations about the role of language in cognition will have to remain speculations.

In fact, it is extraordinarily difficult to know, save in a most superficial way, on the basis of our present knowledge of society, what is the nature of situations that permit control and utilization of the resources of a culture by one of its members and what the cognitive skills are that are demanded of one who would use these resources. It may very well be that the very definition of a subculture could be put into the spirit of Lévi-Strauss's (33) definition of a culture: "What is called a subculture is a fragment of a culture which from the point of view of the research at hand presents significant discontinuities in relation to the rest of that culture with respect to access to its major amplifying tools." By an amplifying tool is meant a technological feature, be it soft or hard, that permits control by the individual of resources, prestige, and deference within the culture. An example of a middle-class cultural amplifier that operates to increase the thought processes of those who employ it is the discipline loosely referred to as mathematics. To employ mathematical techniques requires the cultivation of certain skills of reasoning, even certain styles of deploying one's thought processes. If one were able to cultivate the strategies and styles relevant to the employment of mathematics, then that range of technology is open to one's use. If one does not cultivate mathematical skills, the result is functional incompetence, an inability to use this kind of technology. Whether or not compensatory techniques can then correct functional incompetence is an important, but unexplored, question.

Any particular aspect of the technology requires certain skills for its successful use. These skills, as we have already noted, must also be deployable in the range of situations where they are useful. Even if a child could carry out the planning necessary for the most technically demanding kind of activity, he must not do so if he has been trained with the expectancy that the exercise of such a skill will be punished or will, in any event, lead to some unforeseen difficulty. Consequently, the chances that the individual will work up his capacities for performance in the given domain are diminished. As a result, although the individual can be shown to have competence in some sphere involving the utilization of the skill, he will not be able to express that competence in the relevant kind of context. In an absolute sense, he is any man's equal, but in everyday encounters, he is not up to the task.

The principle cuts both ways with respect to cultural differences. Verbal skills are important cultural amplifiers among Labov's subjects; as many middle-class school administrators have discovered, the ghetto resident skilled in verbal exchanges is a more than formidable opponent in the battle for control of school curriculum and resources. In like manner, the Harlem youth on the street who cannot cope with the verbal battles described by Labov is failing to express competence in a context relevant to the ghetto.

These considerations impress us with the need to clarify our notion of what the competencies are that underlie effective performance. There has been an implicit, but very general, tendency in psychology to speak as if the organism is an information-processing machine with a fixed set of routines. The number and organization of these routines might differ as a function of age, genetic make-up, or environmental factors; but for any given machine, the input to the machine is processed uniformly by the routines (structures, skills) of the organism.

Quite recently, psychologists have started to face up to the difficulties of assuming that all things are equal for different groups of people (concern has focused on difference in age, but the same logic applies to any group comparisons). The study of situational effects on performance has forced a re-evaluation of traditional theoretical inferences about competence. This new concern with the interpretation of psychological experiments is quite apparent in recent attempts to cope with data inconsistent with Piaget's theory of cognitive development. For example, Flavell and Wohlwill (16) sought to distinguish between two kinds of competence: First, there are "the rules, structures, or 'mental operations' embodied in the task and . . . [second, there are] the actual mechanisms required for processing the input and output" (p. 98). The second factor is assumed to be task specific and is the presumed explanation for such facts as the horizontal decalages in which the same principle appears for different materials at different ages. The performance progression through various stages is presumably a reflection of increases in both kinds of competence, since both are assumed to increase with age.

The same general concern is voiced by Mehler and Bever (34). They ask, "How can we decide if a developmental change or behavioral difference among adults is really due to a difference in a structural rule, to a difference in the form of the expressive processes or a difference in their quantitative capacity?" (p. 278). Their own work traces the expression of particular rules in behavior and the way the effect of knowing a rule (having a competence) interacts with dependence on different aspects of the input to produce nonlinear trends in the development of conservationlike performance.

Broadening psychological theory to include rules for applying cognitive skills, as well as statements about the skills themselves, seems absolutely necessary.

However, the extensions contemplated may well not be sufficient to meet all of Labov's objections to inferences about linguistic deprivation. In both the position expressed by Flavell and Wohlwill and by Mehler and Bever, competence is seen as dependent on situational factors and seems to be a slowly changing process that might well be governed by the same factors that lead to increases in the power of the structural rules or competence, in the older sense of the word. Yet in Labov's example, the problem is considerably more ephemeral; Labov gives the impression that the subjects were engaged in rational problem solving and that they had complete control over their behavior. He is claiming, in effect, that they are successfully coping with their problem; it simply is not the problem the experimenter had in mind, so the experimenter claims lack of competence as a result of his own ignorance.

Acceptance of Labov's criticisms, and we think they should be accepted, requires not only a broadening of our idea of competence, but a vast enrichment of our approach to experimentation.

Necessity of a Comparative Psychology of Cognition

If we accept the idea that situational factors are often important determinants of psychological performance, and if we also accept the idea that different cultural groups are likely to respond differently to any given situation, there seems to be no reasonable alternative to psychological experimentation that bases its inferences on data from comparisons of both experimental and situational variations.

In short, we are contending that Brunswik's (8) call for "representative design" and an analysis of the "ecological significance" of stimulation is a prerequisite to research on ethnic and social class differences in particular, and to any research where the groups to be compared are thought to differ with respect to the process under investigation prior to application of the experimental treatments.

Exhortations to the effect that college sophomores with nonsense syllables and white rats in boxes are not sufficient objects for the development of a general psychological theory have produced, thus far, only minor changes in the behavior of psychologists. The present situations seem to require a change.

An illustration from some recent cross-cultural research serves as an illustration of one approach that goes beyond the usual two-group design to explore the situational nature of psychological performance.

Cole, Gay, Glick, and Sharp (13, p. 4) used the free-recall technique to study cultural differences in memory. The initial studies presented subjects with a list of twenty words divided into four familiar, easily distinguishable categories. Subjects were read the list of words and asked to recall them. The procedure was repeated five times for each subject. A wide variety of subject populations was studied in this way; Liberian rice farmers and school children were the focus of concern, but comparison with groups in the United States was also made.

Three factors of the Kpelle rice farmers' performance were remarkable in these first studies: (*a*) The number recalled was relatively small (nine to eleven items per list); (*b*) there was no evidence of semantic or other organization of the material; (*c*) there was little or no increase in the number recalled with successive trials.

Better recall, great improvement with trials, and significant organization are all characteristic of performance of the American groups above the fifth grade.

A series of standard experimental manipulations (offering incentives, using lists based on functional rather than semantic classes, showing the objects to be remembered, extending the number of trials) all failed to make much difference in Kpelle performance.

However, when these same to-be-recalled items were incorporated into folk stories, when explicit grouping procedures were introduced, or when seemingly bizarre cuing procedures were used, Kpelle performance manifested organization, showed vast improvements in terms of amount recalled, and gave a very different picture of underlying capacity. Cole, Gay, Glick, and Sharp (13) concluded that a set of rather specific skills associated with remembering disconnected material out of context underlies the differences observed in the standard versions of the free-recall experiment with which they began. Moreover, they were able to begin the job of pinpointing these skills, their relevance to traditional activities, and the teaching techniques that could be expected to bring existing memory skills to bear in the alien tasks of the school.

Conclusion

The arguments set forth in this study can now be brought together and generalized in terms of their bearing on psychological research that is comparative in nature—comparing ages, cultures, subcultures, species, or even groups receiving different experimental treatments.

The central thesis derives from a re-examination of the distinction between competence and performance. As a rule, one looks for performance at its best and infers the degree of underlying competence from the observed performance. With respect to linguistic competence, for example, a single given instance of a particular grammatical form could suffice for inferring that the speaker had the competence to generate such instances as needed. By the use of such a methodology, Labov demonstrated that culturally deprived black children, tested appropriately for optimum performance, have the same grammatical competence as middle-class whites, though it may be expressed in different settings. Note that negative evidence is mute with respect to the status of underlying capacity—it may require a different situation for its manifestation.

The psychological status of the concept of competence (or capacity) is brought deeply into question when one examines conclusions based on standard experiments. Competence so defined is both situation blind and culture blind. If performance is treated (as it often is by linguists) only as a shallow expression of deeper competence, then one inevitably loses sight of the ecological problem of performance. For one of the most important things about any underlying competence is the nature of the situations in which it expresses itself. Herein lies the crux of the problem. One must inquire, first, whether a competence is expressed in a particular situation and, second, what the significance of that situation is for the person's ability to cope with life in his own milieu. As we have had occasion to comment elsewhere, when we systematically study the situational determinants of performance, we are led to conclude that cultural differences reside more in differences in the situations to which different cultural groups apply their skills than to differences in the skills possessed by the groups in question (13, Chap. 7).

The problem is to identify the range of capacities readily manifested in different groups and then to inquire whether the range is adequate to the individual's needs in various cultural settings. From this point of view, cultural deprivation represents a special case of cultural difference that arises when an individual is faced with demands to perform in a manner inconsistent with his past (cultural) experience. In the present social context of the United States, the great power of the middle class has rendered differences into deficits because middle-class behavior is the yardstick of success.

Our analysis holds at least two clear implications of relevance to the classroom teacher charged with the task of educating children from disadvantaged subcultural groups.

First, recognition of the educational difficulties in terms of a difference rather than a special kind of intellectual disease should change the students' status in the eyes of the teacher. If Pygmalion really can work in the classroom (37), the effect of this change in attitude may of itself produce changes in performance. Such difference in teacher attitude seems to be one prime candidate for an explanation of the fine performance obtained by Kohl (30) and others with usually recalcitrant students.

Second, the teacher should stop laboring under the impression that he must create new intellectual structures and start concentrating on how to get the child to transfer skills he already possesses to the task at hand. It is in this context that relevant study materials become important, although *relevant* should mean something more than a way to motivate students. Rather, relevant materials are those to which the child already applies skills the teacher seeks to have applied to his own content. It requires more than a casual acquaintance with one's students to know what those materials are.

The Soviet psychologist, Lev Vygotsky (43), took as the motto of his well-known monograph on language and thought an epigraph from Francis Bacon: Neither hand nor mind alone, left to themselves, amounts to much; instruments and aids are the means to perfection.[2] Psychologists concerned with comparative research, and comparisons of social and ethnic group differences in particular, must take seriously the study of the way different groups organize the relation between their hands and minds; without assuming the superiority of one system over another, they must take seriously the dictum that man is a cultural animal. When cultures are in competition for resources, as they are today, the psychologist's task is to analyze the source of cultural difference so that those of the minority, the less powerful group, may quickly acquire the intellectual instruments necessary for success of the dominant culture, should they so choose.

References

1. BEE, H. L.; VAN EGEREN, L. F.; STREISSGUTH, A. P.; NYMAN, B. A.; and LECKIE, M. S. 1969. Social class differences in maternal teaching strategies and speech patterns. *Developmental Psychology* 1:726–34.
2. BEREITER, C., and ENGLEMANN, S. 1966. *Teaching disadvantaged children in the preschool.* Englewood Cliffs, N.J.: Prentice-Hall.
3. BERNSTEIN, B. 1961. Social class and linguistic development: a theory of social learning. In *Education, economy and society,* ed. A. H. Halsey, J. Floyd, and C. A. Anderson. Glencoe, Ill.: Free Press.
4. BERNSTEIN, B. 1970. A sociolinguistic approach to socialization: with some references to educability. In *Language and poverty,* ed. F. Williams. Chicago: Markham.
5. BLANK, M., and SOLOMON, F. 1969. A tutorial language program to develop abstract thinking in socially disadvantaged preschool children. *Child Development* 40:47–61.
6. BLOOM, B. S. 1964. *Stability and change in human characteristics.* New York: Wiley.
7. BRUNER, J. S. 1970. *Poverty and childhood.* Merrill-Palmer Institute Monographs.
8. BRUNSWIK, E. 1958. *Representative design in the planning of psychological research.* Berkeley: University of California Press.
9. CALDWELL, B. M. 1970. Infant day care and attachment. *American Journal of Orthopsychiatry* 40:397–412.
10. CAMPBELL, D. 1961. The mutual methodological relevance of anthropology and psychology. In *Psychological anthropology,* ed. F. L. K. Hsu. Homewood, Ill.: Dorsey Press.
11. CAZDEN, C. 1970. The neglected situation. In *Language and poverty,* ed. F. Williams. Chicago: Markham Press.

[2] *Nec manus nisi intellectus sibi permissus multam valent; instrumentibus et auxiliis res perficitur.*

12. CHOMSKY, N. 1966. *Cartesian linguistics.* New York: Harper and Row.
13. COLE, M.; GAY, J.; GLICK, J.; and SHARP, D. W. 1971. *The cultural context of learning and thinking.* New York: Basic Books.
14. DEUTSCH, M. 1967. *The disadvantaged child.* New York: Basic Books.
15. EIFERMANN, R. 1968. *School children's games.* Washington, D.C.: Department of Health, Education, and Welfare.
16. FLAVELL, J. H., and WOHLWILL, J. F. 1969. Formal and functional aspects of cognitive development. In *Studies in cognitive development,* ed. D. Elkind and J. H. Flavell. New York: Oxford University Press.
17. GARFINKLE, H. 1967. *Studies in ethnomethodology.* Englewood Cliffs, N.J.: Prentice-Hall.
18. GAY, J., and COLE, M. 1967. *The new mathematics and an old culture.* New York: Holt, Rinehart and Winston.
19. GLADWIN, T. 1970. *East is a big bird.* Cambridge, Mass.: Belknap Press.
20. GOFFMAN, E. 1964. The neglected situation. In The ethnology of communication, ed. J. Gumperz and D. Hymes. *American Anthropologist* 66(6, pt. 2):133.
21. GREENBERG, J. 1963. *Universals of language.* Cambridge, Mass.: MIT Press.
22. HERTZIG, M. E.; BIRCH, H. G.; THOMAS, A.; and MENDEZ, O. A. 1968. Class and ethnic differences in the responsiveness of preschool children to cognitive demands. *Monographs of the Society for Research in Child Development* 33(1, ser. no. 117).
23. HESS, R. D., and SHIPMAN, V. 1965. Early experience and socialization of cognitive modes in children. *Child Development* 36:869–86.
24. HYMES, D. 1966. *On communicative competence.* Report of a Conference on Research Planning on Language Development among Disadvantaged Children. New York: Yeshiva University Press.
25. JENSEN, A. 1969. How much can we boost IQ and scholastic achievement? *Harvard Educational Review* 39:1–123.
26. JOHN, V. P., and GOLDSTEIN, L. S. 1964. The social context of language acquisition. *Merrill-Palmer Quarterly* 10:265–75.
27. KAGAN, J. 1969. Inadequate evidence and illogical conclusions. *Harvard Educational Review* 39:274–77.
28. KAGAN, J., and KOGAN, N. 1970. Individuality and cognitive performance. In *Manual of child psychology,* ed. P. Mussen. New York: Wiley.
29. KLAUS, R., and GRAY, S. 1968. The early training project for disadvantaged children: a report after five years. *Monographs of the Society for Research in Child Development* 33(4).
30. KOHL, H. 1967. *36 children.* New York: New American Library.
31. KROEBER, A. L. 1948. *Anthropology.* New York: Harcourt, Brace.
32. LABOV, W. 1970. The logical non-standard English. In *Language and poverty,* ed. F. Williams. Chicago: Markham Press.
33. LÉVI-STRAUSS, C. 1963. *Structural anthropology.* Trans. C. Jacobson and B. Grundfest Scharpf. New York: Basic Books.
34. MEHLER, J., and BEVER, T. 1968. The study of competence in cognitive psychology. *International Journal of Psychology* 3:273–80.
35. MISCHEL, W. 1966. Theory and research on the antecedents of self-imposed delay of reward. In *Progress in experimental personality research,* vol. 3. New York: Academic Press.
36. PRICE-WILLIAMS, D. R. A. 1961. A study concerning concepts of conservation of quantities among primitive children. *Acta Psychologia* 18:297–305.
37. ROSENTHAL, R., and JACOBSON, L. 1968. *Pygmalion in the classroom.* New York: Holt, Rinehart and Winston.
38. SCHEGLOFF, E. A. 1968. Sequencing in conversational openings. *American Anthropologist* 70:1075–95.
39. SCHOGGEN, M. November 7, 1969. An ecological study of three-year-olds at home. Nashville, Tenn.: George Peabody College for Teachers.
40. SMILANSKY, S. 1968. The effect of certain learning conditions on the progress of

disadvantaged children of kindergarten age. *Journal of School Psychology* 4(3):68–81.

41. STEWART, W. A. 1970. Toward a history of American Negro dialect. In *Language and poverty,* ed. F. Williams. Chicago: Markham Press.
42. TYLER, S. 1970. *Cognitive anthropology.* New York: Holt, Rinehart and Winston.
43. VYGOTSKY, L. S. 1962. *Thought and language.* Ed. and trans. E. Hanfmann and G. Vakar. New York: Wiley, and Cambridge, Mass.: MIT Press.
44. ZIGLER, E., and BUTTERFIELD, E. 1968. Motivational aspects of changes in IQ test performance of culturally deprived nursery school children. *Child Development* 39:1–14.

27

Education as Social Invention*

I shall take it as self-evident that each generation must define afresh the nature, direction, and aims of education to assure such freedom and rationality as can be attained for a future generation. For there are changes both in circumstances and in knowledge that impose constraints on and give opportunities to the teacher in each succeeding generation. It is in this sense that education is in constant process of invention. I should like particularly to comment upon four changes in our own time that require consideration in thinking about education.

The first of these derives from our increasing understanding of man as a species. As one reads the enormously rich reports of the last decade or two, it is plain that there has been a revolution that forces us to reconsider what it is we do when we occupy man's long growing period in certain ways now familiar as schooling.

A second basis for redefining education is the increase in our understanding of the nature of individual mental growth. There have been profound reorientations in developmental theory in the last generation, changes that have been hastened by studies of normal and pathological

* "Education as Social Invention," by Jerome S. Bruner. Reprinted by permission of the publishers from Jerome S. Bruner, *Toward a Theory of Instruction,* Cambridge, Mass.: The Belknap Press of Harvard University Press, Copyright, 1966, by the President and Fellows of Harvard College. Originally in *Journal of Social Issues,* 1964, Vol. XX, No. 3.

growth, by analyses of the effects of different types of early environments, by studies of the development of language and its impact on thought. All of this work has forced us to reconsider the role of man's symbolic operations.

Third, there is reason to believe that we have come to understand the process of education somewhat more clearly than before. This has been a decade of intense educational experiment involving many of the finest minds of our generation. It has given me pause to see in what measure an eight-year-old can be led to grasp what a poem is, or come to a conception of the conservation of momentum, or arrive slowly but surely at the powerful generality of a quadratic function as a set of sets in which the elements in each set are the same as the number of sets.

Finally, and most obviously, the rate of change in the society in which we live forces us to redefine how we shall educate a new generation. John Dewey's *My Pedagogic Creed,* a movingly concerned document, rests principally upon reflections of the author prior to the first Great War—a yearningly long time ago.

I shall consider each of these matters; but before I do, I must confess some of my own doubts. It is reasonably plain to me, as a psychologist, that however able psychologists may be, it is not their function to decide upon educational goals any more than the ablest general decides whether a nation should or should not be at war. Whatever I know about policy making reinforces the conviction that technicians and scientists often lack the kind of follow-up commitment that is the requisite of wise social policy. I cannot work up much enthusiasm for philosopher kings, psychologist kings, doctor kings, or even mixed-committee kings. The political process—and decisions about the aims of education must work their way through that process—is slow, perhaps, but is committed to the patient pursuit of the possible.

Yet it is also clear that generals do in fact have a strong influence on the politics of war and peace and that scientists have had and will have a powerful influence on our defense and other policies. What is not so clear is the distinction between ends and means, between goals and their implementation. And perhaps it is just as well, for there is an intuitive familiarity that generals have with what is possible and what is not possible in war and in containing its threat, and there is a certain familiarity that psychologists have with how one can get somebody to learn or to pay attention or to stay free of anxiety. While these are not ends in the strict sense, they shape our ends in educational policy as in defense policy. It is, if you will, the psychologist's lively sense of what is possible that can make him a powerful force. If he fails to fill his role as a diviner and delineator of the possible, then he does not serve the society wisely. If he confuses his function and narrows his vision of the possible to what he counts as desirable, then we shall all be the poorer. He can and must provide the full range of alternatives to challenge the society to choice. And now back to the main theme.

How to evaluate education in the light of our newly gained knowledge of man as a species? Let me begin by proposing a view that might best be called evolutionary instrumentalism. Man's use of mind is dependent upon his ability to develop and use tools or instruments or technologies that make it possible for him to express and amplify his powers. His very evolution as a species speaks to this point. It was consequent upon the development of bipedalism and the use of spontaneous pebble tools that man's brain and particularly his cortex developed. It was not a large-brained hominid that developed the technical-social life of the human; rather it was the tool-using, co-operative pattern that gradually changed man's morphology by favoring the survival of those who could link themselves with tool systems and disfavoring those who tried to go it on big jaws, heavy dentition, or superior weight. What evolved as a human nervous system was something, then, that required outside devices for expressing its potential. It was a swift progress. The first primitive primates appeared 5,000,000 years ago and man reached his present morphology and brain size about 500,000 years ago—with the major development of higher hominid to tool user occupying probably less than 500,000 of the years between. From then on, all major changes in the species were, in Weston La Barre's (2) startling phrase, by prosthetic devices, by man's learning how to link himself to amplifiers of his muscles, of his senses, and of his powers of ratiocination.

The British biologist Peter Medawar (3) remarks that it is likely that at about this same point in human history human culture became sufficiently elaborated for evolution to become Lamarckian and reversible rather than Darwinian and irreversible. It is a figure of speech, of course, but Medawar's point is well taken: What is transmitted by the culture is indeed a pool of acquired characteristics, a pool that can get lost just as surely as the Easter Islanders, the Incas, and the Mayas lost whatever skills made it possible for them to leave such splendid ruins to disabled descendants whose genes were probably not one whit changed.

I know that the terms *tool* and *technology* and even *instrument* offend when one speaks of man as dependent upon them for the realization of his humanity. For these words denote hardware, and it is mostly software that I have in mind—skills that are tools. Language is perhaps the ideal example of one such powerful technology, with its power not only for communication but for encoding reality, for representing matters remote as well as immediate, and for doing all these things according to rules that permit us both to represent reality and to transform it by conventional yet appropriate rules. All of this depends on the external resources of a grammar, a lexicon, and (likely as not) a supporting cast of speakers constituting the linguistic community.

Language happens to be a tool of the most general sort, in the sense that it provides direction and amplification for the way we use our muscular apparatus, our senses, and our powers of reflection. But each of these domains also has its skills that are expressed through various kinds of tool using. There are time- and strengthsaving skills for using our muscles, and they are built into the tools we devise for them. There are attentionsaving skills in perception that are imparted and then become the basis for understanding the icons we construct for representing things by drawing, diagram, and design. And there are, finally and most importantly, strain-reducing heuristics to help us figure out things—how to cancel out nuisance parameters, how to use our heads and save our heels, how to make quick but decent approximations, and so on.

Many of these skills are taught in the subtle interaction of parent and child—as in the case of primary linguistic skills. And, as in the case of language learning, where the pedagogy is highly unselfconscious, it is probably true that most of the primitive skills of manipulating and looking and attending are also taught in this way. It is when the society goes beyond these relatively primitive techniques that the less spontaneous instruction of school must be relied upon. At this point the culture necessarily comes to rely upon its formal education as a means of providing skills. And insofar as there has been any innovation in tools or tool using (taking these expressions in the broadest sense), the educational system is the sole means of dissemination—the sole agent of evolution, if you will.

Consider now our understanding of the nature of human ontogenetic development. Several important conclusions stand out. None of them, so far as I know, have been seriously considered in defining the aims and conduct of education.

The first is that mental growth is not a gradual accretion, either of associations or of stimulus-response connections or of means-end readinesses or of anything else. It appears to be much more like a staircase with rather sharp risers, more a matter of spurts and rests. The spurts ahead in growth seem to be touched off when certain capacities begin to develop. And some capacities must be matured and nurtured before others can be called into being. The sequence of their appearance is highly constrained. But these steps or stages or spurts or whatever you may choose to call them are not very clearly linked to age: Some environments can slow the sequence down or bring it to a halt, others move it along faster. In the main, one can characterize these constrained sequences as a series of prerequisites. It is not until the child can hold in mind two features of a display at once, for example, that he can deal with their relationship, as in a ratio.

The steps or stages have been variously described by a variety of investigators working in centers as widely separated as Geneva, Moscow, Paris, London, Montreal, Chicago, and Cambridge, but they seem to have an interesting likeness, even though the proposed dynamism varies. The first stages are relatively manipulative, marked by highly unstable and single-track attention. Knowing is principally knowing how to do, and there is minimum reflection. There follows a period of more reflective functioning in which the young human being is capable of an internal representation, by representative images, of greater chunks of the environment. The high point in this stage is between five and seven. Finally, something very special happens around adolescence, when language becomes increasingly important as a medium of thought. It is evidenced by an ability to consider propositions rather than objects; concepts become more exclusively hierarchical in structure; alternative possibilities can be handled in a combinatorial fashion. There is considerable doubt whether these things have anything directly to do with the onset of physiological adolescence—for there are equally sharp cognitive turning points at the onset of language and at the age five-to-seven turning point without much discernible assist from hormonal tides. And hormonal adolescents in technically less mature societies do not enter this stage.

What comes out of this picture, rough though I have sketched it, is a view of human beings who have developed three parallel systems for processing information and for representing it—one through manipulation and action, one through perceptual organization and imagery, and one through symbolic apparatus. It is not that these are stages in any sense; they are rather emphases in development. You must get the perceptual field organized around your own person as center before you can impose other, less egocentric axes upon it, for example. In the end, the mature organism seems to have gone through a process of elaborating three systems of skills that correspond to the three major tool systems to which he must link himself for full expression of his capacities—tools for the hand, for the distance receptors, and for the process of reflection.

It is not surprising in the light of this that early opportunities for development have loomed so large in our recent understanding of human mental growth. The importance of early experience is only dimly sensed today. The evidence from animal studies indicates that virtually irreversible deficits can be produced in mammals by depriving them of opportunities that challenge their nascent capacities. In the last few years there have been reports showing the crippling effect of deprived human environments, as well as indications that replacement therapies can be of considerable success, even at an age on the edge of adolescence. The principal deficits appear to be linguistic in the broadest sense—the lack of opportunity to share in dialogue, to have occasion for paraphrase, to internalize speech as a vehicle of thought. None of these matters are well understood, save that the principle discussed earlier seems to be operative, that, unless certain basic skills are mastered, later, more elaborated ones become increasingly out of reach. It is in light of this fact that we can understand the increasing difference of intelligence with age between such culturally deprived groups as rural Southern Negroes and more culturally privileged whites. In time, and with sufficient failure, the gap is reinforced to irreversibility by a sense of defeat.

What has been learned about the educational process that may give guidance to our task of redefinition? Very little that is certain, but some extremely interesting impressions that can possibly be converted into testable hypotheses.

The curriculum revolution has made it plain that the idea of readiness is a mischievous half-truth. It is a half-truth largely because it turns out that one teaches readiness or provides opportunities for its nurture, one does not simply wait for it. Readiness, in these terms, consists of mastery of those simpler skills that permit one to reach higher skills. Readiness for Euclidian geometry can be gained by teaching intuitive geometry or by giving children an opportunity to build increasingly elaborate constructions with polygons. Or, to take the aim of the new, second-generation mathematics project,[1] if you wish to teach the calculus in the eighth grade, then begin it in the first grade by teaching the kinds of ideas and skills necessary for its mastery later. Mathematics is no exception to the general rule, though admittedly it is the most easily understood from the point of view of what must be clear before something else can be grasped. Since most subjects can be translated into forms that place emphasis upon doing, or upon the development of appropriate imagery, or upon symbolic-verbal encoding, it is often possible to render the end result to be achieved in a simpler, more manageable form so that the child can move more easily and deeply to full mastery.

The second thing that emerges from pedagogic experiments of the last decade is that cognitive or intellectual mastery is rewarding. It is particularly so when the learner recognizes the cumulative power of learning, that learning one thing permits him to go on to something that before was out of reach, and so on toward such perfection as one may reach. It is a truth that every good athletic coach since the Greek Olympics has known. Teachers also gain pleasure when a student learns to recognize his own progress well enough so that he can take over as his own source of reward and punishment.

A third result of contemporary exploration in teaching is the conclusion

---

[1] See the report of the Cambridge Conference on School Mathematics, *Goals for School Mathematics* (Boston: Houghton Mifflin, 1963).

that educational experiment, in the main, has been conducted and is being conducted in the dark—without feedback in usable form. The substitute for light (or usable feedback) is evaluation after the job has been completed. After the working party has been scattered, the evaluators enter. By then, it is so late in the day that only patching can be done. Indeed, such is the latitude in the choice of criteria for evaluation that something nice can usually be said about practically any course or curriculum. It would seem much more sensible to put evaluation into the picture before and during curriculum construction, as a form of intelligence operation to help the curriculum maker in his choice of material, in his approach, in his manner of setting tasks for the learner.

Finally, one is struck by the absence of a theory of instruction as a guide to pedagogy—a prescriptive theory on how to proceed in order to achieve various results, a theory that is neutral with respect to ends but exhaustive with respect to means. It is interesting that there is a lack of an integrating theory in pedagogy, that in its place there is principally a body of maxims.

As our technology grows increasingly complex in both machinery and human organization, the role of the school becomes more central in the society, not simply as an agent of socialization, but as a transmitter of basic skills. To this we turn next as our final basis for redefining education—the changing society.

In recent years I have wondered, particularly in connection with work in West Africa, why societies are not more mindful of the role of education in shaping their futures. Why in Africa, for example, is the short-term political allure of universal primary education given priority over training a corps of administrators, teachers, and technicians? In many cases, the second is financially precluded by the first, and the long-run result may prove a terrible time bomb as semiliterate youths flock into the new urban Africa with no marketable skills, their familial and tribal boats burned, and no properly trained corps of teachers and civil servants to maintain stability or to teach the untrained.

That is what set me brooding, and while I have no answer to the African problem, I do have some thoughts about our own. They crystallized while reading an essay by the distinguished Italian architect-designer Pier Luigi Nervi (4). Nervi describes the loss in freedom of the architect-designer in an age of technological maturity. You can build a road or a path in any meandering shape you wish, provided the only users are men on foot, or on horse, or in wagons, or in slow cars. But the moment the speed of the vehicle passes a certain critical point, fantasy is constrained and you must conform to the idea of a containing arc. A car traveling at 70 miles per hour cannot turn on a fanciful curlicue.

There was a great deal of public soul-searching at the time of Sputnik as to whether our educational system was adequate to the task ahead. In fact, much new curriculum reform had started before then—out of a sense of the frightening gap between expert knowledge of our technology and public knowledge. I rather suspect that there will never again be such a period of careless or ritualistic regard for public education—but, then, universal public education as a working concept is not yet a century old!

It may well be the case that not only are we entering a period of technological maturity in which education will require constant redefinition, but that the period ahead may involve such a rapid rate of change in specific technology that narrow skills will become obsolete within a reasonably short time after their acquisition. Indeed, perhaps one of the defining properties of a highly matured technology is that there exists a lively likelihood of major technological change within the compass of a single generation—just as ours has seen several such major changes.

I entertained myself and some young students with whom I was working during the summer of 1964 on a social-studies curriculum by formulating Bruner's Rule—critical changes related to the order of magnitude in years away. I used this as an extension of the square law for the retinal angle—that the size of the retinal image is the reciprocal of the square of the distance of an object from the eye. Therefore, the further away a period of time, the longer its duration in order to be discerned! And so:

5×10^9	5,000,000,000	Birth of earth
5×10^8	500,000,000	Vertebrates
5×10^7	50,000,000	Mammals
5×10^6	5,000,000	Primates
5×10^5	500,000	Present man
5×10^4	50,000	Great glacial migrations
5×10^3	5,000	Recorded history
5×10^2	500	Printing
5×10^1	50	Radio / mass education
5×10^0	5	Artificial intelligence

What I learned from my pupils was their conclusion that things were coming thick and fast. Life probably started about 2.5×10^9, so that half the history of the earth was lifeless. Some 99.999 per cent of the earth's life has been manless, and from there on out the record is impressive and awesome. It would seem, indeed, as if the principal thing about tools and techniques is that they beget other more advanced ones at ever-increasing speed. And as the technology matures in this way, education in its very nature takes on an increasing role by providing the skills needed to manage and control the expanding enterprise.

The first response of educational systems under such acceleration is to produce technicians and engineers and scientists as needed, but it is doubtful whether such a priority produces what is required to manage the enterprise. For no specific science or technology provides a metalanguage in terms of which to think about a society, its technology, its science, and the constant changes that these undergo with innovation. Could an automotive engineer have foreseen the death of smalltown America with the advent of the automobile? He would have been so wedded to his task of making better and better automobiles that it would never have occurred to him to consider the town, the footpath, leisure, or local loyalty. Somehow, if change is to be managed, it requires men with skills in sensing continuity and opportunity for continuity. This is a matter to which we shall return shortly.

What may we conclude from all this? It seems to me that four general policies follow from the issues that we have passed in review.

The first has to do with what is taught. It would seem, from our consideration of man's evolution, that principal emphasis in education should be placed upon skills—skills in handling, in seeing and imaging, and in symbolic operations, particularly as these relate to the technologies that have made them so powerful in their human expression.

It is hard to spell out in specific terms what such an emphasis upon skills entails, but some examples might provide a concrete basis for criticism. With respect, first, to the education of the perceptual-imaginal capacities, I can suggest at least one direction to travel. It is in the training of subtle spatial imagery. I have been struck by the increased visual power and subtlety of students exposed to courses in visual design—all differently conceived and with different objectives in view: one for undergraduates given by I. A. Richards at Harvard, another for teachers by Bartlett Hayes at Andover, and a third for city planners given by Gyorgy Kepes and Kevin Lynch at MIT. All of them produced what seemed to me like fresh discrimination in viewing the altered environment of urban America; all provided the students with new models in terms of which to analyze and sort their surroundings. Gerald Holton and Edward Purcell have been experimenting with instruction in visual pattern as a mode of increasing the visualizing subtlety of concentrators in physics—visual subtlety and capacity to represent events visually and nonmetrically. I do not think that we have begun to scratch the surface of training in visualization—whether related to the arts, to science, or simply to the pleasures of viewing our environments more richly. Let me note in passing that Maria Montessori, that strange blend of the mystic and the pragmatist, was groping toward some such conception as this.

At the level of symbolic operation, I think the work of Martin Deutsch (1) with underprivileged children provides an interesting case in point—a conscious effort to lead children to verbal skills, to a sense of paraphrase and exchange. Such an effort surely should not be limited to the underprivileged. The new mathematics curricula illustrate how much can be done in training symbolic skills.

This brings us immediately to a second conclusion. It relates literally to the meaning of the word *curriculum,* a word that derives from a course to be run. It is perhaps a wrong word. A curriculum should involve the mastery of skills that in turn lead to the mastery of still more powerful ones, the establishment of self-reward sequences. It is clear that this can be done in mathematics and science. But it is also the case that reading simpler poetry brings more complex poetry into reach, or that reading a poem once makes a second reading more rewarding. The reward of deeper understanding is a more robust lure to effort than we have yet realized.

A corollary of this conclusion (one I have urged before) is that there is an appropriate version of any skill or knowledge that may be imparted at whatever age one wishes to begin teaching—however preparatory the version may be. The choice of the earlier version is based upon what it is one is hoping to cumulate. The deepening and enrichment of this earlier understanding is again a source of reward for intellectual labors.

The third conclusion relates to change. If there is any way of adjusting to change, it must include, as we have noted, the development of a metalanguage and metaskills for dealing with continuity in change. What these might be is, of course, a moot point, but not completely so by any means. Mathematics is surely the most general metalanguage we have developed, and it provides the forms and patterns in terms of which regularities in nature are comprehended. I find myself forced to the conclusion that our survival may one day depend upon achieving a requisite mathematical literacy for rendering the seeming shocks of change into something that is continuous and cumulative. But, by the same token, there is a second discipline that deals with the search for likeness beneath the surface of diversity and change. It is, of course, the discipline of poetry, the vehicle for searching out unsuspected kinship.

A further speculation about preparation for change is that we are bound to move toward instruction in the sciences of behavior and away from the study of history. Recorded history is only about 5,000 years old, as we saw. Most of what we teach is within the last few centuries, for the records before that are minimal while the records after are relatively rich. But just suppose that the richness of record increases as a function of our ability to develop systems for storing and retrieving information. A thousand years from now we will be swamped. One would surely not dwell then with such loving care over the details of Brumaire or the Long Parliament or the Louisiana Purchase. These are the furbelows of documentary short supply. But there is a more compelling reason to shift away from history toward the social or behavioral sciences.

It has to do with the need for studying the possible rather than the achieved—a necessary step if we are to adapt to change. It is the behavioral sciences and their generality with respect to variations in the human condition that must be central to our presentation of man, not the particularities of his history. This is not to say that we should give up study of the past, but rather that we should pursue such study with a different end in view—the end of developing style. For the development of style, be it style of writing or loving or dancing or eating, requires a sense of contrast and concreteness, and this we do not find in the behavioral sciences.

Finally, it is plain that if we are to evolve freely as a species by the use of the instrument of education, then we shall have to bring far greater resources to bear in designing our educational system. For one thing, if we are to respond to accelerated change, then we shall have to reduce turn-around time in the system. To do this requires greater participation on the part of those at the frontiers of learning. A distinguished mathematician and teacher, John Kemeny, did a survey of high-school mathematics teaching in the mid-1950s and found no mathematics newer than a hundred years old being taught! That has been remedied somewhat since, but the work has hardly begun.

Another resource that must be brought to bear is modern psychology. Something happened to educational psychology a few decades ago that brought it to the low status it now enjoys. The circumstances need not concern us save in one respect. Part of the failure of educational psychology was its failure to grasp the full scope of its mission. It has too readily assumed that its central task was the application of personality theory or of group dynamics or what not. In fact, none of these efforts produced a major contribution to educational practice, largely because the task was not really one of application in any obvious sense, but of formulation. Learning theory, for example, is distilled from descriptions of behavior in situations where the environment has been arranged either for the convenience of observing learning behavior or out of a theoretical interest in some special aspect of learning—reinforcement, cue distinctiveness, or whatever. But a theory of instruction, which must be at the heart of educational psychology, is principally concerned with how to arrange environments to optimize learning according to various criteria—to optimize transfer or retrievability of information, for example. Psychologists must re-enter the field of education in order to contribute to man's further evolution, an evolution that now proceeds through social invention. For it is psychology more than any other discipline that has the tools for exploring the limits of man's perfectibility. By doing so, it can, I think, have its major social impact by keeping lively the society's full sense of what is possible.

Aside from that, it becomes necessary for the various fields of learning to assess the manner in which they contribute to the amplification of mind —the way of doing or experiencing or ratiocinating that is integral to them and that should be part of the way of mind of an educated member of the culture. There are too many particulars to teach and to master. If we are to do justice to our evolution, we shall need, as never before, a way of transmitting the crucial ideas and skills, the acquired characteristics that express and amplify man's powers. We may be sure that the task will demand our highest talents. I would be content if we began, all of us, by recognizing that this is our task as learned men and scientists, that discovering how to make something comprehensible to the young is only a continuation of making something comprehensible to ourselves in the first place—that understanding and aiding others to understand are both of a piece.

References

1. DEUTSCH, M. 1963. The disadvantaged child and the learning process: some social psychological and developmental considerations. In *Education in depressed areas,* ed. A. H. Passow. New York: Teachers College Press.
2. LA BARRE, W. 1954. *The human animal.* Chicago: University of Chicago Press.
3. MEDAWAR, P. 1963. Onwards from Spencer: evolution and evolutionism. *Encounter* 21(3):35–43.
4. NERVI, P. L. 1965. Is architecture moving toward forms and characteristics which are unchangeable? In *Structure in art and science,* ed. G. Kepes. New York: Braziller.

Bibliography: Published Writings of Jerome S. Bruner

1939

Bruner, J. S., and Cunningham, B. The effect of thymus extract on the sexual behavior of the female rat. *Journal of Comparative Psychology* 27: 69–77.

McCulloch, T. L., and Bruner, J. S. The effect of electric shock upon subsequent learning in the rat. *Journal of Psychology* 7: 333–36.

1940

Bruner, J. S., and Allport, G. W. Fifty years of change in American psychology. *Psychological Bulletin* 37: 757–76.

1941

Allport, G. W.; Bruner, J. S.; and Jandorf, E. M. Personality under social catastrophe: ninety life histories of the Nazi revolution. *Charact. Pers.* 10: 1–22.

Bruner, J. S. The dimensions of propaganda: German short-wave broadcasts to America. *Journal of Abnormal and Social Psychology* 36: 311–37.

Bruner, J. S., and Bruner, K. F. The impact of revolution. *Saturday Review of Literature* 24 (36) (December 27): 3–4 ff.

Bruner, J. S., and Fowler, G. The strategy of terror: audience response to *Blitzkrieg im Westen*. *Journal of Abnormal and Social Psychology* 36: 561–74.

Bruner, J. S., and Sayre, J. Shortwave listening in an Italian community. *Public Opinion Quarterly* 5: 640–66.

1943

Bruner, J. S. How much post-war migration? *American Journal of Sociology* 49: 39–45.

Bruner, J. S. OWI and the American public. *Public Opinion Quarterly* 7: 125–33.

Bruner, J. S. Public thinking on post-war problems. *Planning Pamphlet No. 23*, National Planning Association, October.

1944

Bruner, J. S. *Mandate from the people*. New York: Duell, Sloan & Pearce. Translated into French.

Bruner, J. S. Public opinion and America's foreign policy. *American Sociological Review* 9: 50–56.

Bruner, J. S. Public opinion and the next president. *The Nation* (June 17), pp. 704–6.

Bruner, J. S. Public opinion and the peace. In *The second chance: America and the peace,* ed. J. B. Whitten. Princeton: Princeton University Press.

Bruner, J. S. Wanted—more effective management. *Forum and Column Review* (February).

1945

Bruner, J. S. Americans and Britain. *Transatlantic* (London) (January), pp. 23–27.

Bruner, J. S. Le peuple Americain et la paix. *Esprit* (Paris) (August 1), pp. 375–84.

Bruner, J. S. Public opinion and world order. In *Human nature and enduring peace,* ed. G. Murphy. Boston: Houghton Mifflin.

1946

Bruner, J. S. Review of C. A. Siepmann, *Radio's second chance* (1946). *Journal of Abnormal and Social Psychology* 41: 365–68.

Bruner, J. S., trans. and ed. of D. Lazard. Two years under a false name. *Journal of Abnormal and Social Psychology* 41: 161–68.

Bruner, J. S., and Brown, J. L. Contemporary France and educational reform. *Harvard Educational Review* 16: 10–20.

Bruner, J. S., and Korchin, S. J. The boss and the vote: case study in city politics. *Public Opinion Quarterly* 10: 1–23.

Postman, L., and Bruner, J. S. The reliability of constant errors in psychophysical measurement. *Journal of Psychology* 21: 293–99.

1947

Bruner, J. S. International research on social issues: a world survey. *Journal of Social Issues* 3: 38–53.

Bruner, J. S., ed. Toward a common ground: international social science. *Journal of Social Issues* 3(1).

Bruner, J. S., and Goodman, C. C. Value and need as organizing factors in perception. *Journal of Abnormal and Social Psychology* 42: 33–44.

Bruner, J. S., and Postman, L. Emotional selectivity in perception and reaction. *Journal of Personality* 16: 69–77.

Bruner, J. S., and Postman, L. Tension and tension-release as organizing factors in perception. *Journal of Personality* 15: 300–308.

Murphy, G.; Cartwright, D.; and Bruner, J. S. Resources for world-wide research in human sciences. *Journal of Social Issues* 3: 54–65.

Smith, M. B.; Bruner, J. S.; and White, R. W. A group research project on the dynamics and measurement of opinion. *International Journal of Opinion and Attitude Research* 1: 78–82.

1948

Burner, J. S. Perceptual theory and the Rorschach test. *Journal of Personality* 17: 157–68.

Bruner, J. S., and Postman, L. An approach to social perception. In *Current trends in social psychology,* ed. W. Dennis. Pittsburgh: University of Pittsburgh Press. Also trans. into French.

Bruner, J. S., and Postman, L. Symbolic value as an organizing factor in perception. *Journal of Social Psychology* 27: 203–8.

Postman, L., and Bruner, J. S. Perception under stress. *Psychological Review* 55: 314–23.

Postman, L.; Bruner, J. S.; and McGinnies, E. Personal values as selective factors in perception. *Journal of Abnormal and Social Psychology* 43: 142–54.

1949

Bauer, R. A.; Riecken, H. W.; and Bruner, J. S. An analysis of the stability of voting intentions: Massachusetts, 1948. *International Journal of Opinion and Attitude Research* 3: 169–78.

Bruner, J. S., and Postman, L. On the perception of incongruity: a paradigm. *Journal of Personality* 18: 206–23.

Bruner, J. S., and Postman, L. Perception, cognition and behavior. *Journal of Personality* 18: 14–31.

Bruner, J. S., and Smith, M. B. Review of D. Krech and R. S. Crutchfield, *Theory and problems of social psychology. Journal of Abnormal and Social Psychology* 44: 283–88.

Postman, L., and Bruner, J. S. Multiplicity of set as a determinant of perceptual behavior. *Journal of Experimental Psychology* 39: 369–77.

1950

Bruner, J. S. Public opinion and policy-making in the United States. Review of G. Almond, *The American people and foreign policy. World Politics* 2: 560–70.

Bruner, J. S. Social psychology and group processes. *Annual Review of Psychology* 1: 119–50.

Bruner, J. S., and Krech, D. *Perception and personality: a symposium.* Durham, N.C.: Duke University Press.

Bruner, J. S.; Postman, L.; and Mosteller, C. F. A note on the measurement of reversals of perspective. *Psychometrika* 15: 63–72.

1951

Bruner, J. S. One kind of perception: a reply to Professor Luchins. *Psychological Review* 58: 306–12.

Bruner, J. S. Personality dynamics and the process of perceiving. In *Perception: an approach to personality,* ed. R. R. Blake and G. V. Ramsey. New York: Ronald Press.

Bruner, J. S.; Postman, L.; and Rodrigues, J. Expectation and the perception of color. *American Journal of Psychology* 64: 216–27.

Postman, L.; Bruner, J. S.; and Walk, R. D. The perception of error. *British Journal of Psychology* 42: 1–10.

1952

Bruner, J. S.; Busiek, R. D.; and Minturn, A. L. Assimilation in the immediate reproduction of visually perceived figures. *Journal of Experimental Psychology* 43: 151–55.

Postman, L., and Bruner, J. S. Hypothesis and the principle of closure: the effect of frequency and recency. *Journal of Psychology* 33: 113–25.

1953

Austin, G. A.; Bruner, J. S.; and Seymour, R. V. Fixed choice strategies in concept attainment. *American Psychologist* 8: 315. Abstract.

Bruner, J. S., and Rodrigues, J. S. Some determinants of apparent size. *Journal of Abnormal and Social Psychology* 48: 17–24.

Tagiuri, R.; Blake, R. R.; and Bruner, J. S. Some determinants of the perception of positive and negative feelings in others. *Journal of Abnormal and Social Psychology* 48: 585–92.

1954

Bruner, J. S., and Tagiuri, R. The perception of people. In *Handbook of social psychology*, ed. G. Lindzey. Reading, Mass.: Addison-Wesley.

Jones, E. E., and Bruner, J. S. Expectancy in apparent visual movement. *British Journal of Psychology* 45: 157–65.

Matter, J.; Bruner, J. S.; and O'Dowd, D. D. "Response" vs. "principle" in reversal learning. *American Psychologist* 9: 427–28. Abstract.

Miller, G. A.; Bruner, J. S.; and Postman, L. Familiarity of letter sequences and tachistoscopic identification. *Journal of General Psychology* 50: 129–39.

O'Dowd, D. D.; Bruner, J. S.; and Austin, G. A. The effect of error on the identification of familiar sequences. *American Psychologist* 9: 443–44. Abstract.

1955

Bruner, J. S. Freud's legacy. Review of E. Jones, *Sigmund Freud: life and work*. vol. 2: *Years of maturity, 1901–1919*. *Sunday Times* (London) (October 2).

Bruner, J. S.; Matter, J.; and Papanek, M. L. Breadth of learning as a function of drive level and mechanization. *Psychological Review* 62: 1–10.

Bruner, J. S.; Miller, G. A.; and Zimmerman, C. Discriminative skill and discriminative matching in perceptual recognition. *Journal of Experimental Psychology* 49: 187–92.

Bruner, J. S., and Minturn, A. L. Perceptual identification and perceptual organization. *Journal of General Psychology* 53: 21–28.

Tagiuri, R.; Bruner, J. S.; and Kogan, N. Estimating the chance expectancies of diadic relationships within a group. *Psychological Bulletin* 52: 122–31.

Tagiuri, R.; Kogan, N.; and Bruner, J. S. The transparency of interpersonal choice. *Sociometry and the Science of Man* 18: 368–79.

1956

Bruner, J. S. A cognitive theory of personality. Review of G. A. Kelley, *The psychology of personal constructs*. *Contemporary Psychology* 1: 355–56.

Bruner, J. S. Freud and the image of man. *American Psychologist* 11: 463–66. Also in *On Knowing* (1962).

Bruner, J. S.; Goodnow, J. J.; and Austin, G. A. *A Study of Thinking*. New York: Wiley (paperback, Wiley Science Editions, 1962). Translated into Japanese, Hindi, Italian.

Jeeves, M. A., and Bruner, J. S. Directional information and apparent movement. *Journal of Experimental Psychology* 8: 107–13.

Smith, M. B.; Bruner, J. S.; and White, R. W. *Opinions and Personality*. New York: Wiley (paperback, Wiley Science Editions, 1964).

1957

Bruner, J. S. Comment on "Effect of overtraining on subsequent learning of incidental cues." *Psychological Review* 3: 317–320.

Bruner, J. S. Going beyond the information given. In *Contemporary approaches to cognition,* ed. H. Gruber et al. Cambridge, Mass.: Harvard University Press.

Bruner, J. S. Mechanism riding high. Review of K. W. Spence, *Behavior theory and conditioning. Contemporary Psychology* 2: 155–57.

Bruner, J. S. Neural mechanisms in perception. *Psychological Review* 64: 340–58.

Bruner, J. S. On perceptual readiness. *Psychological Review* 64: 123–52.

Bruner, J. S. What it takes to start an idea. In *The creative process,* ed. J. D. Scott. Michigan Advertising Papers No. 1, University of Michigan, Ann Arbor.

Bruner, J. S. What social scientists say about having an idea. *Printers Ink* 260(2) (July 12): 48–52.

Bruner, J. S., and Perlmutter, H. V. Compatriot and foreigner: a study of impression formation in three countries. *Journal of Abnormal and Social Psychology* 55: 253–60.

1958

Bruner, J. S. A colloquy on the unity of learning. *Daedalus* 87(4) (Fall): 155–65.

Bruner, J. S. The Freudian conception of man and the continuity of nature. *Daedalus* 87(1) (Winter): 77–84.

Bruner, J. S. The need for new myths. *The Colorado Quarterly* 7(2), (Autumn): 117–28.

Bruner, J. S. Social psychology and perception. In *Readings in social psychology,* ed. E. Maccoby, T. Newcomb, and E. Hartley. New York: Holt.

Bruner, J. S. Review of F. Bartlett, *Thinking: an experimental and social study. British Journal of Psychology* 49: 160–63.

Bruner, J. S.; Bresson, F.; Morf, A.; and Piaget, J. *Logique et perception.* Paris: Presses Universitaires de France.

Bruner, J. S.; Mandler, J. M.; O'Dowd, D.; and Wallach, M. A. The role of overlearning and drive level in reversal learning. *Journal of Comparative Physiology and Psychology* 51: 607–13.

Bruner, J. S., and O'Dowd, D. A note on the informativeness of parts of words. *Language and Speech* 1: 98–101.

Bruner, J. S.; Shapiro, D.; and Tagiuri, R. The meaning of traits in isolation and in combination. In *Person perception and interpersonal behavior,* ed. R. Tagiuri and L. Petrullo. Stanford, Calif.: Stanford University Press.

Bruner, J. S., and Wechsler, H. Sequential probability as a determinant of perceptual closure. *American Journal of Psychology* 71: 604–5.

Tagiuri, R.; Bruner, J. S.; and Blake, R. R. On the relation between feelings and the perception of feelings among members of small groups. In *Readings in Social Psychology,* ed. E. Maccoby, T. Newcomb, and E. Hartley. New York: Holt.

1959

Bruner, J. S. The art of ambiguity: a conversation with Zen master Hisamatsu. *Psychologia* 2: 101–6.

Bruner, J. S. The cognitive consequences of early sensory deprivation. *Psychosomatic Medicine* 21: 89–95.

Bruner, J. S. The economy of perceiving. *Proceedings of the 15th international congress of psychology, Brussels 1957.* Amsterdam: North Holland.

Bruner, J. S. Learning and thinking. *Harvard Educational Review* 29(3): 184–92.

Bruner, J. S. Myth and identity. *Daedalus* 88(2) (Spring): 349–58.Also in *On knowing* (1962).

Bruner, J. S. A psychologist's viewpoint. Review of B. Inhelder and J. Piaget, *The growth of logical thinking. British Journal of Psychology* 50: 363–70.

Bruner, J. S.; Wallach, M. A.; and Galanter, E. H. The identification of recurrent regularity. *American Journal of Psychology* 72: 200–209.

1960

Bruner, J. S. The anguished quest for identity. *Radcliffe Quarterly* (February), pp. 6–7.

Bruner, J. S. The functions of teaching. *Rhode Island College Journal* 1 (March): 2.

Bruner, J. S. Individual and collective problems in the study of thinking. *Annals of the New York Academy of Sciences* 91: 22–37.

Bruner, J. S. On learning mathematics. *The Mathematics Teacher* 53: 61–69. Also in *On knowing* (1962).

Bruner, J. S. *The process of education.* Cambridge: Harvard University Press (paperback, Random House Vintage Editions, 1963). Translated into Russian, Greek, Urdu, Japanese, Arabic, Spanish, Italian, Czech, Hungarian, Hebrew, Norwegian, Danish, Swedish, German, Polish, Slovak, Hindi, Portuguese, Dutch, Rumanian, French.

Bruner, J. S., and Klein, G. S. The functions of perceiving: new look retrospect. In *Perspectives in psychological theory: essays in honor of Heinz Werner,* B. Kaplan and S. Wapner. New York: International Universities Press.

1961

Bruner, J. S. The act of discovery. *Harvard Educational Review* 31: 21–32. Also in *On knowing* (1962).

Bruner, J. S. Affrontement et défense. *Journal de Psychologie* (France) 1: 33–56. English version, On coping and defending. In *Toward a theory of instruction* (1966).

Bruner, J. S. After John Dewey, what? *Saturday Review* (June 17), pp. 58–59ff. Also in *On knowing* (1962).

Bruner, J. S. Quelques observations sur le choix. *Journal de Psychologie* (France) 3: 271–89.

Bruner, J. S. Preface to W. McDougall, *Body and mind.* Boston: Beacon Press.

Bruner, J. S. Report of the working group on the application of technology to educational and cultural affairs, June 30, 1961. (See 1966 under Elliott, W. Y., for final published form of GETT report.)

Bruner, J. S., and Tajfel, H. Cognitive risk and environmental change. *Journal of Abnormal and Social Psychology* 62(2): 231–41.

1962

Bruner, J. S. Books, courses, and curricula. In *The challenge of change.* New York: American Textbook Publishers Institute.

Bruner, J. S. Introduction: the new educational technology. *American Behavioral Scientist* 4(3): 5.

Bruner, J. S. *On knowing: essays for the left hand*. Cambridge: Harvard University Press (paperback, New York: Atheneum, 1965). Translated into Polish, German, Japanese, Spanish, and Italian.

Bruner, J. S. Preface to L. S. Vygotsky, *Thought and language* (English translation). Cambridge, Mass.: MIT Press, and New York: Wiley.

1963

Bruner, J. S. How we learn and how we remember. *Harvard Alumni Bulletin* 66(4): 163 ff.

Bruner, J. S. Looking at the curriculum. *The Educational Courier* (Toronto) 33(3): 18–26.

Bruner, J. S. Needed: a theory of instruction. *Educational Leadership* 20(8): 523–32.

Bruner, J. S. School for wives. *The Winsor Club Bulletin* 30: 5–8.

Bruner, J. S. Structures in learning. *NEA Journal* 52(3): 26–27.

Bruner, J. S., and Kenney, H. Observations on the learning of mathematics. *Science Education News,* American Association for the Advancement of Science (April), pp. 1–5.

Bruner, J. S., and Olver, R. R. Development of equivalence transformations in children. *Monographs of the Society for Research in Child Development* 28(2) (ser. no. 86): 125–43.

1964

Bruner, J. S. The course of cognitive growth. *American Psychologist* 19: 1–15.

Bruner, J. S. Education as social invention. *Journal of Social Issues* 20(3): 21–33.

Bruner, J. S. Growing. *Proceedings of the 1963 invitational conference on testing problems*. Princeton: Educational Testing Service.

Bruner, J. S. Is well begun half done? *New directions in kindergarten programs: proceedings of the 1963 New England kindergarten conference.* Cambridge, Mass.: Lesley College.

Bruner, J. S. On teaching teachers. In *Undergraduate education: 1964 current issues in higher education,* ed. G. Kerry Smith. Washington, D. C.: Association for Higher Education.

Bruner, J. S. Preface to Z. P. Dienes, *An experimental study of mathematical learning*. London: Hutchinson Educational, Ltd.

Bruner, J. S. Some theorems on instruction illustrated with reference to mathematics. In Theories of learning and instruction. *Yearbook of the National Society for the Study of Education,* ed. E. Hilgard. 63, part 1: 306–35.

Bruner, J. S. A vivid glimpse of the future. Review of F. Brown, *The nongraded high school. Saturday Review* (January 18), pp. 70–71.

Bruner, J. S., and Potter, M. C. Interference in visual recognition. *Science* 144 (3617) (April 24): 424–25.

1965

Bruner, J. S. The growth of mind. *American Psychologist* 20(12): 1007–17. Also as Occasional paper no. 8, Social Studies Curriculum Project, Educational Services, Inc. (1966), and in *The relevance of education* (1971).

Bruner, J. S. Liberal education for all youth. *The Science Teacher* 32(8): 19–21.

Bruner, J. S. Man: a course of study. *ESI Quarterly Report* (Spring-Summer), pp. 3–13. Also in *Toward a theory of instruction* (1966).
Bruner, J. S., and Kenney, H. J. Representation and mathematics learning. *Monographs of the Society for Research in Child Development* 30 (1) (ser. no. 99): 50–59.
Bruner, J. S., and Tajfel, H. A rejoinder. *Journal of Personality and Social Psychology* 2(2): 267–68.
Bruner, J. S., and Tajfel, H. Width of category and concept differentiation: a note on some comments by Gardner and Schoen. *Journal of Personality and Social Psychology* 2(2): 261–64.

1966

Bruner, J. S. The growth of representational processes in children. *Proceedings of the 18th international congress of psychology*, Moscow, 1966.
Bruner, J. S. The infancy of man. *Expanding horizons of knowledge about man: a symposium.* Occasional paper, Yeshiva University, New York.
Bruner, J. S. A look at incongruity. Occasional paper no. 4, University of Cincinnati.
Bruner, J. S. The perfectibility of intellect. In *Knowledge among men* (Smithsonian Bicentennial). New York: Simon & Schuster. Also in *The relevance of education* (1971).
Bruner, J. S. Some elements of discovery. In *Learning by discovery,* ed. L. Shulman and E. Keislar. Chicago: Rand McNally. Also in *The relevance of education* (1971).
Bruner, J. S. *Toward a theory of instruction.* Cambridge, Mass.: Harvard University Press (paperback, Norton, 1968). Translated into German, Rumanian, Danish, Portuguese, Spanish, Swedish, Italian, Japanese & Slovak.
Bruner, J. S. In *Education and training in developing countries: the role of U.S. foreign aid,* ed. W. Y. Elliott. New York: Praeger.
Bruner, J. S. The will to learn. *Commentary* 41(2): 41–46. Also in *Toward a theory of instruction* (1966).
Bruner, J. S., ed. *Learning about learning: a conference report* (Cooperative Research Monograph no. 15, catalog no. FS5.212:12019). Washington, D.C.: U.S. Government Printing Office.
Bruner, J. S.; Olver, R. R.; Greenfield, P. M.; et al. *Studies in cognitive growth.* New York: Wiley. Translated into Japanese, Italian, and German.
Greenfield, P. M., and Bruner, J. S. Culture and cognitive growth. *International Journal of Psychology* 1: 89–107.

1967

Bruner, J. S. The ontogenesis of symbols. In *To honor Roman Jakobson: essays on the occasion of his seventieth birthday,* vol. 1. The Hague: Mouton.

1968

Bruner, J. S. Culture, politics and pedagogy. *Saturday Review* (May 18), pp. 69–72 ff. Also in *The relevance of education* (1971).
Bruner, J. S. Foreword to English translation of *The mind of a mnemonist,* A. R. Luria. New York: Basic Books.
Bruner, J. S. Foreword to *Toward a contemporary psychology of intuition,* M. R. Westcott. New York: Holt.

Bruner, J. S. Gordon W. Allport: 1897–1967. *American Journal of Psychology* 81(2): 279–84.

Bruner, J. S. *Processes of cognitive growth: infancy,* vol. 3. Heinz Werner Memorial Lecture Series. Worcester, Mass.: Clark University Press, with Barre. Translated into Italian.

Bruner, J. S. Review of Jean Piaget, *Six psychological studies* (1968). *New York Times Book Review* (February 11), pp. 6 ff.

Bruner, J. S., and Bruner, B. M. On voluntary action and its hierarchical structure. *International Journal of Psychology* 3(4): 239–255. Also in *Beyond reductionism: new perspectives in the life sciences,* ed. A. Koestler and J. R. Smythies. Alpbach Symposium, Austria, 1968. London: Hutchinson, 1969.

1969

Bruner, J. S. Eye, hand and mind. In *Studies in cognitive development: essays in honor of Jean Piaget,* ed. D. Elkind and J. H. Flavell. New York: Oxford University Press.

Bruner, J. S. Foreword to *Infants and Mothers,* T. B. Brazelton. New York: Seymour Lawrence, Delacorte.

Bruner, J. S. Modalities of memory. In *The pathology of memory,* ed. G. A. Talland and N. C. Waugh. New York: Academic Press.

Bruner, J. S. The nature of learning in childhood. *Rehovot* (Israel), 25th anniversary issue, Weizmann Institute of Science (Winter 1969–70), pp. 40–43 ff.

Bruner, J. S. The origins of problem solving strategies in skill acquisition. Presented at 19th International Congress of Psychology, London, July 1969.

Bruner, J. S. Processes of growth in infancy. In *Stimulation in early infancy,* ed. A. Ambrose. Proceedings of Ciba Foundation-CASDS Study Group, London, November 1967. London and New York: Academic Press.

Bruner, J. S. Up from helplessness. *Psychology Today* 2(8): 30–33 ff.

Greenfield, P. M., and Bruner, J. S. Culture and cognitive growth (revised version). In *Handbook of socialization theory and research,* ed. D. A. Goslin. Chicago: Rand McNally. Also in condensed form as Work with the Wolof: on learning and language. *Psychology Today* (July 1971), pp. 40–43 ff.; and in *The relevance of education* (1971).

1970

Bruner, J. S. Constructive cognitions. Review of U. Neisser, *Cognitive psychology* (1967). *Contemporary Psychology* 15(2): 81–83.

Bruner, J. S. Discussion: Infant education as viewed by a psychologist. In *Education of the infant and young child,* ed. V. H. Denenberg. New York: Academic Press.

Bruner, J. S. Foreword to *Cognitive development: the child's acquisition of diagonality,* D. R. Olson. New York: Academic Press.

Bruner, J. S. The growth and structure of skill. In *Mechanisms of motor skill in development,* ed. K. J. Connolly. Proceedings of Ciba Foundation-CASDS Study Group, London, November 1968. New York: Academic Press.

Bruner, J. S. Poverty and childhood. Occasional paper, Merrill-Palmer Institute, Detroit. Also in *The relevance of education* (1971).

490   BIBLIOGRAPHY

Bruner, J. S. Preface to *Cognitive Studies,* vol. 1, ed. J. Hellmuth. New York: Brunner / Mazel.

Bruner, J. S. Reason, prejudice and intuition. In *The place of value in a world of facts: Nobel symposium 14,* ed. A. Tiselius and S. Nilsson. Stockholm: Almquist and Wiksell (reprinted for Wiley Interscience Division).

Bruner, J. S. The skill of relevance or the relevance of skills. *Saturday Review* (April 18), pp. 66–68 ff. Also in *The relevance of education* (1971).

Bruner, J. S., and Hall, E. Bad education: a conversation with Jerome Bruner and Elizabeth Hall. *Psychology Today* (December), pp. 50–57, 70–74.

Mackworth, N. H., and Bruner, J. S. How adults and children search and recognize pictures. *Human Devlopment* 13(3): 149–77.

1971

Bruner, J. S. Overview on development and day care. In *Day care: resources for decisions,* ed. E. H. Grotberg. Washington, D.C.: Office of Economic Opportunity.

Bruner, J. S. *The process of education* reconsidered. In *Dare to care / dare to act,* ed. R. R. Leeper. Washington, D.C.: Association for Supervision and Curriculum Development.

Bruner, J. S. *The relevance of education*. New York: Norton.

Cole, M., and Bruner, J. S. Cultural differences and inferences about psychological processes. *American Psychologist* 26(10): 867–76.

1972

Bronfenbrenner, U., and Bruner, J. S. The president and the children (editorial). *New York Times* (January 31), p. 41.

Bruner, J. S. The nature and uses of immaturity. *American Psychologist* 27(8): 1–22. Also a longer version is to appear in *The early growth of competence,* ed. K. J. Connolly and J. S. Bruner. Proceedings of the Ciba Foundation Study Group, London, January 1972. New York: Academic Press.

Bruner, J. S. Toward a sense of community. Review of *Children teach children,* Gartner, Kohler, and Riessman. *Saturday Review* (January 15) pp. 62–63.

Bruner, J. S., and Koslowski, B. Visually preadapted constituents of manipulatory action. *Perception* 1(1): 3–14.

Hillman, D., and Bruner, J. S. Infant sucking in response to variations in schedules of feeding reinforcement. *Journal of Experimental Child Psychology* 13(1): 240–47.

Index